W9-BLH-639

ORIENTATION TO THE COUNSELING PROFESSION

ADVOCACY, ETHICS, AND ESSENTIAL PROFESSIONAL FOUNDATIONS

THIRD EDITION

ORIENTATION TO THE COUNSELING PROFESSION

ADVOCACY, ETHICS, AND ESSENTIAL PROFESSIONAL FOUNDATIONS

Bradley T. Erford
Loyola University Maryland

Pearson

330 Hudson Street, NY, NY 10013

Director, Teacher Education & the Helping Professions: Kevin M. Davis
Portfolio Manager: Rebecca Fox-Geig
Content Producer: Janelle Rogers
Content Project Manager: Pamela D. Bennett
Media Project Manager: Lauren Carlson
Portfolio Management Assistant: Anne McAlpine
Executive Field Marketing Manager: Krista Clark
Executive Product Marketing Manager: Christopher Barry

Procurement Specialist: Deidra Smith
Cover Designer: Melissa Welch
Cover Photo: Getty Images/Image by Catherine MacBride
Full-Service Project Management: Sudip Sinha, iEnergizer Aptara®, Ltd.
Composition: iEnergizer Aptara®, Ltd.
Printer/Binder: LSC Communications/Crawfordsville
Cover Printer: LSC Communications/Crawfordsville
Text Font: Palatino LT Pro, 10/12

Copyright © 2018, 2014, 2010 by Pearson Education, Inc. or its affiliates. All Rights Reserved. Printed in the United States of America. This publication is protected by copyright, and permission should be obtained from the publisher prior to any prohibited reproduction, storage in a retrieval system, or transmission in any form or by any means, electronic, mechanical, photocopying, recording, or otherwise. To obtain permission(s) to use material from this work, please visit http: //www.pearsoned.com/permissions/

Acknowledgments of third party content appear on the pages 578–584, which constitute an extension of this copyright page.

Unless otherwise indicated herein, any third-party trademarks that may appear in this work are the property of their respective owners and any references to third-party trademarks, logos or other trade dress are for demonstrative or descriptive purposes only. Such references are not intended to imply any sponsorship, endorsement, authorization, or promotion of Pearson's products by the owners of such marks, or any relationship between the owner and Pearson Education, Inc. or its affiliates, authors, licensees or distributors.

Library of Congress Cataloging-in-Publication Data
Names: Erford, Bradley T., editor.
Title: Orientation to the counseling profession : advocacy, ethics, and
    essential professional foundations/[edited by] Bradley T. Erford, Loyola
    University Maryland.
Description: Third edition. | Boston : Pearson, [2018] | Includes
    bibliographical references and index.
Identifiers: LCCN 2016035763 | ISBN 9780134387796 | ISBN 0134387791
Subjects: LCSH: Counseling—United States. | Educational counseling—United States.
Classification: LCC BF636.6 .O75 2018 | DDC 361/.06—dc23 LC record available at
https://lccn.loc.gov/2016035763

1 16

Print:
ISBN 10:   0-13-438779-1
ISBN 13: 978-0-13-438779-6

This effort is dedicated to
The One: the Giver of energy, passion, and understanding;
who makes life worth living and endeavors worth pursuing and accomplishing;
the Teacher of love and forgiveness.

PREFACE

Orientation to the Counseling Profession: Advocacy, Ethics, and Essential Professional Foundations, Third Edition, provides a comprehensive overview of the major tenets of the counseling profession, including advocacy and multicultural counseling, licensure, professional associations, ethical and legal issues, crisis intervention, consultation, supervision, outcome research, and the counseling process, with diverse applications across the life span, settings, and specialties. By contrast, nearly all introductory counseling orientation texts on the market approach the field from a dated and more generic "helping professions" perspective. New counselor preparation initiatives expose counselors in training to essential current and future practices that help students orient to the future of counseling practice.

NEW TO THIS EDITION

- A new chapter on crisis intervention.
- Alignment with 2016 CACREP standards, current trends in counseling practice and professional orientation, and key issues that need to be addressed by the counseling profession.
- Discussion updates and applications of ACA and ASCA codes of ethics, and Internet or distance counseling practices.
- An increased focus on advocacy counseling, social justice, and technology issues as foundational constructs.
- An increased focus on wellness practices within the counseling profession.
- Nearly half of the references are more recent than 2010.

ORGANIZATION OF THIS TEXT

The content of *Orientation to the Counseling Profession*, Third Edition, is precisely aligned with the 2016 CACREP standards, because CACREP defines the standard of quality in the counselor preparation field. This text helps CACREP-accredited programs meet the CACREP standards and non-CACREP programs provide counselors in training with the most current professional training standards. The text is divided into four sections: "Foundations of Professional Counselor Identity," "Counseling Processes and Approaches," "Client Issues and Advocacy," and "The Effectiveness of Counseling."

Section One, "Foundations of Professional Counselor Identity," provides an in-depth look at the foundational issues in counseling, covering historical and future issues, professional identity, associations, credentialing, and legal and ethical dimensions of practice. Chapter 1, "Becoming a Professional Counselor: Philosophical, Historical, and Future Considerations," by Bradley T. Erford and Gerta Bardhoshi, explores the definition and philosophical underpinnings of the terms *counseling* and *professional counselor*. Key to this understanding is the development of a firm foundation in the knowledge of the numerous historical events and key people that gave rise to the counseling profession. Important issues facing counselors as the profession moves into the future are identified and discussed, including outcome-based research, managed care, multiculturalism, technology, and gatekeeping. Finally, wellness practices within the counseling profession are given a special focus.

In Chapter 2, "Professional Counseling Organizations, Licensure, Certification, and Accreditation," by Joshua C. Watson, Bradley T. Erford, and Grafton T. Eliason, students are introduced to the American Counseling Association (ACA) and its divisions, branches, and professional partners so that students can become familiar with the wide array of professional associations advocating for counselors and clients. This chapter offers a glimpse of the many credentials that professional counselors can earn. An overview of state licensure, national certification, and counselor education program accreditation processes (e.g., CACREP and CORE) is provided to answer student questions early and to make students aware of the choices that exist for future professional credentialing. Various accountability mechanisms found at the state level for educational systems and mental health agencies are also reviewed.

Section One ends with Chapter 3, "Ethical and Legal Issues in Counseling," by Lynn E. Linde and Bradley T. Erford. The chapter is a comprehensive introduction to ethical and legal issues in counseling practice, covering new editions of the ACA and ASCA ethical codes, confidentiality, privilege, subpoenas, malpractice, records and personal notes, child abuse, suicide, HIPAA, FERPA, minor consent, and ethical decision making. A professional counselor must always remember that how one conducts oneself personally and professionally reflects not only on oneself, but also on one's colleagues.

Section Two, "Counseling Processes and Approaches," provides an in-depth review of counseling theories, process, and skills. Chapter 4, "Theories of Counseling," by Bradley T. Erford and Ann Vernon, portrays the nature and quality of the counseling relationship as more significant than any other factor in counseling. Regardless of the setting, and whether they are working with individuals, families, or groups, counselors have a professional responsibility to develop a foundation and clear rationale for their theoretical orientation to serve clients best. Professional counselors operate out of theories that best fit their personal philosophies of human change and the counseling process. Chapter 4 highlights the significance of theory to counseling practice and provides a brief overview of the major theoretical paradigms. Students will also explore their own beginning preferences for theoretical orientation with the intent of continuing their personal and professional exploration to discover their personal style.

Chapter 5, "The Counseling Process," by Donna S. Sheperis, orients students to counseling processes and approaches, providing a brief overview of the stages of the counseling process and approaches to helping clients. The counseling process embodies the art and science of helping. Professional counselors bring their training, experience, and personalities into the process. Once initiated, counseling occurs over a series of stages that includes information gathering and the application of theory to generate relevant goals, treatment, assessment, and termination. In Chapter 5, students beginning the path to becoming professional counselors are encouraged to consider their fit with the process and profession of counseling.

Chapter 6, "Counseling Microskills," by Joseph B. Cooper, provides an overview of the fundamental skills that constitute the key elements of effective helping relationships. The skills in this chapter focus on Ivey, Ivey, and Zalaquett's's (2013) microskills hierarchy. At the heart of this hierarchy is the basic listening sequence, an interrelated set of skills that not only fosters the development of rapport with clients, but also aids in the identification of interventions to help achieve a successful resolution to the clients' presenting concerns. Examples of the skills in use, along with practice exercises to foster individual skill development, are provided.

Section Three, "Client Issues and Advocacy," explores the knowledge, skills, and attitudes required of the counselor when working with clients across the life span and with common presenting problems (e.g., substance use, eating disorders, behavioral difficulties, crisis intervention), as well as multicultural competence, consultation, and supervision. Chapter 7, "Crisis Prevention and Intervention," by Judith Harrington and Charlotte Daughhetee, recognizes that crises, suicide and homicide continue to play increasingly important roles in American society and on the world stage. Suicide and homicide affect us personally as we, family members, friends, and those in extended social networks struggle with the ever-increasing challenges of modern life. The effectiveness of the care given by professional emergency first responders, as well as the effectiveness of ordinary people in responding to their own crises and the crises of those about whom they care, is improved by background knowledge involving current trends in and treatments for suicidal and homicidal impulses.

Chapter 8, "Mental Health and Rehabilitation Counseling," by Catherine Y. Chang, Amy L. McLeod, and Nadine E. Garner, provides a broad overview of the general mental health settings and client issues (i.e., drug and alcohol counseling, mental health counseling, career counseling, and rehabilitation counseling). The field of counseling is becoming increasingly specialized, with certifications and licensures available for addictions counselors (National Certified Addictions Counselor [NCAC]; Master Addiction Counselor [MAC]), mental health counselors (Licensed Professional Counselor [LPC]—term may vary depending on the state), career counselors, and rehabilitation counselors (Certified Rehabilitation Counselor [CRC]). Although these areas are not distinct, and clients may enter counseling with a mental health, substance use, career, or rehabilitation issue, or any combination of the four, it is important for professional counselors to have a basic understanding of each area.

Chapter 9, "School, College, and Career Counseling," by Nadine E. Garner, Jason Baker, and Molly E. Jones, describes the unique characteristics of working as a professional counselor in the increasingly multicultural settings of elementary and secondary schools; college and university campuses; and career counseling.

Chapter 10 "Human Development Throughout the Life Span," by Bradley T. Erford briefly describes developmental characteristics of infancy and toddlerhood (birth to age 3 years); early childhood (ages 4 to 6 years); middle childhood (ages 6 to 11 years); early adolescence, midadolescence, and later adolescence (ages 11 to 24 years); young adulthood (ages 24 to 40 years); middle adulthood (ages 40 to 60 years); and later adulthood (ages 60 years and older). The information in these approximate age categories serves as a basis for examples of interventions that helping professionals can use to facilitate development at several of these stages.

In Chapter 11, "Multicultural Counseling," by Geneva M. Gray, multicultural counseling applications are reviewed to help students integrate principles of cultural diversity into the counseling process from the beginning of their training. This chapter features multicultural applications of identity development and counselor competency (multicultural implications are highlighted throughout the other chapters of the text too). Cultural identity developmental processes and culturally specific information and intervention strategies are presented across the cultural dimensions of socioeconomic status, race, ethnicity, gender, sexual orientation, spirituality, ability level, and age.

Chapter 12, "Assessment, Case Conceptualization, Diagnosis, and Treatment Planning," by Bradley T. Erford, reviews each of these major counseling tenets. Assessment is the systematic gathering of information to address a client's presenting concerns effectively. A case conceptualization reflects how the professional counselor understands the nature of the presenting problems and includes a diagnostic formulation. Treatment plans outline counseling outcome expectations and interventions to meet these expectations.

In Chapter 13, "Supervision and Consultation," by Mark A. Young and Alan Basham, an introduction to supervision and consultation is provided to help students understand the theory and practical applications of these two essential counselor roles. In particular, the chapter helps counselors in training understand how to get the most out of their relationships with supervisors and understand what will be expected of them as future supervisors to the next generation of counselors in training. Models, techniques, types of activities, and important skills used to fulfill the role of consultant or supervisor are presented.

An innovative facet of this text is the integration of advocacy counseling and the introduction of professional advocacy strategies. Chapter 14, "Advocating for the Counseling Profession," by Amy Milsom, answers important questions about advocacy counseling, including: "What does it mean to advocate for the counseling profession?" "Why is professional advocacy important?" "In what ways can professional counselors advocate for the profession?" Counselors can best serve their clients by advocating for a strong professional presence in the public and legislative venues. A positive view of the counseling profession by citizens and legislators helps remove barriers for clients and promotes the worth and dignity of diverse individuals.

In addition, obtaining social justice for clients demands that professional counselors understand and practice advocacy counseling according to the standards developed by the ACA. Chapter 15, "Advocacy Counseling: Being an Effective Agent of Change for Clients," by Donna M. Gibson, proposes that the core purpose of advocacy counseling is to address external barriers that interfere with human development. Although this purpose can be met by advocating for the profession of counseling, it is often met by advocating at the individual client level. Through an examination of the advocacy competency domains (Ratts et al., 2015), specific guidelines are provided on how to increase clients' empowerment and how to be a successful advocacy counselor.

Section Four, "The Effectiveness of Counseling," addresses the crucial issues of accountability and outcome in counseling. The future of the counseling profession lies in the ability of counselors to show that counseling practices are effective in helping clients reach their stated goals. Counselors in training need to learn to conduct needs assessments, outcome studies, and program evaluation to determine what services are needed, and the effects of those services. Chapter 16, "Accountability in Counseling," by Bradley T. Erford, proposes that accountability is a central responsibility of all professional counselors. At its core, accountability shows the effect that a professional counselor has in producing changes in clients and program stakeholders. The process of outcome studies is approached from traditional research methods perspectives and contemporary perspectives, including action research and single-subject research designs.

Counselors also need to realize that a great wealth of extant literature exists to inform their daily counseling practice with clients. This literature is reviewed in Chapter 17, "Outcome Research in Counseling," by Bradley T. Erford, to bolster the students' knowledge of what does and does not work in counseling, and so counselors can use effective counseling interventions. Professional counselors have an ethical responsibility to use counseling methods grounded in theory and empirically validated through research. It is now known that counseling is effective in many forms and for many client conditions. Chapter 17 reviews research on the effectiveness of counseling in several areas: client–counselor characteristics, individual approaches, group approaches, career intervention, and school-based student interventions. This body of information should be used by professional counselors to inform their practice and increase treatment efficacy.

Orientation to the Counseling Profession: Advocacy, Ethics, and Essential Professional Foundations provides a wealth of information on the most foundational and emerging issues of the counseling profession. It was specifically designed to orient counselors in training, regardless of specialty area, to the profession of counseling that we have all dedicated our careers and lives to improving. Enjoy!

SUPPLEMENTAL INSTRUCTIONAL FEATURES

Supplemental to this text are pedagogical tools helpful to counselor educators choosing to use this text as a course text. The companion *Instructor's Resource Manual with Test Bank* contains at least 50 multiple choice questions and 20 essay questions per chapter. Numerous case studies and activities included in the text can stimulate lively classroom discussions. PowerPoint® lecture outlines are also available. Instructor supplements can be downloaded from the Instructor Resource Center at www.pearsonhighered.com.

ALSO AVAILABLE WITH MYCOUNSELINGLAB®

This title is also available with MyCounselingLab—an online homework, tutorial, and assessment program designed to work with the text to engage students and improve results. Within its structured environment, students see key concepts demonstrated through video clips, practice what they learn, test their understanding, and receive feedback to guide their learning and ensure they master key learning outcomes.

- **Learning Outcomes and Standards measure student results.**
  MyCounselingLab organizes all assignments around essential learning outcomes and national standards for counselors.

- **Video- and Case-Based Exercises develop decision-making skills.**
  Video- and Case-based Exercises introduce students to a broader range of clients, and therefore a broader range of presenting problems, than they will encounter in their own pre-professional clinical experiences. Students watch videos of actual client-therapist sessions or high-quality role-play scenarios featuring expert counselors. They are then guided in their analysis of the videos through a series of short-answer questions. These exercises help students develop the techniques and decision-making skills they need to be effective counselors before they are in a critical situation with a real client.

- **Licensure Quizzes help students prepare for certification.**
  Automatically graded, multiple-choice Licensure Quizzes help students prepare for their certification examinations, master foundational course content, and improve their performance in the course.

- **Video Library offers a wealth of observation opportunities.**
  The Video Library provides more than 400 video clips of actual client-therapist sessions and high-quality role plays in a database organized by topic and searchable by keyword. The Video Library includes every video clip from the MyCounselingLab courses plus additional videos from Pearson's extensive library of footage. Instructors can create additional assignments around the videos or use them for in-class activities. Students can expand their observation experiences to include other course areas and increase the amount of time they spend watching expert counselors in action.

ACKNOWLEDGMENTS

All of the contributing authors are to be commended for lending their expertise in the various topical areas. As always, Kevin Davis of Pearson has been wonderfully responsive and supportive. At Aptara, thanks go to the production team (Sudip Sinha, Production Project Manager; Ramesh Rawat, Production Lead). Finally, special thanks go to the outside reviewers whose comments helped to provide substantive improvement to the original manuscript: Maria D. Avalos, University of Texas of the Permian Basin; Laura Choate, Louisiana State University; Pit Kolodinsky, Northern Arizona University; Kara P. Ieva, Rowan University; and Waganesh Zeleke, Duquesne University.

BRIEF CONTENTS

SECTION ONE   **Foundations of Professional Counselor Identity**   **1**

Chapter 1   Becoming a Professional Counselor: Philosophical, Historical, and Future Considerations ■ Bradley T. Erford and Gerta Bardhoshi   3

Chapter 2   Professional Counseling Organizations, Licensure, Certification, and Accreditation ■ Joshua C. Watson, Bradley T. Erford, and Grafton T. Eliason   35

Chapter 3   Ethical and Legal Issues in Counseling ■ Lynn E. Linde and Bradley T. Erford   70

SECTION TWO   **Counseling Processes and Approaches**   **113**

Chapter 4   Theories of Counseling ■ Bradley T. Erford and Ann Vernon   115

Chapter 5   The Counseling Process ■ Donna S. Sheperis   160

Chapter 6   Counseling Microskills ■ Joseph B. Cooper   192

SECTION THREE   **Client Issues and Advocacy**   **217**

Chapter 7   Crisis Prevention and Intervention ■ Judith Harrington and Charlotte Daughhetee   219

Chapter 8   Mental Health and Rehabilitation Counseling ■ Catherine Y. Chang, Amy L. McLeod, and Nadine E. Garner   249

Chapter 9   School, College, and Career Counseling ■ Nadine E. Garner, Jason Baker, and Molly E. Jones   280

Chapter 10   Human Development Throughout the Life Span ■ Bradley T. Erford   311

Chapter 11   Multicultural Counseling ■ Geneva M. Gray   337

Chapter 12   Assessment, Case Conceptualization, Diagnosis, and Treatment Planning ■ Bradley T. Erford   373

Chapter 13   Supervision and Consultation ■ Mark A. Young and Alan Basham   406

Chapter 14   Advocating for the Counseling Profession ■ Amy Milsom   435

Chapter 15   Advocacy Counseling: Being an Effective Agent of Change for Clients ■ Donna M. Gibson   458

SECTION FOUR   **The Effectiveness of Counseling**   **487**

Chapter 16   Accountability in Counseling ■ Bradley T. Erford   489

Chapter 17   Outcome Research in Counseling ■ Bradley T. Erford   520

CONTENTS

About the Editor   *xxvi*

About the Authors   *xxviii*

SECTION ONE   Foundations of Professional Counselor Identity   1

Chapter 1   Becoming a Professional Counselor: Philosophical, Historical, and Future Considerations

■ **Bradley T. Erford and Gerta Bardhoshi   3**

Preview   3

Counseling and Professional Counselors: Where We Are   3

   How Do Counselors Differ from Psychologists and Social Workers?   6

The Philosophical Underpinnings of Counseling   7

How We Got Here: People, Issues, and Societal Forces That Have Shaped the Counseling Profession   9

   1900–1920   9

   1921–1940   15

   1941–1960   17

   1961–1980   18

   1981–2000   19

   2001–Present   20

Where We Are Going   22

   Evidence-Based Practices, Research-Based Practices, and Outcomes Research   22

   Managed Care   23

   Multiculturalism, Diversity, and Social Justice Counseling   24

   Technology   25

   Gatekeeping   26

   Professional Advocacy and Social Advocacy Counseling   26

   Mentoring and Leadership Training   29

   Bonding and Splintering of Facets of the Counseling Profession   29

Developing a Commitment to Career-long Wellness   30

   Summary   34

Chapter 2   Professional Counseling Organizations, Licensure, Certification, and Accreditation

■ **Joshua C. Watson, Bradley T. Erford, and Grafton T. Eliason   35**

Preview 35

Professional Counseling Organizations 35

AMERICAN COUNSELING ASSOCIATION 36

American Counseling Association Divisions 39

AMERICAN COLLEGE COUNSELING ASSOCIATION 40

AMERICAN MENTAL HEALTH COUNSELORS ASSOCIATION 41

AMERICAN REHABILITATION COUNSELING ASSOCIATION 41

AMERICAN SCHOOL COUNSELOR ASSOCIATION 41

ASSOCIATION FOR ADULT DEVELOPMENT AND AGING 41

ASSOCIATION FOR ASSESSMENT AND RESEARCH IN COUNSELING 42

ASSOCIATION FOR CHILD AND ADOLESCENT COUNSELING 42

ASSOCIATION FOR COUNSELOR EDUCATION AND SUPERVISION 42

ASSOCIATION FOR CREATIVITY IN COUNSELING 43

ASSOCIATION FOR HUMANISTIC COUNSELING 43

ASSOCIATION FOR LESBIAN, GAY, BISEXUAL, AND TRANSGENDER ISSUES IN COUNSELING 43

ASSOCIATION FOR MULTICULTURAL COUNSELING AND DEVELOPMENT 44

ASSOCIATION FOR SPECIALISTS IN GROUP WORK 44

ASSOCIATION FOR SPIRITUAL, ETHICAL, AND RELIGIOUS VALUES IN COUNSELING 44

COUNSELORS FOR SOCIAL JUSTICE 45

INTERNATIONAL ASSOCIATION OF ADDICTIONS AND OFFENDER COUNSELORS 45

INTERNATIONAL ASSOCIATION OF MARRIAGE AND FAMILY COUNSELORS 45

MILITARY AND GOVERNMENT COUNSELING ASSOCIATION 45

NATIONAL CAREER DEVELOPMENT ASSOCIATION 46

NATIONAL EMPLOYMENT COUNSELING ASSOCIATION 46

American Counseling Association Regions and Branches 48

Other Essential Professional Counseling Organizations 50

AMERICAN COUNSELING ASSOCIATION FOUNDATION 50

CHI SIGMA IOTA 50

COUNCIL FOR ACCREDITATION OF COUNSELING AND RELATED EDUCATIONAL PROGRAMS 51

COUNCIL ON REHABILITATION EDUCATION 51

NATIONAL BOARD FOR CERTIFIED COUNSELORS 51

Professional Development 51

Benefits of Joining Professional Counseling Organizations 52

ADDITIONAL BENEFITS FOR PROFESSIONAL COUNSELOR MEMBERS 52

THE AMERICAN COUNSELING ASSOCIATION MEMBER SERVICES COMMITTEE 53

ADDITIONAL BENEFITS FOR STUDENT MEMBERS   53

ETHICAL STANDARDS   54

LEGISLATIVE ADVOCACY   54

SUPPORTING THE MISSION OF THE PROFESSION   54

Relationship Between the American Counseling Association and the American Psychological Association   56

Some Key Challenges That Need to be Addressed by Counseling Professionals   56

National Accreditation   58

INTERNATIONAL EFFORTS AT PROGRAM REGISTRY   60

State Accreditation   60

State Professional Certification and Other Credentials   60

State Licensure   61

EDUCATION   62

SUPERVISED EXPERIENCE   62

EXAMINATION   63

AMERICAN ASSOCIATION OF STATE COUNSELING BOARDS   63

License Portability   64

CERTIFICATION/LICENSURE FOR PROFESSIONAL SCHOOL COUNSELORS   64

BENEFITS AND DRAWBACKS OF COUNSELING LICENSURE   65

National Certification   65

Commission on Rehabilitation Counselor Certification   66

Summary   68

Chapter 3   **Ethical and Legal Issues in Counseling**

■ **Lynn E. Linde and Bradley T. Erford   70**

Preview   70

Ethical Standards and Laws   70

AMERICAN COUNSELING ASSOCIATION CODE OF ETHICS   72

THE PRACTICE OF INTERNET OR TECHNOLOGY-ASSISTED DISTANCE COUNSELING   83

AMERICAN SCHOOL COUNSELOR ASSOCIATION ETHICAL STANDARDS FOR SCHOOL COUNSELORS   83

DECISION MAKING USING ETHICAL STANDARDS   85

Additional Sources of Information and Guidance: Courts, Laws, and Regulations   91

COURT SYSTEM   91

STATUTORY LAW   92

STATE AND LOCAL AGENCIES: REGULATIONS AND POLICIES   92

Making Decisions   93

Additional Legal Considerations   95

PROFESSIONAL COMPETENCE   95

"CAN I BE SUED?" AND "WHAT IS MALPRACTICE?"   96

SUBPOENAS   98

Confidentiality   100

LIMITS TO CONFIDENTIALITY   101

CONFIDENTIALITY AND PRIVILEGED COMMUNICATION   102

Minor-Consent Laws   103

Records and Personal Notes   104

EDUCATIONAL RECORDS   104

PERSONAL NOTES   108

The Health Insurance Portability and Accountability Act (HIPAA) of 1996   109

Child Abuse   109

Suicide   110

Summary   112

SECTION TWO   Counseling Processes and Approaches   113

Chapter 4   Theories of Counseling

■ **Bradley T. Erford and Ann Vernon   115**

Preview   115

The Significance of Theory   115

ETHICS OF APPLYING COUNSELING THEORY   116

WHAT MAKES A GOOD THEORY?   117

Theoretical Paradigms   117

PSYCHODYNAMIC PARADIGM   121

HUMANISTIC/EXISTENTIAL PARADIGM   125

BEHAVIORAL/COGNITIVE-BEHAVIORAL PARADIGM   127

FAMILY SYSTEMS PARADIGM   136

EMERGENT THEORIES   142

Applying Theory to Practice   151

VIEW OF HUMAN NATURE   152

GOALS OF COUNSELING   153

ROLE OF THE PROFESSIONAL COUNSELOR   153

TECHNIQUES AND APPROACHES   153

FLEXIBILITY   154

Theoretical Integration   155

INTEGRATIVE VERSUS ECLECTIC COUNSELING   155

WHY AN INTEGRATIVE APPROACH?   156

Summary   159

Chapter 5   The Counseling Process
■ **Donna S. Sheperis   160**
Preview   160
The Professional Counselor   160
   COUNSELOR CHARACTERISTICS   161
   COMMON ISSUES FOR THE BEGINNING COUNSELOR   162
   CLIENT CHARACTERISTICS   164
   CROSS-CULTURAL COUNSELING COMPETENCE   165
   BASIC COUNSELING PARADIGM   166
   THE COUNSELING PROCESS AND STAGES OF CHANGE   166
The Helping Process—The Helping Relationship   168
   THE ART OF HELPING   168
   HELPING AS A SCIENCE   169
   COMMON FACTORS IN HELPING   170
What Brings Clients to Counseling?   171
Initiating Counseling   174
   COUNSELING ENVIRONMENT   174
   HELPING RELATIONSHIP   175
   ROLE OF THEORY   177
Structure of Counseling   178
   INFORMED CONSENT   178
   INFORMATION GATHERING   179
Exploring and Working Together   180
   GOAL SETTING AND POSITIVE COUNSELING OUTCOMES   182
   WHAT HAPPENS WHEN CHANGE DOES NOT HAPPEN?   183
Integration and Termination   185
Becoming a Professional Counselor   188
   PERSONAL STRENGTHS AND CHALLENGES   188
   Summary   191

Chapter 6   Counseling Microskills
■ **Joseph B. Cooper   192**
Preview   192
Essential Counseling Microskills   192
Attending Skills   193
   EYE CONTACT   193
   BODY POSITION   194
   VOCAL TONE   195
Basic Listening Sequence   196
   OPEN AND CLOSED QUESTIONS   197

REFLECTING SKILLS   201

HOW TO REFLECT MEANING   210

Summary   216

SECTION THREE   Client Issues and Advocacy   217

Chapter 7   Crisis Prevention and Intervention

■ Judith Harrington and Charlotte Daughhetee   219

Preview   219

Crisis Theory   219

CONCEPTS   222

RESILIENCE AND POST-TRAUMATIC GROWTH   224

Counselor Safeguards: Professional Burnout, Compassion Fatigue, Secondary Traumatic Stress, Vicarious Trauma, and Transcrisis   227

Crisis Counseling   232

HOW DOES CRISIS COUNSELING DIFFER FROM TRADITIONAL COUNSELING?   232

ETHICAL CONSIDERATIONS   232

Risk Assessment: Suicide and Homicide   234

SIGNIFICANCE OF THE PROBLEM   234

PRINCIPLES OF ASSESSMENT   236

SUICIDE RISK ASSESSMENT   237

CLINICAL INTERVIEW MODALITY   237

HOMICIDE ASSESSMENT   238

INTIMATE PARTNER VIOLENCE   243

CHILD AND ELDER ABUSE   243

Special Topics in Crisis Intervention and Prevention   244

COMMUNITY DISASTERS   244

SCHOOL SYSTEM ADAPTIONS   245

SAFETY CONCERNS   247

Summary   248

Chapter 8   Mental Health and Rehabilitation Counseling

■ Catherine Y. Chang, Amy L. McLeod, and Nadine E. Garner   249

Preview   249

Counseling Career Choices   249

Counseling in Mental Health Settings   250

BACKGROUND   250

COMMUNITY/AGENCY SETTING   251

HOSPITALS   252

CORRECTIONS   254

PRIVATE PRACTICE   255

MARRIAGE AND FAMILY COUNSELORS   257

PASTORAL COUNSELING   257

WILDERNESS THERAPY   258

Mental Health Counseling Issues   259

DEPRESSION   259

ANXIETY   261

EATING DISORDERS   262

ADDICTIONS   263

DRUG AND ALCOHOL TREATMENT APPROACHES   264

ALCOHOL AND DRUG USE ISSUES IN SPECIAL POPULATIONS   266

Rehabilitation Counseling   269

SUMMARY OF REHABILITATION LAWS   270

DISABILITY ELIGIBILITY AND DEMOGRAPHICS   272

ADAPTATION TO DISABILITY   274

REHABILITATION COUNSELING AND TECHNOLOGY   274

VOCATIONAL REHABILITATION COUNSELING   275

MULTICULTURAL AND SOCIAL JUSTICE ISSUES IN REHABILITATION
COUNSELING   276

Summary   278

Chapter 9   School, College, and Career Counseling

    ■ **Nadine E. Garner, Jason Baker, and Molly E. Jones   280**

Preview   280

Counseling in the Schools   280

BACKGROUND   280

ELEMENTARY COUNSELING   281

MIDDLE SCHOOL/JUNIOR HIGH COUNSELING   282

HIGH SCHOOL COUNSELING   283

CURRENT ISSUES AFFECTING ALL SCHOOL COUNSELING SETTINGS   283

MULTICULTURAL AND SOCIAL JUSTICE ISSUES IN SCHOOLS   286

College/University Counseling and Student-Life Services   289

BACKGROUND   289

COLLEGE AND UNIVERSITY COUNSELING   290

STUDENT-LIFE SERVICES   293

COUNSELING COLLEGE AND UNIVERSITY STUDENTS WHO HAVE
A DISABILITY   296

MULTICULTURAL AND SOCIAL JUSTICE ISSUES IN COLLEGE COUNSELING
AND STUDENT-LIFE SERVICES   297

Career Counseling Issues   298

MAJOR THEORIES OF CAREER DEVELOPMENT   299

TECHNOLOGY USE AND CAREER RESOURCES   308

SOCIAL JUSTICE ISSUES IN CAREER COUNSELING   309

Summary   310

Chapter 10   Human Development Throughout the Life Span

■ **Bradley T. Erford   311**

Preview   311

Counseling and Human Development: A life span perspective   311

Infancy and Toddlerhood   314

MOTOR DEVELOPMENT IN INFANCY AND TODDLERHOOD   314

EMOTIONAL DEVELOPMENT IN INFANCY AND TODDLERHOOD   315

COGNITIVE/LANGUAGE DEVELOPMENT IN INFANCY AND TODDLERHOOD   315

Early Childhood   316

SOCIAL DEVELOPMENT IN EARLY CHILDHOOD   316

EMOTIONAL DEVELOPMENT IN EARLY CHILDHOOD   316

COGNITIVE DEVELOPMENT IN EARLY CHILDHOOD   317

DEVELOPMENTAL INTERVENTIONS IN EARLY CHILDHOOD   318

Middle Childhood   319

SOCIAL DEVELOPMENT IN MIDDLE CHILDHOOD   319

EMOTIONAL DEVELOPMENT IN MIDDLE CHILDHOOD   319

COGNITIVE DEVELOPMENT IN MIDDLE CHILDHOOD   320

DEVELOPMENTAL INTERVENTIONS IN MIDDLE CHILDHOOD   321

Adolescence   321

EARLY ADOLESCENCE   321

DEVELOPMENTAL INTERVENTIONS IN EARLY ADOLESCENCE   323

MIDADOLESCENCE   324

DEVELOPMENTAL INTERVENTIONS IN MIDADOLESCENCE   325

LATE ADOLESCENCE (EMERGING ADULTHOOD)   326

DEVELOPMENTAL INTERVENTIONS IN LATE ADOLESCENCE
(EMERGING ADULTHOOD)   327

Early Adulthood   328

THE WORKER IN EARLY ADULTHOOD   328

THE PARTNER IN EARLY ADULTHOOD   328

THE PARENT IN EARLY ADULTHOOD   329

DEVELOPMENTAL INTERVENTIONS IN EARLY ADULTHOOD   329

Middle Adulthood   330

PHYSICAL CHANGES IN MIDDLE ADULTHOOD   330

COGNITIVE CHANGES IN MIDDLE ADULTHOOD   330

KEY DEVELOPMENTAL TASKS IN MIDDLE ADULTHOOD   331

DEVELOPMENTAL INTERVENTIONS IN MIDDLE ADULTHOOD   332

Later Adulthood   332

ACCEPTING LIFE IN LATER ADULTHOOD   333

REDIRECTING ENERGY TO NEW ROLES AND ACTIVITIES IN LATER
ADULTHOOD   333

PHYSICAL CHANGES IN LATER ADULTHOOD   333

COGNITIVE CHANGES IN LATER ADULTHOOD   334

DEALING WITH LOSS IN LATER ADULTHOOD   334

DEVELOPMENTAL INTERVENTIONS IN LATER ADULTHOOD   334

Summary   336

Chapter 11   Multicultural Counseling

■ **Geneva M. Gray   337**

Preview   337

Multiculturally Competent Counseling   337

Key Issues in Multicultural Counseling   340

ETIC VERSUS EMIC DEBATE   340

HOW MUCH OF COUNSELING IS MULTICULTURAL?   340

ASSESSMENT AND TREATMENT   341

EVIDENCE BASED PRACTICES IN MULTICULTURAL COUNSELING   342

Cultural Identity Development and Multicultural Counseling   342

CULTURAL IDENTITY DEVELOPMENT MODELS   344

RACIAL AND ETHNIC IDENTITY DEVELOPMENT   345

FEMINIST IDENTITY DEVELOPMENT   348

SEXUAL IDENTITY DEVELOPMENT   348

SPIRITUAL IDENTITY DEVELOPMENT   349

Counseling Culturally Diverse Individuals   350

SOCIOECONOMIC STATUS AND POVERTY   350

RACIAL AND ETHNIC DIVERSITY   352

GENDER   358

SEXUAL MINORITIES   361

SPIRITUALITY   363

COUNSELING INDIVIDUALS WITH DISABILITIES   367

COUNSELING THE ELDERLY   368

Social Justice in Counseling   368

**Multicultural Organizational Development: Creating a Culturally
Sensitive Environment   369**

Summary   371

Chapter 12   Assessment, Case Conceptualization, Diagnosis, and Treatment Planning

■ **Bradley T. Erford   373**

Preview   373

A Comprehensive Approach to Understanding Client Issues and Designing Plans to Help   373

Assessment   374

TESTING AND THE COUNSELING PROFESSION   375

WHY SHOULD PROFESSIONAL COUNSELORS KNOW ABOUT TESTING?   376

CATEGORIES OF TESTS   376

TYPES OF TESTS   377

QUALITIES TO CONSIDER WHEN EVALUATING TESTS   379

CULTURAL FAIRNESS   381

TECHNOLOGY AND TESTING   381

ETHICAL CONSIDERATIONS   381

TESTING RESOURCES   382

INTAKE INTERVIEWS   382

WHAT IS A MENTAL STATUS EXAMINATION?   383

WHAT ARE THE ELEMENTS OF A SUICIDE ASSESSMENT AND AN EXPLORATION OF INTENT TO HARM OTHERS?   384

BEHAVIORAL OBSERVATION   386

ENVIRONMENTAL ASSESSMENT   386

DEVELOPMENTAL CONSIDERATIONS   387

Case Conceptualization   390

Diagnosis   394

SOCIAL JUSTICE COUNSELING AND ASSESSMENT, DIAGNOSIS, AND TREATMENT   396

BENEFITS OF DIAGNOSIS   397

DRAWBACKS OF DIAGNOSIS   398

Treatment Planning   398

TREATMENT PLANS   399

COMPREHENSIVE MODELS OF ASSESSMENT AND TREATMENT PLANNING   402

Summary   404

Chapter 13   Supervision and Consultation

■ **Mark A. Young and Alan Basham   406**

Preview   406

Use of Supervision and Consultation in Counseling   406

Supervision   409

MODELS OF SUPERVISION   410

SUPERVISION FORMATS   412

SUPERVISION INTERVENTIONS   414

SUPERVISORY RELATIONSHIP   418

Consultation   423

MODELS OF CONSULTATION   424

CONSULTANT ROLES   426

CONSULTATION SKILLS   428

CONSULTATION SETTINGS   429

Summary   432

Chapter 14   Advocating for the Counseling Profession

■ **Amy Milsom   435**

Preview   435

Defining Advocacy   435

Brief History of Counselors Advocating for the Profession   436

Current Counseling Advocacy Agendas   437

Why Advocate?   439

Prerequisites to Effective Advocacy   444

Process of Advocacy   446

IDENTIFY THE PROBLEM   447

ASSESS THE AVAILABILITY OF RESOURCES   447

ENGAGE IN STRATEGIC PLANNING ACTIVITIES   448

TRAIN PROFESSIONAL COUNSELORS TO ADVOCATE   449

IMPLEMENT A PLAN OF ACTION   450

CELEBRATE ACCOMPLISHMENTS   451

Ways to Advocate   451

IDENTIFYING YOURSELF AS A PROFESSIONAL COUNSELOR   451

SERVE YOUR COMMUNITY   452

USE THE MEDIA   454

TECHNOLOGY   454

TARGET POLICY MAKERS   456

Summary   456

Chapter 15   Advocacy Counseling: Being an Effective Agent of Change for Clients

■ **Donna M. Gibson   458**

Preview   458

Advocacy Counseling   458

WHEN TO ADVOCATE   459

ADVOCACY COUNSELING AND INTERVENTION COMPETENCIES   461

COUNSELING AND ADVOCACY INTERVENTION COMPETENCIES: COMMUNITY   469

COUNSELING AND ADVOCACY INTERVENTIONS COMPETENCIES: PUBLIC POLICY   477

COUNSELING AND ADVOCACY INTERVENTION COMPETENCIES: INTERNATIONAL AND GLOBAL AFFAIRS   483

    Summary   485

SECTION FOUR   The Effectiveness of Counseling   487

Chapter 16   **Accountability in Counseling**
■ **Bradley T. Erford   489**
Preview   489
Accountability   489
Using a Counseling Program Advisory Committee   491
Conducting a Needs Assessment   492
    DATA-DRIVEN NEEDS ASSESSMENT   492
    PERCEPTIONS-BASED NEEDS ASSESSMENT   497
Evaluating Programs   504
    SERVICE ASSESSMENT   505
Outcome or Results Evaluation   506
    IMPORTANT ASSESSMENT TERMS   507
    PRACTICAL PROGRAM EVALUATION CONSIDERATIONS   508
    AGGREGATED OUTCOMES   508
    DESIGNING OUTCOME STUDIES   510
    SINGLE-SUBJECT RESEARCH DESIGN   513
    ACTION RESEARCH   516
Reporting Results   516
    ACCOUNTABILITY AND SOCIAL JUSTICE COUNSELING   518
    ACCOUNTABILITY AND TECHNOLOGY   518
      Summary   518

Chapter 17   **Outcome Research in Counseling**
■ **Bradley T. Erford   520**
Preview   520
How Research Assists Counselors: The Importance of and Barriers to Conducting Outcome Research   520
How Effective is Counseling?   527
    FACETS OF COUNSELING THAT CONTRIBUTE TO OUTCOMES   528
Which Client and Professional Counselor Factors Contribute to Successful Outcomes?   531

The Effectiveness of Individual Counseling 533

The Effectiveness of Group Counseling 535

PROCESS ISSUES IN GROUP OUTCOME RESEARCH 535

GROUP COUNSELING WITH CHILDREN 536

The Effectiveness of School-Based Interventions for Children and Adolescents 538

SPECIFIC TYPES OF SCHOOL-BASED INTERVENTIONS 539

Implications for the Future of Professional Counseling 542

COLLABORATE WITH RESEARCHERS 542

ADVOCATE FOR OUTCOME RESEARCH FUNDING 544

INCREASE KNOWLEDGE AND USE OF OUTCOME LITERATURE 544

PUTTING IT ALL TOGETHER: WORKING FOR THE FUTURE 546

Summary 547

References 549

Credits 578

Index 585

ABOUT THE EDITOR

Bradley T. Erford, PhD, LCPC, NCC, LPC, LP, LSP, is a professor in the school counseling program of the Education Specialties Department in the School of Education at Loyola University Maryland. He was the 61st President of the American Counseling Association (ACA) for 2012-2013. He is the recipient of the ACA Research Award, ACA Extended Research Award, ACA Arthur A. Hitchcock Distinguished Professional Service Award, ACA Professional Development Award, ACA Thomas J. Sweeney Award for Visionary Leadership and Advocacy, and ACA Carl D. Perkins Government Relations Award. He was also inducted as an ACA Fellow. In addition, he has received the Association for Assessment in Counseling and Education (AACE) AACE/MECD Research Award, AACE Exemplary Practices Award, AACE President's Merit Award, the Association for Counselor Education and Supervision's (ACES) Robert O. Stripling Award for Excellence in Standards, Maryland Association for Counseling and Development (MACD) Maryland Counselor of the Year, MACD Counselor Advocacy Award, MACD Professional Development Award, and MACD Counselor Visibility Award. He is the editor of numerous texts including: *Orientation to the Counseling Profession* (Pearson Merrill, 2010, 2014, 2018), *Crisis Intervention and Prevention* (Pearson Merrill, 2010, 2014, 2018), *Group Work in the Schools* (Routledge, 2016), *Clinical Experiences in Counseling* (Pearson Merrill, 2015), *Group Work: Process and Applications* (Pearson Merrill, 2011), *Transforming the School Counseling Profession* (1st through 4th editions; Merrill/Prentice-Hall, 2003, 2007, 2011, 2015), *Professional School Counseling: A Handbook of Principles, Programs and Practices* (1st - 3rd editions, pro-ed, 2004, 2010, 2016), *Assessment for Counselors* (1st & 2nd editions, Cengage, 2007, 2012), *Research and Evaluation in Counseling* (1st & 2nd editions, Cengage, 2008, 2015), and *The Counselor's Guide to Clinical, Personality and Behavioral Assessment* (Cengage, 2006); and co-author of eight more books: *Mastering the NCE and CPCE* (Pearson Merrill, 2011, 2015), *35 Techniques Every Counselor Should Know* (Merrill/Prentice-Hall, 1st & 2nd editions, 2010, 2015), *Free Access Assessment Instruments for Common Mental Health and Addiction Issues* (Routledge, 2013), *Educational Applications of the WISC-IV* (Western Psychological Services, 2006) and *Group Activities: Firing Up for Performance* (Pearson Merrill, 2007). He is also the General Editor of *The American Counseling Association Encyclopedia of Counseling* (ACA, 2009). His research specialization falls primarily in development and technical analysis of psycho-educational tests and has resulted in the publication of more than 70 refereed journal articles, 100 book chapters, and a dozen published tests. He was a representative to the ACA Governing Council and the ACA 20/20 Committee: A Vision for the Future of Counseling. He is a past president and past treasurer of AACE, past chair and parliamentarian of the American Counseling Association - Southern (US) Region; past-chair of ACA's Task Force on High Stakes Testing; past chair of ACA's Standards for Test Users Task Force; past chair of ACA's Interprofessional Committee; past chair of the ACA Public Awareness and Support Committee; chair of the Convention and past chair of the Screening Assessment Instruments Committees for AACE; past president of the Maryland Association for Counseling and Development (MACD); past president of Maryland Association for Measurement and Evaluation (MAME); past president of Maryland Association for Counselor Education and Supervision (MACES); and past president of the Maryland Association for Mental Health Counselors (MAMHC). He is a senior associate editor and past associate editor for quantitative research for the *Journal of Counseling & Development*. Dr. Erford has been a faculty member at Loyola since 1993 and is a Licensed Clinical Professional Counselor, Licensed Professional Counselor, Nationally Certified Counselor, Licensed Psychologist and Licensed School Psychologist. Prior to arriving at Loyola, he was a school psychologist/counselor in the Chesterfield County (VA) Public Schools. He maintains a private practice specializing in assessment and treatment of children and adolescents. A graduate of The University of Virginia (Ph.D.), Bucknell University (M.A.), and Grove City College (B.S.), he teaches courses in counseling assessment, lifespan development, research and evaluation in counseling, school counseling, and stress management (not that he needs it).

ABOUT THE AUTHORS

Jason Baker, PhD, LPC, is an associate professor and program coordinator of the master's program in school counseling in the Department of Psychology at Millersville University. He received his doctorate in counselor education and supervision from Regent University. His areas of research interest include rural school counseling, technology in counseling and counselor education, and sustainability efforts and issues in K-12 and higher education settings.

Gerta Bardhoshi PhD, CSC, LPC, is an assistant professor in the counselor education and supervision program in the Department of Rehabilitation and Counselor Education at the University of Iowa. She received her doctorate in counselor education and supervision from the George Washington University. Her areas of research pertain to counselor burnout, school counselor self-efficacy, and program development and evaluation.

Alan Basham, MA, is a retired counselor educator at Eastern Washington University, where he taught in CACREP-accredited school counseling and mental health counseling programs. He is past president of the Washington Counseling Association and the Association for Spiritual, Ethical and Religious Values in Counseling (ASERVIC), a division of the ACA. Alan has written chapters in several texts, co-authored a volume on leadership ethics and teamwork, drafted the ACA's Code of Leadership, and contributed to the ACA's position papers on High Stakes Testing and Test User Qualifications. He is especially interested in integrating spirituality into the counseling process, in applying Native American perspectives, and in creating support systems on university campuses for military veterans and their families as they adjust to college and civilian life.

Catherine Y. Chang, PhD, is an associate professor and program coordinator of the counselor education and practice doctoral program in the Department of Counseling and Psychological Services at Georgia State University. She received her doctorate in counselor education from The University of North Carolina at Greensboro. Her areas of research interest include multicultural counseling and supervision, professional and social advocacy in counseling, Asian and Korean concerns, and multicultural issues in assessment.

Joseph B. Cooper, PhD, LPC, NCC is an assistant professor in the department of counseling at Marymount University in Arlington, Virginia. He received his doctorate in counselor education from the University of North Carolina at Charlotte, and has over 16 years of experience providing individual, family, and group substance abuse and mental health counseling services in the agency, school, and private practice settings. His current research interests include attachment theory, intensive short-term dynamic psychotherapy, and neurophysiology. He maintains a private practice in Washington, DC, and is a guest faculty member for the intensive short-term dynamic psychotherapy program at the Washington School of Psychiatry.

Charlotte Daughhetee, PhD, is a professor of counseling at the University of Montevallo and serves as the Chair of the Counseling, Family Consumer Sciences, & Kinesiology Department. She received her B.S in Early Childhood Education from Indiana University in 1980, her M.Ed. in Counseling from the University of South Carolina in 1988 and her Ph.D. in Counselor Education from the University of South Carolina in 1992. She is a Licensed Professional Counselor (LPC), Licensed Marriage and Family Therapist (LMFT) and a National Certified Counselor (NCC) with over 27 years of clinical counseling experience. She has worked in K12, university, and private practice settings with clients of all ages. Her research interests include counselor trainee evaluation and crisis intervention.

Grafton T. Eliason, EdD, LPC, NCC, is a professor in the Department of Counselor Education at California University of Pennsylvania. He has published on the topics of career counseling, death, dying, and spirituality, and has a special interest in existential philosophy and religion. He received his doctorate in counselor education and supervision from Duquesne University, and he is an ordained Presbyterian minister.

Nadine E. Garner, EdD, LPC, is an associate professor in the Psychology Department and graduate program coordinator of the School Counseling program at Millersville University of Pennsylvania. She is co-author of *A School with Solutions: Implementing a Solution-focused/Adlerian-based Comprehensive School Counseling Program*. Dr. Garner provides training in solution-focused counseling to counselors and educators both nationally and abroad. She also consults with school districts that seek to implement a solution-focused approach into their comprehensive developmental counseling curriculum. As a former K–12 professional school counselor at Scotland School for Veterans' Children, Dr. Garner developed a comprehensive conflict resolution/peer mediation program.

Donna M. Gibson, PhD, LPC, NCC, completed her doctorate in counseling and counselor education at the University of North Carolina at Greensboro and is an associate professor in the counselor education programs at the University of South Carolina. She has served as Member-at-Large for Membership and President of AACE. Her research interests include pedagogical issues in teaching assessment, K–12 career assessment, leadership in school counseling and counselor education, professional identity development in counseling and counselor education, and relational/cultural theory.

Geneva M. Gray, PhD, LPC, is an assistant professor at Argosy University–Atlanta Campus. She received her doctoral degree in Counselor Education and Practice from Georgia State University in 2007. She is a licensed professional counselor in Georgia and provides clinical services for children, adolescents, and families. She has completed research in the areas of addictions, LGBT issues in counseling, and multiculturalism. In addition, Dr. Gray served as past president and past-secretary of the International Association for Addiction and Offender Counselors (IAAOC).

Judith Harrington, PhD, LPC, LMFT, is an assistant professor at the University of Montevallo, AL, and also in full time private practice for 30 years in Birmingham, AL, providing counseling and consultation to individual, couples & families, groups and agencies. She is an approved trainer for assessing and managing suicidal risk curriculum for mental health professionals on behalf of the Suicide Prevention Resource Center at SAMHSA and the American Association of Suicidology. Since 2008, she has instructed the graduate counselor education curriculum on suicide for the University of Alabama at Birmingham and the University of Montevallo. She served for five years on the Standards, Training, and Practices Committee for the National Suicide Prevention Lifeline at SAMHSA. She has served the suicidally bereaved community by facilitating the SOS Bereavement Group for 14 years, and was the first- and twice-elected president of the nonprofit Alabama Suicide Prevention and Resources Coalition (ASPARC). Her state and ASPARC was awarded a three year Garrett Lee Smith Youth Suicide Prevention grant for which, among its many initiatives, she developed the Comprehensive Suicide Prevention Resource Directory for mental health professionals and concerned citizens, found at www.legacy.montevallo.edu.

Molly E. Jones is a graduate student in the School Counseling M.Ed. and certification programs at Millersville University of PA and the graduate assistant for the School

Counseling program and the Center for Sustainability. She holds an undergraduate degree in Psychology from Elizabethtown College

Lynn E. Linde, EdD, is the Senior Director of Professional Affairs at the American Counseling Association. She formerly was the Coordinator of Clinical Experiences in the school counseling program at Loyola University Maryland. She received her doctorate in counseling from The George Washington University. She is a former Branch Chief for Pupil Services at the Maryland State Department of Education. She was the 2009–2010 President of the American Counseling Association and 2012–2103 Treasurer. She was the Southern Region representative to the ACA Governing Council, Past Chair of the ACA–Southern Region, and Past President of the Maryland Association for Counseling and Development, and has served on numerous committees and task forces, including the 2014 ACA Ethics Revision Task Force. She is an ACA Fellow, a recipient of the Carl Perkins Award, and a number of awards from ACA, its entities, and from the State of Maryland.

Amy L. McLeod, PhD, LPC, NCC, is an assistant professor and co-director of training in the Counseling Department at Argosy University–Atlanta. Her research interests include multicultural issues in counselor education and supervision, assessment and diagnosis, women's issues, and crisis and trauma counseling.

Amy Milsom, DEd, NCC, LPC-S, is an associate professor at Clemson University. She earned her doctorate from Pennsylvania State University and is a former middle and high school counselor. Her primary research interests are in the areas of students with disabilities, postsecondary transitions and college readiness, and school counselor preparation.

Donna S. Sheperis, earned her PhD in counselor education from the University of Mississippi. A core faculty member in the mental health counseling program of Lamar University, Dr. Sheperis is a licensed professional counselor, national certified counselor, and approved clinical supervisor with more than 20 years of experience in community counseling and private practice settings. Her primary areas of interest include counselor development, ethics, and supervision.

Ann Vernon, PhD, NCC, LMHC, is professor emeritus and former coordinator of counseling at the University of Northern Iowa; she is also a counselor in private practice, where she works extensively with children, adolescents, and their parents. Dr. Vernon is the former director of the Midwest Center for REBT and vice president of the Albert Ellis Board of Trustees. She is the author of numerous texts, chapters, and articles, including *Thinking, Feeling, Behaving* and *What Works When with Children and Adolescents*.

Joshua C. Watson, PhD, LPC, NCC, ACS, completed his doctoral study at the University of North Carolina at Greensboro and is an associate professor in the counselor education program at Texas A&M University–Corpus Christi, with primary teaching responsibilities in assessment and educational statistics courses. His research interests include counseling student-athletes, wellness, and counselor-training issues. He is a past president of the Association for Assessment in Counseling and Education (AACE) and ACA Governing Council representative.

Mark A. Young, PhD, LMHC, NCC, completed his doctorate at Idaho State University and is currently an assistant professor and director of the marriage and family counseling program at Gonzaga University. His teaching and research interests are in couples and family counseling, supervision, and professional development.

Foundations of Professional Counselor Identity

Section One, "Foundations of Professional Counselor Identity," provides an in-depth look at the foundational issues in counseling, covering historical and future issues, professional identity, associations, credentialing, and legal and ethical dimensions of practice. Chapter 1, "Becoming a Professional Counselor: Philosophical, Historical, and Future Considerations," explores the definition and philosophical underpinnings of the terms *counseling* and *professional counselor*. Key to this understanding is the development of a firm foundation in the knowledge of the numerous historical events and key people that gave rise to the counseling profession. Important issues facing counselors as the profession moves into the future are identified and discussed, including outcomes-based research, managed care, multiculturalism, social justice counseling and advocacy, technology, and gatekeeping. Finally, wellness practices within the counseling profession are given a special focus.

In Chapter 2, "Professional Counseling Organizations, Licensure, Certification, and Accreditation," students are introduced to the American Counseling Association (ACA) and its divisions, branches, and professional partners so that students can become familiar with the wide array of professional associations advocating for counselors and clients. This chapter offers a glimpse of the many credentials that professional counselors can earn. An overview of state licensure, national certification, and counselor education program accreditation processes (i.e., CACREP and CORE) is provided to answer student questions early and to make students aware of the choices that exist for future professional credentialing. Various accountability mechanisms found at the state level for educational systems and mental health agencies are also reviewed.

Section One ends with Chapter 3, "Ethical and Legal Issues in Counseling." The chapter is a comprehensive introduction to ethical and legal issues in counseling practice, covering new editions of the ACA and ASCA ethical codes, confidentiality, privilege, subpoenas, malpractice, records and personal notes, child abuse, suicide, HIPAA, FERPA, minor consent, and ethical decision making. A professional counselor must always remember that how one conducts oneself personally and professionally reflects not only on oneself, but also on one's colleagues.

1

Becoming a Professional Counselor

Philosophical, Historical, and Future Considerations

BRADLEY T. ERFORD AND GERTA BARDHOSHI

PREVIEW

This initial chapter explores the definition and philosophical underpinnings of the terms *counseling* and *professional counselor*. Development of a firm foundation in the numerous historical events and key individuals who gave rise to the counseling profession is vital to understanding it. Important issues facing professional counselors as the profession moves into the future are identified and discussed, including outcome-based research, licensure portability, managed care, multiculturalism, social justice, technology, and gatekeeping. Finally, a section on counselor wellness addresses important self-care practices for optimizing personal and professional functioning.

COUNSELING AND PROFESSIONAL COUNSELORS: WHERE WE ARE

A thorough understanding of the counseling profession's origin and historical progression provides a framework within which the counseling student can increase his or her identification with the profession, gain a sense of pride in the profession, develop an identity as a professional counselor, understand where that identity fits within the professional circles, and be armed with knowledge necessary to advocate for the profession. Perhaps even more important, this understanding ensures the next generation of professional counselors will continue to move forward, not mistaking innovation for history; will anticipate how events will impact the profession; and will be likely to make important contributions to the profession.

In the 1990s, authors (e.g., Gladding, 1996; Heppner et al., 1995) warned that the field of counseling could cease as a specialty or become obsolete if specialization and preparedness did not advance in step with society's needs. Understanding the history of counseling along with its current status seems an appropriate and necessary place to begin, and no better way exists to gain such awareness than first to understand where they came from and how they arrived at this place. A profession without a known history lacks direction and trajectory, and for this reason, counseling students and new professionals must gain a complete understanding of the profession they have chosen. This chapter discusses what counseling is today, the philosophy underlying counseling, the history of the profession, current trends within the field, and the importance of wellness and counselor self-care.

Before delving into the past, a look at the counseling profession's current status, meaning, and philosophy is warranted. While the practice of offering counsel has probably always occurred in some fashion in human society, counseling as a distinct helping profession is relatively new when compared to other mental health disciplines. In addition, the general public, as well as professional counselors, is often perplexed by and has difficulty ascertaining the true meaning, purpose, and intention of what counseling is, what it is not, and how it differs from other closely related helping professions.

The meaning of counseling can be ambiguous for several reasons. First, the word *counseling* has been used broadly to refer to everything from financial consultants and lawyers to home designers and wedding planners. Second, the word has carried different connotations over the years, even within the counseling profession. Finally, the word *counseling* describes many different activities a counselor actually does (e.g., educate, coordinate, advocate, assess). For the sake of clarity, counseling is defined as specific, specialized, and distinguishable from other mental health disciplines by its philosophy, its evolution, and its focus.

About a half century ago, the purpose of a counselor was said "to facilitate wise choices and decisions" or "to promote adjustment or mental health" (Tyler, 1969, p. 10). Clearly, two agendas were represented. This is because counseling largely evolved from the guidance movement and actively differentiated itself from psychotherapy. Historically, **guidance** referred to guiding or helping others make choices about vocation, lifestyle, or education. In contrast, **psychotherapy** assumed a medical model, meaning the person receiving help was somehow ill. The goal of psychotherapy was to alleviate the sickness, with the therapist as expert using information about the client's past to provide insight into thoughts previously kept out of awareness. As can be seen even in this brief discussion, guidance and psychotherapy were concerned with very different things (pro-developmental and remedial, respectively), though they had much in common as well. From these two agendas, modern counseling evolved, its roots grounded in both foundations while its boughs reached into new therapeutic directions. Table 1.1 provides some distinctions between the modern conceptions of counseling and psychotherapy.

The Association for Specialists in Group Work (2007) provides a helpful differentiation between definitions of counseling and psychotherapy in the group work context that carries over nicely to work with individual clients and families. Psychotherapy involves an in-depth, long-term commitment (i.e., 12–50+ sessions) requiring advanced therapeutic training and expertise and addressing serious, long-term, and enduring conditions, such

TABLE 1.1 Historical Distinctions Between *Counseling* and *Psychotherapy*

Psychotherapy	Counseling
Long-term (up to 2 years)	Short-term (less than 6 months)
Medical model	Wellness model
Alleviate symptoms	Improve quality of life
Past is most important	Focus on the here and now
Goal of insight	Goal of change
Therapist as expert	Counselor as collaborator

as personality disorders, complicated bereavement, sexual abuse, and other significant trauma (Erford, 2011). In contrast, counseling applies a process-oriented, theoretically based approach (e.g., humanistic-existential, cognitive-behavioral, psychodynamic, systemic) to address cognitive, affective, and behavioral changes jointly agreed to by the client and counselor, and is usually time-limited (e.g., 6–25 sessions in clinics; 2–10 sessions in schools). Counseling addresses client knowledge and skill needs in areas such as changing family issues, grief and loss, and adjustment to normal developmental challenges. A further helpful contrast is that psychotherapy is entrenched in the medical model, which views the client as ill and the goal of therapy to cure the illness. Counseling focuses on developmental and wellness approaches to help clients cope and compensate for developmental challenges and hurdles, thus redirecting the client's developmental life course in order to attain and maintain wellness. Hopefully, attaining and maintaining wellness will prevent further similar challenges. It is essential for professional counselors to understand the differences between psychotherapy and counseling and between the medical and wellness models so they are better able to express, convey, and advocate for the counseling profession. It is unhelpful to use the terms psychotherapy and counseling synonymously.

In 2005, a collaborative effort among 31 counseling organizations was begun. The effort was called 20/20: A Vision for the Future of Counseling. The 20/20 committee provided the following definition of counseling: "**Counseling** is a professional relationship that empowers diverse individuals, families, and groups to accomplish mental health, wellness, education, and career goals" (American Counseling Association [ACA], 2017). Converging on this definition was no easy task. Bradley T. Erford was a member of the 20/20 Committee and often jokes that it took 31 counseling leaders 24 months to craft a 21-word definition of counseling. In the end, the group converged on a definition that encapsulated what they believed composed the core or essence of counseling. Still, only 29 of the 31 organizations approved adoption of the definition of counseling.

Embedded within this definition, and the broader practice of professional-counseling licensure and certification laws and regulations, are five important elements:

1. Counseling is a profession that requires graduate-level education; necessitates adherence to ethical standards; and encourages licensure, certification, and organizational membership and involvement.
2. Counseling is holistic and concerns itself with treating the entire person—without stepping outside one's area of competence.
3. Counseling focuses on relatively healthy functioning individuals who are experiencing difficulty.
4. Counseling is empirically driven and based on theoretically sound underpinnings and interventions.
5. Counseling involves the facilitation of behavioral, cognitive, and emotional change.

In addition to agreeing on the definition of counseling, the 20/20 committee also gained consensus on issues to advance the counseling profession, deal with strengthening professional identity, present as one profession, develop a licensure portability system, promote client welfare, improve the public perception of the counseling profession, improve the research support for counseling, and focus on counseling students and prospective students.

Counseling also includes various areas of specialty that draw on a refined and advanced accrual of knowledge acquired after the general requirements of a professional counselor's education are met. Specialties under the counseling umbrella include school counseling, college counseling, career counseling, mental health or community counseling, marriage and family counseling, rehabilitation counseling, addictions and offender counseling, and gerontological counseling (American Counseling Association, 2018a).

According to the U.S. Department of Labor's *Occupational Outlook Handbook* (2014), in 2012 there were 635,700 counselors in the United States. Within the field of counseling, subspecialty areas were dispersed as follows: 262,300 school and career counselors; 117,500 rehabilitation counselors; 166,300 mental health counselors and marriage and family therapists; and 89,600 substance-abuse and behavioral-disorder counselors. This compares to 607,300 social workers and about 160,000 psychologists.

How Do Counselors Differ from Psychologists and Social Workers?

As will become clearer in the historical overview later in this chapter, counseling shares a common history with psychology. Many of the theories and techniques professional counselors use to help clients and students meet personal, social, career, and academic counseling goals are the same as those used by psychologists. The emergence of counseling psychology within the field of psychology led to the subsequent emergence of mental health counseling.

The primary differences lie in education and training. Ordinarily, the practice of psychology requires a doctoral degree, whereas the practice of counseling requires a master's degree. That said, much of the basic coursework at the master's level is very similar in psychology and counseling programs. Although similarities in the professions' basic foundations exist, recognized differences in the education and training of these two similar, yet distinct, professions are also present. Because of this, distinctions in practice can frequently be observed as well. Most noticeable is that psychologists tend to focus more heavily on testing and assessment, longer-term psychotherapy, and more serious emotional and personality disorders.

Some of the clinical training for psychologists is usually conducted in an inpatient setting to help psychology trainees gain experience in the treatment of severe psychiatric disorders. While some of the training counselors receive is equivalent to that received by many psychologists, the focus of counselor training is usually approached from a developmental or wellness path—hence the term *mental health counselor*—as opposed to pathology. Finally, both counselors and psychologists are licensed by state regulatory agencies.

Social work and counseling also share many commonalities. In fact, social workers in many ways blazed the trail for counselors in state licensure. For example, licensed clinical social workers (LCSWs) were able to pass state laws and regulations recognizing their title and practice at the master's level years before counselors. In addition, the recent focus among professional counselors on social justice and client advocacy has traditionally been a prominent role of social workers. Although the clinical skills of social workers are in many ways equivalent to professional counselors and psychologists, the training of social workers focuses more heavily on identifying systemic barriers to client success and identifying and accessing resources that will help clients overcome those barriers. Social workers, psychologists, and professional counselors all provide individual and group interventions to clients in private practice, community agencies, and, in many states, schools. Thus, in many ways these three behavioral health professions share common education and training standards, and also practice in similar manners.

Each of these vocations has its own professional associations and licensing boards that advocate on behalf of relevant issues and strive to protect the public. The American Counseling Association (ACA) advocates on behalf of counselors. The American Psychological Association (APA) supports psychologists, and the National Association for Social Work (NASW) champions social workers. That being said, in many states the practices of professional counselors, social workers, and marriage and family therapists are regulated by the same board (e.g., trilateral board). Indeed, common factors research across disciplines shows that the professional practice behaviors among professional counselors, marriage and family therapists/counselors, social workers, and psychologists look very similar, and the approaches and interventions used by these professionals result in very similar outcomes and degrees of effectiveness. Today, counselors often work as members of interdisciplinary teams alongside other mental health professionals to holistically advocate for, diagnose, and treat clients.

THE PHILOSOPHICAL UNDERPINNINGS OF COUNSELING

Despite the similarities in training and practice, the field of counseling continues to distinguish itself separately. The values and beliefs of the counseling profession are distinct aspects that segregate it from other helping professions. In some ways, the philosophy of counseling has changed less than any of the profession's other facets throughout its history. First articulated by Remley (1992) and later documented and expanded on by Hershenson, Power, and Waldo (2003) and Remley and Herlihy (2016), several underlying philosophical assumptions characterize and unite the counseling profession: approaches that emphasize wellness, normal human development, empowerment, and prevention.

Within a **wellness perspective**, the goal of counseling is not just to relieve the client of problematic symptoms (i.e., the medical model, which focuses on curing symptoms), but rather to strive for optimal functioning and health in life. Maslow (1968) referred to this as the process of **self-actualizing**, whereas Rogers (1961) described it as a process of becoming **fully functioning**. Regardless of the phrasing used, both terms focus on striving for a state of satisfaction and reaching one's full potential, instead of on meeting immediate needs and alleviating symptoms. Myers, Sweeney, and Witmer (2000) discussed the use of such a wellness model in counseling and offered the following as areas of concentration within a wellness perspective: **spirituality** (e.g., belief in a higher power, optimism, purpose, worship or meditation, values, and transcendence); self-direction (e.g., worthiness, mastery, rational beliefs, coping, problem solving, creativity, humor, health, self-care, identity); work and leisure; friendship; and love. Through these areas of focus, professional counselors assist clients in striving for their own wellness.

THINK ABOUT IT 1.1

If you were to evaluate yourself in each of these areas of wellness, what improvements might you need to make to truly begin to move toward wellness?

A **developmental perspective** is the second characteristic underlying the basic premise and philosophy of counseling. Professional counselors understand the issues clients bring to the counseling relationship within a human developmental framework. What this means is that many of the problems viewed as pathological by other helping professionals are instead viewed by professional counselors as (a) normal responses to abnormal events, (b) abnormal reactions to normal events, or (c) transitory issues in response to change (Remley & Herlihy, 2016). It is because of this difference in perspective that counselors' approach to treatment is sometimes different from what might otherwise be used by clinicians using a pathology-based model.

Within developmental coursework provided to counselors in training, the timing-of-events model states that reactions to events and change depend heavily on whether the change was expected during that developmental phase of life. Events that occur as expected are considered **on time**, whereas events that occur earlier or later than expected or perhaps not at all are considered **off time**. Crises might result from the unexpected timing of events (Papalia, Feldman, & Martorelli, 2012). For instance, for many individuals, a pregnancy could be a happy and planned event, whereas for a high school student, it might spur a crisis. Similarly, the death of a parent is an event most people experience at some point in their lives. However, for an 8-year-old boy, this event would have additional repercussions because it occurred much earlier than typically expected.

A third focus unique to the counseling philosophy is that of **empowerment**, which is aligned closely with the emerging paradigm of client advocacy (see Chapter 15). Because counselors work within a developmental model, realizing that many issues presented in counseling are normal and temporary, and because wellness is emphasized, professional counselors encourage and foster independence of the client from the helping relationship by teaching clients self-advocacy. In this way, clients can gain the confidence to navigate their future lives and problems without becoming dependent on the counselor each time a new issue arises. **Empowerment** is defined as follows:

> The process by which people, organizations, or groups who are powerless (a) become aware of the power dynamics at work in their life context, (b) develop the skills and capacity for gaining some reasonable control over their lives, (c) exercise this control without infringing upon the rights of others, and (d) support the empowerment of others in their community. (McWhirter, 1991, p. 224)

Empowerment begins within the therapeutic relationship as the professional counselor alters the power differential between counselor and client in such a way that the client becomes an equal partner in the helping process. What occurs within the counseling setting becomes transferable and generalizable to the world outside the counseling setting, helping clients to gain a sense of control over their own lives. At a minimum, professional counselors have a basic understanding that clients are the experts of their own lives and are capable and responsible enough to develop the necessary skills to live independently (Remley & Herlihy, 2016). In some ways related to empowerment, professional counselors also focus on social and client advocacy, multicultural sensitivity, and multicultural counseling competence in our global society. These topics will be addressed in great detail in subsequent chapters of this book.

A tenet of systems theory is that individuals do not operate independently from their environments (Gladding, 2016). Thus, not only does the individual influence the environment, but the environment also influences the individual. Therefore, problems presented for counseling must be viewed within the larger scope and context of the client's worldview. Professional counselors make every effort to understand and conceptualize a client's issues with respect to that client's political, social, familial, and economic context, because these variables surely influence the client's current state. However, the professional counselor does not place blame or responsibility for the client's presenting concerns on these environmental factors; rather, the counselor encourages the client to take responsibility for change within that system.

One final note regarding the philosophy of counseling: Counseling is proactive and preventive, often through education and resources provided to the community. When intervention is necessary, it is preferable that it occur during the early stages of the problem. Because professional counselors believe everyone can benefit from counseling, they also believe individuals experiencing even mild distress should seek help rather than wait until the distress evolves into a true crisis. This belief contributes to the overall wellness perspective rather than advocating for a model of pathology. In essence, the professional counselor understands the client from a developmental model and in relation to his or her environment, works toward wellness, prefers prevention or early intervention, and attempts to empower the client and teach the client how to advocate for his or her current and future needs.

THINK ABOUT IT 1.2

If you could change one thing about the philosophy of counseling, what would you change? How might this one change affect the course of history and the profession as we know it today?

HOW WE GOT HERE: PEOPLE, ISSUES, AND SOCIETAL FORCES THAT HAVE SHAPED THE COUNSELING PROFESSION

Throughout history, every society has found methods beyond the family to provide direction and support to its members as they struggled with questions of who they were or might become. In some instances, the individuals who delivered such guidance were philosophers, physicians, priests, medicine men, or teachers (Erford, 2015a). Before the 1900s, most guidance took the form of giving advice or imparting knowledge. However, with social reform, population changes, educational concerns, and the rise of industrialization came the birth of a profession known as counseling. While the historical events influencing the counseling profession are numerous, only some of the most important events are discussed in detail here and in subsequent chapters. As a supplement, Table 1.2 provides a time line and brief notice of these and other historical events important to understanding the counseling profession's genesis and development. Although not all these people and events are discussed in the text because of space considerations, each has influenced the direction of the counseling profession.

1900–1920

In the late 1800s and early 1900s, the United States was transitioning from a national economy based, in general, on agriculture to an economy increasingly based on manufacturing and industrial processes. As this transition ensued, urbanization and occupational diversity increased, as did national concerns about strengthening industrial education as a way

TABLE 1.2 Counseling Time Line

1907	Jesse B. Davis introduced the first guidance course as part of the school curriculum.
1908	Frank Parsons founded the Vocational Bureau of the Civic Services House.
1908	Clifford Whittingham Beers authored *A Mind That Found Itself,* changing societal attitudes about the mentally ill.
1909	Parsons's *Choosing a Vocation* was published following his death one year earlier.
1909	The Binet-Simon Scale was translated into English.
1909	Sigmund Freud was invited to the United States to present his ideas on neurosis.
1913	The National Vocational Guidance Association, the first counseling association, was founded.
1914	World War I began, and psychological instruments were used for screening purposes.
1917	The Smith-Hughes Act provided funding for vocational education in schools.
1917	Army Alpha and Army Beta tests were designed for the military.
1921	Hermann Rorschach published his projective inkblot test.
1921	Child-guidance clinics were created.
1922	Alfred Adler began using collective counseling, or group therapy.
1927	The Strong Vocational Interest Blank was developed by Edward K. Strong, Jr.
1929	The Great Depression began after the stock market crashed.
1929	The first family and marriage counseling center opened in New York City.
1930s	E. G. Williamson developed the first theory of counseling based on the work of Parsons.
1935	Henry Murray and Christiana Morgan developed the Thematic Apperception Test (TAT).
1935	Alcoholics Anonymous was founded.
1937	Recovery Inc., a self-help group focused on mental illness, was founded.
1938	O. K. Buros published Volume 1 of *Mental Measurements Yearbook*.
1939	The first edition of the *Dictionary of Occupational Titles* (DOT) was published.
1939	The Wechsler-Bellevue Intelligence Scale was introduced.
1939	World War II began in Europe, and counselors were widely used for military classification, screening, and treatment.
1940s	Certification of school counselors was established.
1940	Otto Rank, Alfred Adler, Karen Horney, Erich Fromm, Erik Erikson, and Victor Frankl immigrated to the United States to escape Nazi persecution.
1940	The Minnesota Multiphasic Personality Inventory (MMPI) was published.
1942	Carl Rogers published *Counseling and Psychotherapy,* introducing client-centered therapy.
1946	The National Mental Health Act was introduced.
1948	The first *Occupational Outlook Handbook* was published.
1949	The Graduate Record Exam (GRE) was published.
1949	The Wechsler Intelligence Scale for Children (WISC) was published.
1950	Theory development began to flourish, including systematic desensitization, rational-emotive therapy, transactional analysis, and career development.
1952	The American Personnel and Guidance Association (APGA; which would become the ACA) was formed.
1953	The American School Counselor Association (ASCA) joined APGA as a division.
1957	The Soviet Union (Russia) launched Sputnik, spurring the creation of the National Defense Education Act (NDEA) the following year.

1958	The American Rehabilitation Counseling Association (ARCA) was chartered.
1960s	Existentialism, family systems, and cognitive theories became popular.
1962	C. Gilbert Wrenn, in *The Counselor in a Changing World,* introduced the concept of the culturally encapsulated counselor.
1963	The Community Mental Health Centers Act was enacted, making it possible to build and staff many mental health centers across the United States.
1964	The APGA recommended a branch be formed in every state.
1964	The Civil Rights Act was passed.
1965	The Association for Assessment and Research in Counseling (AARC) was chartered.
1966	The National Employment Counseling Association (NECA) was chartered.
1966	The Education Resources Information Center (ERIC) Clearinghouse was established.
1967	The APA legislation committee proposed a restriction on who could provide counseling.
1972	The Association for Multicultural Counseling and Development (AMCD) was chartered.
1972	The International Association of Addictions and Offender Counselors (IAAOC) was chartered.
1973	The Association for Specialists in Group Work (ASGW) was chartered.
1973	The Southern Association for Counselor Education and Supervision (SACES) established the first counselor licensure committee.
1974	The Association for Spiritual, Ethical, and Religious Values in Counseling (ASERVIC) was chartered.
1974	Congress passed the Family Educational Rights and Privacy Act (FERPA).
1974	The APGA adopted the position paper "Counselor Licensure: Position Statement," calling for licensure legislation efforts in all 50 states.
1974	The American Rehabilitation Counseling Association (ARCA) certified rehabilitation counselors.
1975	Congress passed the Education for All Handicapped Children Act (Public Law 94-142).
1975	Virginia passed the first regulatory act for professional counselors.
1976	The Career Education Incentive Act was provided for career education within schools.
1978	The American Mental Health Counselors Association (AMHCA) was chartered.
1979	The AMHCA certified mental health counselors.
1979	Arkansas passed the second licensure law; Alabama became the third state to achieve licensure.
1983	The American Personnel and Guidance Association (APGA) changed its name to the American Association for Counseling and Development (AACD).
1983	The National Board for Certified Counselors (NBCC) was established.
1984	The Association for Counselors and Educators in Government (ACEG) was chartered.
1986	The Association for Adult Development and Aging (AADA) was chartered.
1989	The International Association of Marriage and Family Counselors (IAMFC) was chartered.
1990	The Americans with Disabilities Act was passed.
1991	The American College Counseling Association (ACCA) was chartered.
1992	The American Association for Counseling and Development (AACD) changed its name to the American Counseling Association (ACA).
1994	More than 19,000 counselors held National Certified Counselor (NCC) certification.

(Continued)

TABLE 1.2 Counseling Time Line (*continued*)

1996	The Association for Gay, Lesbian, and Bisexual Issues in Counseling (AGLBIC) was chartered.
1997	The ACA Governing Council developed a cohesive definition of counseling.
2001	More than 31,000 counselors held National Certified Counselor (NCC) certification.
2002	The Counselors for Social Justice (CSJ) was chartered.
2003	The ASCA published the *ASCA National Model: A Framework for School Counseling Programs.*
2004	The Association for Creativity in Counseling (ACC) was chartered.
2006	The 20/20 committee, 20/20: A Vision for the Future of Counseling, convened for the first time.
2007	Nevada became the 49th state to license professional counselors.
2009	California became the final state to pass a state licensure law.
2010	The Affordable Care Act was signed into law.
2011	The definition of counseling was endorsed by the counseling organizations composing the 20/20 committee.
2014	The Veterans Administration and TRICARE approved independent practice of licensed counselors.
2014	Ohio became the first state to require graduation from a Council for Accreditation of Counseling and Related Educational Programs (CACREP)-accredited clinical mental health counseling program as a condition for counseling licensure.
2015	CACREP and Council on Rehabilitation Education (CORE) announced merger.

to prepare young people to enter the growing opportunities in the workforce. Such goals effectively required the dissemination of information about how people could identify and gain access to emerging jobs. During this time, particularly in urban areas, such information was so differentiated and comprehensive that families and local neighborhoods could no longer be the primary sources of occupational information or the allocation of jobs. More formal mechanisms, including vocational guidance in schools, became necessary (Erford, 2015a).

Societal changes also were occurring regarding views on mental illness. In the late 1800s, a widespread belief claimed that heredity irrevocably determined each individual's fate. Because of this assumption, healthy members of society endorsed containing individuals who were dubbed mentally ill rather than providing "futile" attempts at treatment. However, this established way of thinking gradually began to shift, and mentally ill individuals came to be viewed with consideration of their environment and social context.

Three events within three years led three individuals to separately emerge as leaders and innovators in the development of counseling. In 1907, a school superintendent named **Jesse B. Davis** made a suggestion that was quite progressive for his time. He felt strongly that his teachers should provide a lesson each week focusing on character, problem solving, and prevention in an effort to restore the moral fiber of American society. To facilitate this change, he designated 117 English teachers as vocational counselors (Gladding, 2016).

One year later, a Yale graduate named **Clifford Whittingham** Beers (1908) recounted his time as a patient in a mental health facility:

> I soon observed that the only patients who were not likely to be subjected to abuse were the very ones least in need of care and treatment. The violent, noisy, and troublesome patient was abused because he was violent, noisy, and troublesome. The patient too weak, physically or mentally, to attend to his own wants was frequently abused because of that very helplessness. (p. 116)

Containing this and other horrendous and compelling statements, *A Mind That Found Itself* (Beers, 1908) unequivocally provided the incentive for the **mental-hygiene movement**. This movement was pivotal in shifting society's view of the mentally ill from irrevocably sick individuals to individuals in need of help. The movement helped society focus on early intervention, prevention, and more humane treatment options for people who were mentally ill. Beers purposefully set out to use his written accounts to bring about such a change in societal attitudes. Through affiliations with wealthy and influential individuals, he also created reform through organization and legislation, leading to the establishment of the National Mental Health Association in 1909.

THINK ABOUT IT 1.3

If Clifford Whittingham Beers were committed to an inpatient psychiatric hospital today, how would his experience differ from his experience as a patient in 1903?

Around the same time, a lawyer, teacher, social worker, and engineer amalgamated into one man who became best known as a social reformer. **Frank Parsons**, considered the father of the American guidance movement, was many things before he became the founder of the Vocational Bureau of Boston in 1908, where he served as a vocational counselor and director. He believed growth and prevention were necessary for social reform, and in May 1908, Parsons presented a lecture on his idea for systematic guidance. A few months later, he died, leaving his most important written work, *Choosing a Vocation*, to be published the following year (Tang & Erford, 2016). This book, combined with Parsons' ideas and work while alive, set forth the framework that later became the basis for personality psychology's trait theory, a theory focused on measuring one's personality traits and abilities to better understand which careers might best suit that person.

According to Parsons, when an understanding of one's capabilities and interests is paired with knowledge and facts about different vocations, ideal choices of vocation become evident. In other words, Parsons was the first to propose that to be happy and successful in a particular career, a person must consider one's interests and skills and take into account the qualifications and compensation for the preferred line of work in order to make an informed and rational decision. Together, these three men—Jesse B. Davis, Clifford Whittingham Beers, and Frank Parsons—changed the meaning and formation of mental health care and guidance. Their influence ultimately resulted in the development of the counseling profession.

While great strides were taking place in guidance and mental health care to ultimately form the counseling profession, the field of psychology was advancing as well. Specifically, psychologists were progressing in their understanding of human behavior. Before the turn of the century, **Sigmund Freud**, an Austrian originally trained as a neurologist, began publishing his observations from a single case study. In 1909, Freud was invited to the United States to present his ideas on neurosis at various universities. However, strong resistance to his ideas prevented the inclusion of his work in textbooks for years to come.

Meanwhile, psychology was becoming a social science. In the late 1800s Germany, Wilhelm Wundt was credited with developing the first experimental psychology laboratory, and **William James** modified Wundt's design and incorporated it into practice in the United States. James was interested in the whole person, cognitively, affectively, and behaviorally, and used a laboratory-type setting to gain insight into the reasons for human behavior. Around this time other psychologists, such as G. Stanley Hall, Burrhus Frederic (B. F.) Skinner, and Max Wertheimer, were also crafting their own approaches to understanding how individuals developed and behaved, stressing the importance of gaining knowledge and developing theory through observation and scientific inquiry. Notably, each of these pioneers used the scientific method to gain knowledge in the field and create the scientific underpinnings for a new discipline of study in human behavior.

Not only did Wundt inspire James, but Wundt also influenced the field through his work in measurement, which established data collection as a norm in the field. By evaluating the reaction times of children to various stimuli and standardizing experimental procedures, Wundt contributed greatly to the measurement movement. **James Cattell** became interested in measurable differences between individuals while studying under Wundt. Upon returning to the United States, similar to William James, Cattell incorporated and expanded on what he had learned in Germany. The term *mental test* was first used by Cattell, and he was the first to focus on measuring mental abilities and intelligence. Although Cattell did much to give impetus to the measurement movement, especially as it applied to measuring mental abilities, the first true intelligence test was not published until 1905—hence the term *the 1905 scale*. It is also known as the Binet-Simon Scale, which was later translated, revised, and published in the United States as the Stanford-Binet.

While the Stanford-Binet certainly contributed to the testing (measurement) movement, the need for measuring the emotional and intellectual abilities and deficiencies of large groups of people became most obvious as World War I began. Nearly 1.5 million people needed classification to enter and serve in the U.S. armed services. This need gave rise to the development of large-scale psychological measurement instruments, a process known as psychometrics. Specifically, the Army Alpha and Army Beta tests were developed. The Army Alpha tested English-speaking recruits who could read, and the Army Beta tested illiterate and non-English-speaking recruits. The use of such large-scale testing services created a need for more clinicians equipped to administer and interpret the tests; these individuals later became known as **psychometrists**.

The decade leading up to 1920 included several additional events that have a unique place in the history of counseling and therefore deserve mention. First, in 1913, the National Vocational Guidance Association (NVGA) was founded and, within two years, began publishing a bulletin that would later become the flagship journal for the entire profession of counseling. This bulletin, after several changes in title and focus, became what is now known as the *Journal of Counseling & Development* (since 1984).

The role of the U.S. federal government, in relation to guidance and mental health, has at times been instrumental to the counseling profession. In addition to the government's commissioning of psychological testing for would-be members of the armed services, the Smith-Hughes Act of 1917 established grants to support vocational education in public schools and counselor-training departments at major universities (Zunker, 2015).

Finally, group-counseling formats had already proven their usefulness before 1920. Group counseling was being used in hospitals to aid similarly diagnosed medical patients, in schools to assist in vocational decision making, and with immigrants to assist with adjustment to American culture (Erford, 2011).

1921–1940

As the United States came into crisis, the guidance movement continued to gain acceptance and become more widely used. Simultaneously, the movement came under scrutiny when it became obvious that its focus was too narrow to meet all the needs of society. During the Great Depression (1929 1940), a time of massive unemployment and economic hardship, desperation surrounded the search for employment. At the same time, the very aspect of guidance that had helped to promote and legitimize it also became a point of controversy. Primarily, guidance was criticized for largely ignoring aspects of human development and experience, instead focusing too heavily on testing instruments for the constricted purpose of career placement (Gladding, 2016). With the economy in disrepair, career placement was but one small piece of the puzzle as mental health issues arose for even the most stable of individuals. Still, instrumentation retained center stage in guidance, and instruments such as the Strong Vocational Interest Blank, developed by Edward K. Strong Jr. in 1927, provided much needed standardized support materials for the guidance movement, setting a course that would continue for several decades (Zunker, 2015).

As society changed during the 1930s, so too did the guidance movement. Inspired by educational theorist John Dewey's philosophy of education and his own belief in the testing movement, **E. G. Williamson** developed a theory of counseling known as clinical counseling. He based his theory on the assumption that personality consists of measurable traits related to occupational choices. He tailored his scientific, empirical method to each client, focusing on problem solving and decision making in relation to choosing a vocation. Herein lay the problem, because counseling was still heavily focused on occupational concerns.

In 1921, an increased interest in the mental health of children arose, and child-guidance demonstration clinics were created in many U.S. cities. These clinics were community-established facilities where teams of professionals came together to treat children displaying maladjustment. This movement also took a scientific approach as it emphasized the early detection of emotional disorders through testing and diagnosis. Intervention and treatment involved psychoanalysis or modifying the child's environment.

There were some exceptions to the standard interventions and treatments offered by these child-guidance clinics, however. Relationship therapy, play therapy, and neo-Freudian techniques, for instance, were all beginning to take shape. In one such child-guidance clinic in Rochester, New York, **Carl Rogers**, a clinical psychologist initially trained in psychometrics, developed an interest in the new relationship therapies. Rogers focused on developing his own nondirective and client-centered therapy, heavily influenced by relationship therapies.

In 1922, **Alfred Adler**, the founder of individual psychology, began using a form of group therapy he termed *collective counseling*, which he applied to his work with children and prison populations. He also began using family councils in his treatment of children, allowing him to gain input from and insight into the families while helping them to understand that many problems with children related to existing problems within the family. While Adler was developing these approaches to group counseling, so too was J. L. Moreno in his formulation of the Theater of Spontaneity, a foundation for the creation of Gestalt techniques, encounter therapies, and **psychodrama**, a form of therapy known for role-playing and dramatic self-expression.

In 1929, the first ever marriage and family counseling center was established by Abraham and Hannah Stone in New York City. This marked the beginning of marriage and family counseling as a specialization within the field of counseling. During the 1930s, self-help groups continued to increase in popularity, and, in 1935, **Alcoholics Anonymous** was established as a self-help approach to alcohol addiction. Two years later, Recovery Inc., a self-help group focused on mental illness, was founded. Finally, the once individual-focused theory of psychoanalysis began to be incorporated into group formats, a change that acknowledged the influence of social forces and biology on an individual's behavior (Gladding, 2016).

During the Great Depression, a need existed for counselors to work with unemployed individuals in nontraditional ways. Guidance centers housed within school settings were no longer adequate in scope to meet the needs of society. In response to the Great Depression, society began to understand the importance of the economy and that the chances for improvement were greater if people were successfully matched to careers and were satisfied with their work (Gladding, 2016). Nonschool guidance workers within social agencies came to the forefront of the counseling profession because they were now in the position to create the greatest amount of change within society. Counseling became available to adults and children, and settings expanded to include public schools, colleges, and community sites.

Although the public had become far more aware of and interested in mental health and vocational counseling by the 1940s, the necessary funding from the federal government had not yet been made available. Before the Great Depression, funding had been provided almost exclusively by individual states and various private foundations. However, the federal government's financial role began to change as the Great Depression made it obvious that a need existed for social welfare programs, access to health services, and research on mental health.

In direct response to the Great Depression, the federal government passed legislation designed to aid the unemployed. The Wagner-Peyser Act of 1933 established the U.S. Employment Service. The Civilian Conservation Corps was created in 1933, and the Works Progress Administration was established in 1935. All of these legislative initiatives were designed to provide employment for the masses who could not find jobs during this period. In 1939, the first edition of the *Dictionary of Occupational Titles* was published by the U.S. Employment Service, becoming a much-needed source of information for vocational counselors.

THINK ABOUT IT 1.4

If you could ask one person in the history of counseling a question, who would you ask, what would you ask, and why would you ask that question? How might that person have responded?

1941–1960

World War II uncovered a reality few could deny. More than 1 million men were rejected for military service for psychiatric reasons, alerting the United States to the extensiveness of the mental health problems within its society. Psychiatric evaluations and mental-hygiene clinics became commonplace at recruitment, training, and separation centers in an effort to sort the various servicemen correctly. Many of those who served ended up suffering from what was then called battle fatigue, shell shock, or war neurosis, a condition today known as post-traumatic stress disorder (PTSD). Mental health professionals were able to treat many of these men and return them to active duty. Because of these experiences, the federal government and the general public began to recognize the need for the prevention and treatment of mental health disorders. As a result, the National Mental Health Act of 1946 was enacted, authorizing funds for research and training in the areas of prevention, diagnosis, and treatment of mental health disorders.

As the need for mental health counseling increased, so too did the need for guidance and vocational counseling. Not only were women entering the workforce in record numbers, but returning veterans also needed assistance with reentrance. In addition, the need for rehabilitation counselors became obvious because many veterans were disabled in some capacity and needed assistance with the transition back to a productive and meaningful civilian life.

Along with greater public awareness of the need for mental health services, the 1940s ushered in a new direction in counseling and guidance that differed in theory and practice from the widely used model of E. G. Williamson. Williamson's pervasive approach to counseling consisted of information gathering, evaluation, diagnosis, and treatment. In 1942, Carl Rogers, who a decade earlier was beginning to shape his nondirective approach, published *Counseling and Psychotherapy* to propose his now completed theory of **client-centered counseling**. In contrast to Williamson's method, Rogers focused on the client, viewing the person as the expert on his or her own life and considering the client responsible for the direction of change and growth within counseling. Rogers believed that with the right therapeutic environment and conditions, clients would move in a positive direction. Rogers placed new emphasis on counseling techniques, training and education of counselors, research, understanding the counseling process, necessary conditions for effectiveness, and the goals of counseling. Activity 1.1 will further stimulate your thinking about the approaches of Williamson and Rogers.

ACTIVITY 1.1

A common debate in the 1940s through the 1960s centered on whether the ideas of Williamson (e.g., test them and train them) or Rogers (e.g., accept them and listen to them) were more developed and helpful. First, conduct further research into the ideas of E. G. Williamson and Carl Rogers. Next, after dividing into two groups, have one group espouse the ideas of Williamson and the other group espouse the ideas of Rogers. Debate the importance of their views.

During the 1940s, an influx of European existentialists and neo-Freudians who escaped from Nazi persecution and the Holocaust arrived in the United States. Otto Rank, Alfred Adler, Karen Horney, Erich Fromm, Erik Erikson, and Victor Frankl were among them. Their approaches differed from the prevalent assessment and diagnostic perspective common in the United States, as well as from the behavioral, trait personality, and Freudian psychoanalytic perspectives. The influence of their views helped to shape the growth and acceptance of humanism within the United States and contributed to the work and vision of theorists such as Rollo May, Abraham Maslow, and Carl Rogers.

Developments in the field of counseling after World War II were of extraordinary importance. Beginning in the early 1950s, increased federal funds were made available for training counseling professionals, building facilities, and staffing them. Within this decade alone, the field of counseling began to grow as a distinct entity. First, the American Personnel and Guidance Association (APGA; which would become the ACA) was formed when four entities merged. The founding divisions included the NVGA (now known as the National Career Development Association [NCDA]); the National Association of Guidance and Counselor Trainers (NAGCT; now known as the Association for Counselor Education and Supervision [ACES]); the Student Personnel Association for Teacher Education (SPATE; now known as the Association for Humanistic Counseling [AHC]); and the American College Personnel Association (ACPA). Next, Division 17 (Society of Counseling Psychology) was developed within the APA because some APA members voiced an interest in working with less pathological clients.

Finally, the U.S. government passed the National Defense Education Act in response to the panic created by the Russians' successful launch of the first satellite to achieve Earth's orbit. The surprise of **Sputnik** in 1957 created a fear within Americans that the Soviet Union (Russia) would become stronger than the United States politically because it had proven its superiority with space technology. All over the world, news stories repeated the idea that Americans had failed to produce adequately trained students in math and the sciences, resulting in inferior capabilities when compared with the Russians. In an effort to direct large numbers of students quickly into math and science courses, the U.S. Congress created programs to increase the number of guidance, or school, counselors, who could provide such direction to students (Erford, 2015a; Remley & Herlihy, 2016).

THINK ABOUT IT 1.5

If you could arrange a dialogue, or conversation, between two influential individuals in the history of counseling, who would you choose, and what might they say to one another?

1961–1980

The 1960s and 1970s were a time of rapid societal changes. The unequal rights of racial minorities and women were recognized, and federal and state legislatures passed numerous laws to address these inequities. These efforts continue today. This increased emphasis on addressing social injustices coincided with a concomitant increase in counselors.

During the 1960s and 1970s, such a high demand arose for school counselors that colleges and universities could not keep pace. Rushed training and increased responsibilities led to confusion about the exact role of the school counselor. Leaders within the APGA (now known as the ACA) collaborated to define roles and functions of the school counselor, increasing cohesion and clarity. With the development of a clearer professional identity came the need for guidelines to protect and shepherd the development of the profession of counseling. This need led to accreditation of university programs through the Council for Accreditation of Counseling and Related Educational Programs (CACREP) and the creation of certification and licensing boards.

Toward the end of the 1950s, theory development had begun to flourish; theories included Joseph Wolpe's systematic desensitization, Albert Ellis's rational-emotive therapy (RET, now known as rational-emotive behavior therapy, or REBT), Eric Berne's transactional analysis, and Donald Super's career-development theories. In the 1960s, existentialism, family systems, and cognitive theories evolved. Group-therapy modalities also became common during this time, with the most popular groups being basic encounter groups (i.e., personal-growth groups emphasizing awareness through emotions) and marathon groups (i.e., extended groups lasting for an extended and consecutive period). Human developmental perspectives became popular and were considered a primary focus of the counseling profession as the 1960s began. However, with the Civil Rights movement, the Vietnam War, and the women's movement afoot, other issues and concerns began to take precedence.

In 1963, the Community Mental Health Centers Act promoted the growth of counseling as a field that addressed issues within the community in direct response to increased problems with alcoholism, drug use, marital discord, and family crisis. This important piece of legislation provided funds for community-based mental health programs in an effort to increase prevention and decrease hospitalizations. For the first time in the history of counseling, schools were no longer the primary counseling setting. A necessary response to the impending plans to close large state mental hospitals, this legislation led to the development of crisis centers, drop-in clinics, battered women's shelters, rape-counseling centers, and runaway centers. Similar to what happened in the school counseling profession, community needs overwhelmed the mental health arena; counselors and psychotherapists were undertrained, and sites were understaffed. As the number of mental health professionals grew, these professional counselors actively pursued increased recognition and training.

1981–2000

A growing awareness of pluralism began to take place with an interest in how ethnicity, society, culture, gender, and personal biases affected behavior and treatment. Counseling services in all settings became more specialized, resulting in more stringent educational requirements, more advanced degrees, and licensure and certification.

Toward the end of the 1970s, the APGA had begun to question its vision and purpose, and it was decided that its previous professional identification of guidance and personnel had passed into history. During the 1981 APGA annual convention, the editorial board of the *Personnel and Guidance Journal* held a discussion, later contributing resulting statements for publication within the journal. Samuel Gladding, an influential counselor educator and editor at that time, was quoted as saying:

> APGA's present dilemma stems from a lack of identity. We simply do not know collectively if we are a part of what has traditionally been thought of as guidance . . . or what has emerged vigorously in the last 20 years, counseling psychology. . . . As a profession, it has been difficult for us not to identify ourselves as one or the other. With this difficulty has come confusion, stumbling, and seemingly a lack of direction. (Barclay et al., 1981, p. 132)

In 1983, the APGA changed its name to the American Association for Counseling and Development (AACD) to reflect the changes occurring in the profession and to renew its commitment to the field of counseling. Just nine years later, in 1992, the organization changed its name again to what it uses today, the **American Counseling Association (ACA)**.

2001–Present

During the previous few decades, a fourth force had arisen in counseling (the first force was the psychodynamic approach, the second was the cognitive-behavioral approach, and the third force was the humanistic-existential approach). It has come to be known as the multicultural, or systemic, paradigm. Acknowledging a force in counseling must be a deliberate process because forces must stand the test of time and hold up to historical scrutiny. "All counseling is multicultural counseling" is an oft-repeated phrase echoed in counseling classrooms around the world, and it is clear that the systemic/multicultural paradigm has truly earned a place among the forces of counseling. However, just naming something a force does not make it so. For example, advocacy counseling has risen in prominence, perhaps to the level that some have taken to calling it the fifth force in counseling. The ACA (2003) published the *ACA Advocacy Competencies*, and Chapters 14 and 15 of this book have been dedicated to this important emerging area within the field. Whether advocacy counseling will stand the test of time to become widely referred to as the fifth force of counseling remains to be seen. These advocacy competencies and multicultural counseling competencies (Sue, Arredondo, & McDavis, 1992) were revised and combined in the Multicultural and Social Justice Counseling Competencies (Ratts, Singh, Nassar-McMillan, Butler, & McCullough, 2015).

In 2009, the ACA and related counseling organizations achieved their 30-year push to attain licensure for professional counselors in all 50 states when California passed its legislation. This was a major, milestone achievement for the profession. Of course, when a goal is attained, the landscape shifts, and new possibilities and challenges appear on the horizon.

In quick succession, CACREP education and training standards were declared the industry standard for counselor education programs by the Veterans Administration (VA). All mental health counselors who want to provide services to veterans through the VA or the military's TRICARE program must graduate from a CACREP-accredited mental health counseling program. Until this decision, licensed professional counselors (LPCs) were not allowed to provide these services while practicing independently; that is, LPCs needed to practice under the supervision of an approved provider (e.g., psychologists, social workers, psychiatrists). While this policy is exciting because it represents a coming of age for CACREP standards and parity for independent LPCs, it also excludes many current and future licensees from providing high quality services to enlisted service men and women and veterans unless they meet restrictive criteria. Steps forward are fraught with challenges.

The 20/20: A Vision for the Future of Counseling committee, which was conceived in 2005 by the ACA and the American Association of State Counseling Boards (AASCB) and is composed of 31 counseling organizations, continued to meet until 2013, and derived consensus on issues of importance to the entire counseling profession. After achieving consensus on the definition of counseling and guiding principles, as mentioned earlier, the 20/20 committee turned its attention to the issue of licensure portability.

Each state has its own licensure law and state board that licenses counselors. Unsurprisingly, 50 states (and a handful of territories plus the District of Columbia) passing licensure laws during a 30-year period and within diverse political conditions have created 50-plus different laws. These laws vary on practice title, education/training requirements, and even the scope of practice in which counselors are allowed to engage. Also, a counselor licensed to practice in one state is not allowed to practice in another state without first applying for a license and meeting all legal requirements in that other state. This also means that a counselor could be eligible for licensure in one state but not another, because of different and/or more restrictive educational or training requirements.

The 20/20 committee attempted to standardize licensure laws so counselors could practice in all 50 states and related territories on a common set of licensure requirements—a process known as *reciprocity* among state counseling boards—which would result in licensure portability across state lines. Consider the following point: More than 40 different titles exist for licensed counselors across the United States and its territories. How can the profession expect the public to know who professional counselors are and what they do when its members cannot even agree on what to call themselves? Three 20/20 committee work groups attempted to reach consensus on three building blocks to licensure portability: title, scope of practice, and educational/training requirements. The 20/20 committee and its constituent entities recently agreed to promote the common title *licensed professional counselor* and agreed to a consensus scope of practice, but failed to endorse CACREP as the official training standard. The committee failed to reach consensus, primarily because supporters of Council on Rehabilitation Education (CORE) opposed the move. However, a short time later CACREP and CORE proposed a merger that would finally result in a single accreditation organization for professional counseling programs. This is a huge development, cementing the professional identity of all professional counselors. In 2015, AASCB announced a portability proposal and urged state counseling boards to act on it. Likewise, NBCC, ACES, and AMHCA announced a similar portability plan. At present, few state counseling boards offer reciprocity or portability to LPCs from other states, ostensibly because licensure regulations vary from state to state. Thus, state statutes require all licensees in a state to meet all its requirements.

Finally, while in many ways the counseling profession is maturing and becoming unified, this maturation is also occurring among a number of setting-specific entities within the profession. For example, the American School Counselor Association (ASCA) has grown to more than 25,000 members, and its leadership is focused on promoting the well-being of school counselors. Because the ASCA has its own mission statement and definition of counseling, it would not endorse the broad 20/20 definition of counseling or the committee's principles. Likewise, the American Mental Health Counselors Association (AMHCA) did not support the consensus title *licensed professional counselor* because its constituency is composed of clinical mental health counselors, so the organization prefers the title *licensed clinical mental health counselor* (LCMHC). The purpose of the 20/20 initiative was to unify the counseling profession. While progress was made in this regard among some counseling organizations, instances of splintering within the general field of counseling continue. At the same time, some counseling specialties are consolidating around prescribed identities. For example, ASCA introduced a third edition of the *ASCA National Model* (2012), and CACREP and AMHCA have coalesced around a movement to promote clinical mental health counseling education and training standards for state licensure as a professional counselor.

WHERE WE ARE GOING

It is clear from this historical overview that counseling continues to develop its identity, striving for recognition and respect from the public and legislative representatives, and seeking parity with other mental health professions. An examination of the past helps us understand the rich history of the counseling profession, but it also helps us identify pressing issues on the horizon that will continue to challenge professional counselors in the future. Some of these future challenges include evidence-based and research-based practices and outcomes research, managed care, multiculturalism, technology, gatekeeping, professional and social advocacy, mentoring and leadership, and professional unity.

Evidence-Based Practices, Research-Based Practices, and Outcomes Research

While evidence-based practices, research-based practices, and outcomes research are associated with a number of growing pains, they have thus far proved to be good for the field. A growing effort is under way to narrow the gap between research and practice to train and educate scientist-practitioners. A **scientist-practitioner** is a professional who is adept at integrating scientific research and counseling practice to form a more exact science. An increasing push is being made for more scientists to engage in practice and for more practitioners to also act as scientists. Although this push has been prominent in the past few decades, the scientist-practitioner model actually originated from the APA's Boulder Conference in 1949, again demonstrating that the counseling profession shares much of its history with the psychology profession.

In the 1980s, a review of the existing body of literature revealed a lack of relevant information for counseling practitioners. Thirty years later, Norcross and Lambert (2013) noted an increased emphasis on evidence-based and empirically supported treatments, but still encouraged a continued focus on objective understanding while incorporating therapeutic factors specific to the professional counselor. The struggle to achieve the goal of outcome integration is ongoing. (See Chapter 17 for a summary of counseling outcome literature.)

Counseling interventions must continue to gain empirical support, but many difficult-to-measure human factors account for successful counseling outcomes. Counseling is a complex activity and sometimes is not easily researched. Designing research suitable for such complexity is not the only factor hindering the integration of outcome-based research. Although the burden of proof seems to rest most heavily on those doing the research and disseminating the knowledge, a strong commitment by researchers to produce helpful, practice-enhancing information is not enough. Ideally, master's level counselors themselves also would take part in producing research and, at a minimum, they would be trained thoroughly enough in research methodology to understand the applicability of their findings. Unfortunately, practitioner contributions to the counseling literature have declined over the past 20 years in virtually every counseling journal (Byrd, Crockett, & Erford, 2012a, 2012b; Crockett, Byrd, & Erford, 2014; Crockett, Byrd, Erford, & Hays, 2010; Erford, Clark, & Erford, 2011; Erford, Crockett, Giguere, & Darrow, 2011; Erford, Erford, & Broglie, 2012; Erford, Erford, Broglie, & Erford, 2013; Erford, Miller, Duncan, & Erford, 2010; Erford, Miller et al., 2011). The exception is the *Journal of Mental Health Counseling* (Crockett, Byrd, & Erford, 2012), which still boasts a practitioner author rate of about 20%.

Because attention to a profession's journals can provide an inside perspective on professional concerns and issues current to that profession, a look at several content analyses and editorial notes is warranted. Erford and colleagues began a series of meta-studies of ACA-related journals in 2010 and, to date, have published historical trends and quantitative reviews of *Measurement and Evaluation in Counseling and Development* (Erford, Miller et al., 2010), *Counselor Education & Supervision* (Crockett et al., 2010), *Journal of Counseling & Development* (Erford, Miller et al., 2011), *Adultspan* (Erford, Clark, & Erford, 2011), *Journal of Employment Counseling* (Erford, Crockett et al., 2011), *Journal of Humanistic Counseling* (Erford, Erford, & Broglie, 2012), *Journal of Mental Health Counseling* (Crockett, Byrd, & Erford, 2012), *Counseling & Values* (Erford, Erford et al., 2013), *Journal for Specialists in Group Work* (Byrd, Crockett, & Erford, 2012a), *Journal of College Counseling* (Byrd, Crockett, & Erford, 2012b), *Career Development Quarterly* (Crockett, Byrd, & Erford, 2014), and *Professional School Counseling* (Erford, Gugiere, Glenn, & Schein, 2015). The purpose of these meta-studies was to determine the author, article, and research study characteristics of manuscripts published in counseling journals with an eye toward trends over time in content and methodology. In general, these meta-studies concluded that more articles are being authored by women, mirroring the dramatic change evident in the now female-dominant ranks of counselor educators. The proportion of research articles is increasing, as is methodological and statistical sophistication and average sample size. These are positive developments in the emerging counseling literature.

Managed Care

A second challenge to the field of counseling revolves around the many inherent issues of **managed care**. Beginning in the late 1980s, managed care became a double-edged sword. On the positive side, managed care insists on accountability, potentially provides more and better referrals for professional counselors, potentially provides more employment opportunities for professional counselors, and forces professional counselors to accomplish the positive outcome of delivering effective services. At the same time, managed care focuses on cost-cutting practices, and often substantially limits the number of sessions approved for clients.

Originally developed by the insurance establishment as a means of protecting clients from unnecessary services and fees, managed care has evolved into a system designed to cut costs. Decisions regarding the client's treatment often are made by staff with little or no counseling background. Sometimes, ethical considerations are a concern, especially as they pertain to confidentiality and privacy, freedom of choice with regard to a counselor, and rights to collaborative decision making regarding the course and length of treatment.

Professional counselors often feel pressured to reduce the quality of services they offer to stay within a client's number of allotted sessions, "upcode" a diagnosis (i.e., offer diagnosis of a more severe condition rather that the less severe condition for which the client sought services) to help a client qualify for counseling services, or terminate prematurely a client because of financial necessity. While managed care referrals may offer professional counselors increased employment opportunities, a reduced number of sessions necessitate an increase in the number of clients served annually. Changes within the managed-care system include consideration of coverage for diagnoses outside the fifth edition of the *Diagnostic and Statistical Manual of Mental Disorders* (*DSM-5*) (American Psychiatric Association, 2013), the reference used for criteria necessary in making a diagnosis, as well as the inclusion of more mental health professionals on staffs and boards involved in decision-making processes. At the same time, counselors are adapting by receiving training in brief, solution-focused counseling skills to maintain quality services within a reduced time frame (Glosoff & Schwarz-Whittaker, 2013).

Multiculturalism, Diversity, and Social Justice Counseling

Often referred to as the *fourth force* in counseling (with psychodynamic, cognitive-behavioral, and humanistic-existential being the first three), **multiculturalism** has gained much attention during the past several decades. It remains an essential future focus for the field of counseling because much change and innovation is still needed. Wrenn (1962) first introduced the concept of the **culturally encapsulated counselor**, a term that applies to professional counselors who perceive others through their own narrow cultural lenses without regard for the cultural values and experiences of their clients. Today, counselors are trained to consider clients in relation to their environments, worldviews, and experiences. In addition, in the decades following the first use of the term, social forces, demographic changes, and legislation have provided the impetus for change, while research and scholarship have proliferated, thus expanding professional counselors' understanding and practice in the field.

Despite these changes, much remains to be done. In essence, the multicultural movement seeks to reconceptualize existing theories and techniques to encompass more diverse populations, calling for modifications to espouse a more diversified perspective. Existing treatments have been empirically validated to serve a predominantly white, male, educated, Eurocentric, middle-class population. However, individuals who seek counseling come from all walks of life, ethnic groups, and gender identities. Cultural differences not only take into consideration issues related to race and ethnicity, but also issues related to gender, social class, sexual orientation, age, disability, and religion, among others. Therefore, professional counselors must exercise caution when working with individuals and understand that countless differences and intersections between and among differences exist. Because of these intersections, counseling processes ranging from the beginning stage, establishing a relationship, to the final stage, termination, are lacking in comprehensiveness, exactness, and client goal attainment (Remley & Herlihy, 2016). For example, it stands to reason that the worldviews and experiences of a materially poor, white, heterosexual male will differ substantially from a wealthy lesbian of African American heritage. Understanding the intersections among cultural variables is essential. Social justice advocacy needs for each client will also differ markedly.

Professional counselors can take steps to help ensure ethical multicultural practice. First, self-awareness and self-evaluation are crucial. Counselors must constantly and consistently examine themselves in search of preconceived notions and biases and acknowledge the value-based assumptions they make. It is only with this first step of self-awareness and acknowledgment of biases that counselors can begin to practice from multicultural and social justice perspectives. Second, professional counselors must make every effort to increase their knowledge of the populations and clients they are working with. It is generally assumed that the more information and knowledge one has, the less able that person is to think and view in constricted terms. Finally, professional counselors should seek to translate and appropriately adapt the skills and techniques currently in use to suit culturally diverse clients (Hays & Erford, 2018). Careful consideration must be given when applying standard-treatment methods to vastly different individuals. Multicultural and social justice counseling comprises an important area of current practice and much needed future research. Ratts and colleagues (2015) revised the original multicultural counseling competencies and social justice counseling competencies.

Technology

The fourth future trend concerns the increasing use of technology in counselor education, training, and practice. Beginning in the 1990s, technology and Internet use in counseling began to grow at a tremendous rate. Since that time, the use of technology can be observed in counseling in numerous beneficial ways. Internet searches provide a fast and efficient way for professional counselors, counseling students, counselor educators, and clients to access information on various counseling-related topics; however, the soundness of this information is sometimes questionable. Databases, assessment tools, diagnostic screening, consultation, supervision, education, and referrals are only some of the many appropriate uses of technology in counseling-related ways.

More recently, technological innovations are being used for actual counseling (e.g., audio conferencing, video conferencing, synchronous electronic communication), leading some practitioners, counselor educators, and licensing board members to question the ethical implications of providing counseling services to clients in a nontraditional capacity (see Chapter 3). Some tasks inherent to the counseling process can best be served by using technology, allowing professional counselors greater efficiency in their work. Few would argue that technology is a valuable resource for responsibilities considered clerical in nature, such as data entry, scheduling and appointments, referrals, and contact with community resources. However, relationship building and clinical judgment may be limited when conducted in a nontraditional capacity (e.g., email counseling, bulletin-board counseling, chat-room counseling, e-coaching, voice interactive, video conferencing), rather than in traditional, face-to-face formats. As explained in more detail in Chapter 3, the *ACA Code of Ethics* (2014a) includes an entire section addressing technological issues in counseling, including non-face-to-face counseling, which has tremendous potential to help clients who are from remote regions or who are unable to consistently attend in-person sessions, but at the same time is technology fraught with ethical challenges. In addition, with the proliferation of social media, professionals must be cautious of boundary issues with clients—especially minors and students.

Advocates for using technology for counseling purposes rightly point out that this modality is beneficial because it offers previously underserved subpopulations (e.g., individuals in remote areas, individuals without reliable transportation, individuals with physical impairments or disabilities) easier access to counseling services. This approach can also alleviate some anxiety for clients who perceive a relationship through a computer to be less threatening than a face-to-face relationship. This process may also be beneficial for clients who travel extensively or members of the armed services stationed abroad so that they can participate in family or conjoint counseling sessions.

Having noted the benefits that might have originally spurred the use of technology in counseling, the potential problems should be noted as well. State regulatory boards are coming to grips with the oversight issues. Can they protect their citizens from unethical or unqualified counselors providing Internet-based services to clients residing in different states? The credentials of some people who provide online counseling services are questionable, as is their adherence to ethical practices and quality of services. Many state licensing boards are requiring or considering requiring counselors who provide online counseling services to be licensed in the state in which the client resides in order to protect citizens under state practice laws. In addition, counseling websites accessible today might not exist in six months' time, online confidentiality cannot be ensured, and therapeutic factors and nonverbal behaviors may be difficult to gauge and appreciate fully. Technological innovations such as encryption and secure identification protocols help bolster confidentiality.

Gatekeeping

The fifth future concern is gatekeeping, an issue gaining momentum in the counseling profession. **Gatekeeping** refers to the screening, remediation, and dismissal of counselors in training who are poorly fit for the counseling profession. A student who shows emotional impairment, inappropriate relationship skills, and unethical behavior should be evaluated closely to determine whether these issues are problematic or constitute true impairment. Vacha-Haase, Davenport, and Kerewsky (2004) provide working definitions of *problematic* and *impairment* and delineate between the two. A student who is problematic displays behavior that is unacceptable and inappropriate, whereas an impaired student shows signs of mental illness or emotional distress that would affect and hinder effective functioning as a professional counselor. Gatekeepers should make every effort to differentiate between unacceptable and acceptable behaviors as well as distress that is developmentally normal versus that which is not.

In their classic study on the issue, Gaubatz and Vera (2002) estimate that more than 10% of master's level counseling students are poorly or marginally suited for the field. Of this 10%, faculty members intervene in a little more than half the cases; meaning, approximately 5% of all counseling students granted admission into counseling programs are either remediated or dismissed each school year. This also indicates that another 5% become **gateslippers**, impaired students who receive no intervention and are instead graduated.

When examining key determining factors to the gatekeeping issue, Gaubatz and Vera (2002) found that (a) CACREP-accredited programs have 10% fewer overlooked gateslippers; (b) programs with a larger adjunct-to-faculty ratio have higher numbers of gateslippers; (c) programs with fewer tenured faculty have higher numbers of gateslippers; and (d) programs whose faculty are concerned about being sued by students, are concerned about receiving poor teaching evaluations, or feel pressure from the institution not to screen out problematic students have higher numbers of gateslippers. Having formalized gatekeeping procedures in place was found to be the most important predictor of graduating fewer problematic and impaired counseling students. Gaubatz and Vera stated, "Any program that institutes formalized procedures will reduce the number of deficient students it graduates" (p. 304).

Professional Advocacy and Social Advocacy Counseling

Chapters 14 and 15 address the important issues of professional advocacy and advocacy counseling, respectively. For now, suffice it to say that the prominence of advocacy and advocacy counseling in the years to come hinges on our ability to advocate for parity with other mental health professionals (e.g., psychologists, social workers) on the national, state, and local levels. Professional advocacy helps to promote the counseling profession, but more importantly, serves to protect the public. In addition, it is an essential current and future mission of professional counselors to help every client learn to self-advocate to address societal privileges and inequities leading to mental health and wellness challenges, both individually and collectively. Injustice and unfairness in any aspect of society threaten justice and fairness for all within that societal order.

VOICES FROM THE FIELD 1.1   Advocating for the Counseling Profession: My Path to Becoming an Advocate for the Field of Counseling, by Gregory Pollock

---

I have often thought about how one becomes an advocate for the profession and have come to the conclusion that advocates develop over time. It is my belief that passionate advocates for the profession, much like passionate professional advocates for individual clients, have seen firsthand the inequities within the field of counseling.

It is no longer surprising to come across counselors who have limited knowledge of the present challenges facing the profession of counseling. During presentations I have given on professional advocacy, I have encountered many counselors who were uninformed. This led me to the conclusion that we, as a profession, have not done enough at the grassroots level to make legislative advocacy important within training programs and especially for practicing counselors. It seems that practicing counselors removed from an academic setting are more likely to be disconnected.

When I began my counseling career nearly two decades ago, I was not aware of the need for advocacy efforts for the field. I was naïve about issues that affected the profession. The training I had received had been very focused on helping clients, attending to client issues, and advocating for clients with little or no emphasis on advocating for the profession itself. I have spent a great deal of time wondering why this is the case and have come to the conclusion that many of the professors I had encountered were trained and held identities outside the field of counseling. I had not been aware of the opportunities to join specific organizations related to the field of counseling because they had not been openly discussed and participation in them had not been encouraged at the time of my training.

By the time I entered the workforce as a professional counselor, I had come to believe no differences existed between the many helping professions because all of us were doing the same work and had similar training. Early in my career, however, it became apparent that there were many and profound differences among persons offering services to clients. I found myself working alongside persons who had associate's and bachelor's degrees, and they were performing very similar services. There were also apparent differences in the amounts of training people with whom I was working had received. It was clear that a number of persons in positions of authority, and many of those making hiring decisions, did not have a clear understanding of who counselors were and what specific talents counselors possessed, which led to counselors not being valued as service providers.

I found myself practicing counseling for a number of years without a strong counselor identity. In fact, in the early stages of my career, I didn't know what it meant to be a counselor and I did not know what the important issues were that we faced and needed to work on as a profession. Discouragement began to set in as the inequities became increasingly visible, and I discovered that there were actually many limitations facing counselors, most of which were directly related to a lack of advocacy efforts within the field. I encountered too many situations in which counselors were not valued as meaningful providers of services to clients, and I found myself becoming very discouraged and often wondered why I was doing what I was doing and whether I had made the right career choice.

(Continued)

I continued to struggle with identity issues as a counselor until I began working in a private practice setting with other professional counselors on a regular basis. I found myself recognizing common themes, attitudes, and experiences as I interacted with other counselors. At the same time, I began to see deeper issues related to inequities that counselors were facing. It was shocking to learn about insurance panels counselors were not allowed to serve on and our inability to bill for Medicare reimbursement. Most surprising was the lack of knowledge in the mental health and legislative worlds about what counselors were and could do. I feel that I was insulated from a number of these issues when I was solely working in agencies, because I had not dealt with billing issues or contracting issues with insurance companies. In private practice, there no longer was a cushion of having the billing sheets signed off on by someone who was eligible to bill for the services in question, often a psychiatrist, psychologist, or social worker.

My frustration continued to build, and I continued to question whether I had made the right career choice. The thing I could not get past, however, was the great sense of satisfaction I received from working with clients and seeing their successes. I *knew* I was helping; so to address the barriers and challenges, I began to explore things I could do to remedy some of the issues with which I was frustrated.

My first step was to reach out to a close friend who was actively involved in various counseling organizations. I shared my frustrations and asked what I could do to make a difference. I was given the phone number for the current president of the state counseling association and was encouraged to reach out and explore ways to become involved.

I look back on my initial contact with the president of the state counseling association with amazement. After hearing about the things I wanted to be involved in and the struggles that had led to me contacting him, he offered me the position of chair of the association's Government Relations Committee. I could not think of a better role to serve in, because this position would allow me to push for change and become aware of and educate others about needed changes. It would also afford me the opportunity to teach my colleagues about these important issues.

I am very proud of the progress my colleagues and I have made in advocating for the profession, given the many opportunities we have had to advocate for the profession on the state and national level. I have had a number of opportunities to testify before my state's House of Representatives Judiciary Committee. I have spent countless hours organizing events in the state to encourage counselors to advocate for important issues that affect our ability to practice. I have made contact with several state and federal legislators and have educated them about what counselors do and why it is important to have counselors included in important pieces of legislation, such as Medicare legislation.

In my role as chair of the Government Relations Committee in my state association, I have had the opportunity to become very well versed in public policy and issues facing counselors on the state and federal levels. Looking back, I am shocked at how uninformed I had been as a counselor prior to getting involved. Unfortunately, this is a common condition we need to work on throughout the profession. Many people I have contact with in the profession are not aware of important professional issues, and they have no idea about where to begin to advocate for the profession. This is an area all counselors can focus on by getting involved in state and national organizations and remaining active with those organizations so that each one of us is aware of the issues we need to focus on and advocate for to move our profession forward.

It does not take a great deal of time and effort to advocate for the counseling profession. I realize time is a valuable commodity and that lack of time stands in the way of counselors participating in activities related to professional advocacy. The simple truth is that without our personal and collective efforts, no one will advocate for our profession. For us to effectively advocate, we need to be involved, stay involved, and put in a little time and effort. We can move the profession of counseling forward and make the necessary changes to gain the respect we deserve and achieve parity with other mental health service providers.

Mentoring and Leadership Training

The future of the counseling profession is sitting in graduate counseling programs all around the world. How the profession chooses to mentor and nurture the next generation of professional counselors will in large part determine its destiny. The extent to which students seek out mentoring relationships with highly professional and accomplished practicing counselors and counselor educators will determine their orientation to the counseling profession. For example, a number of ACA divisions and branches have established mentoring programs for student members that match students with qualified mentors. These relationships often last a lifetime and set a firm foundation for achievement and professional practice. For a counselor in training to become truly oriented to the counseling profession, one should become a member of relevant professional associations, including ACA, the ACA state branch, and specialty divisions of practice or passion (see Chapter 2).

Counseling graduates should also pursue state certification/licensure through state entities and national certification through the National Board for Certified Counselors (NBCC). Exposure to professional organizations grounds counselors in traditions, orients counselors to professional practice, and keeps counselors informed of changes affecting practice and future practice opportunities. Belonging to professional associations also sends a strong message to legislators that professional counselors comprise a large, strong, and vibrant voice for the U.S. citizenry that does not hesitate to act in the best interests of all citizens, in particular for the marginalized and oppressed.

Bonding and Splintering of Facets of the Counseling Profession

Growth, development, and adaptation are processes natural to any living organism or system, and so the counseling profession is naturally subjected to these forces of change. In the 60 years since the ACA was formed, several instances of discord have occurred, most recently causing two divisions to threaten to disaffiliate from the ACA and go their own ways as separate organizations; however, it is important to understand that those two divisions are still aligned with ACA in the usual manner.

The two divisions are the ASCA and the AMHCA, two of the largest work-setting organizations (i.e., organizations dedicated to advocating for counselors in a given work setting, such as schools and clinics). Interestingly, the ASCA was the only counseling organization that did not support the consensus principles for unifying and strengthening the profession, and it was one of two counseling organizations—Counselors for Social Justice (CSJ) being the other—that did not support the consensus definition of counseling. This points to some philosophical discord over how the ASCA leadership representing school counselors see the specialty fitting into the overall discipline of counseling. Indeed, all specialty-counseling divisions except the ASCA view their members as counselors who apply the principles and techniques of counseling within different work settings. In contrast, in recent years the ASCA leadership views school counselors as educators who apply the principles and techniques of counseling to their work setting with school-aged children. It should be noted that this view contrasts markedly with CACREP's (2016) perspective and the vast majority of counselor educators who train school counselors. An interesting future challenge to the unification of the counseling profession will be whether counseling organizations splinter off or stick together to accomplish important professional goals, such as legislative initiatives.

A prime example of unification and bonding efforts within the counseling profession is the merger between CACREP and CORE. Finally, the counseling profession will have a single specialty accreditation organization that sets the standard for education and training of all counseling professionals. Coupled with recognition by the U.S government and U.S. Veterans Administration, and approval of several state legislatures as a requirement for licensure, the course for the future revolution of counselor training in the United States is becoming very clear. It is likely that by 2050, nearly every professional counselor licensed in each state will be a graduate of a CACREP-accredited program. This impetus has not come without a good deal of consternation. Graduates from programs that are not currently CACREP accredited often feel uncertain about what this move will do to their professional future. At this point, liberal grandfathering provisions are proposed when any change in state statute occurs, and these grandfathering provisions are supported by CACREP, AASCB, ACA, and NBCC. Still, with change comes uncertainty and anxiety. While no university or counseling program is compelled to seek specialty program accreditation through CACREP, failing to do so in states that require graduation from a CACREP-accredited program for licensure will graduate counselors at a decided disadvantage in the job market.

It is beyond the scope of this chapter to review all the current trends and issues facing the field of counseling. Specific discussions of additional aspects of licensure portability, pharmacotherapy, creativity, spirituality, and assessment are warranted. For now, complete Activity 1.2 to identify trends and issues in society that may affect future generations of counselors. Then enjoy the final section of this chapter on counselor wellness. Your longevity in the counseling profession will depend on it.

ACTIVITY 1.2

With your classmates, make a time line for the next 10–20 years of counseling. Give some thought to where the field has been so as to predict more accurately where you believe the field is going. Include important events, legislation, and key people with regard to the trends discussed above.

DEVELOPING A COMMITMENT TO CAREER-LONG WELLNESS

Just as striving for optimal functioning and health in a client's life is an essential goal of counseling, focusing on counselor wellness is an important professional development goal for professional counselors. It is not an overstatement that counseling can be a difficult profession, fraught with challenges that create both personal and professional demands on practitioners. In order for students and practitioners to maintain their personal and professional energy and remain engaged and effective in their chosen profession, developing specific resources and skills to enhance wellness becomes necessary. Indeed, both the 2016 CACREP Standards and the 2014 *ACA Code of Ethics* emphasize self-care as an essential component of counselor training and ethical practice.

The topic of counselor wellness is not new. Historically, Rogers (1961) emphasized the importance of the counselors' personal characteristics in being able to help clients, and several other models and theories of wellness have embraced a holistic orientation that encompasses the entire person (Dorn 1992; Renger et al., 2000). Although wellness is a highly subjective state pertaining to optimal health and functioning best conceptualized along a continuum, a recent review of existing theories indicates that most wellness models include dimensions pertaining to emotional, intellectual, physical, social, and spiritual wellness (Roscoe, 2009).

Historically, one of the most frequently cited wellness models in counseling literature is the Wheel of Wellness, developed by Sweeney and Witmer (1991), with later expansions by Myers, Sweeney, and Witmer (2000). Grounded in the humanistic counseling principles of Maslow and Adler and based on a conceptualization of wellness as a state of optimal well-being that maximizes one's potential, the model was later renamed the Indivisible Self: An Evidence-Based Model of Wellness (IS-WEL; Myers, Luecht, & Sweeney, 2004). The IS-WEL is composed of 5 components that make up the indivisible self (i.e., Creative, Coping, Social, Essential, and Physical), with an additional 17 evidence-based wellness facets grouped within the 5 components of the self. It is interesting to note that within this model, self-care is a factor conceptualized within the "Essential Self" dimension. A measure of wellness based on this model has also been developed, the Five Factor Wellness Evaluation of Lifestyle (5F-Wel; Myers & Sweeney, 2005), a tool that could prove useful for self-evaluation and clinical supervision practices for emerging and seasoned counselors alike. However, others also suggest incorporating qualitative measures to accurately capture the fluid and highly individual construct of wellness (Roscoe, 2009).

Wellness features centrally in CACREP-accredited counselor education programs, with accreditation standards emphasizing the integration of wellness throughout the curriculum. Specifically, programs are directed to incorporate self-awareness and self-care strategies in the development of counselors in training, especially as they relate to their professional roles (CACREP, 2016). Practicing self-care early may not only prepare counselors-in-training for challenges they will face later on, but may also address the amelioration of current difficulties (Roach & Young, 2007).

While the emphasis on wellness and self-awareness may contribute to higher levels of reported wellness among counseling graduate students (Lambie, Smith, & Ieva, 2009), and an enhanced understanding of the importance of wellness in both personal and professional dimensions (Burck, Bruneau, Baker, & Ellison, 2014), research indicates that students also report significant levels of psychological distress while in their graduate counseling programs (Smith, Robinson, & Young, 2007). The term *wounded healers* has been used in counseling literature to describe those entering the counseling profession whose combined life experiences and personality traits may render them vulnerable, impacting their overall effectiveness (Moorhead, Gill, Barrio Minton, & Myers, 2012). In addition to preexisting difficulties, stressors inherent in counselor training may pose an additional challenge to maintaining wellness (Skovholt, 2001), lending urgency to the application of self-awareness and self-care strategies during counselor training.

So, what are some self-care strategies that may be helpful to counseling students other than practicing general healthy behaviors? A qualitative study conducted by Burck et al. (2014) suggested that counselors in training would benefit from having site supervisors who value and incorporate wellness into clinical supervision. Although there are many avenues for incorporating wellness when training students, Shapiro, Brown, and Beigel (2007) highlight mindfulness practices as a potentially useful tool for emerging counselors. Having a cognitive understanding of the signs of impairment, recognizing personal counseling as a support (Yager & Tovar-Blank, 2007), and initiating self-change projects to enhance wellness based on an initial assessment (Smith, Myers, & Hensley, 2002) are all strategies that can instill a reflective and proactive orientation toward self-care. Other research indicates that obtaining support from others (i.e., faculty, friends, significant others) is also an important strategy for maintaining wellness (Roach & Young, 2007; Witmer & Granello, 2005).

As stressful as graduate counseling work may be, practicing counselors are also faced with a number of difficulties. Being in a profession that is high on empathy demands, ambiguity, and complexity, counselors are tested to practice tolerance and acceptance on a regular basis (Skovholt, Grier, & Hanson, 2001). Research indicates that postgraduate counselors are at an increased risk for anxiety, depression, job stress, and overload (Young & Lambie, 2007). Although the *ACA Code of Ethics* emphasizes the necessity of self-care for professional counselors, regular engagement in self-care can often be a real struggle (Skovholt et al., 2001). The potential consequences of neglecting personal wellness are reflected in the literature in terms of counselor burnout and impairment (see Chapter 7).

Burnout is often conceptualized as the result of experiencing long-term emotional and interpersonal stressors on the job, resulting in a state of emotional exhaustion, cynicism toward clients, and feelings of reduced effectiveness (Maslach, Schaufeli, & Leiter, 2001). Burnout is indeed a significant problem in the mental health field, impacting core outcomes such as work engagement, job satisfaction, overall health and stress, as well as empathy toward clients (Morse, Salyers, Rollins, Monroe-DeVita, & Pfahler, 2012). These factors are often implicated with counselor impairment. Impaired counselors are unable to mitigate their personal issues in order to address client needs, either because of burnout or other factors (e.g., mental or physical illness).

Working in a healthy organization is often a prerequisite for professional wellness (Young & Lambie, 2007). However, becoming aware of interpersonal, organizational, and work-setting variables that may be related to counselor burnout (e.g., emotion-oriented coping, a high caseload, limited resources) can help in employing a proactive approach, as well as initiating personal and organizational change (Bardhoshi, Schweinle, & Duncan, 2014; Oser, Biebel, Pullen, & Harp, 2013; Wilkerson & Bellini, 2006). Skovholt et al. (2001) identify a number of hazards inherent to the counseling profession that have a high potential for depleting practitioner energy. Enhancing self-awareness to avoid common pitfalls (e.g., inability to say no, assuming sole responsibility for solving client problems) is an important practice that bolsters resilience.

Receiving emotional support from colleagues, supervisors, and mentors can also assist practicing counselors with normalizing difficult job-related experiences. Similarly, Bradley, Whisenhunt, Adamson, & Kress (2013) suggest that applying creative approaches in self-care practices (e.g., journaling, drawing) may prove cathartic and help externalize difficulties counselors may be facing. Finally, remaining engaged in the profession through pursuing professional development and growth opportunities, including clinical supervision, can reenergize seasoned counselors and help propel them forward.

On a personal level, engaging in restorative activities including leisure (Skovholt et al., 2001), spending time with family and friends, exercising, and practicing meditation or other mindfulness-based procedures can help professional counselors address individual self-care needs (Lent & Schwartz, 2012). A qualitative inquiry into postgraduate counselors revealed that practitioners equate wellness with maintaining a state of personal and professional balance. This is achieved for counselors through the pursuit of health, relationships, and fun, as well as maintaining self-preservation, self-concept, and supportive professional relationships (Neswald-Potter, Blackburn, & Noel, 2013). Similarly, Lawson (2007) reported that maintaining a sense of humor was a frequently endorsed career-sustaining behavior by professional counselors.

The journey from counseling student to practitioner can be challenging, but it is also ripe with opportunities for personal and professional development and growth. As continuous reflection and awareness are vital in the development of counselors regardless of one's career stage (Rønnestad & Skovholt, 2003), providing counselors with a knowledge base of danger zones, coping techniques, and proactive strategies can promote a life-long practice of self-awareness and self-care. Wellness is one of the cornerstone principles of the counseling profession, and integrating wellness into the training and practice of counselors is an essential component in not only competently meeting the needs of our clients, but also reaching our own potential as professional counselors.

VOICES FROM THE FIELD 1.2   Lack of Self-Care and Lorna Doones, by Nicole Bradley

After completing my master's degree in community counseling, I began working full-time with children and adolescents at a community mental health agency. I was ecstatic to have found a job close to home and to begin working only weeks after graduation. Previously, I had spent years working with children in multiple noncounseling capacities, including daycare, direct care in a residential treatment facility, a center for autism, and school settings. As I tried on the role of professional counselor, I was excited and eager to continue my work with children and use the skills I had worked hard to cultivate over the past two years.

In addition to working with children, self-care had also always been a priority for me. I had been a runner since the age of 11, maintained supportive friendships, and was always conscious about eating healthfully. Despite my attempts to take care of myself, I was not prepared for how emotionally draining counseling could be.

After a year and a half in my first counseling position, I was beginning to feel burned out. I was not running as much as I did previously; I was working through lunch, regularly eating the Lorna Doone cookies I kept in my office; and I was experiencing intense guilt about going home to a safe home, unlike my clients, where I had food, heat, clean clothes, and knew no one would hurt me. Thankfully, I recognized I wasn't pulling on my healthy coping skills and began to make changes in my life. I look back now and reflect on what a valuable learning experience this was for me.

To overcome the stresses of my counseling job, I created rituals. I committed myself to running with my friends a few days a week—as I had previously done—and asked them to help me be accountable to this commitment. To facilitate focus at work, I began taking the lunch breaks I had gotten into the habit of skipping, making the extra effort to call a friend or leave the office area to help take my mind off work and my clients. Finally, probably one of the most important changes I made was the creation of a daily routine to leave my work at work and not bring it into my personal life. Each day before I left the office, I would stand in front of my door after locking it and say to myself out loud, "I am leaving it here until tomorrow." I found that having that concrete behavior at the end of my day really helped me transition into my personal life in a healthier way. Now, did it always work? No! But it did significantly decrease my emotional stress and help me set a work–home boundary. At present, I work clinically and teach master's level counseling courses. I make sure to continue to engage in these self-care strategies as well as others, and I actively promote the importance of self-care to my students.

Summary

The importance of understanding the origination of a profession cannot be overstated. It is crucial to have a clear sense of what the counseling profession is and is not, what influenced it on the way to its existing status, and what issues require current and future attention. Counseling is defined in many ways, but the profession of counseling incorporates a holistic, proactive, preventive, and rehabilitative viewpoint, focusing on facilitating healthy growth, redirecting unhealthy development, and improving the current quality of life.

The philosophy of counseling was discussed as it relates to wellness, developmental, empowerment, and prevention perspectives. Within the wellness perspective, professional counselors focus not only on symptom reduction, but also on improving the client's optimal well-being. Within a developmental perspective, professional counselors understand and view client concerns within a life span development framework, understanding that many reactions are appropriate given that surrounding conditions are temporary. From an empowerment and advocacy perspective, counselors work to encourage and assist clients to gain the confidence and independence to use life skills and exercise control over their lives.

Accounts of the history of counseling typically begin with the landmark contributions of Jesse B. Davis, Frank Parsons, and Clifford Whittingham Beers. Davis designated teachers as guidance facilitators and incorporated character building into class time. Beers exposed the inhumane treatment of mentally ill individuals and worked with influential people to bring about a change in societal attitudes. Parsons was the first to state that to be happy in a career, a person must first consider what he or she is good at.

Guidance and psychotherapy influenced the developing counseling profession. The measurement movement, the use of group formats, the development of counseling theory, World War I and World War II, the rise of humanism, changes in legislation and funding, and movement toward accreditation all helped shape the field. Current trends and issues in the counseling profession include evidence-based outcomes research, managed care, multiculturalism and social justice counseling, technology in counseling, gatekeeping, advocacy, mentoring and leadership, and the splintering and bonding of professional associations.

This chapter provided the profession's historical progression, enabling the counseling student to begin developing a framework within which to increase identification with the profession, gain a sense of pride in that profession, develop an identity as a professional counselor, advocate for the profession, and make important and innovative contributions to the profession.

MyCounselingLab for Introduction to Counseling

Start with the Topic 10 Assignments: *History of Counseling* and then try the Topic 6 Assignments: *Current Trends in Counseling*.

2 Professional Counseling Organizations, Licensure, Certification, and Accreditation

Joshua C. Watson, Bradley T. Erford, and Grafton T. Eliason*

PREVIEW

This chapter highlights the positive role professional organizations have played in the identity development of the counseling profession and in providing various services to counselors and clients. An in-depth examination of the American Counseling Association (ACA) provides readers with an overview of its various divisions, branches, policies, and professional partners as well as its professional development opportunities and other numerous benefits for both counselors and students. This chapter offers a glimpse at the many credentials that can be earned by professional counselors (i.e., state licensure, state certification, national certification) and counselor education programs (i.e., accreditation). Various accountability procedures found at the state level for educational systems and mental health agencies are also reviewed.

PROFESSIONAL COUNSELING ORGANIZATIONS

Professional counselors, working through professional counselor organizations, have achieved a great deal during the past six decades since the creation of the organization known today as the American Counseling Association. The lives of professional counselors and the clients they serve would be quite different if these organizations had never existed. Ponder for a moment how the counseling world might look without the influence and hard work of professional counseling organizations.

Professional counselors would not be licensed in any state. Expectations for ethical professional practice would not exist, and the public would not be protected because practitioners would not be held accountable to various codes of ethics or legal statutes. Third-party reimbursement from health insurance companies would not be possible for professional counselors. The U.S. Department of Veterans Affairs would still exclude rehabilitation and mental health counselors from providing mental health services to veterans of the U.S. armed services. Professional school counselors would continue to find the title *guidance counselor* on the office door while being inundated and preoccupied

*Special thanks to Dr. David Kaplan, Chief Professional Officer of the American Counseling Association, for his contributions to the first two editions of this chapter.

with administrative tasks, leaving the office primarily to take care of lunch and bus duties. Graduate counseling programs, if they existed at all, would consist of fewer than 30 credits, require 100 hours (or fewer) of field experience, and be viewed by other mental health professions as providing far less than a professional level of training.

However, thanks to professional counseling organizations' hard work and efforts, much-needed changes and advancement have been brought to the field of counseling, which has benefited individuals seeking counseling services, professional counselors, and counselors in training. It is incumbent on all professional counselors, counselor educators, and counseling students to join and be active members of counseling associations to advance the profession, demonstrate professionalism, maintain counseling skills, and partake in the many benefits counseling organizations offer.

Navigating through the acronym-rich world of these organizations can be daunting, even for experienced professional counselors. Here is just one dizzying example: The NJAADA is a division of the NJCA, which is a branch of the ACA. It is also a state division of the AADA, which is itself an ACA division. This sentence translates to: The New Jersey Association for Adult Development and Aging (NJAADA) is a division of the New Jersey Counseling Association (NJCA), which is the New Jersey branch of the American Counseling Association (ACA). The NJAADA is also a state division of the Association for Adult Development and Aging (AADA), which is the ACA division that focuses on adult development across the life span (see Figure 2.1). Whew! Got that? To help you sort out the professional associations, this chapter provides a synopsis of major counseling organizations as well as the benefits and services they provide to counseling students and professional counselors.

American Counseling Association

The **American Counseling Association** is the world's largest association for counselors, serving more than 56,000 members in the United States and 50 other countries. The ACA speaks to and for professional counselors across all settings and specialties. The ACA gives

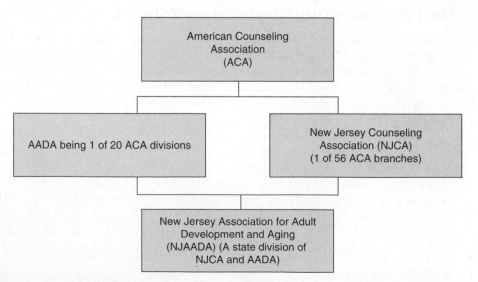

FIGURE 2.1 The relationship between the ACA and its divisions, state branches, and state divisions.

members the opportunity to stay in touch with issues across the entire counseling spectrum; thus, members can benefit from ideas and approaches from areas outside their specialties.

For example, the annual ACA conference offers more than 500 sessions covering more than two dozen counseling specialty areas. At the conference, professional school counselors can attend programs that focus on school counseling, but they can also attend workshops on establishing a private practice, a topic that might not appear in a conference devoted exclusively to school counseling. Career counselors can go to sessions that speak to career development, but they also have the opportunity to attend family-counseling workshops, an area sparsely covered at most career-development conferences. Rehabilitation counselors can find programs on assisting clients with disabilities, but they can also attend sessions on normal human development and abilities. The same type of interactive dialogue and participation is provided in ACA publications, the ACA website (www.counseling.org), online continuing education (CE), webinars, blogs, social networking, and many other services and products.

It is interesting to view the evolution of the counseling profession through the specific titles the ACA has held over the years. The ACA was founded in 1952 as the American Personnel and Guidance Association (APGA). This title reflected the four organizations that came together to form the ACA: the National Vocational Guidance Association, the National Association of Guidance and Counselor Trainers, the Student Personnel Association for Teacher Education, and the American College Personnel Association. It seems clear from reviewing the names of the founding ACA divisions that the roots of the profession are in education and career development.

In 1983, the organization changed its name from the APGA to the American Association for Counseling and Development (AACD). This name change signified the emergence of a professional identity that could be distinguished from other mental health professions, such as psychology and social work. For the first time, *counseling* was in the professional organization's title for the entire world to see. The word *development* was also added to the association's title. The organization's initial focus on career development had blossomed into a niche held by no other helping profession: human development across the human life span that focuses on positive growth rather than pathology.

The most recent name change occurred in 1992, when the AACD dropped the word *development* from its title and became the American Counseling Association. The purpose of deleting the word *development* from the organization's title was to unite and reflect the common link between association members. This sense of unity is clearly articulated in the organization's mission statement: "the mission of the American Counseling Association is to enhance the quality of life in society by promoting the development of professional counselors, advancing the counseling profession, and using the profession and practice of counseling to promote respect for human dignity and diversity" (ACA, 2016). In addition, this change signified a growing recognition that counseling was becoming established as a core mental health profession.

The ACA issues two important publications to all members, *Counseling Today* and the *Journal of Counseling & Development*. *Counseling Today* is a monthly magazine that features award-winning writers and articles on topics of special and general interest to counselors. *Counseling Today* also provides employment advertisements; advertisements from companies offering products for counselors; and monthly columns for students, private practitioners, and others. The *Journal of Counseling & Development* is the ACA's flagship journal. It publishes articles of interest to the entire ACA membership, with topics reaching across all specialties and work settings. Counselors and mental health professionals can benefit

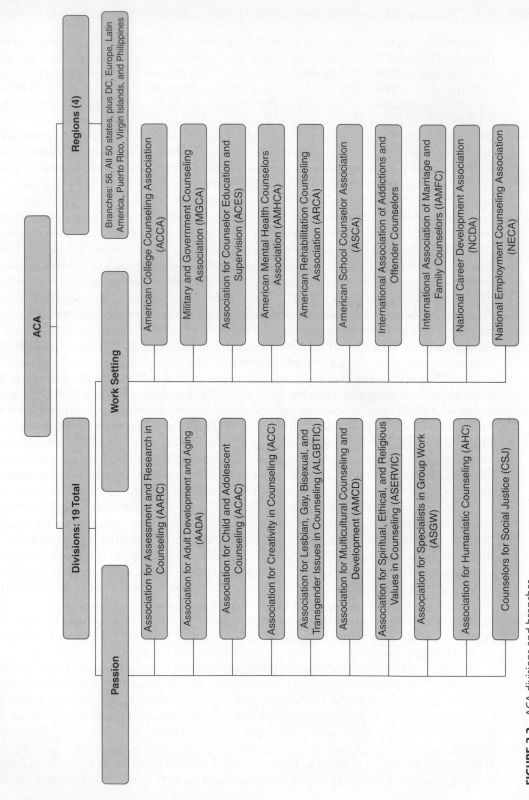

FIGURE 2.2 ACA divisions and branches.

from the journal's informative literature regardless of whether they work in private practice, community or government agencies, hospitals, or an educational setting (i.e., elementary school through college).

AMERICAN COUNSELING ASSOCIATION DIVISIONS

The 20 divisions of the ACA provide professional counselors and students with a unique opportunity to focus on specific areas of interest. The ACA divisions also provide information, resources, and leadership opportunities for their members. Each division elects its own division officers who preside over independent activities and represent an active voice in national ACA governance (i.e., the ACA Governing Council). By joining one or more divisions of the ACA, members gain the opportunity within their divisions to enhance their professional identities and practices.

Divisions can be categorized as belonging to either the *passion* divisions or the *work-setting* divisions (see Figure 2.2). **Passion divisions** focus on areas of expertise and topics of interest. For example, if one is passionate about multicultural and ethnic-minority counseling, in addition to belonging to the ACA, that person might belong to the Association for Multicultural Counseling and Development (AMCD). By being an active member of the AMCD, that person could keep abreast of and remain knowledgeable about all the latest research, theories, and counseling implications for multicultural and ethnic-minority counseling. He or she could also help advance this area of counseling by taking on leadership roles within the organization, promoting the goals and mission of the organization to colleagues and aspiring colleagues, and conducting and sharing his or her own research on these topics with others in the field. Of the 20 divisions within the ACA, 10 are considered passion divisions.

The remaining 10 ACA divisions can be classified as **work-setting divisions**, which focus on the various specialties and specific work settings within professional counseling. For example, in addition to belonging to the ACA, a professional school counselor might also belong to the American School Counselor Association (ASCA) to keep abreast of the latest research, topics, trends, and theories relevant to professional school counselors in the work setting. However, one should not judge a book by its cover or, in this case, an association by its title. Titles alone do not tell the history, mission, goals, and values of an ACA division. Therefore, this chapter explores all 20 divisions in slightly more detail.

VOICES FROM THE FIELD 2.1   The Importance of Joining Professional Associations as a Graduate Student, by Carolyn Berger

---

When I was a new graduate student and one of my professors recommended I join professional organizations, I could not help but get frustrated. I remember thinking, "I'm eating macaroni and cheese for dinner tonight, and I'm supposed to pay to join a counseling club? No thanks." I was already broke, having spent every penny I had to move myself across the country and pay for books, tuition, and living expenses. I didn't see how I could possibly afford membership in any professional organizations, so at first I chose not to join.

As time passed and my financial situation got a little more under control, I learned from a few friends that they were members of the ACA. They shared the benefits of joining and showed me the publications they received in the mail. I was impressed to see the cutting-edge research in

(Continued)

the counseling field within these journals. And the magazines offered great professional advice, even for graduate students. I learned that the ACA and some division websites had career pages that shared tips on resume building and interviewing.

These friends also went to a state conference and told me how helpful it was for them. I finally came to the realization that joining professional organizations would have a big payoff, especially once it came time for me to look for a job. I could attend conferences, network, receive training, hear tips from experienced professionals, and stay abreast of research-based counseling techniques. I started to view joining professional organizations as an investment in my future, and I decided to make doing so a priority. I could not, of course, put this expense above necessities, but I could put it above going out to dinner with friends. I calculated that if I sacrificed eating out one fewer time each month, this change would pay for my yearly ACA dues. I got on the ACA website and signed up. It was a great decision. Toward the end of my master's program, I decided it was time to take a trip to a conference. I applied to copresent at the ACA conference and was accepted. It was my first trip to a conference, and I was excited. While at the conference, I made connections, attended workshops, and heard several excellent speakers. It was an eye-opening experience.

Reflecting back, I have only two regrets: I wish I had gotten involved sooner and that I had submitted more proposals to present at conferences earlier on as a graduate student. Poster presentations are a great way to get acclimated to presenting at conferences. Poster sessions allow you to present research you have conducted without having to present in front of a big audience; instead, you simply talk one on one or in small groups with people who are interested in your topic. Your topic can be based on a project you do in one of your classes, and you can collaborate with peers or a professor who can assist you. Since I had to overcome a fear of public speaking, poster presentations would have been a great place for me to start. Professors had told me about these opportunities, but the information did not truly sink in until I had attended an ACA conference for the first time.

The experience of attending conferences has helped me grow and develop as a professional counselor and as a counselor educator. I continue to develop connections with other professionals, learn new things, explore my areas of interest, and share my own ideas with others. Conferences are invigorating experiences, and I always leave them exhausted but motivated.

In between conferences, I pay attention to the organizations' e-mails, which notify me of news in the counseling field, including training opportunities such as webinars and podcasts. Some organizations have professional chat rooms, too, which I keep an eye on so I can ask questions of and share ideas with other counselors. I also do my best to read the organizations' publications, including magazines, journals, and blogs.

Without these organizations, I would be out of the loop on what is happening in the world of counseling; therefore, I always do my best to stay involved. I encourage you to do the same and to make professional organizations and conferences a priority. If national organizations and conferences are too much of a financial strain for you, research your state's counseling organization and attend its conferences. Don't wait until you graduate. The best time to start is now!

American College Counseling Association

Chartered in 1991, the **American College Counseling Association (ACCA)** focuses on professional counselors who provide services at institutions of higher education. The ACCA fosters student development in colleges, universities, and technical and community-college settings. In addition, the ACCA strives to improve college counseling and ethical practices while promoting communication and cooperation within and among other collegiate institutions and professional organizations. The ACCA's goal is to enhance college students' development and the profession of counseling in the higher education setting (ACCA, 2018). The association publishes the *Journal of College Counseling* and a newsletter, *Visions*. For more information about this work-setting division, visit www.collegecounseling.org.

American Mental Health Counselors Association

Chartered in 1978, the **American Mental Health Counselors Association (AMHCA)** represents clinical mental health counselors. The AMHCA's mission is to use education, advocacy, licensing, and professional development to improve the profession of mental health counseling. The AMHCA not only rallies behind professional mental health counselors, it also "advocates for client-access to quality services within the health care industry" (AMHCA, 2018). The AMHCA publishes the *Journal of Mental Health Counseling* and a newsletter, the *Advocate*. For more information about this work-setting division, visit www.amhca.org.

American Rehabilitation Counseling Association

The **American Rehabilitation Counseling Association (ARCA)**, chartered in 1958, advocates for the counseling needs of individuals with disabilities. The ARCA's mission is focused on promoting excellence in professional rehabilitation counseling, research, consultation, and professional development to enhance the development of individuals with disabilities throughout their lives. The ARCA stresses its equal commitment to eliminating environmental and attitudinal barriers that hinder individuals with disabilities from pursuing opportunities, such as those in education, employment, and community activities. The ARCA publishes a newsletter and scholarly journal, the *Rehabilitation Counseling Bulletin*. For more information about this work-setting division, visit www.arcaweb.org.

American School Counselor Association

Chartered in 1953, the **American School Counselor Association (ASCA)** advocates on behalf of and expands the image and influence of professional school counselors. In addition to advocacy, the ASCA promotes leadership, collaboration, and systemic change in the field of school counseling. The ASCA empowers professional school counselors with the knowledge and skills to help improve student success at school, at home, and in the community. In addition, the ASCA focuses on helping professional school counselors enhance the personal, social, and career-development areas of student life. ASCA members work with students, educators, parents, and community members to provide positive learning environments. The ASCA's mission is to represent professional school counselors from elementary school settings through higher education institutions and to promote professionalism and ethical practices. The ASCA publishes a journal, *Professional School Counseling*, and the *ASCA School Counselor* magazine. For more information about this work-setting division, visit www.schoolcounselor.org.

Association for Adult Development and Aging

"Chartered in 1986, AADA serves as a focal point for information sharing, professional development, and advocacy related to adult development and aging issues; [and] addresses counseling concerns across the lifespan" (AADA, 2018). The **Association for Adult Development and Aging (AADA)** finds ways to improve the standards and services professional counselors provide to adults of all ages by "improving the skills and competence of American

Counseling Association members, expanding professional work opportunities in adult development and aging, promoting the lifelong development and well-being of adults, promoting standards for professional preparation for counselors of adults across the lifespan." The AADA sees creating partnerships with other organizations as a key initiative to improving the standards of care given to adults of all ages. The AADA publishes a journal, *Adultspan*, and newsletter, *Adultspan Newsletter*. For more information about this passion division, visit www.aadaweb.org.

Association for Assessment and Research in Counseling

The **Association for Assessment and Research in Counseling (AARC)** was originally chartered in 1965 as the Association for Measurement and Evaluation in Guidance. Later, it became known as the Association for Assessment in Counseling. In 2003, the organization became known as the Association for Assessment in Counseling and Education, and finally AARC in 2012. AARC advocates for the counseling profession's effective use of assessment and research. The AARC's vision statement proclaims it is an "organization of counselors, educators, and other professionals that advances the counseling profession by providing leadership, training, and research in the creation, development, production, and use of assessment and diagnostic techniques" (AARC, 2016). Its mission is to promote and recognize scholarship, professionalism, leadership, and excellence in the development and use of assessment and diagnostic techniques in counseling. The AARC publishes two important journals, *Measurement and Evaluation in Counseling and Development* and *Counseling Outcomes Research and Evaluation*, and a newsletter, *AARC Newsnotes*. For more information about this ACA passion division, visit www.aarc-counseling.org.

Association for Child and Adolescent Counseling

The **Association for Child and Adolescent Counseling (ACAC)**, chartered in 2013, is the newest ACA division. Designed as an information and support network for counselors who work with children and adolescents, the mission of the ACAC is to promote a greater awareness, advocacy, and understanding of children and adolescents, as defined as the ages from birth to adolescent, among members of the counseling profession and related fields. Members are any counselors working with children and adolescents, including mental health clinicians, school counselors, play therapists, and counselor educators. ACAC members receive a quarterly newsletter highlighting current trends in counseling children and adolescents and updates on upcoming trainings and opportunities for greater involvement. To learn more about this passion division of ACA, visit www.acachild.com.

Association for Counselor Education and Supervision

Originally called the National Association of Guidance and Counselor Trainers, the **Association for Counselor Education and Supervision (ACES)** was a founding association of the ACA in 1952 (American Counseling Association, 2018a). The ACES supports counselor educators and professional counselors who provide supervision. The ACES advocates for quality graduate education and supervision of counselors in all work settings. The ACES is a strong supporter of the accreditation process and professional development, through which it strives to improve education, credentialing, and supervision of counselors. The

ACES publishes a journal, *Counselor Education & Supervision*, and a newsletter, the *Spectrum*. For more information about this work-setting division, visit www.acesonline.net.

Association for Creativity in Counseling

Established in 2004, the **Association for Creativity in Counseling (ACC)** is a "forum for counselors, counselor educators, creative arts therapists and counselors in training to explore unique and diverse approaches to counseling" (ACC, 2018). From art and dance therapy to creativity in psychotherapy, the ACC's goal is to promote greater awareness, advocacy, and understanding of diverse and creative approaches to counseling. The ACC publishes the *Journal of Creativity in Mental Health* and the *ACC Newsletter*. For more information about this passion division, visit www.creativecounselor.org.

Association for Humanistic Counseling

Nicknamed, "the heart and conscience of the counseling profession," the **Association for Humanistic Counseling (AHC)** (previously the Counseling Association for Humanistic Education and Development [C-AHEAD]) has a rich history dating back to 1931. It was founded as the Teachers College Personnel Association, which was dedicated to personnel workers who trained teachers. The name changed in 1946 to the Personnel Section of the American Association of Teacher Colleges and changed again in 1951 to the Student Personnel Association for Teacher Education. In 1952, the Student Personnel Association for Teacher Education joined three other organizations to form the APGA, which later became the ACA. Thus, the AHC is one of the four founding associations of the ACA.

The AHC is based on the philosophical principles of the humanistic approach to counseling, and its mission is to focus on ways to empower and advocate for the client to make a difference. As a result, another important philosophy of this organization is to know the client rather than the diagnosis. The AHC provides its members with a forum to exchange information about humanistically oriented counseling practices. In addition, this organization's mission is to "promote the growing body of theoretical, empirical, and applied knowledge about human development and potential" (AHC, 2018). The AHC publishes the *Journal of Humanistic Counseling* and a newsletter, *Infochange*. For more information about this passion division, visit http://afhc.camp9.org.

Association for Lesbian, Gay, Bisexual, and Transgender Issues in Counseling

The **Association for Lesbian, Gay, Bisexual, and Transgender Issues in Counseling (ALGBTIC)** was originally chartered in 1996 as the Association for Gay, Lesbian, and Bisexual Issues in Counseling. Throughout its existence as a division of the ACA, the ALGBTIC has fought hard to be recognized as an organization to promote awareness rather than an association based on members' sexual orientation. The mission of the ALGBTIC is to provide education to promote awareness, understanding, and equality for clients and counselors of minority sexual orientations. In addition, the ALGBTIC strives to improve standards for and identify barriers to gay, lesbian, bisexual, and transgender counseling. The ALGBTIC identifies issues related to lesbian, gay, bisexual, and transgender clients and advocates for the reduction of stereotypical thinking and homosexual prejudice. The ALGBTIC publishes the *Journal of LGBT Issues in Counseling* and a newsletter, the *ALGBTIC News*. For more information about this passion division, visit www.algbtic.org.

Association for Multicultural Counseling and Development

Chartered in 1972 as the Association for Non-White Concerns in Personnel and Guidance, the **Association for Multicultural Counseling and Development (AMCD)** works to improve cultural, ethnic, and racial understanding in counseling. The AMCD's mission is to advance multicultural issues throughout the counseling profession by enhancing awareness of racial and ethnic diversity in human growth and development, addressing racial and ethnic differences, examining theory development and research, and providing leadership and training (AMCD, 2018). While the AMCD is dedicated to improving ethnic and racial understanding, it also extends its efforts to planning personal-growth activities and creating educational opportunities for culturally diverse populations. AMCD also defends human and civil rights and ensures those rights remain a major focus for the ACA and its divisions. The AMCD publishes the *Journal of Multicultural Counseling and Development* and the *AMCD Newsletter*. For more information about this passion division, visit www.multiculturalcounseling.org.

Association for Specialists in Group Work

The **Association for Specialists in Group Work (ASGW)** was chartered in 1973. The mission of the ASGW is to provide professional leadership in the field of group work, establish group-work standards for professional training, and support research and the dissemination of knowledge in the various aspects of group counseling. In addition, the ASGW strives to foster diversity and dignity in groups, use group process to extend counseling, provide a forum for professional counselors to obtain innovative and developing concepts in group work, and provide modeling of effective group practice. The ASGW publishes the *Journal for Specialists in Group Work* and the newsletter the *Group Worker*. For more information about this passion division, visit www.asgw.org.

Association for Spiritual, Ethical, and Religious Values in Counseling

The creation of this professional association was a twofold process dating back to 1951, when the Catholic Guidance Council was formed as part of the Archdiocese of New York to promote counseling and guidance in parochial schools. The need for this organization spread nationally, which led to the development of the National Conference of Guidance Councils in 1958. During this same period, a small group of counselors, many of whose members were influential in forming the New York diocesan council, attended the 1955 American Personnel and Guidance Association (APGA) annual conference in Chicago and formed the Catholic Counselors in the APGA. In 1961, these two groups merged and created the National Catholic Guidance Conference; however, divisional charter status was not awarded until 1974. Three years later, the charter changed its name to the Association for Religious Values in Counseling. The division was again renamed in 1993 as the **Association for Spiritual, Ethical, and Religious Values in Counseling (ASERVIC)**.

Although this organization has a strong background in Catholic heritage, today ASERVIC is no longer dominated by one specific religious affiliation. Rather, "ASERVIC is devoted to professionals who believe that spiritual, ethical, religious, and other human values are essential to the full development of the person and to the discipline of counseling" (ASERVIC, 2018). As a result, ASERVIC believes in and promotes the infusion of spirituality, ethics, and religious values in counselor training and application. ASERVIC publishes a journal, *Counseling and Values*, and its newsletter, *Interaction*, is an online publication. For more information about this passion division, visit www.aservic.org.

Counselors for Social Justice

The **Counselors for Social Justice (CSJ)**, chartered in 2002, "is a community of counselors, counselor educators, graduate students, and school and community leaders who seek equity and an end to oppression and injustice affecting clients, students, counselors, families, communities, schools, workplaces, governments, and other social and institutional systems" (CSJ, 2018). To accomplish this mission, the CSJ maintains an active support network; implements social-action strategies; challenges oppressive systems of privilege and power; uses online resources to maintain social-justice advocacy; and disseminates information about the inequalities that face counselors, clients, students, and communities. The CSJ publishes the *Journal for Social Action in Counseling and Psychology* and a newsletter, the *Activist*. For more information about this passion division, visit http://counselorsforsocialjustice.com.

International Association of Addictions and Offender Counselors

The **International Association of Addictions and Offender Counselors (IAAOC)** was originally chartered in 1972 as the Public Offender Counselor Association. "Members of IAAOC advocate the development of effective counseling and rehabilitation programs for people with substance abuse problems, other addictions, and adult and/or juvenile public offenders" (IAAOC, 2018). The IAAOC's mission is to provide advancement and leadership in the fields of addictions and offender counseling. This organization supports research, training, prevention, treatment, and advocacy for the addicted and forensic/criminal-justice populations. The IAAOC publishes the *Journal of Addictions and Offender Counseling* and the *IAAOC Newsletter*. For more information about this work-setting division, visit www.iaaoc.org.

International Association of Marriage and Family Counselors

Chartered in 1989, the **International Association of Marriage and Family Counselors (IAMFC)** promotes excellence in the practice of couples and family counseling. "Members help develop healthy family systems through prevention, education, and therapy" (IAMFC, 2018). The IAMFC is notable for its publications, media products, and exploration forum for family-related issues; involving diverse professionals; and emphasizing collaboration. The IAMFC encourages counselors to advocate for the value and dignity of all families. The IAMFC publishes the *Family Journal* and a newsletter, the *Family Digest*. For more information about this work-setting division, visit www.iamfconline.org.

Military and Government Counseling Association

The **Military and Government Counseling Association (MGCA)** (formerly known as the Association for Counselors and Educators in Government or ACEG) was chartered in 1984 as the Military Educators and Counselors Association to support all members of the armed services and their families by providing them with meaningful guidance, counseling, and educational programs. This included individuals and their family members in the following categories: active duty, retired, civilian employees of the Department of Defense, and employees of other government agencies. Members voted in 1994 to change the name of the organization to the Association for Counselors and Educators in Government. Today, the MGCA continues to counsel clients, and their families, who work in local, state, federal, and military-related government agencies. The MGCA publishes the *ACEG Newsletter* as well as the *Journal of Military and Government Counseling*. For more information about this work-setting division, visit www.acegonline.org.

National Career Development Association

Originally founded in 1913 as the National Vocational Guidance Association, the **National Career Development Association (NCDA)** was the first counseling association in existence. The NCDA was one of the four founding associations of ACA. The mission of the NCDA is to "provide professional development, publications, standards, and advocacy to practitioners and educators who inspire and empower individuals to achieve their career and life goals" (NCDA, 2018). The NCDA publishes the highly rated *Career Development Quarterly* and a newsletter, *Career Developments*. For more information about this work-setting division, visit http://ncda.org.

National Employment Counseling Association

Originally chartered in 1966, the **National Employment Counseling Association (NECA)** began as a division of the ACA under the name National Employment Counselors Association. The NECA is committed to offering professional leadership to individuals who counsel those in the employment or career-development setting. The NECA membership expands to a diverse work setting, which includes individuals from private practice; business and industry; community agencies; colleges and universities; and federal, state, and local governments. The NCDA publishes the *Journal of Employment Counseling* and the *NECA Newsletter*. For more information about this work-setting division, visit www.employmentcounseling.org.

Now complete Activity 2.1 to find out more about the ACA, its divisions and other entities, and counseling-related publications and information. Then complete Activity 2.2 to test your memory of the ACA divisions and their expressed missions. Finally, complete Activity 2.3 by picking the three ACA divisions that most interest you.

ACTIVITY 2.1 FINDING CURRENT RESEARCH

It is important for professional counselors to have knowledge of recent issues and findings in counseling. Many professional counseling organizations provide current research and information pertinent to the counseling field. The following are activities that can be done to increase your knowledge base of these up-to-date findings:

1. Some journals can be located at a university library for hard-copy articles and text. More common today, professional journals can be accessed online through the journal's specific website or Psycline (www.psycline.org/journals/psycline.html), an online guide to psychology and social-science journals on the web. Choose a topic of special interest to you as a professional, and find five research articles discussing this topic.
2. Go to your university library, choose a topic of special interest from the text holdings, and read the book.

3. Not all information found on the Internet has been evaluated by an expert in the field. However, this does not mean that there is no beneficial information on the World Wide Web.
   a. Psychwatch.com is an online resource for professionals in psychology and psychiatry. It has numerous links to other counseling disciplines and resources, including online journals, licensure information, and software.
   b. Psychcentral.com is a mental health and psychology website providing peer-reviewed information since 1995. This site has a resource directory of current topics related to counseling and psychology, along with symptom and treatment links to mental health disorders.
   c. Information can also be located at professional organizations' homepages, including the ACA, www.counseling.org, and the ASCA, www.schoolcounselor.org.
4. Using all the information you found during your research of journals, books, and Internet sites, write a short literature review to illustrate the knowledge you have gained from this activity.

ACTIVITY 2.2

Find the division of ACA that best fits each description below. (An answer key is provided at the end of this chapter.)

___ 1. Counselor educators with a humanistic orientation

___ 2. Professional counselors who lead groups

___ 3. Professional counselors who advocate quality services within the health care industry

___ 4. Professional counselors in employment counseling settings

___ 5. Professional counselors who focus on life span concerns and senior citizens

___ 6. Professional counselors who are engaged in societal issues, seeking social action

___ 7. Psychometrists; testing specialists

___ 8. A founding association of the ACA; now concerned with career development

___ 9. Counselors of clients (and their families) in local, state, and federal governments or in military-related agencies

a. Association for Assessment and Research in Counseling (AARC)

b. Association for Adult Development and Aging (AADA)

c. Association for Creativity in Counseling (ACC)

d. American College Counseling Association (ACCA)

e. Military and Government Counseling Association (MGCA)

f. Association for Counselor Education and Supervision (ACES)

g. Association for Lesbian, Gay, Bisexual, and Transgender Issues in Counseling (ALGBTIC)

h. Association for Multicultural Counseling and Development (AMCD)

i. American Mental Health Counselors Association (AMHCA)

j. American Rehabilitation Counseling Association (ARCA)

____10. Emphasizes the need for quality education and supervision of professional counselors

____11. Works to improve cultural, ethnic, and racial empathy and understanding

____12. Professional counselors who work for the full development of the individual through values and religious, ethical, and spiritual issues

____13. Professional counselors promoting healthy family systems

____14. Professional counselors fostering student development in higher education

____15. Professional counselors who focus on substance-abuse issues

____16. Professional counselors who work in the school system

____17. Professional counselors who work with disabled clients

____18. Educates counselors in the area of sexual identity

____19. Counselors specializing in counseling clients under the age of 19 years.

____20. Professional counselors interested in using creative arts with clients

k. American School Counselor Association (ASCA)

l. Association for Spiritual, Ethical, and Religious Values in Counseling (ASERVIC)

m. Association for Specialists in Group Work (ASGW)

n. Association for Humanistic Counseling (AHC)

o. Counselors for Social Justice (CSJ)

p. International Association of Addictions and Offender Counselors (IAAOC)

q. International Association of Marriage and Family Counselors (IAMFC)

r. National Career Development Association (NCDA)

s. National Employment Counseling Association (NECA)

t. Association for Child and Adolescent Counseling (ACAC)

ACTIVITY 2.3

In small groups, determine the three divisions that best fit your career interests and explain to group members the values and interests you possess that make those divisions a good match for you. Do you have professional counseling interests not met by the current ACA division structure? Explain.

AMERICAN COUNSELING ASSOCIATION REGIONS AND BRANCHES

For the purposes of the ACA, the United States and affiliated international organizations are broken into four **regions**: Midwest, North Atlantic, Southern, and Western (see http://www.counseling.org/about-us/divisions-regions-and-branches). The four regional designations allow ACA members who are not members of ACA divisions to have representation through an ACA Governing Council representative.

Branches represent the grassroots of counseling. The ACA has 56 branches (see http://www.counseling.org/about-us/divisions-regions-and-branches), including one for each state, plus the District of Columbia, Europe, Latin America, Puerto Rico, Virgin Islands, and the Philippines. (Note: Some branches are currently inactive.) Branches provide something that a national organization cannot: a local connection. Branches enable professional counselors to network with other professional counselors in their town, county, state, or territory through local and state conferences and workshops. Branches are in touch with the issues that are pertinent to their particular states and so can target resources, training, and advocacy to a specific need or issue.

For example, the Illinois Counseling Association provides members with specific information on health insurance companies that provide counselor reimbursement in the Chicago area. The Kentucky Counseling Association provides information on how to find a school counseling position in Kentucky. The Texas Counseling Association has a referral bank where state residents can find association members who are practitioners. The Maine Counseling Association, through its branch division the Maine School Counselor Association, links to a vital resource for school counselors in Maine, including the Maine Comprehensive School Counseling Program Model. Often, local or statewide services such as these are of greatest importance to resident counselors and students in training and beyond the scope of national association missions. Branch associations fill these needs.

Branches also play a vital role in advocating for state legislation that is in the best interest of counselors, clients, and the public. A great example concerns now-defeated legislation in Indiana that would have restricted the use of more than 200 tests and inventories to only licensed psychologists and would have prevented counselors from using these instruments in mental health centers, rehabilitation agencies, or independent practice. The bill might have been signed into law by the governor of Indiana if not for a coalition formed by the National Board for Certified Counselors (NBCC) and the Fair Access Coalition on Testing (FACT), consisting of professional counselors, social workers, test publishers, marriage and family therapists, and other professional groups. This coalition was able to convince the governor not to sign the bill. As a result, counselors in Indiana can continue to provide assessment services within their scopes of practice and training to residents of Indiana.

In another example, the ACA, AMHCA, and NBCC helped counselors in Nevada form a coalition to pursue licensure, and, in 2007, Nevada became the 49th state to achieve that goal. The California Coalition for Counseling Licensure, with the financial backing of the NBCC and ACA, achieved licensure for professional counselors in California in 2009. As a result of the hard work and efforts of local state branches and national organizations like AMHCA, NBCC, and ACA, professional counselors can now become licensed in all 50 states and the District of Columbia.

VOICES FROM THE FIELD 2.2   Getting Involved: Joining and Promoting Professional Counseling Organizations, by Kelly Duncan

I checked the box.

This seemingly simple task performed while filling out the evaluation for the first state branch conference I attended as a new professional counselor has had a profound impact on my professional and personal life. The box at the bottom of the evaluation form asked if I would like to get involved with my state counseling association, and I checked yes.

I realize now that this relatively simple act in my mid-20s propelled me into a lifetime of professional involvement with and service to the profession of counseling. This involvement has spanned local, state, regional, national, and international levels, which has allowed me to advocate for the profession I love and form relationships with colleagues all over the world.

Because my own involvement has affected me in this way, I continually look for opportunities to mentor other young professionals in hopes that they, too, might have the chance to enhance their journeys. It is difficult to put into words the many ways this involvement has enriched my life, but I know it has created a confidence in me that has allowed me to have the courage to embrace new experiences and take risks. It has permitted me to travel, which has expanded my worldview. My involvement has provided me with opportunities to advocate for a profession I love and for people who might not have a way to advocate for themselves.

I know that my life's journey would have been very different had I not checked the box that day. I'm certainly glad I didn't miss the opportunities that checkmark brought my way.

OTHER ESSENTIAL PROFESSIONAL COUNSELING ORGANIZATIONS

The ACA partners with other professional organizations to provide its members with various resources, such as the ACA Foundation, a charitable foundation. All professional counselors are committed to academic excellence and high standards within the counseling setting. As a result, additional relationships exist within the counseling world among a foundation to support counselor and client well-being (American Counseling Association Foundation [ACAF]), an honor society for counselors (Chi Sigma Iota [CSI]), university accreditation for counseling programs (Council for Accreditation of Counseling and Related Educational Programs [CACREP] and National Council on Rehabilitation Education [CORE]), and a national counseling certification organization (NBCC), each of which is briefly introduced.

American Counseling Association Foundation

The **American Counseling Association Foundation (ACAF)** encourages and supports counselor well-being and the well-being of those whom counselors serve. This foundation was established in 1979. Since its inception, the ACAF has supported counseling students with essay competitions; honored outstanding educators and practitioners; published a free weekly column, the *Counseling Corner*, in approximately 300 U.S. newspapers; and used the Growing Happy and Confident Kids project to reach out to elementary school students to help them deal with and develop skills to face the problems that plague our schools (e.g., bullying, violence, substance abuse, gangs). The ACAF established the Counselors Care Fund, which reached out to counselors and branches affected by Hurricanes Katrina and Rita. The ACAF remains a professional partner of ACA through tax-deductible gifts from corporations, individuals, foundations, and ACA divisions and branches. Many professional counselors donate gifts to the ACAF to promote this charitable work.

Chi Sigma Iota

Chi Sigma Iota (CSI) is the counseling profession's official honorary society. Founded in 1985, this independent membership organization distinguishes the outstanding contributions of individuals to the profession and recognizes spectacular leadership, scholarship, research, advocacy, and achievement in counseling. Numerous universities sponsor local chapters of CSI. For further information, visit www.csi-net.org.

Council for Accreditation of Counseling and Related Educational Programs

Created in 1981 by the ACA, the **Council for Accreditation of Counseling and Related Educational Programs (CACREP)** is an independent council that accredits institutions with graduate-level counselor-preparation programs. To ensure quality training in the field of counseling, CACREP promotes high standards, imparts rigorous and objective reviews of established programs, and works with other credentialing organizations. For further information, visit www.cacrep.org.

Council on Rehabilitation Education

Formed in 1971, the Council on Rehabilitation Education (CORE) accredits graduate programs that prepare rehabilitation counselors. The CORE Registry also recognizes undergraduate programs in rehabilitation and disabilities studies. To ensure quality training in the field of rehabilitation counseling, CORE promotes high standards and rigorous and objective reviews of established programs. For further information, visit www.core-rehab.org/index.html. In 2013 CACREP and CORE entered into an affiliation agreement allowing CORE to become a corporate affiliate of CACREP. As a result of this agreement, clinical rehabilitation counseling programs could now seek joint accreditation through CACREP and CORE. CACREP and CORE further announced a merger that is scheduled to commence July, 2017.

National Board for Certified Counselors

The **National Board for Certified Counselors (NBCC)** is a voluntary, nonprofit, nongovernmental, independent corporation that advances professional counselor credentials. To help counselors advance their credentialing, the NBCC administers the national certification process; identifies counselors who have chosen to become nationally board certified; and manages the certification examination and specialty certificates for addictions counselors, clinical mental health counselors, and school counselors. Much more information regarding the NBCC follows later in this chapter. See also www.nbcc.org.

PROFESSIONAL DEVELOPMENT

Regardless of the professional work setting, continuing education (CE) and professional development are musts for professional counselors to stay current in their knowledge and provide the most up-to-date treatments to the clients they serve. Whether to obtain certificate or license renewal, to increase occupational opportunities, or for career development, continuing education is a reality that stretches well beyond the receipt of a graduate degree, state licensure, or national certification. Having to obtain licenses and certifications guarantees that professional counselors will need ongoing continuing education and professional development training because the licensing or certifying entities require it.

The purpose of professional development is to help the professional counselor maintain or increase counseling knowledge and skills. Continuing professional development can be costly and time-consuming, so the ACA and its divisions and branches offer high-quality and affordable continuing education courses presented by experts in an assortment of subject areas, allowing participants to partake at their own convenience.

The ACA offers continuing education courses online and through webinars. Participants who have access to the Internet can obtain online continuing education credit at times most convenient to their busy schedules. The ACA offers members four ways to obtain online continuing education credit. First, the ACA offers three-credit and five-credit online courses with corresponding examinations. Second, the ACA offers an individual the capability to read articles in the *Journal of Counseling & Development* and take corresponding examinations for continuing education credit. The ACA also offers the option to read from selected ACA book chapters and take corresponding examinations for continuing education credit. Third, the ACA now offers continuing education credit for its podcasts and webinars. Finally, ACA members receive a "CE of the month" message. The ACA warns, however, that before enrolling in online courses, a professional counselor should confirm that online credits are accepted by his or her state licensure board or certification body. Recently, the ACA began offering webinars, which are live streaming presentations on various topics for continuing education credit. Although most state licensure boards and certification renewal bodies accept online courses for continuing education credit, not all do at this time.

Finally, national, state, and regional conferences provide an opportunity for counseling professionals to contribute to the field through presentations and to expand their knowledge base as educators and practitioners. For example, continuing education contact hours can be earned at the ACA annual convention. During this convention, the ACA offers the ACA Learning Institute, where more than 40 skill-building workshops are offered during the two-day preconvention time period. In addition, the ACA offers the annual conference content sessions every spring, where more than 400 educational opportunities are available for professional counselors and mental health practitioners. Numerous other professional counseling organizations at the state and national levels offer myriad opportunities for professional development.

BENEFITS OF JOINING PROFESSIONAL COUNSELING ORGANIZATIONS

Professional counseling organizations have developed benefits and services to best meet the needs of their members. Counselors are kept informed of current issues and updates in the profession through publications, including books, journals, newsletters, web pages, and Listservs. Members of the ACA receive the quarterly *Journal of Counseling & Development* and the professional monthly magazine *Counseling Today*. Many organizations provide grants, awards, and scholarships through foundations supporting students, research, mentoring, advocacy, service, and humanitarian efforts in the counseling field. In addition, employment listings are often provided for state and national opportunities. Assistance in job searches, resume writing, interviewing skills, and occupational trends might be included.

Additional Benefits for Professional Counselor Members

The ACA considers its professional members, counselors and counselor educators, to be the linchpin to helping clients and students meet the daily challenges they face. As a result, the ACA and its divisions and branches are dedicated to providing members with resources, products, information, and services to help them find success. The ACA also trusts its professional members to make important decisions about the future of counseling and the ACA by encouraging them to run for elected offices and serve on committees. The ACA keeps its professional members abreast of the information, ideas, and experiences created at the annual conventions by publishing the information on *VISTAS Online*. Finally, the ACA offers its professional members multiple opportunities to receive continuing-education credit and teach courses for others to obtain their continuing education credits.

The American Counseling Association Member Services Committee

In today's world, where personal liability lawsuits have become commonplace, insurance companies serve an essential role. As a result, the ACA has teamed up with an independent corporation to promote quality insurance coverage and services for ACA members and groups in the human-development professions. Whether counselors work with individuals, families, or difficult populations, such as sex offenders, this insurance offers broad professional liability coverage. Master's level graduate student members of ACA are provided professional liability insurance free of charge as a member benefit; CACREP requires graduate students to have professional liability insurance during practicum and internship experiences.

The ACA also uses licensed insurance underwriters and agents to write and provide insurance for professional counselors, students, multidisciplinary groups, business owners, and nonprofit organizations. Options consist of auto, homeowners, and group life and health plans, which include disability income, business overhead expenses, term life, customized major medical, catastrophic major medical, short-term major medical, hospital protection, accidental death and dismemberment, dental, long-term care, and Medicare supplemental insurance.

Additional Benefits for Student Members

The ACA and its divisions and branches recognize that students are the future of the counseling profession and provide students with the resources to begin a career in counseling. Students are offered opportunities through the ACAF Graduate Student Essay Contest. All runners-up and the first-place winner receive a one-year membership to the ACA. The first-place winner also receives a monetary award. Another competition offered to students is the Ethics Case Study Competition. Graduate students at both master's and doctoral levels are given the opportunity to think critically about and analyze a probable ethical case, generate an appropriate ethical decision, and make a plan to respond to the decision.

In conjunction with the ACAF, the ACA offers the Ross Trust Graduate Student Scholarship Competition. The competition begins every fall and is for students studying to be professional school counselors in elementary, middle, or high school. Fifteen scholarships are awarded yearly, of which 10 are for master's level students and 5 are for doctoral students. Another benefit is having ACA Connect available to student members as a way to communicate with other professional counseling students locally, nationally, and internationally.

Divisions and branches of the ACA also offer student and professional-member benefits and opportunities. For example, the ASCA offers its members professional liability insurance, the *ASCA School Counselor* magazine, the *Professional School Counseling* journal, annual conference discounts, access to the ASCA website and online resources, government contacts, and level-specific message boards. An accounting of the membership benefits of

ACA, its 20 divisions, and its 56 branches would require an entire book. Many students and professionals find joining associations relevant to their location and professional aspirations to be a smart decision *and* a great investment in their future and that of the profession (see http://www.counseling.org/about-us/divisions-regions-and-branches).

Ethical Standards

Professional organizations have been instrumental in setting professional and ethical standards for counselors and counselor education programs. Ethical codes work to standardize guidelines for professional practice, continually evolving to meet contemporary needs and issues (see Chapter 3). Ultimately, both counselors and clients benefit. In addition to liability insurance, professional organizations often provide specific services such as ethical or legal consultation for counselors.

Legislative Advocacy

National and state organizations work diligently to advocate politically for the counseling profession. In many cases, success has been the result of a unified effort on the part of professional counseling organizations and their members. It is important to continue to represent the interests of the profession and to positively influence public policy and legislation regarding the field of counseling. The ACA has an Office of Public Policy and Support and a standing committee known as the PP&L (Public Policy and Legislation).

Supporting the Mission of the Profession

As you can tell from the information on organizations presented so far, many exciting opportunities for professional involvement exist. Of course, joining a professional association costs money, and joining numerous organizations costs more money. So a question new counselors often ask is, "Which organizations should I belong to, and which credentials should I pursue?"

Many professional counselors, and especially students, join the ACA and their state branches. This gives professionals contact with the associations that serve all counselor interests at the state and national levels. Many also join a work-setting division (e.g., school counselor, mental health counselor, career counselor); pursue national certification, such as the national certified counselor (NCC) certification; and state licensure or certification, which are often needed to engage in private practice or work for nonprofit agencies or school systems.

Joining professional organizations and pursuing professional credentials shows your commitment to professional standards, places you in contact with like-minded professionals at the national and state levels, and keeps you informed of important work and legislative issues. Counselors who are passionate about certain counseling specialties (e.g., assessment, social justice, multiculturalism) often join the national divisions and state affiliates that serve those causes. There are numerous opportunities to get involved, attend professional development events, and advocate on the part of your clients and profession. Getting involved in professional organizations and pursuing professional credentials are the best ways to develop and maintain your professional identity and serve the best interests of your clients and students.

Now complete Case Study 2.1. What to Join!

CASE STUDY 2.1

What to Join, What to Join?!

Most counseling programs encourage students to join professional organizations in the field. This usually leads to the counseling student asking what would be the best organizations to join.

Mike was a student studying school counseling at a state institution in Pennsylvania. He was a conscientious student with a high GPA who wanted to participate in the counseling field at a meaningful level while still a student. When Mike met with his advisor, they discussed a number of pertinent options. Mike saw the long list of possibilities and felt overwhelmed with the number of choices. The first step was to help Mike focus on the most appropriate places to begin, including which professional counseling organizations usually offer a discounted rate for student membership. This information was a bit of relief for Mike, who, like other students, had to consider financial factors when making choices.

An additional benefit that may be offered by parent organizations, such as ACA, or larger divisions, like ASCA, is free liability insurance for student members who are placed in practicum, field education, or internships. This increases savings.

At the national level, Mike decided to purchase student memberships in ACA and ASCA, although there were other divisions within ACA that could be chosen at time of registration. Mike was advised to review the list of divisions to see if he felt a strong sense of interest in any of them. Mike said that he would consider the Association for Multicultural Counseling and Development (AMCD) as an option because he felt multicultural counseling was an important part of his counseling focus.

Mike was also encouraged to join some entity at the state level, which would allow him to attend meetings and conferences to become more involved in the counseling profession at a state and regional level. He could network with other professionals already established in the field and he could also begin the process of advocating for the counseling profession at a local level. He found that Pennsylvania had two state organizations with student memberships: the Pennsylvania Counseling Association (PCA) and the Pennsylvania School Counselors Association (PSCA). Each state usually has similar organizations.

Because of Mike's high GPA, his advisor encouraged him to also join Chi Sigma Iota: Counseling Academic Honor Society International (CSI). This would provide an excellent opportunity to become part of an honors organization within the university and on an international level. He would get to know other counseling students with similar interests. CSI also promotes advocacy and charitable projects within the chapters' communities. Mike was happy with these choices and thought they added an important component to his counseling experience.

Now, break into small groups with other counseling students.

1. Review the professional organizations offered to counselors and counseling students.
2. What are the advantages to joining professional organizations?
3. Which organizations would you prefer to join and why?
4. Discuss your responses with the group.

RELATIONSHIP BETWEEN THE AMERICAN COUNSELING ASSOCIATION AND THE AMERICAN PSYCHOLOGICAL ASSOCIATION

The ACA is the national association for all counselors, regardless of specialty area, and serves the interests of all professional counselors. The American Psychological Association (APA) is the national association for all psychologists, regardless of specialty area, and serves the interests of all psychologists. The two associations often work in concert to accomplish legislative or professional goals shared in common, but "turf war" issues sometimes arise between counselors and psychologists. Because psychological associations at the national and state levels have existed longer than counseling associations, they are often better known by the public and better respected by legislators.

"Turf war" battles continue to occur in some states. In the late 1990s through 2008, psychologists in Maryland and Indiana attempted to restrict the use of psychological tests by professional counselors, whom they deemed as a class of professionals "unqualified" to administer, score, and interpret competently the tests' results, even though the professional counselors in those states met the standards of the established licensure boards and test publishers. The psychologist advocates in those states claimed such restrictions protected the public from harm, even though no claim of harm resulting from the use of psychological tests was ever made against a licensee of either state. Despite the claims of protecting the public, such restrictions were clearly aimed at supply-and-demand economics and restraint of trade, as stated in several opinions by the Maryland Attorney General's Office.

These are only a few of the numerous reasons to join and maintain membership in counseling organizations and to pursue professional credentials. Without strong professional organizations, the rights of professional counselors would be jeopardized, as would the protection of the public.

SOME KEY CHALLENGES THAT NEED TO BE ADDRESSED BY COUNSELING PROFESSIONALS

As an emerging profession, counseling still has numerous issues to address. Many of the more conceptual issues were addressed at the end of Chapter 1 and are discussed in subsequent chapters. A lengthy treatise of these issues is beyond the scope of this text. In truth, a new set of issues evolves every decade or two, is identified and focused on by professional organizations and legislators, and, it is hoped, successfully resolved. The following brief discussion does not offer an exhaustive list of issues, but it does give readers some insights into the types of issues currently on the minds of leaders in the profession.

Professional identity has been a key issue for the field for a long time and is likely to continue to be wrangled over for the next decade at least. Several of the authors in this text were involved in 20/20: A Vision for the Future of Counseling, an initiative undertaken by the ACA and 30 other counseling associations and entities to identify and address issues of pressing importance to the future of the counseling profession—issues that need to be resolved by 2020. As mentioned in Chapter 1, the 20/20 committee has agreed on a definition of counseling and principles for unifying and strengthening the counseling profession. It also attempted to address the issue of licensure portability, which would allow counselors to transfer their practice licenses between states when they move.

Professional identity is a huge issue that will continue to evolve. A side effect of our profession's emergence is that its affiliated associations have become a loose consortium of entities, which in some cases has led to a loosening of ties and bonds between the ACA and some of its divisions. All national divisions are autonomous entities and have historically shared a convergent purpose, mission, and activities. However, not all division leaders see or desire the counseling profession to be a unified one.

For example, in 2003, after repeated warnings of bylaws violations, the ACA Governing Council voted to serve a notice of revocation of the charters of two of its larger divisions, ASCA and AMHCA. Even though the divisions soon reestablished compliance and their charters were actually never revoked, the damage caused by the intraprofessional conflict lingers. In fact, the issue reemerged in 2009.

To this day, some school counselors and mental health counselors believe the ASCA and the AMHCA disaffiliated from the ACA, even though they did not. Some still do not see the counseling profession as a unified profession, an identity issue that will need to be resolved in the near future.

Work-setting divisions will need to determine their members' professional identifications. Are their members professional counselors who work and apply the principles and techniques of counseling in different work settings? Or are their members so specialized in their practices that they are not professional counselors but are instead individuals who have core identities other than counseling and happen to use counseling principles and techniques during the discharge of their duties (e.g., how a psychiatric nurse identifies first and foremost with the nursing profession)? This is a critical issue of our time. In fact, the ASCA leadership has proposed that school counselors are first and foremost educators who happen to do counseling in a school setting, discordant with the philosophy of CACREP (2016) and the vast majority of counselor educators who train school counselors.

History has taught us that unity often coalesces during times of threat, and, fortunate or not, there are no serious threats to dismantle the counseling profession at this time. Indeed, between 2009 and 2012 the profession accomplished two long-held goals. First, California became the final state to issue licenses for professional counselors. Within a period of about a quarter century, 50 states and several territories had passed professional counselor licensure laws. Second, the ACA has long advocated for professional counselors to achieve parity with psychologists and social workers with third-party insurance-reimbursement providers, including governmental programs. Counselors recently came closer to this goal by obtaining TRICARE parity (i.e., became independent providers of mental health services to veterans).

The current difficulties in the area of parity stem from the profession's relatively recent embodiment. Much of the country's original legislation was written before professional counselors existed. As pieces of legislation come up for renewal or refunding by governmental agencies and legislatures, some lawmakers, often at the urging of constituents who represent competing mental health service providers, resist revising provider status to add professional counselors to the list of qualified providers.

Many new challenges are on the horizon. Counseling programs already have two accrediting organizations (i.e., CACREP and CORE), and a merger between these organizations would lead to further unification of the profession. Also, a number of for-profit counseling registries have emerged that offer a "credential" to anyone who meets the minimum standards and is willing to pay the annual fee. Counselors in training are advised to exercise care when pursuing credentials and to be sure that any credentials procured come from reputable sources—ordinarily professional counseling associations and organizations.

Emerging professional issues (e.g., online counseling) will continue to be addressed through vehicles such as position papers and the ACA Code of Ethics. Doing so requires the support of legislative advocacy and a dedication to the mission of the profession: to serve the mental health and wellness needs of all members of society, especially those who are marginalized or oppressed.

An element critical to the future of the counseling profession is the effective transitioning of student members and their energy and excitement into professional membership in the ACA and its specialty divisions. Students and new professionals are looking for a stable professional home through mentoring and networking. Finding ways to address member needs through electronic means is one initiative. In recognition of the internationalization of counseling, the ACA is exploring how to collaborate with and increase international memberships in a culturally and economically sensitive manner and provide continuing education to members around the world. The ACA (and other counseling organizations) has clear strategic plans to address these and other issues influencing the future of the counseling profession, but the support and efforts of professional counselors are needed to accomplish the agenda items.

The education, training, and recognition of highly qualified counselors is the responsibility of counselor educators, counselor supervisors, and of the professionals and organizations that develop and administer accreditation and credentialing processes. The remainder of this chapter introduces the reader to the accreditation and credentialing processes that govern the profession and raise the quality of counselors to meet high standards of professionalism.

NATIONAL ACCREDITATION

Accreditation is pursued by a university, college, or educational institution to demonstrate compliance with high professional, educational, or training standards developed by an independent professional review board. Accreditation is one way for counselor education programs at institutions of higher education to show that quality education and training are being imparted to students. Many students look at a school's accreditation status when applying to graduate counseling programs. This is not to say that only accredited programs are of high quality; nevertheless, programs that have achieved accreditation demonstrate attainment of and adherence to high professional standards.

Two major types of accreditation exist in the United States. Institutional accreditation involves a general review of operational and curricular practices at an entire university, college, or school. Specialized accreditation focuses on a particular program or field of study, such as counseling, teacher education, or medicine. Accreditation enhances an institution's reputation. It requires programs to undergo periodic self-examination, continuous assessment, and quality improvements to adhere to and exceed standards. Institutions often pursue accreditation because it allows access to federal funding and student loans. Two accrediting organizations of primary interest to counselors and counseling programs are CACREP and CORE.

CACREP, established in 1981, accredits graduate counselor-preparation programs in the United States by setting high educational training standards, influencing and advancing the professional preparation of future professional counselors to serve in a complex and diverse society. CACREP (2016) has had a tremendous impact on the counseling profession. More than 640 programs in more than 280 U.S. universities have achieved CACREP accreditation, and nearly all state licensure boards and the NBCC have modeled their educational requirements on the CACREP required curriculum.

CACREP reviews programs offering master's degrees in addiction counseling; career counseling; clinical mental health counseling; clinical rehabilitation counseling; college counseling and student affairs; school counseling; and marital, couple, and family counseling. CACREP also reviews doctoral degree programs in counselor education and supervision. CACREP (2016) follows a process of program review and approval that features six steps: (1) self-study and application, (2) initial review, (3) on-site visit, (4) team report, (5) institutional response, and (6) accreditation decision. Accreditation decisions include (a) full eight-year accreditation, (b) two-year provisional accreditation (minor deficiencies to address in a follow-up report), or (c) denial of accreditation.

The CACREP board undertakes a standard revisions process every eight years to continuously improve the responsiveness of accredited programs to diverse professional and societal changes. The CACREP board is composed of 11 professional members and 2 public members, but it relies on more than 300 trained volunteers who serve as initial reviewers or conduct on-site reviews.

Many university counseling programs are housed in departments of education that might undergo accreditation by external accrediting organizations. For example, many schools or departments of education undergo accreditation by the Council for the Accreditation of Educator Preparation (CAEP), formerly known as the National Council for Accreditation of Teacher Education (NCATE). CAEP insists that counseling programs within CAEP-accredited institutions align with CACREP standards (2016), indicating again the influence and respect CACREP holds within the United States as the leader in setting high standards for counselor education training programs. Learn more about CACREP by visiting its website at www.cacrep.org.

Another accrediting organization in the field of professional counseling is the **National Council on Rehabilitation Education (CORE)**, which was established to evaluate higher education programs in the field of rehabilitation counseling. CORE was established in 1971 and promotes standards for rehabilitation counseling programs, including mission and objectives, program evaluation, general curriculum requirements, knowledge domains, educational outcomes, clinical experience, administration and faculty, and program support and resources. CORE board members are appointed by the National Rehabilitation Counseling Association, National Council of Rehabilitation Education, ARCA, and Council of State Administrators of Vocational Rehabilitation; two public members are also appointed by the CORE board. Rehabilitation counseling programs are evaluated by the 15- to 20-member Commission on Standards and Accreditation, and these evaluations are reported to the CORE board for decisions. For national certification in the field of rehabilitation counseling, other than clinical rehabilitation counseling programs jointly accredited by CACREP and CORE, CORE is the accrediting body, not CACREP. CACREP and CORE announced a merger to take effect in 2017. Complete Activity 2.4 to investigate the accreditation of your college or university.

ACTIVITY 2.4

Investigate the accreditation of your college or university. Which accrediting bodies have been involved? Many different accreditation entities accredit the college or university, various departments, and programs. After determining which organizations accredit the college or university, also research whether any other accrediting bodies recognize your department or program of study. What must your college or university do to be in compliance?

THINK ABOUT IT 2.1

What is the importance of regular reviews of standards for counselor education programs?

International Efforts at Program Registry

Almost all CACREP-accredited universities are within the United States although a couple of them have been located in Canada and one is in Mexico. A number of counseling programs around the world have asked CACREP to develop accreditation standards for international universities. However, CACREP's standards and process were developed for the U.S. university system and therefore are not necessarily directly applicable to universities with diverse cultures and languages in nations around the world. For example, some nations do not educate counselors at the bachelor's level, let alone require a master's degree to practice counseling. In addition, counseling is not a term used widely around the world, although most nations have some individuals who practice something closely related to counseling.

CACREP recognized that counseling programs across diverse cultures, nations, educational systems, and languages needed some form of quality-assurance procedures for the entry-level preparation of counselors. To address this need, CACREP developed a registry system that recognizes counseling programs from diverse nations that adhere to culturally appropriate accreditation standards. This program is known as the International Registry of Counsellor Education Programs (IRCEP). IRCEP is not an accrediting body, but it does recognize international programs that meet basic standards of program quality and help them prepare for future accreditation.

STATE ACCREDITATION

Similar to CACREP, state agencies can approve higher education counseling programs. When a state gives its approval, it is simply saying the college or university has met the minimum requirements for the statewide standards for all programs at degree-granting institutions. However, accreditation exceeds this endorsement; it assures the public that an institution of higher education meets high levels of quality that other colleges and universities of the same type recognize as quality standards.

Many states accredit graduate-level school counseling programs in conjunction with national accreditation processes. For example, CAEP, which accepts CACREP accreditation standards and decisions, might coordinate a visit to a college or university with a state's department of education. While each entity makes an independent decision, the standards used are often similar. Similarly, the Maryland State Department of Education has a Division of Certification and Accreditation with three areas: certification (teacher and professional personnel, such as school counselors), nonpublic-school approval, and program approval for all degree-granting institutions operating in Maryland.

STATE PROFESSIONAL CERTIFICATION AND OTHER CREDENTIALS

Credentialing in the counseling world occurs when professionals demonstrate they have met high standards of education, knowledge, and experience. Out of necessity, credentialing laws and regulations for the counseling profession have been left to state legislatures and other regulatory agencies. Credentialing procedures might differ in different states as a result. However, there are some commonalities, primarily as a result of advocacy efforts by professional counseling organizations.

Gladding (2016) pointed out that there are four levels of credentialing procedures, ranging from least prestigious to most prestigious: inspection, registration, certification, and licensure. **Inspection** is an examination by state agencies to determine whether professional counselors are practicing in a way that is conducive to public safety, health, and welfare standards. This inspection is often done with professional counselors who are employed by state agencies. During an inspection, personnel are interviewed and program case notes and agency procedures are scrutinized.

The next type of state credential is **registration**. To qualify for a registry, one's state legislature must have passed a law that allows professional groups to document or list the individuals within the profession who have met specific standards. Generally, those standards include certification. Registries are often published, giving the public a resource. In addition, listing one's name on the registry provides a means for advertisement of services.

Certification for title restrictions is provided for individuals within a given profession who have met higher standards than others within the same professional group. Higher standards often involve completing a graduate program, working a specific number of hours or years within the field, and passing an examination to show competency in the given area. Take, for example, the lucrative world of number crunching. Accountants and financial analysts alike can work in the financial industry, but only individuals who have met the specific high standards may use the title *certified public accountant* (CPA) or *certified financial analyst* (CFA). These titles are not reciprocal, because each title requires different procedures and examinations. If one has met the high standards for the CPA and the CFA, one can use both titles.

The same is true for the field of counseling. For example, many volunteers or professionals within the mental health profession, with little or much training, may work with clients with addictions. However, only professionals who have met the high standards of the certification process may use the title *certified addictions counselor*. Professionals meeting these specific standards apply for this certification from a professional certification board.

STATE LICENSURE

Licensure is another level of state credentialing procedures, and it is the most prestigious. Licensure is the process by which individual state legislatures regulate the title, practice, or both of an occupational group. It differs from certification in that it is governmentally sanctioned and not trade sanctioned. Professional licensure laws restrict or prohibit individuals who have not met state-specified qualifications from practicing in the field or using the title of the profession in any way. As a profession, counseling began pushing for licensure in the 1970s. Beginning with Virginia in 1976, every state and the District of Columbia eventually adopted a counseling licensure law, California becoming the last to do so. The adoption of counseling licensure laws regulating the title and scope of practice has resulted in increased visibility of professional counselors among the helping professions, in managed care organizations, and to the general public (Hawley & Calley, 2009).

Licensure laws vary by state. In many states, the licensure laws are written as practice acts, while some are written as title acts. **Practice acts** prohibit the practice of professional counseling without first obtaining licensure. These acts are designed to ensure public health, safety, and welfare. In states where practice acts are in place, individuals must successfully complete all specified education, training, and examination requirements before becoming licensed. Nearly every state has adopted some form of practice act for the licensure of professional counselors (American Counseling Association, 2014b).

Title acts restrict the use of a professional title to individuals granted licensure by their appropriate state credentialing agencies. In other words, various individuals or groups of practitioners may engage in counseling and counseling-related activities without being licensed (e.g., psychologists, social workers). However, only individuals who have successfully completed all state licensing requirements can call themselves **licensed professional counselors** (or some related title). Many states have licensure laws that function as title and practice acts.

Also, title acts in different states could result in professional counselors being referred to by different titles or names. For example, in Pennsylvania, the title is *licensed professional counselor*, whereas in Pennsylvania's neighbor to the south, Maryland, the title is *licensed clinical professional counselor*. And in Pennsylvania's neighbor to the north, New York, the title is *licensed mental health counselor*. Different state legislatures draft different bills leading to different laws. This is one of the reasons why the portability of licensure from one state to another is so important to the future of the profession, not to mention why it is so confusing to make sense out of the "alphabet soup" that follows some professionals' names. (For example, consider *Bradley T. Erford, PhD, NCC, LCPC, LPC, LP, LSP. PhD* represents Erford's Doctor of Philosophy in counselor education from the University of Virginia; *NCC* stands for *national certified counselor*, issued by the NBCC; *LCPC* stands for *licensed clinical professional counselor* from Maryland; *LPC* stands for *licensed professional counselor* from Virginia; *LP* stands for *licensed psychologist* from Pennsylvania; and *LSP* stands for *licensed school psychologist* from Virginia.)

To become licensed, individuals must satisfy their respective state's licensing requirements. Although these requirements vary by state, they all include some combination of educational background, supervised counseling experience, and the successful passing of a comprehensive counseling-practice examination.

Education

Applicants for licensure are required to complete a master's degree in counseling at an accredited college or university before applying for licensure. The minimum number of semester hours required is 48, with most states now requiring at least 60 semester hours of graduate study. In addition to the number of hours required, many state licensing boards include specific coursework that must be included in one's graduate training, ordinarily aligning with the CACREP educational standards.

Supervised Experience

In addition to earning the appropriate academic degree, licensure applicants must document their supervised counseling experience. State requirements range from 2,000 to 4,500 hours of supervised experience. In most cases, these hours are to be accumulated within a specific time frame (e.g., two years). These hours typically include time spent in individual counseling, group counseling, case staffing, record keeping, and face-to-face supervision. Supervised experience usually means the work experience must be conducted concurrently with individual, triadic, or small-group face-to-face supervision with a qualified supervisor licensed by a state board to practice counseling (e.g., a licensed professional counselor), or a related mental health service (e.g., psychology, social work).

Some state counseling boards are considering requiring that applicants for licensure as professional counselors receive supervision specifically from licensed professional counselors to orient the applicants to the profession and help shape their professional identities. Furthermore, some states are requiring applicants to receive supervision from board-qualified supervisors (e.g., Mississippi). Board-qualified supervisors often have to document specific training and years of supervision experience to be recognized by the state licensing board as someone who can supervise those seeking licensure. These proposed practices make a lot of sense from the professional-identity perspective, but they might not always be in the best interest of counselors. True, no one is better equipped to help orient and supervise a mental health counselor than another experienced mental health counselor supervisor and mentor. Even so, experienced, qualified, and willing supervisors might be difficult to locate, and other licensed mental health professionals (e.g., licensed psychologists, licensed clinical social workers, psychiatrists) might be just as experienced and capable as supervisors and mentors.

Examination

All states require licensure applicants to pass a comprehensive examination on the practice of professional counseling. To standardize licensure testing, all states that regulate counseling adopted a policy in 2000 to use an examination prepared by the NBCC. Depending on the state in which an applicant is seeking licensure, this test could be either the National Counselor Examination (NCE) or the National Clinical Mental Health Counselor Examination (NCMHCE).

American Association of State Counseling Boards

The American Association of State Counseling Boards (AASCB) maintains responsibility for the licensure and certification of counselors in the United States (American Association of State Counseling Boards, 2017). Currently, the AASCB works with all 50 states, the District of Columbia, Guam, and Puerto Rico, to establish licensure, create common standards, develop national portability of licensure, and serve as a useful clearinghouse for tracking and documenting unethical counselors from state to state. To facilitate license portability, or the ability to transfer one's license automatically from one state licensing board to another, the AASCB has devised two formulas for state licensure. The first formula consists of 48 semester hours and a master's degree in counseling or a related field; coursework consistent with CACREP standards and guidelines; 3,000 hours of post-master's supervised experience with at least 1,900 hours of direct client contact; 100 hours of clinical supervision; and passage of the licensure examination as recognized by the member state. The second formula consists of 60 semester hours and a master's degree in counseling or a related field; coursework consistent with CACREP standards and guidelines with additional coursework in a specialty area; 4,000 hours of post-master's supervised experience with at least 2,500 hours of direct client contact; 5 years of counseling experience in clinical counseling; and passage of the licensure examination as recognized by the member state.

The AASCB allows extra years of experience to compensate for deficits in coursework, supervision hours, and additional testing requirements. The AASCB continues to work with states to unify the state counseling licensure procedure expectations.

LICENSE PORTABILITY

Although the AASCB is working hard to unify the field of counseling, because of different state standards and procedures for licensure, the counseling profession currently does not have a portability agreement for licensed professional counselors. **Portability** refers to the ability of professionals to move their licensed status from state to state. In the past, a licensed counselor moving from one state to another would have to apply for standard-entry licensure in the new state regardless of any license or licenses previously held or level of training and experience. Some states have begun addressing this issue by reaching reciprocity agreements with partner states. In these cases, states with similar licensing requirements agree to accept each other's licenses as long as the appropriate fees are paid in the new state.

Because certification, registry, and licensure requirements and procedures differ from state to state, it is important to research what is required. Misuse of qualifications, title, and status are subject to legal penalties, generally misdemeanor violations, which can be imposed by certification, registry, and licensure boards. To avoid misdemeanor offenses and the potential of losing the legal ability to practice, it is important to research what is required, especially when relocating. For current information about individual state requirements, as well as information for the District of Columbia, Guam, and Puerto Rico, consult the professional counselor board website from the desired jurisdiction. Then complete Activity 2.5 to explore the licensure requirements in your state.

ACTIVITY 2.5

What are the licensure requirements for professional counselors in your state? How many hours of graduate study and supervised clinical experience must an individual have to apply for licensure? What comprehensive examination must he or she pass? Once you have researched your own state, select another state you might consider working in. How are the licensure laws similar between the two states? How are they different?

Certification/Licensure for Professional School Counselors

State governments are given power by the U.S. Constitution to regulate the educational system within their own jurisdictions, leaving ultimate power and authority to reside with the state boards of education. As a result, states establish and implement certification and licensure standards for teachers, administrators, and other personnel, including professional school counselors. Usually, this is done either by the state department itself, using an approved program approach upon which a recommendation for the program results in licensure, or by a division created within the state department, which oversees the credentialing of prospective educators and education personnel. This division ultimately determines if individuals are qualified to perform in the public schools.

In many states, professional school counselors are certified (in some states called licensed) by the state department of education to provide counseling services in public schools, similar to the way teachers and principals are certified. Such procedures assure the public that the professionals working with students have met the minimum criteria and standards of education and training.

Benefits and Drawbacks of Counseling Licensure

The adoption of counseling licensure laws by every state would seem to indicate that licensure is a benefit to the public and the counseling profession. Proponents of licensure often cite the safeguarding of client welfare, professional accountability standards, and increased accessibility of services as a few of the major benefits of licensing counselors (Corey, Corey, Corey, & Callanan, 2014). In addition, the benefits to counselors consist of third-party reimbursements and advertisements. Licensure also has intangible rewards, such as the internal drive to achieve at the highest level within one's profession. However, some see little benefit in licensing counselors. The drawbacks of licensure include its promotion of "turf war" among the mental health disciplines, the costs required to acquire and maintain licenses, the geographical limitations it places on practicing counselors, and the lack of any true research evidence supporting its existence.

THINK ABOUT IT 2.2

Do you believe the enactment of counseling licensure laws has benefited the public and the counseling profession or limited counseling's growth?

NATIONAL CERTIFICATION

National certification of professional counselors is administered by the **National Board for Certified Counselors (NBCC)** which was established in 1982 and has become the world's largest counselor certification system, certifying more than 55,000 professional counselors in all 50 states and 40 countries worldwide. National certification is voluntary. Counselors who wish to become nationally certified voluntarily submit their credentials to the NBCC, which determines whether they have met the preset, specific standards required to attain the national certified counselor (NCC) credential, which is basically a general-practice certification. Requirements for the NCC include specific educational coursework, documented experience, endorsements by qualified professionals, and a passing score on the National Counselor Examination. Beginning January 1, 2022, individuals seeking to obtain national certification through NBCC will need to have an earned master's degree or higher from a CACREP-accredited counseling program.

The NCE is a 200-item written test of the knowledge, skills, and abilities necessary for providing professional counseling services (NBCC, 2018). The NCE is not limited to individuals pursuing national certification; it has also been adopted by many state licensure boards as a required element of the state licensure process. The content areas represented on the NCE are the core curricular areas required by CACREP (i.e., professional orientation and ethical practice, social and cultural foundations, human growth and development, career and lifestyle development, helping relationships, group work, assessment, and research and program evaluation), but these curricular areas have been cross-referenced with five work-behavior domains (i.e., fundamentals of counseling, assessment and career counseling, group counseling, programmatic and clinical intervention, professional practice issues). Of the 200 items on each administration of the NCE, 160 are scored and 40 are under field test development. The NBCC sets a criterion-referenced passing/cutoff score for each administration.

The NCE is used to assess individual performance of those who voluntarily submit to the examination and cannot be used by counselor education programs as a program evaluation device. For the purpose of program evaluation, an NBCC affiliate (the Center for Credentialing and Education) prepares and administers the Counselor Preparation Comprehensive Examination (CPCE), which is currently used as a program evaluation tool by more than 380 counselor education programs in U.S. colleges and universities.

When a professional counselor becomes an NCC, the counselor can pursue national certification in a specialty area, such as school counseling (**national certified school counselor [NCSC]**), clinical mental health counseling (**certified clinical mental health counselor [CCMHC]**), or addictions counseling (**master addictions counselor [MAC]**). Each specialty certification sets additional educational, examination, and experience requirements. The NBCC also offers an **approved clinical supervisor (ACS)** certificate.

Additionally, the NBCC promulgates and enforces the *NBCC Code of Ethics*, which sets standards for the ethical behavior of all NCCs. The NBCC also developed and distributes the *Standards for Ethical Practice of Internet Counseling*, which covers Internet counseling relationships; confidentiality in counseling relationships; and legal considerations, licensure, and certification (see Chapter 3). The NBCC also publishes its own journal, the *Professional Counselor*. Finally, the NBCC is a founding member of the Fair Access Coalition on Testing, a nonprofit organization that advocates for the appropriate access to and use of tests by competent professionals. The NBCC has been instrumental in advocating and achieving numerous victories for professional counselors in the United States on various issues, from testing to licensure to incorporation of counselors as service providers within third-party payer networks.

ACTIVITY 2.6

Explore the NBCC (www.nbcc.org) website to identify recent developments in the counseling profession.

COMMISSION ON REHABILITATION COUNSELOR CERTIFICATION

The oldest of all the national counselor certifications is the **Commission on Rehabilitation Counselor Certification (CRCC)** (see www.crccertification.com), which issues the certified rehabilitation counselor (CRC) credential. The CRCC is not affiliated with the NBCC. The CRCC was established in 1974 with the purpose of assuring the public that professionals in the field of rehabilitation counseling met the quality standards within the profession and practice (Commission on Rehabilitation Counselor Certification, 2018). To obtain this national certification, applicants must take the certification examination. Beyond this, however, applicants may choose one of six different paths for the remainder of the certification process.

The first path involves completion of a master's degree program that is fully accredited by CORE. In addition, an applicant must have participated in a supervised internship consisting of either a 480-hour quarter system or a 600-hour semester system. The second path is identical to the first path but makes a provision for a student who graduated from a program that was not accredited by CORE. In this case, the applicant must have an additional year of supervised experience under a CRC and present a letter stating he or she is in good standing. The third path to national certification is for an applicant who, similar to an applicant choosing the second option, did not graduate from an accredited college but also did not have an internship experience. In this case, the applicant is required to complete a two-year internship under the supervision of a CRC.

The fourth path is designed for a student enrolled in an accredited master's degree program for rehabilitation counseling. In addition to the accredited program, the student must have 75% of his or her course work finished, part of which is the internship under the supervision of a CRC, and provide a letter from the CRC stating he or she is in good standing. However, certification will not be granted until after the master's degree program is complete. The last two options are for applicants who are not U.S. citizens and for applicants who hold doctorates in rehabilitation counseling. In these situations, applicants must ensure they have met the requirements from one of the other four options.

Upon completion of this national certification process, a counselor is granted certification for five years. For recertification, an applicant must complete 150 contact hours of approved CE credit. Otherwise, the counselor must go through the examination process again.

CASE STUDY 2.2

What to Pursue, What to Pursue?!

Mike was an excellent school counseling student at a state school in Pennsylvania. He had a high GPA and participated in a number of professional organizations and Chi Sigma Iota. He met with his advisor prior to his graduation to discuss future plans. His most pressing question was which credentials, certifications, and licenses he should pursue. This is something every counseling student must address, and though there may be differences from state to state, this case provides a general example of what to consider.

The first thing noted by Mike's supervisor was that the school counseling program he attended was both nationally accredited by CACREP, and state accredited by the Pennsylvania Department of Education. This is important to consider because it affects both the ability to secure specific credentials and the time in which those credentials might be procured. Because the program was CACREP accredited, Mike could take the National Counseling Exam (NCE) prior to graduation. This exam is required to become a Nationally Certified Counselor (NCC) through the National Board for Certified Counselors (NBCC). CACREP accreditation also allows the student to obtain his NCC upon graduation, without having to pursue supervised work experience over time after graduation.

At the state level, because Mike fulfilled the requirements of the PA Department of Education accredited school counseling program, he was able to graduate with a state certificate in School Guidance Counseling. Pennsylvania grants Pre-K–12 certification;

however, the grade level certification may differ from state to state. There is a national trend moving toward Pre-K–12 certification.

In addition to national- and state-level certifications in counseling and school counseling, Mike's program met the course requirements to become a Licensed Professional Counselor (LPC) in Pennsylvania. Pennsylvania requires a 60-credit master's degree in counseling, a passing score on the NCE, and 2 years of supervised work experience following graduation. Licensure requirements may differ slightly from state to state. In this case, Mike hopes to find a job in the field of school counseling and pursue 2 years of supervised work experience so that he can obtain his LPC credential in PA. With these three credentials in hand, Mike will have many opportunities in the field of counseling. He can later look at more specialized credentialing, certifications, or licenses through continued education.

Discuss which credentials, certifications, and licenses are available to you and most important for your success in the counseling field.

What is required in your state based on your program?

Develop a plan of success for your journey as a professional counselor.

Summary

We hope you are now aware of the importance of membership in professional organizations. But which should you join? We would like to suggest that you become a member of, at minimum, three associations: the ACA, at least one ACA division, and your state ACA branch. We also recommend that you become an NCC and obtain licensure in your state. This will cover all your professional bases and maximize your employment opportunities.

These organizations keep you informed and educated about trends and new practices across the entire counseling profession, keep you updated in your specialty area, and provide you with local networking opportunities with advocates for counseling issues in your state or territory. Does joining these counseling organizations cost a bit of money? You bet. Should you do it anyway? Absolutely! It is the price we all pay for the elevation over the past few decades of counseling into a fully acknowledged and comprehensive profession. Would you expect your physician to be a member of the American Medical Association and your lawyer to be a member of the American Bar Association? Of course. So, too, do our clients expect to be able to reap the benefits of having counselors who have memberships in professional counseling organizations.

Accreditation of institutions of higher education involves a commitment to high curricular and organizational standards. CACREP and CORE are the primary accreditation organizations for counselor education programs. CORE accredits rehabilitation counseling programs, and CACREP accredits master's degree programs in career counseling; college counseling; clinical mental health counseling; marital, couple, and family counseling/therapy; school counseling; student affairs; and doctoral degree programs in counselor education and supervision. Credentialing involves the voluntary submission of evidence of a professional counselor's education and experience for comparison with a set of standards and passing an examination of the knowledge and information required for practice as a professional counselor. Verification of counselor credentials can entail inspection, registration, certification, and licensure. National certification is conducted by the NBCC, which also administers the NCE.

The licensing of professional counselors is a state-governed process. Individuals wishing to practice as licensed professional counselors must satisfy all the licensing board requirements for their respective states. These requirements include graduate coursework in counseling and related areas, supervised clinical experience, and passing scores on the states' designated comprehensive examinations. Since counseling licenses are not portable, professional counselors should familiarize themselves with the requirements of any states they might relocate to in the future. Accreditation, national certification, and state licensure serve to construct a strong foundation for the establishment of quality counselor-education training programs and continuous professional development so the public not only is protected from harm by unqualified practitioners, but also is well served by highly qualified professional counselors.

Answer Key

Activity 2.2   1. n, 2. m, 3. i, 4. s, 5. b, 6. o, 7. a, 8. r, 9. e, 10. f, 11. h, 12. l, 13. q, 14. d, 15. p, 16. k, 17. j, 18. g, 19. t, 20. c.

MyCounselingLab for Introduction to Counseling

Try the Topic 11 Assignments: *Licensure and Credentialing.*

3 Ethical and Legal Issues in Counseling

Lynn E. Linde and Bradley T. Erford

PREVIEW

This chapter addresses some ethical and legal issues in counseling. As a professional counselor, you must always remember that how you conduct yourself personally and professionally reflects not only upon yourself, but also upon your colleagues. Knowledge and understanding of the issues reviewed in this chapter are only a starting point. Keep up-to-date with the laws, ethics, policies, and procedures that govern professional practice. The implementation of your professional responsibilities will require your undivided attention every day of your professional life.

ETHICAL STANDARDS AND LAWS

The cornerstone of the counseling relationship rests upon the public's trust in the services provided. Each professional counselor has an enormous responsibility to uphold the public trust and must seek high levels of training, education, and supervision in the ethical application of counseling practices. This is particularly essential in a profession such as counseling because counselors usually work with clients and students as lone professionals, often with little oversight and behind closed doors in confidential circumstances. Attention to ethical and legal issues is thus crucial.

One of the greatest challenges facing most professional counselors daily is how to appropriately handle the many different ethical and legal situations they encounter. Because of the nature of counseling, professional counselors must be prepared to help clients who present a variety of challenges. It is often difficult to know all one needs to understand and do. Numerous resources and sources of information can help guide professional counselors as they strive to assist clients in an ethical and legal manner. The professional associations for counselors have created ethical standards for professional behavior and provide a wealth of current information, resources, and training. Federal and state governments continually enact laws and regulations that affect counselors, including the judicial branch, in which courts hand down decisions that directly affect counselors' behavior. In addition, state boards of education and local school systems create policies, guidelines, and procedures that professional school counselors must follow.

Professional counselors are sometimes confused by the difference between ethical standards and laws and what one should do when these seem to be in conflict with each other. It might be helpful to take a look at the origin of both ethical standards and laws.

Ethical standards are usually developed by professional associations to guide the behavior of a specific group of professionals. According to Herlihy and Corey (2015), ethical standards serve three purposes: to educate members about sound ethical conduct, to provide a mechanism for accountability, and to serve as a means for improving professional practice. Ethical standards change and are updated periodically to ensure their relevance and appropriateness.

Ethical standards are based on generally accepted norms, beliefs, customs, and values. The **Code of Ethics** published by the American Counseling Association (ACA; 2014a) is based on six moral principles of autonomy, justice, beneficence, nonmaleficence, fidelity, and veracity (Linde, 2015). **Autonomy** refers to the concept of independence and the ability to make one's own decisions. Professional counselors need to respect the right of clients to make their own decisions based on their personal values and beliefs and not impose the counselors' values on clients. **Justice** means treating each person fairly, but it does not mean treating each person the same way. Rather, counselors should treat clients according to each client's needs. **Beneficence** refers to doing good or what is in the best interests of clients. In counseling, it also incorporates the concept of removing conditions that might cause harm. **Nonmaleficence** means doing no harm to others. **Fidelity** involves the concepts of loyalty, faithfulness, and honoring commitments. This means that professional counselors must honor all obligations to clients. The final principle is **veracity**, which means being truthful in one's professional actions with clients and others; this sixth principle was added in the 2014 revision.

Laws are also based on these same, generally accepted norms, beliefs, customs, and values. However, laws are more prescriptive, have been incorporated into code, and carry greater sanctions or penalties for failure to comply. Laws and ethical standards exist to mandate the appropriate behavior of professionals within a particular context to ensure that the best interests of clients are met. When laws and ethics seem to be in conflict with each other, the professional counselor must attempt to resolve the conflict in a responsible manner (Cottone & Tarvydas, 2007). Professional counselors must make their clients aware of any conflicts and their ethical standards. Because there are greater penalties associated with laws, professional counselors will often follow the legal course of action when no harm will come to clients. Many ethical standards recognize that other mandates must be followed and suggest that professional counselors work to change mandates that are not in the best interests of their clients. Activity 3.1 provides an opportunity to explore the nuances of an ethical/legal conflict.

ACTIVITY 3.1

Consider a situation in which the law and ACA ethical standards are in conflict with one another (such as when a minor child comes for confidential counseling, but the parent holds the confidence and privilege, or when a minor child comes for substance use or reproductive counseling he or she is entitled to under the law, but he or she is engaging in dangerous behaviors in these regards). Role-play with a peer how you might approach your client in explaining the conflict and your ethical standards. What might you do to begin working toward changing legal mandates that are not in the best interest of your client?

Within the ACA, there are multiple codes of ethics. The ACA has its *ACA Code of Ethics* (2014a), to which its members must adhere. In addition, several divisions have their own codes of ethics, including the American School Counselor Association (ASCA) and the American Mental Health Counselors Association (AMHCA). Some associations, such as the Association for Specialists in Group Work and the Association for Assessment in Counseling and Education, have developed standards or guidelines for best practices. **Best-practice guidelines** are not ethics per se but do recommend practice standards that professional counselors should strive to uphold. These codes of ethics and guidelines parallel the ACA's Code of Ethics but speak more directly to their specialty areas. For example, the ASCA's Ethical Standards for School Counselors discusses what ethical behavior consists of in a school setting.

Many professional counselors belong to multiple organizations, each of which might have its own code of ethics. They might also hold credentials from organizations or state credentialing boards that have a code of ethics as well. Many counselors are national certified counselors (NCCs), a credential offered by the National Board for Certified Counselors (NBCC), which also has a code of ethics. It is often hard to know which code takes precedence. While each professional will have to make that determination individually, there are two general guidelines. First, what is the setting in which one is practicing, and is there a particular code that applies specifically to that setting? Second, in what capacity (e.g., licensed professional counselor, marriage and family therapist, certified school counselor) is the professional operating? For the most part, these codes are similar, and all concern behaving in an appropriate professional manner; operating in the best interests of the client; and practicing within the scope of one's education, training, and experience. If a professional counselor is doing all of this, the existence of multiple codes of ethics should not be a significant issue.

American Counseling Association Code of Ethics

The ACA revises its *Code of Ethics* about every 10 years. The seventh and most recent revision took effect in March 2014. There are numerous significant changes from the 2005 *ACA Code of Ethics* to the 2014 *ACA Code of Ethics*. Parts of the *ACA Code of Ethics* have been updated to reflect the current thinking and practice in the field, and several new issues have been added. The 2014 *ACA Code of Ethics* added a new section that specifically addresses distance counseling, social media, and technology issues. The new code also addresses issues with which counselors have been grappling, such as at what point does someone become a client, under what conditions may the counselor refer a client, the role of values in counseling, and clarity regarding how counselors think about our relationships with our clients. The glossary was expanded and includes additional terms. Now complete Think About It 3.1 to consider the current societal issues that might affect the writing of the next *ACA Code of Ethics*.

THINK ABOUT IT 3.1

Society changes over time, affecting the practice of counseling. What are some foreseeable changes spurred by societal or technological issues that might influence current clinical practice or influence the next revision of the ACA Code of Ethics?

The ACA Code of Ethics serves six main purposes:

1. The *Code* sets forth the ethical obligations of ACA members and provides guidance intended to inform the ethical practice of professional counselors;
2. The *Code* identifies ethical considerations relevant to professional counselors and counselors-in-training;
3. The *Code* enables the association to clarify for current and prospective members, and for those served by members, the nature of the ethical responsibilities held in common by its members;
4. The *Code* serves as an ethical guide designed to assist members in constructing a course of action that best serves those utilizing counseling services and establishes expectations of conduct with a primary emphasis on the role of the professional counselor;
5. The *Code* helps support the mission of ACA;
6. The standards contained in this *Code* serve as the basis for processing inquiries and ethical complaints concerning ACA members. (p. 3)

The 2014 *ACA Code of Ethics* (see https://www.counseling.org/knowledge-center/ethics/code-of-ethics-resources) addresses the responsibilities of professional counselors toward their clients, colleagues, workplace, and themselves by delineating the ideal standards for conducting counselors' behavior. All members are required to abide by the *ACA Code of Ethics*, and action is taken against any member who fails to do so. In effect, since these are the standards of the profession, all professional counselors are held to the *ACA Code of Ethics* by the mental health community, regardless of whether they are members of the ACA. The revised *Code* places increased emphasis on the client as the focus of counseling. Additionally, for the first time, the professional values for the counseling profession are enumerated in the Preamble of the *Code*; these values form the conceptual basis for the ethical principles also outlined in the Preamble.

The *ACA Code of Ethics* is divided into nine areas: (A) the Counseling Relationship; (B) Confidentiality and Privacy; (C) Professional Responsibility; (D) Relationships with Other Professionals; (E) Evaluation, Assessment, and Interpretation; (F) Supervision, Training, and Teaching; (G) Research and Publication; (H) Distance Counseling, Technology, and Social Media; and (I) Resolving Ethical Issues. Each of these areas details specific counselor responsibilities and standards.

The *ACA Code of Ethics* discusses respecting one's client and the background each client brings to the counseling setting; maintaining professional behavior with clients and other professionals; practicing with the best interests of the client in mind; practicing within the limits of one's training, experience, and education; and the use of social media and technology in counseling. The last section provides direction for members resolving ethical dilemmas. Highlights from each of these areas are summarized below, but at this point, readers should locate the actual ACA *Code of Ethics* on the ACA website and peruse it in detail.

SECTION A: THE COUNSELING RELATIONSHIP   Section A covers all areas related to the nature of the relationship with the clients and includes the subtopics of client welfare, client rights, clients served by others, personal needs and values, managing and maintaining boundaries and professional relationships, extending boundaries beyond conventional parameters, sexual intimacies with clients or their family members, multiple clients, group work, fees and bartering, termination and referral, and end-of-life issues. In summary, professional counselors must always put the best interests of their clients first and ensure that clients understand the extent and limitations of counseling. The *ACA Code of Ethics* (2014a) adds language to this section to make it clear that counselors must avoid imposing their personal values and may not refer a client based on any of the counselor's personally held beliefs, values, or behaviors. One of the most significant changes is the use of the term "extending counseling boundaries" to replace the terminology previously used of "harmful and beneficial relationships," which had replaced the term "dual relationships" in the 1995 *ACA Code of Ethics*. This new terminology reflects the reality that there may be times when a counselor needs to go beyond the conventional counseling boundaries for the good of the client, but must first take all appropriate professional precautions such as consultation, informed consent, and documentation. This section also prohibits a counselor from having a personal virtual relationship with current clients and continues the prohibition on having a sexual or romantic relationship with clients or their family members for five years; this includes in-person and electronic relationships. Counselors should refrain from having an in-person or electronic relationship with former clients, their romantic partners, or family members if there is the potential of harm to the former client.

Continued emphasis continues to be placed on critical issues, including general client welfare and avoiding harm, appropriate termination of services, fees and bartering, and informed consent. The informed consent provision is particularly important because many state counseling boards now require written consent so clients can choose a counseling relationship with a qualified provider from an informed consumer position. Section A.2.b specifies that informed consent includes, but is not limited to, "purposes, goals, techniques, procedures, limitations, potential risks, and benefits of services; the counselor's qualifications, credentials, and relevant experience, and the use of technology; . . . the intended use of tests and reports, fees, and billing arrangements"; the right to confidentiality and limitations; the continuation of services should the counselor become incapacitated; "obtaining clear information about their records"; participating in ongoing treatment planning; and the right to refuse treatment at any time along with the potential consequences for doing so. In addition, the code addresses the need to balance assent from minors and others incapable of giving consent without the assent of parents and family members who hold the legal rights of consent, protection, and decision making on their behalf. Table 3.1 provides a sample informed consent that addresses these salient points.

TABLE 3.1 Professional Disclosure Statement*

Bradley T. Erford, PhD
Address
Telephone Numbers & E-mail

I welcome you as a new client, and I look forward to working with you. The purpose of this form is to let you know about my approach to counseling, what you can expect from counseling, and my background. This form will also give you an opportunity to give consent for counseling or assessment services.

I have been a licensed professional counselor since 1988. I earned my bachelor's degree (BS) in biology from Grove City College (PA), my master's degree (MA) in school psychology from

TABLE 3.1 Professional Disclosure Statement* (*Continued*)

Bucknell University (PA), and my PhD in counselor education from the University of Virginia. I am a member of the American Counseling Association, and I am a licensed clinical professional counselor (LCPC), which allows me to practice mental health counseling in Maryland. My LCPC state license was issued by the Board of Professional Counselors and Therapists in Baltimore, MD. I also am a national certified counselor (NCC), which is a designation given by the National Board for Certified Counselors (NBCC).

My Practice of Counseling

I specialize in working with children, adolescents, and their families. I provide psychoeducational assessment as well as individual, group, and family counseling. I am particularly experienced in working with individuals presenting disruptive, anxious, and depressed behaviors; individuals experiencing learning, divorce, or grief adjustment difficulties; and those in need of stress management.

In my view, the relationship of feelings and thoughts to behavior is crucial to understanding the issues that affect being successful in life. I use a variety of strategies that can help people make sense of their world, strategies that are mostly humanistic and cognitive-behavioral in nature; that is, they are strategies based on the notions that people often experience personal difficulties because of relationship issues and that the way people think about and see themselves and the world influences how they feel and behave. You will be encouraged to engage in strategies to address these issues both during and between our sessions.

Individual counseling offers you a chance to express ideas and concerns to understand your situation better and learn new ways to solve problems. However, there are risks and limitations to counseling. At times, you might experience feelings that are uncomfortable and hard to face. I often compare this process to taking medicine: It might not taste great, but it also might be good for you in the long run. I will do my best to provide an accurate and fair assessment and diagnosis that will help guide our treatment planning and goal setting. We will also discuss this assessment/diagnosis and your resulting treatment plan/goals throughout the counseling process. Counseling is a collaborative process done with your best interests in mind, and the ultimate goal is for you to reach your goals and a level of healthy and independent personal functioning.

Termination

Of course, you have the right to refuse or terminate treatment at any time. Should you believe either of these options is appropriate, I hope you will discuss the potential benefits and risks associated with your decision with me. If at any time I become unavailable to continue providing services to you as a result of incapacitation or other cause, I will help transition you to another mental health care provider who can either continue treatment or ensure appropriate referral so your best interests are served.

Confidentiality and Limits

Everything you discuss with me will be kept confidential by me except matters pertaining to (a) harm to self or others; (b) suspicion of physical abuse, sexual abuse, or neglect of minors, persons with disabilities, and the elderly; (c) legal activity resulting in a court order; (d) your written request that I disclose information; and (e) anything else as required by law. For those matters, legally and ethically, I would have to break confidentiality and involve others. Except for these conditions, any written information or report I possess cannot be shared, orally or in writing, with another individual or agency without your express written permission. Tests are administered and reports are produced to facilitate personal diagnosis and treatment. Of course, I would share information with any other professional or agency you wish, provided you sign a written release-of-information form, which I can provide to you. In contrast, you may share results from written reports or sessions at your discretion because confidentiality applies to my communications, not yours.

(Continued)

TABLE 3.1 Professional Disclosure Statement* (*Continued*)

Ethical Standards of Practice and Licensure Information

Legally, I adhere to United States and Maryland statutes, including HIPAA provisions. You have a right to a copy of your file and to inspect and amend the file as appropriate. Ethically guiding my behavior is the ACA Code of Ethics, published by the American Counseling Association in Alexandria, VA; the ethical code of the NBCC; and the Code of Ethics adopted by the Maryland Board of Professional Counselors and Therapists.

Fees and Cancellation Policy

As far as counseling/assessment session fees are concerned, I charge $____ per hour. This same rate applies to time spent on providing special services, such as court appearances. Cost for a standard psychoeducational assessment is $_____, which includes a written report and up to one hour for a feedback/interpretation consultation session. I do not participate with third-party payers, such as managed care organizations and insurance companies. By signing this form, you are agreeing to pay this fee on the day the service is provided. Missed appointments without a 24-hour notice will have to be paid for, except for genuine emergencies.

I have attached a business card to this letter. If I am unavailable during or after business hours, you can leave a message, and I will get back to you as soon as possible. In the event of an emergency, call 911 or go to the nearest emergency room. I am usually available through email at (email address). As part of this consent agreement, please indicate below the manner(s) in which you prefer to be contacted by me in case the need arises. Check all that apply, and fill in the applicable contact information.

___ Telephone: _____ Is it all right to leave a message? (circle) yes / no

___ Email: _____

___ Postal mail (address): _____

I hope you will find this counseling experience to be successful and, in some ways, enjoyable. I thank you very much for taking the time to read this. Please sign below to indicate your consent to pursue counseling or assessment services.

Bradley T. Erford, PhD, LCPC, NCC   LC#
Contact Information:
Board of Professional Counselors and Therapists   4201 Patterson Avenue
Baltimore, MD 21215-2299   410-764-4732
Note: You do not have to sign this; you have the right to refuse counseling or psychoeducational assessment.

I, _____, fully understand what I have just read and offer my consent for counseling or psychoeducational assessment, free of any pressure to do so. Here is my signature and the date of the signature (that expires one year from now).

_____   _____

Signature   Date

_____   _____

Signature of a custodial parent or legal guardian is   Date
required when the counseling patient is a minor

*This information is required by the Board of Professional Counselors and Therapists, which regulates all licensed clinical professional counselors in Maryland. You can contact the Board of Professional Counselors and Therapists at 4201 Patterson Avenue, Baltimore, MD 21215-2299 or 410-764-4732.

Section A also includes standards for serving the terminally ill and facilitating end-of-life decisions; the ACA was one of the first national associations to address these issues. In doing so, the ACA directs counselors to receive adequate supervision; seek multiple professional collaborations; and help clients exercise self-determination, establish high-quality end-of-life care, and participate maximally in decision making. Finally, the 1999 ACA Ethical Standards for Internet Online Counseling was integrated into A.12, broadening the code to address issues related to technology in providing counseling services, record keeping, and research applications.

SECTION B: CONFIDENTIALITY AND PRIVACY   Section B covers all areas related to the confidentiality rights of clients and discusses the limits to confidentiality. It includes the subtopics of multicultural/diversity considerations, the client's right to privacy, confidentiality when working with groups and families, working with minor or incompetent clients, all aspects of record keeping, and case consultation. This section clarifies the confidentiality rights of deceased clients and discusses the issues of confidentiality when counseling families. Changes included reinforcing the confidential nature of records kept in any medium and the need for counselors to keep records as appropriate to their practice.

Within this section, there are several notable changes from the 2005 Code. First, Section B creates the expectation that counselors will keep records necessary for professional services. The term "records kept in any medium" is used to be inclusive of whatever records are kept and includes such things as artwork, music, and all other records from counseling. In Section B.2.c the issue of contagious and life-threatening diseases is clarified and counselors no longer need to confirm the diagnosis prior to potentially disclosing a client's status; however, counselors must continue to adhere to all state laws.

VOICES FROM THE FIELD 3.1   Managing Boundary Issues in Counseling, by Victoria E. Kress

As I pulled into my driveway, I noticed someone lying in the grass on my front lawn. My initial thought was, *That's strange.* I went into the house and peered out the window only to realize the person in the grass was one of my clients. My next reaction was, *Wow, this is creepy. Do I call the police? Do I go and talk to her? How did she know where I live? Why is she on my lawn?* Sadly, in graduate school, no one had taught me what to do when situations like this arise.

When in doubt, peer supervision is always the way to go. So I called my friend who is a counselor, but she didn't answer the phone. I thought about calling the state counseling board to consult, but it was a Saturday so no one would be answering the phones. I considered reviewing my ethics textbook from graduate school, but I knew the answer couldn't be found there.

Knowing this client was unpredictable and volatile, worst-case scenarios started going through my head: *Is she going to attempt suicide on my lawn? Is she going to harm me and my dog?* As I pondered my options, she left. She ostensibly wanted me to know that she had been there, and once that end was met, she was able to leave.

What to do next? Naturally, I decided to address the issue with my client. "Tell me about what was going on when you were lying on my lawn Saturday." She was coy in her explanation of why she was at my home, but I was direct in my response. I set boundaries with her and explained the importance to her—and to me—of her honoring those boundaries. We discussed

(Continued)

that if she couldn't navigate those boundaries and regulate her emotions around our relationship, we would need to explore finding a counselor with whom she could have a more successful counseling relationship. Because her core issues were related to self- and other boundaries, the experience did provide good fodder in helping her work toward reaching her goals. Thankfully, she did not return to my lawn.

SECTION C: PROFESSIONAL RESPONSIBILITY Section C continues to place emphasis on issues such as facilitating access to services, practicing in a nondiscriminatory manner, professional competence, advertising and soliciting clients, professional qualifications, public responsibility, and adhering to the *ACA Code of Ethics*. Standard C.2.g addresses counselor impairment. Professional counselors must be alert to signs of personal impairment and should refrain from providing or offering services if an impairment could potentially harm a client. If a problem reaches the level of professional impairment, the professional counselor should seek out assistance. Professional counselors are now also required to assist supervisors or colleagues in recognizing impairment and, if necessary, provide assistance, intervention, or consultation.

Standard C.2.h further addresses the issue of counselor impairment or subsequent termination of practice. This new standard states that a counselor should follow a prepared plan for the transfer of files and clients when he or she leaves a practice. In particular, a counselor needs to designate a specific colleague, or *records custodian*, and create a proper plan for file and client transfer in the case of his or her incapacitation, termination of practice, or death.

Standard C.6.e continues to emphasize that professional counselors must use techniques, modalities, and procedures that have scientific or empirical foundations and are grounded in theory. If not, counselors should note their procedures or techniques to be "unproven" or "developing." The potential risks and ethical considerations of the procedures or techniques should be explained to clients, and counselors should take all necessary steps to protect clients from any potential harm. Counselors are still required to monitor their effectiveness and take any necessary actions to improve as professionals.

The most significant addition to this section is C.6.e, Contributing to the Public Good. Counselors are expected to provide services to the public for which there is little or no financial benefit for the counselor. But the concept of *pro bono publico* was expanded to include services such as providing professional development, sharing of professional information, and other such services to the profession in addition to low- or no cost services to clients.

CASE STUDY 3.1

Ethics Case Study: Sarah, by Nadine Hartig

At a community mental health agency, I had been providing individual counseling services to a 26-year-old woman, "Sarah," for six weeks when she came in and disclosed that she had had sex with a male mental health professional. I felt a bit stunned when Sarah opened the session by disclosing this potentially unethical relationship, but I tried very hard to be present for my client.

She continued to share information and disclosed that she had seen this professional for services and met him because of their professional relationship; he was her former therapist. However, Sarah was very clear that she did not want to disclose who the person was, what type of services were provided, or when the services were provided. She stated, "I don't want to give you any identifying information, because I don't want anything bad to happen to him." She only shared this situation with me because she was feeling very hurt that he hadn't responded to her text messages and phone calls after she felt like they had physically and emotionally connected.

I was incredibly troubled by this information. Sarah was a survivor of physical and sexual abuse and had struggled with an eating disorder, drug addiction, sexual addiction, and significant interpersonal problems. She had been suicidal in the past, and I consistently monitored her for suicidal ideation. I felt an incredible burden to keep her safe and routinely sought consultation about her case. In addition, she had a very difficult time setting boundaries with others, particularly with men. She routinely engaged in sexual activity she later regretted, feeling used and worthless from these interactions. These feelings of worthlessness quickly escalated into feelings of hopelessness and suicidality, and I was worried this relationship would lead to a downward spiral for Sarah.

I struggled with this case on many levels. One, I felt caught in a double bind: I was gravely concerned that an impaired mental health professional in the field was taking advantage of clients and doing harm, and I was unable to identify this person. Yet, I was ethically and legally mandated to protect my client's right to privacy and respect her wishes not to share identifying information. Two, I was troubled that Sarah's predicament was symptomatic of her past history, and I needed to ensure her safety. Three, while a part of me wanted to press her for information about the professional, I was quite aware that our rapport was precarious at best, and I wanted to maintain the therapeutic relationship, particularly during this situation.

My first step in resolving this dilemma was to get through the session without being judgmental and without making any promises to the client I couldn't keep (e.g., not reporting the professional). My second step was to immediately document all the necessary information so I wouldn't forget any important details. My third step was to seek supervision. During supervision, my supervisor and I reviewed the laws and ethical codes and determined I was not able to make a report to the state licensure board. We also processed my feelings of helplessness with the situation and frustration with this unknown mental health professional. Processing my feelings was immensely helpful to me so I could keep my feelings in check during my sessions with the client.

In my next session with Sarah, I shared my concerns about her history, safety, and vulnerability, and I was clear that if I did receive identifying information about this person I would need to make a report. I believe my honesty modeled boundaries within our relationship and gave her a clear understanding of my possible course of action. Sarah continued to see me for counseling, and I was never given information about his identity.

1. How would you feel about the ethical dilemma caused by needing to keep the community and other clients safe from the mental health professional and the legal mandate to respect your client's privacy?
2. How would you process your emotions about this client and the mental health professional?
3. What would you do in this situation?

SECTION D: RELATIONSHIPS WITH OTHER PROFESSIONALS   Section D stresses the importance of interaction and relationships between counselors and other professionals. Professional counselors should become knowledgeable about their colleagues and develop positive working relationships and communication systems. The 2014 *ACA Code of Ethics* reinforces the concept that professional counselors often may be part of interdisciplinary teams; it continues to delineate counselors' responsibilities as part of teams. The term interdisciplinary is intentionally retained to reflect the variety of teams of which one might be a part, including treatment and other therapeutic teams, as well as educational and work teams.

Professional counselors are reminded to be respectful of differing approaches to counseling services and the traditions and practices of other professional groups (Standard D.1.a). Inclusion of Standards D.1.b-d specifically addresses interdisciplinary relationships and teamwork. Professional counselors must work to develop and strengthen relationships with interdisciplinary colleagues. Professional counselors must also keep focused on how best to serve their clients when working in team environments. To do so, counselors can contribute to and partake in decisions that could potentially affect the well-being of clients by the use of the values, experiences, and perspectives of the counseling profession and other disciplines. Standard D.1.d reminds counselors that when working in interdisciplinary teams, they are responsible for clarifying the ethical and professional obligations of individual members and whole teams. Professional counselors are encouraged to attempt to resolve ethical concerns initially within their teams. If resolutions cannot be made within their teams, counselors should pursue other means to address the concerns consistent with the well-being of their clients.

SECTION E: EVALUATION, ASSESSMENT, AND INTERPRETATION   Section E covers standards related to the assessment of clients, the counselor's skills, and appropriateness of assessment. It includes the subtopics of general appraisal issues, competence to use and interpret tests, informed consent for appraisal, releasing information, proper diagnosis of mental disorders, test selection, conditions of test administration, diversity in testing, test scoring and interpretation, test security, obsolete tests and outdated test results, test construction, and forensic evaluations. The word *assessment*, which has a more integrative and broader connotation than *tests*, is used in this section. The section recognizes that assessment is only one part of the overall counseling process and that professional counselors must take into account cultural, social, and personal factors.

Historical and Social Prejudices in the Diagnosis of Pathology (Standard E.5.c) emphasizes that professional counselors should be aware of social and historical prejudices in the pathologizing and misdiagnosis of specific individuals and groups. In addition, counselors should be cognizant of the role of mental health professionals in the continuation of these problems. Not only does the *ACA Code of Ethics* take into consideration historical factors, it also has changed to reflect the current trends in counseling.

The inclusion of Section E.13 Forensic Evaluation: Evaluation for Legal Proceedings denotes the increased presence of professional counselors in legal proceedings and subsequent legal matters. This section outlines the primary obligations of counselors, the details of informed consent for forensic evaluation, and the necessity to avoid potentially harmful relationships in regard to forensic evaluations. The primary obligation of professional counselors conducting forensic evaluations is to generate objective findings that are supported by appropriate techniques and information. Counselors are entitled to form their own professional opinions, but they must define any limitations in their testimonies or reports.

SECTION F: SUPERVISION, TRAINING, AND TEACHING   Section F is revised and expanded in certain content areas, such as supervisory relationships, student welfare and responsibilities, and counselor educator responsibilities. Focus still remains on fostering professional relationships and creating appropriate boundaries between supervisors and their students. The ethical obligations of both parties are clearly set forth; counselors should be accurate, honest, and fair during the training and assessment of students.

Areas of focus include: counselor supervision and client welfare, counselor supervision competence, supervisory relationships, supervisor responsibilities, counseling evaluation and remediation, responsibilities of counselor educators, student welfare and responsibilities, evaluation and remediation of students, roles and relationships between educators and students, and multicultural/diversity competence in counselor education and training programs. As with Section A, Standards F.3.a and F.10.a are included to address use of the concept of extending conventional boundaries between counselor educators or supervisors and students. Significant changes to teaching include requiring counselor educators to provide instruction only in their areas of competency, provide direct assistance with field placements, and provide career assistance to students. Revisions also include explicit responsibilities for gatekeeping for students and supervisees. The revisions to this section are numerous; you are encouraged to consult the 2014 *ACA Code of Ethics* in depth.

SECTION G: RESEARCH AND PUBLICATION   The revised code recognizes that independent researchers who lack access to an institutional review board might design and conduct research programs; these researchers are bound by the same ethical principles and federal and state laws as other researchers. To make appropriate safeguards available to research participants, such independent researchers are advised to seek out and consult with researchers who are acquainted with institutional review board procedures.

Topics include the disposal of research documents and records of relationships with research participants when interactions are intensive or extended. Professional counselors are obligated to take appropriate steps to destroy any documents or records that contain confidential data or might identify research participants within a reasonable period after the completion of a research study or project. Section G.3 outlines the restrictions on relationships with research participants—including nonprofessional relationships, sexual or romantic interactions, and sexual harassment—and includes both in-person and electronic relationships.

Finally, the publication section of the 2014 Code of Ethics maintains Standard G.5.b, which specifically states that professional counselors should not plagiarize or present another person's work as their own. In addition, the standard concerning professional review of documents presented for publication is expanded to include making valid publication decisions, reviewing materials in a timely manner, avoiding biases, and evaluating only those documents that fall within one's field of competency.

SECTION H DISTANCE COUNSELING, TECHNOLOGY, AND SOCIAL MEDIA   Based on Section A.12 from the 2005 *ACA Code of Ethics*, technology in counseling is deemed to be such a critical area that a separate section has been created. Section H reinforces the concept that counseling may no longer be limited to in-person, face-to-face sessions and now includes a variety of modalities. Technology is ever evolving; counselors are encouraged to become knowledgeable about these resources, the benefits of using technology, and their place in counseling. Counselors must also understand the challenge to confidentiality that technology poses and the ethical and legal requirements of its use.

Section H.1 addresses knowledge and legal considerations. Counselors who use any form of technology must become knowledgeable about technology, as well as the ethical and legal issues related to its use. Clients have the right to decide whether to use technology in the counseling relationship, and the specific issues related to technology must be part of the informed consent and disclosure processes. Clients must be made aware of the limitations to confidentiality when using technology (H.2.c). Further, H.2.d requires that counselors use appropriate encryption standards when using technology. When employing distance counseling, social media, or other technology, counselors must be able to verify the identity of the client and explain the benefits and limitations of the technology's use (H.3, H.4).

Maintaining professional boundaries takes on added importance when counselors employ technology, distance counseling, and/or social media. Section H.4.b requires that counselors establish professional boundaries with clients. Section H.6.b requires that counselors keep their professional and personal virtual presence on social media separate. Section H.6.c mandates that counselors respect the privacy of their client's presence on social media and must be given consent by the client prior to viewing any information about their client through social media or on the web. Further, H.6.d urges counselors to take precautions to avoid disclosing information about their clients through public social media. In summary, Section H recognizes the evolving nature of the counseling relationship and the role of technology, social media, and distance counseling, but provides mandates to protect clients' confidentiality and ensure that the use of these modalities is in their best interests.

SECTION I: RESOLVING ETHICAL ISSUES   This final section addresses the expectation that counselors will behave in an ethical and legal manner and provides information regarding the need to be knowledgeable about ethical and legal issues. Counselors are expected to act if another professional is suspected of behaving unethically. Section I outlines the procedures to be followed. Standard I.1.c states that if a conflict between ethical responsibilities and laws arises, professional counselors should make known their commitment to the *ACA Code of Ethics* and work to alleviate the conflict. Counselors may follow legal requirements, regulations, or other legal authority if the ethical conflict cannot be resolved in this manner.

Standard I.2 covers the details needed by professional counselors to report a suspected ethical violation. When informal resolution is inappropriate for an ethical violation, or the issue is not correctly resolved, professional counselors are directed to take further action, such as seeking out voluntary national certification bodies, state or national ethics committees, state licensing boards, or any suitable institutional authorities. This standard is not applicable if a professional counselor has been retained to review the work of the counselor who is in question or if it would violate any confidentiality rights.

Standard I.2.f states that professional counselors absolutely should not deny a person's advancement, admission to academic programs, employment, promotion, or tenure based only upon that person having made an ethics complaint or being the subject of an ethics complaint. This standard provides some protection against unfair discrimination for counselors who have made ethics complaints or been the subject of complaints.

The Practice of Internet or Technology-Assisted Distance Counseling

Technology-assisted distance counseling is on the rise, compounding government agencies' oversight challenges to protect the public. This category of counseling services includes telephone-based, email-based, electronic-chat-based, and video-based services that are either synchronous (real time) or asynchronous (staggered or gaps in time between client and counselor responses). Distance counseling holds great promise for allowing access to services by homebound clients, clients without transportation capabilities, and clients living in rural locales or other areas that make face-to-face counseling on a regular basis challenging. Before engaging in technology-assisted distance counseling, professional counselors should check existing statutes in both the states in which they are licensed to practice and the locations in which the potential clients reside. Some state regulatory boards require counselors to hold licenses in clients' states of residence. Such requirements allow boards in clients' home states to serve as primary arbiters in any consumer complaints or disputes.

While a number of professional associations and state licensing boards are developing ethics and standards of practice for technology assisted distance counseling, the NBCC has taken the lead and constructed best-practice guidelines for Internet counseling (see www.nbcc.org/Assets/Ethics/internetCounseling.pdf). The NBCC (2012) provides a taxonomy for and definitions of forms of counseling practice and offers helpful standards related to the counseling relationship and confidentiality related to Internet counseling.

Because of the emergence of technology-assisted distance counseling and the ethical and legal challenges inherent in the application of these new technologies to counseling, professional counselors engaging in these activities must be well trained in the specific technologies and well informed about the associated legal and ethical issues in the jurisdictions of practice.

American School Counselor Association Ethical Standards for School Counselors

In addition to the ACA, other counseling organizations have established codes of ethics. The ASCA (2010) has developed a parallel set of ethical standards that specifically addresses counseling practice in schools. As in the ACA's standards, these standards discuss putting the client's best interests first, treating each student as an individual and with respect, involving parents as appropriate, maintaining one's expertise through ongoing professional development and learning, and behaving professionally and ethically. There are seven sections in the *ASCA Ethical Standards for School Counselors*. They are designed to guide the ethical practice of professional school counselors, provide self-appraisal and peer-evaluation information, and inform stakeholders of responsible counselor behaviors. Although many of the provisions overlap with the *ACA Code of Ethics* explained above, what follows is a discussion of additions, extensions, and clarifications provided in the ASCA code. (Note: The ASCA Ethical Standards are currently being revised as this book goes to press.)

A. RESPONSIBILITIES TO STUDENTS   School counselors are concerned with and make available to students comprehensive, developmental, data-driven programs that address the academic, career, and personal-social needs of all students. They respect and accept the diverse cultural and individual values and beliefs of students and do not impose their own values on students or students' families.

Professional school counselors disclose the limits of confidentiality and gain informed consent as appropriate. Confidentiality and informed consent are challenging issues when dealing with minor children. School counselors involve important persons and support networks; counselors consider laws, regulations, and policies as appropriate to ensure that parents/guardians are active partners in their minor children's school experiences. School counselors acknowledge and support parents' legal and inherent rights. When students participate in small-group counseling experiences, school counselors notify parents/guardians. As with adult clients, a student's right to confidentiality is surrendered when the student presents serious and foreseeable harm to self or others.

Professional school counselors use brief, solution-focused approaches when possible and strive to maintain an appropriate professional distance from students so as not to engage in dual relationships that would jeopardize the effectiveness of the primary counseling relationships. School counselors especially avoid online social-networking relationships with students through various communication mediums. School counselors also take steps to ensure that students understand the nature of, and how to report the occurrence of, cyberbullying.

School counselors separately store sole-possession notes used as memory aids and destroy these notes when the students to whom they refer transfer to other schools or school levels (i.e., elementary to middle, or middle to high school) or graduate. If notes might possibly be needed in future court proceedings, school counselors use best judgment in the maintenance of these sole-possession records. The issue of sole-possession notes is covered in more detail later in this chapter.

B. RESPONSIBILITIES TO PARENTS/GUARDIANS   School counselors establish appropriate collaborative relationships with parents and respect parental rights and responsibilities. Unless prevented by court order, school counselors honor parental requests for student records and periodic reports. This especially applies to noncustodial parents who might ask for periodic performance reports that custodial parents might choose not to provide. Legally, noncustodial parents are allowed access to their students' information unless a judge has ordered otherwise.

C. RESPONSIBILITIES TO COLLEAGUES AND PROFESSIONAL ASSOCIATES   Professional school counselors understand their schools' *release-of-information* processes and that parents of minor children must provide written permission for any releases. School counselors work with their supervisors/directors and counselor educators, as appropriate, to implement data-driven, competencies-based comprehensive school counseling programs.

D. RESPONSIBILITIES TO SCHOOL, COMMUNITIES, AND FAMILIES   As advocates for all students within the school community, school counselors notify appropriate officials of conditions that systematically limit the effectiveness of school counseling programs or other curricular components. School counselors also engage in community partnerships to obtain resources that support their comprehensive programs and promote student success. School counselors advocate for the hiring of only qualified and appropriately trained school counselors and accept employment only for positions for which they are qualified.

E. RESPONSIBILITIES TO SELF   As do all counselors, school counselors function within the boundaries of their training and experience. They are responsible for maintaining physical and mental self-care and wellness and engaging in continuous personal and professional growth throughout their careers. This presumes that school counselors will remain current with research and practice innovations in broad areas that influence school counseling practices (e.g., advocacy, cultural competence, technology, leadership, assessment data). Recall that as counselors become more experienced, the standards-of-care expectations on them increase. Thus, as school counselors become more experienced, the expectations for their ethical and legal performances also increase. School counselors use culturally inclusive language, create equity-based programs that promote the performance and achievement of all students, and maintain current membership in professional associations.

F. RESPONSIBILITIES TO THE PROFESSION School counselors follow legal and policy dictates regarding conducting research and program evaluation. They clearly articulate that what they say and write as private individuals represents only themselves and not the views of their schools or profession. School counselors also do not use their school counselor positions to recruit clients for private practice.

Professional school counselors do provide mentoring and support to school counselors in training, ensuring those candidates have professional liability insurance and that university counselor supervisors conduct at least one on-site visit for each practicum or internship student so they can observe and evaluate each candidate in person.

G. MAINTAINANCE OF STANDARDS This final section provides school counselors with specific guidance on how to handle ethical dilemmas in the field and with colleagues. It is important that school counselors work through appropriate channels and take steps to remedy ethical challenges. Colleagues who behave in an unethical manner are problematic, and their behavior needs to be addressed when evident. Ethical codes and hearing committees also often serve an educative function to promote high standards and good practice. These procedures are relatively common across ethical codes of conduct and will be addressed more comprehensively in the next section.

Decision Making Using Ethical Standards

The ACA, ASCA, and other professional counseling organizations have developed guides to ethical decision making that can be used when a professional counselor is concerned about a particular situation and needs to determine if an ethical dilemma exists. The ACA's model involves seven steps: (a) identify the problem, (b) apply the *ACA Code of Ethics*, (c) determine the nature and dimensions of the dilemma, (d) generate potential courses of action, (e) consider the potential consequences of all options and choose a course of action, (f) evaluate the selected course of action, and (g) implement the course of action (Forester-Miller & Davis, 1996).

Stone (2013) has taken the ACA model and applied it to the school setting. As Stone and others caution, professional counselors using either of these models or any other ethical decision-making model would not necessarily come to the same conclusion. There is seldom one correct way of handling any given situation, and each counselor brings a different background, belief system, and values to each dilemma. However, if the counselor reflects on ethical principles and continues to practice with these in mind, it is likely that the dilemma can be resolved in the client's best interests.

Remley and Herlihy (2016) suggested four self-tests to consider before a decision is made: First, in thinking about justice, would you treat others this same way if they were in similar situations? Second, would you suggest to other counselors this same course of action? Third, would you be willing to have others know how you acted? Fourth, do you have any lingering feelings of doubt or uncertainty about what you did? If you cannot answer in the affirmative to the first three tests and in the negative to the fourth test, perhaps the proposed decision is not ethically sound. It is always appropriate and ethically sound to consult with a colleague when working through a dilemma to ensure all aspects of the issue have been examined and all possible problems have been discussed. Now read and respond to the situations in Case Study 3.2. Next, Activities 3.2 through 3.4 will help you integrate the information on ethical and legal issues in counseling and apply ethical decision-making principles to numerous scenarios.

CASE STUDY 3.2

Ethical Decision Making

For each numbered situation, indicate whether the person's behavior is ethical (E) or unethical (U) and cite the *ACA Code of Ethics* standard or standards that apply. The person in question in each scenario is underlined.

Situation #1: Judy, a counselor educator at a university, has a colleague named John who is opening a private practice in addition to his teaching job. John is building his client caseload by offering special supervisory rates to recent graduates of the university counseling program in exchange for providing supervision the graduates need for licensure.

E   U   Standard(s) _____

Situation #2: A rehabilitation counselor is conducting a research study. Because raw data includes confidential information about individual participants, the counselor deletes all identifying data about the participants before giving the material to the secretary for computer entry.

E   U   Standard(s) _____

Situation #3: Larry Adams has a PhD in history and is a university professor. He also has a master's degree in counseling and is an LPC. He plans to open a part-time private practice and has business cards printed that read, "Dr. Larry Adams, Individual and Group Counseling."

E   U   Standard(s) _____

Situation #4: A woman enters into a counseling relationship with a male professional counselor at a mental health center after finishing a treatment program for alcohol addiction. The woman has a history of violent behavior when intoxicated. She maintains her sobriety for several months. But one evening, obviously intoxicated, she calls the counselor and threatens to kill her mother. Despite the client's incoherence, the counselor discerns that she has a gun. The counselor calls the client's mother but is unable to reach her and then calls the police.

E   U   Standard(s) _____

Situation #5: A <u>residence-hall director</u> who is responsible for hall discipline at a university dormitory has a master's degree in counseling. He is approached by students living in his hall who say they would like to address some personal concerns and want him to be their counselor. The residence-hall director arranges weekly sessions for counseling with the students.

E   U   Standard(s) _____

Situation #6: A male <u>professional counselor</u> works daily in a mental health center with clients who are taking medications. A client who is taking Prozac for treatment of depression tells the counselor she continues to be quite depressed. The counselor says, "No problem. You might need to have your medication changed. I'll arrange that." Then he refers the woman to the staff psychiatrist.

E   U   Standard(s) _____

Situation #7: A <u>professional counselor</u> has been encouraging a client to get involved in more social activities to get her out of her house more often. One day, the client unexpectedly shows up at an art class the counselor is enrolled in, saying she signed up for the same class. The counselor decides to continue taking the class.

E   U   Standard(s) _____

Situation #8: A <u>professional counselor</u> has been working with a married couple. The spouses decide to divorce. Between sessions, the couple has an argument and the husband moves out of the house. The wife obtains a restraining order because she fears her husband will harm her or their children, as he has in the past. The husband calls the counselor and threatens to bomb the house if his wife does not allow him to see their children. The husband sounds rational but definitely wants to get even with his wife. The counselor believes the husband is just spouting off, so does not contact or warn the wife or the authorities.

E   U   Standard(s) _____

Situation #9: <u>Sharon</u>, a counselor in private practice, receives a phone call from a former friend and sexual partner. He tells her he is grieving the death of his father and requests counseling from her. Because Sharon specializes in grief counseling and has not dated the man for more than a year, she agrees to counsel him.

E   U   Standard(s) _____

Situation #10: A female <u>graduate student</u> in counseling is doing her internship in a community agency. The administrators tell her not to inform clients that she is a student intern. They explain that clients might think they are getting second-class

(Continued)

service if they know their counselor is in training. The administrators contend that clients are paying (on a sliding scale) for services they receive and that it would not be psychologically good to give them any information that might cause them to believe they are not getting the best help available. The student does as she is told.

E   U   Standard(s) _____

Situation #11: Robert requests counseling from a <u>professional counselor</u> in private practice. He indicates that he and his wife are involved in marriage counseling as a couple through an agency in town. Robert says he is undecided about continuing the marriage and would like to sort out his feelings and reach a decision. He intends to continue couples counseling in the meantime. The professional counselor agrees to provide counseling to Robert without requesting permission to contact the marriage counselor.

E   U   Standard(s) _____

Situation #12: A <u>professional counselor</u> has administered a personality inventory to a Mexican American client. The counselor is aware that this inventory contains several race-sensitive items but has decided to use it anyway because this partic-ular client seems so well acculturated.

E   U   Standard(s) _____

Situation #13: A <u>family counselor</u> in a mental health clinic has been having weekly sessions with two parents and their adolescent child, a juvenile offender who is about to be released from a detention center. In the past, the juvenile was known to be extremely dangerous and violent and had made generalized state-ments of hostility but with no intended or identifiable victim. The counselor took no action to block his release.

E   U   Standard(s) _____

Situation #14: A <u>professional school counselor</u> is working with a student who is distressed about her family situation, which involves the use of crack cocaine. The counselor has no training in drug counseling. He continues working with the student even though a local family service center has an excellent, free program for teenagers with parents who abuse substances.

E   U   Standard(s) _____

Situation #15: As a private practitioner, a <u>professional counselor</u> decides not to purchase malpractice insurance and proceeds to practice without it.

E   U   Standard(s) _____

Situation #16: A <u>high school counselor</u> is contacted by a teacher who reports that Diane, a student in her English class, has written a poem about death. When the teacher talked with Diane, she threatened to kill herself. The counselor calls Diane into her office, and Diane admits to being deeply despondent and wanting to end her life. Diane begs the counselor not to tell her parents or anyone else. The counselor is concerned for Diane's safety, so she calls her parents to tell them of Diane's suicidal ideation.

E   U   Standard(s) _____

Situation #17: A <u>professional counselor</u> is seeing a client who had been sexually abused as a child. The client expresses frustration that she cannot remember the earliest incidents of abuse and insists that hypnosis would help her break through this barrier. Although the counselor has no specific training in hypnosis, she agrees to purchase a hypnosis audiotape and attempt the procedure with the client.

E   U   Standard(s) _____

Situation #18: Steve reveals to his <u>professional counselor</u> that he is infected with HIV. After the counselor explores the situation a bit, Steve tells his counselor he is embarrassed, confused, and finds it difficult to talk about his condition. Steve admits that he engages in unprotected sexual relations and does not disclose his condition to his partners. The counselor agrees to continue providing counseling services to Steve only if his client gives a verbal agreement that he will not have sexual relations with others until he is less confused.

E   U   Standard(s) _____

Situation #19: Joe, a 23-year-old college student, was convicted of illegal possession of a controlled substance and is now serving a two-year probation sentence. He is seeing a <u>college counselor</u>. Joe's probation officer contacts the counselor and requests a report. Although Joe has not signed a release of information, the counselor complies, fearing that not doing so might cause the probation officer to file a negative report on Joe with the court.

E   U   Standard(s) _____

Situation #20: Before seeing a family for counseling, a <u>professional counselor</u> gives the parents a written document explaining the process of counseling. After reading the informed-consent document, the parents sign it and bring the family to counseling. The informed-consent document is not given to or described to the children.

E   U   Standard(s) _____

ACTIVITY 3.2

As a future professional counselor, write a reflection on (a) your ethical decision-making process (emphasizing self-awareness and analysis of the various codes of ethics) and (b) how your personal and cultural values might influence your counseling practice.

ACTIVITY 3.3

Mark the appropriate column for each sentence stem below. How ethical is it for a professional counselor to

	Almost Never	Rarely	Sometimes	Usually	Almost Always
1. barter with a client for services?					
2. invite a client to a personal party or social event?					
3. provide counseling to a friend who is in a crisis?					
4. accept a gift from a client if the gift is worth less than $10?					
5. accept a gift from a client if the gift is worth more than $50?					
6. accept a client's invitation to a special event?					
7. go out for coffee with a client after a counseling session?					
8. become friends with a client after termination of the counseling relationship?					
9. give your home phone number to a client?					
10. share personal experiences as a member of a self-help group when a client is in attendance?					
11. occasionally hire a client to baby-sit?					

ACTIVITY 3.4

Consider what you have learned so far about the *ACA Code of Ethics* (2014a) and other ethics information contained in this chapter as you answer the following questions:

1. Are the code's ethical standards sufficiently comprehensive and specific to guide you in working with diverse client populations? Are you aware of any subtle biases you might have against individuals who are different from you? How can you guard against racial and sexual stereotyping in your counseling relationship with clients?
2. How can you recognize when you are meeting your personal needs at the expense of a client? Do you think it is possible to continue your work as a professional counselor if you do not meet your own needs? Can you think of any values you

hold that you might impose on certain clients? If you became aware of personal problems that were negatively affecting your work, what would you do?

3. What might you want to tell clients about the exceptions to confidentiality? Do you think that informing clients about the limits to confidentiality increases or decreases trust? What are your thoughts about confidentiality as it pertains to contagious, fatal diseases? What are your thoughts about confidentiality as it pertains to clients who are minors?

4. Under what circumstances might you consult with another professional regarding your ethical obligations to a client? How can you determine when a client's condition represents a clear and imminent danger to the client or others? How can you assess the degree of danger?

5. When might you make use of assessments as a part of the counseling process? What factors do you need to take into account in selecting, administering, scoring, and interpreting assessments? What are the ethical considerations in assessing diverse client populations?

6. How can appropriate relationship boundaries between counselor educators and students be determined? Which ethical, professional, and social-relationship boundaries between counselor educators and students do you think are important? Which ethical, professional, and social-relationship boundaries between supervisors and supervisees do you think are important?

ADDITIONAL SOURCES OF INFORMATION AND GUIDANCE: COURTS, LAWS, AND REGULATIONS

While the ethical standards provide an important foundation for guiding counselor behavior, there are many other sources of information with which professional counselors must become familiar if they are to maintain the highest standards of ethical and legal behavior. These other sources include the courts, laws, and regulations.

Court System

Professional counselors are affected by three main types of laws: **statutory law**, which is created by legislatures; **constitutional law**, which results from court decisions concerning constitutional issues; and **common law**, which results from other court decisions. There are 51 U.S. court systems—the court systems for the 50 states and the federal system. Both state and federal courts can enact decisions affecting counselors, and their systems are composed of tiers. The structure of state court systems varies but generally consists of trial courts that include courts of special jurisdiction, such as juvenile courts or small claims courts, and courts of appeal.

All states have a court that is the final state authority to which cases may be appealed. The name of this court varies among states. For example, Maryland and New York call their highest courts the Court of Appeals; West Virginia calls its the Supreme Court of Appeals; some other states call theirs superior court. One must be careful when reading state-court decisions to note which court rendered the decision, because high-court names are inconsistent across states. Cases from the highest court in each state may be appealed directly to the U.S. Supreme Court. Decisions from state courts are binding only on individuals living in that state, but they may serve as precedent for a similar case in another state.

The federal court system is a three-tiered system. Approximately 100 U.S. district courts form the basis of the federal system. These courts hear cases that involve federal law, disputes between citizens from different states that involve more than $75,000, and cases in which the United States is a party. There are 13 federal courts of appeals. Decisions from the circuit courts of appeals are binding only on the states within a ruling court's jurisdiction. However, a decision from one court may influence the decision rendered by another court when the same issue arises. Cases from the circuit courts of appeals may be appealed to the U.S. Supreme Court, the highest court in the United States.

Statutory Law

Statutory law is the body of mandates created through legislation passed by the U.S. Congress and state legislatures. Many of the health, mental health, and education structures, and policies that govern their implementation, are found within these mandates. The federal government has the authority to pass legislation related only to the powers specified in the U.S. Constitution. Numerous laws have been enacted that affect professional counselors. Most legislation influencing counselors is passed by state legislatures and concerns two types of legislation: state legislation to implement federal legislation and new, state-specific legislation. State laws may be more restrictive than federal legislation, but they may never be less restrictive. To explore how laws affect the counseling practice, complete Activity 3.5.

ACTIVITY 3.5

Go to your state's legislative website. Peruse the bills and laws relevant to professional counselors that have been passed recently. How will these affect your practice?

State and Local Agencies: Regulations and Policies

Most state departments of mental health, which ordinarily house licensing boards (e.g., a board of professional counselors), can enact regulations that are binding upon the practice of counseling within their states. Likewise, most state departments of education have the ability to enact regulations that are binding on the school districts within their states. The regulations often encompass areas not addressed through other state legislation or add detail to state legislation and may include implementation plans and more specific definitions. State agencies also develop policies, which are often detailed explanations of how to implement a specific law. Last, state agencies may also issue guidelines, which are suggestions about how to address specific issues. In contrast to regulations and policies, guidelines are not mandates and do not have to be followed. However, because they do represent agencies' current thinking regarding particular issues, local policies generally do not deviate too far from them.

Although it is not a regulation, a state attorney general's **opinion** or advice of counsel is often incorporated into an agency's policies or guidelines. This guidance is frequently in response to a new court case, law, or request of a state agency. The advice or opinion is the attorney general's interpretation of what that law or case means for the agency or agencies affected and usually suggests what the agency or agencies need to do to comply.

Local school systems and agencies may also develop their own policies, procedures, and guidelines. School systems, in particular, often take state regulations and policies and rewrite them to reflect their specific local situations; these are often adopted by the local boards of education. Local mental health departments or agencies may also define state policies and procedures further to reflect their jurisdiction-specific needs. Finally, individual schools or centers may have additional policies or guidelines in place for certain issues that further direct professional school counselor actions.

Importantly, professional counselors functioning in private practice or agencies other than school systems are not bound by the policies or guidelines developed by the schools, just as professional school counselors are not bound by the policies or guidelines developed by state agencies without school oversight or authority. To explore how school or agency policies, procedures, and guidelines affect the counseling practice, complete Activity 3.6.

ACTIVITY 3.6

Access a local school's or agency's policies, procedures, and guidelines. Become acquainted with unfamiliar policies and procedures that will directly affect your practice as a professional counselor.

MAKING DECISIONS

Failure to understand the law, and by extension policies, procedures, and guidelines, is an unacceptable legal defense. It is incumbent on the professional counselor to become familiar with all the various sources of information and guidance that are available to perform one's responsibilities in an ethical and legal manner. There are many ways of maintaining current information.

In most work settings, with the exception perhaps of private practice, professional counselors have supervisors or other individuals in authority who can help them become familiar with setting-relevant regulations, policies, and guidelines. Most schools and many community agencies have administrative manuals that incorporate all these sources of information into continually updated binders. The ACA newsletter, *Counseling Today*, highlights issues and important, timely topics in counseling, as do other professional journals and newsletters. Many commercially available newsletters cover recent court rulings and their impacts in different work settings.

The Internet has become a valuable tool for accessing current information and resources, although one must be careful to authenticate this information. Guillot-Miller and Partin (2003) identified more than 40 sites that include information relevant to ethical and legal practices for professional counselors. The professional associations for counselors and other mental health professionals, institutions of higher education, state and federal government agencies, government-funded organizations, and professional and legal publishers all continuously update their websites and are good sources of current information. Activity 3.7 directs you to explore the sources of information helpful in maintaining an ethical and legal practice.

ACTIVITY 3.7

Access applicable sources of information that will guide your decision making as a professional counselor. What sources are available to you so you can continuously update your knowledge of ethical and legal guidelines and information?

Sometimes mandates seem to be in conflict with each other. In such cases, common sense should prevail. There might be a therapeutically logical reason to follow one particular mandate rather than another one. Professional counselors should follow the logical course of action and document what they do and why. For example, if a counselor is working with a suicidal teenage client but believes telling the client's parents would perpetuate an abusive situation, the counselor should handle the situation as an abuse case and inform child protective services about the suicidal behavior. In addition, if a particular policy, guideline, or regulation is not in the best interests of the clients in the counselor's work setting, as per the profession's ethical standards, the counselor should work to change the mandate.

Two other issues are sometimes confusing for professional counselors. The first concerns the different ways in which counselors in different settings operate. Some mandates cover all counselors, particularly mandates that are the result of federal or state legislation or court cases. For example, child abuse and neglect laws apply to all counselors regardless of the settings in which they work. However, the implementation of some mandates, particularly as they are influenced by policies and guidelines, could look different in different settings.

Schools have perhaps the greatest number of mandates under which staff must operate, yet professional school counselors seldom need permission to see students (Remley & Herlihy, 2016), particularly if their schools have approved comprehensive developmental programs. A mental health counselor employed by an outside center or agency but working either in a school or in a school-based health center needs signed, informed consent forms to see the same students. In some cases, local school systems have mandated opt-in programs, which require signed informed consent forms for students to participate in different aspects of the comprehensive guidance programs. In such cases, professional school counselors working in nearby systems or schools may operate differently, perhaps using opt-out programs in which all students participate unless a parent or guardian expressly (in writing) forbids a student from participating. For additional practice in adhering to agency or school policies and professional ethics, complete Activity 3.8.

ACTIVITY 3.8

Depending on your intended work setting, construct one of the following forms:

1. Develop an informed consent form relevant to your work setting.
2. Develop an opt-in or opt-out form for use in a school program.
3. Develop an informed consent form for use with parents and children in a community or private-agency setting.

A second issue concerns professional counselors who hold multiple credentials. A counselor may work as a professional school counselor but hold state certification or licensure and work as a mental health counselor outside of school. The counselor might need permission to do something as a professional school counselor but not need permission as a mental health counselor, or vice versa. Under which set of mandates should the counselor operate?

The answer to both these issues is the same: an employee must follow the mandates that apply to his or her work setting. A professional counselor is required to operate under the mandates of the system that employs him or her or, in the case of a volunteer, the mandates of the entity under whose auspices he or she is working. If a counselor is employed by an agency or a private practice, he or she must follow the mandates of that entity. If a counselor is employed by a school system as a counselor, he or she must follow the mandates of the local school system. Teachers who have degrees in counseling or other related mental health degrees who continue to be employed as teachers do not have the same protections as counselors, because they are not employed in a mental health capacity. They need to check the policies of their school systems carefully to see if they are covered by any protections, such as confidentiality.

ADDITIONAL LEGAL CONSIDERATIONS

In developing an ethical stance, professional counselors must take all the aforementioned sources of information into account. There are several other influences that must be considered as well (Herlihy & Corey, 2015; Stone, 2013). Each counselor brings to every counseling relationship the sum of his or her experience, education, and training. Each counselor brings to a setting that which makes him or her unique—the counselor's values, morals, and spiritual influences. Who a professional counselor is strongly influences the stances he or she takes on issues. Professional counselors must continually be aware of how their own beliefs and values impact the ways they think about issues, clients and their needs, and options they perceive to be available. Professional counselors must also continually examine their behavior in light of cultural bias and multicultural understanding. When deciding on a course of action regarding a client, a counselor must always try to do what is in the best interests of the client.

Professional Competence

In addition to being knowledgeable about mandates, as was previously discussed, there are further steps professional counselors should take to ensure ethical and legal behavior. Several of these are mentioned in the *ACA Code of Ethics* (2014a), but it is important to reemphasize them. As reported by Cottone and Tarvydas (2007), professional counselors should adhere to the following directives:

- Maintain professional growth through continuing education. While counselors must attend continuing education opportunities to renew national credentials, state credentials, or both, it is important to stay current with the theories, trends, and information about clients and different populations.
- Maintain accurate knowledge and expertise in areas of responsibility. Information changes so quickly that professional counselors must ensure they are providing quality and effective services to their clients. One way of achieving this goal is through

professional development, but counselors may also gain information through reading, consultation with colleagues, supervision, and other means.

- Accurately represent credentials. As stated in the ethical standards, professional counselors should claim only the credentials they have earned and only the highest degree in counseling or a closely related mental health field. Counselors who hold doctorates in nonmental health fields should not use the title *doctor* in their work as a counselor. This is a particular problem in school settings where counselors might earn doctorates in administration and supervision, or related fields, but continue to work as counselors and use the title *doctor* in their jobs. Counselors should not imply in any way that their credentials allow them to work in areas in which they are not trained.

- Provide services only for which you are qualified and trained. The easiest way for professional counselors to get into trouble professionally is to provide services for which they are not qualified, either by training or by education. This is particularly true when using counseling techniques. Counselors should have training in using a particular technique before using it. Reading about a technique is not equivalent to implementing it under supervision. Also, professional counselors should not try to work with clients whose problems go beyond their expertise. If professional counselors are put in a situation in which there are no other counselors to whom to refer the client, the counselor should consult with colleagues and ask for supervision to ensure the effectiveness of the counseling.

"Can I Be Sued?" and "What Is Malpractice?"

Can you be sued? Yes, of course. Anyone can be sued for almost anything, particularly in our litigious society. The more important question is, *Will you be found guilty?* The answer to this question is much more complex.

If professional counselors fail to exercise *due care* in fulfilling their professional responsibilities, they can be found guilty of **civil liability**—that is, committing a wrong against an individual. **Negligence** may be found if the wrong committed resulted in an injury or damage—in other words, if the duty owed to the client was breached in some way that caused damage to the client. However, in counseling, it is more likely counselors will be sued for malpractice. **Malpractice** is the area of tort law that concerns professional conduct. Malpractice is professional misconduct in the application of skills or performance in the discharge of professional duties. Generally, for a counselor to be held liable in tort for malpractice, four conditions have to be met (Stone, 2013): (a) a duty was owed to the plaintiff (client) by the defendant (counselor); (b) the counselor breached the duty; (c) there is a causal link between the breach and the client's injury; and (d) the client suffered some damage or injury.

A professional counselor's failure to report an abuse case is an example of negligence. The counselor had a duty to the client and failed to fulfill that duty. In contrast, malpractice is contingent upon the client suffering owing to the counselor's lack of skill or inappropriate behavior. A counselor treating a client with an eating disorder through hypnosis when the counselor is not trained in the use of hypnosis is an example of malpractice. The situation becomes further complicated if this technique is not recognized as effective for treating eating disorders.

The standard of practice will be used in any liability proceeding to determine if the professional counselor's performance was within accepted practice. The standard of practice answers the question "While performing a professional counseling service, was the counselor's treatment of the client or level of care consistent with the counselor's level of learning, skill, and ethics that ordinarily would be expected and possessed under highly similar circumstances by other reputable counselors?"

The **standard of practice** will be established through the testimony of peers. These peers, who are called expert witnesses, are considered to be experts in the field under question. For professional school counselors, the expert witnesses would be other school counselors (Stone, 2013). For rehabilitation counselors, the expert witnesses would be other rehabilitation counselors. For mental health counselors, the expert witnesses would be other mental health counselors. The standard is an ever evolving level of expectation and is influenced by two major factors: education and experience. The standard is not an absolute one but a variable one. It will be much higher for a professional counselor who has practiced for many years and pursued advanced graduate training or professional development than it will be for a counselor in the first year of practice immediately after graduate school. The more training and experience a counselor possesses, the higher the standard to which the counselor will be held accountable. The assumption is that a professional counselor should know more each year he or she practices through experience and training and thus should be held to a higher standard with each additional year. Using this standard of practice, a counselor will usually be found guilty of malpractice if one or more of the following situations occur:

- The practice was not within the realm of acceptable professional practice.
- The counselor was not trained in the technique used.
- The counselor failed to follow a procedure that would have been more helpful.
- The counselor failed to warn or protect others from a violent client.
- The counselor failed to obtain informed consent.
- The counselor failed to explain the possible consequences of the treatment.

Sexual misconduct is the primary reason liability actions are initiated against professional counselors. School staff, counselors, and other mental health professionals have been accused of committing sexual abuse or misconduct. It might be that other problems, such as failure to use a more appropriate technique, are actually more common. However, most clients lack the ability to recognize therapeutic problems and might just have a general sense that it isn't working or helping and choose to terminate.

Although the number of professional counselors who are sued is increasing, the number still remains small. In schools, parents are more likely to request their children not be included in certain school-counseling program activities or to complain to the principal or central administration about a program or behavior. In rare cases, parents might sue. Most cases against school counselors have been rejected by the courts (Linde, 2015). In school or agency settings, violating or failing to follow mandates would get a professional counselor in trouble faster than almost any other behavior. Depending on the counselor's action, the professional counselor could be reprimanded. In extreme cases, the counselor's employment might be terminated. In clinics and agencies, few counselors are sued over professional practice issues; counselors are more often sued because of sexual conduct or illegal activities.

Professional counselors also must be knowledgeable about their communities or schools. They might have a legal right to implement certain programs or conduct certain activities, but if the community or school is not supportive of those activities, the counselors are going to face opposition.

When a professional counselor is faced with any legal action, the first thing the counselor should do is call a lawyer. Then the counselor should tell a counselor supervisor, if he or she has one. Most agencies, clinics, practices, and schools are accustomed to dealing with such legal issues and might even have a procedure for what needs to be done. A professional counselor should never attempt to reason with the client or contact the client's lawyer without advice of counsel. The counselor should not provide any information to or discuss the case with anyone except his or her lawyer or the person designated to help the counselor. Just as professional counselors advise clients to get professional mental health help when they have personal problems, counselors must get legal help when they have legal problems.

Subpoenas

Many professional counselors will receive a **subpoena** at some point in their professional careers. The most common cases counselors, and particularly professional school counselors, receive subpoenas about include custody disputes, child abuse or neglect allegations, and special education disputes. In most cases, the client an attorney is representing believes the counselor might have some information that will be helpful to the case. Professional counselors need to pay attention to subpoenas because they are legal documents. At the same time, counselors must consider whether the information being requested is confidential, because professional school counselors might be limited in what they can share. Under no circumstances should the counselor automatically comply with the subpoena without discussing it first with the client, the client's attorney, or both, and the agency's or school system's attorney. Professional counselors should take the following steps when they receive a subpoena (Linde, 2015):

1. Contact the client or the client's attorney and ask for guidance (*exception:* not if the client is suing the counselor). If you work for a school system, contact the school system's attorney to seek guidance.
2. If the above-mentioned parties advise you to comply with the subpoena, discuss the implications of releasing the requested information.
3. Obtain a signed informed consent form to release the records. That form should specify all conditions of release: what, to whom, and so forth.
4. If the decision is made not to release the records, the attorney should file a motion to quash (or, in some areas, ask for a protective order). This would allow you to not comply with the subpoena.
5. Maintain a record of everything you and the attorneys do. Keep notes regarding all conversations and copies of any documents pertaining to the subpoena.

An attorney who wants information may ask a judge to issue a court order. A **court order** permits the release of confidential information but does not mandate its release; that is, a court order allows a professional counselor to use his or her judgment regarding whether to release confidential information. If the release of confidential information is damaging to the client, the counselor should not release the requested materials. However, if both a subpoena and a court order are received, the counselor must release the required information with or without the client's consent (unless a motion to quash is filed). Failure to do so could result in the counselor being held in contempt of court. Still, even though required to release confidential information, the counselor should release only the information relevant to the case and required by the judge. In other words, it is not likely the judge would order the release of an entire client file.

On the surface, these situations can seem confusing. That's why it's important to remember two things when receiving subpoenas: (a) do not panic, and (b) do consult an attorney. Subpoenas are legal documents, but counselors have enough time to consider the implications to their clients of releasing the information and to seek legal advice. Lawyers are legal professionals who can help counselors sort through the issues, comply with legal mandates, and protect the confidential relationships the counselors have with their clients.

VOICES FROM THE FIELD 3.2   Garnering a License, by James R. Rough, executive director/Ohio Counselor, Social Worker and Marriage and Family Therapist Board

---

Many licensure applicants struggle to navigate the licensure process because of a lack of understanding or knowledge of state laws and rules and regulatory-board-related processes. What follows are several examples of licensure-related problems I commonly see:

1. Graduates with master's degrees in counseling get jobs and hold themselves out as licensed counselors because they passed the National Counselor Examination (even though they are not yet licensed in their states).
2. Students attend Council for Accreditation of Counseling and Related Educational Program-accredited programs and assume this accreditation automatically provides them licensure, when in fact many states have additional coursework or training requirements.
3. Students complete their internships in settings that are not acceptable to regulatory boards (e.g., a school setting), or they do mostly case management and little clinical work.
4. Licensure applicants with felony convictions try to get licensed and/or counsel with a license but cannot get licenses or find jobs.

In regard to the first problem, what is the difference between a licensed professional counselor and a graduate of an approved master's counseling program? A licensed professional counselor can legally call oneself a counselor and perform services for fees, while an unlicensed graduate with a master's degree cannot. To practice without an actual license is a violation of the law in most states and can result in disciplinary action being taken.

In regard to the second problem, graduates who want to be licensed counselors need to know the laws in the states in which they want to practice. Each state has its own law—rules regarding which degrees lead to counselor licensure—and scope of practice for services counselors can perform.

For example, in Ohio the most common problem out-of-state graduates encounter is a need for additional clinical coursework for Ohio licensure because of the state's 20-semester-hour clinical coursework requirement. In addition, Ohio requires the completion of an advanced assessment course focused on the use of assessment instruments in diagnosis and treatment planning.

The best way to find answers to questions about such situations is to visit the NBCC's State Board Directory web page (www.nbcc.org/directory). The directory links to the states' websites, which offer application forms and other needed information.

Proper research of the licensure requirements in the states in which applicants wish to seek licensure will invite easier licensure experiences. Applicants must do due diligence to find out this information, even if they want to remain in the states in which their graduate programs are housed. When it comes to licensure, the five Ps most certainly apply: Prior planning prevents poor performance.

CONFIDENTIALITY

For clients to feel free to share sometimes sensitive and personal information during counseling sessions, they must believe they can trust their professional counselors not to share what is disclosed during sessions with anyone else without their permission. This sense of trust and privacy, called confidentiality, is essential for counseling to be successful. **Confidentiality** is the cornerstone of counseling and is what separates the counseling relationship from other relationships in which information is shared. Confidentiality belongs to the client, not to the counselor. The client always has the right to waive confidentiality or to allow information to be shared with a third party.

Counseling minors presents particular challenges to the issue of confidentiality. Every state sets the age of majority; for most states, it is 18 years of age. Most (noncollege) students are minors and are not legally able to make their own decisions. Minors have an ethical right to confidentiality, but the legal rights belong to their parents or guardians (Remley & Herlihy, 2016). Most states protect counselor–client confidentiality. Approximately 20 states protect professional-school-counselor–student confidentiality through statutes (Cottone & Tarvydas, 2007), but many include significant restrictions.

Professional counselors often ask what to do if parents want to know what is discussed during counseling sessions with their minor child. Legally, parents have the right to know what is being discussed. However, the child might not want the information to be shared with his or her parents. Section B.5.b, Responsibility to Parents and Legal Guardians, of the ACA Code of Ethics states the following:

> Counselors inform parents and legal guardians about the role of counselors and the confidential nature of the counseling relationship. Counselors are sensitive to the cultural diversity of families and respect the inherent rights and responsibilities of parents/guardians over the welfare of the children/charges according to law. Counselors work to establish, as appropriate, collaborative relationships with parents/guardians to best serve clients. (ACA, 2014a, p. 7)

This statement leaves professional counselors with a dilemma. To resolve this dilemma, Remley and Herlihy (2016) suggested the counselor first discuss the issue with the child to determine if the child is willing to disclose the information to his or her parents. If the child does not want to disclose the information, the counselor should try to help the parents understand that the best interests of the child are not served by disclosure. If this does not work, the counselor should schedule a joint meeting with the parents and child to discuss the issue. If the parents are still not satisfied, the counselor might have to disclose the information without the child's consent.

Some professional counselors would suggest that this type of situation could reflect some deeper family issue. While the parents or guardians have a legal right to the information, there might be an underlying "family secret" the parents do not want known, and the counselor should be sensitive to any difficulties the child might be exhibiting. Or this situation might be the result of cultural differences, and the counselor needs to be sensitive to the family's traditions and beliefs.

Many professional counselors suggest that at the beginning of the first session of each new counseling relationship, the professional counselor should discuss confidentiality with the client, explain what it means, and point out the limits of confidentiality. Some counselors choose to hang signs on their office walls that outline this information to reinforce what is discussed in the first session. While this issue seems simple on the surface, in reality, it is a very complex issue that has generated a significant amount of research and professional discourse. As the use of technology increases in counseling settings, the discussions will continue and expand. There are significant challenges to keeping electronic information confidential.

Limits to Confidentiality

According to section B.1.b of the *ACA Code of Ethics* (2014a, p. 6), "Counselors respect the privacy of prospective and current clients." Section B.1.c states, "Counselors protect the confidential information of prospective and current clients. Counselors disclose information only with appropriate consent or with sound legal or ethical justification." Section B.1.d states, "At initiation and throughout the counseling process, counselors inform clients of the limitations of confidentiality and seek to identify situations in which confidentiality must be breached." There are several instances, however, in which counselors must break confidentiality. These are delineated in Section B.2. The most important of these is the **duty to warn**. When a professional counselor becomes aware that a client is in danger of being harmed, such as in instances of abuse or suicide, or when the client is likely to harm someone else, the counselor may break confidentiality to tell an appropriate person.

The basis for the duty-to-warn standard began with the 1974 Tarasoff case in California (*Tarasoff v. Regents of the University of California*, 1976). In this case, the client, a graduate student, told his psychologist about his intent to kill a girl (named Tatiana Tarasoff) who had rejected his advances. The psychologist told the campus police and his supervisor but did not warn the intended victim or her family. The graduate student murdered Tarasoff. In the ensuing case, the Tarasoffs sued the UCLA Board of Regents and others, noting that had the university notified the Tarasoffs or their daughter directly, the tragedy might have been prevented. After the trial and several levels of appeal, the majority of the California Supreme Court ruled that the psychologist had a duty to warn a known, intended victim. This case established the legal duty to warn and protect an identifiable victim from a client's potential or intended violence and has formed the basis of many other court decisions across the United States. The *ACA Code of Ethics* (2014a), Section B.2.a, now reads, "The general requirement that counselors keep information confidential does not apply when disclosure is required to protect clients or identified others from serious and foreseeable harm or when legal requirements demand that confidential information must be revealed." (p. 7). It is important to note that Texas does not require the duty to warn.

In the ensuing decades, some cases have extended the duty-to-warn standard to include types of harm other than violence and foreseeable victims in addition to identifiable victims. Several other situations constrain the limits of confidentiality, as delineated in the *ACA Code of Ethics* (2014a, p. 7):

- *Subordinates* Confidentiality is not absolute when subordinates, including employees, supervisees, students, clerical assistants, and volunteers, handle records or confidential information. Every effort should be made to limit access to this information, and the assistants should be reminded of the confidential nature of the information they are handling.
- *Interdisciplinary Teams* The client should be informed of the treatment team and the information being shared.

- *Consultation* The professional counselor always has the right to consult with a colleague or supervisor on any case. In such instances, the counselor should provide enough information to obtain the needed assistance but should limit any information that might identify the client.
- *Groups and families* In group or family counseling settings, confidentiality is not guaranteed. The counselor might state that what goes on in the sessions is confidential, and the members might agree. However, because there is more than one client in the group, it is impossible to guarantee confidentiality.
- *Third-party payers* Information will sometimes have to be sent to a mental health provider, insurance company, or other agency that has some legitimate need for the information. The counselor must secure the client's permission to disclose this information.
- *Minors* There are special considerations regarding confidentiality and minors; these are discussed in detail in the next section.
- *Contagious, life-threatening diseases* In contrast to the duty-to-warn standard, the *ACA Code of Ethics* states that the counselor is justified in disclosing information about a client to an identifiable third party if that party's relationship with the client is such that there is a possibility of him or her contracting the disease and the client does not plan on telling the third party. The word used is *justified*, not *should* or *must*. This wording leaves it up to the counselor to decide if the third party is at risk and must be warned.
- *Court-ordered disclosure* Subpoenas and court orders were previously discussed. Even if ordered to reveal confidential information by a judge, a counselor should limit what he or she reveals to only what is relevant to the court proceeding and required by the judge so the counselor can protect the confidential client–counselor relationship. A lawyer is a legal professional who can help a counselor comply with the law while maintaining his or her ethical obligations.

In summary, confidentiality is a very complex issue, but it is essential to the effectiveness of counseling. Clients have an ethical right to confidentiality, and counselors must make every effort to ensure this right. There are specific cases, however, in which it is not only permissible but essential that a counselor break confidentiality to protect a client or others from a client.

Confidentiality and Privileged Communication

The term *confidentiality* is used in discussions about counseling, whereas the term **privileged communication** is the legal term used to describe the privacy of counselor–client communication. Privileged communication exists by statute and applies only to testifying in a court of law. When it exists, the privilege belongs to the client, who always has the right to waive the privilege and allow the counselor to testify. In other words, if the client holds privilege and orders the counselor to testify on the client's behalf, the counselor cannot refuse to testify on the basis of privileged information.

Clients have an ethical right to confidentiality, and the ethical standards for the mental health professions detail the boundaries of confidentiality. Privileged communication is more limited; federal, state, and local mandates determine its parameters. Whether a counselor–client relationship is covered by privileged communication varies widely across jurisdictions. Even within a jurisdiction, a counselor in private practice might be covered by privileged communication, while school counselors who work in that same jurisdiction might not be. It is essential that counselors become familiar with their local mandates and policies to determine the extent to which privileged communication applies to their situations. Think About It 3.2 provides an opportunity to think ahead and consider how you would handle circumstances when confidentiality might need to be compromised.

THINK ABOUT IT 3.2

What precautions will you take as a professional counselor to forewarn your clients about the possible limits to confidentiality? Consider how you would approach a client if a breach of confidentiality is necessary. Then practice this approach with a peer.

MINOR-CONSENT LAWS

Each state has a **minor-consent law** that allows certain minors to seek treatment for certain conditions, usually involving substance abuse, mental health, and some reproductive-health areas. These laws are based on the federal regulation 42 U.S.C. §§290dd-3; 42 C.F.R. Part 2, which references the confidentiality of patient records for drug- and alcohol-abuse assessment, referral, diagnosis, and treatment. The law further prohibits the release of these records to anyone without the client's informed consent and includes clients younger than age 18, even if they are in school and living with their parents or guardians.

Over the past few decades, there has been a movement to increase the number of student-assistance teams and student-assistance programs in schools. These teams usually consist of an administrator, one or more student-services professionals (e.g., professional school counselor, school social worker, pupil personnel worker, school psychologist, school nurse), and teachers, and they might include a substance-abuse assessor from a local agency or a similar professional. School staff members may refer a student who is suspected of having a substance-abuse problem to this team. The team is trained to deal with substance-abuse issues and, if its members believe a student has a substance-abuse problem, have the student assessed and referred for appropriate assistance.

The controversy surrounding this program concerns the role of parents or guardians in this process. Under federal law, a student may go from referral through completion of treatment without his or her parents' or guardians' knowledge. Substance-abuse professionals are divided regarding whether it is possible to treat teens successfully who abuse substances without family involvement in treatment. Other professionals have concerns about the ability of young adolescents to seek treatment without any family knowledge or involvement.

As this federal law has been incorporated into state statutes, states have taken different approaches to deciding to whom and for what this law applies. Generally, the patient must be old enough to understand the problem, the treatment options available, and the possible consequences of the problem and treatment options. Some states have no age limits and maintain that a minor has the same capacity as an adult to consent to certain services. Some states have decided on a specific age at which a minor may consent to mental health treatment, reproductive or substance-abuse services, and treatment for sexually transmitted diseases and HIV/AIDS.

According to the Guttmacher Institute's *State Policies in Brief* report entitled "An overview of minor's consent law" (2015), various states handle minor-consent issues differently (see http://www.guttmacher.org/statecenter/spibs/spib_OMCL.pdf). There is also some question as to the applicability of this law to school settings. The laws clearly cover medical personnel and certain conditions. A school nurse is covered, but a professional school counselor or school psychologist might not be covered. To assure compliance, it is critical that professional counselors become familiar with the minor-consent laws in the states in which they work. A state law might allow a professional counselor to address reproductive issues and substance abuse without parental consent or notification, but a local policy might prohibit such counseling. The law might cover minors seeking advice or treatment, or both. If a minor is not seeking help, the law might not apply, and the counselor would need to follow other policies or procedures in dealing with these issues.

Legal issues aside, this is the law that raises a tremendous number of ethical issues for professional counselors. Numerous professionals have difficulty with the ability of young adolescents, in particular, to access these services without family involvement. Should a professional counselor help a 13-year-old with a substance-abuse problem seek treatment without the child's family knowing? How successful would the adolescent's recovery be? What about a 15-year-old who is abusing drugs and engaging in risky sexual behaviors? What is the counselor's ethical responsibility in such cases?

The problem this law presents for many professional counselors is that it allows them to assist adolescent clients legally but might conflict with their personal beliefs. Some professionals believe that behaviors such as these cause harm to the client and thus they have a duty to warn, which supersedes all other responsibilities. Some professional counselors work with the adolescent to help the adolescent involve his or her family, whereas others believe that telling the family will work against the adolescent obtaining help. Another issue is that many parents do not realize that a child can seek treatment in these areas without parental consent. Parents will be understandably angry and distrustful when they discover their child has a sexually transmitted disease or is abusing substances and the professional counselor knew but did not tell them about it. Professional counselors need to be prepared to deal with the aftermath of such discoveries. They need to think through their positions on these issues carefully and be honest with clients about their beliefs. Professional counselors should not wait until they are faced with a situation to figure out where they stand on the issue. To consider this likely scenario, complete Activity 3.9.

ACTIVITY 3.9

How might you address parents who are understandably angry over a minor-consent issue and are now distrustful of you as their child's professional counselor? What precautions might you take to avoid this situation?

RECORDS AND PERSONAL NOTES

Educational Records

Educational records include all records of a student's achievement, attendance, behavior, testing and assessment, school activities, and other information the school collects and maintains. Schools frequently divide student records into cumulative records, health records, special education records, and confidential records, including psychological evaluations. This division of records is done for the convenience of the school; all these records are considered to be a part of the educational record. The only exceptions are personal notes, reports to child protective services about abuse or neglect, and, in some states, reports from law enforcement agencies regarding students' arrests for reportable offenses.

The inspection, dissemination, and access to student educational records must be in accordance with the **Family Educational Rights and Privacy Act (FERPA)** of 1974. This law, often referred to as the Buckley Amendment, applies to all school districts, Pre-K–12 schools, and postsecondary institutions (colleges) that receive federal funding through the U.S. Department of Education (FERPA, 2008). Nonpublic schools that do not accept federal funding are exempt from this law.

FERPA has several provisions. The first provision requires that schools or systems annually send a notice to parents or guardians regarding their right to review their children's records and to file complaints if they disagree with anything in the records. The system has 45 days in which to comply with the parents' request to review the records. There are penalties, including loss of federal funding, for any school or system that fails to comply.

Second, the law limits who may access the records and specifies what personally identifiable information can be disclosed without informed consent—that is, what constitutes directory information, or public information. Under FERPA, individuals accessing educational records must have an educational interest considered legitimate under the law. This includes a new school when a student transfers. The sending school may send the records without a parent's consent but should make every attempt to inform the parent that it has done so. The major exception relates to law enforcement; the school must comply with a judicial order or lawfully executed subpoena. The school must also make whatever information is needed available to the school's law enforcement unit. In emergencies, information relevant to the emergency can be shared (see www.ed.gov/print/policy/gen/guid/fpco/ferpa/index.html). All states and jurisdictions have incorporated FERPA into state statutes and local policies, with some variance among aspects such as what constitutes directory information.

The right of consent transfers to a student at age 18 or when the student attends a postsecondary institution. However, the law was amended to give parents additional rights for their dependent children who are in postsecondary institutions. If a student is a dependent under Internal Revenue Service (IRS) rules, information can be given to the parent. Noncustodial parents have the same rights as custodial parents, unless their rights have been terminated or limited by the courts. Stepparents and other family members who do not have custody of the child have no rights under FERPA, unless the court has granted authority.

The **Protection of Pupil Rights Amendment (PPRA)** of 1978, often called the Hatch Amendment, gives parents additional rights. It established certain requirements when surveys are given to students in Pre-K–12 schools; it does not apply to postsecondary schools because students can consent on their own. If the survey is funded with federal money, informed consent must be obtained for all participating students if students in elementary or secondary schools are required to take the survey, and questions about certain personal areas are included. It also requires informed parental consent before a student undergoes any psychological, psychiatric, or medical examination, testing, or treatment or any school program designed to affect the personal values or behavior of the student. The Hatch Amendment also gives parents the right to review instructional materials in experimental programs.

The **No Child Left Behind Act (NCLB)** of 2001 included several changes to FERPA and the PPRA and continued to increase parents' rights. The changes apply to surveys funded either in part or entirely by any program administered by the U.S. Department of Education. The NCLB made minor changes to the seven existing categories concerning surveys and added an additional category. The PPRA now includes the following requirements:

- Schools and contractors must make instructional materials available for review by the parents of participating students if those materials will be used in any Department of Education-funded survey, analysis, or evaluation.
- Schools and contractors obtain written, informed parental consent before students' participation in any Department of Education-funded survey, analysis, or evaluation if information in any of the following areas would be revealed:
  - Political affiliations or beliefs of the parent or student
  - Mental and psychological problems of the family or student
  - Sex behavior or attitudes
  - Illegal, antisocial, self-incriminating, or demeaning behavior
  - Critical appraisals of other individuals with whom the student has close family relationships
  - Legally recognized privileged or analogous relationships such as those of lawyers, ministers, and physicians
  - Religious practices, affiliations, or beliefs of the student or parent/guardian (newly added)
  - Income other than such information required to determine eligibility or participation in a program (NCLB, 2001)

The new provisions of the PPRA also apply to surveys not funded through the U.S. Department of Education programs. These provisions give parents the right to inspect, on request, any survey or instructional materials used as part of the curriculum if created by a third party and involving one or more of the eight aforementioned areas. Parents also have the right to inspect any instrument used to collect personal information that will be used in selling or marketing. Parents always have the right to deny permission or to opt their child out of participating in any activity involving the eight previously delineated areas. The PPRA does not apply to any survey that is administered as part of the Individuals with Disabilities Education Improvement Act (2004).

As can be seen from the previous discussion, there are many constraints on schools in relation to assessing, testing, and surveying students. Because individual school systems, districts, or colleges might have defined this legislation further, it is essential that professional counselors become familiar with the requirements of the policies and procedures for their specific school systems.

The word *parents* has been used in the preceding discussion about student records. The law does recognize the right of students ages 18 and older to access their own records and accords them the same rights as parents of students younger than age 18. However, the law does not specifically limit the rights of parents whose children are 18 years of age or older to access their child's records, particularly in cases in which the child is still living at home and is an IRS-recognized dependent of the parents. The law also gives noncustodial parents the same rights as custodial parents. Unless there is a court order in the child's file that limits or terminates the rights of one or both parents, both parents have the same access to the child's records. School personnel also must provide copies of records such as report cards to both parents if requested.

The word *parent* is used to reference the legal guardian of the child, who might not be the biological or adoptive parent of the child but some other legally recognized care-giver. Stepparents and other family members have no legal right to the student's records without court-appointed authority, such as adoption or guardianship. This is particu-larly problematic in situations in which a relative provides **kinship care**—that is, the relative has physical custody 24 hours a day, 7 days a week, but no legal custody of the child. Legally, this person has no educational decision-making rights for the child and cannot access the child's records or give consent. Drug epidemics, incarcerations, and HIV/AIDS have created a situation in which millions of children younger than 18 years of age are involved in informal kinship-care situations. Kinship care might be the best situation for these children, but these situations present significant legal implications for schools.

Outside agencies may not access the records of any student without the signed con-sent of the parent or legal guardian. Some states have worked out interagency agreements wherein a parent signs one form that designates what records may be shared with which agencies, making individual forms unnecessary. Local policies dictate whether signed informed consent is needed to share information at school team meetings, such as student assistance programs, individualized education programs (IEP), or student-services meet-ings, when the agency personnel are regular members of the team.

VOICES FROM THE FIELD 3.3   Client Records: A Common Ethics Problem, by William L. Hegarty, JD

For 15 years, I have been the chief investigator for the Ohio Counselor, Social Worker and Mar-riage and Family Therapist Board. During my time with the board, I have investigated every issue imaginable (e.g., counselors having sex with clients, counselors having sex with clients' family members, counselors borrowing money from clients, insurance fraud, counselors acting outside the scope of their practices). One issue that has been a constant yet steadily growing problem over the years is proper record keeping. Recently, the board has seen a sharp rise in counselors backdating case files. This backdating is usually an effort to correct a mistake when the record was originally created. Sometimes, however, the record is backdated to make it appear as though services were offered on a date on which they were not. The backdating of records is not lawful. In some states this is considered falsifying records and possibly even insurance fraud. Depending on the type of record falsified, this practice might also invite federal prosecution. A licensed professional counselor can go back into a file to add or amend a note, but the file's date then has to reflect the date the note was added or amended as well as the original date the document was created.

Another problem we are seeing with records is the outright creation of false case notes. These cases almost universally involve licensed professional counselors who provide home-based counseling services as an employee of an agency. We are increasingly seeing counselors who do not go to scheduled home-based sessions yet create case notes as if they had. These faux sessions

(Continued)

are then submitted for billing purposes. These actions are illegal and harm clients, since the clients are not receiving the necessary services. Furthermore, these instances also reduce the amount of services these clients can obtain since they use the clients' entitlements. I have seen agencies have to repay tens of thousands of dollars due to the falsification of notes. The rise in occurrence of this type of situation might be related to the increased agency productivity pressures being place on counselors; that is, agencies are urging counselors to provide an increasing number of billable hours.

Another issue related to record keeping is their legibility. When records are illegible, client care is compromised. In some client files, the treatment plan, client goals, and client statements are totally illegible. When I inquire about the utility of an illegible file, I tend to get blank stares before the realization settles in that the file is of no functional use.

While record-keeping case violations are not as sensational as, say, sexual violations, they are extremely common. Most of these issues can be avoided with proper supervision and peer review within an agency setting. All counselors must police themselves to ensure they are devoting the appropriate amount of time to keeping their records accurate, timely, and comprehensible by those who might need to review them.

Personal Notes

Personal notes are notes written by professional counselors to serve as an extension of their memories; they are an impression of the client or session. These notes must remain in the sole possession of the maker and cannot be shared with anyone except a substitute maker. A substitute maker is someone who takes over for a counselor in the counselor's position, in the same way a substitute teacher takes over for a regular teacher. In the case of school counselors, a substitute maker is not the counselor who becomes responsible for the child the next year or in the next school.

Personal notes must remain separate from the educational or clinical record. When any information in the personal notes is shared, it is no longer confidential. If professional counselors keep their personal notes in their offices, they should keep them separate from all other records and secure them, such as in a locked file cabinet. Some counselors keep them in their cars or houses, but this is unnecessary unless there are problems with security in the counselor's office.

As technology becomes more common in counseling offices, professionals might prefer to keep their personal notes on the computer. This is not a good idea, unless the counselor can absolutely guarantee that no one can access the program or break through network firewalls. Even keeping the notes on a portable electronic storage system is questionable. Stories of computer hackers breaking codes and paralyzing websites for hours are frequently reported in the news. Even a laptop can easily become a private diary, facing the same security risks as paper files, or perhaps fewer when it comes to password-protected files and encryption options. It is preferable to keep notes separate and not tell anyone they exist, even if there is nothing of particular interest in them. The information is confidential, and the professional counselor needs to ensure its security.

Information from the notes can be shared only in cases in which there is a clear duty to warn or when a judge requires that confidentiality be broken and the information be shared, such as in court-ordered testimony. Activity 3.10 is meant to stimulate your thinking over how you will handle personal notes pertaining to clients.

ACTIVITY 3.10

How might you store your personal notes as a professional counselor? What precautions would you take to keep them secure? If subordinates are involved, what precautions would you take to ensure confidentiality?

THE HEALTH INSURANCE PORTABILITY AND ACCOUNTABILITY ACT (HIPAA) OF 1996

The **Health Insurance Portability and Accountability Act (HIPAA)** of 1996 required that the U.S. Department of Health and Human Services adopt national standards for the privacy of individually identifiable health information, outlined patients' rights, and established criteria for access to health records. The requirement that the U.S. Department of Health and Human Services adopt national standards for electronic health care transactions was also included in this law. The Privacy Rule was adopted in 2000 and became effective in 2001 (U.S. Department of Health and Human Services, 2002). The Privacy Rule set national standards for the privacy and security of protected health information. The rule specifically excludes any individually identifiable health information that is covered by FERPA. Health records in schools that are under FERPA are specifically excluded from HIPAA.

In educational settings, the situation is not that simple, particularly in the area of special education. Many schools receive mental, physical, and emotional health assessments of students that have been conducted by outside providers whose practices are covered by HIPAA regulations. In previous years, such assessments and reports automatically became part of the educational record. This might no longer be the case, particularly if the provider requests that the report not be disclosed again. As HIPAA continues to affect the sharing of health information, agencies and school systems must develop policies and procedures to address any potential conflicts between FERPA and HIPAA. Professional counselors must be aware of these issues and any additional policies, regardless of whether they are employed at schools, universities, agencies, or in private practice.

CHILD ABUSE

Another issue for professional counselors that has clear legal mandates is child abuse and neglect. Efforts to recognize and intervene in child abuse cases began in the late 1800s and were modeled on the prevention-of-cruelty-to-animals laws. In 1961, *battered child syndrome* was legally recognized, and by 1968, all 50 states had laws requiring the reporting of child maltreatment. In 1974, the National Child Abuse Prevention and Treatment Act became a federal law. The act was later reauthorized with changes and renamed the **Keeping Children and Families Safe Act** of 2003. The law defined **child abuse** as physical or mental injury, sexual abuse or exploitation, negligent treatment, or maltreatment of a child younger than age 18 years or the age specified by the child-protection law of the state in question by a person who is responsible for the child's welfare within circumstances that indicate the child's health or welfare is harmed or threatened.

The law is clear regarding who must report cases of child abuse and neglect. Every health practitioner, educator, human-services worker, and law enforcement officer must report suspected abuse or neglect, generally within 24 to 72 hours of first "having reason to suspect" (Keeping Children and Families Safe Act, 2003). It is incumbent on the individual who first suspects the abuse or neglect to call child protective services to report. The oral report must be followed up by a written report in most cases. States have slightly different procedures for reporting; some states allow 7 days for submission of the written report and identify different agencies to which the report must be made. What does not change is the legal mandate to report.

There is no liability for reporting child abuse, even if a subsequent investigation determines no evidence that abuse or neglect occurred, unless the report is made with malice. Most states do have serious penalties for failure to report, however. These penalties could include loss of certification or license, disciplinary action, or termination of employment.

Parents or guardians have no rights to information during this process. The agency, school, or other entity making the report should not inform the parents that a report is being made. It is the responsibility of the department of social services and the law enforcement agency to contact the parent and conduct the investigation. It is critical that professional counselors understand the federal, state, and local laws and procedures regarding cases of child abuse and neglect and follow the procedures exactly. The individual submitting the report does not have to prove that abuse has occurred; it is enough to have reason to suspect it.

A professional counselor is sometimes put in an awkward position when he or she is not the first person to suspect abuse, but the staff member who does is not willing to make the report and asks the counselor to do it. In such cases, if the staff member will not make the report, the professional counselor should do it but should apprise the agency administrator of the circumstances surrounding the report. Regardless of who submits the report, the client will need support and assistance throughout the process. Activity 3.11 pertains to handling cases of potential abuse and neglect.

ACTIVITY 3.11 HANDLING SUSPICIONS OF ABUSE OR NEGLECT

Become familiar with local or state processes for reporting suspicions of abuse or neglect to child protective services. What might you do if another professional or staff person in your building or agency approaches you about his or her suspicion of child abuse or neglect?

SUICIDE

For many years, the standard that was used in the counseling profession for dealing with potential suicide cases was based on the Tarasoff case, which was previously discussed. As a result of the Tarasoff case ruling, professional counselors had a duty to warn if there was a foreseeable victim. According to Remley and Herlihy (2016), subsequent court decisions interpreted the case differently; some judges in some jurisdictions ruled that the duty exists even when there is no foreseeable victim, if individuals are unintentionally injured by the dangerous client—classes of persons of which the victim is a member, bystanders, and other individuals. Generally, when dealing with a potentially suicidal client, the professional counselor conducts a lethality assessment, determines the seriousness of the threat, and, based on the seriousness of the threat, decides whether the duty to warn is applicable.

The Eisel case in Maryland changed the standard for many professional school counselors. In that case, two middle school students became involved in Satanism and became obsessed with death and self-destruction. Friends of Nicole Eisel went to their school counselor and told the school counselor that Nicole was thinking about killing herself. That counselor consulted with Nicole's school counselor. Both professional school counselors spoke with Nicole, who denied thinking about killing herself. Shortly thereafter, on a school holiday, Nicole's friend, who attended another school, shot Nicole and killed herself in the park behind the school. Steven Eisel, Nicole's father, sued the school, the school system, and the professional school counselors. The circuit court dismissed the case. Eisel appealed to the court of appeals. Its October 29, 1991, decision stated:

> Considering the growth of this tragic social problem in the light of the factors discussed above, we hold that school counselors have a duty to use reasonable means to attempt to prevent a suicide when they are on notice of a child or adolescent student's suicidal intent. (*Eisel v. Board of Education*)

Based on the facts of this case as developed to date, a trier of fact could conclude that the duty included warning Eisel of the danger to his daughter. The case was remanded back to the circuit court to decide the issue of liability for the school system and the professional school counselors. The case concluded eight years after it began and found that the school and professional school counselors had acted appropriately given the circumstances, their training, and the policies in place at the time.

The court's decision had a major impact on professional school counselors in the state of Maryland. In actuality, this decision removed the counselor's ability to determine whether duty to warn is applicable. As a consequence, professional school counselors in Maryland must always tell the parent whenever there is any indication from a child or someone else that the child is thinking about suicide, regardless of the seriousness of the threat. They must also inform the principal or the principal's designee. Many of Maryland's school systems now apply this procedure to all student-services personnel employed by the school system, and other states have implemented similar provisions and policies.

Although this case is legally binding only on professional school counselors in Maryland, it has become the standard by which subsequent cases have been decided in other states. Professional school counselors must be aware of the policies within their school systems. The courts clearly are ruling in favor of duty to warn as opposed to counselor discretion. Professional counselors practicing outside schools should abide by state statute and policy, but deciding to warn when there is any reason to suspect the client is a danger to himself or herself or others is probably a good practice in almost all circumstances, particularly when the client is a minor.

Summary

If one were to survey practicing counselors regarding the "hot issues" in counseling, the list would likely include eating disorders, HIV/AIDS, self-mutilation, autism spectrum disorder, bullying, harassment, changing family structures, mobility, cultural diversity, sexual orientation, depression, loss and grief, individuals with special needs, emotional disturbance, gangs, and a host of other topics. So how does a counselor help a 21-year-old who believes he is gay? Or a 16-year-old who is starving herself to death? Or an incarcerated parent who wants the professional counselor to read his letters to his children because the mother will not let him have any contact with his children?

Here are some final words of wisdom to help guide you as a professional counselor:

- Always document in writing what you did and why you did it.
- If you did not follow a policy, document why you did not (e.g., not calling the parent in a suicide case because it was handled as an abuse case).
- Know federal, state, and local laws, regulations, policies, and guidelines.
- Consult with a colleague or supervisor when you have questions or doubts.
- Read and use resources.
- Consult with a lawyer when appropriate.

Professional counselors must be prepared to deal with these issues and more every day of their professional lives. Many of these areas do not have clear laws, regulations, court cases, or policies to guide counselors toward legal and ethical behavior. Professional counselors need to try to do what is in the best interests of their clients and to help their clients see what that is. They must advocate for their clients, because, frequently, professional counselors are the only support clients have. Professional counselors must never stop believing that what they do makes a difference in the lives of their clients.

MyCounselingLab for Introduction to Counseling

Try the Topic 7 Assignments: *Ethical and Legal Considerations.*

SECTION TWO

Counseling Processes and Approaches

Section Two, "Counseling Processes and Approaches," provides an in-depth review of counseling theories, process, and skills. Chapter 4, "Theories of Counseling," portrays the nature and quality of the counseling relationship as more significant than any other factor in counseling. Regardless of the setting, and whether they are working with individuals, families, or groups, counselors have a professional responsibility to develop a foundation and clear rationale for their theoretical orientation to serve clients best. Professional counselors operate out of theories that best fit their personal philosophies of human change and the counseling process. Chapter 4 highlights the significance of theory to counseling practice and provides a brief overview of the major theoretical paradigms. Students will also explore their own beginning preferences for theoretical orientation with the intent of continuing their personal and professional exploration to discover their personal style.

Chapter 5, "The Counseling Process," orients students to counseling processes and approaches, providing a brief overview of the stages of the counseling process and approaches to helping clients. The counseling process embodies the art and science of helping. Professional counselors bring their training, experience, and personalities into the process. Once initiated, counseling occurs over a series of stages that includes information gathering and the application of theory to generate relevant goals, treatment, assessment, and termination. In Chapter 5, students beginning the path to becoming counselors are encouraged to consider their fit with the process and profession of counseling.

Chapter 6, "Counseling Microskills," provides an overview of the fundamental skills that constitute the key elements of effective helping relationships. The skills in this chapter focus on a microskills hierarchy. At the heart of this hierarchy is the basic listening sequence, an interrelated set of skills that not only fosters the development of rapport with clients, but also aids in the identification of interventions to help achieve a successful resolution to the clients' presenting concerns. Examples of the skills in use, along with practice exercises to foster individual skill development, are provided.

4 Theories of Counseling

BRADLEY T. ERFORD AND ANN VERNON*

PREVIEW

The nature and quality of the counseling relationship is more significant than any other factor in counseling. So why do professional counselors study theories? Whether working with individuals, families, or groups, regardless of the setting, professional counselors have a professional responsibility to develop a foundation and clear rationale for their theoretical orientation to serve clients best. Professional counselors operate using theories that best fit their personal philosophies of human change and the counseling process, but they also choose approaches that effectively address the client's issues. Developing a personal theoretical orientation is a career-long process that begins during professional training. In this chapter, the significance of theory to counseling practice is explored, and a brief overview of the major theoretical paradigms is presented. You will also begin to explore your own initial preferences for theoretical orientation with the intent of continuing your personal and professional exploration to discover your personal style.

THE SIGNIFICANCE OF THEORY

Theories ground us as professional counselors. They provide a means to understand what we are doing, how we are serving clients, and how to explain counseling to clients. People entering counseling are generally not interested in hearing a detailed description of their counselor's philosophical beliefs about the nature of the counseling relationship and human change. Rather, they are seeking guidance about the change process and how the professional counselor can help accomplish that goal. Theories represent clients' realities and what we know to be important and effective elements of the counseling relationship (Hansen, 2006a). Professional counselors must have a firm sense of the counseling process alongside their own philosophies about what works in counseling and how individuals change and grow. A firm understanding of your beliefs about counseling can help you explain the process to clients, helping them understand the nature of counseling and what can be expected (Gladding, 2016). This road map for counseling can help you generate new ideas with a client to determine the best course of action and the means to reach goals.

Theories provide a framework for conceptualizing client problems and determining a course of action in counseling (Halbur & Halbur, 2014). For example, a professional counselor who operates from a cognitive-behavioral standpoint would identify a client's struggle with bulimia as faulty logic and plan a course of treatment to reshape thoughts and behaviors. A psychodynamic-oriented professional counselor would view the issue

*Special thanks to Dana Heller Levitt and Alissa Darnell for their contributions to previous editions of this chapter.

through the lens of the client's past and spend counseling time uncovering early triggers and sustaining factors for the disorder.

Ethics of Applying Counseling Theory

One theory does not fit all clients. A successful approach with one client might be a complete disaster with another. Professional counselors have an ethical responsibility to be culturally competent and to address each client's needs as such. There is no cookie-cutter, one-size-fits-all approach to counseling. Despite what some clients might be seeking, professional counselors do not have a handbook of problems and solutions. Professional counselors instead must use their understanding of theory to provide the best possible services to clients. Operating from a clear theoretical framework also means being flexible with that approach to know when it will not work. Case Study 4.1 provides an opportunity to explore some of the theoretical underpinnings of your counseling approach.

CASE STUDY 4.1
Frames of Reference

A second-grade girl is referred for counseling. Recently, she has been having difficulty staying on task during class and difficulty making friends. Her parents were never married and no longer live together. Her teacher reports that the girl came to her the previous day and mentioned something about other students making fun of her because she does not have a "real" family.

1. As a professional counselor, how would you establish rapport?
2. What types of questions would you ask her during the first session?
3. What strategies would you employ to begin solving some of the problems she is having?
4. If the student were a 21-year-old male, Asian college student, what types of alterations would you make to your approach and strategies? Answer questions 1–3 again.
5. If the client were a 42-year-old woman returning to college or graduate school who has a history of distractibility and poor peer relations, how might you change your approach and strategies? Answer questions 1–3 again.

From an ethical standpoint, professional counselors must be clear about their professional orientation to serve clients best. As discussed in Chapter 3, the American Counseling Association (ACA) *Code of Ethics* (2014a) provides guidelines for professional and ethical counseling practices. All professional counselors and counselors in training are expected to abide by the principles stated in the *ACA Code of Ethics*. Sections of the *ACA Code of Ethics* pertain specifically to learning and practices associated with theories. Professional counselors must be aware of new trends and best practices in the profession. Professional counselors must also be competent in the use of the theories they choose to employ in counseling and must have a firm foundation for the work they perform with clients.

Closely related, and perhaps one of the most fundamental aspects of professional and ethical practice, is continual counselor self-reflection. **Self-awareness** is crucial to counselor development. Professional counselors must regularly assess their beliefs about the counseling process and their effectiveness with clients. By this manner of self-awareness, professional counselors can determine and strengthen their theoretical beliefs and practices. Activity 4.1 encourages exploration and refinement of your theoretical approach by exploring the approaches used by practitioners in the field.

ACTIVITY 4.1 THEORY IN PRACTICE

Interview three practicing counselors about their theoretical orientations. Discuss with them the importance of theory in their current work, how they came to embrace particular theories, and the relationship of those theories to their personal philosophies. Do counselors tap different theories when working with individuals, groups, or families?

What Makes a Good Theory?

In their classic text, Hansen, Stevic, and Warner (1986) suggested five components of a good counseling theory. The theory is (1) clear and easily understood; (2) comprehensive; (3) explicit and heuristic, generating further research; (4) specifically geared to help clients reach their desired outcomes; and (5) useful to practitioners. Theories must be sound to be plausible to professional counselors. Literally hundreds of theories exist, with more emerging each decade (Ivey, Ivey, & Zalaquett, 2013). All of these theories can be overwhelming to beginning counselors who are trying to do what is in the best interests of their clients. Professional counselors need a means of organizing the information about theories, applying what works, and building on natural helping capabilities.

Intentionality, making conscious and intentional decisions, is a necessity in applying the basic helping skills (Halbur & Halbur, 2014). Skill application is both art and science. Technical expertise, while important, will not always make you the most effective professional counselor. A firm, philosophical understanding of the counseling profession and practice, and knowledge of the research behind what you do, will help you in your selection of and adherence to a theory that best fits your natural style of helping. Considering theories with respect to their common elements can help you determine what works best for whom and, most notably, for you as the counselor.

THEORETICAL PARADIGMS

Through self-awareness, professional counselors strengthen their approaches and learn new ways to work with clients. Theoretical orientation usually remains relatively constant through counselors' development given the connection to personal philosophy. Changes that occur tend to be within the general categories of theories, referred to as **paradigms**. These paradigms are a means of grouping theories based on common characteristics. Multiple theories exist within each paradigm. Table 4.1 provides summary characteristics of the five most prominent paradigms and Table 4.2 summarizes the techniques and multicultural considerations of the important theories ordinarily associated with each paradigm. Each of these paradigms will be explained in detail throughout the remainder of the chapter.

Theories can be described as having specific and common factors. **Specific factors** are the unique characteristics of a given theory. They are elements that distinguish one theory from another and are often the basis of association with a theory. For example, the

TABLE 4.1 Theoretical Paradigms: Theories and Theorists

Paradigm	Major Theories	Prominent Theorists
Psychodynamic	Psychoanalysis	Sigmund Freud
	Adlerian	Alfred Adler
	Ego Psychology	Carl Jung
Humanistic/Existential	Person-Centered	Carl Rogers
	Existential	Victor Frankl, Irvin Yalom, Rollo May
	Gestalt	Frederick (Fritz) Perls
Behavioral/Cognitive-Behavioral	Behavioral	John Watson, B. F. Skinner, Albert Bandura, John Krumboltz
	Cognitive	Aaron Beck
	Cognitive-Behavioral Therapy	Donald Meichenbaum
	Rational-Emotive Behavior Therapy	Albert Ellis
	Reality Therapy and Choice Theory	William Glasser
Systems	Family Systems	Murray Bowen, Virginia Satir
Emergent	Narrative	Michael White, David Epston
	Constructivist	George Kelly
	Feminist	
	Interpersonal Psychotherapy (IPT)	

TABLE 4.2 Summary of Theoretical Paradigms: Techniques and Multicultural Considerations

Paradigm	Principles	Techniques	Multicultural Considerations
Psychodynamic	Predetermined	Free association	Ego and past cultural identity development
	Relationship of events and current functioning	Interpretation	Id, ego, superego development
	Bring unconscious into conscious	Dream analysis	Limited views of women
		Analysis of transference	
Humanistic/ Existential	Innate goodness of people	Counseling relationship	Attention to individual's unique perspective
	Self-actualization	Empty chair	Lack of structure
	Freedom and responsibility	Genuineness, empathy, unconditional positive regard	Limited attention to external factors
	Finding meaning	Role-play	Common values of love, death, anxiety
	Anxiety	Role reversal	
		"I" statements	
Behavioral/ Cognitive-Behavioral	Changing behavior, negative thought patterns, beliefs	Specify automatic thoughts	Understanding beliefs as identity

TABLE 4.2 Summary of Theoretical Paradigms: Techniques and Multicultural Considerations (*Continued*)

Paradigm	Principles	Techniques	Multicultural Considerations
	ABCDEs of REBT	Homework	Structure
	Disputing irrational beliefs	Thought stopping	Caution when challenging belief systems
		Cognitive restructuring	
		Token economy	
Systems	Family provides framework for understanding individual	Genograms	Identity patterns
	Differentiation of self	Questioning	Caution when attempting to change multigenerational patterns
		Coaching	Resistance to external input on family
		"I" position	
		Detriangulation	
Emergent Narrative	Retell story to create favorable outcomes	Deconstruct problems	Many cultures emphasize storytelling
	Person is not the problem	Externalize problems	High-level processing required
		Miracle question	
		Sparkling moments	
Constructivist	Personal reality	Card sort	Insight required
	Personal construct	Identify constructs	Challenges test beliefs and principles
		Repertory	
Feminist	Application of feminist principles: equality, empowerment	Gender role analysis	Addresses shared experiences of oppression
	Mutuality	Empowerment	Political action might be against belief
	Androgyny	Egalitarian relationship	Limited application with men
		Sociocultural exploration of gender	
Interpersonal psychotherapy	Improve interpersonal functioning, social network	Therapeutic alliance	Flexible and adaptable to unique individuals
	Attachment, social, and communication theories	Communication analysis	
	Present focus	Interpersonal incidents	
		Content and process affect	
		Role-playing	

empty-chair technique (i.e., having the client dialogue with a person not present) is a specific facet of Gestalt, a humanistic/existential theory. Disputing irrational beliefs is specific to Albert Ellis's rational emotive behavior therapy (REBT) and the behavioral and cognitive-behavioral paradigm. **Common factors** are characteristics that appear in most, if not all, theoretical perspectives. For example, a therapeutic alliance and a healing setting that promotes client trust through professional counselor competence are common factors. A coherent rationale and set of procedures are also common to all theories. These are important principles to keep in mind as you review the major paradigms and begin to formulate your approach to counseling. To illustrate further the application of theoretical principles, consider the case of Terry in Case Study 4.2, then answer the questions posed. We will return to this case throughout our discussion of the paradigms and theories.

The following discussion of theories and paradigms is broad in nature. You are encouraged to read further about theories in the references provided throughout this chapter, and to research in greater depth the specific theories of interest.

CASE STUDY 4.2
The Case of Terry

Terry is a 23-year-old graduate student in microbiology. Terry recently relocated to the area to pursue graduate study after completing her undergraduate degree at a small college near her hometown. Now living two states and hundreds of miles away from her family, Terry feels that she is experiencing her independence for the first time.

Terry first became interested in science when she received a science kit for her seventh birthday. Her parents encouraged her to study science throughout high school and pushed her toward a major in biology when she entered college. Terry has heard on more than one occasion that she is the family's "only hope for a doctor." As first-generation immigrants to the United States, Terry's parents feel that their only daughter must be successful to prove their culture's ability to compete in an American environment.

Terry was referred to counseling following the midterm period of her first term in graduate school. Her roommate discovered numerous cuts on her arms and reported that Terry had seemed down over the past few weeks. When she finally agreed to see a professional counselor, Terry reported that she did not perform well on her midterm exams and was questioning whether she could make it in graduate school. She was concerned about disappointing her parents and bringing shame to her family. Considering the case of Terry, write your initial reactions to her presenting issues for counseling. Specifically:

1. What is the problem?
2. Who is involved in Terry's dilemma?
3. How is the dilemma affecting Terry?
4. What would you hope to see as the goal of counseling for Terry?
5. What might counseling entail?
6. How would you know that counseling is complete?
7. How does your conceptualization attend to Terry's culture?

Keep your responses in a convenient location as you review the remainder of the chapter. These responses may relate to your emerging theoretical orientation.

Psychodynamic Paradigm

At the time of his work, Sigmund Freud was considered revolutionary in his thinking and conceptualizing of the problems experienced by people, primarily women. Today, many theories are based upon Freud's work, either additive to what he developed or created as an alternative explanation (in reaction) to a theory heavily focused on the past and the subconscious mind. For this reason, the psychodynamic paradigm serves as an introduction and foundation to the other paradigms of counseling theories.

Theories that fall under the psychodynamic paradigm are based largely on insight, unconscious motivation, and personality reconstruction. The psychodynamic paradigm holds that most issues clients face are the result of unresolved issues from their early development. The focus in counseling from a psychodynamic framework is on the relationship of past events with current functioning. In the case of Terry, the professional counselor might question how childhood messages of expected success are affecting her current performance in graduate school and the subsequent feelings she experiences. The psychodynamic approach is very analytic in nature and might require a good deal of time to uncover past issues and make headway into current and future functioning.

PSYCHOANALYSIS   Freud's psychoanalytic theory is probably the most widely recognized theory in the psychodynamic paradigm. Many people might have the image of a wise therapist sitting behind a couch on which a client lies and contemplates the meaning of past events. Many popular media depictions do little to ameliorate this stereotype and might perpetuate the public's beliefs about the nature of counseling in general. Although this image might have been the form of psychoanalysis in early renditions of the theory, much has changed since Freud's groundbreaking approach to counseling to challenge the means by which professional counselors with a psychoanalytic orientation help their clients.

Freud believed that personality is completely formed in childhood and that challenges later in life are the result of unresolved conflicts. Consistent with the idea that theories emerge from our personal philosophies and experiences, Freud's background demonstrates his emphasis on childhood and the family. The eldest of eight siblings of an authoritarian father, Freud was particularly close to his mother. His upbringing and religious affiliation (a Jew in Vienna, Austria, in the mid-to-late 1800s) limited his career aspirations to medicine or law. One might see the basis of Freud's intense self-analysis and his subsequent theories of personality dynamics based upon his own life experiences.

In psychoanalysis, the personality is perceived as being composed of three parts: the **id**, or pleasure principle; the **ego**, or reality principle; and the **superego**, or morality principle (conscience). Conflict among these structures creates anxiety in the individual. The subsequent anxiety is often managed by the ego by employing **defense mechanisms**. These mechanisms help the individual to cope with the anxiety and not be overwhelmed. Defense mechanisms can be either adaptive or damaging. For example, Terry could be turning her frustrations with her parents' expectations inward and harming herself rather than expressing these feelings to her parents. This process of projecting unwanted emotions on oneself in this case is maladaptive in the sense that Terry is being harmed physically and emotionally.

The goal of psychoanalytic counseling is to bring unconscious drives into consciousness and develop insight into intrapsychic conflicts. Techniques such as free association, interpretation, dream analysis, and analysis of resistance and transference may be employed to assist in the development of insight. As might be expected (and often a criticism of this approach), this process can be quite lengthy and time-consuming.

The psychoanalytic counselor is like a blank screen. Listening, analyzing, and attending to **transference** (i.e., a client projects feelings for another person onto the counselor, such as when the client perceives the counselor to be a father figure) and **countertransference** (i.e., a counselor reciprocates by engaging in interactions with the client similar to what the client experienced in a primary relationship, such as when the counselor behaves as the parent figure would toward the client who perceives the counselor to be a father figure) issues are essential to successful counseling in the psychoanalytic approach. The therapeutic relationship takes the form of the professional counselor as expert, teaching the client about the intrapsychic processes occurring.

Concepts such as defense mechanisms and transference seem to be relevant for individuals from various backgrounds. The culturally sensitive counselor might encourage individuals from ethnic and racial minority groups to develop an overall ego identity as well as a cultural identity. It is also important for psychoanalytic counselors to address their own potential biases and recognize how countertransference could unintentionally play a part in the counseling process. A limitation for multicultural counseling in psychoanalysis is in the area of gender issues. Women are seen as inferior to men because they do not resolve the Electra complex as completely as it is thought that men resolve the Oedipus complex. This concept and other similar concepts, such as penis envy, have been largely discredited and discontinued. For independent study on psychoanalysis, consult the following foundational resources:

Freud, A. (1936). *The ego and the mechanisms of defense* (J. Strachey, Trans.). New York, NY: International Universities Press.
Freud, S. (1900/1955). *The interpretation of dreams* (J. Strachey, Trans.). London, UK: Hogarth.
Freud, S. (1923/1933). *New introductory lectures on psychoanalysis* (W. J. H. Sprott, Trans.). New York, NY: Norton.
Freud, S. (1923/1947). *The ego and the id* (J. Strachey, Trans.). London, UK: Hogarth.

ADLERIAN COUNSELING   Alfred Adler, a student of Freud, developed his theory as a result of disagreement with many of the principles his mentor proposed. Adler commended Freud's work on dream interpretation, yet the generalizations Freud drew from dreams and his emphasis on sexual trauma and development did not resonate with Adler. Herein lies another example of the need to formulate a specific, personally relevant theory of counseling. Adler left Freud's tutelage to develop his approach of focusing on the whole person. This holistic viewpoint approached the client as a whole, indivisible being who is capable of growth and seeks social interests and connections with others. Similar to Freud, Adler emphasized the role of childhood in personality development and problem (and solution) formation.

Adler's work has been widely used yet not widely researched or developed. Adler's work is best known for its emphasis and analysis of birth order and sibling relationships. Traces of Adler's work are evident in the wellness movement in the counseling profession. Commonly used Adlerian-based techniques include use of "I" messages, acting "as if," and "spitting in the client's soup."

The Adlerian concept of social interest supports the theory's focus on cultural sensitivity. **Social interest** means individuals are encouraged to move beyond themselves to learn about and understand different cultural groups and how the individuals could contribute to the greater society. Cultures that emphasize the family find that many Adlerian concepts fit with their value systems. However, limitations exist where emphasis is placed on changing the autonomous self and in the exploration of early childhood experiences. Some clients might find it inappropriate to reveal family information or might not want to delve into the past because they might not see the connection to current pressing concerns. For more information regarding Adlerian counseling, the following resources could be useful:

Adler, A. (1927). *Understanding human nature.* Greenwich, CT: Fawcett.
Adler, A. (1964). *Social interest: A challenge to mankind.* New York, NY: Capricorn.
Adler, A. (1969). *The practice and theory of individual psychology.* Patterson, NJ: Littlefield, Adams.
Dreikurs, R. (1953). *Fundamentals of Adlerian psychology.* Chicago, IL: Alfred Adler Institute.
Sweeney, T. J. (1998). *Adlerian counseling: A practitioner's approach* (4th ed.). Muncie, IN: Accelerated Development.

OTHER PSYCHODYNAMIC THEORIES   Jungian theory (also referred to as ego psychology) and object-relations theory are other approaches that fit within this paradigm. Although many principles of these theories are used today, modern adaptations of psychoanalysis and Adlerian counseling are seen more often in practice. To study a foundational work by Carl Jung, refer to Jung, C. G. (1961), *Memories, dreams, reflections,* New York, NY: Vintage. Table 4.3 provides a listing of strategies and techniques aligned with the psychodynamic paradigm.

TABLE 4.3 Psychodynamic Strategies and Interventions

- Analysis of transference and countertransference
- Analysis of private logic
- Parent or teacher consultations
- Encouragement
- Analysis of Adlerian goals of misbehavior (attention, power, inadequacy) and building of social interest through group activities
- Teaching "I" statements and other skills
- Encouraging insight into unconscious aspects of the problem through creative processes
- Adlerian play therapy to discover the child's lifestyle and private logic
- Teaching parents techniques for encouraging the child
- Family constellation and family atmosphere
- Lifestyle analysis
- Striving for significance and belonging
- Focusing on natural and logical consequences
- Early recollections to understand the child's behavior patterns
- Adlerian family counseling for family to learn to operate cooperatively
- Varying activities between play and talking/interviewing
- Using metaphor and exploration of developmental themes highlighted in movies, television, and books
- Focusing on helping the client become more self-aware through the use of pictures, stories, and metaphors
- Helping the client to accept responsibility for the life choices that come with adulthood and to avoid regression toward childhood, where decisions were made on his or her behalf

(Continued)

TABLE 4.3 Psychodynamic Strategies and Interventions (*Continued*)

- Assisting with adult identity formation in a culturally sensitive fashion
- Exploring recurrent themes in a child's fantasies and play
- Using play therapy techniques to understand the current emotional state of the student
- Teaching how to act "as if"
- Free association
- Determining events of childhood that could have a larger impact later in life
- Empty chair
- Role-playing
- Using sand-tray play and puppets to help younger children project angry feelings outside of themselves
- Trying a projection game, such as Parallels with Animals, in which the counselor asks the child what different animals look, act, and sound like when they are angry (Vernon, 2006)
- Using incomplete sentences to draw out the client's spontaneous answers.
- Psychoeducational lessons/handouts on self-understanding
- Recognizing feelings and basic motivations
- Mutual storytelling
- Drawing a tree and making a branch for each person the client feels he or she can trust
- Analysis of avoidance (e.g., refusing to come to school)
- Talking about the fears and worries that might be embedded in the unconscious
- Relationship of events to current functioning
- Dream analysis
- Analysis of ego development (fragile ego, under- or overdeveloped superego)
- Analysis of anxiety and defense mechanisms (especially avoidance)
- Discerning patterns of similar behavior by family members
- Interpreting the reason for behavior based on dialog, drawings, or dreams
- Exploring relationships between current behavior and past or current life events
- Attachment assessment and introduction of stable adult figure
- Exploring relationship with teachers perceived as safe or unsafe
- Exploring unconscious themes through use of a time line to chart significant life events
- Orally exploring the client's past and how it affects current behavior
- Using various art mediums, such as drawing or sculpture, to allow clients to explore and work through early childhood stressors
- Listing positive things about self to draw on strengths, encourage and build self-esteem
- Analysis of relationship with father and mother throughout childhood
- Assisting in achieving industry versus inferiority and identity versus role confusion
- Using expressive techniques to uncover unconscious struggles
- Uncovering and processing attachment issues, childhood conflicts, and motivations for behavior
- Exploring conflicts regarding maintaining power/status quo in classroom
- Processing childhood interests and experiences and how one views family and self roles
- Exploring use of emotion (e.g., anger) to mask hurt
- Analysis of immature/neurotic defenses (e.g., projection, regression, acting out, splitting, devaluation, displacement, rationalization, intellectualization)

Humanistic/Existential Paradigm

In contrast to the subconscious focus in the psychodynamic paradigm, the humanistic/existential paradigm is relationship-oriented. Rather than focusing on an individual's unresolved conflicts in the past, the focus here is on current and future functioning. Humanism and existentialism are similar in the belief that human nature is fundamentally good and people have the freedom and responsibility to grow and develop.

Humanists believe that goodness and worth are qualities people possess. In the journey toward self-actualization, it is believed that people are purposeful, active, and capable of determining their own behavior. Similarly, existentialists place emphasis on the importance of anxiety, freedom, values, responsibilities, and finding meaning in one's actions (Gladding, 2016). Another parallel between humanists and existentialists is that both underline the importance of the client–counselor relationship. The professional counselor must enter the client's subjective world to focus on client perceptions of the presenting issue.

PERSON-CENTERED Person-centered therapy, developed by Carl Rogers (1951, 1961), is a major theoretical approach in the humanistic framework. Over time, this approach has also been identified as nondirective, client-centered, and Rogerian. According to Rogers, the primary motivating force of humans is **self-actualization**, the tendency to move in the direction of growth, adjustment, socialization, independence, and self-realization.

Because people have the basic need for high self-regard, they attempt to organize their internal and external experiences into an integrated self. During this process of self-actualizing, unhealthy psychological or social influences could hinder an individual from realizing his or her potential as an integrated, productive self. In other words, conflicts develop when individuals' basic needs and their needs to obtain approval from others are inconsistent. Terry, for example, is experiencing conflict between her basic need for self-actualization and her need for approval from her parents. The professional counselor working with Terry must be present and congruent to assist her in moving toward the discovery of her true self.

Rogers (1957) identified three essential characteristics a professional counselor must employ for a therapeutic relationship to be established: genuineness (or congruence), unconditional positive regard, and empathy. **Genuineness** is displaying honesty, sincerity, and directness while avoiding any personal or professional façade. **Unconditional positive regard** is defined as the professional counselor's ability to accept every aspect of the client's personality while remaining nonjudgmental and nonevaluative toward the client's feelings, thoughts, and behaviors. **Empathy** is the ability to understand the client's world in the way the client understands it. With Terry, the professional counselor must be open to hearing Terry's experiences and must acknowledge her challenges with the situation, regardless of personal opinion. Creating a nonthreatening, anxiety-free relationship would allow Terry to resolve conflicts and reach self-understanding.

Person-centered counseling has had a significant impact in the area of human relations with diverse cultural groups. Many countries have adopted person-centered concepts in counseling as well as cross-cultural communication and education. Multicultural limitations include lack of structure, difficulty translating core conditions to practice, and focus on internal evaluation rather than external evaluation (Corey, 2012). The following resources provide more information about person-centered counseling:

Rogers, C. (1942). *Counseling and psychotherapy.* Boston, MA: Houghton Mifflin.
Rogers, C. (1951). *Client-centered therapy.* Boston, MA: Houghton Mifflin.
Rogers, C. (1961). *On becoming a person.* Boston, MA: Houghton Mifflin.
Rogers, C. (1980). *A way of being.* Boston, MA: Houghton Mifflin.

EXISTENTIAL   Existentialism stems from Søren Kierkegaard, a 19th-century philosopher who focused on the pursuit of becoming an individual. There are many contributors to existentialism as a therapeutic approach, including Ludwig Binswanger, Fyodor Dostoyevsky, Friedrich Nietzsche, and Abraham Maslow. In more recent years, notable figures in existential psychotherapy include Rollo May, Victor Frankl, and Irvin Yalom.

The essence of existentialism is that humans are believed to have the capacity for self-awareness and the freedom and responsibility to make choices that would bring about meaning in their lives. However, along with this freedom comes the reality of living with the consequences of those choices, which could lead to **existential anxiety**. May (1977) asserted that normal anxiety can be healthy and motivational.

Frankl (2006) maintained that despite negative conditions, individuals can preserve their own independent thinking, spiritual freedom, and opportunities for choice. In contrast, an individual who sees life as meaningless and without value would be in what Frankl termed an **existential vacuum**. A well-functioning person is an individual who authentically experiences reality and expresses needs in a way that is not determined by others. Terry might not be in an existential vacuum, but she might be questioning the meaning of her current experiences. As she has her first taste of freedom, it is important that Terry explore her choices and needs as self-determined rather than as parent determined.

Other than concentrating on the client–counselor relationship, there is no systematic way existential counselors help others. Still, Yalom (2002) was able to emphasize three significant qualities within the existential counseling process: (a) helping clients attend to the **here and now** (i.e., being present in the current moment), (b) being open and authentic with clients, and (c) cautiously using self-disclosure.

Specific goals in existential counseling include making clients sensitive to their existence, identifying characteristics unique to each client, assisting clients in enhancing interactions with others, helping clients pursue meaning in life, and promoting present and future decision making that will affect clients' directions in life. Few specific techniques are offered in an existential approach. All interventions are undertaken with the intention of assisting clients to find meaning in their actions.

The existential focus on love, suffering, anxiety, and death, all of which are the universal elements of human life, makes this theory applicable cross-culturally. In contrast, a limitation of multicultural existential counseling involves the emphasis on self-determination and the lack of focus on the environment and the social context. Some clients could feel powerless in the face of external realities, such as discrimination, racism, and oppression. Refer to the following resources for more information on existential counseling:

Frankl, V. (2006). *Man's search for meaning.* Boston, MA: Beacon.
May, R. (1953). *Man's search for himself.* New York, NY: Dell.
May, R. (Ed.). (1961). *Existential psychology.* New York, NY: Random House.
Yalom, I. D. (1980). *Existential psychotherapy.* New York, NY: Basic Books.

GESTALT THERAPY   Gestalt therapy began in response to the reductionist emphasis in theories of counseling, such as psychoanalysis and behaviorism, which attempt to break an individual's personality or behavior into understandable parts. In contrast, **Gestalt therapy** promotes the idea of wholeness. Frederick (Fritz) Perls and his wife, Laura Perls, were the major theorists associated with this school of thought.

Similar to person-centered counseling, Gestaltists believe that people have the tendency to move toward wholeness or self-actualization. Emphasis is placed on the present as indicated by Laura Perls's (1970) statement: "To me, nothing exists except the now. Now = experience = awareness = reality. The past is no more and the future is not yet. Only the *now* exists" (p. 14).

In contrast to psychoanalysis, which focuses on predetermined and unconscious forces, the Gestalt view of human nature is antideterministic: People can become responsible, grow, and change from past events. For example, Terry is experiencing difficulties in her life that are a result of her earlier thoughts, feelings, or experiences. This phenomenon is otherwise referred to as **unfinished business**—in Terry's case, asserting her own interests. The role of the Gestalt counselor is to provide an atmosphere that allows Terry to identify and pursue what she needs to grow. Being honest as well as deeply and personally involved with Terry would allow the counselor to help Terry redirect energy in more positive and adaptive ways of functioning.

Gestalt counselors also directly confront clients with their inconsistencies. They focus on the polarities within people and push clients to correct misconceptions, to genuinely express emotions, and to take responsibility for change. Gestalt techniques include exercises and experiments such as empty chair, role-playing, role reversal, dream analysis, and the use of "I" statements (Erford, 2015b). Other characteristics of Gestalt counseling that help clients develop and become mature in the now include awareness of nonverbal and verbal expressions and shedding neurotic tendencies. Laura Perls (1970) identified five layers of neurosis that were thought to impede a client's ability to be in touch with himself or herself. Only when individuals reach the final, or explosive, layer can they be truly authentic and in touch with themselves and others.

Gestalt counseling can be viewed as a culturally sensitive theory because the experiments employed by professional counselors could encourage clients to integrate the polarities that exist between the cultures to which they belong. Gestalt techniques can also be tailored to fit with a client's distinct perception and interpretation of his or her own cultural framework. However, because Gestalt counseling has an individualistic focus, it might be a conflict for people from cultures that emphasize group values. Table 4.4 provides strategies and techniques aligned with the humanistic/existential paradigm. Consult the following resources for further study of Gestalt therapy:

Perls, F. (1969). *Gestalt therapy verbatim.* Moab, UT: Real People Press.
Perls, F. (1972). *In and out of the garbage pail.* New York, NY: Bantam.
Polster, E., & Polster, M. (1973). *Gestalt therapy integrated: Contours of theory and practice.* New York, NY: Brunner/Mazel.
Zinker, J. (1978). *Creative process in Gestalt therapy.* New York, NY: Random House.

Behavioral/Cognitive-Behavioral Paradigm

Clients seek action. Terry wants to act to change her current dilemma. The behavioral or cognitive-behavioral paradigm is the most action-oriented of the theoretical groupings.

TABLE 4.4 Humanistic/Existential Strategies and Interventions

- Therapeutic conditions (genuineness, unconditional positive regard, empathy)
- Model active listening, congruence, unconditional positive regard, and empathy with family
- Use role-play and reverse role-play to assist client in finding meaning of current behavior while encouraging responsibility
- "I" statements
- Focus on the present, immediacy
- Use active listening and reflection of feelings
- Focus on building relationships
- Provide opportunities for empathy and safe exploration of thoughts, feelings, and behaviors
- Encourage self-awareness and decision making, leading to acceptance of self and others
- Gently confront inconsistencies
- Teach family members to focus on the here and now; take responsibility for their own thoughts, actions, feelings, and sensations; and accept personal responsibility for change
- Teach family members to substitute the use of *won't* for *can't* and the use of *what* and *how* for *why*
- Teach parents to use self-esteem building activities with their children
- Encourage self-exploration and self-discovery through a warm, supportive, affirming therapeutic relationship
- Through the client–counselor relationship, the client can learn to accept himself or herself and begin the journey toward self-actualization
- Provide support around goal setting
- See counseling as a way of *being with*, rather than *doing to*, the client
- Culturally sensitive play therapy techniques could be used, giving children the opportunity to *play out* rather than *talk out* feelings
- Show appreciation for student uniqueness
- Focus on choice, taking responsibility for actions, and the present and future
- Redirect energy or actions
- Focus on the person a client desires to be through art-therapy techniques (mask activity)
- Avoid using desks to be more personal than authoritative
- Respect the client regardless of acting-out behaviors
- Create a job or role for the client to feel a sense of meaning
- Have the client create a memory box to feel a sense of accomplishment and connection when he or she adds to the box
- Examine anxiety and behavioral issues related to safety, belonging, and personal and global responsibilities and freedom (to classmates, classroom, school, community)
- Create a mentoring relationship for the client
- Minimal encouragers and few questions
- Establish a relationship based on acceptance and trust
- Use puppets and expressive art therapies for social issues and familial issues
- Use reflective play therapy to process anxiety
- Be cautious about counselor self-disclosure
- Music and art as adjunctive techniques
- Help parents and staff understand the student's perspective

TABLE 4.4 Humanistic/Existential Strategies and Interventions (*Continued*)

- Role-play potential scenarios relevant to responsible and irresponsible behavior
- Identify emotions and appropriate expression
- Examination of anxiety and behavioral issues and a sense of belonging to classmates, classroom, school, and community
- Informal "lunch bunches" with student and potential friends to foster relationships among peers and sense of accomplishment and connection
- Redirect energy or actions
- Encourage client to write a letter to his or her ideal self
- Use humor to lighten the mood
- Explore significant changes, both good and bad, in the client's life
- Help to find meaning by having client work with even younger clients
- Develop self-awareness
- Consultations with familial environments and guardians
- Frame client understanding of self in the context of community
- Help client to find a place through a major life transition
- Develop activities that correct behavior but with respect and regard for the client as an individual
- Explore parent feelings toward clients and any incongruence
- Help to provide a sense of belonging by creating a special role for the client (i.e., mentor younger students, special job to complete daily)
- Help the client to work through the feelings of being stuck, which can accompany transitions
- Explore life scripts
- Allow client to analyze ads for messages
- Consider clients' roles in society and the meaning of their choices
- Explore conflict regarding future plans
- Provide decision-making models for present and future use
- Explore scenarios using the empty-chair technique
- Explore the meaning of place in the world at this time
- Identify and resolve incongruence

Clients are guided to pursue specific, tangible changes in behavior and thought. From a practical standpoint, many beginning professional counselors are drawn to this paradigm because of the many tools and techniques it employs. In addition, professional counselors and clients alike can more readily observe progress in counseling from this perspective.

BEHAVIORAL COUNSELING   John B. Watson was one of the first advocates for **behaviorism** because he was able to establish that human emotions were acquiescent to conditioning. Over time, behaviorism has incorporated various ideas, practices, and theories. Other theorists associated with this approach include Burrhus Frederic (B. F.) Skinner, Joseph Wolpe, Hans Eysenck, Albert Bandura, and John Krumboltz.

Behavioral theory focuses on how to reinforce, extinguish, or modify a wide range of behaviors. Specifically, it emphasizes the association between feelings and environmental stimuli and the learning or unlearning of behaviors accordingly. Professional counselors are mainly concerned with the science of observing behavior with the resulting consequence of whether to reward positive behavior or extinguish negative behavior. This is accomplished by eliminating the cause or condition that triggered the behavior. Terry might be presented with alternatives for handling the emotional and academic stresses she faces, with the goal of developing a new set of more adaptive behaviors that can be used in everyday situations. A specific behavioral technique is the **token economy**, which calls for a client to gain or lose tokens based on whether he or she is moving toward or has reached a mutually agreed-upon target behavior. Other behavioral techniques include the use of the Premack principle (i.e., do what you don't want to do before you do what you do want to do), behavioral contract, time out, response cost, and overcorrection (Erford, 2015b). Techniques based on social-learning theory include modeling, behavior rehearsal, and role-play.

Another behavioral approach involves the stimulus-response model. This model applies **classical conditioning**, or learning through the association of two stimuli. The best-known example of this model is from Ivan Pavlov, a Russian physiologist, and his laboratory experiments with dogs. He found that when he paired two stimuli, food and the sound of a bell, the dogs would eventually associate the sound of the bell with food and begin salivating in response to the bell before the food was served. Similarly, certain human emotions, such as phobias, develop because of paired associations. Once these associations are learned, they can be unlearned and replaced in a procedure referred to as counterconditioning or systematic desensitization.

The nature of the client–counselor relationship in behavioral counseling differs dramatically from the humanistic/existential approaches. Behavioral counselors function as active teachers, reinforcers, and facilitators who help clients learn, unlearn, or relearn specific ways of behaving. It is also common for professional counselors to enter into the client's environment to instruct people who are a part of helping the client's change process. Beyond the use of reinforcers, behavioral counselors can use other techniques, including systematic desensitization, assertiveness training, implosion and flooding, contingency contracts, and aversive techniques. The ideal outcome of most behavior-modification programs is to have the client's new behavior continue after the program has terminated (**response maintenance**) and to have the desired behavior generalized to environments outside the counseling setting.

Behavioral counseling has advantages for individuals who are from cultures that do not focus on the experience of catharsis. For example, emphasis is placed on specific behaviors the client wants to change and the development of problem-solving skills. Behavioral counseling takes into account an individual's environmental conditions that could be contributing to psychological problems, such as sociocultural, political, and social influences. A limitation exists when professional counselors fail to recognize conditions beyond the individual, such as Terry's cultural emphasis on family. Other resources on behavioral counseling include:

Bandura, A. (1969). *Principles of behavior modification.* New York, NY: Holt, Rinehart & Winston.
Skinner, B. F. (1953). *Science and human behavior.* New York, NY: Macmillan.
Watson, J. B. (1925). *Behaviorism.* New York, NY: Norton.

COGNITIVE-BEHAVIORAL In the 1970s, many professional counselors recognized that behavioral approaches were too limited and saw value in combining them with cognitive approaches. Aaron Beck developed cognitive therapy, an approach that focuses on recognizing and changing negative thoughts and maladaptive beliefs into more realistic and constructive thoughts and beliefs. The essence of cognitive therapy is to focus on the cognitive content or automatic thoughts associated with an individual's reaction to an event. Beck asserted that psychological problems were derived from common processes, such as making incorrect inferences on the basis of incorrect information, being unable to distinguish between reality and fantasy, and faulty thinking. In short, he maintained that how people think basically determines how they feel and behave.

Donald Meichenbaum is one of the founding theorists of the cognitive-behavioral-therapy (CBT) approach. Similar to Beck, Meichenbaum thought that helping people change the way they talk to themselves so they use more constructive cognitions was central to the counseling process. The maladaptive self-statements that affect individuals' behaviors are termed *cognitive distortions*. The following are nine ways of mentally assessing a situation: all-or-nothing thinking, catastrophizing, labeling and mislabeling, magnification and minimization, mind reading, negative predictions, overgeneralization, personalization, and selective abstraction (Gladding, 2016).

The CBT counselor collaborates with the client by sharing the responsibility of selecting goals and bringing about change. Specific techniques, such as specifying automatic thoughts, assigning homework, thought stopping, and cognitive restructuring, are useful in identifying and challenging distorted thoughts. With Terry, the professional counselor might address her all-or-nothing perception of success with being a doctor and being accepted by her parents. Homework might include exploration of others' career decision making to challenge cognitive distortions. There are dozens of CBT techniques; they are usually active, time limited, and structured (Erford, 2015b). Consult the following resources for further study on cognitive and cognitive-behavioral counseling:

Beck, A. T. (1976). *Cognitive therapy and emotional disorders.* New York, NY: New American Library.
Beck, A. T. (1987). *Love is never enough.* New York, NY: Harper & Row.
Meichenbaum, D. (1977). *Cognitive behavior modification: An integrative approach.* New York, NY: Plenum.

RATIONAL EMOTIVE BEHAVIOR THERAPY Rational emotive behavior therapy (REBT) is a comprehensive form of therapy in that it includes a reciprocal relationship between thoughts, feelings, and behaviors. Albert Ellis, the founder of REBT, assumed that people contribute to their psychological problems by how they interpret life circumstances and events, and although people have the capacity to think logically and rationally, it is also very typical for them to think irrationally and behave in self-destructive ways because of their tendency to distort facts, make assumptions, and think in other illogical ways. In other words, while people have a tendency to move toward growth, self-preservation, happiness, and self-actualization, they also have a propensity for self-destruction, intolerance, self-blame, and avoidance of actualizing growth potentials. Ellis stressed that the way people feel is based on the way they think, so the key to effective therapy is to minimize strong negative emotions and self-defeating behaviors by helping people change their thinking. Challenging irrational beliefs and replacing them with rational and effective beliefs is central to REBT.

The REBT counselor helps clients identify irrational ideas in the form of demands against self, others, or the world because these beliefs contribute to their disturbed behavior

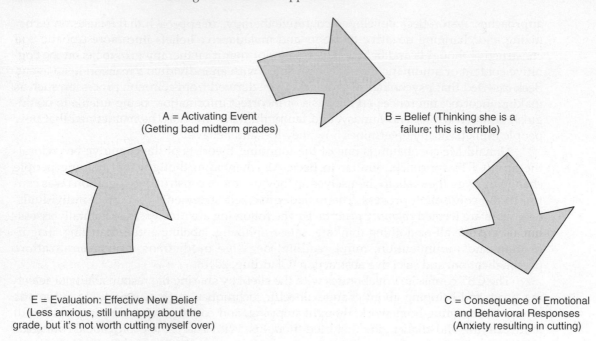

A = Activating Event
(Getting bad midterm grades)

B = Belief (Thinking she is a
failure; this is terrible)

E = Evaluation: Effective New Belief
(Less anxious, still unhappy about the
grade, but it's not worth cutting myself over)

C = Consequence of Emotional
and Behavioral Responses
(Anxiety resulting in cutting)

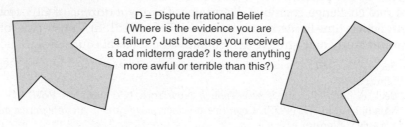

D = Dispute Irrational Belief
(Where is the evidence you are
a failure? Just because you received
a bad midterm grade? Is there anything
more awful or terrible than this?)

FIGURE 4.1   The ABCDEs of REBT in Terry's case.

and emotions. The counselor teaches clients how to challenge their dysfunctional beliefs by using logical, empirical, functional, and philosophical disputing techniques. Then the counselor helps clients learn how to replace their irrational beliefs with more rational alternatives. One way to accomplish these goals is to use the ABCDEs of REBT (see Figure 4.1). The letter *A* (Activating Event) represents the activating experience. *B* (Belief) represents what the person believes about the experience. *C* (Consequence) refers to the subsequent emotional and behavioral response to *B*. *D* (Dispute) represents disputing irrational beliefs. *E* (Evaluation) refers to the development of effective new beliefs. In addition to disputing, other specific techniques that may be used in REBT include: humor, changing one's language, rational-emotive imagery, role-playing, cost-benefit analysis, shame attack exercises, reframing, homework assignments, and numerous other cognitive, emotive, and behavioral techniques.

The cognitive-behavioral counseling approach, and REBT in particular, has advantages from a cultural perspective. Specifically, because REBT emphasizes self and other-acceptance, REBT counselors are intrinsically accepting of all clients, regardless of religious or cultural practices. Furthermore, REBT counselors do not dispute clients' diverse beliefs, values, or practices, but do help them examine how those beliefs or practices work for them. A limitation to these approaches exists when the professional counselor does not fully understand the cultural background of the client. It is important for professional counselors to proceed with sensitivity and caution when challenging beliefs, values, and ideas. For more information on REBT, refer to the following resources:

DiGiuseppe, R., Doyle, K. A., Dryden, W., & Backx, W. (2014). *A practitioner's guide to rational emotive behavior therapy* (3rd ed.). New York, NY: Oxford.

Dryden, W., & Branch, R. (2008). *The fundamentals of rational emotive behaviour therapy* (2nd ed.). West Sussex, UK: Wiley.

Ellis, A. E. (1994). *Reason and emotion in psychotherapy: A comprehensive method of treating human disturbances* (rev ed.). New York, NY: Carol.

Reality Therapy and Choice Theory.   William Glasser developed choice theory, which is based on the assumption that all behavior is purposeful and is a choice. Glasser (2000) contended that most people do not have a clear understanding of why they behave as they do; they choose behaviors they think will help them cope with frustrations caused by dissatisfactory relationships, which constitute many of the problems people have.

Also central to choice theory is that humans make choices based on the physiological need of survival and four psychological needs: love and belonging, power, freedom, and fun (Glasser, 2000). Survival relates to how to maintain good health and a satisfying life. Love and belonging signify the importance of involvement with people and the need to love and be loved. Power refers to the need to be in charge of one's life and to have a sense of accomplishment and achievement. Freedom is the need to make choices. And fun is the need to laugh, experience humor, and enjoy life. Individuals attempt to control their world to satisfy these five basic needs, which differ in degree. Importantly, choice theory is Glasser's theoretical explanation of his approach, and reality therapy is the counseling application of choice theory.

Reality therapy stresses the present, thereby helping people solve current problems. Instead of emphasizing feelings, the focus is on thinking and acting to initiate change (Glasser, 2000). Reality therapy, whether employed in an individual or group setting, is active, didactic, and directive. It teaches clients to look at whether their actions are getting them what they want, examine their needs and perceptions, and make a plan for change.

One of the basic premises of reality therapy is that connections and interpersonal relationships are very important, which leads to wide applicability of reality therapy to groups. With this in mind, a primary role of a counselor is to establish a good relationship with the client by engaging in warm and caring interactions, but the counselor must also engage in direct and confrontational interactions as appropriate.

According to Glasser (2000), counselors must be responsible individuals who can fulfill their own needs in order to help others do the same. Furthermore, they must be mentally and emotionally mature, supportive, involved, accepting, and respectful of all. Professional counselors can serve as role models of responsible behavior and help clients to assume responsibility for their own actions. Professional counselors help clients find effective ways to meet their needs and to develop specific action plans that will help clients make the changes needed to attain their goals. Counselors are active, teaching and encouraging clients to take control of their lives by thinking and acting differently. Of course, professional counselors need to develop their own styles so they can employ them with sincerity. It is critical that professional counselors demonstrate openness to their own growth and a willingness to explore their own values with the clients or students.

Wubbolding (1991) identified four techniques commonly employed in reality therapy: humor, paradox, skillful questioning, and self-help procedures. According to Wubbolding, humor helps clients to develop an awareness of a situation and should be used only after considering the timing, focus, and degree of trust. Paradox, wherein clients are asked to perform the problematic behavior under certain circumstances while restraining the behavior's expression under all other circumstances, can be effective for some clients but should be used cautiously in school settings. Skillful questioning involves using open-ended questions to help clients explore issues. It is also important to focus on positive behaviors that clients would like to target.

Advantages of reality therapy are that it stresses accountability and includes a structure that helps individuals develop action plans for change. In addition, choice theory is straightforward, flexible, and a relatively brief approach to counseling. Clients learn to accept responsibility for their behaviors, realize that they can control themselves but not others, and develop their problem-solving abilities. Clients also learn how to engage in self-evaluation and deal with present concerns in a supportive environment. Limitations to this approach include the deemphasis on feelings and lack of exploration of the past. Counselors are cautioned against being too simplistic and acting as moral experts. For more information on reality therapy, refer to the following resources:

Glasser, W. (1965). *Reality therapy.* New York, NY: Harper & Row.
Glasser, W. (2000). *Counseling with choice theory.* New York, NY: HarperCollins.
Wubbolding, R. E. (1990). *Expanding reality therapy: Group counseling and multicultural dimensions.* Cincinnati, OH: Real World.
Wubbolding, R. E. (1991). *Understanding reality therapy.* New York, NY: HarperCollins.

Solution-Focused Brief Counseling (SFBC).   Brief counseling approaches have become increasingly popular since the 1980s due to managed care and other accountability initiatives. Brief counseling approaches go by many names, but currently the most prominent counselor-related orientation is called solution-focused brief counseling (SFBC). SFBC is difficult to categorize under a specific paradigm and could easily be placed under the emergent-theories category. However, given the action-oriented, brief strategies employed in SFBC, it has been included here under the behavioral/cognitive-behavioral paradigm.

SFBC is a social-constructivist model underlaid by the observation that clients derive personal meaning from the events of their lives as explained through personal narratives. Counselors who use SFBC value a therapeutic alliance that stresses empathy, collaboration, curiosity, and respectful understanding, but not expertness. De Shazer (1988, 1991) and O'Hanlon and Weiner-Davis (2003) are often credited as scholarly and theoretical forces behind the prominence of SFBC, which de-emphasizes the traditional therapeutic focus on a client's problems and instead focuses on what works for the client (i.e., successes and solutions) and exceptions in the client's life during which the problems are not occurring. Berg and Miller (1992, p. 17) summed up the SFBC approach very nicely by proposing three basic rules on which counselors using SFBC operate: (a) "If it ain't broke, don't fix it"; (b) "Once you know what works, do more of it"; and (c) "If it doesn't work, don't do it again." It is easy to see the basic appeal of this commonsense approach to counseling.

Walter and Peller (2014) proposed five assumptions that expand on these three basic rules: (a) concentrating on successes leads to constructive change; (b) clients can realize that for every problem that exists, exceptions can be found during which the problem does not exist, effectively giving clients solutions to their problems; (c) small, positive changes lead to bigger, positive changes; (d) clients can solve their own problems by exposing, detailing, and replicating successes during exceptions; and (e) goals need to be stated in positive, measurable, and active terms. Sklare (2014) successfully applied SFBC to children and adolescents using the rules and assumptions above to focus on changing student actions rather than their insights. Sklare concluded that insights do not lead to solutions; successful actions lead to solutions.

Five techniques are commonly associated with SFBC (Erford, 2015b): scaling, exceptions, problem-free and preferred future dialogue, miracle question, and flagging the minefield. *Scaling* is a commonly used technique when counseling individuals of nearly any age and from any theoretical perspective. Basically, scaling presents clients with a 10-point (or 100-point) continuum and asks clients to rate what they are currently feeling, for example, sad (1) or happy (10), calm (1) or irate (10), hate (1) or love (10), and unmotivated (1) or motivated (10). Scaling is helpful in gauging a client's current status on a wide range of issues. It is even more helpful when it is reused periodically to gauge the progress of a client. Scaling is a very quick and helpful assessment technique with wide applicability in counseling.

Exceptions (Erford, 2015b) are essential to the SFBC approach because exceptions provide the solutions to a client's problems. A professional counselor probes and questions a client's background in search of times when the problem wasn't a problem, determining exceptions, and providing the client with alternative solutions to act upon. *Problem-free and preferred future dialogue* is the technique that allows a counselor to turn a counseling intervention from a problem-focused environment into a solution-focused environment. A counselor who uses SFBC holds the core belief that when clients focus on problems they become discouraged and disempowered and any insights clients might gain into the origins and sustenance of their problems are not therapeutically valuable. A complementary belief is that finding exceptions/solutions to problematic circumstances encourages and empowers clients, leading to actions and successes. The *miracle question*, meanwhile, helps to reconstruct the way clients perceive problematic circumstances into visions for success, which motivates clients to pursue the actions that will lead to successes.

The final technique is a treatment-adherence technique called *flagging the minefield* (Erford, 2015b). Treatment adherence is critical in any field in which individuals seek and receive help. Many, even most, receive the help they seek, but then they do not follow the treatment regimen, for whatever reason, basically guaranteeing the treatment will not be effective. For example, a patient might go to a doctor to address a medical condition but then not follow the doctor's advice. If medication is prescribed, the patient might not have the prescription filled or might not take the medication according to the doctor's directions. Flagging the minefield is a technique ordinarily implemented during termination that facilitates clients' thinking about situations during which the positive outcomes and strategies learned during counseling might not work. It encourages them to think ahead of time about what should be done to persevere and succeed in those circumstances. Treatment adherence is a critical issue in counseling; what good is all that hard work and effort to alter problematic thoughts, feelings, and behaviors if clients will return to problematic functioning shortly after termination?

SFBC is a culturally respectful approach to working with clients of diverse backgrounds because it discourages diagnoses, focuses on clients' personal frames of reference, and encourages clients to integrate and increasingly use actions that have already been shown to be successful fits for their personal frames of reference. The SFBC approach proposes that the client is the leading expert on what works for the client and the counselor's role is to help the client recognize what the client knows already works. The professional counselor then encourages the client to alter actions and cheerleads for the client's successes. SFBC approaches are particularly appreciated by clients who prefer action-oriented, directive interventions and concrete goals. SFBC is one of the more effective cross-cultural approaches because it embraces clients' personal values, beliefs, and behaviors and does not try to dispute or alter them. As a brief review of the theoretical approaches described so far, complete Activity 4.2. Table 4.5 provides strategies and techniques aligned with the behavioral/CBT paradigm. For more information on SFBC, refer to the following resources:

> De Jong, P., & Berg, I. K. (2002). *Interviewing for solutions* (2nd ed.). Pacific Grove, CA: Brooks/Cole.
> de Shazer, S. (1988). *Clues: Investigating solutions in brief therapy.* New York, NY: Norton.
> de Shazer, S. (1991). *Putting difference to work.* New York, NY: Norton.
> Metcalf, L. (1998). *Solution focused group therapy: Ideas for groups in private practice, schools, agencies, and treatment programs.* New York, NY: Free Press.

ACTIVITY 4.2

Numerous action concepts and approaches are discussed in the first three paradigms. Test your knowledge by matching the following theorists with their important concepts (The answer key is at the end of the chapter):

___ 1. Adler	A. Wholeness
___ 2. Freud	B. Social interest
___ 3. Meichenbaum	C. Self-actualization
___ 4. Ellis	D. Spiritual freedom and choice
___ 5. Frankl	E. Interpretations of life events
___ 6. Perls	F. Defense mechanisms
___ 7. Rogers	G. Cognitive distortions

Family Systems Paradigm

In contrast to the counseling approaches discussed so far, the systems approach focuses on the interactive perspective or the communication patterns within the client's family system.

TABLE 4.5 Behavioral/CBT Strategies and Interventions

- Positive reinforcement
- Token economy
- Premack principle
- Behavior charts
- Behavior contracts
- Disputing irrational beliefs
- Cognitive restructuring
- Specifying automatic thoughts
- Analysis of negative self-talk and practice positive self-talk
- Visual imagery
- Modeling
- Behavioral rehearsal
- Role-playing
- Time out
- "Picture in your mind," what would it look like if . . .
- Exceptions
- Miracle question
- Overcorrection
- Response cost
- Flagging the minefield
- Behavioral play therapy
- Parent/guardian or teacher consultations
- Brainstorming
- Bibliotherapy/biblioguidance
- Recognizing and disputing negative thoughts and beliefs, replacing them with rational self-talk
- Thought stopping
- Behavioral homework
- Develop action plans for change
- Identify positive behaviors and exceptions to the problem and strive to do more of the positive behaviors
- Scaling
- Teach family about basic needs (survival, autonomy, control, belonging)
- Responsibility
- Teach parents about the common irrational beliefs of children and parents
- ABCDEs of REBT
- Analyze the client's shoulds, oughts, musts, catastrophizing, and awfulizing
- With children younger than age eight, focus on concrete skills, such as problem solving and behavior rehearsal
- With older children, the therapeutic alliance is essential to help the child *buy in* to the therapeutic process and establish goals for behavioral change

(Continued)

TABLE 4.5 Behavioral/CBT Strategies and Interventions (*Continued*)

- Develop coping strategies
- Consider contextual/environmental factors
- Use guided imagery/relaxation
- Develop behavior intervention plans
- Use scaling questions to address degree of catastrophizing
- Positive reframing to challenge negative predictions
- Assess triggers through drawing, role-play, puppets, or sentence completion
- Postulate different points of view
- Practice healthier self-talk
- Use "picture on paper"
- Examine a recent situation in which the client made a bad choice and ask him or her to tell you what a better choice would have been
- Set up a reward system for completed class work and homework
- Develop coping strategies
- Use psychoeducation groups (e.g., friendship building, conflict resolution, emotional regulation)
- Use positive feedback focusing on resources
- Reframe weaknesses into strengths
- Journal or draw about feelings and thoughts
- Understand one's perceptions of the issue and how those perceptions lead to feelings and actions
- Address negative predictions
- Functional behavior assessment
- Instruct parents to assist in helping the student change the behavior
- Assign a job to foster a sense of belonging and responsibility
- Clients can be taught the stages of change (Prochaska & DiClemente, 1982), with emphasis placed on timing and choice to modify behavior
- Build on perceived strengths and use culturally relevant examples
- Help clients understand that people think and therefore feel differently
- Teach about choice theory and help the student make a list of some of the good and poor choices made that have contributed to the current situation
- Monitor the student to determine compliance with writing homework down and coming to school prepared
- Adopt a strengths-based approach that emphasizes successes rather than failures
- Make situationally intelligent decisions based on the context and salient cultural factors
- Consideration of the consequences of behavior can help to manage and direct thinking and actions to meet personal goals
- Collaborate to set up clear and tangible goals
- Explore realities of impact of behaviors/circumstances on future life plans (e.g., relationships, family planning)
- Facilitate an increasing awareness of reality testing to discover how the world works

In other words, the family provides the framework for understanding how the client behaves and functions in interpersonal relationships. There are many pioneers in family therapy.

Murray Bowen developed one of the most comprehensive views of human behavior of any approach to family therapy. The essence of Bowen's model is **differentiation of self**, which is the ability to maintain one's individuality in the face of group influences, such as the pressures of a person's family (Nichols, 2013). Bowen asserted that clients have less emotional autonomy than they imagine and that clients are more dependent and reactive than we realize. Bowenian theory explains how the family, as a multigenerational structure of relationships, shapes the interaction of individuality and togetherness using six concepts: differentiation of self, triangles, emotional cutoff, nuclear family emotional process, multigenerational transmission process, and societal emotional process (Bowen, 1966, 1976).

Normal family development is thought to occur when anxiety is low, family members are well differentiated, and partners are emotionally sound within their families of origin. This becomes difficult because most people leave home during the adolescence-to-adulthood transformation. The result often is that adults react with adolescent sensitivity in their relationships with their parents and with others who interact in a way that is reminiscent of their parents (Nichols, 2013). This is evident in Terry's struggle to communicate her anxiety and pressure to her parents. Bowen believed that individuals are likely to repeat problematic behaviors in their own families that have been passed down from past generations unless they explore and resolve these patterns (*intergenerational transmission*).

To help family members identify intergenerational patterns, and to help members differentiate from one another, a professional counselor must remain calm, neutral, and objective and be differentiated from his or her own family. A Bowenian counselor might work with all members of a family, although it is not necessary because it is believed that changing just one family member directly impacts the entire family system. Specific techniques that may be used include genograms, asking questions, going home again, detriangulation, person-to-person relationships, differentiation of self, coaching, and the "I" position (Gladding, 2016; Nichols, 2013).

A **genogram** can be an appropriate tool for professional counselors to use to identify cultural aspects that influence family members' behaviors. A genogram is a visual depiction of family structure. Lineage, nature of relationships, and interactional patterns are displayed and analyzed with the counselor to better understand the client's current family system. The genogram helps individuals and families to see the relationships between familial patterns and present behaviors. Also, evidence suggests that differentiation can be applied to individuals from different backgrounds. In contrast, some concepts might be limited in their application to people from diverse backgrounds. For more information regarding genograms, refer to McGoldrick, M., & Gerson, R. (1985), *Genograms in family assessment*, New York, NY: Norton. Table 4.6 provides strategies and techniques aligned with the family systems paradigm. For more information regarding family systems counseling, refer to the following resources:

Bowen, M. (1972). On the differentiation of self. In J. Framo (Ed.), *Family interaction: A dialogue between family researchers and family therapists* (pp. 111–173). New York, NY: Springer.

Bowen, M. (1976). Theory in the practice of psychotherapy. In P. J. Guerin Jr. (Ed.), *Family therapy: Theory and practice* (pp. 42–90). New York, NY: Gardner Press.

Bowen, M. (1978). *Family therapy in clinical practice.* New York, NY: Aronson.

TABLE 4.6 Family Systems Strategies and Interventions

- Caregiver or teacher training for dealing with relevant behavioral, academic, and social issues and family dynamics
- Play therapy
- Parent/guardian or teacher consultations
- Teacher training on helping children cope with relevant issues
- Reach out to caregivers to engage them in school
- Explore the family system through development of a genogram to identify behaviors and patterns passed down
- Coaching
- "I" position
- Teach family members to recognize harmful communication patterns
- Assist in building each family member's self-esteem
- Teach family members differentiation by modeling "I" statements
- Focus on familial relationships and times when the family successfully overcame difficulties
- Emphasize strengths, community, and resources
- Educate parents on signs, process, and interventions related to issues (e.g., bullying, divorce)
- Focus on interpersonal relationships
- Family as framework for understanding individual
- Use parent skills training for promoting family connectedness and involvement
- Analysis of family rules and expectations
- Evaluation of family communication style
- Exploration of family conflict-management techniques
- If family members are unavailable, ask clients what they would be doing or saying if family members were there
- Highlight strengths in the existing system
- Use metaphors and narrative to indirectly guide clients to healthier ways of behaving and coping
- Miracle question
- Sparkling moments
- Exploring interpersonal incidents
- Role-playing
- Exceptions
- Flagging the minefield
- Provide resources in the community to support the family
- Teach individuality despite family pressure
- Collaboration with parents about expectations
- Counseling for siblings and/or parents
- Parent education about school support systems available
- Education and collaboration with school personnel to assist clients
- Assess family needs
- Teach caregiver skills to support developmental needs, consistency, and availability and explore alternative solutions

TABLE 4.6 Family Systems Strategies and Interventions (*Continued*)

- Autobiography/time line of family events through sand, art, or play
- Family sculpting
- Analyze family dynamics
- Referral to local agency for family intervention
- Identify triggers
- Assess basic needs of family
- Build a pattern of communication conducive to emotional expression
- Identify key school and community persons who can assist the family in getting an evaluation for client
- Consult with faith-based and community leaders for assistance
- Community member participation in career day
- Get students involved in job-shadowing programs
- Teacher training on exposing all students to the college option
- Educate families on the change in family dynamics common in transitional situations
- Link with community resources to support family stability and locate extracurricular activities
- Discuss triangulation and work toward detriangulation
- Help the client to differentiate between self and family and to develop mature peer relationships
- When working with parents, try to reframe misbehavior using a developmental and emotional context
- Use family dynamics as framework for understanding the situation
- Communication analysis
- Try to learn what values are important to the client's family
- Assist client in discussing feelings with parents
- Consult with parole officers, community counselors, and other community-service agents working with the client
- Determine client's perceived and actual role in the family, school, and community
- Facilitate healthy peer relationships and connections with mentors
- Revisit discipline policies that continue to affect client's academic progress
- While the student must follow the school protocol, explore ways that school staff, students, and parents can reinforce success
- Encourage adolescent to explore "going home again" and work on differentiation from emotional reactivity in family of origin
- Support the client through identity development
- Help the family to understand changing parent–child relationships and the need for independence that defines adolescence
- Connect the family to resources to support the client in pursuing postsecondary options
- Work with parents to identify possible community resources to assist in understanding client behavior
- Identify cultural beliefs and values that will help contextualize client behavior

Emergent Theories

The theories included in the previously discussed paradigms have the distinct quality of being supported and implemented over time. Theories take time to develop and become empirically validated for use in the profession. A fifth paradigm of counseling theory includes the theories that are newer, or emerging, in the profession. Many can fall into this paradigm, including postmodernism (Hansen, 2006a), decisional counseling (Ivey et al., 2013), motivational interviewing, narrative or constructivist approaches, and feminist counseling.

Some emergent theories were developed for specific purposes. For example, motivational interviewing is an approach designed to work with individuals struggling with chemical dependency. Many emergent theories have been criticized for lacking empirical evidence that the approach works. Some (e.g., feminist) have even been viewed as lacking specific techniques and being more of a philosophy. In defense of philosophy, Hansen (2006b) has posited that it is a philosophical perspective that makes us most effective as professional counselors. In addition, theories take time to develop.

Professional counselors want to avoid the "conference syndrome" approach of applying any new theory they hear or read about in professional-development opportunities. Instead, a more systematic approach to learning about newer theories as they are emerging is proposed, seeing what fits within one's personal style of counseling, and applying principles as opportunities arise and theories become more solidified. For the purposes of this chapter, and to avoid overwhelming the reader, only four emergent theories in counseling are addressed: narrative, constructivist, feminist, and interpersonal counseling. However, many more emergent theories exist and are becoming more popular, including mindfulness-based cognitive therapy (MBCT), dialectical-behavior therapy (DBT), and acceptance and commitment therapy (ACT).

NARRATIVE THEORY Terry has a story to tell. She has created a story about her life and present situation, one that she might say needs to be retold. The professional counselor can help Terry to see and create success by helping her to retell her story of wanting to fulfill parental expectations and continual concerns about measuring up to her potential into a story that more accurately fits her desires. Such is the nature of narrative counseling: Help clients to retell the stories of their lives to create outcomes that better reflect what they would like to be (Monk, Winslade, Crocket, & Epston, 1997).

One way to conceptualize narrative counseling is to consider a book with many chapters. We can read a book and think we know how it will end in the final chapter. As a metaphor for our lives, we might be comfortable with the opening chapter and a few in between, but we might be dissatisfied with the contents of the book as a whole. Rather than looking to change the problems, a narrative approach suggests rewriting the chapters themselves to create a better perspective on the problems that lie therein. In essence, narrative counseling holds that we are the authors of our own lives (White & Epston, 1990).

Michael White and David Epston are the primary individuals associated with narrative counseling. The concepts of the theory are originally derived from family counseling. White and Epston (1990) drew from family therapy expert Gregory Bateson, who suggested that the means for change is to compare one set of events in time with another. In counseling practice, the goal of narrative counseling is to develop alternative stories for one's life. The counselor would help Terry identify what she would truly like her life to be like, evaluate the possibilities, and determine what must occur in the interim to make this story a reality. The counselor would want Terry to understand that she or her parents are not the problem; rather, the problem itself is the problem. Narrative counseling can assist Terry to shift her perspective of the problem and create a new outlook (story) for her life and circumstances.

The narrative counselor asks many investigative questions to understand what underlies the story and one's self-perception. Techniques used in narrative counseling are encompassed within this idea of questioning and investigating as it relates to retelling one's story. The narrative counselor helps to deconstruct problems, externalizing and separating them from the person and avoiding blame and self-recrimination (Monk et al., 1997). The professional counselor seeks exceptions to the story, times when the outcomes of one's actions are inconsistent with what one says or does in the story. These exceptions are referred to as **sparkling moments**, the positive shifts that begin to occur when one can exert control over the problem and begin to create a new story (White & Epston, 1990).

The client and professional counselor work together *against* the problem to identify more favorable stories (Monk et al., 1997). From a cultural standpoint, narrative therapy is consistent with the storytelling nature of some ethnic populations. For example, the Chinese culture is built upon a series of stories handed down from generation to generation and appearing in the form of mythical beliefs. For individuals who come from cultures where storytelling is a part of their practice, narrative therapy can feel familiar and productive. The shift to identifying one's role in changing stories can be challenging, and the narrative counselor must exercise patience and caution to deconstruct problems and not beliefs.

Narrative theory tends to provide an overarching and organizing vision of the problem as separate from the person. This approach can be empowering and eye-opening. Narrative therapy requires a level of insight from the client to be able to tell and then retell the story. For more information on narrative theory, refer to the following resources:

White, M., & Epston, D. (1989). *Literate means to therapeutic ends*. Adelaide, Australia: Dulwich Centre Publications.

White, M., & Epston, D. (1990). *Narrative means to therapeutic ends*. New York, NY: Norton.

VOICES FROM THE FIELD 4.1   Narrative Therapy with Children Who Have Been Abused, by Victoria E. Kress

When counseling children and adolescents who have been abused or traumatized, I like to integrate strength-based approaches, such as narrative therapy, with evidence-based treatments for addressing trauma, such as trauma-focused cognitive-behavioral therapy. Narrative therapy presupposes clients possess the inner strengths and resources needed to resolve their own problems. Meanwhile, the counselor's job is to develop, identify, and apply clients' strengths. Children who have been abused often feel a deep sense of shame, guilt, and/or embarrassment and can benefit from approaches that are inherently empowering.

(Continued)

One technique I often use with this population in individual and group counseling is called *Letters from the Future*. In this activity, clients are asked to imagine they are writing letters to themselves (in the present) from a future time when they are much older and wiser. Clients are invited to provide suggestions, advice, and words of hope and wisdom to themselves from this future state.

When I do this activity in a group setting, I often have group members each write a Letter from the Future to a Friend (i.e., a friend inside the group, outside the group, or a fictitious person) who has recently experienced sexual abuse. Group members are invited to provide wisdom, encouragement, and direction to their friends. What follows is a letter written by a 12-year-old African American girl who was sexually abused by her mother's boyfriend for two years. She wrote this Letter from the Future to a Friend during her third session of a group I had facilitated for adolescents who had been sexually abused:

> *Dear Friend,*
> *Hi. How are you doing? Well . . . fine? I would like to share something about the sexual abuse which was when I was raped. It was painful, so I talked to my mom about the abuse. It helped but it still hurts but I see I am going strong anyways. And the man is in jail for what he did to me and I thank God for that. I have had the wisdom to talk to people, but before I didn't do that. And even though you have lost a little part in you, I hope that you will keep your self-confidence and always love yourself because whatever happened to you is not your fault. So keep up the good work and keep up having the words of good courage. So keep your mind POSITIVE and look ahead. You have to not do drugs and drink because that is not going to help you neither. When you want to do those things you need to talk to your good friends and to your mom and your counselor. You have to keep going to church and believe God will help you get through this too. Because he will. I promise.*
> *Well, bye-bye. See you soon. And just remember, stay POSITIVE and STRONG.*

In providing advice from a future orientation, the client was able to identify positive coping skills (e.g., the value of talking about her experiences, using her spirituality and faith to ground herself, avoiding substances as a coping mechanism, engaging in positive self-talk, avoiding self-blame) and ways she could evolve and grow secondary to her abuse experiences. A counselor can give a client guidance and suggest adaptive ways of coping, but ultimately the counselor's goal is to help the client connect with and internalize these resources on his or her own. This narrative-therapy technique provides an opportunity for clients to readily connect with solutions and answers to their struggles that fit within their values and beliefs. Sometimes, getting out of the present can help people better connect with solutions and more adaptive realities.

CONSTRUCTIVIST THEORY   Is one person's perception of a problem another person's reality? How do we derive meaning from our lives, and how do we make sense of this reality? Constructivist theory, based upon the work of George Kelly's (2013) **personal constructs**, suggests that people create their own meaning and realities based upon personal experiences. Constructivism holds that people create their own meaning, and it is the job of the counselor to respect and work with that reality, not to contradict or deny it (Hansen, 2006a).

Terry believes she must be a successful scientist to please her parents. She is operating under the belief system that success is equal to parental approval. She also believes people should have personal responsibility for upholding the expectations of a culture.

The constructivist counselor would see that Terry is operating under a set of personal constructs, or belief systems, that guide her actions and goals. Personal constructs, as defined by Kelly (2013), are self-beliefs. They guide us in determining the courses of action, the people with whom we associate, and the decisions we make about our own lives. The process of identifying and integrating these personal constructs is at the heart of constructivist counseling.

The constructivist counselor is inquisitive. Constructivism is often paired with narrative techniques, such as storytelling and searching for alternative explanations to problems. The goal of constructivism is to create and construe personal reality actively through the examination of personal constructs. The professional counselor and client work collaboratively to identify constructs and their origins. Often, clients do not emerge with specific strategies to handle situations but instead focus on personal learning and examination of how they are living authentic lives based on these identified constructs.

One specific technique that stands out from this theory is the use of a **card sort**. The card sort is a means of organizing beliefs into categories to help illustrate the organization of one's system of understanding and operating (Kelly, 2013). The constructivist counselor might help the client to develop a repertory test or grid to illustrate and organize belief systems. For example, Terry might be assisted to determine the major beliefs she has created about family, career, success, and failure. The professional counselor and Terry might identify the basic belief systems to explore further how the counselor and client are operating in Terry's interactions and decisions regarding her future. In doing so, Terry would develop insight and explore the meaning she places on her constructs and the actions she takes to find meaning in her life.

Similar to narrative theory, constructivism requires significant client insight and a higher level of processing than many traditional approaches. The theory could have limitations in its cross-cultural application because some cultures expect adherence to their principles. Clients engaged in constructivist counseling are questioning and at times even challenging fundamental belief systems. In Terry's case, the exploration of personal constructs might reveal that culture is not as strong a belief to her as it is to her parents. This could contradict her culture's expectation of respect for parents and elders and might challenge Terry to create a new perspective of her situation. Conversely, proponents of constructivist counseling hold that the exploration of beliefs can be the ultimate goal of the theory and can work effectively with most cultures. Resources for further reading about constructivist counseling include the following:

Kelly, G. A. (1955). *The psychology of personal constructs: A theory of personality.* New York, NY: Norton.
Neimeyer, G. (1992). *Constructivist assessment: A casebook.* Newbury Park, CA: Sage.

FEMINIST COUNSELING   A feminist approach to counseling has been greatly criticized as challenging fundamental cultural beliefs. Yet feminist counselors operate from the basic philosophy of feminism and support, respect, and highly value the role of culture in one's life.

The feminist philosophy espouses the equality and rights of women. The feminist movement began during the 1800s and the (slavery) abolitionist movement, wherein women were fighting for their voices to be heard (Wood, 2010). The feminist movement continued through voting rights (suffrage), and what is more commonly perceived as the start of feminism, the women's rights movement of the 1960s. The principles of feminism held that women should be perceived as equals with men, have equal rights for employment and opportunities, be given certain inalienable rights to make their own choices, and essentially be treated with a fundamental human respect.

Because of this history, one often perceives feminist counseling as benefiting (or being provided by) only women. Much of the literature regarding feminist counseling suggests a woman-centered focus. Chester and Bretherton (2001) identified six themes in feminist counseling from their research with practicing professional counselors: woman-centered, egalitarian, feminism as belief, feminism as action, critique of patriarchy, and a positive vision of the future. Gilbert (2010) further asserted elements of feminist counseling to include empowerment, androgyny, and mutuality within the counseling relationship. The latter citation emphasizes the importance of equality in counseling and in one's life and carries a more universal position that can benefit women and men. Gender sensitivity in counseling might be a more accurate (and perhaps more palatable) position in applying feminist principles to men in counseling (Bartholomew, 2003).

How feminist counseling appears to the observer is less known. The fact that this approach is an application of feminist principles makes it difficult to identify key feminist counseling theorists. We could look to the work of Carol Gilligan, a preeminent theorist on women's development, Judith Jordan and her colleagues at the Stone Center, and others who all have had important roles in the creation and proliferation of feminist approaches to counseling. The feminist counselor values the female as well the male perspective—ideally, the role of gender in our lives (Bartholomew, 2003).

A **gender role analysis** is one of the primary techniques used from this perspective. The gender role analysis is a means of examining with clients the messages they received about what it means to be male or female, from where these messages were derived, and how they have been employed and are affecting one's functioning (Bartholomew, 2003). Gender role analysis may address another important principle of feminist counseling: androgyny.

Based on the pioneering work of Sandra Bem (1981), androgyny challenges the traditional gender roles for men and women. **Androgyny** contends that we should value individual characteristics for what they are, regardless of a predefined category. Professional counselors addressing androgyny see that stereotypically masculine and feminine roles are valuable within each individual. A woman who is aggressive in the workplace and athletic with her peers might also be very sensitive and caring with her partner. Feminist counselors employ gender role analysis to examine these roles and to help the individual put them in a historical and societal context (Hoffman, 2001). The client is encouraged to see that all these attributes create his or her uniqueness. It is often society's views that perpetuate his or her belief that he or she is somehow aberrant or unacceptable (Chester & Bretherton, 2001). Feminist counseling also addresses the societal perceptions and the means by which the individual can take action to implement change. Attaining this sociocultural perspective, taking action, and achieving a degree of assertiveness are the goals of feminist counseling.

The sociocultural history and viewpoint of feminism contribute to the multicultural sensitivity of this approach in counseling. Feminism has a rich history of working toward equality. Pioneers such as bell hooks and Alice Walker in the 1970s proposed that feminism addressed the concerns of only white, upper-class women (Wood, 2010). Current feminist movements emphasize and work toward equal rights for all, focusing on issues of gender, race, ethnicity, and other cultural variables.

One criticism of the feminist theory is the push for political action. Critics argue that suggesting individuals must see personal issues as political and engage in social change imposes the professional counselor's values, which might be inconsistent with one's cultural beliefs. We advocate instead that feminist counselors simply suggest the societal context of issues and explore what, if any, role clients would like to have in shaping the understanding of client issues from a broader perspective.

Terry's case could be an example of the cultural context and challenges from a feminist perspective. Terry is attempting to fulfill her parents' wishes for her success, a message that might suggest cultural values of parental respect and collectivism. A professional counselor might also wonder about messages Terry received about what it means to be female in her culture and in her family. Are there expectations that she will unquestioningly accept her role as a daughter and follow her parents' career aspirations for her? Terry's pursuit of a career in science is nontraditional for women in the United States (even in the 21st century), although science and technology careers are becoming more common in immigrant families that educate women. From a feminist counseling perspective, a gender role analysis might include an exploration of Terry's role in a predominantly male field. This would be completed without bias or suggestion that Terry must stay in or leave the profession. Instead, there would be an exploration of what this means to Terry in terms of being female and her identity as a whole. In other words, how does Terry perceive herself and her presenting concern through a gendered lens? Additional resources regarding feminist counseling include the following:

Bem, S. L. (1993). *The lenses of gender.* New Haven, CT: Yale University Press.
Brown, L. S. (1994). *Subversive dialogues: Theory in feminist therapy.* New York, NY: Basic Books.
Enns, C. Z. (1997). *Feminist theories and feminist psychotherapies: Origins, themes, and variations.* New York, NY: Haworth.

INTERPERSONAL PSYCHOTHERAPY Interpersonal psychotherapy (IPT), originally developed for adults with depression, is time limited and specifically focuses on interpersonal relationships. Goals of IPT include helping clients improve their relationships, or their expectations about them, and their social support systems to alleviate their presenting distress. For IPT, the view of human nature is based on the assertion that psychological symptoms are connected to interpersonal distress (Stuart & Robertson, 2012). This approach is derived from three theories: (a) attachment theory, (b) communication theory, and (c) social theory.

Attachment theory is based on the premise that individuals have the intrinsic drive to form interpersonal relationships, a result of the need for reassurance and the desire to be loved. Attachment theory describes the way individuals form, maintain, and end relationships and hypothesizes that distress occurs as a result of disruptions in an individual's attachment with others. Problem areas specifically addressed by IPT include interpersonal disputes, role transitions, and grief and loss.

While the attachment theory is useful in understanding the broader, or macro, social context, the **communication theory** works on a micro level, describing the specific ways in which individuals communicate their attachment needs to significant others. In other words, maladaptive attachment styles lead to specific ineffective communications. The result is that the individual's attachment needs are not met.

Social theory contributes to IPT by placing emphasis on interpersonal factors and how those factors contribute to depression or anxiety. One's social support system might be disturbed as a result of an individual's maladaptive response to a particular life event. The level of social support one has directly influences how one handles interpersonal stress. Social theory hypothesizes that poor social support is a fundamental factor in the development of psychological distress (Stuart & Robertson, 2012).

There are three main goals of counseling for IPT: (a) relieving the client's disturbing psychological symptoms; (b) examination of conflict, loss, and transition in the client's relationships; and (c) establishing the client's needs to aid in more effective use of his or her social support system. In contrast to CBT, where the focus is on the client's internal cognitions, IPT concentrates on interpersonal communication. Where IPT might touch on cognitions, they are not the primary targets. Likewise, CBT and the other theories of counseling might touch on interpersonal issues, but they are not the focus.

In contrast to analytically oriented theories, which tend to focus on early life experiences in relation to current psychological distress, IPT has a present, here-and-now focus that helps the client improve his or her current communication and social support systems. In light of its time-limited approach and its here-and-now focus, IPT aims to resolve psychological distress and improve interpersonal communication rather than to change the underlying cognitions.

The IPT counselor uses the client–counselor relationship to develop insight into the client's interpersonal functioning and to assess the client's attachment style. In the case of Terry, the professional counselor first would need to establish a therapeutic alliance with Terry to understand her experiences with school and the pressure from her parents. Together, the counselor and Terry would examine Terry's communication patterns and her social support system. What does Terry need to improve her here-and-now interpersonal relationships to build a more effective social support system? What about Terry's attachment style and communication patterns with her parents needs to be addressed?

Common techniques of IPT include establishing a therapeutic alliance, communication analysis, describing interpersonal incidents, using content and process affect, and role-playing. Because IPT has a solid theoretical foundation and a solid structure, it can be useful for clients from diverse backgrounds. The process and content of IPT counseling are flexible and adaptable, and IPT highlights the unique needs of individuals. IPT takes into account the components of several theoretical paradigms and creates a unique approach to address the individual needs of the client. Consult the following resources for further reading on IPT:

Bowlby, J. (1969). *Attachment*. New York, NY: Basic Books.

Kiesler, D. J. (1996). *Contemporary interpersonal theory and research: Personality, psychopathology, and psychotherapy*. New York, NY: John Wiley & Sons.

Sullivan, H. S. (1953). *The interpersonal theory of psychiatry*. New York, NY: Norton.

Weissman, M. M., Markowitz, J. C., & Kleman, G. L. (2000). *Comprehensive guide to interpersonal psychotherapy*. New York, NY: Basic Books.

Table 4.7 provides strategies and techniques aligned with the emergent-theories paradigm. Complete Activity 4.3, Think About It 4.1, and Case Study 4.3 to begin considering what you would do as a professional counselor and how your decisions fit within the theoretical perspectives. The next section of this chapter addresses the means by which you can apply theory in your counseling practice.

TABLE 4.7 Emergent Strategies and Interventions

- Miracle question
- Sparkling moments
- Empowerment
- Communication analysis
- Interpersonal incidents
- Role-playing
- Reading stories (bibliotherapy)
- Creating drawings
- Storytelling
- Provide client with age-appropriate information about various aspects of issues
- Deconstruct the problem-laden story, identify unique outcomes, and help clients co-author a new story that is strength based
- Externalize the problem and work against the problem
- Celebrate success
- Address attachment issues
- Here-and-now focus
- Work on communication skills and accessing social support
- The process of change results from dialogue between counselor and family members
- Empower each family member to re-author a more successful story
- Focus on communication skills, building friendships, and development of personal goals
- If the client and family desire it, attend to development of identity and fluency in both the mainstream and native cultures
- Examination of interpersonal relationships
- Social-support-system analysis and improvement
- Motivational interviewing
- Narrative therapy to deconstruct and externalize problems
- Examine personal constructs
- Identify and improve personal support systems
- Fill-in-the-blank exercises
- Sentence stems
- Word-sort activities
- Coat of arms
- Listen to client's story without blame
- Explore gender roles
- Empower client in healthy ways to decrease feelings of helplessness
- Use content of current situations to process affect
- Parent/student collaboration building and negotiating
- Caregiver/teacher training for dealing with relevant behavioral, academic, and social issues
- Explore family, school, and community dynamics

(Continued)

TABLE 4.7 Emergent Strategies and Interventions (*Continued*)

- Have the client write a short story about how the client successfully accomplished a goal
- Bibliotherapy about other clients' experiences that are similar
- Explore alternative explanations to problems
- Question and challenge the status quo
- Focus on resiliency factors
- Mentoring
- Encourage client to self-advocate and be competent and confident
- Scaling to determine needs and levels of anxiety
- Use expressive therapies (art, music, play) to tell life stories
- Stress reduction and mindfulness
- Psychoeducational and support groups to construct new realities
- Assist the client in developing positive social networks
- Assist the client in creating a story about the situation and identifying a more favorable outcome
- Break problems down into pieces
- Assess ability to "code switch" (between value codes) in the school environment, if applicable
- Explore beliefs and attitudes toward working with diverse students
- Help school staff ponder multicultural considerations and biases regardless of racial self-identification
- Analyze client expectations of teachers and what life events have shaped client expectations or concerns about school staff
- Read stories about different careers and issues
- Create drawings to understand career interests
- Focus on positive relationships with peers and adults
- Provide clients with age-appropriate information about various issues
- Improve interpersonal relationships by rehearsing behaviors to achieve desired goals
- Identify someone in the client's life who would be the least surprised to see the client planning for the future
- Shape application of discipline policy
- Identify cultural strengths the client and family bring to the school
- Identify cultural strengths and capital within the family and community and harness these strengths to gain support and encouragement for parenting the student
- Share stories about people the student might be aware of, their learning processes, and how they pursued their careers

THINK ABOUT IT 4.1

Review your previous perceptions of Terry's case. How do your beliefs about her situation and how you might approach counseling align with the counseling paradigms discussed in this chapter?

ACTIVITY 4.3

Match the component with each of the emergent theories identified. Expand upon your understanding by applying concepts from Terry's case (Answer key at the end of the chapter).

___ 1. Family systems	A. Personal constructs
___ 2. Narrative	B. Clients are more dependent and reactive than we realize
___ 3. Feminism	C. Develop alternative stories for one's life
___ 4. Constructivism	D. Highly value the role of culture in one's life
___ 5. Interpersonal psychotherapy	E. Relationships are key to development and wellness

When considering Terry's case, what specific issues do each of these theories indicate?

CASE STUDY 4.3

The Picture in Your Mind, by Barb Carlozzi

A 42-year-old Caucasian woman was in counseling to deal with her anger toward her husband who had left her and their two children and married a woman 10 years her junior. It had been 8 years since the divorce, and though the client wanted to get past her anger, she just couldn't let it go. She said, "I just never thought this would happen to me. I'm really angry with him for what he's done to our family." After a discussion about the specifics of this latter statement, the counselor asked the woman to describe how she had always imagined her family would be. At this point, the client began to cry, saying, "I just always pictured a whole, happy family." Some tears later, she explained, "I guess that's it. I hate that phrase 'broken family.' I think I'm over his leaving me, but what I've really been angry about is that I have a broken family. Letting go of that ideal family and what we've lost is just so sad."

Process Questions

1. Naming the problem can, in itself, be therapeutic. This client has identified her struggle as a lost assumption about the nature of her family. As the counselor, what would you say next to this client? What function would your statement serve?
2. What emotions and cognitions do you anticipate this client would encounter while processing her reaction to having "a broken family"?
3. Describe an approach or intervention that might help this client get past her feelings of anger and sadness.

APPLYING THEORY TO PRACTICE

These discussions of the various counseling paradigms offer a sampling of the many theories that exist. The information provided can be very challenging to digest. And it can be even more challenging to determine what fits you as a professional counselor. After reviewing paradigms and considering culture, counselors must begin to apply theory in their counseling practice. As a beginning counselor, what are the critical components of your approach?

A means of organizing thoughts about theory selection is to consider whether the underpinnings of a theory align with your basic beliefs about counseling. The elements of a theory highlight the specific and common factors, personal philosophy, and multicultural considerations discussed in this chapter. But to be philosophically aligned with a paradigm or theory, you should consider each of the following elements: view of human nature, goals of counseling, role of the professional counselor, and the techniques or approaches used.

View of Human Nature

How do people change? What motivates people to behave, think, and feel in the ways they do? What do you believe will best help someone grow and develop? These are important questions to ask yourself when considering your own **view of human nature**. The manner in which you believe individuals change will be directly related to the counseling theories to which you subscribe. For example, if you believe personality is more or less fully constructed in childhood and change can occur only through regression back to those times, you might be more suited to one of the psychodynamic theories. Conversely, if you believe people are self-determined and control their own destinies, a humanistic/existential approach might be a better match.

Regardless of varying beliefs about how people change, practitioners across settings can agree that change happens only when one is ready to engage in the process. The pioneering work of Prochaska and DiClemente (1982) proposed stages of the change process to explain the manner in which individuals move through changes in thought, behavior, or emotion. Their work originally studied smoking cessation in an adult population and has since been adapted to many issues and populations. Table 4.8 outlines Prochaska and DiClemente's five **stages of change** and how they might appear in counseling practice.

TABLE 4.8 Stages of Change

Stage	Description	Application in Practice
Precontemplation	No intent to change Unaware that problem exists	Identify problem as others have presented it to the individual; create ownership
Contemplation	Awareness of problems, but not yet committed to act to change	Weigh pros and cons of problem and solutions
Preparation	Intent and commitment to take action	Address fears, impact of possible change in life
Action	Modify behavior, experiences, or environment to overcome problems	Discuss experience of the change and subsequent feelings Consider means to sustain change
Maintenance	Prevent relapse and sustain gains achieved through change	Monitor and discuss new approach to problem

Adapted from "Transtheoretical Therapy: Toward a More Integrative Model of Change," by J. O. Prochaska and C. C. DiClemente, 1982, *Psychotherapy: Theory, Research, and Practice, 20*, pp. 161–173.

Goals of Counseling

A second important aspect in applying theory to practice is the perceived goals of counseling. Clients might enter counseling wanting immediate answers to difficult problems. But professional counselors are not prone to give direct advice or be problem solvers. Instead, we give individuals the tools they need to manage their own problems and encourage them to use the tools in future situations. An overarching goal of all counseling is to help individuals more effectively manage problems in everyday living.

At first glance, the identification of an overarching goal of counseling might seem to answer all our questions about this subtopic. However, further examination shows that theories describe goals for what counseling should accomplish. Person-centered counselors believe counseling should result in greater self-awareness, behaviorists want to see physical evidence of change in actions, and REBT-oriented counselors assert that changes in thinking and behavior are the ultimate goals of the counseling experience. Your personal beliefs about what individuals should gain from their time in counseling will dictate your determination of approach.

A word of caution: Many new counselors jump to the conclusion that it is their role to determine specific goals for their clients. Specific goals, such as to stop smoking, build a healthy romantic relationship, stay out of prison, or get into college, must be established by the individual seeking counseling. Goal setting is a collaborative venture between professional counselors and clients. The emphasis on elements of goals and the manner in which counseling can assist in reaching them is determined by counselor orientation.

Role of the Professional Counselor

Relative activity or passivity as a professional counselor will help apply theory to practice. As you have read, theories differ in their perceptions of the roles professional counselors play in the therapeutic process. For example, one could be collaborator, expert, equal, or indifferent. The professional counselor's role must be consistent with the other elements of theory and can in great part be determined by the counselor's personality and style of interaction. Some professional counselors teeter on the edge of offering advice, whereas others utter only a few words during their time with clients.

Techniques and Approaches

Professional counselors entering the profession might be drawn to approaches that outline specific techniques to be used with clients. For this reason, we have seen many professional counselors begin with a cognitive-behavioral orientation and gradually shift to approaches that offer more flexibility in the process. This phenomenon might be due in part to the level of ambiguity we are willing to endure as we enter into new situations. So much of what we do as professional counselors cannot be found in a how-to manual. We do not have guidelines suggesting, for example, that if a client states his disdain for his mother, we should offer him the opportunity to role-play a preferred interaction with her. We must instead rely on what seems to be consistent with our beliefs about counseling as outlined in the other elements of theory selection.

Some theories are heavily laden with techniques, whereas others are amorphous in providing general guidelines about approaches. As you review the theories, ask yourself what stands out to you as the most meaningful and effective. As you enter into the professional counselor role, ask yourself what you consistently notice about your approach. Are you drawn to certain techniques? Do you work more effectively when you can rely on a general approach and employ specific techniques as needed? A guide to understanding and applying techniques to counseling practice is Erford's (2015b) *40 Techniques Every Counselor Should Know* (Pearson Merrill).

Flexibility

Beginning to apply theory to practice requires contemplation of the aforementioned elements. Applying theory also requires flexibility. No two counseling interactions are alike. What works well with one individual may fall flat with another. As we will discuss shortly, few professional counselors operate from truly purist perspectives; instead, they combine principles that fit best with their goals, beliefs, and desired roles in counseling. Selecting a theory relies on a careful examination of your own personal style. The focus questions presented in Think About It 4.2 are intended to assist you in considering your counseling style and application of theory. After working through Think About It 4.2, complete Activity 4.4.

THINK ABOUT IT 4.2   Focus Questions on Theory Application

Answer the following questions as honestly as possible as they relate to each element of theoretical orientation. Consider your own beliefs and preferences as you answer the questions.

View of Human Nature

1. How do people change?
2. Are people able to change (self-determined), or is our destiny determined for us?
3. What motivates people to change?

Goals of Counseling

1. What are common goals for all people in counseling?
2. What is the possibility of change as the result of counseling?
3. What can be reasonably accomplished in the context of counseling?

Role of the Professional Counselor

1. How do you perceive the relationship between professional counselor and client? Equals? Expert to client?
2. To what extent are you willing to let the client dictate the direction of the session, and to what extent do you believe the professional counselor should determine the counseling focus?
3. To what degree should professional counselors provide guidance through personal disclosure and perspective?

Techniques and Approaches

1. What tools do you believe are most helpful in communicating with clients?
2. Which basic counseling skills (e.g., reflecting feeling, challenging) are most appealing to you in counseling?

> 3. *What do you believe would be most beneficial to you if a professional counselor were to help you with a present concern?*
>
> *Review your answers to the above-listed questions. Compare them with the information in Tables 4.1 and 4.2 to delineate which theories might be most appealing to you as you enter into your counseling practice.*

ACTIVITY 4.4

Research a specific theory to discover the basic elements of the theory (e.g., the way of looking at human nature, techniques, goals). You might wish to begin your research with the references listed after each theory discussion in the chapter.

- What types of clients and presenting problems would most likely benefit from the use of this theory?
- For what types of clients and presenting problems would this theory be inappropriate?
- Would you use this theory? Explain.

THEORETICAL INTEGRATION

With so many sound theories from which to choose, it can be challenging to select just one. Many professional counselors, as previously stated, rely on more than one theoretical perspective. **Theoretical integration** is the synthesis of the best aspects of several theories with the belief that doing so will produce richer and more meaningful outcomes. Professional counselors operating from an integrative perspective combine the best of what works for them with intentionality. While employing diverse perspectives and techniques, the integrative counselor holds fast to one underlying, foundational theoretical orientation. For example, we might at our core believe and operate from the existential standpoint of finding meaning in life and searching for ultimate existence. Yet working with adolescents in an alcohol treatment facility might require that we employ person-centered techniques to build rapport and behavioral techniques to demonstrate change required for discharge. At our core, however, remains the fundamental belief system of existentialism, which guides the use of supplemental approaches.

Integrative versus Eclectic Counseling

We are intentional in differentiating integrative and eclectic modes of counseling. **Eclecticism**, in contrast to theoretical integration, is more haphazard in nature. The eclectic counselor is a technical expert, relying on knowledge of approaches and applying what seems to fit at a given time. Eclectic counselors select approaches based on client presenting issues and symptoms. Eclectic counselors use techniques from several areas without regard for theory (Cutts, 2011). There is a lack of a unified or guiding theory for the professional counselor employing this approach. In many ways, eclecticism feels safe for beginning counselors who feel they are flying by the seat of their pants every time they face a new client and presenting issue. A challenge with an eclectic approach is a lack of organized understanding of which principles of a foundational theory are most appropriate to a given client. Without the complete knowledge of a guiding theory, it is difficult to know which pieces of the theory to extract and which to apply. While it is tempting to take the eclectic approach, always consider more fully what you believe about counseling and use that as your guide.

Why an Integrative Approach?

Despite the myriad research efforts to demonstrate best practices in counseling, there is ironically a lack of consensus on a single most effective theory. Professional counselors rely instead on the "it depends" mentality of counseling. Not to be confused with eclecticism, theoretical integration offers the professional counselor flexibility in working with various issues and presenting concerns. There exists a level of responsibility to meet clients where they are when they enter counseling. Also, you must be sure that what you do matches what clients need. Professional counselors can remain authentic in so doing, because the application of elements of theories differs based on one's underlying belief systems. Theoretical integration offers at its core a guiding theory; this guiding theory assists the counselor in making informed decisions about how to proceed in counseling while maintaining flexibility in the techniques used to assist the client in reaching goals (Cutts, 2011).

One must also acknowledge the limitations of a purist approach. As discussed earlier, professional counselors work in settings with specific requirements for their clients. For example, community mental health agencies often require that individuals reach counseling goals and implement change within a limited time. How is a psychodynamically oriented counselor to work under such managed care dictates? One answer could be simply to maintain the fundamental principles of psychodynamic approaches in selecting cognitive-behavioral strategies to employ in practice. In a school setting, where counseling time limits per individual are even more restrictive, existentially oriented counselors can help youth explore what is most meaningful in their lives by challenging them to face issues and work in the present-focused framework of reality therapy or Gestalt theory.

Integrative counseling was developed initially to help clarify conceptual understanding of theories and their applications (Norcross & Goldfried, 2005). Being an integrative counselor requires the individual to be knowledgeable. Familiarity with the many theories, or at minimum their paradigms, is required to determine consistency in applying varying techniques to support a counselor's foundation. A guiding theory at the core of an integrative approach is necessary in conceptualizing client presenting issues and determining a general direction for counseling (Cutts, 2011). Additionally, exploring one's own beliefs about counseling, as discussed in the previous section, builds a better foundation on which to add supporting approaches. Counseling is a profession valued for its flexibility and ability to see multiple dimensions of a problem. Professional counselors must put these abilities into practice by employing what works best to meet a client's needs. Complete Activity 4.5 to explore your personal integrated approach to counseling.

ACTIVITY 4.5 MY INTEGRATED ORIENTATION

Indicate the various theories you believe will be part of your integrated style of counseling. Consider not only which theories appeal to you for their consistency in beliefs, but also how they will be used. For example, what do you assume to be your

FIGURE 4.2 Core: Belly; Theory: Existential; Tools: Hands; Supplemental theories: Person-centered and CBT.

FIGURE 4.3 My Integrated Theory Core: _____ _____; Tools: _____ _____; Supplemental theories: _____ _____ _____.

core, guiding theory? As illustrated in Figure 4.2, a humanistically oriented counselor, one might identify the core of existentialism at the midsection, or belly, of the figure because one might operate from the "gut" in counseling. One might tend to use hands as a counselor and supplement the work with approaches in person-centered therapy and CBT. On what part of the figure do you identify the core? Of course, your integration must be consistent. Using a core existential approach and supplementing it with psychodynamic eyes would not be effective because of the very different philosophies of these two theories. Place your own core theory at your own identified core on Figure 4.3.

As you complete and review your integrated theory, provide a rationale for how these different theories work well together. How do their philosophies complement one another? How is the overall approach depicted here consistent with your own personal beliefs? How is the overall approach depicted here consistent with your beginning beliefs about the counseling process and change?

VOICES FROM THE FIELD 4.2   How My Counseling Theory Has Informed My Practice, by Randall M. Moate

---

I recall quite clearly the first day of my counseling theories class in my master's degree program. After taking a look at the syllabus and glancing in the textbook, I wondered, *How in the world will this stuff ever help me?* The material seemed interesting in an academic sense but far removed from what I envisioned counseling to be. I thought, *Real counselors probably don't spend time thinking about this stuff!*

(Continued)

Through my development as a practicing counselor, I have developed a deep appreciation for the importance and utility of connecting with a counseling theory. Reflecting back on my development as a counselor, I can see that cultivating a solid theoretical foundation has been invaluable to me. In fact, I cannot envision what it would be like to practice *without* having a counseling theory to work from. The following paragraphs briefly detail how I have come to appreciate and use a counseling theory in my work.

As I began reading about the various theories, I approached each as I would a first date. I tried to keep an open mind about things, not have any serious expectations, and then see where things went from there. Needless to say, there were several bad first dates, but also some pretty good ones. Eventually, I came across a theory that was the perfect fit for me—love at first sight, you might say. I recall nodding my head frequently as I read about the theory, saying to myself, *This totally makes sense to me*, and *I have always looked at the world in this way*. At this point, I wasn't exactly sure how I would use my theory, but I did feel a sort of kinship with it. I felt reassured that there were other likeminded counselors out there.

As soon as I met with my first *real* client in practicum, the utility of espousing a counseling theory or approach became readily apparent to me. I noticed that during a 50-minute counseling session, my client had a lot of information he wanted to share with me. I also noticed our conversation wasn't linear and my client took several different tangents. At times, I felt like my head was spinning and that the session was moving very fast. What allowed me to persevere through this experience was having my theory to help filter and organize what was being said. My theory functioned like a personal assistant in session. It helped me to organize and prioritize all that was being said.

Typically, when I begin working with a new client, the first couple of sessions seem to go by rather quickly. In general, my clients tend to want to focus on their presenting problems, share their stories, and have me deeply listen to what they have to say. This generally seems to be a good starting point for our therapeutic relationship as we build trust, rapport, and understanding. However, as we continue our work together, questions start to tug at the back of my mind: How is our work together going? Do we have a direction and focus in session? Am I helping the client achieve his or her goal(s)? Am I doing a good job?

I am able to fall back on my counseling theory to help me answer these questions. My theory helps to provide a context I can use as a measuring stick to evaluate how I am doing as a counselor and whether I am helping my clients make progress. I also frequently find myself reflecting on the following questions: Who am I as a counselor? How do I help people? What are my strengths and weaknesses? During times of doubt and stress, I find answering these questions to be sustaining and comforting. This process helps me to reaffirm who I am as a counselor, how the process of change occurs, and what I hope to achieve as a counselor. My counseling theory, in part, influences how I answer these questions. Rather than being left on my own to sort through these things, I have the bulwark of my theory to fall back on.

I have come to regard a counseling theory as a lens through which I see the world. After several years of practicing from a counseling theory, it has become integrated with who I am as both a professional and a person. Looking back over my education experiences, my theoretical development was critical to my development as a counselor. Starting as a student who was skeptical of the real-world utility of counseling theories, I have become very appreciative of all the ways in which theories support the work I do as a counselor.

Summary

In this chapter, we discussed the significance of studying theories of counseling. As mentioned, it is the counselor's ethical responsibility to understand theory and to employ techniques with flexibility that are sensitive to the client's needs. The case of Terry as well as the activities provided throughout this chapter help to encourage the reader to apply theory to personal practice by focusing on human nature, goals of counseling, the role of the counselor, and techniques employed with flexibility.

Given the vast array of theories to choose from, this chapter attempted to compartmentalize many theories and their specific factors into larger, more cohesive paradigms. The five major paradigms discussed include psychodynamic, humanistic/existential, behavioral/cognitive-behavioral, systems, and emergent. By providing examples of the major theoretical paradigms in counseling, we emphasized the fundamental principles of each theory and attempted to familiarize counselors with the common factors in these theories. Without evidence of a single most effective theory, most professional counselors today employ an integrative approach. Integrative approaches rely on the application of theories that work best with a client, attempt to synthesize different treatment strategies to best serve the unique needs of the client, and foster growth and development in the personal philosophy of the counselor.

Determining a counseling theory is an involved and lengthy process. The five paradigms discussed in this chapter act as a foundation from which you can base additional learning about the counseling theories as you enter into practice. Before settling on a specific theory, we strongly encourage beginning counselors to reflect upon their beliefs about themselves, human nature, and counseling. Aside from the ethical and professional responsibilities for using theory in practice, understanding how counseling works will better prepare you to help clients. A unique perspective on your client's issues, which is embedded in your beliefs about how people change and develop, will enable you to select appropriate interventions to assist clients to reach their goals. An intentional counselor is a successful counselor, employing a unique integration of personal characteristics and counseling theories.

Answer Key

Activity 4.2 1. b, 2. f, 3. g, 4. e, 5. d, 6. a, 7. c.
Activity 4.3 1. b, 2. c, 3. d, 4. a, 5. e.

MyCounselingLab for Introduction to Counseling

Try the Topic 5 Assignments: *Counseling Theory*.

5 The Counseling Process

Donna S. Sheperis*

PREVIEW

The counseling process embodies the art and science of helping. The client makes the decision to receive services, creating an opportunity for the counseling relationship to begin. Professional counselors bring their training, experiences, and personalities into the process. Once initiated, counseling occurs over a series of stages that include information gathering, application of theory to generate relevant goals, treatment, assessment, and termination. Students beginning the path to becoming a professional counselor are encouraged to consider their fit with the process and profession of counseling.

THE PROFESSIONAL COUNSELOR

The profession of counseling provides clients opportunities for healing with a focus on client autonomy and empowerment. Counseling opportunities occur over a range of settings, including private practices, schools, colleges, and community agencies or clinics. Counselors in training often try to envision what it will be like to work with clients. Regardless of the setting, the counselor and client develop a powerful relationship to facilitate change. Professional counselors put forth diligent effort to enter this profession and must recognize that there are unique dimensions of being a professional counselor directly related to effectiveness and the counseling environment. To become effective, professional counselors must examine the nature of being a professional counselor as well as some of the important factors of the therapeutic alliance.

Students enter graduate programs in an effort to secure a degree in counseling. However, students must do more than reach degree status to practice the profession of counseling; they each must truly *become* a counselor. Professional counselors are in a unique position to engage in the powerful process of healing with clients. They establish intense relationships with clients willing to become vulnerable in their presence. The prominent dimensions of counseling, established by theory, research, and practice, are the aspects of *becoming* a counselor that are aspired to by students entering graduate programs.

How does one embody the role of the professional counselor? One of the most significant factors affecting the lives of clients is the makeup of the professional counselor. All of us have personality characteristics that will influence our counseling.

The professional counselor is central to the counseling process and works with the tools of the profession in the same manner that a surgeon uses medical tools. Counseling

*Special thanks to Cyrus Marcellus Ellis for his outstanding contribution to the first two editions of this chapter.

theories and techniques are instruments anyone can read about just as medical tools are instruments anyone can hold. However, skilled surgeons can use these instruments in ways individuals without training and discipline cannot; likewise, skilled professional counselors can use their training and discipline in ways untrained individuals cannot. Activity 5.1 provides an opportunity to consider your fit with the profession of counseling.

ACTIVITY 5.1

Consider what you bring to the role of the professional counselor. You have an initial session with a client. Complete your client's following sentence:
"I just left my new counselor's office. My counselor is _____, and I know I will benefit because _____."

The professional counselor is a special individual who recognizes the need to shape academic training and skills into a fine instrument. The skills of the professional counselor are composed of an active placebo and specific counselor characteristics (Kottler, 2010), cross-cultural counseling skills, and a basic counselor paradigm (Hackney & Cormier, 2012).

Counselor Characteristics

What motivates you to be a professional counselor? A fundamental question from classmates as well as from friends and family might emerge early in your counselor training: Why do you want to be a counselor? It is an interesting question that might not have a direct answer. In fact, for many, the words are hard to find. Is it a matter of money, esteem, self-help, prestige, giving back, or rescuing or saving others? The motivation to become a counselor can pull on any number of the ideas presented here as well as a host of other personal and professional reasons. It is important for each counselor in training to consider what motivates him or her to work with human beings who are seeking relief from a variety of life events that have the capability to inhibit growth and personal empowerment. Why are you beginning this journey?

Most counseling theories discuss human behavior in terms of motivation, which a variety of life events can influence. Historically, existential thought focused on the famous questions, Who am I? Why am I here? Why do I exist? These kinds of existential questions reside, each in their own way, in the minds of people who attempt to determine a life path. For counselor trainees, the reasons behind beginning an endeavor that calls for so much personal as well as professional growth and change is an important one to consider. Psychoanalytical theorist Carl Jung asserted that the overall persona and behavior we each display to the world is an action of our collective unconscious, which Jung describes as the reservoir of all that has happened to us over the course of our lives (Hunt, 2012). Examining ourselves through this concept can start the process of determining if we are motivated to be in the counseling profession and able to help all people gain personal empowerment and overall wellness. Looking at the work of DiCaccavo (2002), we see that many beginning counselors enter counseling programs because they (a) are driven to help others from a faith-based perspective, (b) were helped by professional counselors in their own lives,

(c) believe themselves to be good listeners, (d) believe they have good advice to offer others, or (e) have been caregivers and nurturers most of their lives. Perhaps one of these reasons or a mix of these ideas is related to your reasons for becoming a professional counselor. Wampold (2011) did a thorough review of existing literature to provide us with the characteristics of an effective counselor. As you review this list, consider how well you fit with each of these qualities. Effective counselors:

- have a number of interpersonal skills, including empathy, emotional expression, and acceptance, that are visible to others.
- use nonverbal behaviors to create a sense of safety and trust for clients.
- form a therapeutic bond and alliance with clients.
- are able to explain the client's concerns and symptom distress in a way the client can understand.
- provide consistent and functional treatment plans for clients.
- instill hope in the client by being knowledgeable about the treatment.
- are flexible.
- are comfortable with discomfort and difficult material.
- communicate hope for success and engage the client's strengths in the process.
- understand the culture and context of the client.
- are self-aware.
- work to grow professionally and personally through continuing education and supervision.

You need to discover your reasons for seeking to become a professional counselor because you will be an active component of the change process for your clients. Make sure that your instrument, which is composed of your presence, skills, and abilities, is particularly sharp and is used to achieve the best possible outcome for your clients.

VOICES FROM THE FIELD 5.1

I look back on my career and I clearly remember what I was saying and doing with my first clients. I cringe sometimes when I think about the things I was trying to do. I know today I would do things differently. The thing that eases my mind is that I remember clearly that I began each counseling interaction with an attitude of wanting to help the person in front of me. I used every skill I had at the time with the intention to help each client the best way possible.

Common Issues for the Beginning Counselor

Whether in practicum or internship class, beginning counselors working with clients face a number of challenges. Rønnestad and Skovholt (2003) stated that beginning counselors have a significant learning curve to work through. They have to adjust to real-world conditions (e.g., clients who don't match what was taught in school). Novice counselors frequently struggle to address the ambiguity of the session, the nonlinear, illogical, and nonsequential manner of the counseling hour. More advanced counselors can use intuition and experience to assist in conceptualizing client issues, while many novice counselors struggle to digest vast amounts of information from client interaction.

Beginning counselors commonly struggle with the transition from school-based learning to applying their academic training to clients with issues that fall outside their academic preparation. Beginning counselors struggle with their understanding of their role as a counselor when working with clients. Many counselors can recall what was taught to them in their training, but the reality of a "real" client sitting in front of them can provoke a great deal of anxiety in the counselor and derail them from focusing on the positive factors of the counseling environment. Many beginning counselors tend to forget to develop the counseling relationship, choosing instead to try to "fix" the client's problem, often in an attempt to reassure a sense of counseling competence.

Consider this regarding the counseling process: Kottler (2010) described the notion of there being an **active placebo** at work for professional counselors. The active-placebo concept refers to the fact that counselor and client expectations play a major role in the helping process—as great a role as the actual theories and techniques used in the helping process. Kottler recognized that there are four things that assist professional counselors in their attempts to intervene in the lives of clients. The professional counselor's dress, manner, setting, and style of helping are present in interactions with the public, and if these match the client expectations of what a professional counselor *is*, clients begin to believe that counseling might work for them.

Counselors in training who arrive at this understanding recognize that the active placebo is at work during every moment of their professional lives. In fact, it ought to shape the way in which you conduct your practice, the way in which you are seen by the public, and the manner by which you approach clients and their counseling needs, as well as the way in which you establish your counseling environment.

The active placebo is influenced by more than the explicit expectations of the relationship. Multicultural considerations play essential roles in our personal relationships with others, and they are present in the professional counseling relationship as well. Consider your style of relating to others, especially when you meet someone new. Do you tend to be gregarious or reserved? Do you tend to be assertive or deferential? What differences do you notice in your interactions with individuals of the same gender and with individuals of the opposite gender? It is likely that your responses to these questions are influenced, in part, by cultural dynamics.

Much of your personal style of interaction is known to you; that is, you are aware of how you are received by those you meet. However, all of us have blind spots. You are not always aware of your mannerisms and styles of relating that draw others toward you or turn others away from you. Now is the time in your professional development to gather information about your relationship style. Complete Activity 5.2 to explore the active placebo and your relational style.

ACTIVITY 5.2 ACTIVE PLACEBO EXERCISE

Write down how you currently approach personal and professional activities. Do you have a particular manner for personal interactions and a different manner for professional interactions? Explain. Ask a classmate to comment on your manner in class and other aspects of your behavior. What do you need to do to develop an active placebo that would convince the public you represent the counseling profession?

Counselor characteristics are also an important part of the therapeutic dynamic. **Counselor characteristics** refer to the personality and the approach of the counselor. Kottler (2010) stated that the professional counselor must to be "vibrant, inspirational, and charismatic"; "sincere, loving, and nurturing"; and "wise, confident, and self-disciplined" (p. 3). These personal characteristics are essential to motivate and connect with clients struggling with issues ranging from developmental problems to multiple levels of dysfunctional coping mechanisms. Take a minute to consider your own personality and characteristics that will influence your work as a counselor by reading Think About It 5.1 and then completing Activity 5.3.

THINK ABOUT IT 5.1

Counseling is heavily influenced by the personal characteristics of the counselor. What traits and skills do you possess that will make you an effective professional counselor?

ACTIVITY 5.3 COUNSELING CHARACTERISTICS EXERCISE

Consider Kottler's list of essential counselor characteristics. Think about your life, and describe times when you have been:

Vibrant
Inspirational
Charismatic
Sincere
Loving
Nurturing
Wise
Confident
Self-disciplined

Client Characteristics

Equally important for beginning counselors is recognizing the characteristics of our clients. Clients possess a great number of characteristics that are as active in the counseling process as are the characteristics of the professional counselor. Paul Pedersen once spoke openly about recognizing that clients enter treatment with a thousand voices. No, he did not mean that clients are hearing voices. He meant that clients have a number of voices active in their consciousness as they enter the counseling relationship. Clients do not enter counseling as soon as things are not working out the way they wish. Often they enter treatment after making a number of attempts to solve their issues without success. Once they become aware of their inability to address their issues they look at the counseling process as a representation of their inability to work through their issues.

Frankel and Levitt (2008) indicated that counselors need to be aware that clients entering counseling tend to be apprehensive, timid, and guarded. When beginning treatment, they can be disengaged or withdrawn or can decrease their overall intention to address issues related to their presenting problem. Clients can display resistance (to be discussed later in this chapter) as well as employ increased storytelling as a means to distract the counselor from exploring emotionally charged and clinically relevant dialogue in the counseling session. Emotional discomfort from various life events *experienced* by clients lead to apprehension and guarded communication by clients upon entering counseling.

Cross-Cultural Counseling Competence

Cross-cultural counseling competence is an essential ingredient in counselor preparation. At its very essence, every counseling interaction is cross-cultural in nature. Two (or more) unique individuals enter into the counseling relationship with their own cultural perspectives and experiences. The relationship these individuals create is independent of previous relationships, yet will be influenced by those previous relationships. Some of this impact is discussed later in terms of transference and countertransference. At its most basic level, each counselor–client dynamic is a culture unique unto itself.

Counselors in training prepare for the multicultural practice of professional counseling. Graduate programs may emphasize student understanding of diverse cultures through stand-alone multicultural courses, or programs may infuse multiculturalism throughout the curriculum. Murphy and Dillon (2014) suggest three guidelines for multicultural best practice based on their understanding of the multicultural literature:

1. As clinicians, we need to be aware of our own ethnic, gender, and cultural heritage.
2. We need to acquire knowledge about the cultures and customs of the clients with whom we work.
3. We need to use this self-awareness and knowledge to devise flexible strategies for intervention that are effective and congruent with our client's values. (pp. 39–40)

We all have a diverse collection of thoughts and feelings that are not homogeneous to people who may closely match our own racial, class, gender, or ethnic makeup. Each individual brings a lifetime of perceptions and apperceptions that affect each other in the counseling process. This impact, which defines the multicultural dynamic of the relationship, serves to help or hinder the counseling relationship. Your job as counselor is to continually assess the relationship between what is going on in the client's life, in the session, or in your response to the client and the cultural forces at play. Activity 5.4 provides a cross-cultural exercise to sensitize you to the power of descriptive labels.

ACTIVITY 5.4 YOUR PERSONAL CULTURAL FRAME OF REFERENCE

Make a list of words you have used and you have heard that describe people who are racially and ethnically similar to you. Then make a list of words you are familiar with that describe people who are different from you, including members of a different gender and socioeconomic class.

1. Which words do you perceive as coming from feelings of fear, anger, or anxiety?
2. Which words indicate solidarity, understanding, and social justice?

(Continued)

3. How can you put more words to work in your counselor training that build connections with people who are different from you?
4. Now take a moment to consider how you are unique. How do you define your own culture?
5. Consider your demographic factors and the type of family in which you were raised, your current relationships and lifestyle, and characteristics unique to where you live. Write a one-page description of the unique culture that defines you.

Basic Counseling Paradigm

As discussed in the integrative counseling portion of Chapter 4, ultimately, the journey of discovery leads each professional counselor to an end result, the establishment of his or her own **basic counseling paradigm**. A basic counseling paradigm is the manner by which the professional counselor can understand the human condition in all of its various forms. A view of the basic counseling paradigm of the profession has been proposed by Hackney and Cormier (2012), who recognized that professional counselors work within the role of human growth and development. Professional counselors serve as the experts on how people may need prevention-based services (e.g., drug prevention, relationship training, premarital counseling) as well as remediation services (e.g., recovery counseling, couples counseling, anger management counseling) across the life span.

Hackney and Cormier's (2012) view serves as a foundation for recognition that theories, techniques, and interventions are guided by the notion that humans have the capacity to live functional lives, but occasionally may need additional coping skills to address particular aspects of their lives. It is important that counselors formalize their thoughts on the nature of change. What causes client problems, and how are people best helped? Use Activity 5.5 to begin this thought process.

ACTIVITY 5.5 BASIC COUNSELING PARADIGM EXERCISE

Explain how people become healthy, unhealthy, and in need of assistance. How do people get better? Is it because of their thoughts, feelings, relationships, behaviors, or some combination of these? Explain. Match your thoughts to how general counseling theories propose that people are healthy or unhealthy. What does this say about how your understanding of the human condition is developing?

The Counseling Process and Stages of Change

In order to begin the discussion of the counseling process, look at the change process. The previous chapter introduced you to the stages of change model, or the transtheoretical model (TTM), which approaches the concept of change through stages (Norcross, Krebs, & Prochaska, 2011). Using this model, change begins before we really even realize it. Recall that in the Precontemplation stage, clients are not yet considering change. It may be that they have not experienced consequences for maladaptive behaviors, they have given up on trying to change, or they are in what we commonly refer to as "denial." Because of this, counselors will rarely see clients in this stage unless they are seeking services for another problem or concern. For example, a client may present with marital difficulties without any real understanding of how alcohol use is creating a problem within the marriage. A counselor's place of employment may also allow an opportunity to work with clients in the Precontemplation stage. For example, clients in a correctional or shelter setting may begin counseling in the Precontemplation stage. As a result, counselors are able to help clients see areas of change that they are blind to in the course of working with them.

In the Contemplation stage, when clients are actively considering making changes to maladaptive behaviors, the counseling process can begin in earnest. This is a stage where people can better evaluate the pros and cons of changing, but, without intervention or momentum, would become stuck and not make a change. Counselors have the opportunity to provide that intervention or momentum. For example, a client who is unhappy in his current job can see the benefits of sending out resumes and interviewing but has not taken action yet. If no action is taken, the client may become stuck in this stage. If the client is working with a counselor, these actions may take on new meaning.

The third stage in the transtheoretical model is Preparation, which happens when clients intend to take action and may have already taken steps toward action. Often, the third stage occurs during the counseling process. The Preparation stage is a wonderful time for a counselor to work with a client because the client is motivated and ready for change. Movement in the Preparation stage results in the fourth stage, or Action. Action is when clients take real steps toward making change. Support from the counselor is essential during this time as it is easy for the client to lose momentum. This is a stage where clients often discontinue counseling. Having taken action, they often see no point in continuing services in the final stage of change, the Maintenance stage. However, clients in the end stage have a chance to work to retain new patterns that have resulted from the changes they have made. The counselor's role in the counseling process changes with each stage. However, it is important to note that the client's role changes as well.

We have talked about what the counselor brings to the relationship and the stages of change through which clients may progress. Now we can take a look at what the client brings to the relationship. Client characteristics are as numerous as clients. First, it is important to know whether clients have sought counseling before. Have they experienced positive benefits as the result of counseling? If so, they may have a positive belief in the outcome of the current counseling experience, also known as efficacy.

Second, some clients are heavily motivated toward change while others may be reluctant or even resistant. How interested they are in change, often referred to as a help-seeking attitude or motivation, is a variable that affects counseling outcome. Third, what symptoms are they presenting? How much distress are they in? These are important considerations because researchers have found that clients with high symptom distress, who are further along in the change process (e.g., have a greater readiness for change), and who have not previously been in counseling have a high predicted success rate in counseling (see Hummel & Lichtenberg, 2001; Friedlander, Lambert, & de la Peña, 2008). Clients with this combination of variables show a greater decrease in the symptoms they presented with at the onset of counseling than do clients without these characteristics. Does this mean that if a client has been in counseling before that you are destined to be unsuccessful? Of course not. But it is helpful to identify what characteristics are known to offer the best advantage.

THE HELPING PROCESS—THE HELPING RELATIONSHIP

What do you think it means to be a helper? Many of us become counselors because of the desire to help others. Perhaps we were helped by someone over the course of our lives and that has inspired us to become helpers as well. If you have ever received help at a difficult time in your life, or if you have ever given help to someone at a difficult time, you may recognize that the match in relationship between the one giving help and the one receiving help is instrumental. It is this helping relationship that serves as a focal point for counselors in training. Likely at some point in your own life you have experienced the benefit of change. For Think About It 5.2, consider change in light of your personal circumstances.

THINK ABOUT IT 5.2

Reflect upon a time when you developed awareness or insight that precipitated change in your life. What were the motivating circumstances? What support structures and challenges were in place?

Sharfstein (2005), in a commentary on the power of healing through relationships, recognized that people with serious mental health issues can be assisted through the power of relationships. Sharfstein ended by recognizing that, "relationships, love, [and] connectedness is what makes life worth living" (p. 213). Sharfstein's commentary is important as we discuss the helping relationship. Professional counselors can get so wrapped up in professional functions such as crisis work, treatment planning, and client stabilization that they forget that many clients are seeking some sort of connection with another human being. In the healing process, clients seek to feel joined with and part of the world around them. What has drawn you to this profession of healing? Take a moment to reflect on your desire to help by engaging in Think About It 5.3.

THINK ABOUT IT 5.3

Why do you want to help people? What experiences have you had helping others? What experiences have you had being helped?

The Art of Helping

Professional counselors have been trained in the **art of helping** and are able to recognize issues in clients that are detrimental to their overall well-being (Young, 2013). As you continue your professional growth toward being a full-fledged member of the counseling profession, it is important that you recognize some key dimensions of being a helper to individuals in need of help.

So let's revisit the question, what do you think it means to be a helper? For some, being a helper means that you are a benevolent person who works very hard to provide assistance to people who may need clothing, food, or shelter. For others, it may mean that you take care of people who need help because it comes easy to you. You may extend yourself to others who may need money or someone to talk to when they are expressing difficult personal issues.

The ability to help others may be the motivating force that supports one's decision to become a professional counselor. Many of us were helpers all of our lives. We may have helped our parents, our siblings, other family members, and, most especially, we may have been the "counselor" for our friends throughout junior high, high school, and college. When you sit and reflect on why you would open your own emotional well-being to another's struggle, discomfort, and personal pain, is your answer, "I want to help"? Here is the doorway to the art of helping—determining why you want to be a helper, and why you want to study how to become a helper.

As a helper intent on practicing the art of counseling, here are some questions for you to reflect on as you approach your training: (a) What does it mean to be a good helper? (b) What would I have to gain from my training to understand the process of helping? (c) What do I bring to my counselor training that will allow me to be a good helper? (d) What parts of my being can get in the way of being a good helper?

These questions mirror comments from Kottler (2010), who recognized that the art of helping others comes from our ability to be in touch with our passion and desire to be in a relationship with another human being. The art of helping others lies within our ability to form a relationship with another human being because we have made a commitment to self, an examination of personal motives for wanting to help others, and a realization that the helping process involves being present and attentive to clients through a variety of clinical approaches and techniques. Kottler stated that professional counselors are people who possess unique characteristics, such as being a vibrant, inspirational, charismatic, loving individual able to be present and available for clients. Debate exists within the counseling community on whether we are **scientist-practitioners** or practitioner-scientists (see Chapter 17). Does research drive our interventions with clients? Isn't research itself driven by practice? The answer to both of these questions is yes; this is a profession that requires the interplay of art and science. We have explored what it means to be an artist within the counseling profession. What about science?

Helping as a Science

Counselors enter into a profession driven by science. Many will work in agency, mental health, or school settings where counselors must validate the need for and efficacy of services. In order to work and be competitive in this data-driven world, counselors must understand the importance of science to what we do. Early on, Haring-Hidore and Vacc (1988) explained the essence of the science of helping for professional counselors. In your introductory course, your professor may cover many of the eight core areas specified by the Council for Accreditation of Counseling and Related Educational Programs (CACREP, 2016), one of which is research. Research uses the scientific method, or science. All professional counselors, regardless of specialty area, should use scientific methodology to make practice-based decisions. The American Counseling Association *Code of Ethics* (American Counseling Association, 2014a) requires professional counselors to use research-based practices.

Evidence-based treatment is a focus for counselor training, helping to bridge the gap between the objective science and the subjective art of the profession. In other words, counselors use scientifically validated methods, tools, and techniques in work with clients.

The **science of helping** means that treatment decisions are informed by research and best practices. Much of the science of counseling is learned in a graduate program, but counselors must continue to be consumers of research through journals, workshops, and continuing education opportunities to stay abreast of the current trends. In doing so, counselors also have opportunities to participate in the development of evidence-based treatment through research.

A form of research often used in counseling settings is action research. **Action research** (see Chapter 16) is a practical research approach intended to collect information, address a specific problem, and generate solutions. It informs best-practice decisions for counselors and is one method of helping to discover what is working with clients. By its nature, action research is responsive to a particular need or situation. For example, a counselor in a school may be interested in the perceptions of the teachers she works with on her role as a school counselor. She may survey the teachers to determine if their perceptions match her true job duties. If they do not, she may focus on communicating her role to her colleagues and improve the working relationship. As you read Think About It 5.4, what are the thoughts and feelings you have about research?

THINK ABOUT IT 5.4

How do you feel about reading and conducting research? If you could conduct a research study that would answer burning questions you have about counseling, what questions would you want answered?

Common Factors in Helping

Counseling combines the art of understanding and "being with" another person with the research basis of what works. Much of the research in helping professions has centered on answering the question, What makes the difference in the client–counselor relationship? In other words, what are the common factors in helping that facilitate change regardless of theoretical approach of the counselor or stage of change of the client?

One common factor is a shared belief in how the problem originated. Counseling is more effective when both the counselor and the client perceive the etiology of the presenting problem from the same perspective. For example, a client suffering from depression believes that his thoughts cause his depression and enters counseling looking to change those thoughts. This client will respond better to a cognitive-behavioral therapy approach than clients who believe that external forces or genetics cause depression (Wampold, Imel, Bhati, & Johnson-Jennings, 2007).

Another common factor relates to cultural understanding. Many counselors mistakenly believe that matching the client and the counselor culturally results in improved outcomes. The reality is that it is not the matching of culture that makes the difference. The true common factor that improves outcome is having a counselor who understands and attends to important client cultural considerations (Ito & Maramba, 2002).

Finally, it is the insight the counselor develops and is able to communicate to the client regarding the client concerns that is one of the most salient factors in successful counseling. Here, the word *insight* refers to "obtaining a functional understanding of one's problem, complaint, or disorder through the process of psychotherapy" (Wampold et al., 2007, p. 119).

The counselor's ability to understand the client's problem and translate that understanding through verbal and nonverbal communication, use of theory, development of shared treatment goals, and cultural awareness constitutes a common factor that transcends any one theoretical orientation. Your training as a counselor is heavily focused on increasing these very skills and abilities as you learn the science of techniques, theories, and treatment interventions that you are then able to convey to the client through the use of the art of counseling, otherwise represented as your "presence."

Practitioners understand the art and science of counseling, appreciate the role of theory, and apply current research to treatment models to serve clients best. The goal of professional counselors is to create an environment conducive to client change. What becomes equally important is what actually brings a client in to begin the counseling process.

VOICES FROM THE FIELD 5.2   Trust in the Process and Yourself, by Nicole Bradley

---

For me, one of the more difficult aspects of becoming a counselor was learning to trust in the counseling process and myself. As a new counselor, I knew that I had the knowledge and skills to work in the counseling profession, but I questioned if I was being helpful and effectively implementing the knowledge and skills I had gained throughout my training.

During one of my first counseling sessions, I met with a 16-year-old female client who was "forced" to come to counseling by her mom. Session after session, she glowered at me, arms crossed, making no eye contact except for the occasional eye roll. The harder I tried to connect with her and help her feel comfortable in opening up, the more it felt she pulled away from me. Before each session with this client, I would think to myself, "What am I doing wrong?" I began feeling anxious before all my sessions with her and questioned everything I said and did within the sessions. Although things improved a bit, I never felt as though we had the counseling relationship I had read about in my books, or had come to expect, as essential for client change to occur. Consequently, I found that my anxiety with her began to generalize to other clients, and I started questioning if I was being helpful to anyone. I wondered if I had been on the wrong path and thrown away two years of my life studying to become a counselor.

After working with this client for 6 or 7 months, I decided to leave my current position and started to prepare my clients for the transition. At this juncture, the client began opening up and bringing up topics and material that we had discussed in previous sessions months earlier during the eye-rolling, shoulder-shrugging period. In addition, at our last session, the client hugged and thanked me for all of "my help" and asked if she could continue to see me at the new agency where I would be working. The client then discussed the changes she had made in her life and once again brought up topics and skills we had discussed much earlier. I learned from this experience that, sometimes, client change is not something tangible; it isn't always something we can see or even feel. Most important, I learned that I needed to trust the counseling process and myself. We never know what seeds we are planting with our clients or how they will come to fruition.

WHAT BRINGS CLIENTS TO COUNSELING?

As we grow as professional counselors, we think about our practice in various ways. We wonder what our challenges will be. We wonder what opportunities will arise. We wonder where we will work and what our clients will be like. We wonder what brings clients to counseling.

Clients enter into counseling to address a host of concerns. A consequence of being a complex human being includes facing the challenges of living, many of which may cause us to have a need for a professional counselor. Not only does life possess the potential for all of us to find our way to a professional counselor, but when we add the additional dimensions of racism, classism, gender inequities, ability differences, ageism, intolerance of differing sexual issues, medical difficulties, lack of individual value, unfulfilling jobs, poor relationships, death, fear, lack of love, and poverty, we may want to ask: Why aren't more people seeking out professional counselors on a daily basis?

As we face the pressures of life and the many difficult conditions that living can create for anyone, it becomes clear that the inability to cope with life is the driving force for someone to seek counseling. When clients' temporary fixes fail, and their inability to cope becomes apparent (e.g., too much sex; abusing alcohol; too much smoking; avoidance of issues; isolation; continuous crying or never crying; too much spending; losing their car, house, or job), they make a decision whether or not they will call or ask for a referral for counseling. You will likely help many different types of clients, and some client types will be specialty areas for you. Use Activity 5.6 to consider the client populations you are currently drawn to serve.

ACTIVITY 5.6 HELPER EXERCISE

Write down the types (e.g., populations) of clients you would like to specialize in helping as a professional counselor. What makes you want to help each population? What would you receive from helping such people?

Write down whom (e.g., types, populations) you would not want to help. What makes these groups of people outside of your reach when it comes to providing help? What are the reasons you tell yourself for not wanting to help a particular group of people? How does this work with or against your active placebo, counselor characteristics, or view of the human condition?

Counselors in training can easily assume that clients recognize their own issues and then sit down with a host of options before them to select a professional counselor. Counselors may also assume that clients have the ability to call their health maintenance organization (HMO) or other medical plan and ask for a referral and make their initial appointment and then meet the professional counselor and begin treatment. Certainly there are cases where clients recognize their need for assistance and seek out and select their professional counselor without much delay or hesitation. For the most part, however, potential clients have a hard time requesting help; they go through various steps when making the decision to seek counseling.

Although counseling is a necessary service and is generally supported by the community, many potential clients still feel a sense of shame or weakness when thinking of seeing a professional counselor (Sheu & Sedlacek, 2002). Across gender, race, and cultural lines, going to a professional counselor can be viewed as a failure, not manly, reserved for the weak-minded, or a place where only women go to work out their problems.

Potential clients also attempt to answer their own questions about the benefits of going to a professional counselor based on what they have heard (apperceptions), what they believe about professional counselors (connotations), and, for some, their past experiences with professional counselors (perceptions). In addition, real life makes it hard for potential clients to come into counseling. People may think that a time of distress and maladaptive coping is not a good time to enter into counseling. They may believe that, because of life events, "I don't have time for counseling!"

Although counselors are trained to think that opting for counseling can be a liberating experience, many people see appointments and intake requirements as an additional hardship that they may be better off not incorporating into their hectic lives. All of these dimensions of a person's life provoke potential clients to sift through their fears and doubts about counseling to make a decision to make an appointment and seek help. It is important to address the fact that we *are* our clients. As humans first, and professional counselors second, we are no more immune to these life challenges than are the individuals who seek our services. In fact, most professional counselors would argue that receiving counseling is a prerequisite for providing counseling because it helps us to empathize with the client role.

Case Study 5.1 presents just some of the questions going through the minds of potential clients. While there is some variability with the kinds of answers that could be given, these are concerns that our potential clients struggle with when trying to decide if they will enter into a counseling relationship. Once committed, they can begin the process of counseling. What would it take for you to enter (or reenter) counseling? Use Activity 5.7 to consider your relationship with counseling.

CASE STUDY 5.1

Empathizing with Clients

This case is about you! Assume that you need to establish a relationship with a professional counselor for a personal concern of your choice. To increase your empathy further, answer the following questions:

1. *Could you give up two and a half hours each week for 15 weeks?* (Counseling is more than the 50-minute session; you must travel there and back, fill out paperwork, and sometimes see additional people.)
2. *If you were to see a professional counselor, would you have to miss work?*
3. *Would you have to attempt to move your schedule around?*
4. *Would you have to worry about people knowing where you are going?*
5. *If you are a graduate student going to school at night and have family responsibilities, who would take care of those issues while you were going to your counseling appointments?*

ACTIVITY 5.7 THE "WHAT BRINGS YOU TO COUNSELING?" EXERCISE

List three experiences in your life that were or could have been addressed in counseling. What led you to seek counseling or kept you from seeking counseling in those situations? If you were going to a counseling session today, what would you want to address? Think about a time when you have been frustrated about something. What did you want from the people you talked to about the frustration? How does it feel when others tell you what you need to think, feel, or do when you are frustrated?

Theorists over the years have considered counseling as a process that occurs in stages. To facilitate an understanding of the counseling process, these stages are discussed in terms of the elements inherent in initiating the relationship, exploring and working together, and integration and termination.

INITIATING COUNSELING

Initiating counseling sets the tone for the working relationship between the client and the professional counselor. During this initial stage, the professional counselor makes a personal connection with the client, defines the process of counseling, and makes a plan for working together. A primary goal at this stage is to create a climate for change. This climate is affected by numerous variables including the setting and structure of counseling. Initiating counseling provides a foundation for establishing the helping relationship necessary to effect change.

Counseling Environment

Counseling occurs in schools, community agencies, organizations, colleges, private practices, and other environments conducive to establishing a helping relationship and providing services. The **counseling environment** refers to the combination of external physical conditions and counselor characteristics that affect the growth and development of clients. The concept of the counseling environment reveals the importance of establishing a safe arena for counseling. Professional counselors are responsible for creating an accepting environment, both physically and interpersonally, that is as free from anxiety and distraction as possible.

Setting up a counseling office is a process and it requires a clear focus and understanding about how you wish to present yourself to others. In a sense, your office is an extension of your counseling posture. Depending on where you work, you may not have a lot of control in certain areas such as flooring, lighting, walls, and furniture. Although you may not be able to always have your heart's desire regarding your office setup and décor, there are some things to keep in mind.

VOICES FROM THE FIELD 5.3

I remember my first office—what a great feeling. I remember wanting to hang my diplomas on the wall and other documents that demonstrated my "right" to be in that office. I remember wanting to demonstrate my pride in my accomplishment and in my profession by displaying everything I had. I wanted clients to know that I had my credentials. I wanted my office to be so great by what people saw that they would somehow be better from just walking in the door. When my colleagues saw what I did with my office, to my surprise they didn't think I did a good job. Instead, they thought I went overboard. They thought my personal touches might discourage clients because I am displaying so much and they have so little. Ultimately they asked me to think about why I have so much in my office. As a result of this new awareness, I made some changes to my environment to better serve my clients.

Offices can communicate a lot about your personality and can give a client a sense of who you are. Recall the active placebo. Knowledge of who you are can help clients before you actually begin providing services. Your office is a part of that active placebo and it is important to be aware of your environment by establishing an office that communicates warmth and caring. A constant discussion among counseling professionals is, To what depth should personality show in the way offices are set up? Many counseling professionals think an office ought to be somewhat neutral, so clients get a sense that they can be themselves. Others think that adding some personal affects in your office allows you to come across as a real person and not someone who is disconnected and distant. Offices that display personal items like pictures, religious symbols, vacations, and family can be interpreted differently by each client. At times, clients may ask you about what they see in your office and become curious about you beyond the counseling hour. This dynamic can be uncomfortable for some counselors and provoke additional strain on developing the counseling relationship. Caution ought to be taken when deciding to display certain items that may be overly controversial in nature, especially along sociopolitical lines. It is a good rule of thumb to consider the clientele served and the reasons behind choices for decorating an office.

Counseling generally is most successful in situations that afford the client privacy and offer a setting conducive to intimate conversations. Although the physical environment is important, effective counseling requires interpersonal skills. The initial appointment provides the opportunity for work to begin, but ultimately, **relational competence**, or the ability to establish and maintain the helping relationship, is integral to counseling.

Helping Relationship

To better understand the role that the helping relationship plays in the counseling process, it is beneficial to understand the nature of interpersonal relationships in general. Human relationships develop through the exchange of information. You get to know someone by learning bits of information and giving information about yourself. When you meet someone for the first time, you often exchange names, hometowns, majors, and other information that describes you. As you grow closer to someone, you may share hopes, dreams, fears, and insecurities. We make decisions about how much we tell others based on whether it is appropriate to the relationship. Some people learn a great deal about us, while others know very little. However, virtually without exception, the exchange of information is reciprocal; that is, we tend to tell others things about us that they are willing to tell us about themselves. Rarely would we tell someone intimate details of our lives if they do not reciprocate and tell us those things about themselves.

Yet that is exactly what clients are asked to do when they enter into a counseling relationship. Clients disclose personal and private information to professional counselors as a necessary part of the process. That disclosure, in a nonreciprocal relationship, violates all of the relationship rules clients have established in their other relationships. What that means for us as professional counselors is that to engage clients successfully in the helping relationship, we have to make it safe for clients to tell us things they normally would not tell another person. Historically, professional counselors have been called "professional inviters of self-disclosure" (Jourard, 1971, p. 15). Creating an environment for successful healing requires professional counselors to relate differently to clients than do others in the clients' lives. It is the responsibility of the counselor to greet and interact with the client in such a way as to minimize anxiety and maximize opportunity for healing (Sperry, Carlson, & Kjos, 2003). When have you felt comfortable disclosing to others? Think About It 5.5 asks you to consider disclosure from a personal perspective.

THINK ABOUT IT 5.5

Has there ever been a time when you found yourself telling someone more than you expected? What was happening at the time? What caused you to tell this person these things? What was it like? How did you feel afterward? What, if any, consequences were there because of your disclosure?

Egan (2013) proposes a three-stage model for helping that is geared toward helping clients manage the problems of living. He asks that the client and counselor address three main questions: What is going on, what do I want instead, and how might I get to what I want? Egan's counseling approach focuses on helping clients identify their challenges and devising ways to live more effectively. The clients maintain the power in the relationship as the directors of their own lives, and the counselor uses the power of the relationship, along with specific counseling skills, to assist the clients.

As the client approaches the presenting problem, the counselor uses empathy and active listening skills to facilitate the story. The counselor helps the client identify any blind spots and focus or prioritize the concerns. This initial stage of the helping relationship is considered exploratory in nature.

Egan (2013) conceptualizes the next step, which is related to the question "What do I want instead?" as being aware of possibilities. During this stage of the relationship, the counselor may participate in collaborative brainstorming or serve as a challenger to test the possibilities available to the client. When the client settles on a direction of action, the counselor's role is to help the client develop a plan of action.

During the final action phase, the counselor engages the client in brainstorming again. This additional round of brainstorming has to do with strategies and possible ways of getting to the preferred reality. Action planning results in steps the client can take to reach the goals set in counseling.

Professional counselors work as healers with clients, creating "opportunities for clients to explore issues, take stock of their situations, and make preliminary plans toward self-actualization" (Schmidt, 2002, p. 66). As previously discussed, the personality of the professional counselor is as important to this process as almost any other component of healing (Kottler, 2010). The therapeutic relationship is vital to the healing process. Thirty percent of therapeutic outcome is associated with the interpersonal relationship between the professional counselor and the client (Sperry et al., 2003). In other words, how one interacts with the client is essential to the process of healing.

The professional counselor creates a **climate for change** through the setting and structure of counseling as well as the interpersonal relationship. Counselors create opportunities for reflection and growth by facilitating the client's awareness of possibilities and alternatives. Professional counselors encourage the client's sense of responsibility for acting on one or more of these alternatives (Capuzzi & Gross, 2013). The insight and awareness cultivated in counseling become opportunities; opportunities become choices and actions; these choices and actions create the changes through which healing occurs.

One of the fallacies related to becoming a counselor is that counselors are advice givers. Many of us come into the profession because we have been sought after by friends and family for our ability to problem-solve and give advice. Creating a climate for change is not

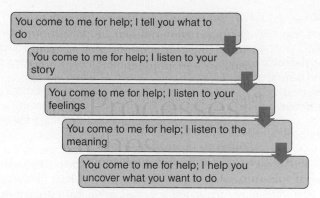

You come to me for help; I tell you what to do

You come to me for help; I listen to your story

You come to me for help; I listen to your feelings

You come to me for help; I listen to the meaning

You come to me for help; I help you uncover what you want to do

FIGURE 5.1 The movement from advice to healing.

advice giving. In fact, most beginning counselors go through the process illustrated in Figure 5.1 from advice givers to listeners to healers.

Role of Theory

To set the stage for successful counseling, a professional counselor must practice from a foundation rooted in theory. Chapter 4 provided a good foundation in theory. But it is insufficient to understand only the techniques and interventions of counseling; professional counselors must also be able to conceptualize why the interventions work. **Theory** helps clarify why we do what we do during counseling. In other words, techniques and interventions are how we counsel, but theoretical orientation drives the choices made by the counselor. Theory impacts the counseling process in that the choice of theory influences the type of counseling needed and provided.

Whether practicing from a humanistic, cognitive-behavioral, integrative, or other paradigm, there is an element common across theoretical orientations. Within counseling theory, the concept of empathy is always present. **Empathy** has been defined as a trait and a state (Hofelich & Preston, 2012). People have the ability to experience empathy as a trait—that is, to place ourselves in the shoes of another and take on that person's worldview or perspective. In addition, we have the ability to convey empathy behaviorally through our words and nonverbal behaviors. This state allows others to understand that we are experiencing them, that we see their perspective.

Professional counselors possess and practice the elements of empathy as we provide services to clients. We rely on a cognitive understanding and practical application of the tenets of one or more theories to provide clients with the opportunities for reflection, growth, and change vital for clients to be successful in counseling.

VOICES FROM THE FIELD 5.4   Different Strokes for Different Folks, by Nicole Adamson

---

The first time I met with a 16-year-old female student at the alternative school, we talked about clothes, hair, and weekend plans. I knew better than to ask her, "What kind of difficulties are you experiencing?" Because of her alternative school placement and legal history, I suspected that she

(Continued)

would not respond well to this type of counseling approach. However, the first time I met with a self-referred teenage girl from a private high school, I asked her about her current struggles, she explained her suicidal thoughts, and we began to uncover the hidden feelings of pain and neglect she was experiencing.

The next time I met with the student at the alternative school, we spent time listening to music, and began to discuss ways she related to the violent, painful lyrics in some of her favorite songs. She shared that her father was in prison, and explained the adversity she faced with the responsibility of caring for her mother and three younger siblings. My second meeting with the student from the private school involved her family as well. We discussed her enmeshed relationship with her mother and the resentment she harbored for her father and brother. Both clients gained significant insight about themselves in relation to their families and the world around them.

Over the course of each counseling relationship, both students were able to identify sources of strength in their own lives and ways that they could overcome the difficulties they faced. Eventually, we were able to begin identifying long-term goals for the clients' lives and applied these same strengths and resources to their future difficulties. Although each counseling process was unique and individualized, both relationships involved an initial meeting, several working sessions, future planning, and termination. When I accepted that each counseling relationship would be different, I was able to truly appreciate the art and creativity involved in the counseling process.

STRUCTURE OF COUNSELING

Let's assume the professional counselor has developed a theoretical grounding; can facilitate helping, healing, empathic relationships; and is operating in a setting conducive to counseling. Now what? The next step in the counseling process is to establish the structure of counseling. **Structure**, explicitly stated and implicitly defined, gives clients and professional counselors a framework within which the practice of counseling can occur. Clients naturally enter counseling with some trepidation regardless of the extent to which they want help. Anxiety is normal when confronted with a counseling need, and helping clients understand what to expect from the process helps to address that anxiety (Cochran & Cochran, 2006). Some elements common to providing clients with the structure and expectations of counseling include assuring informed consent, including discussing fee arrangements, agreeing on frequency and duration of sessions, and explaining what the process will actually look like.

Informed Consent

In Chapter 3, you were introduced to professional ethics in counseling. The ethical counselor has a number of mandates to follow in initiating, developing, maintaining, and terminating the counseling relationship. This section will focus on one critical aspect of that process, informed consent. As you are aware, professional counselors are ethically bound to provide clients with **informed consent** (American Counseling Association, 2014a). Generally, informed consent occurs in the first session and as frequently as necessary thereafter to ensure that clients are aware of and understand their rights and responsibilities within the counseling relationship. Perhaps the most important issue covered in informed consent is confidentiality and its exceptions. This topic was covered in Chapter 3 in detail.

Another topic to be covered in informed consent is the fee charged by the professional counselor for services, including when payment is expected, and whether or not the counselor files the client's insurance. Professional counselors who are comfortable with discussing privacy, confidentiality, and the benefits and risks of counseling may find themselves uncomfortable discussing fees with clients. Money is a difficult topic for most people to discuss, and counselors are no exception (Berger & Newman, 2011). The informed consent process, including a written agreement with clients, can actually ease that reluctance by making it clear and explicit from the beginning of the relationship.

A crucial element in the business of counseling is the frequency and duration of sessions. Most individual sessions last 50–60 minutes, but some sessions may last longer; for example, group sessions are frequently 90 minutes in length. Will the client have weekly appointments? How will appointments be scheduled? What if the client needs to cancel or change an appointment? These issues are best addressed at the beginning of the counseling process. Once clarified, the client and professional counselor can begin to explore fully the reasons for coming in for services. You have probably reviewed copies of informed consent agreements for counseling. Have you considered what you will include in your own practice? Activity 5.8 allows you to begin to put your ideas about informed consent on paper. When your draft is complete, compare it with your classmates' drafts, and see if there are other areas you would like to include. To add to this experience, take a few minutes to try to explain the informed consent document to your classmates as if they were clients. Becoming comfortable with the language of informed consent takes practice, but it is an integral part of the counseling process. Now complete Activity 5.8.

ACTIVITY 5.8 INFORMED CONSENT EXERCISE

Begin to write your own informed consent form. What will it look like when you are ready to see clients? How will you describe yourself? What will you expect of clients? What scheduling and fee arrangements will you propose?

Information Gathering

Most professional counselors employ some form of an intake or psychosocial history in the initial session. An **intake** is simply a means of obtaining comprehensive information about a new client. Relevant information to gather in the first session varies from setting to setting (see Appendix I of Erford, 2013, for a sample intake interview). However, typical areas of an intake or psychosocial history include:

- Client contact information—name, address, referral source, telephone numbers, emergency contact.
- Basic demographic information—age, gender, marital status.
- A general overview of why the client is seeking services at this time—what brings the client to counseling? Why now?
- A description of the history of the presenting concern—how long has this been occurring? Has it ever been any better or worse?
- Family background, including family of origin and family of creation—what was the client's childhood like? What is the current family structure? Does the client have children?

- Any abuse history—have there ever been times when someone has taken advantage of the client physically or sexually?
- Medical history—does the client have any diagnosed medical disorders? Is the client on any current medications? Has the client ever been hospitalized and if so, for what? At what age were the developmental milestones of walking and talking met? Were there any major childhood accidents or injuries? What about alcohol or drug use?
- Level of education—how far did the client go in school? Did he or she fail or repeat a grade?
- Present and past occupational status—is the client currently employed? What is the client's occupational history?

Professional counselors generally also include their impressions and recommendations at the conclusion of the intake. These observations set the stage for treatment planning and goal setting. As stated previously, we are our clients. Use Activity 5.9 to conduct an intake on the client you know best—yourself!

ACTIVITY 5.9 INTAKE EXERCISE

Address, for your own situation, the questions standard to a traditional intake or psychosocial history as outlined in this chapter. Write out your responses to these questions. What might a professional counselor see as significant in your responses?

Once the counseling structure is established, information has been gathered, and a helping relationship has begun, the client and professional counselor begin to explore more deeply the presenting concerns and establish a working relationship conducive to change.

EXPLORING AND WORKING TOGETHER

Throughout this chapter, we have examined the role of the professional counselor and elements of the art and science of counseling. The foundation is set, and the client has entered into counseling. How do we go about the business of counseling? What does the counseling relationship look like?

In the next chapter, you will learn some of the essential nuts and bolts of counseling: counseling skills. The verbal responses of counselors, techniques, nonverbal responses, treatment objectives, and intentionality affect the dynamics of the counseling relationship. As we prepare to address goal setting and client outcome, it is also crucial to explore the relationship levels inherent in the counseling process. Whether in individual, group, or family settings, there exists the real relationship between the client and the counselor and more subtle factors influencing the relationship.

The real relationship is the overt, explicit relationship between the client and the counselor. It includes what is clear, known, and unequivocal about the dynamic between the parties. Although such obvious relationship factors are important, they do not capture some of the more implicit subtleties that occur when complex human beings are in relationships. You may already be aware that communication is not only about what you say (e.g., clear, explicit, overt content), but also how you say it (e.g., subtle, implicit, deeper meanings). The same is true in the counseling relationship. The client and the counselor need more than techniques and textbook counseling responses to effect change. The real relationship is influenced by many additional factors, including transference, counter-transference, and the working alliance.

Transference is a term you have probably heard before. Put simply, **transference** occurs when a client's emotions from a previous experience are projected, displaced, or *transferred* onto the counselor and the counseling relationship. This assignment of feelings to the counselor is unconscious and unrelated to the client's actual feelings about the counselor or counseling. Transference includes thoughts or beliefs that are projected into the counseling relationship as well. A classic example of transference is the adolescent client who "parentifies" his adult female counselor because she embodies similar traits, which may be as simple as age and gender, to his mother.

Countertransference occurs when the projection of beliefs, emotions, or experience is from the counselor to the client. We are aware that as counselors we respect our client's values and cultural ways of being, yet we recognize that we cannot operate without our own value set and personal history. You may be of the opinion that as a professional, you will be able to check your personal "stuff" at the door of your counseling office and prevent it from affecting the relationship. Realistically, that is impossible.

As professional counselors who are also human, we acknowledge the certainty of countertransference in the client–counselor relationship. Imagine being a new professional, fresh out of traditional undergraduate and graduate school, who is approaching work with clients. You are assigned a case in your university counseling center of a woman in her mid-30s who has returned to school to better her employment opportunities and earning potential. A single mother, she has had a string of failed relationships that have interfered with her job stability. You discover that her current relationship is violent at times, and she has fled to the local domestic violence shelter on two occasions to escape her boyfriend's temper.

Many professional counselors facing such a client would find themselves wondering what keeps the client in the relationship. Treatment goals related to protecting her safety and making healthy relationship choices are indicated. If, as the counselor, you had a history of your mother having been in and out of violent relationships, you may carry feelings of fear, shame, anger, or resentment that affect the feelings you have toward this client. You may find yourself being more directive and perhaps critical of her choices. You may find yourself judging her or comparing her to your mother. Although you may believe you have the client's intentions at heart, your personal history would cloud your own objectivity and clarity. Such lack of clarity is an example of the impact of countertransference and an excellent point for counseling supervision. Although largely unconscious, the realities of transference and countertransference are present and affect the real relationship between the client and the counselor.

Another element of the counseling relationship is the **working alliance**. It is generally accepted that the working or therapeutic alliance is crucial to success in counseling (Patterson, Anderson, & Wei, 2014). This alliance is essentially a collaborative environment in which the client and counselor can work and transcends theoretical orientations. The working alliance relies heavily on the interpersonal skills of the counselor and can be a predictor of a successful counseling experience. Professional counselors who are warm, inviting, and interpersonally sensitive may have a natural ability to form a working alliance with clients.

Graduate training programs often offer classes in facilitative skills to teach these basic interpersonal techniques that are empirically supported as beneficial to the counseling relationship. Assessment tools have been developed to measure the working alliance between the client and the counselor. Such measures include the Working Alliance Inventory and the Barrett-Lennard Relationship Inventory. The factors of relationship, transference, countertransference, and the working alliance all affect the ability of the client and counselor to explore and work together.

Much of the relationship is established in the early sessions that direct the course of counseling. During initial sessions, crucial information is gathered that leads to the development of a **treatment plan** or protocol. Anchored in the relationship between the client and the counselor, this assessment of needs and formulation of goals provides the foundation for the counseling work to be done during this stage.

Goal Setting and Positive Counseling Outcomes

Conducting an initial assessment via the intake process was previously discussed in the context of initiating the counseling relationship. A treatment agenda or plan typically emerges from this intake or psychosocial history. A treatment plan should be a standard practice of professional counselors and include overarching goals for counseling that are developmentally appropriate for the client's situation (Patterson et al., 2014). Treatment planning is not an easy task because it requires a complex assessment of the presenting concerns of the client and the theoretical foundation, experience, and ability of the professional counselor.

In addition, periodic assessment of client progress is essential to effective helping. If progress is occurring, do treatment goals need to be altered? Often what seems like the overarching treatment objective for a client changes as more details emerge, and the professional counselor develops a greater understanding of the client's desires and abilities. Ultimately, it is critical to view treatment planning as an ongoing process, rather than a single end product.

How do we know that we are effective as professional counselors? How do we know that our work, reflective powers, and clinical skills have assisted clients in a positive way? How do we know change is occurring? To assess this, we must recognize that change is a process, not a product. Continued assessment is crucial to understanding where the client is in the change process. Treatment goals need to be specific enough to provide a measure of change that the professional counselor and the client can identify, evaluate, and alter as needed. When a goal is reached, and change is noted, it should be celebrated within the client–counselor relationship because a primary responsibility within the counseling relationship is to assess the efficacy of treatment and note any positive counseling outcomes (PCOs). When professional counselors speak of treatment efficacy and PCO, we are talking about how well we have intervened in the lives of clients and been able to resolve the client's need for counseling (Hackney & Cormier, 2012).

Treatment efficacy is not necessarily tied to PCO. It is possible for professional counselors to use effective treatment practices and at the end of the therapeutic relationship not have achieved PCOs in their clients. Instead, treatment efficacy is an issue of truly understanding the maladaptive nature of the human condition and applying theories and techniques to assist clients to reengage their lives in an adaptive way. Treatment efficacy relates to how well you are able to gain knowledge and skills in approaches emanating from affective, behavioral, cognitive, interpersonal, and somatic theories (Hackney & Cormier, 2012). Treatment efficacy also involves the application of this knowledge and skill set.

It is incumbent upon all professional counselors to understand the integrative nature of issues that confound human beings and lead them to seek treatment. Treatment efficacy is constantly challenged as counselors reflect upon and review treatment plans and practices for completeness and consistency or the approach to the client's pathology or issue. Counselors are most effective when they do three things: (a) recognize the best practices available for the issue; (b) become true consumers of research concerning the issue intervened in; and (c) recognize the special skills of the counselors' approach and the particular limitations of clinical paradigms.

Likewise, **positive counseling outcomes (PCOs)** are related to treatment efficacy, but they are not always a result of sound treatment approaches. PCO is a phrase that clinicians use to describe the nature of their intervention and how well their clients have responded to their treatment. Although a PCO is subjective, many colleagues (e.g. Hackney & Cormier, 2012; Oxman & Chambliss, 2003) view PCOs as encompassing the following: (a) clients leave the counseling relationship better able to address the issues that brought them into counseling; (b) clients gain increased insight into their life and the ways in which their life provokes adaptive or maladaptive coping abilities; (c) clients develop a plan (written or verbal) that involves their knowledge of their cues for relapse; and (d) treatment goals are achieved.

When clients have a PCO, it is evidenced in appreciable ways; for example, clients have stopped smoking, or they are not as depressed as they were before they came into treatment. But the reality is that there will be times when client outcomes are not as positive.

What Happens When Change Does Not Happen?

Change is never guaranteed. The best counseling plans, similar to the best professional counselors, do not always result in a client's goals being accomplished. Numerous factors are related to this possibility. To address these factors, let us consider that successful counseling is grounded in capitalizing on opportunity, the relational competence of the client and the professional counselor, and initiative (i.e., the expectation and desire to change).

Opportunity is compromised when clients fail to attend or are chronically late for regularly scheduled appointments (Cochran & Cochran, 2006). Although a structure may be established early in the helping relationship, the structure is not valid if it is not followed. Successful professional counselors are skilled at comfortably discussing changes made to the structure by the client. We realize that it may be the professional counselor who has been absent or late, but we are hopeful that the professional counselor would be more attentive to the needs of the client than that, and would avoid falling into such a trap.

Relational competence is a two-way street. The most proficiently skilled counselors may not be able to reach clients with whom they cannot seem to relate. Personality being crucial to the process, not all professional counselors can reach all clients. You have likely experienced being taught by many qualified, intelligent professors in your college career, and yet it is equally likely that you have learned more from some than others. Why? Those were the instructors you were better able to relate to and with whom you had a more productive learning experience. This same inevitability between teachers and students is true for counselors and clients. What happens when the counselor is approached by a client whose treatment needs are outside of the counselor's boundaries of competence? Think About It 5.6 asks you to consider how you would handle such a situation.

THINK ABOUT IT 5.6

A client comes to you for counseling about a specific issue about which you have no experience or training. How do you express this to the client and facilitate a referral?

Finally, there is the concept of initiative, or conversely, **resistance**. Often, professional counselors assume resistance is the exception, rather than the norm, but realistically some level of resistance is to be expected in all client–counselor relationships. No matter how desirous the client is of help and change, the risk inherent in the process taps our most human defense mechanisms. Sometimes that resistance may be overt, while at other times, it may be more subtle. As we consider the concept of resistance, reflect on the following questions:

- What concerns would you seek counseling to address?
- What might make you uncomfortable seeking counseling services?
- What counselor characteristics would inhibit your willingness to share intimate concerns?
- What cultural influences are present in this concept of resistance?
- As you reflect on your responses, what do you need to consider about your own style of helping that will maximize client initiative?

In the practice of counseling, voluntary and involuntary participants in the counseling process can present as unwilling or reluctant clients. The involuntary clients who may be court ordered or otherwise placed into counseling against their wishes are less likely to join willingly in the process. Professional counselors in such situations are best served by anticipating anger and defensiveness and viewing the emergence of such as an expected development within the counseling dynamic (Leahy, 2012). Openly discussing the circumstances surrounding the counseling relationship is key because professional counselors merely exacerbate the problems that stem from resistance when they pressure clients into participating.

Resistance is to be expected, but it may also be culture-bound. For example, prison inmates receiving counseling services are likely to be resistant and not trusting of the counselor or the process. Although a measure of resistance is expected in a corrections environment, individuals of chronically oppressed cultures (e.g., African American, Hispanic American) show more resistance to counseling than do their white counterparts (Hays & Erford, 2018). Culturally influenced resistance manifests as the result of differences in language, socioeconomic class, and culture-specific value systems. Including cultural resistance in the counselor's approach to working with clients would minimize the impact such resistance has on the process of counseling.

More subtle forms of resistance include the initial defensiveness experienced by clients who begin to reveal secret, difficult, or shameful things to the professional counselor. Frustration and embarrassment may be masked as resistant behaviors as the client becomes less verbal or willing to participate in dialogue about such matters. Clients may be late for, cancel, or miss appointments to avoid the work that constitutes counseling (Cochran & Cochran, 2006). In all situations of resistance, whether subtle or more overt, professional counselors have a variety of options.

In general, it is best to expect and reframe resistance as another way that your client is communicating with you. Resistance to certain topics tells you that you have entered into risky territory for that client, and those topics should be addressed more sensitively. Resistance does not give you license to avoid a particular topic, however, because often the areas that are most sensitive are the areas that need the most work. Understanding client reactions is key to meeting them at their point of need so as to work best with them within their perspective. Relying on the basic skills of attending to your client, creating an open nonjudgmental climate, and showing patience throughout the process increases the client's trust in the professional counselor and the counseling process, thereby reducing resistance.

Some professional counselor behaviors increase client resistance. Giving advice, solving problems prematurely, and relying on questions as the basis of the relationship may be well intended on the part of the professional counselor, but destructive to the therapeutic relationship. Professional counselors who have trained long and hard to earn their degrees, license, or certification sometimes approach their work with a certain formality. To minimize resistance, it is suggested that you be flexible with your interaction style and "[l]ower your rank" (Schmidt, 2002, p. 71). Meet the client at his or her level. Formal addresses such as Mrs. Smithers or Dr. Starkey serve only to elevate and distance you from the client. Use of the professional counselor's first name, regardless of age, is encouraged to bridge this gap between the client and the counselor.

INTEGRATION AND TERMINATION

The ultimate goal of counseling is for professional counselors to work themselves out of their jobs with their clients. Does this mean the profession of counseling is on its way out? Absolutely not! The professional counselor is working with each client to facilitate new learning that is applied and integrated into the client's daily functioning. When that occurs, a natural point of **termination** in the client–counselor relationship presents itself. When a client has developed necessary insight to incorporate real change, and there are no other demands present, the counseling work has come to completion.

While it sounds ideal to reach a point of conclusion in counseling as a result of having met previously agreed upon goals, it can in fact be quite challenging. The counseling relationship is, by its very nature, an intimate one. We generally do not walk away from intimate relationships without some measure of anxiety. Likewise, clients may feel anxious about being "set free from the nest" to manage life without your support. This termination anxiety arises out of a real sense of loss experienced by the client, who has grown to trust and perhaps depend on you as the counselor.

Client termination anxiety may manifest in several ways. Clients may develop new and significant problems as they anticipate the end of the relationship. As a result of feelings of insecurity, they may regress into old patterns of dysfunctional behavior that require continued counseling intervention (Welfel & Patterson, 2005). Clients may experience real sadness or grief around the loss of their relationship with you as a person. Clients often struggle with termination despite their knowledge that it is healthy and desirable. However, not all clients struggle with termination. In general, the end of the counseling relationship is viewed as a positive event by the client and the professional counselor. To illustrate the challenges of termination, consider Case Study 5.2.

CASE STUDY 5.2

Flo, a 43-year-old woman, entered into a counseling relationship with you 9 months ago to deal with the effects of her recent separation after a 17-year marriage. Flo did not want the separation and was devastated by her husband's departure. Childless, she struggled with why her husband left, how to manage her time and her home without him, and feelings of rejection. She reported sleep and appetite disturbance, poor job performance, and isolating herself from her friends. You worked with her on a weekly basis in individual counseling to address her social fears, her feelings of inadequacy, and her anger at her now ex-husband. During this time, she returned to her previous level of functioning on her job, began sleeping more soundly, showed improved eating habits, joined a weekly professional woman's club, and began socializing again with her friends.

Upon assessing her treatment plan, you both concluded that Flo was making significant progress and was no longer experiencing the symptoms that brought her into counseling in the first place. After determining that you would cut back on the frequency of sessions in an effort to transition her out of services, Flo returned to her next appointment and shared with you her fears about terminating counseling. She stated, "I have come so far and I may not make it on my own! Why can't I continue in weekly counseling just in case I have problems that I can't handle on my own?" Consider your responses to the following questions:

- What are the benefits of continuing to work with Flo?
- What are the drawbacks?
- What areas do you see a need to discuss with her?
- What are your feelings about continuing to work with Flo?

Although the focus of Case Study 5.2 is on the client response to termination, professional counselors are not immune to their own anxiety related to this stage in the counseling process. If we are lucky as professional counselors, we will find our work with clients to be personally and professionally rewarding. We will like our clients, we will celebrate their successes, and we will miss them when we are no longer working with them. These termination issues will be difficult for us, but may not be as difficult as another form of termination issue such as the client who prematurely terminates the relationship with us.

Clients will miss appointments, drop out of counseling prematurely, or even declare that the counselor is not a good fit for them. As much as we understand the basis for premature termination on the part of the client, it is still difficult to accept that there is someone whom we have been unable to help optimally. In ideal circumstances, both client and counselor will appreciate and acknowledge the need for termination and plan accordingly for its inevitability.

Termination is simply one of the stages of the counseling process. Professional counselors can take several steps to facilitate termination in the most helpful manner possible. Attending to the client's needs and establishing clear follow-up appointments allows the client to participate in the natural ending of the relationship and establish closure. Reviewing the progress in counseling with a focus on the progress made is key (Welfel & Patterson, 2005). Celebrating the successes and changes as a result of counseling acknowledges the client's efforts and growth. Finally, considering what might lead to a return to counseling, and how the client can go about doing so, empowers clients as they leave your care.

Professional counselors can establish effective working relationships with clients, identify the core concerns, develop appropriate treatment plans, and work from a core foundation of theory to facilitate change with their clients. Gaining the academic and inter-personal skills necessary to become an effective professional counselor takes diligence and effort on the part of the counseling student. In addition, determining if this career path is appropriate for you is part of what an introduction to the counseling profession course addresses.

VOICES FROM THE FIELD 5.5 **Working Within Multiple Systems While Remaining Focused on the Client's Welfare, by Amanda M. Evans**

I worked with a 14-year-old adolescent female who was referred by children's services because of allegations of violent and aggressive behavior. The client was referred to me because those allegations were determined to be unfounded by children's services and the local police.

The client stated that she was an athlete, maintained an A average in school, planned to attend college to become a veterinarian, and had an interest in enlisting in the National Guard to assist with college tuition. The client identified her strengths as "hard working, a good friend, and smart." She reported a desire to participate in counseling to improve her relationship with her mother. Alone, the client presented as appropriate and respectful, and reported a desire to initiate a healthy relationship with her mother. When we invited the client's mother into our session, the mother blamed the client, became argumentative and yelled frequently. I attempted to develop a crisis plan to use when an argument ensued. The mother indicated that she had no interest in discussing a crisis plan. Throughout this portion of the counseling session the client's nonverbal behaviors appeared blunted; she was tearful and withdrawn. A pattern emerged that was repeated in additional sessions. Alone, the client was interactive, appropriate, and insightful. With her mother, the client almost appeared to shut down. I observed the mother become angry, verbally aggressive, and accusatory.

After reviewing the *Diagnostic and Statistical Manual* (DSM) criteria, client reports, personal observation, and client file, I diagnosed the client with a V-code (61.20)—Parent–Child Relational Problems. In the agency where I worked, a V-code would allow me to continue to see the client despite the absence of mental health symptomology. In addition, knowing that this client had an interest in pursuing higher education and possibly military enlistment, I determined that a V-code would provide the forum to discuss and understand the family dynamics without affecting the client's future goals.

Upon sharing the diagnosis with the client and her mother, the client's mother became agitated and insulting. She said that her daughter clearly had "bipolar disorder" and that I was wrong in my diagnosis. I reminded the client's mother that, based on the presenting problem, children's services request, and client reports, my role was to assist the client, which might include interventions to improve family dynamics, verbal communication, and conflict resolution. I reminded the mother and client that they had the right to seek a second opinion, but that my observations of the client did not support a diagnosis of bipolar disorder. It was at this time that the client's mother refused to continue participating in counseling sessions; however, the client chose to continue working with me.

Throughout the next several months, the client pleaded for strategies to remain with her mother, fearing that placement in foster care would damage her peer relationships in junior high

(Continued)

school. Thus, we began working on establishing autonomy. Because children's services was involved in the case and abuse could not be determined, my goal was to assist the client in managing her living situation. We focused on identifying healthy relationships, self-confidence, resolving conflict, and developing independent living skills. I terminated counseling with the client 6 months after our initial appointment. She continued to remain actively involved both athletically and academically in her school. The client reported a "better" relationship with her mother, in part because the client was more prepared in responding to her mother's somewhat irrational behavior. Finally, the client reported better self-understanding and a more peaceful internal state.

This case illustrates the importance of maintaining the client's welfare, despite the client's clearly complicated living situation. My role was to support the client even if that meant upsetting her mother. It can be difficult working with adolescents when multiple stakeholders (e.g., parents, guardians, school personnel) attempt to influence the counseling relationship or outcome. I believe that this counseling relationship was successful because the client was willing to learn skills to help her manage a difficult home life at such a young age. I wish that I would have been more successful with the client's mother, but hopefully by modeling professional behaviors, educating her on my role as a counselor, and not judging the mother's reaction to me, I have planted the seed within the mother to consider counseling for herself when *she* is ready.

BECOMING A PROFESSIONAL COUNSELOR

Many professional counselors enter into the profession for personal reasons. They may have a desire to help others, have had a personally satisfying experience with counseling in the past, be intrigued by how people change, or any combination of reasons. How do you know if the profession is a good fit for your talents, interests, and abilities? Choosing a new field of study as a skilled helper requires students to participate in a discernment process.

Personal Strengths and Challenges

Counselors usually enter into this profession with a natural style of helping on which they can build. Successful professional counselors develop a skill set that includes their personal strengths and addresses their challenges. You will benefit from examining your own ability to provide opportunity and direction for clients without succumbing to a need to rescue them from their struggles. As a professional counselor, you will grow in your treatment efficacy as you recognize that your own ability to address any of your personal unresolved life events aids in your ability to help others. You will, it is hoped, exude a sense of humor, be flexible, and participate in ongoing supervision and wellness efforts. You will observe your comfort with strong emotion and develop a sense of ease when faced with the distress of others. Another self-check in the discernment process will be your ability to develop, create openness with, and have capacity for intimate relationships.

As a student choosing the counseling field, you will find it necessary to judge wisely the fit between you and the profession. What are your areas of growth? How do you open yourself to the process of not only earning a degree in counseling, but truly becoming a counselor? Your attention to this discernment process will allow you to develop fully throughout your career as a professional counselor. Now complete a final reflection (Activity 5.10) on the counseling process.

ACTIVITY 5.10 A FINAL REFLECTION

Throughout this chapter you have been asked to reflect on your understanding of the profession of counseling, the art and science of counseling, and your role as a counselor. As both gatekeepers and gate openers for this profession, we desire to pave the way for students to become professional counselors and offer you this final reflection opportunity. With this culmination activity, take some time to pull all the bits and pieces together and consider in a discerning way your hopes, strengths, and challenges in becoming a professional counselor. Begin with the following suggestions:

- First, seek your own best counsel by spending time in reflection where you listen to your inner voice, gut feeling, or true self that is your personal source of wisdom.
- Talk with others; claim your talents and strengths; and seek counsel from your instructors, your personal counselor, and your peers about your abilities.
- Listen to your gut—where do you feel pleased and certain? About what do you feel unease or discouragement?
- Above all, trust in who you are, and be mindful that life is unfolding for you in terms of what is best for you. As you attend to the information, cues, and signs around you, the choices about your life path will become clearer.

During this time of mindfulness, consider the following questions:

1. How is my awareness of the dynamics of counseling changing through my exposure to graduate study?
2. How confident am I in my ability to acquire and use the skills involved in the art and science of counseling?
3. How are my understanding of, awareness of, and commitment to the fundamental principles of the profession developing?
4. How are my comfort with, and capacity for, intimate relationships changing?

These questions are intended to help you judge wisely the fit between you and the counseling profession and to help you make decisions about opportunities for growth within this discipline. If you encountered answers that you found difficult, exposed areas that you were uncomfortable with, or found matters you were reluctant to consider, these reactions might be an indication that you need to work harder at your choice of counseling as a profession and seek further help in your studies. Reactions that included a sense of peace and determination regarding your professional choice will aid you as you continue in your degree program. Welcome to the profession!

VOICES FROM THE FIELD 5.6   Empathy and Patience, by F. Robert Wilson

During my training as a counselor and psychotherapist, I wanted to develop techniques for producing healthful change for my clients. My training supervisor advised me that the keys to success in relationship building and in the art of therapy were empathy and patience. My supervisor advised me . . . a client taught me.

(Continued)

After her intake, the nurse who prepared my client's initial paperwork and scheduled her for her first appointment with me said, "She's a handful." How true. My first appointment with her was memorable. I intended to conduct a thorough diagnostic interview; she dominated the conversation. She was belligerent, demanding, and loquacious. I wanted to discuss our therapeutic approach; she made it clear: she wanted medications. I got enough information from her to understand she certainly needed help with mood management and with maintaining sobriety. With that initial diagnosis, we set some general goals for counseling and I gave her an appointment to see our psychiatrist to be evaluated for pharmacotherapy. She agreed to come back to see me.

We began weekly appointments. She proved to be both a difficult and an intermittent client. In session, she ranted about dramatic episodes with predatory men, untrustworthy women, "book smart" but "street stupid" teachers, rigid and unsympathetic employers, and racist police officers. Occasionally, she grieved about telephone fights with her mother and the difficulties she had with her son. With each session came a new crisis. From time to time, I offered gentle confrontations or tentative interpretations. She would have none of it. So, I listened, and I listened, and I listened. A pattern developed: after six to eight meetings, she would disappear for a period of time, only to return with new stories of crisis and conflict. Often, I wondered whether I was doing her any good at all.

Months grew to years. Despite my worry about whether I was helping her, she was dependable in her irregularity. In the fourth year of our relationship, after being gone for several months, she appeared and spoke with a formidable singleness of purpose: "I'm not going to talk to you today! You book me an appointment for next week; make it two hours. And you bring your notebook!" She turned and walked out. I booked the appointment.

When we met the next week, she opened our session by saying, "I been bullshitting you for four years! I don't tell my business to Black people, why am I going to tell my business to some old White guy? I'm not going to bullshit you anymore. I've had it with those women in my recovery meetings. They have their own sobriety to worry about. None of them are recovered enough to be a sponsor. I did my first three steps but I have to have someone to sponsor my Step Four. I have got to get on with getting on. Hang on to your ass—you're going to be my sponsor."

And, I heard about it all. About being born in poverty housing. About loving her father and dying inside when her mother ran him off. About hating her sister because she had the light skin and the good hair. About insults and humiliations. About being pregnant when she was still but a child. About her baby being "everybody's baby" because she was too young and wild to care for it. About predators and betrayals, gangs and cops, and surviving in the streets with a knife in her pocket, a knife in her shoe, and a knife down her bra. About high times and bad choices. About finding God and finding sobriety. About finding a new city, finding a job, and finding a home. I heard about it all.

From that point on, our counseling sessions were more like conversations and less like rants. A fierce defender of her autonomy, she rarely asked my opinion, but she began to let me lay a gentle hand on her pain. She didn't bristle at tentative interpretations or cautious confrontations. She used our sessions to talk herself through the environmental and emotional explosions in her life: her longstanding physical ailments and recurrent medical emergencies, her continuing struggles to manage her emotionality and impulsivity, her continuing longing for and disappointment in not being able to reconnect with her son, her struggles to forgive her mother and sister and others for their contributions to her painful childhood, and her struggles with sobriety and her needing but not freely trusting the women in her recovery group.

In a counseling session years later, one day she said, "I gave this city too many years of my life. Maybe someday I'll try somewhere else." I knew she meant, "Good bye." Of course, when I asked, she denied it. Shortly thereafter, she vanished for the last time. Yes, my supervisor had advised me, but this client taught me, as no other had before: Counseling *is* empathy and patience.

Summary

The professional practice of counseling requires training, experience, and an understanding of the complex nature of interpersonal relationships. The client–counselor relationship is affected by environmental concerns such as the setting and reason for services as well as the personality characteristics of the professional counselor. Expectations that the client and the counselor bring to the counseling opportunity constitute an active placebo and affect the process as much as the training, experience, setting, and personality traits of the professional counselor.

Professional counselors hold a basic competence in cross-cultural work. They have an understanding of the basic counseling paradigm under which they operate and are able to integrate cultural influences within this model of helping. This paradigm is foundational for professional counselors in that it is grounded in their view of human nature and how people change, their theoretical orientation, techniques, and choice of interventions.

As helpers, professional counselors practice both the art and the science of helping. The art of helping refers to our ability to recognize client concerns and create a climate for change. This intuitive sense is a focus of our graduate training, while being reinforced and expanded through experience with a diverse client population. In addition, there is a science of helping. As scientist practitioners, we realize the importance of research-driven methods to help our clients best. Whether actual researchers or simply intelligent consumers of our colleagues' research, professional counselors address the art and the science of the counseling profession.

Clients enter counseling for numerous reasons and with many barriers that would keep them from the process. Professional counselors establish an environment and style conducive to creating a therapeutic relationship. Theoretical grounding and an understanding of the interpersonal skills and empathy required to meet clients at their point of need combine to create the greatest opportunity for positive counseling outcomes (PCOs).

The counseling relationship begins with the necessities of informed consent and the information-gathering or intake process. Using the legal and ethical foundation of informed consent, professional counselors set the structure for the work. Intakes or psychosocial histories provide the initial information needed to develop relevant treatment goals with the client. These goals are regularly assessed, with the ultimate goal being to come to a point of termination of services when the work from counseling has become integrated in the client's life. There are challenges within the counseling relationship, however, that may manifest as resistance or even termination anxiety.

For the beginning professional counselor, it is critical to understand that one does not simply receive a degree in counseling; rather, one *becomes* a professional counselor. Students who are beginning this process of becoming a counselor are encouraged to consider the concepts presented in this chapter and text in light of how they see themselves fitting within the profession. A thoughtful discernment process is beneficial throughout graduate training and will set the stage for a productive and satisfying career as a professional counselor.

MyCounselingLab for Introduction to Counseling

Try the Topic 3 Assignments: *Characteristics of the Effective Counselor.*

6 Counseling Microskills

JOSEPH B. COOPER

PREVIEW

This chapter provides an overview of the fundamental skills that constitute the key elements of effective helping relationships. The skills in this chapter focus on the microskills hierarchy (Ivey, Ivey, & Zalaquett, 2013). At the heart of this hierarchy is the basic listening sequence, an interrelated set of skills that not only will foster the development of rapport and a therapeutic alliance with clients, but also will aid in the identification of interventions to help achieve a successful resolution to the client's presenting concerns. Examples of the skills in use and practice exercises to foster individual skill development are provided.

ESSENTIAL COUNSELING MICROSKILLS

This chapter delineates the basic foundational skills involved in effective helping relationships. These skills are the foundational tools on which the success of interventions with a client could depend. They help create the necessary conditions from which positive change can take place. They provide the client with alliance-building constructs, such as empathic understanding, genuineness, and acceptance, and greatly facilitate the development of a safe therapeutic environment.

In addition, these skills aid in establishing rapport with a client. **Rapport** refers to a harmonious or empathic relationship. In helping relationships, the development of rapport starts with the initial contact and continues throughout the counseling process. The professional counselor's primary concern should be fostering this rapport to develop a cohesive and supportive relationship with the client. The development of rapport is crucial for individuals seeking counseling because this might be a client's first encounter with a professional counselor, and this interaction could either encourage or discourage the client from seeking counseling in the future or following up for subsequent counseling sessions.

This chapter focuses on the microskills hierarchy (Ivey et al., 2013). Microskills represent a set of verbal and behavioral responses that facilitate the process of counseling and alliance formation regardless of professional counselors' theoretical orientations. In other words, the skills are atheoretical. This means that these skills are not representative of, or limited to, a specific theory. They can be used across various psychotherapeutic approaches. For example, Gestalt, cognitive-behavioral, and psychodynamic counselors might all use, at one time or another, the technique of *open questions*. However, it is really the specific type of counseling approach, as well as the intention of the counselor, that determines the type, timing, and frequency of the skills used.

Finally, for some students, discussion of these skills might seem like a redundant review of the basic skills taught in a previous skills course. For others, this might be the first presentation of the skills. Either way, it is important to be aware of and practice effective skills continuously because they are the hallmark of effective counseling, and there is always the possibility of implementing ineffective skills over time.

Ivey et al. (2013) present these skills as a hierarchy that is organized within a systematic framework. At the bottom of the hierarchy are the basic attending skills, such as patterns of eye contact, body language, and tone of voice. A bit farther up the skills hierarchy is the basic listening sequence, which includes questioning, paraphrasing, summarizing, and reflection of feelings. Each of these basic skills is reviewed and is paired with practical examples of the skill in use.

ATTENDING SKILLS

Good communication involves more than just verbal content, because professional counselors communicate using more than just words. Much communication occurs nonverbally. The next time you are engaged in conversation with someone, take a moment to pay attention to all the nonverbal cues your partner is giving you. What does his or her facial expression say to you? What is conveyed by the look in his or her eyes? Does he or she have a closed or open body stance? Although important in social relationships, these attending skills are even more important in the counseling relationship.

Bedi (2006) surveyed clients who had received counseling and asked them to identify the specific counselor behaviors that most helped to form a working alliance. Following validation and education, clients ranked nonverbal gestures, presentation, and body language as the most important alliance-building factors. These nonverbal attending behaviors communicate a counselor's interest, warmth, and understanding to the client and include such behaviors as eye contact, body position, and tone of voice.

Eye Contact

Maintaining good **eye contact** is how a professional counselor conveys interest, confidence, and involvement in the client's story (Egan, 2013). Through eye contact, clients know a counselor is focusing on them and is fully committed to the helping process. For clients who have difficulty with closeness, making eye contact can be an important vehicle of change.

Good eye contact is not the same as staring your client down. There should be natural breaks in eye contact; eye contact should be more like an *ebb and flow* as you collect your thoughts and listen to your client's story. Also, it is essential to be sensitive to differences in how eye contact is expressed across cultures. For example, although direct eye contact is usually interpreted as a sign of interest in the middle-class European American culture, some Asian and Native American groups believe direct eye contact is a sign of disrespect (Ivey et al., 2013) Some African Americans might maintain greater eye contact when talking and less eye contact when listening. Many African American males do not look directly into the eyes of an authority figure, because in the black cultural context, avoiding eye contact shows recognition of the authority–subordinate relationship (Bounds, Washington, & Henfield, 2018). Also, for clients who are unduly fragile or under much stress and pressure, direct eye contact could increase their levels of anxiety.

How do you determine how much eye contact to maintain with your client? There is no universal rule or criterion for what is considered either appropriate or inappropriate eye contact; as already noted, this varies among cultures. A good rule of thumb to follow is to maintain a moderate amount of eye contact while monitoring your client's level of comfort and to adjust your eye contact accordingly (Young, 2013). Also, it is helpful for you to become aware of your own nonverbal attending behavior, so you can understand how this behavior might affect the counseling relationship. Use Activities 6.1 and 6.2 to gain a deeper understanding of your own attending behaviors.

ACTIVITY 6.1 EYE CONTACT

Pair up. Name one person the *listener* and the other the *speaker*. Have the speaker talk about anything of interest for about 5 minutes. During this time, have the listener maintain eye contact as he or she normally would in everyday conversation. After 5 minutes, take some time to process the experience. What feedback does the speaker have regarding the listener's level of eye contact? Was it too much? Darting? Too little? Empathic? What was most comfortable? Based on the feedback, do the exercise again. This time, though, have the listener try to incorporate some of the feedback received about the level of eye contact. Process the activity again, and then switch roles.

ACTIVITY 6.2 NONVERBAL MIRRORING

The purpose of this exercise is to become aware of how your clients might perceive your overall pattern of nonverbal communication (Okun & Kantrowitz, 2014). In this exercise, break up into pairs facing one another. Name one person the *communicator* and the other the *mirror*. For the next 5 minutes, the communicator can talk about anything he or she wants. Throughout this time, the mirror is to silently mirror the communicator's gestures, facial expressions, eye contact, and movements. The mirror does not attempt to "interpret" the message that is being sent by the communicator; he or she is only to mirror the perceived nonverbal cues. At the end of the 5 minutes, process this experience with each other. Then switch roles and repeat. What was it like to see your nonverbal cues mirrored back to you? Did you learn anything about how you come across to others? Is there anything you would want to change, increase, or decrease?

Body Position

As with eye contact, **body position** should convey to the client your interest and involvement. Face the client and adopt an open, relaxed, and attentive body posture; this position will assist in putting your client at ease. Counselors should not cross arms and legs and should not sit behind a desk or other barrier. In addition, Egan (2013) recommends the professional counselor should slightly lean in the upper body toward the client, because this communicates that the counselor is listening to the client and is interested in what the client has to say. Slouching in the chair or leaning away from the client could be perceived by the client as a lack of interest or boredom on your part.

Finally, the physical distance between you and your client should be taken into consideration; getting too close can be overwhelming and uncomfortable, whereas too great a distance can make you appear aloof and might be awkward for the client. Although in Western cultures the average physical distance for conversation is typically two to four feet, this *comfort zone* will vary from client to client (Young, 2013). When in doubt, a good idea is to let your client decide the distance by offering to let your client arrange the chairs at an individual comfort level. Counselors should also be aware of client and counselor personal-space issues and set up personal-space boundaries.

Vocal Tone

Have you ever been engaged in conversation with someone and found yourself becoming increasingly anxious and tense, regardless of the topic? The next time this happens, pay attention to your partner's tone of voice, because you might be unconsciously responding to the emotional tone conveyed in your partner's voice. Emotions are frequently conveyed via **tone of voice**. The pitch, pacing, and volume all can have an effect on how a client responds emotionally to a professional counselor. There is much to be said for a calm and soothing voice in times of distress, especially when the client is in a crisis situation. Do not underestimate the power of this attribute. Your control and calmness might be a great benefit to your client.

Your voice can do much to create a soothing and anxiety-regulating atmosphere for the client. Learn to use your voice as a therapeutic tool. For instance, if your client is unduly agitated, it is often effective to speak more slowly and in a soothing tone because this will help your client to slow things down and begin to focus. Also, to convey a sense of empathic understanding, it can be beneficial to give emphasis to the specific words used by your client. This technique of giving increased vocal emphasis to certain words or short phrases is called **verbal underlining** (Ivey et al., 2013). For example, consider the difference between *You were very hurt by your husband's actions* and *You were **very** hurt by your husband's actions*. In the latter sentence, the counselor places the emphasis on the word *very* to help reflect the intensity of the client's experience. Activity 6.3 will help facilitate a greater awareness of the vocal subtleties in the spoken word.

ACTIVITY 6.3 VOCAL TONE

In small groups, assign one person to be the *speaker*. Instruct the speaker to talk in a normal tone of voice for a few minutes about anything of interest. Have the other group members close their eyes as they listen to the speaker, paying close attention to the speaker's tone of voice, pacing, and volume. After 2 or 3 minutes, stop and have the members give the speaker feedback on the speaker's vocal qualities. What were their reactions to the speaker's tone, volume, accent, and rate of speech? After this processing, repeat the exercise. This time, though, have the speaker adjust his or her tone, volume, and/or pacing. How do the members respond to the speaker's changes to his or her vocal qualities? What emotional responses from the members corresponded with the speaker's various vocal tones? Finally, have the members imagine themselves as clients in counseling. What types of vocal qualities would they prefer to hear?

VOICES FROM THE FIELD 6.1   Listen with Your Eyes!, by JBC

My supervisor once told me to work on "listening with my eyes." What did he mean?

The content of a client's story—what he or she tells you, when something happened, what he or she did next, and so on—is very important. But if that is all you focus on, you'll be missing a wealth of nonverbal communication. Paying attention to *how* a client says something as well as his or her *shifts in posture* when talking about a certain issue, *eye contact* with you (or breaks in contact), subtle *body movements* and their timing, etc., can communicate so much about how a client feels and what he or she believes is important.

If you practice listening with your eyes, your understanding and rapport with clients can grow exponentially. Give it a try. By attending to your client's attending behavior, you can tap into a whole different world of communication.

Finally, Egan (2013) developed a useful conceptual framework to aid in remembering the nonverbal listening process as described above. He used the acronym *SOLER* to describe these skills. Skill Practice 6.1 describes this framework.

SKILL PRACTICE 6.1

Name of Skill: SOLER

Definition: A set of nonverbal listening stances used in active listening to demonstrate your involvement with your client (see below).

Purpose of Skill: To convey to your clients a stance of "being with" them, both psychologically and physically. Helps to convey genuineness and respect toward your clients while putting them at ease.

Tips: Reflect to yourself the extent that your posture communicates availability and openness to your clients, and adjust accordingly. Observe yourself on video during counseling role-plays. Relax!

SOLER:

S: Squarely face your clients. Sitting facing clients gives the impression of attentiveness and involvement.

O: Open posture. An open posture can show that you are available to listen, while crossed hands or legs can convey unavailability. Sitting with your hands either by your side or resting on your lap if you are writing things down is appropriate.

L: Lean (slightly) toward your clients to convey your interest and involvement with them.

E: Eye contact: Maintain appropriate and culturally sensitive eye contact to convey your interest and involvement.

R: Relaxed. Try to be relaxed and natural with your clients. This helps to put them at ease. Fidgeting or maintaining a rigid stance can convey the impression you are not comfortable with your clients.

BASIC LISTENING SEQUENCE

The **basic listening sequence** represents a set of interrelated skills used to achieve three overarching goals: (a) to obtain an overall summary and understanding of the client's presenting issue, (b) to identify the key facts of the client's situation, and (c) to identify the core emotions and feelings the client is experiencing (Ivey et al., 2013). In short, these skills allow you to understand the structure of your client's story. Through the use of these skills, not only will you convey empathy, respect, warmth, and congruence to your client, you will also be setting the foundation for your understanding of the client's issues and the development of subsequent interventions to help achieve a successful resolution to those issues. The skills involved in the basic listening sequence include open and closed questions, paraphrasing, reflection of feelings, reflected meaning, and summarizing. An explanation and overview of these skills, examples of each skill in use, and some brief exercises to help you practice these basic listening skills are provided.

Open and Closed Questions

Questioning is a primary skill that allows professional counselors to gather important and specific information about clients. Questions allow us to make accurate assessments of clients' issues and guide and focus clients so we can make the most effective use of counseling sessions. However, the use of questioning can be a double-edged sword. Used inappropriately, questioning can impede communication and block client disclosure. Drilling clients with questions can assume too much control by the professional counselor. Bombarding clients with questions could confuse and frustrate them and increase their levels of anxiety.

Professional counselors definitely do not want counseling sessions to sound like interrogations. The counselor must be careful to pace the questions appropriately to guard against increasing the client's stress level. Professional counselors need to be aware of how to use questions appropriately and pay close attention to the types of questions used to gather information. The two types of questions examined here are open and closed questions.

OPEN QUESTIONS Open questions usually elicit fuller and more meaningful responses by encouraging the client to talk at greater length. Open questions typically begin with *what*, *how*, *could*, *would*, or *why* and can help begin an interview, draw out the client's story, or bring out specific details (Ivey et al., 2013). With open questions, the client can choose the content and direction of the session. Open questions give more control to the client. Consider the following examples of open questions:

1. **To begin an interview:** *What would you like to talk about today? How can I be of help to you today? What have you come in to discuss today?*
2. **To elicit details:** *What would be an example? What do you mean by "just give up?" What do you usually do when you are feeling down?*
3. **To enrich and deepen:** *What else can you tell me about that? What were your feelings when that happened? What else is important for me to know?*

As you can see from the examples, these questions allow room for the client to respond in myriad ways. How he or she responds depends on the needs and intentions of the client in the here and now of the counseling session. Herein lies the power of open questions: The client, and not the counselor, has the choice to determine the content and the direction of counseling.

Be careful when using *why* questions and questions that are leading in nature. Questions that begin with *why* often cause the client to intellectualize and can lead to a discussion of reasons, or to the client rationalizing his or her problems, when what we really want him or her to do is explore the deeper meaning and feelings behind the issues. In addition, *why* questions can cause the client to become defensive and to feel put on the spot. When this happens, it is common for the client to become more guarded and shut down. For example, think back to a time when you were a child and your parents asked, "Why did you do that?" How did you feel, and what was your reaction to them? Take a moment to consider the responses *Why do you hate yourself?* and *You say you hate yourself. Help me understand that.* Which of these approaches would you prefer your professional counselor use?

Another roadblock to the use of effective questions involves questions that are leading in nature. A leading question often contains a hidden agenda because its answer or expectation is already *embedded* within the question. Although well intentioned, these types of questions place too much power in the hands of the professional counselor and tend to push the client in a preconceived direction. Here are a couple examples of leading questions: *You didn't really want to kill yourself, did you? Don't you think that if you stop drinking, you will feel better?* Notice how the answers are already contained within the questions. Try to guard against using leading questions. Professional counselors want to hear a client's story as the client understands and experiences it. Open questions allow the chance to achieve this end without imposing values and expectations on the client.

CLOSED QUESTIONS   Closed questions can be used when professional counselors need to obtain specific concrete information and get all the facts straight. **Closed questions** typically elicit *yes* or *no* responses or specific factual information, such as the number of drinks a client consumes in a week or the age a client first began experiencing symptoms. In this respect, closed questions are useful and necessary in professional counseling because the counselor must often gather specific information to aid in the assessment of the problem and the development of a treatment focus (James & Gilliland, 2012). Consider the following examples of closed questions:

- Are you thinking of killing yourself?
- When did these symptoms begin?
- Do you have a family member or friend to call on when you are feeling overwhelmed?
- How old were you when your parents divorced?
- On average, how many days a week do you drink?

As can be seen from these examples, closed questions are good for obtaining the necessary details to aid in assessment and intervention. However, one must guard against the overuse of closed questions. Use of too many closed questions can cause the client to shut down and become passive because, in essence, you are training the client to sit back and wait for the next question to answer. A good rule of thumb to follow is to move from the general to the specific in your assessment. In other words, begin with open questions (i.e., general), and as you gather information and hear the client's story, move to more closed questions (i.e., specific) to obtain the specific details important for the assessment and the subsequent intervention plan. Another good rule of thumb is to never ask a question to which you do not need the answer.

The following dialogue provides a brief example of how the professional counselor uses a blend of open and closed questions to obtain important information about Janice, who recently discovered that the company she works for will be closing operations, which will leave her without an income.

JANICE: I've gotten to where I can't even focus at work. My mind just races, and I can't stop thinking about everything.

COUNSELOR (C):   You say your mind is racing and you are having lots of thoughts. Tell me more about some of the thoughts you have been having. (*Open statement/question to facilitate exploration and information gathering*)

JANICE:	That I will never be happy with another job and that I have wasted my time working for this company. I also wonder how I can ever find another job at my age. This is really painful to consider.
C:	You wonder if you will find a satisfying job again and want so much for this pain to go away. (*Empathic paraphrase*) Tell me more about some of the feelings you have been experiencing. (*Open statement/question*)
JANICE:	Mainly down—angry and depressed. I feel this tremendous pain inside my chest—very hurt and sad I guess. I just don't know what my life is going to be like in a few months, and that is scary.
C:	You're feeling very hurt and also worried about your future. It is scary. Janice, can you tell me when you began experiencing these symptoms? (*Closed question to identify time line of symptoms*)
JANICE:	I would say about three months ago, when I found out my company was going out of business. But really, my symptoms have gotten much worse over the last month.
C:	You say they have gotten worse over the last month. What do you make of that? (*Open question to identify client's understanding of her progressing symptoms*)
JANICE:	Well, when I first found out about this, I would talk a lot with my friends and family. But I felt like they were getting sick of hearing me complain all the time, so lately I have just been trying to tough it out and deal with it on my own.
C:	And is this the first time you have sought counseling for this?
JANICE:	Yes.

As this example demonstrates, the professional counselor began with open questions to encourage exploration and to help identify the client's thoughts (e.g., "I will never be happy with another job") and feelings (e.g., anger, grief, fear) associated with the impending loss of her job. The professional counselor then moved to closed questions to obtain more specific information regarding the duration of her symptoms and her experience in counseling.

OPEN VERSUS CLOSED QUESTIONS   As mentioned earlier, professional counselors often need to use closed questions to identify and bring out specific details to aid in assessment and treatment planning. However, one can often obtain the same information by asking open questions; try to refrain from moving too quickly into a closed-questioning approach, unless you are unable to obtain the information otherwise. Consider the following examples of closed questions and their open-question counterparts:

CLOSED: Were you afraid?
OPEN: What feelings did you experience?
CLOSED: Are you concerned about what you will do if your husband returns?
OPEN: How do you think you *might* react if your husband returns?
CLOSED: Do you see your drinking as a problem?
OPEN: What concerns do you have about your drinking?

Notice in these examples that a subtle change in the questions' wording to make them more open is likely to bring out all the information, and more, the professional counselor needs to know. Complete Activity 6.4 for some additional practice. Then complete Think About It 6.1 and Skill Practice 6.2.

THINK ABOUT IT 6.1

When is it appropriate to use closed questions? How would you decide, based on the content of your client's narrative, whether to ask a question, or to use a reflecting skill?

ACTIVITY 6.4 CREATING OPEN QUESTIONS

Change the following leading questions from closed to open questions.

1. Why did you quit your job?
2. Do you think you should stop using drugs?
3. Do you get eight hours of sleep a night?
4. Did you feel angry with him?
5. Can you tell me about other ways you can cope with your anger?

SKILL PRACTICE 6.2

Name of Skill: Questions (Open and Closed)

Definition: Skill used to gather important information and to guide and focus the session. Two types are open questions and closed questions.

Purpose of Skill: To gather information, begin a session, encourage elaboration, elicit examples, focus the session, and encourage the client to communicate and open up. Questioning also aids in assessment, treatment planning, and goal setting.

Tips: Be careful of using "why" questions, or questions that are leading. Do not ask too many questions in a row. Only ask a question for which you need the answer.

Examples: "What are some examples of times when you lost your cool?" (*Open question*)

"At what age did you first begin having panic attacks?" (*Closed question*)

Appropriate Use	Inappropriate Use
Counselor (C): Tell me what brings you in today. (*Open lead*)	Counselor (C): "How's it going?" (*Open question, yet a poor way to open a session. Conversational tone instead of a therapeutic tone.*)
John: Well, I have been using alcohol a bit too much lately, and my wife has been worried about my drinking, too. So, we thought it best to come in and see if I needed to get some help.	John: Things have been better. I have been using more alcohol lately, and my wife has also been worried about my drinking. So, I thought it best to come in and see if I needed to get some help.
C: So your use of alcohol recently has been a concern for you and your wife. (*Paraphrase*) In what ways is it a concern for you? (*Open question*)	C: Does your wife drink too? (*Closed question, not relevant at this time in the session*)

John: Well, I used to drink about two times a week, but lately I have been drinking almost every day! It usually starts when I get home from work, and I drink up until I go to bed.

C: And how much alcohol are you consuming each time you drink? (*Closed question to elicit relevant information about his use of alcohol*)

John: (Sighs) I'm embarrassed to say this, but I often will drink six or seven drinks at a time now. Usually beer. I just have trouble stopping after a couple.

C: So you are finding it difficult to stop after one or two drinks, and feeling ashamed about this. (*Reflection of feeling related to his alcohol intake*)

John: I really do.

C: In addition to what you have said, what else concerns you about your drinking? (*Open question to elicit more information*)

John: Well, my wife said that she cannot live with a drunk. And I was so hung over the other day that I called in sick to work. This was the second time this month I have called in sick from being so hung over.

C: So your drinking is really affecting important areas of your life. (*Paraphrase*) What do you hope to achieve in our work together? (*Open question*)

John: Nope, but she thinks I drink too much. And maybe she's right.

C: Why do you think you drink too much? (*"Why" question can cause defensiveness*)

John: I don't know. Maybe I don't drink too much and she is blowing things out of proportion!

C: Do you think your wife might need some therapy too? (*Closed leading question, not relevant and focused on the wife*)

John: Probably, she is a pretty uptight person. Maybe she should start drinking some!

C: Did your parents have a drinking problem? (*Closed question, not relevant at this time. We still have no idea about the specifics of our client's alcohol use.*)

John: Mmmm, maybe. (*Client is becoming closed off due to overuse of closed, leading questions*)

C: Do you notice you are being vague with me? (*Closed question, in the form of a confrontation. This can increase client's defensiveness.*)

John: Not really. I am not sure what my parents have to do with this.

Reflecting Skills

The **reflecting skills** represent a set of interventions used to help stimulate clients' explorations of their thoughts and feelings related to the presenting problems. Reflecting skills serve many important purposes. At the most basic level, they are a form of active listening that conveys to the client your interest in and understanding of what the client might be struggling with. These skills allow you to convey empathy, genuineness, and acceptance to the client, and this facilitates the creation of a sense of safety. They also stimulate a deeper exploration and understanding of the problem, so the client can examine the issues more objectively. The reflecting skills covered in this chapter are paraphrasing, reflecting feelings, reflected meaning, and summarizing.

PARAPHRASE   A professional counselor feeds back to a client the essence of what has just been spoken in a **paraphrase**. By paraphrasing, the counselor reflects the content and thoughts of the client's message. In other words, the professional counselor is mirroring back to the client, in a nonjudgmental way, an accurate understanding of the client's communication and the implied meaning of that communication. A paraphrase is a reflecting skill used to convey empathic understanding and to facilitate the exploration and clarification of the client's problems (Young, 2013).

The counselor should ensure that the paraphrased information is accurate by checking in with the client. For example, after your paraphrase, you might simply ask, *"Is that about right?"* This checking in also allows for the building of a collaborative relationship between you and your client and conveys your interest and care in accurately understanding his or her message. Inaccurate paraphrasing without affirmation by the client could inaccurately define the primary presenting problem, which could change the direction of the session or interfere with the development of the most appropriate treatment plan for the client. Young (2013) proposed that reflecting skills fulfill numerous important functions, including being:

- a verbal way to communicate empathy;
- a form of feedback that enables the client to confirm or reject the impression he or she has been giving;
- a way to stimulate further exploration of what the client has been experiencing; and
- a way to capture important aspects of the client's story that might have been overlooked or covert. (pp. 106–107)

The paraphrase, if used appropriately, is a powerful counseling tool. Appropriate use means a professional counselor must have the ability to take the essence of a client's statement and reflect back the client's thoughts and facts in the *counselor's own words*. When the paraphrase is used accurately, the client continues to explore and elaborate. Do not parrot back to the client word for word what has been said. Parroting back would be a simple restatement, not a paraphrase. For example:

JOAN: I feel so put down and disrespected by my husband. He is just like my father in a lot of ways. He was verbally abusive and full of anger. I never really felt important to him. Why do I let men treat me this way?

C: Your husband is like your father in a lot of ways.

In the above paraphrase, the professional counselor simply parrots back what the client has said, which adds little and keeps the focus superficial. A better response might be the following:

C: Although you are trying to understand this pattern of hurt and disappointment you have experienced from the important men in your life, it sounds like you are also blaming yourself for this.

To facilitate your skill development in using the paraphrase, you might find it helpful to first identify the key words or themes that capture the essence of your client's concern. When you have the key content in mind, try to translate it into your own words.

Consider the following examples of client statements, possible key themes or words, and resulting paraphrases:

EXAMPLE 1

Client: I am so fed up with my marriage. I try and try to get through to him, and he just shuts me out.

Possible key themes or words: *Fed up, being shut out, failed efforts to connect*

Paraphrase: You are at your wit's end with this. Despite your efforts to connect, you come up against a closed door. Is that correct?

EXAMPLE 2

Client: Exactly, and that is why I have been thinking about leaving him. I know I deserve much better, but I just keep going back to him. I can't seem to make that first move.

Possible key themes or words: *Leaving her husband, being stuck, hesitation, self-worth*

Paraphrase: Although a part of you knows this is not the way you want to live your life, it is still difficult to break out of this cycle.

As demonstrated by the examples, identifying the key words or themes can aid in your ability to develop accurate paraphrases that convey the essence of your client's meaning without coming across as superficial. Use Activity 6.5 to practice your paraphrasing skills. Then complete Skill Practice 6.3.

ACTIVITY 6.5 PARAPHRASING

Below are some client statements. Try to identify the key themes or words. Then, based on the key words, develop a paraphrase of the client's statement.

1. I don't know what to do with my life. I hate my job, and everything seems so meaningless. I can barely muster the energy to get out of bed in the morning. Sometimes, I just want to sleep for days.
2. I am still in shock that my husband is having an affair. I really can't believe it. I thought we had the perfect marriage. How could I have been so stupid not to see this was happening? I feel like such a fool.
3. I can't tell if I am coming or going. I can't sleep, I have nightmares, and I feel like a zombie throughout the day. I am so tense my body aches. No matter what I do, it just keeps getting worse.

VOICES FROM THE FIELD 6.2   Fighting My Instincts, by JBC

Clients often come to counseling in crisis. They might feel overwhelmed or confused, think they are going crazy, or, in more serious cases, feel suicidal or homicidal. In these situations, our tendency is to try to fix the problems by being overly directive, giving advice, or drilling such clients with questions.

However, I have found that doing the opposite is key. In other words, using reflecting skills in these situations can go a long way toward helping clients become more emotionally regulated with you. Simple paraphrases, reflecting feelings, and reflecting meaning can help clients to feel understood, accepted, and safe. And I have found that clients are more likely to take the risk of changing when they feel safe with you.

SKILL PRACTICE 6.3

Name of Skill: Paraphrase

Definition: Reflecting skill used to repeat back a distilled version of the facts and thoughts of a client in a nonjudgmental way.

Purpose of Skill: To convey empathic understanding and facilitate the exploration of the client's problems. To identify aspects of the client's experience that may not be stated explicitly.

Tips: Identify the key words or themes of your client's narrative. Do not parrot. Translate paraphrase into your own words. "Check-in" for accuracy.

Examples: "You want to learn ways to better assert yourself. Correct?"

"Your father's death was unexpected."

Appropriate Use	Inappropriate Use
Susan: When I started using drugs, I just dismissed her (best friend) from my life and stopped talking to her, and as I got clean, I recently tried to reconnect to her, to be friends again, but she didn't seem interested.	Susan: When I started using drugs, I just dismissed her (best friend) from my life and stopped talking to her, and as I got clean, I recently tried to reconnect to her, to be friends again, but she didn't seem interested.
Counselor (C): So when you started getting sober, you wanted to reestablish a healthy relationship to your old friend, yet you found her to be hesitant to do so. (*Paraphrase reflects content and keeps the focus on the client*)	Counselor (C): When you started using drugs, you dismissed your friend. (*Parroting—simply repeats content and does not add anything. Keeps the focus "surface"*)
Susan: Yes, exactly. She was not very interested in that, and so I just wanted to go out and start drinking again.	Susan: Yes but she was not very interested in that, and so I just wanted to go out and start drinking again.
C: When you experienced her as being distant with you, this brought up those old urges to use again. (*Paraphrase and keeps the focus on the client*)	C: And your friend didn't realize how her behavior makes you want to use again (*Focus is on the friend and not the client. This is speculating about someone not in the room.*)
Susan: It really did. This is part of my disease. I started to think, "she should be over it by now." My expectation is that "you need to get over it!"	Susan: I know. And I think, "she should be over it by now." My expectation is that she needs to get over this!

C: So you were feeling angry toward her when you experienced her as distant (*Reflection of feeling related to specific event and keeps the focus on client*)	C: That must be tough when she acts this way (*"Tough" is vague and does not convey a specific feeling. Overall unclear intervention and keeps focus on her friend and not the client.*)
Susan: Yes! I felt angry toward her because she didn't want to be bothered! This is a problem I have that I need to change. I just hold on to resentments and having trouble letting go.	Susan: Yes it is tough for me. I just hold on to resentments.
C: So being able to "let go" and move past resentments is something you really want to work on. (*Paraphrase— highlighting positive goal and therapeutic task*)	C: You hold on to things. (*Minimal paraphrase and a vague general comment. Needs to be more specific to the content client has presented.*)
Susan: Absolutely. I think that is one area I have, for so long, really struggled with. I just hold on and hold on, getting more and more upset with people.	Susan: I guess so. What do you mean?
C: This pattern has been around for a long time for you. (*Paraphrase*)	C: You hold on to things, you hold on to resentments and such, and you can't seem to get over it, and you keep finding that other people are misunderstanding you and you get upset (*Paraphrase is too long and confusing*)
Susan: It has. I remember being this way even in middle school.	Susan: Yea, some people drive me crazy.

REFLECTING FEELINGS   A wealth of research attests to the usefulness of accessing and working with feelings and emotions in counseling (Greenberg & Pascual-Leone, 2006). Naming and identifying a client's feelings can serve many important functions. By **reflecting feelings**, a professional counselor can help the client become aware of the emotions experienced in relation to the issue at hand. Reflecting feelings can bring the client to higher levels of self-awareness and can deepen self-disclosure (Young, 2013). In addition, reflecting feelings can have a positive impact on the therapeutic relationship, and a convincing amount of research has shown the quality of therapeutic relationship to be one of the strongest predictors of counseling outcomes (Horvath, Del Re, Fluckiger, & Symonds, 2011).

It is not the specific theoretical approach of the helper but the strength of the therapeutic relationship that is more associated with the successful achievement of the client's counseling goals (Erford, 2015c; see Chapter 17). The therapeutic relationship is characterized by an experience of mutual liking, trust, and respect between the client and the helper. In addition, such helper qualities as accurate empathy, unconditional positive regard, and genuineness greatly contribute to the development of the helping relationship (Young, 2013). As with the paraphrase, reflecting feelings can promote the development of accurate empathy and help to create a safe environment for the client.

To reflect feelings, the counselor must be able to recognize and put words to the feeling states observed in the client. What is the best way to practice this? One way is to work on becoming more aware of your own feelings and being able to identify and name your feelings accurately. In turn, this awareness will help you to recognize and accurately name the feelings the client might be experiencing. For example, in my counseling-skills class,

TABLE 6.1 Core Feelings and Related Continua

Core Feeling	Continuum of Core Feeling
Joy	*Pleased, pleasant, happy, cheerful, euphoric, ecstatic, overjoyed, elated*
Anger	*Frustrated, annoyed, irritated, aggravated, bitter, irked, mad, irate, furious, enraged*
Shame/Guilt	*Embarrassed, guilty, mocked, humiliated, shamed, responsible, mortified*
Sadness	*Sad, glum, unhappy, down, blue, hurt, downhearted, grieving, somber, mournful, despondent*
Fear	*Anxious, afraid, uptight, worried, tense, agitated, apprehensive, frightened, panicked, terrified, frantic*
Disgust	*Sickened, revolted, put-off, disgusted, repelled, revulsion, nauseated*
Excitement/Interest	*Bored, interested, curious, engrossed, fascinated, delighted, jubilant, thrilled*
Surprise	*Amazed, shocked, stunned, shaken, puzzled, astonished, perplexed*
Calm	*Relaxed, satisfied, peaceful, soothed, safe, comfortable, tranquil, at ease*

I will walk around the class and ask each student to tell me how he or she is feeling *right now*. The most common responses I receive are "fine," or "okay." Notice, however, that these are not feelings and do not provide me with any understanding of what my students might be really feeling. Then I explain the importance of being able to identify and name correctly not only the core feelings we all experience as humans (e.g., anger, sadness, fear, surprise, joy, love, disgust), but also the moment-to-moment feeling states that represent the finer shadings of the core emotions. For example, some of the finer shadings of anger are irritation, bitterness, rage, frustration, and sullenness. By increasing your feeling awareness and feeling vocabulary, you will be able to identify and respond more easily and correctly to a client's feelings. Table 6.1 provides a cursory listing of some of the core feelings we all experience, and the finer shades that help us to better understand human emotions.

A common mistake in reflecting feelings is to either overshoot or undershoot the feeling expressed by the client (Young, 2013). **Undershooting** is when the professional counselor reflects a feeling that is less intense than the feeling expressed by the client, and **overshooting** is just the opposite. The counselor overshoots when he or she reflects a feeling that is more intense than the feeling expressed by the client. For example, if a client says, "My sister showed up 20 minutes late for dinner last night. This is typical of her; she always makes us wait," and your reflection of feeling is, "Wow, you felt *enraged* at your sister," you are probably overshooting the feeling. Conversely, if your response is, "You must feel slightly annoyed with your sister," you are probably undershooting. A more precise reflection might be, "You felt angry at your sister for being late again." We want to adequately mirror what our clients are feeling and not minimize the feelings or make them more than they really are.

How do you identify the feelings your client is experiencing, especially if the feelings are not explicitly stated? These feelings may also be found in the context of the client's communication or inferred from the client's nonverbal behaviors (e.g., facial expression, posture). To identify feelings, it is important to attend not only to what is being said, but also to *how* it is being communicated. Consider the following practical tips (Evans, Hearn, Uhlemann, & Ivey, 2011; Ivey et al., 2013):

1. **Identifying a client's feelings**
   a. Pay attention to the affective component of the client's communication.
   b. Pay attention to the client's behavior (e.g., posture, tone of voice, facial expression).
   c. Use a broad range of words to identify the client's emotions correctly.
   d. Silently name the client's feeling(s).

2. **Steps for reflecting a client's feelings**
   a. Use an appropriate introductory phrase (e.g., *sounds like, looks like, you feel, it seems*).
   b. Add a feeling word or emotional label to the phrase (e.g., *It sounds like you are angry*).
   c. Add a context or brief paraphrase to help anchor or broaden the reflection (e.g., *you feel* _____ *because* _____). This context should add the link or meaning for the perceived feeling (e.g., *It sounds like you are angry at your father because of his refusal to put you in his will*).
   d. Pay attention to tense. Present-tense reflections can often be more powerful than past-tense reflections (e.g., you *feel* angry versus you *felt* angry).
   e. Do not repeat the client's exact words (i.e., parroting).
   f. Reflect mixed emotions when appropriate (e.g., *You are feeling both angry and hurt about your father's behavior toward you*).
   g. Check out the accuracy of the reflection of feeling with the client (e.g., *Am I hearing you correctly? Is that close? Have I got that right?*).

For example,

MIKE: I just sit around the house wondering what to do. We used to spend time with my wife's friends, but now that she is gone, there is no one for me to spend time with. I really miss them, and my own friends seem so busy. I would hate to bore them with my problems.

COUNSELOR: You are feeling both sad and lonely right now, and you are concerned you might be a burden on your own friends. Is that about right? (*Reflection of feeling with check for accuracy.*)

MIKE: Yes, I don't want to bring everyone down with all my problems.

There is one last point to consider when reflecting feelings. If you are presented with a client in a crisis state, you should guard against going too far with uncovering feelings or keeping the primary focus on feelings because this could exacerbate the client's crisis state by overwhelming him or her with emotion. In such cases, strive for a balance of skills to build rapport. And when you do reflect feelings, be sure to keep the focus directly related to the client's presenting concerns (James & Gilliland, 2012). Complete Think About It 6.2, Activity 6.6 and Skill Practice 6.4 to practice identifying feelings so you can develop accurate reflections of feelings.

THINK ABOUT IT 6.2

How comfortable are you with feelings—both your own and those of others? Are there certain feelings you tend to avoid? If so, how might this affect your work as a counselor?

ACTIVITY 6.6 REFLECTING FEELINGS

Read each vignette, and identify the feelings embedded within the client's communications. When you have identified the feelings, develop your own reflection of the feelings.

1. I don't know what to do. My husband keeps working late into the night, and I feel like I never get to see him. When we do get some time together, he is moody and reserved. To make matters worse, I saw a charge on our credit card statement to a local hotel. I think he might be having an affair.
2. Ever since I was mugged, I've been having a hard time. Because of the nightmares, I can't sleep at night and am exhausted all during the day. On top of that, I am panicky and nervous all the time. I worry I might be losing my mind.
3. I can't believe what my father did. He stole all the money from the trust fund Grandmother had willed to my brother and me. I have been calling him day and night, and he will not return my calls. I might have to get a lawyer, but I don't know how I am going to afford it. Why would he do this to us?

VOICES FROM THE FIELD 6.3   Reflection of Feeling, by Larissa Carpenter

When used appropriately, reflection of feeling can create an immediate increase in rapport, helping clients to feel validated and understood. I find it helpful to pay close attention to the client's body language, facial expressions, and tones of voice in assessing what feelings the client is trying to communicate to me. I also try to attend to and match the intensity of the emotion the client is conveying, taking care never to minimize a feeling that might be strongly experienced. Clients often express a strong positive response when both the feeling and its intensity are reflected accurately.

SKILL PRACTICE 6.4

Name of Skill: Reflection of Feeling

Definition: Reflecting skills are used to reflect the feelings and emotional experience of your client. The feelings can be either directly stated by the client, or inferred through content or nonverbal cues.

Purpose of Skill: Conveys empathic understanding, builds the alliance, and facilitates the exploration and processing of the client's emotions. Aids clients in identifying their emotions.

Tips: Pay attention to client's nonverbal cues (tone of voice, facial expression, body posture). Strive for accuracy—don't overshoot or undershoot feeling; pay attention to affective component of client's narrative. Silently ask, "Given what my client is saying, how might I feel?" Add context to anchor the feeling.

Examples: "You feel angry about your demotion at work"

"You are feeling hopeful this relationship might be the one"

Appropriate Use	Inappropriate Use
Monica: I'm really having a problem with my husband lately.	Monica: I'm really having a problem with my husband lately.
Counselor (C): Tell me about that . . . (*Open lead*)	Counselor (C): So, you are feeling like your husband is causing problems (*"Feeling like" is not a feeling, but a thought. The reflection is off-base by blaming the husband.*)
Monica: It is the way he deals with stress. When he is stressed out, he gets extremely controlling around the home and with me, and I start getting uptight too!	Monica: Not always, it is just the way he deals with stress. When he is stressed out, he gets extremely organized and controlling around the home, and I start getting uptight too!
C: So when he gets overly controlling like this, you react by feeling anxious yourself. (*Reflection of feeling—anxiety*)	C: You feel uptight. (*Parrot reflection—adds no context/feeling link*)
Monica: I do, and then I notice my stomach always starts to get upset, like I want to throw up.	Monica: I do, and then I notice my stomach starts to get upset.
C: When you feel anxious and tense, your stomach also reacts with nausea. (*Reflection of feeling—linking anxiety to physical symptoms*)	C: Are you eating a balanced diet? (*Closed question is off topic*)
Monica: It really does, every time. And then he will lecture me and talk down to me too, like I am a child (angry look on her face).	Monica: I believe I do. Anyway, then he will often lecture me and talk down to me too, like I am a child (angry look on her face).
C: And you also feel angry at him because you don't like being lectured to. Is that correct? (*Reflecting feeling anger-based on both content and facial expression, and check-in for accuracy*)	C: I bet you feel enraged being treated like a child. (*Overshooting feeling*)
Monica: Absolutely. I hate it. It really hurts because I never feel close to him anymore (looks down, sad affect).	Monica: Not enraged, but I don't like it, it really hurts, because I don't feel close to him anymore (looks down, sad affect).
C: As you say this, I see a sad look on your face. In addition to anger, it looks like you are also feeling sad and hurt about this. (*Using immediacy to reflect mixed feelings*)	C: If I were you, I would feel a little bad about that. (*Minimizing feeling, "bad" is not a specific feeling. Counselor is telling the client how she should feel versus reflecting the feeling back.*)
Monica: (Nods head and begins to cry.)	Monica: Maybe so.
C: This is a very painful feeling right now. (*Empathic attunement by mirroring painful feeling*)	

REFLECTING MEANING   As humans, we are continually making meaning about our lives. Questions such as *What is the purpose of my life?* and *What really means the most to me right now?* are ones you have probably asked yourself at one time or another. Although meaningfulness is often associated with the life-changing events in our lives, such as the death of a loved one, divorce, or the loss of a job, even the little events in our lives are imbued with meaning.

Moreover, the meanings we attribute to the events, and not the events themselves, determine the impacts the events have on our lives (Seligman, 2009). For example, let's say you are seeing two clients who both work for the same company and who just found out their contracts will not be renewed next year due to budget cuts. The first client might become very depressed or suicidal, interpreting this life event as a personal failure. Meanwhile, the second client might be relieved and see this event as a unique opportunity to find a new direction in life. As you can see, the meaning people make of life events is often the driving force of human behavior. This is why reflection of meaning is such an important skill, because it really tries to capture the essence of how a client makes meaning about his or her life and how this information can be used to identify the focal point for the client.

You can think of reflection of meaning as a way to help clients go deeper into their stories and begin to see how the meanings they construct are significant in shaping their views about themselves, others, and the world. If a paraphrase captures what happened in a client's story and a reflection of feeling captures the client's emotional experience, then the reflection of meaning seeks to answer the question, *What did it mean to you?* For example, let's say a client named Susan comes to you and says, "I am so upset. I just found out they are cutting funding to our program, and I am being laid off. I have two weeks to find a new job, and I have no idea what to do. My children will be devastated because I will not have any money to buy their Christmas gifts." You have a number of choices for interventions here. If you paraphrase, you might say, "You just found out you are being laid off, and this will make it very difficult for you to provide Christmas gifts for your children." A reflection of feeling might be, "You are feeling angry and hurt that your job position is being taken away so suddenly." Both are decent reflections regarding the client's statement, but could you go deeper? Ask yourself, *What does this really mean to the client?* or *What is really important to her about this event?* and try to reflect the answer back to her. You might say, "I also get the sense that the loss of your job is painful because your children mean so much to you and it is important for you to provide for them and be able to bring joy into their lives." See how this statement—in contrast to paraphrasing and reflecting feeling—captures the essence of her issue? This statement invites the client to go deeper to further explore how this event affects her sense of self and what is most important to her.

Because meaning represents a cluster of thoughts and feelings grouped around a central theme or underlying construct that aids in organizing one's experience, reflecting meaning can help our clients work through their thoughts and feelings to better find themselves and the directions in which they want to go (Ivey et al., 2013).

How to Reflect Meaning

Reflecting meaning can be a difficult skill to master, because it often requires you to read between the lines and look for what is implicit in the client's story. Most clients will not come right out and tell you the meaning of events, so you will often have to rely on your best intuition or hunch (Young, 2013). But as with any other skill, reflecting meaning can be learned and mastered, and the examples and suggestions below can help to develop your reflection-of-meaning skills.

First, it is useful to know some key words that will help you begin to discern the meaning of your client's narrative. These words are *value, beliefs, importance,* and *meaning* (Ivey et al., 2013). As you listen to your client's story, ask yourself, *What does this mean to my client?* or *What is really important to or valued by my client?* This will help you to uncover some of the meaning in your client's narrative. Let's return to the previous example of Susan. Ask yourself, *Given what she has just told me, what are her core values underlying this job loss?* Answers could include commitment, being a good parent, responsibility, safety, care, and concern for her children. Thus, you now have some ideas to go on to aid you in making a reflection of meaning. Using these ideas, you might say, "The safety and care of your children is of the utmost importance to you."

Second, Young (2013) suggests using a formula to aid in learning how to reflect meaning. This formula is very similar to the reflection-of-feeling formula, which is *You feel* _____ *because* _____. In the first blank, you place the feeling, and in the second blank, you place the paraphrased content or context. For example, *You feel devastated because your parents found drugs in your room.* The formula for reflecting meaning is very similar, except the second blank reflects the underlying meaning instead of the paraphrased content. Thus, the reflection-of-meaning formula is *You feel* (specific feeling) *because* (the personal meaning). In an example of the parents finding drugs in the client's room, first ask yourself, *What does this mean to the client?* or *What values are at play here?* Answers could include trust and respect. Now plug these answers into the reflection-of-meaning formula: *You felt devastated when your parents found the drugs because you jeopardized their trust in you.* This statement relies on the hunch that the client's parents' trust is what is important to him or her.

Third, Seligman (2009) suggests professional counselors differentiate between a reflection of feeling and a reflection of meaning. Recognizing the links between a client's meaning, thoughts, and feelings will help you present that information to the client. Consider the following examples:

Client experience 1: Her best friend has died.

Reflection of feeling: You feel grief and pain.

Reflection of meaning: You have lost someone who was an important part of your life.

Client experience 2: Her boyfriend canceled a weekend trip with her.

Reflection of feeling: You feel angry and hurt.

Reflection of meaning: Your time with your boyfriend means a lot to you.

Client experience 3: His parents found drugs in his bedroom.

Reflection of feeling: You feel ashamed.

Reflection of meaning: You value your parent's trust and respect.

Finally, you can also use open questions with your client to help elicit meaning as you work to develop your ability to reflect meaning. This is especially helpful with clients who are not really verbal or open about themselves. Open questions can take different forms, but their overall purpose is the same, which is to aid in the client's identification and exploration of meaning. Here are some examples (Ivey et al., 2013):

1. What about this situation has upset you?
2. What does this mean to you?
3. What values underlie your actions?
4. What are some reasons you think that happened?
5. What are some examples of the values that are important in your life decisions?
6. What about this is most important to you?

As you can see from the preceding examples, numerous ways exist to discern meaning in a client's narrative. Skill Practice 6.5 is an example of a client in crisis who has not been able to sleep and who is also suffering from severe anxiety. He requested an emergency counseling session. Here the counselor probes for and attempts to reflect meaning to him. As you read, pay attention to the client's responses to the counselor's interventions to identify whether the interventions were on target.

SKILL PRACTICE 6.5.

Name of Skill: Reflection of Meaning

Definition: Reflecting skill used to reflect the personal meaning and impact of an event that the client is sharing.

Purpose of Skill: Takes the focus of the session to a deeper level. Helps clients to identify how they create meaning around life events, and the impact this has on shaping their unique worldview.

Tips: Be patient and let the client's narrative unfold. Ask to yourself, as you listen to your client's narrative: "What is it that is meaningful or important to my client right now?"

Examples: "You feel angry because your father has been distant, and being close to him is important to you."

"You are feeling ashamed because you believe you have failed in your role as a supportive husband."

Appropriate Use	Inappropriate Use
MIKE: I just can't sleep at night anymore. My mind races and races all night. I feel like I am going crazy.	MIKE: I just can't sleep at night anymore. My mind races and races all night. I feel like I am going crazy.
C: What are some examples of the thoughts you are having when your mind is racing? (*Open question*)	C: Do you think you are "crazy?" What does "crazy" mean to you? (*Leading questions, double-barreling question. Counselor needs to wait and gather more information first from his client.*)
MIKE: Well, basically, I just feel so insecure with my girlfriend. I worry she will break up with me, and even though I know it is irrational, I just can't shake the feeling that she will.	MIKE: Well, I don't know. I mean, I just feel all out of sorts these days, and can't get my mind to slow down.
C: And this is causing you to feel so much anxiety and worry that you have not been able to sleep. (*Reflection of feeling*)	C: And not slowing down and "out of sorts" means you are going crazy? (*Not a reflection of meaning. Closed question using the word "mean" to lead the client.*)
MIKE: Exactly, and I am sure it is related to past relationships, too. Almost every girlfriend I've had has cheated on me. I just have difficulty trusting women.	MIKE: I am not sure. . . . I really just have a problem trusting women. (*Client tries to help counselor get back on track.*)
C: It seems like trust and security in a relationship are very important to you. (*Reflection of meaning*)	C: I wonder if this means there could be a problem with trusting me as well? (*Closed, leading question, not a reflection of meaning. Counselor needs more information first.*)
MIKE: They really are. And I want to trust her, but she has been more aloof and distant with me lately. And when that happens, I find these old insecurities coming back, even though she says everything is fine.	MIKE: I don't know about that. I feel pretty relaxed with you. But, I just have been dealing with a lot of stress, and my girlfriend is very aloof.

C: What does it mean to you when you find her being distant? (*Open question probing for meaning*)

MIKE: That she does not respect me or is not concerned about me. It seems like I am not that important to her. It really gets me angry, too.

C: So in a relationship, care and respect from your partner are core conditions for you. (*Reflection of meaning*)

MIKE: Yes.

C: And when you do not experience these needs from your partner, you become angry and worry the relationship is going to come to an end because it also brings up some old relational wounds. (*Brief summary*)

MIKE: I know; it really is all about respect and security, and I am not getting that from her right now.

C: And I wonder if this means you tend to blame others for your insecurities? (*Leading question that is based on little context or information. Counselor is blaming the client.*)

MIKE: I don't think so. The fact is, she does not respect me or is not concerned about me. It seems like I am not that important to her. It really gets me angry, too.

C: So you are feeling a little bit confused about all of this. (*Inaccurate and vague reflection of feeling.*)

MIKE: Mmmmm, I am not sure. I feel confused right now.

C: And so what this means is that you feel insecure too, and this is what makes you feel "crazy" inside. (*Ignores client. Counselor presses his own agenda on the client.*)

MIKE: I don't know; it really is all about respect and security, and I am not getting that from her right now.

In this example, the counselor started with an open question followed by a reflection of feeling. The client responded positively to these interventions and provided the counselor with more information, allowing the counselor to infer meaning and reflect meaning back to the client. This was followed by a meaning question to continue to elucidate the meaning behind the client's presenting problem. Based on his positive response and the fact that he continued to explore and open up more, we can infer that the counselor's interventions were on the mark. This example also highlights an important sequence to keep in mind when reflecting meaning. Begin first by asking open questions and using minimal encouragers to obtain the specifics of the client's story, and then make an effort to reflect feelings. From there, you can ask yourself, *Why is my client telling me this now?* or *What does this mean to him or her?* When you have enough of the story, you can attempt to reflect meaning. Take your time. Often, meaning has to unfold before you can reflect it back with accuracy, and using your microskills paves the way for this to happen.

VOICES FROM THE FIELD 6.4   Reflecting Meaning, by JBC

Reflecting meaning often requires you to make a hunch about meaning and reflect it back to your client. It requires you to reflect something that is often not explicitly stated. Many beginning counselors are hesitant to do this, because they believe they are putting words in their clients' mouths. But keep this in mind: Your client's response to your reflection will let you know whether your reflection of meaning hit the mark. In my experience, clients light up, widen their eyes, and agree with you when your reflections of meaning are on target. And they continue talking. When you are off base, though, their reactions are flat at best. Interventions that are on the mark create energy and movement in the session, whereas those that are off the mark leave the session feeling stagnant.

SUMMARIZING   The final skill in the basic listening sequence is summarizing. By **summarizing**, a professional counselor can begin to put together the key themes, feelings, and issues the client has presented. By distilling the key issues and themes and reflecting them back to the client, the counselor can begin to help the client make sense of what might have originally seemed to be an overwhelming and confusing experience. In addition, when a client is feeling overwhelmed and is flooded with anxiety, he or she often goes in many directions and on many tangents, making it difficult for the professional counselor to keep up. When this occurs, brief summaries are often useful to help refocus the client and reintroduce some structure to the session, which helps to modulate the client's (and counselor's) anxiety.

When should a professional counselor summarize? Although much depends on the client and the content being discussed, Evans et al. (2011) offered useful guidelines to help determine when a summary is in order: (a) when your client is rambling, confused, or overly lengthy in comments; (b) when your client presents numerous unrelated ideas; (c) to provide direction to the interview; (d) to help move from one phase of the interview to the next; (e) to end the interview; and (f) to provide an opening to the interview by summing up the prior interview.

When making a summary, you do not have to report back to the client every single detail disclosed. This would require a prodigious memory. The key is to capture the important elements, content, feelings, and issues and reflect them back to the client in a concise manner. There are three common types of summaries.

1. **Focusing summaries** are often used at the beginning of the session to pull together prior information the client has given and to provide a focus for the session. For example: *Last time we met you were having trouble sleeping, you were having nightmares, and you were feeling panicky throughout the day. We identified some coping skills and relaxation exercises for you to use. Tell me how that has worked out for you so far.*
2. **Signal summaries** are used to signal to the client that you have captured the essence of his or her topic and that the session can move on to the next area of concern. This helps to provide structure and direction to the session. For example: *So before we move on, let me make sure I understand things correctly. You discovered your husband is having an affair . . .*
3. **Planning summaries** help to provide closure and are used to recap the progress, plans, and any recommendations or agreements made. These summaries are good for ending the session on a positive note and to provide a sense of direction for the client. For example: *"Let's take a look at what we have covered today. Ever since you were mugged, you have been having panic attacks and nightmares. We covered some coping techniques and relaxation exercises for you to practice between now and the next time we meet . . ."* (Young, 2013, p. 149–151)

To put it all together, here is one more example of a summary statement: *Let me see if I understand you correctly. Yesterday you found out your son has been using cocaine for the past 6 months and has stolen money from you on a number of occasions. You are experiencing a mixture of feelings, especially shock and anger, and you are worried he might turn out to be an addict as your father was. However, you are determined to do all you can to not let that happen to him. Let's discuss some possible directions we can go from here.*

This summary captures key issues and feelings without being too wordy and offers a transition for the counselor and the client to begin identifying some action steps to take.

The following example dialogue between Heather and the professional counselor demonstrates the skills of paraphrasing, reflection of feelings, and summarizing:

HEATHER: I really thought things were going well with my husband, so this came as a complete shock when I found out about the affair.

C: You were really blindsided by this. (*Paraphrase*)

HEATHER: Exactly! And I have been trying to push away the pain, but I can't seem to stop thinking about it. I just want to strangle him for putting me through this.

C: Even though you want so much for the pain to go away, it is still there, especially your hurt and anger toward him. (*Paraphrase with a reflection of feeling*)

HEATHER: Yes, and sometimes I can't tell which is worse, my anger or just the hurt I am going through. I sometimes lie in bed at night and wish something terrible would happen to him. I am not saying I want to kill him or anything, but I just want him to suffer like I am suffering.

C: And this reflects the intensity of your grief right now, wanting to see him suffer, too. (*Reflection of feeling*)

HEATHER: Very true.

C: So in essence, you never expected something like this to happen to you. You were blindsided, and this came as a complete shock. You are feeling very angry and hurt about what has happened, and it has been difficult for you to tough it out and push away the pain and grief you have been feeling. Is that about right? (*Summary with check for accuracy*)

VOICES FROM THE FIELD 6.5   Applying Microskills to the Real World, by Nicole Adamson

---

When I first began to learn the basic counseling skills, I loved to practice them at school and with my family and friends. I used to provide knowledge and advice to my loved ones, and through my training, I was able to generate gentle challenges and explore their private logic. I was pleased with my ability to help others in this unique way, and one of my closest friends was obviously pleased as well. Every time we got on the phone to chat, she brought up a recurring problem, and I was inclined to practice my skills. Each time we met to have lunch or go shopping, she dominated the conversation with her distress. I began to notice that I was unable to tell her about any of my own worries or concerns.

After a couple months of this pattern, I realized I had gotten myself into a tough situation. I wanted to help my friend with her difficulties, but I did not want to be her counselor; I wanted to be her friend! I realized I was going to need to separate my friendships from my professional relationships, and I explained to her that I was no longer going to exercise my counseling skills with her. Although it took some time, we were able to return the relationship to a cooperative friendship in which we both talked freely about our lives. However, I began to feel some guilt about not using my counseling skills to help her in the best way I knew how.

Although it was necessary to reduce the use of my counseling skills in my personal relationships, I realized I can never turn off my counselor knowledge. So I practiced regulating it. When

(Continued)

my friend was experiencing great distress, I would identify discrepancies and confront her irrational beliefs. But most of the time, I just used my empathic listening skills sprinkled with some humor and strategic commentary to help my friend get through her difficulties. In this way, we never explored her difficulties to the extent that my own needs were ignored. I found that this balance of maintaining a relaxed friendship while still staying true to my counselor roots has allowed me to flourish as a helper in my professional and personal relationships.

Summary

In this chapter, the basic counseling skills used by professional counselors were reviewed. Use of these skills aids in the development of the counseling relationship with the client and greatly facilitates the creation of a safe therapeutic environment. The nonverbal attending behaviors, such as eye contact, body position, and tone of voice, communicate interest, warmth, and understanding to the client. In short, be sure to face the client and adopt an open, relaxed, and attentive body posture while maintaining culturally appropriate eye contact with the client. The counselor's tone of voice should be steady and clear and should be used to convey a sense of safety, warmth, and security for the client.

The skills covered in the basic listening sequence include open and closed questions, paraphrasing, reflection of feelings, reflected meaning, and summarizing. The basic listening sequence allows the gathering of important information about the client's issues and facilitates the development of trust and rapport. Finally, the basic listening sequence allows the professional counselor to pull together the key issues to begin the collaborative process of determining a plan of action for the client. Open and closed questions are the skills used to gather information, aid in assessment, and

provide a focus and direction to the session. Paraphrasing is a reflective skill used to mirror back to the client, in a nonjudgmental way and in one's own words, an accurate understanding of the client's communication and the implied meaning of that communication. Similar to paraphrasing, reflection of feelings is a reflective skill used to convey to the client an understanding of the client's emotional experience. Through this awareness, reflecting feelings can bring the client to higher levels of self-awareness and can deepen self-disclosure. Reflecting meaning goes even deeper to explore and highlight what is most important to the client, the meaning of the events in the client's life and how that meaning affects the client's sense of self and others.

Finally, summaries put the pieces together to begin to help the client make sense of what might have originally seemed an overwhelming and confusing experience. Summaries can also help keep the session focused, give direction to the interview, and provide closure to the session by reviewing the progress, plans, and any recommendations or agreements made. The basic skills covered in this chapter are fundamental for effective counseling. Using these skills appropriately creates the necessary conditions from which positive change can take place.

MyCounselingLab for Introduction to Counseling

Try the Topic 3 Assignments: *Characteristics of the Effective Counselor.*

SECTION THREE

Client Issues and Advocacy

Section Three, "Client Issues and Advocacy," explores the knowledge, skills, and attitudes required of the counselor when working with clients across the life span and with common presenting problems (e.g., substance use, eating disorders, behavioral difficulties, crisis intervention), as well as multicultural competence, consultation, and supervision. Chapter 7, Crisis Prevention and Intervention," recognizes that crises, suicide, and homicide continue to play increasingly important roles in American society and on the world stage. Suicide and homicide affect us personally as we, family members, friends, and those in extended social networks struggle with the ever-increasing challenges of modern life. The effectiveness of the care given by professional emergency first responders, as well as the effectiveness of ordinary people in responding to their own crises and the crises of those about whom they care, is improved by background knowledge involving current trends in and treatments for suicide and homicide impulses.

Chapter 8, "Mental Health Counseling," provides a broad overview of the general mental health settings and client issues (i.e., drug and alcohol counseling, mental health counseling, career counseling, and rehabilitation counseling). The field of counseling is becoming increasingly specialized, with certifications and licensures available for addictions counselors (National Certified Addictions Counselor [NCAC]; Master Addiction Counselor [MAC]), mental health counselors (Licensed Professional Counselor [LPC]—term may vary depending on the state), career counselors, and rehabilitation counselors (Certified Rehabilitation Counselor [CRC]). Although these areas are not distinct, and clients may enter counseling with a mental health, substance abuse, career, or rehabilitation issue, or any combination of the four, it is important for professional counselors to have a basic understanding of each area.

Chapter 9, "School, University, and Career Counseling," describes the unique characteristics of working as a professional counselor in the increasingly multicultural settings of elementary and secondary schools; college and university campuses; and career counseling.

Chapter 10 "Human Development Throughout the Life Span," briefly describes developmental characteristics of infancy and toddlerhood (birth to age 3 years); early childhood (ages 4 to 6 years); middle childhood (ages 6 to 11 years); early adolescence, mid-adolescence, and later adolescence (ages 11 to 24 years); young adulthood (ages 24 to 40 years); middle adulthood (ages 40 to 60 years); and later adulthood (ages 60 years and older). The information in these approximate age categories serves as a basis for examples of interventions that helping professionals can use to facilitate development at several of these stages.

In Chapter 11, "Multicultural Counseling," applications are reviewed to help students integrate principles of cultural diversity into the counseling process from the beginning of their training. This chapter features multicultural applications of identity development and counselor competency. Cultural identity developmental processes and culturally specific information and intervention strategies are presented across the cultural dimensions of socioeconomic status, race, ethnicity, gender, sexual orientation, spirituality, ability level, and age.

Chapter 12, "Assessment, Case Conceptualization, Diagnosis, and Treatment Planning," reviews each of these major counseling tenets. Assessment is the systematic gathering of information to address a client's presenting concerns effectively. A case conceptualization reflects how the professional counselor understands the nature of the presenting problems and includes a diagnostic formulation. Treatment plans outline counseling outcomes expectations and interventions to meet these expectations.

In Chapter 13, "Supervision and Consultation," an introduction is provided to help students understand the theory and practical applications of these two essential counselor roles. In particular, supervision helps counselors-in-training understand how to get the most out of their relationships with supervisors and helps counselors-in-training understand what will be expected of them as future supervisors to the next generation of counselors-in-training. Models, techniques, types of activities, and important skills used to fulfill the role of consultant or supervisor are presented.

An innovative facet of this text is the integration of advocacy counseling and the introduction of professional advocacy strategies. Chapter 14, "Advocating for the Counseling Profession," answers important questions about advocacy counseling, including: "What does it mean to advocate for the counseling profession?" "Why is professional advocacy important?" "In what ways can professional counselors advocate for the profession?" Counselors can best serve their clients by advocating for a strong professional presence in the public and legislative venues. A positive view of the counseling profession by citizens and legislators helps remove barriers for clients and promotes the worth and dignity of diverse individuals.

In addition, obtaining social justice for clients demands that professional counselors understand and practice advocacy counseling according to the standards developed by the ACA. Chapter 15, "Advocacy Counseling: Being an Effective Agent of Change for Clients," proposes that the core purpose of advocacy counseling is to address external barriers that interfere with human development. Although this purpose can be met by advocating for the profession of counseling, it is often met by advocating at the individual client level. Through an examination of the advocacy competency domains, specific guidelines are provided on how to increase clients' empowerment and how to be a successful advocacy counselor.

7

Crisis Prevention and Intervention

Judith Harrington and Charlotte Daughhetee

PREVIEW

Crises occur in a variety of settings for a variety of reasons. Responses to crises can come in various forms and can include multiple levels of complexities. In this chapter, basic frameworks for assessing and conceptualizing crises are presented, along with a discussion of how crisis intervention may differ from traditional counseling. Specific emphasis is given to suicide and threat assessment. The effectiveness of the care given by professional emergency first responders, crisis counselors, as well as the effectiveness of ordinary people responding to their own crises and the crises of those about whom they care, is improved by background knowledge involving current trends in and treatments for suicidal and homicidal impulses and the aftermath if it occurs.

CRISIS THEORY

Cole, Hayes, Jones, and Shah (2013, p. 472) define a **crisis** as "an event outside the range of normal human experience which would be markedly distressing to anyone." It is imperative that all professional counselors have knowledge of crisis intervention since crisis events happen in every setting. Crises can include expected events such as an anticipated death, or an unexpected event such as a tornado or a murder. Jackson-Cherry, McGlothlin, and Erford (2018) stressed that three components are needed for an incident to be considered a crisis: (a) a precipitating event, (b) a perception of the event that leads to subjective distress, and (c) diminished functioning when the distress is not alleviated by customary coping resources. Crises can include traumatic events, distress over personal problems, developmental transitions, and psychopathology (Sandoval, 2013). Whatever the nature of a precipitating crisis event, it is essential that counselors be prepared and knowledgeable about appropriate crisis prevention and counseling interventions.

VOICES FROM THE FIELD 7.1   Assessing Clients in Crisis, by Doreen S. Marshall

The assessment and management of clients in crisis is an essential competency for professional counselors to develop given the nature of our work. In particular, familiarizing oneself with the language of suicide assessment—knowing what questions to ask and how to ask them comfortably—may be the most important skill a counselor can develop. New counselors often fear that asking directly

(Continued)

about suicide may have a negative impact on the client or the counseling relationship, a myth that often hampers prevention efforts. It is vital that new counselors explore their reactions to working with suicidal clients before they are faced with a client in crisis so that they may respond in a caring and competent way.

One way to increase your competency is to learn more about suicide and suicide risk from the professional organizations that support the understanding of suicide and suicide prevention. The American Association of Suicidology (AAS; www.suicidology.org) is an interdisciplinary organization that includes mental health and public health professionals, researchers, crisis center volunteers, students, and others affected by suicide in prevention efforts. AAS hosts an annual conference that highlights the latest research related to suicide prevention, intervention, and aftercare. The American Foundation for Suicide Prevention (AFSP; www.afsp.org) is dedicated to understanding and preventing suicide through research, education, and advocacy. Each year, AFSP hosts an International Survivors of Suicide day where those who have lost family and friends to suicide come together to support one another and learn more about the experience of suicide. The Suicide Prevention Resource Center (SPRC; www.sprc.org) is a federally funded center that provides information and training to those wishing to learn more about suicide prevention and supports state prevention efforts. Each of these organizations is actively involved in prevention efforts and encourages professional counselors to take an active role in suicide prevention.

According to Parikh and Morris (2011), the development of crisis theory originated in the wake of the Cocoanut Grove nightclub fire of 1942. Three psychiatrists, Eric Lindemann, Alexandra Adler, and Gerald Caplan, worked with and studied the fire survivors and their families. Their work refined the use of grief counseling and also led to an understanding of what would become known as post-traumatic stress disorder (PTSD). Most importantly, Caplan identified the crisis as the effect of the event and not the event itself (Jackson-Cherry et al., 2018). That is, in the case of the Cocoanut Grove fire, the fire itself was not the crisis but the grief and trauma reactions experienced by survivors and family members following the fire constituted the crisis. In particular, Caplan put forth the view that a crisis is a state of disequilibrium that an individual experiences after a precipitating event. Individuals in a state of crisis may require external resources and support to find balance again. Sandoval (2013) states that the breakdown of coping that occurs during the state of disequilibrium is the point at which crisis intervention is needed, and the advancement of client emotional, cognitive, and problem-solving coping is the desired outcome of crisis intervention.

Ultimately, there is the opportunity for crisis survivors to experience personal growth following a crisis. Successful resolution of crisis events can enhance an individual's confidence, self-efficacy, and problem-solving skills when faced with future crises. Conversely, inability to cope with crisis and a history of feeling overwhelmed can lead to lack of a sense of empowerment in future stressful events (Corey & Corey, 2016). Therefore, the importance of appropriate crisis intervention cannot be overstated if survivors of crisis are to restore functioning and rebuild their lives.

The concept of **psychological first aid (PFA)** is a significant element of crisis theory and intervention. Ruzek, Brymer, Jacobs, Layne, Vernbert, and Watson (2007, p. 17) define PFA as "a systematic set of helping actions aimed at reducing initial post-trauma distress and supporting short and long-term adaptive functioning." The purpose of PFA is to provide support directly following a trauma event and offer immediate assistance as well as to mitigate subsequent and long-term effects from the trauma. There are eight core actions associated with PFA: (a) contact and engage affected individuals, (b) provide comfort and safety, (c) stabilize and calm, (d) assess and gather information, (e) address immediate needs, (f) connect client with social supports, (g) provide information on coping, and (h) link client to services for the future. PFA supports crisis survivors in the immediate aftermath of a crisis and provides support for initial recovery and long-term restoration of wellness. While more research is needed on the efficacy of PFA, there are indications of its helpfulness. Development of specific PFA resources and guidelines show promise (Hambrick, Rubens, Vernberg, Jacobs, & Kanine, 2014).

Crisis counseling support is usually galvanized as soon as possible following a crisis event, as research indicates that immediate intervention is critical to long-term favorable outcomes. Dyregrov and Regel (2012, p. 273) support early intervention and state "Early intervention may help in forming adequate appraisals and counteracting misunderstandings and misperceptions, whereas not intervening may lead to the consolidation of maladaptive thoughts and behaviors." They recommend early intervention for crisis survivors; however, they note that clinical judgment should be used in ascertaining the appropriate intervention for each circumstance. Additionally, they state that while early intervention is crucial, it is best to wait at least six hours before deeply delving into the emotional details of a trauma event with a client. Initially, it is more helpful to clients to present factual information before encouraging affective expression. Later, counselors trained in crisis intervention can work to help clients put the trauma event into context through discussion that develops a clear account of their experience. During this process, professional counselors can challenge feelings of guilt and blame while promoting self-care and social support.

The **ABC-X model** and Double ABC-X crisis model come from family systems research but can be adapted to individuals in crisis (Jackson-Cherry et al., 2018) and are helpful in conceptualizing client reactions to crisis. Originally developed by Reuben Hill after World War II, these models further the stance that the interactive response to a precipitating event is the true crisis, and not the event itself. In the ABC-X model, A is the event, B is the family's resources, and C is the meaning attached to the event. The X of the model is the disequilibrium experienced by the family as a result of the interface among the event, client resources, and the meaning attached to the crisis. The **Double ABC-X model** addresses the existence of accumulated unresolved issues and stressors that a family may be facing at any given time (Jackson-Cherry et al., 2018). Thus, individuals and families who enter a crisis with fewer resources and more accumulated stress will have greater difficulty in recovery than individuals and families who have financial and psychological resources and also have fewer current and prior stressors in their lives.

All clients experience adaptation in response to crises and stressors, and while some responses to crisis are maladaptive, other individuals are able to adapt in a life-enhancing manner. The positive enhancing growth and changes individuals gain through dealing effectively with stressors and crisis events is known as **bonadaptation**. Appropriate and timely crisis intervention can promote bonadaptation in clients who experience a crisis. Now expand your understanding of bonadaptation by completing Think About It 7.1.

THINK ABOUT IT 7.1

Have you experienced bonadaptation? Have you experienced a crisis in your past that, upon reflection, had the silver lining of leading to greater understanding and enhancement of your life skills and positive worldview? What internal or external resources helped you positively adapt to crisis circumstances?

Concepts

Stress.   According to the Centers for Disease Control and Prevention (CDC, 2018, para 2), **stress** can be defined as:

> a condition that is often characterized by symptoms of physical or emotional tension. It is a reaction to a situation where a person feels threatened or anxious. Stress can be positive (e.g., preparing for a wedding) or negative (e.g., dealing with a natural disaster).

Everyone experiences stress during their lives, but stress can become problematic when prior coping mechanisms are no longer effective in managing the stress. While stress is a factor in crisis theory, stress does not necessarily equal a crisis. Boss (2002) distinguishes between stress and crisis by pointing out that stress is a continuous variable and can be measured. In contrast, crisis is dichotomous: one is either in crisis or not in crisis. Stress therefore is accumulative, and long-term stress may lead to physical and psychological problems.

According to the National Institute of Mental Health (2017), stress can come from the demands of daily living, changes (both good and bad), and sudden crisis events. Not all stress is bad. In fact, stress responses in our body give us bursts of energy that are essential to survival as in the classic fight-or-flight phenomenon. Our bodies react to perceived threats with an increased heart rate, rapid breathing, release of hormones, and heightened awareness. If an individual is being chased by a bear, these physical responses aid in either fighting the bear or running from it. These days, very few of us encounter wild animals, but our modern day human tendency to ruminate over life's demands is experienced by the body as a threat and the body reacts similarly in order to facilitate a fight or flight situation. Over time, when stress is chronic, these same physical responses can wear our bodies down; inhibit normal functioning; and lead to long-term physical and mental health problems including digestive problems, sleeplessness, headaches, anger, depression, and even compromised immunity.

Jackson-Cherry et al. (2018) noted that stress involves change and hence, the need for adaptation to new circumstances. Stress that is perceived negatively is called **distress**, and stress that is a result of positive changes is known as **eustress**. Whether the changes are negative or positive, the individual must adapt to the changes. The degree of effort this will take depends on how the stressor is interpreted by the individual as well as the resources and support an individual possesses. Increased stress creates disequilibrium, and by accessing internal and possibly external resources, the individual can come back to a state of balance without reaching a crisis state. However, lack of resources and an inability to counter stress in a life-enhancing manner can lead to long-term physical and mental stress-related problems. Stress is to be expected in life and can provide strength and motivation to tackle problems and difficulties. When one becomes overwhelmed by stress, physical and mental health concerns will arise. Dealing with stress on an ongoing basis can be facilitated by intentional wellness activities including diet, exercise, and attention to symptoms that can indicate a medical problem. Moreover, the importance of perspective cannot be overstated. How one interprets circumstances is critical to stress management. Positive self-talk and strength-based actions will mitigate stress effects and stimulate constructive action.

Trauma.   The American Counseling Association (ACA) (2018b) points out that the word **trauma** comes from the Greek word for wound. In the physical sense, trauma refers to bodily wounds that need medical attention in order to heal. Failure to address a physical wound might lead to infection or possibly gangrene and ultimately widespread systemic dysfunction throughout the body. Serious wounds cannot be ignored and must have attention before healing can begin. **Psychological trauma** refers to emotional and mental wounds that challenge one's beliefs, security, thoughts, and feelings and undermines one's ability to cope. As with physical trauma, those experiencing psychological trauma need assistance as they move toward equilibrium and stabilization following a crisis event. Ignoring psychological trauma will likely result in more serious emotional and psychological consequences later.

Clients may have experienced a variety of traumatic events, including emotional, physical, or sexual abuse; rape or sexual assault; intimate partner violence (IPV); exposure to war or terrorist acts; serving as a first responder to crisis events; involvement in an automobile accident; or a natural disaster. Traumatic events result in feelings of fear, helplessness, loss of control, loss of connection with others, and a loss of meaning. **Post-traumatic stress disorder (PTSD)** is a *Diagnostic and Statistical Manual of Mental Disorders* (American Psychiatric Association, 2013) classification that includes four main categories of symptoms: (a) hyperarousal, (b) intrusion, (c) avoidance, and (d) negative alterations in mood or cognitions. Hyperarousal refers to the persistent expectation of danger and may include a heightened startle response and sleep disturbance. Intrusive symptoms include vivid nightmares and flashbacks. Children may re-create the traumatic event through play. Emotional numbness, dissociation, and use of drugs and alcohol to dull pain associated with trauma are examples of constrictive symptoms.

Approximately 3.5% (7.7 million) of U.S. adults experience PTSD each year. Women are more likely to experience PTSD than men. Although clients may experience a traumatic event resulting in PTSD at any age, the median age of onset for PTSD is 23 years (National Institute of Mental Health, 2015). Goals of trauma work include empowerment of the client, reestablishment of safety and structure, mourning the losses resulting from the traumatic experience, and reconnecting with systems of social support. When working with minority clients, it is important to address the influences of oppression and discrimination in connection with the traumatic event. Counselors should also be aware of the potential for post-traumatic growth. Individuals who experience post-traumatic growth are able to find deeper meaning and purpose as a result of coping with trauma and loss (Sheikh, 2008).

Coping.   **Coping** can be thought of as the actions we use to deal with stressful or intimidating circumstances. Sandoval (2013) states that failure to cope is at the core of a crisis and, therefore, helping clients cope is a major objective in crisis counseling. A client's history of coping with negative life situations can predict a client's ability to cope with a current crisis. Failure to cope in the past indicates a lack of skills to respond to negative situations. It also suggests that the client may have a great deal of accumulative stress that is likely to impede the ability to respond to current challenges. Ursa and Koehn (2015) noted that the perceptions of the nature of coping vary. "It may be either a predetermined structure based on a person's internal resources and character or a dynamic process that considers interpersonal, intrapersonal, and situational factors" (p. 251). Coping involves both cognitive and affective resources. When faced with a concern, individuals may respond in a problem-solving manner (cognitive) or they may look to find ways to soothe emotions related to the difficulty. Coping is a complex concept. "[C]oping involves action, avoidance, emotion management, and altering thoughts and beliefs; it varies by individual and within individuals depending on the circumstances" (p. 252). Maladaptive coping such as cutting or the use of substances can exacerbate restoration after a crisis and counselors should be alert to nonproductive coping strategies. Therefore, when providing crisis intervention, counselors should assess clients on current and historical functioning and coping practices as well as contextual factors that may indicate internal and external resources for managing crisis circumstances.

Resilience and Post-Traumatic Growth

A rhetorical question for consideration related to crisis, trauma, loss, or human suffering is, *If two identical persons experienced identical crises or traumatic events, why would one languish and the other thrive?* Central to this question is the exploration of internal capacities and qualities related to resilience, hardiness, and the capacity to adapt to adversity. Much research and attention has been given to resilience and hardiness related to the trajectory of adjustment, adaptation, and well-being of persons who have been traumatized or victimized by crises of all kinds. Perhaps this is due to the heightened nature of global interdependence between nations and the response of governments to help each other following devastating disasters. Or it could be a result of many years of international conflict and the integration of lessons learned from previous wars when serving the traumatized military personnel and civilians. A third possible cause is the increasing knowledge and technology related to the understanding of trauma (Van der Kolk, 2006) wherein scholars, clinicians, leaders, and victims have collaboratively studied how and why some people fare better than others after crises. Additionally, new but related concepts such as post-traumatic growth or post-traumatic resilience have begun to interest researchers and clinicians who study and serve trauma-afflicted persons (Posttraumatic Growth Research Group, 2014). Figley and McCubbin (1983), known for their classic work related to crisis and catastrophes, focused on similar constructs of hardiness, resilience, and posttraumatic growth.

Hardiness is composed of the 3 Cs: attitudes of *commitment* (vs. alienation), *control* (vs. powerlessness), and *challenge* (vs. security) (Maddi, 2004). Hardiness enhances health and performance. Stress-hardy individuals are committed to a cause or course of action, have an internal locus of control that increases self-efficacy, and view obstacles and barriers as challenges to overcome. Similarly, **resilience** entails adaptation to adversity and stressors, such as relational, financial, or workplace problems. People who are resilient have a well of resources (e.g., social capital, immune system, spirituality, financial capital) that allow them to bounce back from adversity. Importantly, resilience is not something individuals either have or don't have; it is a continuum of resources brought to bear when coping with or compensating for challenges. Anyone can develop and improve personal resilience (American Psychological Association, 2015). Finally, **post-traumatic growth** reflects positive changes resulting from struggles with a major life crisis. Humans have the capacity to encounter significant trauma and change in radically new and positive ways. This is a theme that has played out throughout human history in various literary works and spiritual traditions (Post-traumatic Growth Research Group, 2014).

Vocabulary terms and constructs that are often considered together in the literature alongside these constructs include other terms such as self-efficacy, locus of control, sense of coherence, and dispositional optimism. Additionally, McCubbin and Patterson (1983) generated an extension of the ABC-X model to include the Family Adjustment and Adaptation Response model to explain further how not all adversity survivors are destined to high levels of bonadaptation. They may "recover" or accommodate their adversities to eventual states referred to as maladjustment, bonadjustment, maladaptation, and bonadaptation.

Snyder (2000) also offered an interesting view related to outcome research when examining which mental health approaches and theory-oriented applied practices were most effective. In short, Snyder isolated "hope theory" as a constant that appeared across several hundred successful mental health counseling approaches and techniques. Snyder considered self-efficacy an important variable linked to efficacious counseling outcomes. His thinking behind hope theory was that if the client believes that counseling will work, and if the client has qualities related to self-agency, then these are significant elements in successful outcomes. There once was a quietly effective advertisement promoting an addiction treatment center on television with an image of a phone. The narrator asserted . . . *the healing begins the moment you call.* This statement captures fittingly what Snyder believed was the key ingredient in hope theory. In other words, many clients report that they begin to feel better immediately upon making the call to begin counseling, or after going to only one session. It is their hope and belief that counseling works; their self-agency or self-efficacy is a strong variable in promoting positive outcomes. By contrast, professionals may have heard from clients who articulated statements like, "Counseling doesn't work" or "I've tried this before, but to no avail" or "There's really nothing that can change my circumstances." These, of course, *may* be assessed to have lower levels of self-efficacy, or may attain levels of adaptation lower than bonadaptation.

Wolin and Wolin (1993), in their classic research on qualities related to resilience, wondered about the question posed above, *If there were two persons with exactly the same narratives, why would one individual fare well and perhaps even thrive while the other languishes?* Though it is unlikely that there are very many identical persons with *exactly* the same life experiences, we can look at, for example, survivors of tornado destruction from the same neighborhood, and examine factors that contributed to one individual's better or worse prognosis. The ABC-X model purports that one's *perspective* of the difficulties, interfaced with the amount and types of stressors, and available or limited resources, will mitigate the damaging effects of the disaster, and that A, B, and C influence the trajectory of stabilization and recovery. Counselors and clients may not be able to change certain stressors or generate certain resources, but the perspective (i.e., the C in the ABC-X model) is the "wild card" within which many gains may be leveraged through counseling. Wolin and Wolin identified seven resiliencies from their research, traits that may be said to inform the C, the perspective or adaptability of victims of adversity (see Table 7.1).

Knowledge of these topics related to hardiness, resilience, self-efficacy, and post-traumatic growth provides valuable inroads into understanding clients' imminent well-being or the obstacles affecting recovery from crises, traumatic events, loss, and suffering. How could a counselor use this information and know empathically when to introduce these notions into counseling? In brief, a counselor can listen for signs of resilience beginning with

TABLE 7.1 Seven Resiliencies from *The Resilient Self* (summarized from Wolin & Wolin, 1993)	
Insight	The habit of asking tough questions and giving honest answers
Independence	Drawing boundaries between yourself and troubled parents; keeping emotional and physical distance while satisfying the demands of your conscience
Relationships	Maintaining intimate and fulfilling ties to other people that balance a mature regard for your own needs with empathy and the capacity to give to someone else
Initiative	Taking charge of problems; a taste for stretching and testing yourself in demanding tasks
Creativity	Imposing order, beauty, and purpose on the chaos of troubling experiences and painful feelings
Humor	Finding the comic in the tragic
Morality	An informed conscience that extends your wish for a good personal life to all humankind

the first session during intake, history gathering, and assessment. Direct questions and listening for the client's language may yield some insights:

• What hardships has the client endured previously?
• What was the aftermath of those hardships?
• How did the client or the client's family become different afterward?
• How recently (or long ago) did these hardships take place?
• What was learned as a result of the crisis?
• With sufficient time, is life better, worse, or about the same as before?
• What motto (book title, movie title, phrase, caption, etc.) best describes this part of one's life story?

An illustration might be to recall the "motto" or perspective that Rose Kennedy provided when she was asked how she endured all of the nonnormative "Kennedy tragedies." Her reply was often, "God would never give me more than I can handle." Another person with a similar history of accumulated losses might say, "What doesn't ruin me will make me stronger," "I never knew that I could be this durable," or "It could have been much worse." An example of a less adaptive perspective or clue into an individual's resilience or capacity for post-traumatic growth might be a statement like, "This was never supposed to happen to me," or "I'll never survive this." The counselor might conceptualize some of these responses into treatment goals, later assessments, progress checks, and outcome-planning in the course of counseling.

One father who experienced a devastating loss of his son to a boating tragedy, upon initial counseling sessions, presented with high levels of trauma-specific symptoms. He had attempted to rescue his teen and nearly drowned himself, but tragically lost his son to the powerful currents. He grieved inconsolably for months about his inability to rescue or recover his son. After five years, he was still inconsolable and articulating that he "knew" he was a "bad father" whom everyone blamed, and who should die now. With multiple losses of other family members during his five-year bereavement, he had not had a memorial service for his son; he could not go to the funerals of other family members; and he became agoraphobic, preferring to be inside at home for fear of running into his son's friends and their parents in the community. The father's sad and painful experience might best be characterized by the tenets of the Double ABC-X model and transcrisis, discussed in greater detail in later sections of this chapter.

Post-traumatic growth and the "radiance of resilience" may not be a possibility for all. The qualities of hardiness and resilience may not seem enough to counteract compounded or chronic strains, or multiple and interlocking crises, due to many factors that complicate and contribute to protracted suffering. In the case of the father, obstacles to his adaptation were multiple: he felt responsible for taking his son with his friends to the coast on the spur of the moment; he developed a perspective that he did not know enough about boating, even though he had been licensed and had been boating since a teen himself; he accused himself of not being a strong enough swimmer, even though he was fit and strong, albeit no match for the powerful tide; he struggled with the unfinished business of initially not being able to know if his son was dead or alive and later upon acceptance of certain death, although not having his son's remains; he yearned for his son, his only child; he was stagnant in the ambiguous loss (Boss, 2006) of losing his son's body but not his psychological relationship with him; he was alone in the chilling avoidance or absence of any conversations with the other parents or friends about the tragedy; he sequestered himself absent any ritual or memorial to honor his son; he writhed with a phobic response to attending the multiple funerals of other loved ones; and he deteriorated in the extreme social isolation that set in.

The Post-traumatic Growth Research Group (2014), the Resilience Research Centre (2018), and others provide valuable and tempered cautionary notes about how to understand and empathically use resilience and post-traumatic-growth language with clients. It would be highly insensitive to expect the father to respond well to any talk of resilience and growth when the progression of his pain toward relief was so complex and labored. Other approaches and techniques for clients like the father might be better applied, such as treatments recommended for post-traumatic stress, eye-movement desensitization reprocessing (EMDR), dialectical behavior therapy for emotional stabilization, cognitive-behavioral therapy, pharmacological support, and even gentleness and patience.

By contrast, for clients who demonstrate even small indications of self-efficacy, a history of demonstrated strength and buoyancy in the face of adversity, or who are obvious candidates for exploration of resilience and post-traumatic growth, the counselor has a rich set of constructs to explore with them in the realm of resiliency and post-traumatic growth.

COUNSELOR SAFEGUARDS: PROFESSIONAL BURNOUT, COMPASSION FATIGUE, SECONDARY TRAUMATIC STRESS, VICARIOUS TRAUMA, AND TRANSCRISIS

Most if not all ethical codes for mental health practitioners directly or indirectly address the need for clinicians to practice the craft of counseling and psychotherapy free of impairment and with attention to their own wellness and self-care. For example, the *ACA Code of Ethics* (2014a) exhorts:

> Counselors monitor themselves for signs of impairment from their own physical, mental, or emotional problems and refrain from offering or providing professionals services when impaired. They seek assistance for problems that reach the level of professional impairment, and if necessary, they limit, suspend, or terminate their professional responsibilities until it is determined that they may safely resume their work. (p. 9)

The American Association for Marriage and Family Therapy (AAMFT, 2012), in its section on Professional Competence and Integrity, states that clinicians will seek assistance or ". . . appropriate professional assistance for their personal problems or conflicts that may impair work performance or clinical judgment." In addition to the ACA's *Code of Ethics* (2014a) and the AAMFT's *Code of Ethics* (2012), other codes emphasize this message of the burden of responsibility not only to caring for oneself and one's longevity in the field, but also to safeguarding the public's trust in mental health services (AMHCA, 2010; ASCA, 2010; CACREP, 2016). In his classic book, *The Wounded Healer*, Nouwen (1979) provided an alternative recommendation from a nonregulatory point of view on the need to heal from one's own woundedness when ministering to others.

This section underscores the importance of this ethical and clinical obligation when serving the public but with special emphasis on self-care when working within a milieu of conditions that may result in potential burnout, compassion fatigue, secondary traumatic stress and vicarious trauma. The terms connote images of demanding work or overwork, overextension of resources, and personal impact on the self. For persons less familiar with burnout, compassion fatigue, and vicarious traumatization the terms resonate as somewhat similar concepts, but the incidence of and response to them are distinguishable. Newell and MacNeil (2010) provided a comprehensive overview of these concepts and how to confront them. These latter terms are closely associated with working with client populations that have experienced trauma, while burnout is derived from more general work conditions. Newell and MacNeil cautioned educators, agency supervisors, and practitioners alike to refrain from thinking of these concepts as synonyms or interchangeable; rather, they occur and are resolved with varying strategies.

Professional burnout involves physical, emotional, psychological, and spiritual exhaustion stemming from chronic exposure to client suffering (Newell & MacNeil, 2010). Fundamentally, burnout involves deterioration of motivation due to exposure to work environment stress (Manhas & Bakhshi, 2011) caused by long-term emotional demands within the work environment that results in physical, emotional, and mental exhaustion. Job burnout is cumulative and progressive, and frequently a change in job, work environment, or even a vacation can help to substantially reduce burnout.

Compassion fatigue is a syndrome sometimes experienced by helping professionals who constantly treat clients in crisis or otherwise experiencing pain and suffering. Compassion fatigue stems from the emotional and physical fatigue from constant use of empathy (Newell & MacNeil, 2010; Rothschild, 2011). Compassion fatigue accumulates over time, while vicarious trauma and secondary traumatic stress onset is more acute (Newell & MacNeil, 2010). This term is understood in relationship to not only the amount of empathic energy depleted in direct care, but also the amount of administrative stress endured, such as bureaucratic hurdles, agency stress, billing hassles, and juggling executive or organizational duties with clinical duties. Compassion fatigue involves feelings of deep sympathy and sorrow for clients experiencing suffering or misfortune, along with strong desire to help alleviate the client's suffering (ACA, 2015).

Secondary traumatic stress involves vicarious physical or emotional stress/traumatization from knowledge about a significant other experiencing a traumatizing event and stress resulting from wanting to help the victim (Newell & MacNeil, 2010). While secondary traumatic stress is sometimes experienced by counselors, more often it is experienced by relatives or close acquaintances of trauma victims. Signs of secondary traumatic stress are outwardly manifested and observed in a person, as contrasted with internal changes in thought about assumptive beliefs about the world.

Vicarious traumatization is distinguishable from secondary traumatic stress because it stems from a cognitive processing change after direct and chronic exposure to trauma populations, altering the individuals' perceptions, beliefs, and cognitions about trust, safety, and control (Newell & MacNeil, 2010). Indicators of vicarious trauma are internally experienced, such as experiencing changes about one's assumptive beliefs about the world. Vicarious trauma occurs when counselors connect with clients' pain and feel the cumulative impact of that pain (ACA, 2015).

Crises often last from days to a number of weeks. Myer, James, and Moulton (2010) surmised three typical results from a crisis: (a) return to normalcy after stabilization; (b) attain a better-than-before state of functioning wherein the crisis resulted in a change, a paradigm shift, or a contextual shift of coping and priorities; or (c) settle into a residual state of crisis that is long term and lingering with or without PTSD. This third characterization results in **transcrisis**. It may be accompanied by transcrisis points that are irregular, unpredictable, and nonlinear, with debilitation or even fatal outcomes. There can be individual or institutional transcrises. The phenomenon is mentioned here not only to invite further reading to better serve clients, but also to assist counselors in recognizing that, in the absence of a differential diagnosis of PTSD, transcrisis work may have similar effects on the helper as compassion fatigue, secondary traumatic stress, or vicarious trauma.

What happens to professional counselors when they are overexposed to conditions resulting in burnout, secondary traumatic stress, compassion fatigue, or vicarious trauma? The following identifies a few views of outcomes of these professional hazards, followed by ideas for how to prevent or heal from these deleterious exposures.

Barrett (2015) presented a view based on her extensive work with trauma survivors and victims of violence alongside her work as a consultant and clinical supervisor to mental health professionals who found themselves in need of regulated remediation. Her extensive observations informed her view that traumatized clients often presented for counseling with depleted energy in the emotional, intellectual, physical, spiritual, and sexual domains, and reported gaining energy in the counseling transmission process. While clients may have benefited, the clinicians working without careful vigilance of their own energy reserves depleted their sources of emotional, physical, intellectual, spiritual, and sexual generativity. When counselors' energy sources became depleted, the risk was greater for problems at work, problems at home, impaired judgments and actions, and a threat to longevity and vitality. Barrett has trained and consulted within the profession on this matter with vigilance about how to provide the best care while not emptying the resource well of the service provider.

Van Dernoot Lipsky and Burk (2009) wrote of the trauma exposure response and identified 16 potential and diminishing outcomes: (a) feeling helpless and hopeless, (b) a sense that one can never do enough, (c) hypervigilance, (d) diminished creativity, (e) inability to embrace complexity, (f) minimizing, (g) chronic exhaustion or physical ailments, (h) inability to listen and/or deliberate avoidance, (i) dissociative moments, (j) a sense of persecution, (k) guilt, (l) fear, (m) anger and cynicism, (n) inability to empathize or numbing, (o) addictions, and (p) grandiosity or inflated sense of importance related to work. Counselors or clinical supervisors who see these phenomena in their functioning easily should be able to reason how any of these could result in harmful effects on clients through the professional's diminished performance.

When unattended stress and cotraumatic effects begin to permeate the working relationships between clients and clinicians, there may be a crossing of lines from stress and occasional overwhelming feelings into impairment, a condition that imperils the core ethical principles of do no harm (malfeasance) and basic regard for beneficence. The ACA Taskforce on Counselor Wellness and Impairment defined **impairment** as follows:

> Therapeutic impairment occurs when there is a significant negative impact on a counselor's professional functioning which compromises client care or poses the potential for harm to the client. Impairment may be due to 1) Substance abuse or chemical dependency; 2) mental illness; 3) personal crisis (traumatic events or vicarious trauma, burnout, life crisis); or 4) physical illness or debilitation. (ACA, 2015)

When counselors become impaired in any way, it is not only a problem for clients or the counselor, but also a systemic problem for the profession and the public. Counselors are encouraged by our ethical codes to informally convey to the supposedly impaired colleague our concerns about potential ethical violations, and this may be a fear-arousing or even anger-arousing proposition for colleagues when it involves personal self-care. That said, there are a plethora of options and resources to assist or prevent impairment for the clinician both in-office and out-of-office.

Rothschild (2006) has written and trained extensively worldwide about ways in which the counselor in the office can diffuse the drain on empathy. She provides ideas about how to temper the intense and exclusive focus on the client and the traumatic narrative. Rothschild gives examples of how to modify attending skills, SOLER responding, and the provision of more and more deepened empathy that most mental health counselors were trained to do. For example, a counselor may use a notepad as a symbolic barrier on one's lap, held upright, to block the immediate transfer or ownership of the trauma. Or as a variation on this, "put on the brakes" with one's foot or leg muscles as a biophysical way to alter the exchange of information. A counselor might look up at the ceiling in reflective thought as contrasted with always mirroring the client with the deep gaze of empathic eye contact. Other ideas might be to have living things in one's office such as plants or fish in an aquarium. Even secret symbols for strength and immunization from traumatic content transmission might be possible by wearing a special piece of jewelry or article of clothing. Rothschild's work should be consulted for a clearer rendering of her recommendations.

Clinicians can use scheduling structures to attenuate their exposure to stress. For example, if the counselor has five active trauma clients, he or she may try to spread them across several days of the work week to prevent back-to-back sessions. Also identifying the "best day of the week or the best time of the day" is another way to diffuse the exhaustive effects of clients' narratives. Can you see the "hardest" case in your caseload at 4:00 on Friday afternoons? A similar time management strategy may have to do with when phone calls are returned. One colleague established as a self-care plan that she would check voicemails early in the morning and throughout the day, but never after seeing her last client at night. She found that when she checked messages at the end of a long day, she was prone to taking the worries of the call home with her; it interfered with her family life, and she did not rest well. Early calls worked much better. As an example of personal self-care, this can be generalized to other strategies, such as taking breaks throughout the day, literally or figuratively washing one's hands in between sessions, and so on. Another in-session strategy is to ensure practice within one's scope of competence. Being well-trained in doing trauma work is akin to having a well-maintained automobile that works efficiently even when overly exerted. There are innumerable resources on effective and best practices in the field of traumatology. Rothschild (2011) herself offers a good resource with *Trauma Essentials: Go To Guide,* as did Curran (2010, 2013). Training and reading is readily available for clinicians to further develop their expertise and thus reduce the perils of assuming trauma symptoms from clients.

Out-of-session self-care practices are also plentiful. Professionally based resources include having one's own counselor, support group, clinical consultant, peer consultation group, friends and allies in professional associations, and even measured leadership on association boards for which there are dividends and personal health rewards. Other self-care strategies are in the world away from the clinical or professional setting. These may best be found in one's personal friendships; on a vacation; in the kitchen; or at the yoga center, fishing hole, comedy club, movie theater, pool, beach, mountain, music festival, poetry reading, walking trail, bike path, good book, mindfulness or meditation center, massage therapist's office, manicurist's or stylist's station, or anywhere else relaxation and rejuvenation may wait. Get the picture? No matter how important you are to your clients, you cannot be maximally helpful if you are drained of energy and burned out.

The many thousands of mental health professionals might share at least one thing in common. We were probably drawn to the field with a great keenness for how to sit with people in their pain. We might be highly motivated by altruism and humanitarianism. Our lives are immeasurably enriched intellectually, emotionally, and spiritually to work in the presence of healing that comes from suffering. Many clients triumph over their adversities, and often we feel the radiance of resilience and post-traumatic growth. However, self-care is a professional imperative. May your well be deep and your longevity sustained. Table 7.2 provides a listing of helpful resources for counselor self-care. Now complete Activity 7.1.

TABLE 7.2 Resources for Counselors to Safeguard from Burnout, Compassion Fatigue, and Vicarious Trauma

Altman, D. (2011). *One minute mindfulness: Fifty simple ways to find peace, clarity, and new possibilities in a stressed out world.* Novato, CA: New World Library.

Borysenko, J. (2001). *Inner peace for busy people: 52 simple strategies for transforming your life.* Carlsbad, CA: Hay House.

Fanning, P., & Mitchener, H. G. (2001). *The 50 best ways to simplify your life.* Oakland, CA: New Harbinger.

Louden, J. (2005). *The woman's retreat book: A guide to restoring, rediscovering, and reawakening your true self in a moment, an hour, a day, or a weekend.* San Francisco, CA: HarperOne.

Mathieu, F. (2011). *The compassion fatigue workbook: Creative tools for transforming compassion fatigue and vicarious traumatization* (Psychosocial Stress Series). New York, NY: Routledge.

O'Hanlon, B. (2005). *Thriving through crisis: Turn tragedy and trauma into growth and change.* New York, NY: Perigee.

Van Dernoot Lipsky, L. & Burk, C. (2009). *Trauma stewardship: An everyday guide to caring for self while caring for others.* San Francisco, CA: Berrett-Koehler.

Wicks, R. J. (2008). *The resilient clinician.* London, UK: Oxford University Press.

Weiss, L. (2007). *Therapist's guide to self-care.* Oxford, UK: Oxford University Press.

ACTIVITY 7.1

Professional counselors who work with clients who have experienced a traumatic event can experience vicarious traumatization. Self-care is essential for professional counselors who deal with these issues. Generate a list of personal resiliency characteristics and self-care activities you can practice to restore personal wellness.

CRISIS COUNSELING

How Does Crisis Counseling Differ from Traditional Counseling?

According to the ACA (2015), there are basic protocols of crisis counseling, such as establishing rapport, letting clients tell their story, identifying major problems, assessing for safety issues, dealing with emotions, exploring alternatives, developing an action plan, and making referrals if needed. With the exception of a specific focus on safety and meeting basic immediate needs, these protocols generally mirror the manner in which counseling is conducted in a noncrisis type of session. Just as in all types of counseling endeavors, responders to crisis situations should be well versed in theory, intervention, and protocol. Moreover, crisis counselors ought to be collaborative and work closely with first responders and other crisis team members. Chapter 6 stated that the fundamental microskills of attending, listening, open questions, and reflection are essential components of counseling. The use of silence also can be very powerful for clients in crisis. Additionally, the ACA stated that the general goals of crisis counseling relate to safety, stability, and connection with resources and supports, with the chief objective of restoring a client's sense of empowerment and mastery.

Corey and Corey (2016) highlight guidelines for crisis counseling that include ensuring client safety; empathically exploring how the crisis affects clients emotionally, cognitively, and behaviorally as they tell their story; fostering resilience; and monitoring for dangerous behavior. Additionally, they advise that crisis counselors help identify social support and help clients determine action plans. Thus, crisis counseling, while encompassing basic counseling skills, theory, and constructs, is a unique venture that has become an integral part of counselor training and an expected core competency.

Ethical Considerations

Remley and Herlihy (2016) stressed the importance of managing a crisis situation from a legal and ethical perspective in order to avoid harm to clients. It is crucial for crisis counselors to comprehend the unique circumstances of a crisis and be aware of appropriate crisis counseling procedures. Additionally, it is imperative that counselors have multicultural knowledge, awareness, and skills related to various cultural factors during crisis counseling. The effect of culture on client reactions to crisis cannot be overstated, and must be at the forefront of the counselor's awareness during crisis assessment and intervention. It is critically important that counselors are careful not to impose their personal values on clients who are in crisis. Now complete Think About It 7.2.

THINK ABOUT IT 7.2

Clare is doing disaster mental health in a community that has been struck by a tornado. While talking with a family who has lost everything, she is overcome with emotion and compassion and states, "Let's join hands and pray." She immediately notices that the family is very uncomfortable with this suggestion. Discuss Clare's reactions to the situation and the ethical issues around her prayer suggestion.

Legal issues related to privacy are sometimes problematic in crisis situations but it is important to understand that there are provisions within laws to address emergencies and crises. For instance, the Family Educational Rights and Privacy Act (FERPA), was passed in 1974 and protects student record privacy. FERPA allows parents and students 18 years and older to access their educational records and also gives them the right to amend educational records. It safeguards the privacy of student educational information. Schools may be reluctant to release information in emergency situations, but according to the National Center for Education Statistics (NCES):

> In an emergency, FERPA permits school officials to disclose without consent education records, including personally identifiable information from those records, to protect the health or safety of students or other individuals. At such times, records and information may be released to appropriate parties such as law enforcement officials, public health officials, and trained medical personnel. (NCES, 2018, para 3)

It is important that school officials carefully document the reasons why they believed the release of information was necessary to protect others.

The Health Insurance Portability and Accountability Act (HIPAA) of 1996 also addresses the need for release of information in the event of a crisis. Initiated by the outbreak of Ebola in the United States, the U.S. Department of Health and Human Services (2014) issued a bulletin to clarify how private information could be shared in emergency situations. The HIPAA Privacy Rule protects the privacy of patients' health information, but the U.S. Department of Health and Human Services notes:

> The HIPAA Privacy Rule protects the privacy of patients' health information (protected health information) but is balanced to ensure that appropriate uses and disclosures of the information still may be made when necessary to treat a patient, to protect the nation's public health, and for other critical purposes. (para 2)

While they stress that privacy is not set aside during an emergency, the need to protect the public health and prevent harm is cause to release private medical information.

Legal and ethical guidelines do not disappear during times of crisis; however, there may be justification to adjust aspects of common practice in order to protect individuals and the larger public. Best practice in counseling necessitates that counselors are well versed in professional, legal, and ethical issues. Part of that knowledge base should be how emergency and crisis situations can be handled in a legal and ethical manner.

RISK ASSESSMENT: SUICIDE AND HOMICIDE

Working with a potentially violent or self-injurious client generates fear and alarm among clinicians. What are the best methods for preventing death and tragedy? Dealing with clients with suicidal and homicidal ideation shares similarities in ethical, legal, and clinical ways in that the professional counselor is obligated to prevent harm; extend duty-to-protect or duty-to-warn responses to family or other intended victims; and assess risk for lethality, specificity, and intent. Dealing with clients with suicidal and homicidal ideation presents differences in that while the incidence of homicide is unfortunately high, the incidence of suicide is much higher. Also, the aftermath following completed homicides and suicides often creates traumatic crises for loved ones and other survivors. Homicide is a human-made crisis that an assailant does to another or others, while suicide is quite upsetting for survivors of the loss because some may view it as a "choice," making its aftermath distressing in different ways. Furthermore, when thinking of recent and tragic events at Virginia Tech, Sandy Hook, Charleston, Aurora, Chattanooga, and countless other incidents of homicide in schools, movie theaters, churches, and workplaces, it is often questionable whether the assailants in these catastrophes were of sound mental health.

Kleespies (2000, 2009, 2014), an expert in mental health emergencies, stated that there are four occasions requiring clinicians' careful assessment and management of clients' potential to hurt, disable, or kill oneself or another: (a) when one may be suicidal; (b) when one threatens potential harm toward another; (c) when a defenseless individual such as a child, an elderly person, or a person with limited abilities is threatened with victimization; and (d) when a cognitive, medical, or physical condition renders a person so impaired in judgment that he or she is unable to prevent oneself from enacting violence.

An article by Schmitz, Allen, Feldman, Gutin, Jahn, Kleespies et al. (2012) on the need for improved training for mental health professionals to better assess and manage suicidal risk found "serious gaps" in needed competence development within the field. This section will focus specifically on providing clinicians-in-training an overview of some of the concepts germane to the assessment of suicidal and homicidal risk to prevent harm, death, or disabling injuries to a client or other individuals. Further reading and training on treatment and management of care and of risk is recommended.

Significance of the Problem

Suicide and homicide are viewed both as significant mental health problems and problems within the public health domain. It is widely agreed that prevention of suicide and homicide is the responsibility of all members of society and that communities and institutions (e.g., schools, law enforcement, medical care, government) are stakeholders in successful prevention initiatives. This is important for mental health professionals to understand because one lone counselor or even a team of clinicians (e.g., counselor, case manager, psychiatrist) cannot unilaterally prevent suicide or homicide. Mental health professionals may consider the importance of their roles not only in the counseling office, but in prevention and advocacy with partners.

Suicide is the 10th leading cause of death across all age groups, resulting in the deaths of 41,149 U.S. citizens in 2013 (Centers for Disease Control and Prevention, 2015a). Within specific age brackets, suicide was the 2nd leading cause of death for young adults aged 15–34 years, and the 3rd leading cause of death for youth aged 10–14 years in 2013. The rate of suicide, or deaths per 100,000 in specified populations nationwide is 13.0 (Drapeau & McIntosh, 2015). One of the many at-risk groups includes members of the military community (i.e., active, returning military, Reservists, and National Guard) for whom the rate of suicide in 2013 was 13.4 per 100,000 (Navy), 14.3 per 100,000 (Air Force), 23.0 per 100,000 (Army), and 23.1 per 100,000 (Marine Corps) (Smolenski, Reger, Bush, Skopp, Zhang, & Campise, 2015). All of these rates were higher than the general population, rate of 13.0 per 100,000 in 2013.

Other risk groups for which suicide rates are high include survivors of previous suicide attempts; males; white males; Native Americans; lesbian, gay, bisexual, transgender, and questioning; and elderly persons aged 65 years and older. While public health officials tend to focus on large sample groups, and "rate groups" of 100,000 at a time, counseling professionals have a sample size of one (at-a-time) when working with a single at-risk client. Though epidemiologists provide helpful generalizable information about risk and special care that should be extended to known vulnerable populations, it is important to remember that, with a one-person sample—the client in the clinician's office—anyone can become suicidal at any time for any reason, with any method, with any combination of risk factors. Of great concern also for the public and the clinical community alike are the more than 494,169 people with self-inflicted injuries treated in U.S. emergency rooms in 2013 (CDC, 2017).

Homicide is also a painful, traumatic, and costly mental health problem, and a public health problem. In 2013, the 16th leading cause of death in the United States in all age brackets was homicide, with 16,121 lives lost to murder, occurring at a rate of 3.5 per 100,000 (CDC, 2017; Drapeau & McIntosh, 2015). Among the top 10 causes of death in the United States in 2013 in the under-44 age group, homicide took the lives of 11,760 persons, which was 73% of all reported homicides. But as age decreased, homicide rates increased. Homicide was the 3rd leading cause of death for children ages 1–4, youth 15–24, and young adults ages 25–34. Homicide was the 4th leading cause of death in the nation for children ages 5–9, and the 6th leading cause of death for youth ages 10–14 and adults 35–44 (National Vital Statistics System, 2015).

Suicides and homicides result in billions of dollars of economic impact to persons close to the tragedy in terms of complicated bereavement, lost time from productive work and functioning, elevated risk for post-traumatic stress, prolonged and complicated bereavement, and even suicide or violence later. Nonfatal attempts, deaths from suicide, and violent individuals who murder others create an alarming number of clinical demands for survivors of attempts, surviving families and friends (referred to as survivors of suicide or homicide loss), and the professionals who serve them. When viewed systemically, the toll of suicide and homicide on families, community groups, and professionals is staggering. The myth that some members of the public and mental health professionals believe, "*If he(she) really wants to do it, there's little you can really do to prevent it,*" is an abdication of sound evidence-based practices, best practices, and standards of care (QPR Institute, 2010).

Evidence-based practices and best practices are important standards to adhere to in the treatment of individuals who are suicidal or homicidal. Mental health professionals should not be led by personal thoughts, feelings, attitudes, or beliefs rooted in unexamined opinion, religion, moral values, or philosophy that are in contradiction to best practices when caring for an at-risk client (Harrington, 2013a). Rather, providers of clinical care should be trained and prepared to assess for risk using clinical judgment that is consistent with current best practices and empirically based techniques. For example, the CDC now recommends that terminology used to describe suicide death should not include the terms "committed suicide" or "completed suicide." Rather, "died from suicide" is the standard of practice (Crosby, Ortega, & Melanson, 2011) thus establishing suicide as an illness-caused form of death with multifactorial causes resulting in fatal debilitation. This is in stark contrast to earlier views of suicide as a "choice" or as a sin or selfish act, all notions rooted in opinions, attitudes, perceptions, and values, and divergent from evidence-based and best practices.

Principles of Assessment

There are at least four main integrated methods that clinicians should consider when implementing a risk or threat assessment protocol. The counselor should become familiar with and use the clinical interview and in-session dialogue to collect information. When appropriate, the clinical interview might include a collateral interview such as collecting information from a family member or someone close to the at-risk individual. Second, it is advisable to have written "paper and pencil" risk assessments that yield valid and reliable results that either the counselor administers directly to the client or the client completes and the counselor scores. There are dozens of administrable assessments available and an agency or practice would determine the best fit for such a test based on client population, scoring, cost, ease in administering, etc. Third, for any assessment that reveals even low risk, clinicians might use consultation with a third party about the findings of the interview and scored measures. That consultant might be a colleague, a supervisor, a psychiatrist, a suicide specialist, or some other qualified mental health professional. The methods mentioned above would support the concept known as "triangulation" in data collection. This is akin to "inter-rater" reliability practices wherein more than one assessment is better than one. Three methods, persons, or forms of assessing for risk generally produce a more reliable and robust set of data upon which further treatment decisions can be made. A fourth consideration for assessment would be the "approach method." Some notable experts in the field have conducted extensive research and have formed their own theory-driven methods or approaches upon which clinicians can model their assessment protocols. A few such approaches in suicide risk assessment have been developed by Shea (2011), Jobes (2006), Rudd (2006), and Rudd, Joiner, and Rajab (2004), to name a few. AAS and SPRC each have one- or two-day curricula designed to train clinicians to assess and manage suicide risk, and these would be a good overview for learning how to conduct suicide risk assessment.

Finally, it is sensible to plan on multiple assessments in an ongoing fashion with each client who presents risk. These ongoing assessments may occur weekly or less frequently depending on the acuteness of the risk and response to treatment and counseling. Assessment of risk and treatment of risk are intertwined in that the professional counselor will continue to reassess for risk as a regular part of ongoing treatment, and findings from the assessment will yield valuable information about treatment needs and treatment design. For example, the counselor may ask "Do you have thoughts of suicide every minute of every day?" (example of the symptom amplification technique; Shea, 2011), and the client may respond "No, not all the time. . . . just when my kids go to their father's for the weekend." The clinician will then have assessed the frequency of thoughts of suicide and also identified a high-vulnerability zone for which extra safety planning would be done as a function of managing the risk. Another example illustrating the need for ongoing assessment as a companion of treatment is when a client with a chemical dependency enters detoxification, perhaps reluctantly, in a suicidal state of mind. The team may assess and manage the risk capably, but this should not be the end of assessment. Some persons with addictions may achieve sobriety quickly, but perhaps months later begin to realize what a mess of things the addiction has caused, a circumstance requiring reassessment (Center for Substance Abuse Treatment, 2009).

Suicide Risk Assessment

The Substance Abuse and Mental Health Services Administration (SAMHSA), the National Suicide Prevention Lifeline (NSPL), and the SPRC are all government-funded partners collaborating with other prevention allies such as the AAS, AFSP, and the National Action Alliance for Suicide Prevention, among others. These collaborators and other expert researchers likely represent the most current sources for evidence-based practices, best practices, and customary practices for counselors who work with at-risk persons.

In the best practices curriculum, *Assessing and Managing Suicidal Risk for Clinicians* (SPRC, 2016) developed by a committee of experts and co-implemented by AAS and SPRC, clinicians are instructed to understand and adhere to the *Core Competencies for Mental Health Professionals*. Among the 24 core competencies identified, the most relevant to risk assessment considered here include the (a) identification of acute (imminent or emergent) risk contrasted with the identification of chronic risk; (b) determination of the level of risk, including low, moderate, or high level of potential lethality; (c) the analysis of risk factors contrasted with warning signs; and (d) identification of protective factors that may buffer the level of risk.

Clinical Interview Modality

Due to the cursory overview of this chapter, trainees are advised to review the plethora of written "paper and pencil" assessments available for consideration and purchase. A list of these assessment tools is provided in the Comprehensive Suicide Prevention Resource Directory by the Alabama Suicide Prevention & Resources Coalition (ASPARC, 2014; see www.asparc.org). The "approach method" is available for further identification in Jobes (2006), Rudd (2006), Rudd et al. (2004), and Shea (2011).

As a primer to the interview risk assessment, it is advisable that, as a part of an intake interview or items on intake paperwork, counselors routinely ask clients questions related to recent or current thoughts of suicide. This is especially true for any counselors providing distance counseling or technology-assisted counseling, who are advised, before establishing a contract for counseling, to do a "fitness-for-distance-counseling" assessment (American Mental Health Counselors Association, 2015; Barrett, 2015). More specifically, clinicians should be familiar with the dynamics related to interview-style identification of (a) warning signs as contrasted with risk factors; (b) acute risk as contrasted with chronic risk; (c) low, moderate, or high indicators of risk; and (d) protective factors or buffers that may mediate the risk. Risk factors are like "markers" for *possible* or potential risk, and warning signs are more *probable* indicators, behaviorally, that someone is staging a plan to attempt suicide or to die.

The AAS (2018) provides a comprehensive list of chronic and acute indicators that a counselor can use as a checklist in interviewing and identifying the type of risk. **Acute risk** indicates that there is a strong probability that someone will be injured or dead within 24 hours or so. However, a "zone of high vigilance" during acutely risky times is needed. For example, if the client says, "*My birthday is next week, and I can assure you, I will not be turning 40,*" then it may be deemed more acute and not chronic for several days (not only

24 hours). **Chronic risk** can be a long-term presence of risk that may or may not necessitate urgent care, immediate hospitalization, or immediate intervention. Other treatment considerations may be more fitting. Counselors working with clients who are chronically suicidal can be equally as worried about the client, but chronic risk affords a little more time to do counseling that gets at the heart of any hopelessness and risk.

Jobes (2006) indicated that chronically suicidal persons often have more problems relationally; while acutely suicidal persons may have recently experienced a defeat, failure, embarrassment, humiliation, or loss. Importantly, a chronically at-risk person can become acutely at-risk and vice versa. Low, moderate, and high risk are related to the presence of a plan for suicidal action and how clearly or diffusely defined the method is; availability of means; the lethality of the means or method selected; certainty of a timetable for the attempt; whether or not there is a chance for intervention; if intoxication is indicated; and the degree of ambivalence present (i.e., more ambivalence = lower risk; less ambivalence = higher risk). Several mnemonic devices or acronyms are available for the interview-style assessment. Acronymic interview guides are presented in Table 7.3.

Homicide Assessment

Homicide is defined as the willful killing of one person by another person (Harrington & Daughhetee, 2018). The complex etiology related to the incidence of homicide in the United States includes but is not limited to attitudes toward vulnerable persons; habituation to media images of violence and murder; attitudes toward mental health needs; limited cultural, economic, or financial support for early diagnosis and intervention with potentially violent persons; cultural norms about gun ownership; and other factors. For example, homicides that occur in intimate partner violence (IPV) are attributable to one set of factors, while a young man who murders a Bible Study group at a church is linked to other factors. This is contrasted with a reentering military soldier who assaults a base or a government agency, which results from a very different set of factors.

Counselors may erroneously assume that the likelihood of working with a homicidal client may be confined to forensic settings; however, all counselors must be vigilant about a potentially homicidal client who may seek mental health care in any counseling setting, including schools, churches, treatment centers, hospitals, private practices, community agency settings, workplaces, and homes. While suicide assessment and intervention is challenging, it is perhaps less complex than homicide assessment in at least one important way: our profession's duty to protect and duty to warn potential victims of imminent or foreseeable harm.

Just as every sign or indicator of possible suicide risk should be taken seriously, so should statements and comments by clients who may be only expressing an idiom or a colloquialism, such as, "I'm going to kill my son the next time he gets a speeding ticket." A counselor is advised to appropriately inquire about the level of rage and the meaning and intent of the expression, as contrasted with assuming it is an expression of speech or merely an exasperated message.

Risk factors and what epidemiologists know about the incidence and profiles of assailants are important parts of an initial risk assessment. As with suicide, risk factors are like "markers" for *possible* violent behavior, but not necessarily predictions that violence or murder will happen. If a client presents with no risk factors stated or obviated, there is no assurance that he or she could not become violent in the future (Harrington & Daughhetee, 2018).

TABLE 7.3 Mnemonic Devices and Acronyms for the Suicide Risk Assessment Interview

AAS (2006) Juhnke, Granello, and Lebrón-Striker (2007)	Patterson, Dohn, Bird, and Patterson (1983)	McGothlin (2008)	Sankaranarayanan (2013)	*Streed, (2011)
I Ideation	S Sex: Male	S Are you **s**uicidal?	M **M**ental issues: depression, anxiety, agitation, guilt, shame, delusions	S **S**ignificant others (loss or absence of), **S**upport systems (lacking or inexplicable drop out from); **S**uicide preoccupation (gestures, threats, attempts); **S**eparating from life; **S**hame-avoidance; **S**uccorance
S **S**ubstance abuse	A **A**ge: Older	I **I**deation	A **A**ttempts at self-destruction	U "**U**nsuccessful" previous attempts
	D **D**epression	M **M**eans	N **N**o positive support from family, peers	I **I**nquiring about death and/or afterlife, **I**dentification with others who have died from suicide, **I**mpulsivity, **I**solation for attempt
P **P**urposelessness		P **P**erturbation		CI **C**hronic **I**llness, injury, family instability; **C**ommunicated **I**ntent; **C**ognitive **I**ssues
A **A**nxiety	P **P**revious Attempt(s)	L **L**oss, actual or perceived	T **T**riggering stressors	D **D**emographics; **D**epression; **D**ichotomous thinking; **D**isorientation; **D**rug abuse; **D**elusional experiences

(Continued)

TABLE 7.3 Mnemonic Devices and Acronyms for the Suicide Risk Assessment Interview (*continued*)

AAS (2006) Juhnke, Granello, and Lebrón-Striker (2007)	Patterson, Dohn, Bird, and Patterson (1983)	McGothlin (2008)	Sankaranarayanan (2013)	*Streed, (2011)
T Trapped	**E** Ethanol abuse	**E** Earlier attempts	**H** Hopelessness	**A** Age, Abuse history, Abasement, Anger, Alliances not/poorly formed, Anomic preoccupation, Anniversary of significant event, Alcohol abuse, Altruistic integration into a group/cause
H Helpless	**R** Rational thinking loss		**I** Ideas and Intent	**L** Lifestyle in turmoil, Love for life is ended, Lack of purpose, Legal issues, Loss, Loneliness
	S Social supports lacking	**S** Substance abuse	**S** Substance abuse	
W Withdrawal	**O** Organizes plan	**T** Trouble-shoot client's problem-solving ability		
A Anger	**N** No spouse or partner	**E** Emotion (hopeless, hapless, worthless, loneliness, depression)	**I** Illness, chronic pain	
R Reckless	**S** Sickness	**P** Parents or family history, exposure	**S** Suicide in the family history	
M Mood change		**S** Stress and life events	**N't** Suicide Note	
			F Final arrangements, saying goodbye, giving away possessions	

TABLE 7.3 Mnemonic Devices and Acronyms for the Suicide Risk Assessment Interview (*continued*)

AAS (2006) Juhnke, Granello, and Lebrón-Striker (2007)	Patterson, Dohn, Bird, and Patterson (1983)	McGothlin (2008)	Sankaranarayanan (2013)	*Streed, (2011)
			A	
			Access to means	
			I	
			Isolation	
			R	
			Recent psychiatric hospitalization; **R**egret surviving an attempt	

*Clinicians are urged to read the original sources about these interview constructs for the full meaning and interpretation of the conditions and constructs associated with each. This is especially true for Streed, which provides multiple elements for each letter in the acronym along with additional factors related to "suicide by cop."

Some risk factors for adult males include a history of mental illness, family violence, job instability, impulsivity, and insecurity (Klott & Jongsma, 2015). When in the context of intimate relationships, men who are potentially homicidal may exhibit possessiveness, rage, and a need for control. Adolescent males who may become violent have profiles that include legal problems and juvenile delinquency histories, academic difficulties, substance abuse, family of origin violence and chaos, parental norming or approval of violence and abusive behavior, availability of and access to guns, diagnosis of conduct disorder, and poverty (Loeber et al., 2005).

Female adolescent assailants often have a history of legal and delinquency problems, substance abuse, poor parental supervision, association with peers who exhibited similar difficulties, anger management problems, and mood disorders (Roe-Sepowitz, 2007). Finally, safety advocates also link a history of cruelty to animals as a strong possible correlate to violence toward people (Humane Society of the United States, 2011). The Humane Society report provided data about a co-occurring history of violence toward animals and humans: (a) of persons arrested for animal crimes, 65% had committed battery; (b) of a small subject sample of murderers, 45% had committed animal torture as teens; and (c) of seven school shootings between 1997 and 2001, all involved boys with a history of performing cruelty against animals.

While such potential predisposing risk factors are noteworthy, the clinician should especially take into consideration other indicators such as motive, intent, and the means and capability to carry out the violent plan. Similarly to suicide risk factors and warning signs, very specific and behaviorally indicated actions take on more urgency and higher probability of enactment. Remember: risk factors are possibilities; warning signs (specific and behavioral indicators) are probabilities. O'Toole (2000), of the National Center for the Analysis of Violent Crime (NCAVC), offered guidance to assessors of homicidal threat: One should learn as much about the details, the specificity of the plan, the intended victims, the achievability of the plan, the access to the methods to murder, any recent triggers

TABLE 7.4 National Center for the Analysis of Violent Crime Levels of Threat of Homicidal Behavior (summarized from O'Toole, 2000)

	Potential for harm	Specificity	Preparation	Achievability	Likelihood
Low	Minimal risk to a victim or public safety	Vague, indirect	Inconsistent	Lacks realism	Unlikely to be carried out
Medium	Threat could be carried out but not entirely realistic	More direct, more concrete than low threat	Client has given thought to how to enact the threat	Some specific details (time and place) but far from a detailed plan	Some preparatory steps have been taken, but preparations are veiled or ambiguous
High	Threat poses imminent and serious danger to the safety of others	Threat is direct, specific, and plausible	Concrete steps have been taken to prepare (e.g., research, rehearsal)		

or "last straw" to activate the homicidal plan, and the client's emotional lability. As mentioned earlier, Kleespies (2009) cites psychological impairment as a potential emergency.

The NCAVC established three levels of threat: low, medium, and high. Table 7.4 provides a brief review of these levels. See O'Toole (2000) for greater detail into how to assess risk and the constructs that factor into threat level measurement.

In summary, mental health professionals should consider how and what they assess when determining the risk or threat level for suicidal or homicidal behavior. "How" they will assess may include clinical interviews, paper-and-pencil measurements, consultation, approach-based assessment, and reassessment or multiple assessments over time with the at-risk client. "What" they will assess will include risk factors, warning signs, acuteness of risk or chronicity of risk, the level of risk (i.e., low, moderate, or high), and what protective factors might reduce the potency of the risk factors. Many clinicians and experts may assert that there are no two suicide or homicide scenarios that are alike, and in the same vein, there are no two suicide risk or homicide assessment protocols or experiences that are alike. It is incumbent upon the professional counselor to be familiar with the concepts presented in this chapter while also deepening one's training and using acceptable clinical judgment and treatment protocols. Now complete Case Study 7.1.

CASE STUDY 7.1

Richard is a 55-year-old, middle-class white man. He began counseling to help cope with work-related stress. Richard has been divorced for 15 years and does not have any family living in his home state. Richard reports drinking alcohol on occasion, approximately two to three liquor drinks every 2 weeks. When Richard arrives for his third session, you notice he is slightly disheveled and appears unusually anxious, with rapid and pressured speech. He paces around the room, and you notice the smell of alcohol on his breath. Richard discloses that he was fired from his job today. He feels that he will never find a job that compares to his last job because of his age. When you ask Richard if he has thoughts of hurting himself, he begins to cry and then punches the wall. He says that he would not kill himself because he would not give his boss the satisfaction of knowing he drove him to suicide.

- What additional questions would you ask Richard?
- What risk factors can be identified?
- What ethical issues should be considered?
- Is it safe to allow Richard to leave your office unaccompanied?

Intimate Partner Violence

According to the CDC (2015b), more than 10 million women and men experience violence from their partners each year. Intimate partner violence (IPV) has major physical and psychological effects on the abused partner, including a loss of sense of self, depression, and PTSD (Ursa & Koehn, 2015). The classic cycle of violence theory was put forth by Walker (1979) in three phases. Phase I involves a tension building where the abused partner is "walking on eggshells" and desperately trying to appease the abusing partner and keep the situation from escalating. Phase II involves an acute battering incident usually triggered by some external event. Phase III is the "honeymoon phase" during which the abuser asks for forgiveness and may bring the abused partner gifts. Promises are made that it will never happen again. McLeod, Muldoon, and Jackson-Cherry (2018) note that the existence of the honeymoon phase may make it difficult for abused partners to acknowledge that they are in an abusive relationship.

McLeod et al. (2018) identified common crisis issues that counselors should address when working with IPV cases. First of all, the need for medical attention to physical injury is crucial and clients should be given information on medical resources. Second, counselors must work with clients to establish their safety and find a safe place where they will be protected from further harm. Counselors should also assess for suicidal and homicidal ideation and intent. Reporting IPV to law enforcement is another consideration. Many times abused partners will not want to report; however, if there are children in the home who are witnessing the abuse, it falls within mandatory reporting conditions and counselors may need to contact authorities. The first step in assessing for IPV is to build rapport and create a safe atmosphere for disclosure. Once the client has disclosed, the counselor should address issues of lethality of the abuse and also any other illegal behaviors in which the abusing partner may be engaging. A thorough history of abuse can help in the evaluation of current risk. Finally, the client and counselor should develop a safety plan using resources such as shelters.

Child and Elder Abuse

In 2013, there were 678,932 cases of child maltreatment reported to child protective services agencies in the United States (CDC, 2015a). Child abuse is underreported and it is believed that lifetime abuse occurrence is one in four children. Child maltreatment cases fall within the following categories: physical abuse, sexual abuse, psychological or emotional abuse, and neglect. Professional counselors are mandated reporters in all 50 states, meaning counselors must report suspected abuse. The laws related to failure to report differ among states and professional counselors are urged to be familiar with reporting laws in their jurisdiction. Signs of physical child abuse include unexplained injuries, bruises, burns, or other injuries that do not match the explanation given.

Sexual abuse signs might include knowledge beyond the child's years about sexuality, pregnancy, sexually transmitted infections, genital injury, and sexual acting out. It is difficult to see visible signs of sexual abuse in children and the most common way that that sexual abuse comes to light is when a child discloses to a trusted adult. Thus, the need for good rapport and creating a safe environment for children to disclose is paramount. Emotional and psychological abuse is also difficult to ascertain. Emotionally abused children may withdraw socially and may exhibit low self-esteem, lack of confidence, depression, and anxiety. Neglect signs can include inadequate clothing in cold weather, dirty clothing, hunger, poor hygiene, lack of medical and dental care, and lack of supervision. Parental behavior that is callous or uninterested may also indicate maltreatment. As mandated reporters it is counselors' legal and ethical duty to report suspected child abuse and neglect.

According to the Administration on Aging (2014), all 50 states have in place some type of mandatory reporting law for elder abuse. Professional counselors should become familiar with the specific reporting laws in their state. Elder abuse includes physical abuse, sexual abuse, neglect, exploitation, emotional abuse, abandonment, and self-neglect (e.g., when the individual is no longer able to provide self-care). Kohl, Sanders, and Blumenthal (2012) pointed out that older adults are often dependent upon others for care and sometimes those are the very people who abuse and take advantage of the elder adult. One in five elder adults have been financially defrauded. While family members are sometimes the instigators of financial exploitation, there has been an increase in fraudulent activity by nonfamily individuals who prey on the elderly with false sweepstake winning schemes, magazine sales, and fake charities. The elderly are also vulnerable to con artists who trick them into revealing bank and credit card information. Often, the family members of these victims are unaware that the elder adult has been swindled until it is too late. The Administration on Aging (2014) provides a list of warning signs for elder abuse:

- Bruises, pressure marks, broken bones, abrasions, and burns
- Withdrawal from activities, depression, decrease in alertness
- Injuries around genital areas
- Bed sores, poor hygiene, and weight loss
- Belittling behaviors by the spouse
- Strained relationship or arguments with the caregiver

Just as with the protection of children, counselors have a legal and ethical responsibility to protect elder adults and report suspected abuse, exploitation, and neglect.

SPECIAL TOPICS IN CRISIS INTERVENTION AND PREVENTION

Community Disasters

A community-wide disaster is an event that upsets the structure and function of a community as property is destroyed and lives are disrupted. Community disasters include natural disasters such as floods or wildfires, as well as human-activated disasters like terrorist attacks or oil spills. The extent of damage a community disaster inflicts is a mixture of the threat exposure of the event and how susceptible the population is to the crisis. The availability of resources to bounce back from disaster is a major factor in recovery. Due to lack of resources, poverty-stricken communities often struggle to rebound from catastrophe and may not have articulated disaster management procedures and protocols.

Communities tend to have a shared reaction to disasters. Jackson-Cherry and Erford (2018) noted that "a collective trauma occurs on a community wide level whereby communities either join together and prevail or fragment and possibly create isolation and further conflict." (p. 249). Therefore, it is essential that communities engage in emergency management planning and training, preferably with both public and private participation and support. Chen, Chen, Vertinsky, Yumangulov, and Park (2013) found that partnerships between public and private organizations can help create communities that are resilient in the face of crisis. The social capital of trust, built through alignment of goals and cooperation in the past, is particularly helpful in promoting an appropriate community response to crisis. Emergency management teams of first responders, community leaders, and community resources are critically important. Such teams should meet and engage in drills on an ongoing basis so that they are prepared when disaster strikes. Included in these drills should be procedures for collaborating with federal entities such as the Federal Emergency Management Agency (FEMA) and the U.S. Department of Homeland Security.

School System Adaptions

When a crisis affects a school, the professional school counselor is a vital leader in the response. School crises can include death of a student or teacher, violent incidents within the school, deaths from the community that are distressing to the school population (e.g., a deadly car wreck involving well-known community members), or a fire that destroys the house of a student. School crises also include widespread natural disasters and national events. Since schools are often the center of a community, a crisis occurring off campus can have a profound effect on the students, faculty, and staff of a school (Erford, 2018). Any of the aforementioned crises can cause shock and a sense of despondency within the school community and culture; therefore, it is imperative that professional school counselors are well-versed in crisis intervention and prevention. The end goal of school crisis intervention is to return the school to its pre-crisis level of functioning, and help students return to some sense of normalcy.

After a crisis affects a school, it is customary to hear the phrase "counselors will be available." Therefore, professional school counselors should expect that they will be on the front line of any crisis that befalls their schools and communities. Depending on the nature and severity of the crisis, professional school counselors may need to bring in additional counselors from their school system and from neighboring school systems. Counselors from community agencies may also be called in for assistance (Davis, 2015). The ASCA (2013) states that school counselors are vital resources in crisis situations and collaborate with local mental health resources, first responders, and law enforcement. It is almost certain that every school counselor will have to deal with crises; forethought and preparation for a variety of potential crises can facilitate an appropriate response when a school faces emergency situations. Therefore, Erford (2018) emphasized the importance of FEMA's recommendations of mitigation and prevention of crises in schools, which include knowledge of the building and community, coordination and communication with leaders both in the school and in the region, as well as regular needs assessments to refine the school safety plan.

A crucial aspect of crisis preparation in schools is the formation and training of a Crisis Response Team. According to Brock (2013), in school settings crisis response teams are primarily school-based and include personnel whose roles best fit the qualifications for an Incident Commander, Operations Chief, Planning Chief, Logistics Chief, and Finance/Administration. Additionally, district-level teams and regional teams are also important, especially when dealing with widespread disasters. Schools should develop crisis plans and procedures that should be reviewed on a yearly basis by school faculty and staff so that everyone knows his or her role and tasks when a crisis occurs and can respond promptly (Erford, 2018).

Davis (2015) emphasized the importance of the school counselor's knowledge of the school and relationship with students, faculty, and staff. Cole et al. (2013) studied the long-term effects of crisis on school staff and found that staff reactions can last for years after the event. They stress the need for longtime support and use of coping strategies for school staff following traumatic events in order to foster resiliency and healing. Davis (2015) stressed that since others will be looking to them for comfort and support, it is particularly important for professional school counselors to maintain calm during crisis events. Therefore, it is vital for school counselors to be very intentional about self-care as a professional matter of utmost importance both during a crisis and as an ongoing professional responsibility.

Colleges and universities must also be prepared to deal with a wide range of crises. As in Pre-K–12 settings, the faculty and staff of a higher education institution should be knowledgeable about crisis plans and procedures (Erford, 2018). In recent decades, the necessity for systematic threat assessment has been evident in work and educational environments. Best practice in higher educational institutions includes the formation of a threat assessment team that includes input from faculty, staff, and students. Meloy, Hoffman, Guldimann, and James (2012) stated that "Threat assessment is concerned almost wholly with the risk of targeted violence by a subject of concern, and has a behavioral and observational policing focus" (p. 257). They identified behavioral warning signs that could be used to gauge the threat from an individual. Warning behaviors provide evidence of increased risk which is acute, dynamic and toxic, and often help the crisis professional determine whether an individual poses a threat. These include behaviors that would indicate that an attack is being planned; fixation on a person, group, or cause; a desire to identify with military or combatants; increasing violent acts; or a vague leakage of warnings to others followed by increasingly direct threats to targets. It is evident that crisis intervention planning and training for all personnel is essential in educational settings, particularly when assessing potential threats of violent activity. Now complete Case Study 7.2.

CASE STUDY 7.2

Catalina is a 16-year-old Latina girl who was referred by a teacher at the Catholic high school she attends. Catalina typically earns very good grades and has never been in trouble at school. In the past month, her grades have declined dramatically. She has been sitting by herself in the cafeteria at lunch. She spends most of her time after school in her bedroom by herself and often cries herself to sleep. After two sessions, Catalina tells you that she stole some liquor from a local store and has started drinking to cope with her sadness. She also reveals that she is cutting on her arms and stomach with a razor blade. Five minutes before the session ends, Catalina bursts into tears and tells you that she was raped by a male neighbor. She says that her life is ruined. She begs you not to tell her parents that she is no longer a virgin.

- Do you think Catalina is at risk for suicide?
- What risk factors are present?
- What ethical issues should be considered?
- How would you handle this situation?

Safety Concerns

An aspect of crisis intervention that is often overlooked is the need for crisis counselors to be aware of their surroundings and be attentive to their personal safety. Safety issues can be related to a dangerous physical environment following a natural disaster or the safety concerns of working with high-risk or dangerous clients. Therefore, an aspect of crisis intervention is the need for precaution related to the personal safety of both clients and counselors. It is important for crisis counselors to be mindful of safety concerns and protocols in emergency situations and to proactively train and prepare for a safe and secure counseling environment (Daughhetee, Jackson, & Parker, 2018). This includes the need for collaboration and cooperation with local authorities and other first responders. Through training and conscientious planning, responder and client safety can be maintained.

Counselor safety can be compromised in a variety of ways. When meeting with high-risk clients who are a danger to self and/or others, the professional counselor must be attentive to client nonverbal behaviors and assess for suicidal and/or homicidal intent. Daughhetee et al. (2018) stated that professional counselors must be aware of safety when setting up their offices. There should be a clear path to escape and office policies should include some type of emergency communication to other staff in the event the client becomes dangerous. Clients who have a history of violence, stalking, or impulsive behavior can pose a threat to counselors, and office protocols should include safety and escape plans in the event of a violent outburst.

Counselors who work alone in an office or from their homes are particularly vulnerable and must be meticulous in their new client screening processes. Despenser (2007) maintains that sole private practitioners are particularly exposed to danger due to their isolation. In attempts to grow their practices, sole practitioners may be too eager to take on new clients without properly screening them first. They are particularly vulnerable when taking on clients who were not referred from another professional. Despenser is very clear that counselors must listen to their inner warning bells and not take on new clients if their intuition indicates discomfort.

Finally, the safety and well-being of crisis counselors is in many ways contingent on the counselors' self-care practices. While self-care is always important in mental health work, it is particularly crucial when conducting crisis counseling. As mentioned earlier in this chapter, burnout and vicarious trauma are very real factors in crisis response and it is an ethical imperative that counselors monitor their own mental health and intentionally engage in self-care activities. Now complete Case Study 7.3.

CASE STUDY 7.3

Melton is a 70-year-old African American man who started coming to counseling after his wife died two months ago. Melton and his wife were married for 50 years, and he reports difficulty getting through each day without her. Melton has two adult children who live about two hours away; they visit on holidays, but are not particularly present in his life. Melton reports that he has been sleeping about 16 hours per day for the past week. He is tearful during the session. He tells you that he has stopped going to church and has not worked in his garden all week. What's the point, he says, his wife was the one who really liked doing those things. Melton also reveals that he has stopped taking his blood pressure and diabetes medication. He says that he does not want to be on this Earth any longer than he has to be.

- Do you think Melton is at risk for suicide?
- What risk factors are present?
- What ethical issues should be considered?
- As Melton's counselor, what is your next step?

Summary

Counselors in every setting will have crisis events that they must be able to address. In recent decades, the counseling profession has recognized the importance of training and professional development in crisis intervention and management, and skills in crisis counseling are considered essential for every professional counselor.

The actual crisis is not the precipitating event itself, but rather the reaction such an event generates within the people who experience it. Early research in crisis response led to increased understanding in post-traumatic stress, client disequilibrium following crisis, and the importance of Psychological First Aid in the immediate aftermath of a crisis. Models such as the ABC-X and Double ABC-X help to clarify the role that resources, meaning, and accumulated stress play in an individual's or a family's ability to cope with crisis and respond to the event in either a maladaptive manner or more life enhancing bonadaptive way. Client stress, trauma, resiliency, post-traumatic growth, and coping are all factors to consider when conducting crisis counseling.

Additionally, counselors must be alert to signs of burnout, compassion fatigue, and vicarious trauma within themselves during crisis intervention. Intentional self-care is a crucial aspect of best practice in crisis counseling.

Crises can impact individual clients, organizations, schools, or communities. A vital skill in all crisis intervention is the ability to assess the risk of harm to self or others within a client. It is important for counselors to be aware of current best practices in risk assessment and follow established protocols for determining an individual's risk of suicide, homicide, abuse (child and elder), and domestic violence. When a crisis befalls an entire community, organization, workplace, school, or university, crisis preparedness is essential. The best way to prepare for larger system crisis is to develop a crisis team that is well trained and up to date on crisis management procedures and can work collaboratively with first responders. Counselors well prepared in crisis intervention can provide timely help and mitigate long-term effects of a crisis event.

8 Mental Health and Rehabilitation Counseling

CATHERINE Y. CHANG, AMY L. MCLEOD,
AND NADINE E. GARNER

PREVIEW

This chapter provides a broad overview of two specialty areas in the field of counseling: mental health counseling and rehabilitation counseling. Mental health and rehabilitation counselors work in a wide variety of treatment settings and serve clients with diverse clinical concerns. This chapter explores various treatment settings and counseling issues in order to provide counselors in training with an understanding of available career options as well as applicable multicultural and social justice issues central to the counseling profession.

COUNSELING CAREER CHOICES

Counseling is defined as "a professional relationship that empowers diverse individuals, families, and groups to accomplish mental health, wellness, education, and career goals." (Kaplan, Tarvydas, & Gladding, 2014, p. 366). This definition makes it clear that all professional counselors share certain common goals and characteristics. At the same time, the field of counseling also has distinct specialty areas. For example, the Council for Accreditation of Counseling and Related Educational Programs (CACREP, 2016) provides standards for entry-level specialty areas in addiction counseling; career counseling; clinical mental health counseling; clinical rehabilitation counseling; college counseling and student affairs; marriage, couples, and family counseling; and school counseling. The National Board of Certified Counselors offers the following specialty certifications: Certified Clinical Mental Health Counselor, Master Addictions Counselor, and National Certified School Counselor. Finally, the American Counseling Association has 20 divisions, each focusing on a particular specialty area or interest in the field of counseling. Counselors should have a basic understanding of each specialty area since client issues typically do not neatly fall into only one category. For example, clients may enter counseling with a mental health issue and a substance abuse issue or a career issue and a rehabilitation issue. In this chapter, we will explore mental health counseling and rehabilitation counseling. Other counseling specialty areas are addressed in other chapters in this book.

In addition to considering which specialty area(s) of practice is most appealing, counselors in training must consider the treatment setting in which they wish to practice. The experiences that a professional counselor will have on the job are largely shaped by the setting in which counseling occurs. It is essential, during one's graduate program, to carefully explore the special features of these settings, including the diverse counseling career choices within each.

Graduate students who take the initiative to investigate the realities of their intended counseling setting have distinct advantages over students who do not acquire this knowledge. They will be equipped to make an informed decision about their future career plans. They will also appear more attractive to potential employers during the interview process by conveying their understanding of the counselor's role and asking important clarifying questions about the specifics of the position.

Knowledgeable professional counselors are less likely to accept a position and then make the shocking discovery that they are not well matched for the demands of their career choice. They can also avoid the extra expense and time of having to return to school to be trained as a counselor in a different setting, which in some cases could amount to getting an unexpected second master's degree.

Ultimately, well-informed graduates become productive counselors who have an excellent chance of experiencing real job satisfaction in their professional roles. They choose to work in a setting that allows them to use their talents in ways that contribute to their clients' progress toward personal growth and wellness.

COUNSELING IN MENTAL HEALTH SETTINGS

The field of mental health counseling encompasses a broad spectrum of settings, serving diverse audiences. Community/agency, hospital, corrections, private practice, pastoral counseling, and wilderness therapy are six distinct areas where mental health counselors are employed. Complete Activity 8.1 to help you develop your own working definition of mental health counseling.

ACTIVITY 8.1 DEVELOPING A WORKING DEFINITION OF MENTAL HEALTH COUNSELING

Visit the website of the Council for the Accreditation of Counseling and Related Educational Programs (CACREP) (www.cacrep.org), which provides an extensive description of mental health counseling. From the information given, develop your own working definition of mental health counseling.

Background

For most of America's history, the dominant setting for addressing mental health concerns involved state psychiatric hospitals. These institutions primarily served patients with chronic or severe mental illness. By the middle of the 20th century, psychotropic drugs were used to control psychotic behavior, anxiety, and depression with greater effectiveness, enabling otherwise dependent adults to function in the community. Community-based mental health programs began to grow as a consequence of the legislative initiatives of the 1960s, expanding the settings for treatment beyond state-run psychiatric hospitals.

In 1986, the National Institute of Mental Health (NIMH) created the category of "mental health counselors." This fifth category of mental health practitioners was added to what existed since its inception in 1940: psychiatry, psychology, social work, and nursing.

In 2002, President George W. Bush created the President's New Freedom Commission on Mental Health (President's New Freedom Commission on Mental Health, 2003). The commission members were charged with a yearlong study of the national mental health delivery system in order to make recommendations toward transforming a system that has been criticized as "fragmented, disconnected, and often inadequate" (p. 1). Although the president's initiative received mixed reviews by the American public, the initiative did underscore the need for a mental health system that is recovery-oriented in nature, and one that is more accessible and functional for all consumers. In an effort to further increase the accessibility of the mental health and substance abuse services, the *Mental Health Parity and Addiction Equity Act of 2008* (H. R. 1424—117) requires insurance providers to provide the same level of benefits coverage for mental health and substance abuse issues that is provided for medical and surgical issues (Feldman, 2013). The *Mental Health First Aid Act of 2015* (S. 711/H.R. 1877) provides funding for training in how to recognize the common symptoms of mental health and substance abuse issues, how to de-escalate a mental health crisis situation, and how to make a referral to a qualified mental health treatment provider.

These legislative efforts highlight the increasing national attention to the importance of the mental health and substance abuse issues. Mental health counselors are at the forefront of addressing these needs. Counselors today have more career opportunities than ever. In fact, O*NET predicts 64,000 new job openings for mental health counselors between 2012–2022, which represents projected job growth of 22% or more (O*NET, 2015).This is an exciting time for trained mental health counselors.

Community/Agency Setting

The community/agency setting is a broad setting that offers a host of career opportunities. The types of **community/agency settings** include government agencies (e.g., increasingly funded directly by states or counties as opposed to the federally funded programs of the 1960s) and privately funded, community-based clinics. According to the National Mental Health Services Survey, approximately two-thirds of mental health agencies are private, nonprofit organizations; 24% of mental health agencies are funded and operated by federal, state, and local government; and 10% are private, for-profit organizations (SAMHSA, 2014a). Community and agency settings provide treatment to client populations with serious and chronic mental illness and substance abuse issues as well as clients with less severe pathology. Community/agency settings provide professional counselors trained as generalists a viable starting point for their career. As beginning counselors gain work experience and understanding about their preferences, they may develop a specialty area. Examples include providing treatment to juvenile sexual offenders, families and children, the homeless population, clients with substance abuse issues, and survivors of intimate partner violence.

VOICES FROM THE FIELD 8.1   Mental Health Counseling, by Greg E. Bechtold

I had no idea what I was getting into when I began working as a drug and alcohol counselor for court-committed juveniles. Not only was I counseling adolescent males for drug and alcohol use, I was also dealing with anger, depression, suicidal thoughts, family dysfunction, and about a million

(Continued)

other issues that came along with the package. Throughout my first year, there was a persistent underlying question ringing in my head: How can I possibly counsel someone who does not seem to have any intention of changing?

Believe it or not, that question is also connected to my greatest reward. I am able to see my clients gradually change their behaviors, attitudes, and thoughts. I have the privilege of helping a client move through the process of change, which is definitely a challenge, but that is what I love about it. Every day is something new. Clients progress and regress, laugh, cry, yell, goof off, and work hard. Misbehavior is to be expected. It is my job to learn how to effectively intervene and help my clients find alternative strategies to reach their goals.

After eight years at our facility (and several promotions), I feel confident in my skills and abilities, but I am constantly looking to improve them. I also need to keep up-to-date on current trends such as drugs of abuse, drug selling, gangs, current laws and regulations regarding crime, gun use, and fatherhood. This job can be very rewarding and, at times, it can be extremely frustrating. When I entered this field, I had to make a commitment. It's not about me anymore. Parents, the probation system, and the community entrust me to work with adolescents, many of whom would be labeled as "difficult clients." Drug use is typically just the tip of the iceberg. During 6 to 12 months of treatment, I am ultimately responsible for the life of a child. Does it get any more serious than that?

Hospitals

Hospitals, inpatient or hospital-based treatment facilities, provide 24-hour care to clients in acute crisis situations. Clients who are suicidal or homicidal may require **inpatient treatment** to ensure their safety and the safety of others. Clients with mental illnesses such as schizophrenia or bipolar disorder may need inpatient treatment to deal with psychosis or manic episodes. Inpatient treatment may also be necessary for clients who have severe eating disorders and are at risk medically. Clients with substance dependence issues may need inpatient detoxification to reduce the medical risk associated with withdrawal symptoms. In inpatient treatment settings, clients receive care from a team of psychiatrists, nurses, professional counselors, and social workers. In the past, 28-day inpatient programs were common. As a result of restrictions imposed by managed care companies, most inpatient programs have been restructured to provide shorter-term stabilization to clients in crisis.

The partial hospitalization (or partial hospital) setting is also referred to as day treatment. A **partial hospital/day treatment** program can be located in either a freestanding facility or a hospital-based facility that operates for at least 20 hours per week (United Healthcare, 2014). It is designed to provide clients with a transitional step between an acute psychiatric episode and their readiness to reenter work, school, and/or home environments (Yanos, Vreeland, Minsky, Fuller, & Roe, 2009). Depending on the client's situation, a partial hospital/day treatment program can be an increase from a less intensive level of care, or a decrease from a more intensive level of care, such as an inpatient or residential treatment program. Counselors in partial hospital/day treatment settings generally provide intense, often group-based services during the weekdays, lasting from morning to early afternoon. Counselors in this setting may work with clients of all ages, ranging from children to senior adults who struggle with serious psychological distress, including behavior disorders, abuse, addictions, anger management, anxiety, autism, bipolar disorder, depression, trauma, personality disorder, and schizophrenia. Depending on the severity of their conditions, clients may work with counselors daily or several times per week until they can gain better control of their mental health.

Clients whose psychosocial functioning has become severely impaired by the symptoms of a mental health condition (but are not at immediate risk of serious harm to self or others) often benefit from the structure and monitoring that counselors can provide in a partial hospital/day treatment program (United Healthcare, 2014). The counselor's two main goals in a partial hospital/day treatment program are to reduce the chances that clients will need to be hospitalized or readmitted to a hospital setting, and to help clients successfully reenter their work, school, and/or home lives. Counselors use a recovery-oriented, hopeful focus by helping clients develop coping skills, social skills, illness management skills, and healthy lifestyle skills (Yanos et al., 2009). Where appropriate, the counselor encourages the client's family and social supports to participate in some of the treatment.

Residential treatment programs provide intensive therapy and a structured living environment for clients struggling with mental health and substance abuse and dependency issues. Clients who typically enter residential treatment programs may have previously been stabilized in an inpatient setting or may require the structure provided by a residential treatment program because of several episodes of mental health and substance abuse issues. Clients may live at a residential treatment facility (which may also be referred to as a halfway house, three-quarter-way house, or recovery residence) for several months while they are developing increased coping skills and focusing on recovery. Some residential programs allow clients to work part-time during treatment.

Intensive outpatient treatment is appropriate for clients who are functioning at a high level but need more intensive treatment than outpatient counseling is able to provide. Intensive outpatient treatment typically meets for 2 to 3 hours a day for 4 to 6 weeks and includes group counseling, family counseling, individual counseling, and support group meetings. Most clients are able to work or attend school full-time while in this type of treatment program.

Outpatient treatment typically consists of weekly or biweekly sessions of 1 hour in length with a professional counselor. Clients may also attend weekly outpatient groups. Outpatient treatment is appropriate for working with clients on a variety of issues. A referral to a more intensive level of treatment may be necessary when a professional counselor determines that a client is not making progress, is having increased difficulty functioning on a daily basis, or is in danger of harming him- or herself or someone else. It is essential for professional counselors to be aware of the mental health resources available in their community. Activity 8.2 helps you develop your resource list.

ACTIVITY 8.2

Investigate what mental health resources are available in your community. Where could a client go to receive free or low-cost counseling services? Where would you refer a client in crisis? Where could a non-English-speaking client go for counseling? Keep a list of these resources to use in your future work as a professional counselor.

VOICES FROM THE FIELD 8.2   Determining an Appropriate Level
of Care, by Amy L. McLeod

It is essential that counselors are able to determine the appropriate level of care or treatment setting for their clients. In order to do so, counselors must be able to accurately assess clients' symptoms and levels of functioning. The first step to accurate assessment is building rapport with your
clients and emphasizing that you are gathering information in order to know how to help them,
not to judge them. When you are working with a client whose cultural background varies from
your own, additional attention should be given to building rapport and establishing trust. When
gathering information about what your client is experiencing, use open-ended questions when
possible, ask clarifying questions, and pay attention to areas that need additional exploration. For
example, if a client reports drinking 1 to 2 drinks per day, ask how much alcohol each drink contains. There is a big difference between two five-ounce glasses of wine and two bottles of wine,
but both may be described as two drinks by a client.

Counselors should also be aware of what types of client issues warrant more intensive treatment. A counselor should recognize the limitations of the treatment they are able to provide in
their particular work setting and know when to make a referral to a more or less intensive treatment setting. An updated list of mental health and substance abuse resources in the community
is an essential tool for all counselors.

Corrections

Corrections is part of the field of criminal justice. Professional counselors who work in
corrections may work in the prison setting, the court, or the community. They may be
directly employed by a department of corrections or they may work for a private agency
that serves the department's needs. The clients served by counselors in this setting undergo
a process similar to the following: When an arrest is made for a nonviolent criminal offense,
the suspect is held in jail to await trial. At this point, a mental health professional may be
called into the courts to do an assessment, called a court-ordered evaluation. To perform
this role, a minimum of a master's degree and licensure or certification is generally
required. If the evaluation indicates that a mental health or substance abuse treatment
program is warranted, the nonviolent offender may be sentenced to a diversion program
in lieu of incarceration. **Diversion programs** shift the court's focus from punishment to
rehabilitation and divert potential inmates from incarceration in overcrowded prisons to
treatment facilities within the community. Diversion programs aim to address underlying
mental health and substance abuse issues that contribute to criminal behavior. The probation department supervises the sentencing to a diversion program, where treatments such
as counseling occur.

Progressive judiciary systems recognize the value of comprehensive treatment–based
diversion programs that address behavioral change; these systems have established drug
courts and mental health courts to deal efficiently with the offender's treatment needs,
taking into account overcrowded prisons. Professional counselors can play an active role
throughout the process. They counsel during probation, conduct group and individual
counseling to incarcerated inmates, or counsel offenders on parole.

The needs of incarcerated inmates often focus on dealing with prison life. Counselors
must realize that they are not necessarily perceived as being helpful by their clients and

may be seen as part of the punitive system. Nevertheless, an advantage to counseling in a corrections setting is that clients must consistently participate in individual and group counseling and complete assigned tasks because their alternative is prison. In contrast to private practice, these clients cannot choose another counselor or neglect paying for the service, so counselors are free to do their best work from beginning to end. Counselors interested in alternative programs need to understand the program, the counselor's role, the political environment, and the funding sources to make informed career decisions.

Private Practice

Professional counselors and counselors in training often imagine that maintaining a private practice would be an appealing and glamorous career choice; however, both the advantages and challenges of this setting need to be carefully considered. Some of the benefits of establishing a private practice include autonomy regarding decision making, the ability to design a creative work schedule, the ability to select your theoretical approach, the opportunity to become a specialist in one or more treatment areas of interest, and the potential to build a profitable business (Harrington, 2013b). The challenges of maintaining a private practice are many, including developing marketing strategies to generate enough client referrals, bearing the financial responsibility for all aspects of the practice, addressing barriers to services for lower socioeconomic (SES) clients, and managing the business end of the practice (Colburn, 2013; Harrington, 2013b). When discussing the advantages and disadvantages of private practice, long-term mental health counselor and private practitioner, Harrington writes:

> In spite of the challenges that private practice presents, the opportunities it offers for a deeply meaningful and gratifying professional life can eclipse them. While the expenses may be high and the earning potential unpredictable, there are many unquantifiable benefits associated with the identity of private practitioner. These dividends may be intangible, or indescribable, but many colleagues consider them to be bonuses to conventional remuneration and fringe benefits. What are some of the qualitative rewards? It is a privilege to walk with persons in their suffering, to sit for hours at a time with the magic and mystery of the human condition, to be continually intellectually stimulated and emotionally stirred, to be energized when clients make strides or experience victories over their circumstances, and to regularly find joy in one's work. (Harrington, 2013b, p. 195)

Similar to the broad area of community/agency counseling, the private practice setting offers professional counselors the ability to work with a diverse population of clients who present an array of therapeutic concerns. A counselor who contemplates opening a private practice may envision carving out a specialty area such as child and adolescent development, couples and family counseling, women's issues, grief counseling, or trauma counseling. However, to build a client and referral base in the hopes of becoming financially successful, private practitioners are likely to find that, at least in the early stages of developing a practice, they must be willing to expand their service offerings to reach a wide range of potential clients. Ideas for diversifying service offerings in private practice include partnering with noncounseling referral sources (e.g., divorce attorney to obtain marriage and family counseling referrals), providing testing and assessment services, offering clinical supervision to counselors working toward licensure, providing organizational consultation services, serving as an adjunct instructor at a local university, or providing technology supported counseling (Colburn, 2013). Of course, developing a new specialty area requires training, supervision, and consultation. Counselors who are considering private practice are not alone; many counseling organizations offer support and resources on establishing and maintaining a successful private practice.

**VOICES FROM THE FIELD 8.3   Private Practice,
by David C. Hill**

I took the "big jump" and purchased a 2,300-square-foot house for my private practice. I rent to five part-time practitioners, all of whom were once my students or colleagues. This is definitely the single most rewarding aspect of my private practice, specifically, the fact that I have been able to facilitate the professional and career development of my truly gifted associates. The key piece of advice here for a master's student is to affiliate yourself with professionals (faculty members or other licensed practitioners) who have private practices such that you will find doors of opportunity opening for you in the world of private practice. In this endeavor, develop networks by joining local provider associations (social work, addictions counseling, psychology, counseling). This provides opportunities for consultation, supervision, and referrals.

There are a number of important issues to address in considering whether or not you should make part-time or full-time private practice one of your professional goals. They include: (a) Should you rent or buy property? (b) How will you purchase professional liability insurance? (c) What will be the source of your referrals? (d) Who will provide supervision and/or consultation for you on difficult clinical issues? (e) What will be your risk-management plan for situations that occur "after hours" and involve crises such as threats of suicide, homicide, intent to perpetrate abuse? (f) How will you handle the issue of third-party payment (e.g., insurance and publicly funded treatment such as Medicare and Medicaid)? Will you seek to be accepted by them as an approved provider of reimbursable services? (g) How will you manage the federal, state, and local tax issues that confront all small business owners? (h) What licenses or certificates will you need, and what will you need to do in order to earn them? (i) How will you meet the continuing professional education requirements involved in licensure as well as the ethics codes of our various helping professions? (j) How will you meet the expectation of most professional organizations, which suggests that those in the "helping professions" should provide some of their services pro bono? These questions may strike the aspiring private practitioner as somewhat daunting, even overwhelming. For me, personally, answering all of them provided a succinct summary of the key challenges of maintaining a private practice.

The rewards have been many and more than compensate for these challenges. I mentioned the highest reward above: mentoring and supervising my students who have now become accomplished service providers in my practice. The opportunity to serve clients, child protection caseworkers, recovering addicts, children, adolescents, and the family court system has also been very inspiring. One major endeavor that presented itself was to become an expert witness in the family court for child protective services cases involving the possible termination of parental rights. This is difficult work, but the openness of judges, attorneys, clients, and caseworkers to the information derived from my psychological evaluations has been very affirming. Many of them have offered unsolicited words of appreciation for my testimony and assistance. In addition, I have learned as much from my clients as they have from me over the years, and for this I am very grateful. I think that the opportunity to work with clients is a gift and an invitation from them to enter their worlds and understand them in ways that others cannot. If, in the process, I can facilitate their journeys along life's convoluted pathways, then I feel even more gratified.

Marriage and Family Counselors

Of the various types of credentials that counselors may pursue as they work in mental health settings, some specialize in **marriage and family counseling** as a counseling career choice. Marriage and family counselors are present in all mental health settings as well as in many settings outside the mental health arena. A study of American and Canadian marriage and family counselors reported that 52% were in private practice; 13% worked in private, nonprofit agencies; and 6% were employed at a college/university, public social service agency, hospital, medical center, outpatient clinic, business/industry, public school, home, faith-based setting, correctional facility, or military facility (Bradley, Bergen, Ginter, Williams, & Scalise, 2010). The remaining 29% of the sample did not report a specific work setting.

Individuals in the helping professions who are interested in obtaining the marriage and family counseling credential often have backgrounds in psychology, psychiatry, social work, nursing, pastoral counseling, or education. The marriage and family counseling credential is regulated in most states by requiring candidates to graduate from an accredited program, complete supervised clinical experience, and pass a state licensing exam or the national examination for marriage and family counseling (American Association for Marriage and Family Therapy, 2012).

The guiding principle for marriage and family counselors is a family systems perspective, in which individuals (e.g., clients or identified patients) are influenced by their family's pattern of behaviors. Marriage and family counselors examine and treat the set of relationships within which the individual functions (American Association for Marriage and Family Therapy, 2012). When they work with individuals, couples, families, and groups, marriage and family counselors most frequently use cognitive-behavioral therapy (CBT), Bowen family systems theory, solution-focused brief therapy (SFBT), structural therapy, strategic therapy, and experiential therapy (Bradley et al., 2010). Marriage and family counselors typically practice short-term counseling, which concludes after an average of 12 sessions (American Association for Marriage and Family Therapy, 2012).

Pastoral Counseling

Pastoral counseling is a unique counseling career choice that appeals to counselors who would like to integrate spirituality and psychology when counseling clients. Although its professional origins began as religious or spiritual counseling, pastoral counseling has evolved into what is also known as **pastoral psychotherapy**, which intentionally integrates theology and the behavioral sciences (American Association of Pastoral Counselors, 2017). Pastoral counselors provide the same services as other mental health practitioners and are committed to serving clients without imposing their own religious or spiritual beliefs on them. The term *pastoral counseling* can be confusing to consumers seeking counseling services because it has at least two distinct meanings. Sometimes the term refers to a pastor who also provides counseling; however, pastors usually take only one or two counseling courses (McMinn, Staley, Webb, & Seegobin, 2010). Pastoral counseling, as it is described in this chapter, refers to the profession of pastoral counseling, as outlined and credentialed by the American Association of Pastoral Counselors (AAPC), an interfaith organization representing more than 80 faith groups, including the Protestant, Catholic, and Jewish faiths (American Association of Pastoral Counselors, 2017).

To earn the credential of pastoral counselor, candidates usually have a graduate degree in ministry/theology and another graduate degree in counseling/psychology. They then complete hours of postgraduate supervised experience and must pass a licensing or other exam, depending on the state in which they intend to practice. Doering (2009) explained pastoral counseling in the following way:

> [W]hat makes us unique in the field of mental health is that we draw upon our theological education to understand our own spirituality, and the spirituality of those we counsel. In contrast, spiritually-oriented practitioners who do not draw upon a formal theological education face the limitations of being theologically naïve when they counsel spiritually or religiously committed clients. (p. 7)

In recent years, pastoral counselors have become more visible and accessible to the public because they have extended their services to community settings beyond their traditional role in hospitals (Blevins, 2009). Pastoral counselors may use the new theories and research emerging from the field of neuroscience as they relate to the spiritual experience in recovery, especially with clients who are struggling with addiction (Sandoz, 2010b). Pastoral counseling with clients who are addicted to substances or processes connects well with the 12 Step Program of Alcoholics Anonymous (AA), which also emphasizes the spiritual dimension in the recovery from addiction (Sandoz, 2010a).

Wilderness Therapy

Wilderness therapy programs, also referred to as **outdoor behavioral health care programs (OBHs)**, provide a novel and challenging opportunity for at-risk adolescents who may have resisted counseling in other settings. Substance abuse and behavioral disorders (e.g., attention-deficit/hyperactivity disorder [AD/HD], oppositional defiant disorder [ODD]) are likely to be the most prevalent mental health issues that counselors in wilderness therapy settings will treat (Russell, Gillis, & Lewis, 2008). Wilderness therapy programs require adolescent clients to get out of their comfort zones and confront their problem behaviors. Adolescents receive traditional counseling in a wilderness environment, where they live with other at-risk youth. They engage with their peers in physically demanding activities that require them to build trust; use problem-solving skills; and develop self-reliance, self-confidence, and an internal locus of control (Hill, 2007).

Adolescents in wilderness therapy programs often develop a close working relationship with their counselors because they allow themselves to be vulnerable to the unknown demands of the wilderness as well as to group activities that are perceived to be risky. Counselors use Adlerian counseling, reality therapy, and behavioral therapy, frequently incorporating metaphors from the wilderness to help adolescents make connections to their own struggles (Hill, 2007). Counselors are generally not the wilderness guides who lead the adolescents on their activities; counselors usually are responsible for conducting the initial assessment, developing the treatment plan, involving the family before and after the wilderness component, facilitating individual counseling and groups in the wilderness, helping adolescents transfer their learning to their home environments, and providing aftercare programs. Now complete Activity 8.3.

ACTIVITY 8.3 INTERVIEWING A PROFESSIONAL COUNSELOR

Now that you have learned about some of the various career opportunities that are available to mental health counselors, deepen your understanding by interviewing a counselor working in a community/agency, hospital, corrections setting, private practice setting, pastoral counseling, family counseling, or wilderness setting. Spend as much time as you can at the site. Write a report that includes a description of the counselor's role, the overall counseling program, the mission of the setting, and the referral procedures. Include any other information that the counselor thinks you should know about the setting and your own personal observations and impressions.

MENTAL HEALTH COUNSELING ISSUES

According to the National Survey on Drug Use and Health (SAMHSA, 2013) an estimated 43.7 million (18.6%) Americans ages 18 years and older experience some form of mental illness over their lifetime. Another 20.7 million adults (8.8%) struggle with a substance use disorder. The Substance Abuse and Mental Health Services Administration (SAMHSA, 2014b), predicts that by 2020, worldwide mental health and substance abuse disorders will cause more disability than all physical disorders combined. In order to effectively serve their clients, counselors must be knowledgeable about a wide range of mental health issues, including but not limited to depression, anxiety, eating disorders, post-traumatic stress disorder (PTSD), and addictions. In addition to client issues, this section briefly discusses the role of diagnosis in counseling, although a more lengthy treatise on assessment, diagnosis, and treatment of mental and emotional disorders can be found in Chapter 12.

Depression

Major depressive disorder, commonly referred to more generally as depression, is one of the most common client issues a counselor encounters. Nearly 15 million, or approximately 7%, of adults in the United States experience depression annually. Women are more likely to experience depression than men. The median age of the onset of depression is 32 years; however, clients of any age may present to counseling with symptoms of depression (National Institute for Mental Health, 2018).

Depression is characterized by persistent feelings of sadness or irritability (see Case Study 8.1). Clients with depression may report feeling empty or numb and may be tearful during sessions. Clients with depression may also report a loss of interest in hobbies, work, and sexual activity. Sleep disturbance is another common feature of depression. Some depressed clients may have difficulty falling or staying asleep, whereas others sleep more than usual. Clients who are depressed may report feeling exhausted or completely drained all of the time. Clients with depression may report difficulty with concentration or feeling unable to think clearly. Feelings of excessive guilt or worthlessness are also common symptoms of depression. Appetite may increase or decrease during a depressive episode (American Psychiatric Association, 2013). Isolating from family and friends, crying spells, feelings of hopelessness, and neglecting personal hygiene may also occur during an episode of depression. It is important to note that in order to meet the criteria for depression, symptoms cannot be caused by an underlying medical condition or the effects of a medication or drug. Look at Case Study 8.1 and answer the questions. Additionally, culture can dramatically influence the manner in which depressive symptoms are expressed. Activity 8.4 may help you broaden your vocabulary of feeling words to enhance cultural sensitivity and emotional expression. Clients from some cultures may report headaches, problems of the heart, or feelings of guilt or imbalance, all of which may signal depression.

CASE STUDY 8.1

Sienna, an 18-year-old white female, recently moved four hours away from her parents to attend college on a scholarship. When her parents visit her for the first time, they are surprised to see that Sienna has lost about 15 pounds of body weight. Her dorm room is in a state of disarray. When they inquire about how school is going, Sienna becomes tearful and reports she has been missing a lot of class because of oversleeping.

1. Do you think Sienna may be struggling with depression? Explain.
2. What symptoms does she exhibit?
3. What other information would you want to know about Sienna?

ACTIVITY 8.4 INCREASE YOUR FEELING WORD VOCABULARY

Generate a list of as many feeling words as possible for each of the following categories of emotions: mad, sad, glad, and scared. Think about the intensity of each word. How can a vast emotional vocabulary improve your work with clients? Were some feeling categories easier to generate words for than others? How might your cultural group membership influence your ability to generate feeling words or express different emotions?

Sometimes a client may become so depressed that he or she considers taking his or her own life through suicide. According to the most current report from the American Association of Suicidology (2015), 41,149 people in the United States ended their lives through suicide in 2013. Suicide was the 10th leading cause of death in the United States in the total population and the 2nd leading cause of death for young adults ages 15–24 years. Rates of suicide vary among different cultural groups. For example, males are four times more likely to complete suicide than women (78%; 32,055 out of 41,149 completed suicides in 2013), with white males being the highest risk category. Women are three times more likely than men to attempt suicide (American Association of Suicidology, 2015). Lesbian, gay, bisexual, and transgender (LGBT) youth are also in a higher risk category for suicide attempts (American Association of Suicidology, 2016).

Counselors must be prepared to assess for suicide risk and take actions to protect clients from harming themselves when necessary. When conducting a suicide risk assessment, counselors should ask directly if the client is having thoughts of hurting themselves or taking their own life. Counselors should also assess for a suicide plan, access to means to follow through with the plan, and the intent to follow through with the plan. Counselors must be aware of acute risk factors, including direct suicidal statements; talking or writing about death; and attempts to gain access to a means of suicide, particularly a firearm. Clients who have previously made a suicide attempt are also in a high-risk category. The following mnemonic, IS PATH WARM, can assist counselors in remembering risk factors for suicide (American Association of Suicidology, 2015): **I**deation; **S**ubstance abuse; **P**urposelessness; **A**nxiety; **T**rapped; **H**opelessness; **W**ithdrawal; **A**nger; **R**ecklessness; **M**ood changes.

Although it is not possible to predict with absolute accuracy when a client will make a suicide attempt, these risk factors assist counselors in identifying clients who may need immediate crisis intervention. Remember, if a client is an imminent risk of harm to him- or herself, counselors are ethically able to break confidentiality in order to protect the client. This may mean calling 911 and notifying family and friends. It is even possible to have a client involuntarily hospitalized if the client is an imminent risk of harm to him- or herself but refuses treatment. When dealing with a client in crisis, it is important to follow an ethical decision-making model and consult with a supervisor or trusted colleague. It is important to conduct suicide risk assessments with clients on an ongoing basis. Just asking about suicide once during an initial intake session is not enough.

Anxiety

Anxiety disorders are commonly encountered client issues. In the United States, 18.1% of the adult population struggles with an anxiety disorder. Women are 60% more likely to experience an anxiety disorder than men, and anxiety disorders are more common among white Americans than among other racial groups in the United States (National Institute of Mental Health, 2015). The DSM-5 (American Psychiatric Association, 2013) specifies the diagnostic criteria for numerous anxiety disorders, including separation anxiety disorder, selective mutism, specific phobias, social anxiety disorder, panic disorders, agoraphobia, generalized anxiety disorder, substance- or medication-induced anxiety disorder, anxiety due to a medical condition, and unspecified anxiety disorder. The generic term **anxiety** is typically used to refer to generalized anxiety disorder, which typically develops in adolescence or early adulthood, and is characterized by excessive or constant worry, restlessness, irritability, and disturbed sleep. Clients struggling with anxiety may report a lump in their throat, sweating hands, a racing heart rate, and an upset stomach. Anxiety may be triggered by exposure to specific stimuli, such as being around a large group of people, or it may be experienced in a more generalized manner. Some clients experience panic attacks, which may include shortness of breath and chest pains. Sometimes, feelings of anxiety and panic are so intense that people mistake a panic attack for a heart attack and go to the emergency department. Deep breathing can reduce stress and anxiety. Activity 8.5 presents a breathing exercise that you can teach clients who are experiencing anxiety.

ACTIVITY 8.5

Deep breathing, guided imagery, and progressive muscle relaxation exercises promote wellness and can help reduce symptoms of anxiety. Practice a basic deep breathing exercise to see how you feel. Sit up straight and close your eyes. Inhale deeply and slowly. Hold the breath for 3 seconds and exhale slowly. Repeat 10 times. How do you feel?

Eating Disorders

Eating disorders affect women and men across ethnic groups. Counselors should be aware that eating disorder symptoms and symptom-related distress vary substantially among cultural groups (Franko, Becker, Thomas, & Herzog, 2007). A primary factor contributing to the development of eating disorders is the media's emphasis on the idea that to be attractive or of worth one must be thin. The development of an eating disorder may also be influenced by family dynamics, requirements of a sport, or a history of abuse. Three common types of eating disorders are anorexia nervosa, bulimia nervosa, and binge eating disorder.

Anorexia nervosa is characterized by restricted food intake resulting in a lower body weight than what is minimally acceptable for health, a fear of gaining weight coupled with behavior that interferes with weight gain, distorted perceptions of body size and body shape, and an underestimation of the effect of low body weight on overall health and functioning (American Psychiatric Association, 2013). Clients with anorexia may drastically restrict their food intake. An estimated 0.9% of women and 0.3% of men struggle with anorexia nervosa during their lifetime (Hudson, Hiripi, Pope, & Kessler, 2007).

Bulimia nervosa involves binge eating and inappropriate compensatory measures to prevent or reduce weight gain (American Psychiatric Association, 2013). Compensatory measures, also referred to as purging behaviors, may include forced or spontaneous vomiting; the use of diuretics, diet pills, and laxatives; and excessive patterns of exercise (see Case Study 8.2). An estimated 1.5% of women and 0.5% of men experience bulimia nervosa during their lifetime (Hudson et al., 2007).

Binge eating disorder involves eating large quantities of food in a short period of time and feelings of being unable to control food intake. Clients who struggle with binge eating disorder may experience shame, guilt, and distress. Binge eating disorder is distinct from bulimia nervosa in that no compensatory measures are involved (American Psychiatric Association, 2013).

THINK ABOUT IT 8.1   Social Media and Mental Health

Social media allows people to communicate and connect through the use of technology. Social media can be used to combat loneliness and feelings of social isolation or for more destructive purposes including cyber bullying and body shaming. Do you think social media has more of a positive or negative impact on mental health? Consider the impact of social media on various cultural groups. How will you plan to address the connection between social media and mental health in your future counseling practice?

CASE STUDY 8.2

Veronica was a star soccer player in high school and college. After college, Veronica gained 15 pounds. She decided that, to maintain an attractive body, she needed to increase her level of exercise. Veronica now wakes up at 4:00 a.m. every morning to exercise for 2 hours before going to work. After work, Veronica works out for another hour and a half with one of her friends. Veronica has also started taking fat-burning pills that she purchased at a nutritional supplement store.

1. Do you think Veronica has an eating disorder? Explain.
2. What symptoms are present?
3. What other information would you want to know about Veronica?

Addictions

Consider the following cases. Preston is a 20-year-old, white, male college student. He goes out drinking with friends 4 to 5 nights a week. His friends enjoy laughing at his wild behavior when he is drinking and describe Preston as the life of the party. Preston typically drinks until he passes out. Sometimes when he wakes up in the morning, he cannot remember what happened the night before when he was drinking. Often, he has unprotected sex with young women he meets at bars.

Ty is a 45-year-old, working-class African American man. He works two jobs to support his family. Ty smokes marijuana daily and occasionally uses crack cocaine. Recently, he tested positive for marijuana on a random drug screen at work. His employer is requiring him to seek substance abuse treatment to keep his job.

Luella is a 55-year-old, retired Latina schoolteacher. She has never used illegal drugs or alcohol in her life. Two years ago, she was in an automobile accident and was prescribed pain medication by her physician. She still takes the medication daily and has had to increase the dosage. Sometimes she wakes up in the middle of the night sweating, trembling, and feeling nauseated. She has to take the pain medications to make these symptoms subside.

These cases describe examples of typical client issues you may encounter as a professional counselor. Which, if any, of these clients have a problem with substance use? How do you know if a client needs help with these issues? **Substance use disorder** is a pattern of substance use that is maladaptive, and creates significant distress and impairment (American Psychiatric Association, 2013). Clients with a substance use problem may continue to use the substance despite social and interpersonal problems or legal consequences related to the substance. In addition, individuals who meet the criteria for substance use disorder may use substances in physically hazardous situations and fail to fulfill major role obligations at work, school, and/or home. Clients with substance use disorders frequently use more of a substance than they intended to use and are unable to reduce or control use of the substance. These individuals spend a great deal of time using the substance and reduce their participation in important social, occupational, or leisure activities.

Tolerance is another characteristic of substance use disorder. **Tolerance** occurs when the effect of a particular dosage of a substance is lessened because of repeated exposure to the substance (Hasin, Hatzenbuehler, Keyes, & Ogburn, 2006). In other words, one would have to increase the dosage of a substance to achieve the same effect that was once achieved using a smaller dosage.

Withdrawal is also a marker of substance use disorder (American Psychiatric Association, 2013). **Withdrawal** indicates physical dependence on a substance. If the substance is not present in the body, an individual with substance dependence may experience symptoms such as increased irritability, sleep disturbance, headaches, fever, nausea, vomiting, diarrhea, tremors, seizures, strokes, or even death. An individual may take the substance in order to relieve these symptoms (Hasin et al., 2006).

Approximately 35% of adults struggle with some type of substance disorder in their life-time. Substance disorders are more prevalent among men than women. Approximately 20% of men struggle with alcohol use disorder, and 11.5% of men struggle with drug use disorders in their lifetime, compared with 8% and 5% of women, respectively. Rates of substance use disor-der are the highest among adults in early and middle adulthood and generally decrease with age (National Comorbidity Survey Replication, 2005). Activities 8.6 and 8.7 are designed to bring awareness of how the media portrays substance use and the impact of these messages. Activity 8.8 provides an opportunity for self-reflection on personal substance use.

ACTIVITY 8.6

For 2 days, count the number of advertisements or references to alcohol and cigarettes you hear and see in the media. Write a one- to two-page reaction paper discussing your thoughts, feelings, and insights regarding how the media portrays substance use and the impact of these messages.

ACTIVITY 8.7

Watch a movie that focuses on substance abuse. Some examples are *The Lost Weekend* (1945), *Clean and Sober* (1988), *The Basketball Diaries* (1995), *Leaving Las Vegas* (1995), *28 Days* (2000), *Traffic* (2000), *Blow* (2001), *Candy* (2006), and *The Departed* (2006). Process your thoughts, feelings, and reactions to the portrayal of substance use in the film.

ACTIVITY 8.8

Try this experiential activity to increase your empathy for clients with substance abuse and dependency issues. Identify which mood-altering substances (except for legally prescribed medications) or activities play a role in your life. These substances and activities may include alcohol, marijuana, cigarettes, caffeine, shopping, gambling, exercise, sugar, and sex. Engage in a 2-week period of complete abstinence from all self-identified mood-altering substances and activities, and keep a daily journal of this process. How did you feel physically? What was the most challenging part of remaining abstinent? Were you able to remain abstinent? How will this experience affect your work as a professional counselor with clients who abuse substances?

Drug and Alcohol Treatment Approaches

There are three primary approaches to the treatment of drug and alcohol use disorders: the medical model, 12-step model, and strengths-based approach.

MEDICAL MODEL   Proponents of the **medical model** view addiction as a chronic and progres-sive disease, similar to diabetes or heart disease. Research provides evidence that a biological basis or genetic predisposition for addiction exists. Treatment based on the medical model may include **detoxification** or medical stabilization, reduction of withdrawal symptoms, the prescription of medications, and intensive therapy designed to increase coping skills and prevent **relapse,** or the return to substance use (van Wormer & Davis, 2008). Total **abstinence**, or restraint from substance use, is the goal of treatment based on the medical model. Many hospital and community settings ascribe to the medical model of substance abuse treatment.

TWELVE-STEP MODEL   **Alcoholics Anonymous (AA)** is the original **12-step program**. Founded in 1935 by a stockbroker and a surgeon with alcohol problems, AA has grown to be the largest recovery program in the world, with approximately 2 million members in 175 countries (Alcoholics Anonymous, 2016). AA is a self-supported organization for men and women who desire to live a sober life. The 12-step model of AA includes a spiritual component, but the model is not affiliated with any religion or religious organization. Members of AA attend meetings, up to several times a day, where they share their stories and offer support for one another. Members of AA believe that they can be in **recovery** from alcoholism, but they will always be addicted to alcohol, and they must take sobriety one day at a time for the rest of their lives. Recovery not only involves abstaining from substance use but also involves a process of psychological and emotional healing. Social support and coping strategies are considered essential aspects of recovery (Laudet, 2008). Numerous other 12-step programs have been developed to help people with addictions to substances other than alcohol and addictions to behaviors, including Narcotics Anonymous (NA), Crystal Meth Anonymous, Gamblers Anonymous, Overeaters Anonymous (OA), and Sex and Love Addicts Anonymous. Al-Anon is a program for family members of alcoholics. The 12-step model is compatible with the medical model of treatment. Activity 8.9 aims to familiarize you with 12-step meetings and helps you gain a better understanding of what clients may experience while attending these meetings. This activity can also help develop empathy for clients.

ACTIVITY 8.9

Identify and attend an open 12-step meeting or support group in your area. Write a one- to two page reaction paper to the meeting. Discuss your thoughts, feelings, reactions, comfort level, and any other insights you gained from the experience. The following websites may be helpful in locating a local 12-step group: Alcoholics Anonymous, www.aa.org; Narcotics Anonymous, www.na.org; Gamblers Anonymous, www.gamblersanonymous.org; Al-Anon/Alateen, www.al-anon.alateen.org; Crystal Meth Anonymous, www.crystalmeth.org; Sex and Love Addicts Anonymous, www. slaafws.org; Overeaters Anonymous, www.oa.org.

STRENGTHS-BASED APPROACHES   **Strengths-based treatment** approaches are an alternative to the medical model. The goal is **harm reduction**, or minimization of the social, legal, and medical problems associated with unmanaged addiction (Logan & Marlatt, 2010; van Wormer & Davis, 2008). Total abstinence is considered one among many methods of harm reduction. Learning to control substance use is also considered a valid goal of treatment. Other characteristics of strengths-based treatment approaches include an emphasis on personal choice of the client; viewing the client as a competent person with many positive assets; the cultivation of hope, meaning, and a sense of accomplishment; and the development of a social support system. Now complete Activity 8.9 to gain deeper insights into substance use counseling.

VOICES FROM THE FIELD 8.4   Adapting Mindsets for Effective Addictions Counseling, by Brenda J. Edwards

---

Working as a counselor in the substance abuse field requires a capacity for one to be open to "uncharacteristic" thinking and the behaviors that ensue. When first starting to work with clients dealing with substance abuse issues, an initial response is that it makes perfect sense that a client will change or terminate a behavior that contributes to negative and often adverse consequences.

Consequences such as DUIs, incarceration, loss of child custody, loss of employment, etc., would appear sufficient enough to warrant a change in or termination of alcohol- and drug-using behaviors. Yet one quickly learns that this is often not the case. One also learns that a client using and abusing substances has now "tainted" or changed his or her ways of making sense of the world.

As a beginning counselor, coming to terms with what should make sense, yet doesn't make sense, is essential. However, arriving at this point requires a competence to first listen to the client's story and then seek to understand how that client now makes sense of his or her world, subsequent to substance abuse.

More importantly, one must understand that, although you can comprehend that a client's world would be much better without use or abuse of alcohol and drugs, the client's ability to reach this comprehension is now "colored" by the effects of alcohol and drugs. So strive to develop patience for distorted ways of thinking and being in the world. Better yet, have a knowledge base of the effects of alcohol and drugs on the human capacity.

ACTIVITY 8.10

Learn more about what it is like to work with clients with a drug or alcohol problem by interviewing an addictions counselor. Find out why the professional counselor chose to work in the addictions field, what treatment approach he or she ascribes to, what advice he or she would have for a beginning counselor considering entering the addictions field, what challenges he or she has faced as an addictions counselor, and what aspects of working as an addictions counselor are most rewarding.

Alcohol and Drug Use Issues in Special Populations

ADOLESCENTS   Adolescence is a developmental period during which young people attempt to establish independence from their parents, strengthen peer relationships, and develop their own identities. During this period, many adolescents experiment with alcohol and drugs (Burrow-Sanchez, 2006; van Wormer & Davis, 2008). According to the Centers for Disease Control and Prevention (2014), 80% of high school seniors have used alcohol, 46% have used marijuana, and 8% have used cocaine.

Substance use in adolescence is particularly concerning because the adolescent brain is continuing to develop and mature. Substance use can have a long-term impact on brain functioning (Foltran, Gregori, Franchin, Verduci, & Giovannini, 2011). In addition, early age of first use of alcohol and drugs is a risk factor for the development of substance dependence and other psychological disorders later in life (van Wormer & Davis, 2008).

Substance abuse in adolescence is linked with higher rates of unprotected sex, sexual assault and rape, teen pregnancy, physical violence, and car accidents. For these reasons, prevention is critical. **Prevention** efforts include alcohol and drug education programs and programs designed to increase coping and social resistance skills. Activity 8.11 introduces a professional association focused on helping clients with substance use difficulties. Activity 8.12 helps you gain awareness and knowledge of the adolescent culture.

ACTIVITY 8.11

Learn more about the division of the American Counseling Association (ACA) for professional counselors interested in addictions: the International Association of Addictions and Offender Counselors (IAAOC). Investigate the IAAOC website, at www.iaaoc.org, and read about the history, mission, and current goals of the IAAOC.

ACTIVITY 8.12

Establishing trust and building a therapeutic relationship with adolescent clients can be challenging. Using your client's language is a great way to build rapport. Use the Internet and any other available resources to generate a list of as many slang or street names for drugs as possible. Study the list so that you are familiar with the words adolescent and adult clients may use to talk about drugs.

CULTURALLY DIVERSE CLIENTS   Racial, ethnic, and cultural minority clients are underserved by traditional approaches to addictions treatment. Minority groups typically experience greater consequences of substance use, including higher rates of drug- and alcohol-related deaths and higher rates of incarceration for substance-related activities (van Wormer & Davis, 2008). When working with culturally diverse clients, it is crucial to address issues of oppression and discrimination, and how these experiences relate to substance use. The professional counselor should also discuss the client's level of acculturation, level of education, socioeconomic status, spiritual and religious beliefs, and cultural values and norms (Lassiter & Chang, 2006; van Wormer & Davis, 2008). The professional counselor should strive to establish a collaborative relationship with the client and explore cultural explanations for the cause of substance abuse and dependency. Treatment should address the client's beliefs about the cause of the problem and may include integrating family and community resources or working with a traditional healer from within the client's culture (Lassiter & Chang, 2006). As a professional counselor, one should always be aware of the cultural appropriateness and implications for any intervention. The purpose of Activity 8.13 is to assist in viewing interventions through a cultural lens.

ACTIVITY 8.13

Review the 12 steps of AA and similar organizations. What are your reactions? What cultural groups do you think the 12 steps would be the most and least appropriate for? Why?

Another underserved group that can be considered its own cultural group is individuals with disabilities. Not all mental health counselors have received sufficient training to work competently with people who have various disabilities. Current research is focusing on improving counselors' expertise in serving people with disabilities. Strike, Skovholt, and Hummel (2004) studied mental health counselors' self-assessments of their competence in working with people with disabilities, specifically in the areas of self-awareness, perceived knowledge, and perceived skills. Their findings show that the more disability-related counseling experiences that counselors have, the higher their levels of perceived disability competence. In the next section, we will discuss issues related to disabilities and rehabilitation counseling. Table 8.1 lists professional organizations, publications, and websites for mental health counseling.

TABLE 8.1 Professional Organizations, Publications, and Websites for Mental Health Counseling

The **American Counseling Association (ACA)** publishes the *Journal of Counseling & Development*; www.counseling.org. The ACA offers multimedia resources relevant to each counseling specialty. The ACA has numerous divisions representing specialty areas, which counselors may also join. Each state has a branch of the ACA, and many branches maintain divisions of specialty areas as well.

American Mental Health Counselors Association (AMHCA); www.amhca.org

Council for the Accreditation of Counseling and Related Educational Programs (CACREP); www.cacrep.org

President's New Freedom Commission on Mental Health (2003). *Achieving the promise: Transforming mental health care in America* (Publication No. SMA 03-3832): www.mentalhealthcommission.gov/reports/FinalReport/toc.html

Marriage and Family Counseling:

The **American Association for Marriage and Family Therapy** (AAMFT) publishes the *Journal of Marital and Family Therapy (JMFT)*: www.aamft.org

The **Association of Marital and Family Therapy Regulatory Boards (AMFTRB)** is responsible for the regulation of marriage and family therapists in their respective jurisdictions. The AMFTRB uses the standardized MFT National Exam, which assists state boards of examiners in evaluating applicants for licensure or certification in marriage and family therapy: www.amftrb.org

The **American Association of Pastoral Counselors (AAPC)** publishes *Sacred Spaces: The e-Journal of the American Association of Pastoral Counselors*: www.aapc.org

Wilderness Therapy (Outdoor Behavioral Health Care Programs):

Association for Experiential Education (AEE) publishes the *Journal of Experiential Education*: www.aee.org

National Association of Therapeutic Wilderness Camping (NATWC) publishes the *Journal of Therapeutic Wilderness Camping*: www.natwc.org

Outdoor Behavioral Healthcare Industry Council (OBHIC): www.obhic.com

Wilderness Therapy Treatment Programs: www.wildernesstherapy.org

REHABILITATION COUNSELING

Is rehabilitation counseling a specialty of counseling, or is it a separate profession requiring separate training? This question has been around as long as rehabilitation counseling and continues to be debated today. The parent organizations of the two professional rehabilitation counseling associations reflect this disparity. The American Rehabilitation Counseling Association (ARCA) is a division of the American Counseling Association, and the National Rehabilitation Counseling Association (NRCA) is a professional division of the National Rehabilitation Association. In addition to these two professional organizations, until 2015 there were two accreditation bodies, the Council for Accreditation of Counseling and Related Educational Programs (CACREP) and the Council on Rehabilitation Education (CORE) that accredited counseling programs. CACREP accredits master's and doctoral-level programs in counseling and its specialties (i.e., addiction counseling; career counseling; clinical mental health counseling; marriage, couple, and family counseling; school counseling; student affairs and college counseling). Missing from this list of specialties is rehabilitation counseling. CORE accredits undergraduate and graduate programs in rehabilitation counseling. In 2015, CACREP and CORE announced that they had signed a Plan of Merger Agreement. The merger will become effective in 2017, with CACREP taking responsibility for the mission of both organizations. This merger represents a step toward unified standards as well as a recognition that all counselors need to be knowledgeable about disability issues. Give rehabilitation counseling some further thought by completing Think About It 8.2.

THINK ABOUT IT 8.2

How do you view rehabilitation counseling? After researching the websites of ARCA, NRCA, and other resources, do you consider rehabilitation counseling a specialty of counseling or a distinct profession? Provide arguments to support your view.

The current definitions of rehabilitation and rehabilitation counseling seem applicable regardless of whether you view rehabilitation counseling as a specialty within the counseling profession or as a distinct profession. **Rehabilitation** refers to "the process of evaluation of a person with impairments, and the interventions aiming at that person's social participation" (Blouin & Vallejo Echeverri, 2012, p. 9). **Rehabilitation counseling** "is a systematic process which assists persons with physical, mental, developmental, cognitive, and emotional disabilities to achieve their personal, career, and independent living goals in the most integrated setting possible through the application of the counseling process" (Commission on Rehabilitation Counselor Certification, 2018, p. 1). **Rehabilitation counselors** "are committed to facilitating the personal, social, and economic independence of individuals with disabilities. In fulfilling this commitment, rehabilitation counselors work with people, programs, institutions, and service delivery systems" (Commission on Rehabilitation Counselor Certification, 2018, p. 1). According to the Americans with Disabilities Act of 1990, **disability** means: "(a) a physical or mental impairment that substantially limits one or more of the major life activities of such individual; (b) a record of such an impairment; or (c) being regarded as having such an impairment" (U.S. Equal Employment Opportunity Commission, 2008). The World Health Organization views disability as an interaction "between individuals with a health condition (such as cerebral palsy, Down syndrome, depression) and personal and environmental factors (such as negative attitudes, inaccessible transportation and public buildings, and limited social support)" (World Health Organization, 2011, p. 7). The American Community Survey (ACS) categorizes disabilities into one of six categories: hearing disability, visual disability, cognitive disability, ambulatory disability, self-care disability, and independent living disability (Erickson, Lee, & von Schrader, 2014).

In addition to a shared definition, rehabilitation as a specialty and rehabilitation as a distinct profession share a common philosophy and goal (Patterson, 2009). The goal of rehabilitation counseling is to facilitate the independence, integration, and inclusion of people with disabilities. Rehabilitation counseling is a systematic process that may use many interventions, such as behavioral, social, psychological, and vocational counseling; collaborating with the client in the formulation of a treatment program; consulting and collaborating with other professionals and services; and supporting the client toward self-advocacy (Commission on Rehabilitation Counselor Certification, 2017). The rehabilitation philosophy is integrated into the rehabilitation counseling *Scope of Practice*, which outlines the core assumptions of the statement and the underlying values of rehabilitation counseling. The underlying values include the following:

- Value of independence, integration, and inclusion of all people with disabilities in employment and in their communities
- Belief in the dignity and worth of all people
- Commitment to equal justice and advocacy work in the support of individuals with disabilities
- Emphasis on holistic practice
- Recognition of the assets of the person
- Commitment to a comprehensive service plan that includes the consumer and the rehabilitation counselor (see Commission on Rehabilitation Counselor Certification, 2017).

VOICES FROM THE FIELD 8.5   **Rehabilitation Counselors and Client Recovery, by Brad Smith**

During my inpatient spinal cord rehabilitation, I was required to meet with a rehabilitation counselor once per week. At the time, I felt at peace with my situation. I did not think I really needed to talk with a counselor. But after meeting with him, I realized how good it felt to just talk to someone about my situation and about my goals for the future. We talked about my passion for endurance sports and how I could get involved with sports for people with disabilities. We also talked about resources for things that may come up as a result of a spinal cord injury, such as bladder control and skin issues. Working with a rehabilitation counselor was an important part of my recovery and growth.

Summary of Rehabilitation Laws

Although the current definition of rehabilitation counseling is comprehensive and includes personal, career, and independent living goals, the early roots of rehabilitation counseling were based in the vocational area and were closely linked with the State-Federal Rehabilitation Program. The relationship between rehabilitation counseling and the State-Federal Rehabilitation Program is intertwined with legislation regarding financial support, education, civil rights, and the treatment of people with disabilities. Rehabilitation counseling evolved primarily from legislation. Because the primary emphasis of rehabilitation counseling is to empower clients to gain independence, improve their quality of life, and earn a living wage, professional counselors must become familiar with legislation on rehabilitation. Some of the major pieces of legislation that influenced the rehabilitation movement include the following (O'Brien & Graham, 2009; Patterson, Bruyére, Szymanski, & Jenkins, 2012):

- The War Risk Insurance Act of 1914 provided rehabilitation and vocational training to veterans who were injured during their military service.
- The Smith-Hughes Act of 1917 began the vocational rehabilitation movement by providing funding for vocational education.
- The Smith-Fess Act of 1920 provided counseling, training, prosthetic appliances, and job placement for individuals physically disabled from industrial injuries.
- The Vocational Rehabilitation Program of 1935 became a permanent part of the Social Security Act.
- The Barden-LaFollette Act of 1943 broadened the eligibility for disabilities to include individuals with mental illness and retardation, and expanded services for physical restoration.
- The Vocational Rehabilitation Act of 1954 (also known as the Hill-Burton Act), and subsequent amendments in 1965, 1967, 1968, and 1973, authorized services for the severely disabled; extended eligibility status to include individuals who are disadvantaged by reason of age, education, ethnicity, or other factors; provided funds for graduate training and research; improved facilities at rehabilitation settings; and provided funding for new construction of rehabilitation facilities. It also provided annual evaluations of eligibility.
- The Rehabilitation Acts of 1973 and 1974 emphasized services to individuals with severe disabilities and involved the consumer in the rehabilitation process with the establishment of the individual written rehabilitation plan (IWRP).
- The Education for all Handicapped Children's Act of 1975 mandated that all states must provide education for all disabled children (age 3 to 21 years) with the rule of least restrictive environment.
- The Rehabilitation, Comprehensive Services, and Developmental Disabilities Act of 1978 created the National Institute of Handicapped Research and the National Council on the Handicapped. It also provided for independent living services.
- The Americans with Disabilities Act of 1990 prohibited discrimination against individuals with disabilities in employment, transportation, public accommodations, and activities at state and local governments.
- The Individuals with Disabilities Education Act of 1991 and 2004 was an extension of the Education for all Handicapped Children's Act of 1975. These acts extended services to include brain injury and autism and transitional services.
- The Ticket to Work and Work Incentives Improvement Act of 1999 provided health care and employment preparation and placement services for individuals with disabilities.
- Americans with Disabilities Amendment Acts of 2008, while still upholding ADA's definition of disability, made it easier for individuals to establish a disability and

expanded the definition of major life activities (U.S. Equal Employment Opportunity Commission, 2008).

- The Workforce Innovation and Opportunity Act 2014 (WIOA) assists job seekers' access to employment, education, training, and support services (U.S. Department of Labor, 2017). This act has significant implications for disabilities programs.

VOICES FROM THE FIELD 8.6   Rehabilitation Counselors Make a Difference, by Tracy Roberts

---

Working as a rehabilitation counselor provides me with the very rewarding opportunity to journey with clients who have a suspected or diagnosed disabling condition. As their rehabilitation counselor, a part of my role includes working with them to meet their personal and professional goals. Adjustment and grief counseling, knowledge of medical aspects, psycho-education, functional and vocational needs analysis, accommodations advocacy, resource identification, and cost management are all integral parts of my very comprehensive field. The disabilities themselves may be acquired, traumatic, or even catastrophic, but no matter the scope of the disability, they affect the individual, the family, and our very communities. My work thus far has brought me closest to the stories of those living with disorders of thought and mood, low vision and vision loss, spinal cord injury, and blast and combat-related mild traumatic brain injury and posttraumatic stress disorder.

As a rehabilitation team member, I must provide recommendations and integrate those of other mental health professionals to serve the best interest of the client. As an independent practitioner, I encourage, inform, and empathize with clients in their quest for optimal health and wellness. I gratefully heed this calling because not only am I continuously learning but also am daily touched by the strength, courage, and spirit of people with disability challenges who seek to most fully engage life.

Disability Eligibility and Demographics

Since the early days of working primarily with the State-Federal Rehabilitation Program and with rehabilitation facilities and rehabilitation hospitals, the settings of rehabilitation counseling practice have expanded to include locations in the public and private sectors. Rehabilitation counselors can be found in private rehabilitation and insurance companies, substance abuse agencies, employee assistance programs, Pre-K–12 schools, and college and university disability services offices. In addition, "disabilities" is now seen as an umbrella term for impairments, activity limitations, and participation restrictions (World Health Organization, 2011). Regardless of the disability (e.g., physical, mental, cognitive) and the setting (e.g., private or public sector) for services, for individuals to receive services they must have an identifiable and diagnosed disability.

The eligibility for rehabilitation counseling services related to a disability varies depending on the funding source, residence of the client, and other factors. For an individual to be eligible for state or federal rehabilitation services, the individual must have a physical or mental disability that is stable or slowly progressive, the impairment cannot be acute or of an emergency nature, and the impairment must be documented on file. In addition, the impairment must hinder the individual from employment, and the employability of the individual must benefit from rehabilitation service (U.S. Department of Health and Human Services, 2018).

Today, people with disabilities who need rehabilitation services are viewed by professional counselors as active consumers of services who have choices of counselors and services. This perspective represents progress from the more traditional viewpoint of the medical model, which tended to regard people with disabilities as passive recipients who must accept a treatment that is prescribed without their input. Sales (2007) advocates for a collaborative approach to counseling known as the **empowerment model of rehabilitation counseling**: the counselor treats the client as the expert on his or her abilities and disabilities, and the client is encouraged to identify counseling goals.

The shift to considering people with disabilities as active consumers, and as individuals who should be identified as "people" instead of by the disability that they have, is also reflected in the use of **"people first" language**. To project a social model instead of a medical model (which would describe the person as a "patient"), rehabilitation counselors may identify their clients not only as "clients," but also by the descriptions of "a person who needs services," "a consumer," or "a person who has a disability" (as in "a person who has schizophrenia" instead of "a schizophrenic").

More than one billion individuals, or 15% of the world population, experience some form of disability, with 110 million to 190 million individuals experiencing significant difficulties in functioning (World Health Organization, 2011). In 2013, the prevalence of disability for all people in the United States was 12.6% (39,187,600 individuals). The prevalence of disability for people aged 5 to 15 years was 5.3% and increased to 50.7% for people aged 75 years. In regard to gender, females of all ages have a slightly higher prevalence rate (12.7%) of disabilities compared with males (12.4%). There were also differences based on race for working-age people (age 21 to 64 years). The prevalence rate for whites was 10.7%; for black/African Americans, 14.1%; Asians, 4.6%; Native Americans, 18.4%; and persons of some other race, 10.1% (Erickson & von Schrader, 2012). The prevalence rates for disabilities within the United States saw a slight increase from 2012 (12.1%). The global rate for disabilities is also increasing, largely due to the aging of the population, increases in instances of chronic health conditions, and improved methodologies for assessing disabilities. Table 8.2 provides a listing of rehabilitation counseling resources.

TABLE 8.2 Professional Organizations, Publications, and Websites for Rehabilitation Counseling

American Psychological Association (APA) Division 22 (Rehabilitation Psychology) publishes the journal *Rehabilitation Psychology*: www.div22.org/index.php

American Rehabilitation Counseling Association (ARCA) is a division of the ACA and publishes a newsletter at www.arcaweb.org

Commission on Rehabilitation Counselor Certification (CRCC): www.crccertification.com

Council on Rehabilitation Education (CORE): www.core-rehab.org

International Association of Addictions and Offender Counselors (IAAOC) is a member association of the ACA: www.iaaoc.org

International Association of Rehabilitation Professionals (IARP) publishes the Rehabilitation Professional http://www.rehabpro.org/

National Rehabilitation Association (NRCA) publishes the *Journal of Applied Rehabilitation Counseling* http://nrca-net.org/

Adaptation to Disability

The onset of **chronic illness and disability (CID)** has a profound and life-changing impact on the individual as well as on their families. The psychological and social consequences of CID can have damaging effects on daily functioning, so it is essential that rehabilitation counselors are knowledgeable about models of psychosocial adaption to CID (Livneh & Bishop, 2012) in addition to traditional theories of counseling. According to Livneh and Parker (2005), stage-phase models, linear-like models, pendular models, and interactive models are the four most frequently cited theoretical frameworks for psychosocial adaption to CID. Stage-phase models posit that individuals progress through predictable stages and phases. Linear-like models similar to the stage models conceptualize adaptation to CID as a linear process; however, linear-like models include other determining factors such as CID related characteristics, personality attributes, and environmental factors. Pendular models seek to account for the "swings between predisability and postdisablity identities or between illness and health…to portray the process of psychosocial adaptation to permanent disability as a series of gradual changes in self-identity along a pendular trajectory (Livneh & Parker, 2005, p. 18). Finally, the interactive models of psychosocial adaption account for the complex interaction factors both internal (e.g., type and severity of CID, self-concept) and external (e.g., social environment, physical environment) to the individual.

Rehabilitation Counseling and Technology

The use of technology to assist individuals with disabilities is referred to as **assistive technology (AT)**. Through AT, persons with disabilities gain greater independence, diminish functional limitations, increase employment opportunities, and gain greater access to mainstream society in their daily lives (Brodwin, Boland, Lane, & Siu, 2012). AT is defined as "any item, piece of equipment, or product system, whether acquired commercially off the shelf, modified, or customized, that is used to increase, maintain, or improve functional capabilities of individuals with disabilities (Scherer, 2000, p. 185). A few examples of AT include voice recognition technology, pointing and selective devices, and independent power mobility.

Voice recognition technology (VRT) enables individuals to control a task or device using their voice. VRT can be used to control wheelchairs and computers. In order for VRT to work effectively, the individual must have high cognitive abilities, attention, memory, consistency of speech, and control over background noise. Pointing and selective devices extend the area of physical control for the individual. Examples include head sticks, mouth sticks, and light beams. Independent power mobility includes motorized wheelchairs and scooters. Before determining which power mobility device is best for the person with disabilities, it is important to assess the goals, needs, and abilities of the client (Brodwin et al., 2012).

In addition to the ATs discussed above, there are ATs to aid individuals with visual impairments, hearing impairments, and communication limitations. In selecting the AT to assist the person with a disability, it is essential that the rehabilitation counselor consider the human–technology interface. If there is not a good fit between the AT device and the individual, abandonment is risked. In order to maximize the human–technology interface, consider the goals of the client, needs of the client, environmental factors, and compatibility of the AT and the client (Brodwin et al., 2012). Table 8.3 provides some helpful AT resources.

TABLE 8.3 Assistive Technology Websites
AbleData database for products. http://abledata.com/
Do-IT provides resources for people with disabilities. http://www.washington.edu/doit/
Rehabilitation Engineering and Assistive Technology Society of North American (RENSA). Professional organization focused on increasing access to technology for people with disabilities.

Vocational Rehabilitation Counseling

All of the people with disabilities described in this section on rehabilitation counseling may find that part of their comprehensive rehabilitation plan includes working with a vocational rehabilitation counselor. The primary goal of **vocational rehabilitation** is for people with disabilities to secure competitive employment, meaning that the individual with the disability is engaging in meaningful career development instead of merely job placement. Vocational rehabilitation counselors are also case managers who design individualized and comprehensive services in collaboration with their clients. They advocate for the use of assistive technology, consumer choice, and participation for their clients.

Person-focused counseling is a key to addressing individual client needs effectively, beginning with understanding the individual's unique circumstances and his or her perspectives on those circumstances. Vocational rehabilitation counselors plan services in partnership with the individual receiving services so that the individual eventually is empowered to initiate the needed services. Counselors must continuously assess progress, consult with agencies, and coordinate the services needed with an aim toward securing meaningful employment. Case Study 8.3 is a real-life example of a partnership between a vocational rehabilitation counselor and an individual with a disability. The case shows the importance of focusing on a client's strengths, believing that the client has the ability to transform his or her life, and supporting the client on his or her journey toward independence.

VOICES FROM THE FIELD 8.7   Rehabilitation Counseling, by Edward T. Markowski

---

Rehabilitation counselors are social activists and address issues of stigma, discrimination, and access for all individuals. We incorporate various strength-based theories, use holistic approaches during our assessments, and examine and attempt to address societal barriers that could deter successful outcomes.

With financial assistance from the Rehabilitation Services Administration, I was able to pursue and obtain a degree in rehabilitation counseling and work toward my goal of addressing the welfare of the human condition. I found the field to be rich with inspirational practitioners and leaders in research, theory, and policy. I learned that the implementation of rehabilitation services has grown beyond the traditional models of vocational placement. It continues to expand and develop and is one of the fastest growing occupations.

Since completing my education, I have attained licensure as a clinical professional counselor and have worked as a counselor, vocational evaluator, and rehabilitation director. Through my experiences, I have worked with adults, children, and elderly individuals from a variety of cultures

(Continued)

and socioeconomic backgrounds, and with disabilities such as cerebral palsy, traumatic brain injuries, cancer, developmental disorders, mental illnesses, amputations, spinal cord injuries, multiple sclerosis, HIV/AIDS, and posttraumatic stress disorder. I have been touched by the courage and strength of my clients as they have worked toward their goals of employment and independence. These teachers have expanded upon the foundation that my education provided, and it is with great joy and privilege that I continue in this profession.

CASE STUDY 8.3

The Case of Max, the Engineer Who Found His True Passion in Life

This case was related by Thomas Neuville (personal communication, July 7, 2008), an associate professor of special education and a former vocational rehabilitation counselor. As a rehabilitation counselor, Thomas met Max (not his real name) after Max became blind in a car accident. Max had been a successful tire engineer by profession, but he could not continue in his job after the accident. Thomas also learned that Max's true love was working with wood. Before the accident, Max had a cabinetmaking hobby, but he never pursued it professionally because he did not think that he could make a living out of it.

Max's workshop sat dormant after he became blind, but one of the things that Thomas realized was that his client loved cabinetmaking so much that he probably would do anything to get back to it, even with his disability. Max had the engineering knowledge that he needed to adapt the tools in his workshop to be able to use them: He designed a way to set up guiding devices on the circular saw so that he could create the cabinets, even though he could no longer see. Thomas's approach to working with Max was to "never think that I had the solution." As Thomas said, "I had no idea how to do these things, but I knew that [Max] knew."

Thomas engaged Max in the solution—in this case, one of business buildup, by forming a business partnership with him. Once Max redesigned all of his tools, they put a business plan together to market the product. After a year, Max was able to continue with the business independently.

Although Max was initially depressed about his blindness, with Thomas's support he was able to transform his life and follow a lifelong dream to have his own cabinetmaking business. Max said that he would never have had the opportunity to pursue his true passion in life without the accident. Thomas's ability to form a business partnership with his client is not typical of all vocational rehabilitation counselors in all settings, but in Thomas's situation, he was given a budget and a certain number of people with whom to work. He had the flexibility and independence in his job to help his clients achieve success in a variety of ways.

Multicultural and Social Justice Issues in Rehabilitation Counseling

In recent years, a multicultural approach to counseling people with disabilities has emerged in the counseling literature and in counseling training programs: A **minority model of disability** was proposed (Strike et al., 2004). Considering disability to be part of the minority model that represents ethnic and racial groups is a change in the social perspective. The inclusion of disability in the minority model recognizes that people with disabilities have experienced stigma, prejudice, discrimination, and marginalization. Pruett and Chan (2006) discussed how essential it is for educators in rehabilitation counseling programs to encourage their students to examine the negative attitudes that they may hold toward people with disabilities or toward certain specific disability groups, even though students may be able to articulate the profession's egalitarian views of people with disabilities.

As one can see from the previous statistics on the prevalence rate for disabilities, there is a difference based on race. It is expected that the number of disabilities will increase and that the increase will generally come from persons in racial and ethnic minorities (World Health Organization, 2011). Given the increasing number of disabilities within ethnic minority groups, rehabilitation counselors must increase their focus on multicultural issues and work toward becoming multiculturally competent. Persons of color who have a disability must be considered from both perspectives: as a person with a disability and as a person connected to his or her culture. Taylor-Ritzler et al. (2010) found that ethnically diverse individuals with disabilities in the Vocational Rehabilitation system reported experiences of oppression in their daily lives. According to Lee and Matteliano (2009), ethnic minorities with disabilities have a growing need for rehabilitation, and yet despite this growing need they tend to be underserved. Given these findings, it is important to acknowledge that people of color with a disability are members of two groups that have historically been marginalized and that they are at risk for experiencing double discrimination.

This increased recognition of the importance of acknowledging diversity issues within rehabilitation counseling is reflected in the *2010 Code of Professional Ethics for Rehabilitation Counselors* by the Commission on Rehabilitation Counselor Certification (CRCC, 2010) and *A Guide to Cultural Competence in the Curriculum: Rehabilitation Counseling* by the Center for International Rehabilitation Research Information and Exchange (Nochajski & Matteliano, 2008; Lee & Matteliano, 2009). Recognizing the importance of integrating cultural competency education in the rehabilitation training program, CIRRIE developed a curriculum guide to provide faculty access to resources, case studies, and activities that promote cultural competence. In their revised code of ethics, the CRCC addresses cultural diversity throughout the code. The glossary defines cultural diversity as encompassing "age, color, race, national origin, culture, disability, ethnicity, gender, gender identity, religion/spirituality, sexual orientation, marital status/partnership, language preference, socioeconomic status, or any basis proscribed by law" (Commission on Rehabilitation Counselor Certification, 2010, p. 35). The codes also include a new standard and requirement for cultural competence. These revised codes clearly set up the expectation that culturally competent rehabilitation counselors are aware of their own values and biases and that they will develop interventions and services that not only consider the client's cultural heritage but also recognize barriers due to their cultural background (Cartwright & Fleming, 2010; Commission on Rehabilitation Counselor Certification, 2010).

Rehabilitation counselors working with ethnically diverse clients with disabilities will also want to become familiar with the *Multicultural and Social Justice Counseling Competencies (MSJCC)* (Ratts, Singh, Nassar-McMillan, Butler, & McCullough, 2015). These are a revision of the Multicultural Counseling Competencies (MCC) developed by Sue, Arredondo, and McDavis (1992). The MSJCC provide a framework for implementing multicultural and social justice competencies into counseling theories, practices, and research. The MSJCC highlight the intersection of identities and the dynamics of power, privilege, and oppression that is present within the counseling relationship. This is most relevant for ethnic minorities with disabilities because this framework allows the rehabilitation counselor to consider both the ethnic culture and the disability culture of the client. The MSJCC also include four developmental domains: counselor self-awareness, client worldview, counseling relationship, and counseling and advocacy interventions.

Despite the added complexity of considering cultural background and disability background, it is essential that professional counselors consider both these identities when providing services. Weed and Field (2012) provided a general outline as a starting point for working with minority clients with disabilities, and this guideline is echoed by Cartwright and Fleming (2010). They recommend a self-assessment that includes awareness of one's own cultural background (especially in relation to one's biases regarding disability issues) and a client assessment that includes determination of the client's support system, evaluation of the client's acculturation level, and insight into the client's worldview.

Summary

In this chapter, a broad overview of mental health counseling and rehabilitation counseling was provided. Mental health and rehabilitation counselors work in a variety of treatment settings and serve clients with diverse clinical issues. The authors discussed various treatment settings and counseling issues.

Professional counselors working in mental health settings can be found in community/agency settings, hospitals, corrections settings, private practice, pastoral counseling settings, and wilderness therapy programs. It is probable that in all of these settings, professional counselors will begin their careers as generalists—seeing a variety of clients with wide-ranging concerns—and then perhaps develop a specialty area as they become more experienced and as the work setting allows.

Commonly encountered mental health issues (i.e., depressive disorders, anxiety disorders, eating disorders, posttraumatic stress disorder and addictions) were discussed. The importance of professional counselors being prepared to address crisis situations adequately, including clients with suicidal and homicidal ideations, was underlined. Professional counselors were advised to consult relevant legal and ethical codes regarding handling a client crisis. Descriptions of various treatment settings and criteria for identifying which type of setting may be most appropriate for clients at various levels of functioning were also presented.

Counselors working in hospitals or prison settings may deal with people whose problems require intensive intervention where they are confined to that particular setting. The professional counselor's work may be primarily preventive, with the professional counselor's role being to educate groups of workers at their place of employment on topics such as smoking cessation or the benefits and application of stress management techniques.

Rehabilitation counselors work in many of the same settings as mental health counselors; however, their focus is on assisting people who have a recognized disability. Rehabilitation counselors support their clients in functioning as independently as possible and help clients to secure meaningful employment; therefore, it is essential for rehabilitation counselors to be knowledgeable of the various frameworks for understanding adaptions to disability. Regardless of the setting and clinical issue chosen, it is imperative that as a professional counselor you gain additional knowledge in these specialty areas as well as become culturally competent. Professional counselors must carefully consider what constitutes a good match between their own preferences and competencies when choosing the setting in which they will practice their profession.

MyCounselingLab for Introduction to Counseling

Start with the Topic 4 Assignments: *Counseling in Mental Health and Private Practice* and then try the Topic 8 Assignments: *Family Counseling*.

Try the Topic 16 Assignments: *Substance Abuse* and then the Topic 12 Assignments: *Multicultural Considerations*.

9 School, College, and Career Counseling

Nadine E. Garner, Jason Baker, and Molly E. Jones

PREVIEW

This chapter describes the unique characteristics of working as a professional counselor in the increasingly multicultural settings of elementary and secondary schools, college and university campuses, and career counseling settings. Each section concludes with the contact information of related professional organizations, publications, and websites for further exploration.

COUNSELING IN THE SCHOOLS

Background

In the early 1900s, the counselor's role in the schools was to help students find employment. As the United States became involved in World War I, counselors emphasized testing young men to place them in the armed forces. By World War II, a counselor was also viewed as someone who could offer counseling services for a student's greater personal development. A series of federal education acts in the ensuing decades provided the resources for counselors to serve students more fully in the areas of academic and career development. By the end of the 20th century, the role of the professional school counselor was propelled into a new era by two major contributions to the field: (1) the comprehensive developmental counseling curriculum, and (2) the creation of national standards for school counseling programs.

Gysbers and Henderson (2012) and Myrick (2010), in earlier editions of their texts, originally outlined the comprehensive developmental counseling curriculum, which assisted counselors in designing and delivering a curriculum that considered the developmental needs of children at all grade levels. The **ASCA** *National Standards for School Counseling Programs* (Campbell & Dahir, 1997) helped unify the profession on a national level by providing standards that would be relevant to all school counseling programs. These standards defined three categories on which counselors need to focus (i.e., academic development, career development, personal/social development), regardless of whether the professional school counselor worked at the elementary, middle, or high school level. In 2014, ASCA (American School Counselor Association) replaced the national standard with the publication, *Mindsets and Behaviors for Student Success*.

Elementary Counseling

Elementary school counselors work with students from kindergarten through grade 5, ordinarily with a primary emphasis on developmental issues and prevention strategies. Counselors assist children in making the adjustment to the school setting by helping them understand basic social and academic skills. Parents and teachers use counselors as consultants regarding student behavior and classroom management. In addition to using traditional counseling methods, elementary counselors use other methods to engage children in counseling. Play therapy techniques can help children participate more fully in the counseling process through the language of play. Puppets, role-plays, drawing, and bibliotherapy (the use of books and stories in counseling) are expressive arts methods that counselors can use with younger students, especially children who are less verbal. Voices from the Field 9.1 explains how elementary school students can be positively affected by the work of a sensitive counselor.

VOICES FROM THE FIELD 9.1   Elementary School Counseling, by Jason Baker

In reflecting on the time that I have spent as an elementary school counselor, I am humbled by my many opportunities to affect the lives of others and exalted by children's willingness to share their lives with me. In this way, elementary school counseling is similar to the other levels of school counseling. That is, I spent quite a bit of time working either one on one or in small groups directly with the students in the schools I served. I also frequently served as an advocate for children on my caseload by attending individualized educational plan (IEP) meetings, community program meetings, or other meetings where I felt like I would be able to advocate for the needs of a child I knew.

In many other ways, the job of the elementary school counselor is vastly different from that of school counselors at other levels. As an elementary counselor in a rural school setting, I served as the counselor for four different school buildings, which were geographically separated by approximately 20 miles and culturally separated by many different viewpoints and values. This proved to be an additional challenge to the job, as I attempted to address programmatic needs across the various schools in an ecumenical and enthusiastic manner. In comparing my vision of elementary school counseling in graduate school to my actual experience of the job, I think I was most surprised by the fact that there was a fair amount of flexibility in the job. In many ways, this was very good. I enjoyed being able to work with teachers and administrators to determine the programmatic needs of the school. I worked to develop a comprehensive school counseling program, as this idea at the elementary level was fairly novel to this particular district. I really enjoyed creating lessons for different age groups. There is a dramatic difference between addressing bullying with kindergarteners (think puppets!) and fifth-graders (think popular lingo!). This really kept the job interesting and reflective, as it only takes one use of the word *resolution* in a classroom of vacantly staring first-graders to realize that you really have to be adaptive and attentive to the needs of various age groups.

Reaching out to children by accepting where they are developmentally, and watching them grow over these formative years are very gratifying parts of this job. When I first met Anna, she was an 8-year-old, socially withdrawn, and terrified young girl who moved into the school district from out of state. She drew a picture of herself and shared self-descriptive adjectives with me such

(Continued)

as "ugly," "mean," and "stupid." I supported Anna for several years by working one on one with her, consulting with teachers, and meeting with her parents. Her teacher came to me one afternoon and shared a new picture that Anna, now 11 years old, had drawn. Her picture showed a smiling girl—with many friends—who felt good about her schoolwork. As an elementary school counselor, I was humbled to realize that, though I was far from the only person who played a role in this young girl's transformation, my unique role in the school allowed me to help her progress. Obviously, not every individual situation has such dramatically positive outcomes; nevertheless, I feel that the job of the counselor offers me the ability to share a few steps in the journey of life with children—and the years from ages 6–12 years provide some uniquely interesting and rewarding times to share these steps.

Middle School/Junior High Counseling

Middle school counselors work with children in grades 6 through 8, helping them make the transition from elementary school to middle school, and then later from middle school to high school. In these transitions, middle school students have to adapt to different teachers, complicated schedules, and making and losing friends. Counselors need to be aware of the great degrees of variation in physical and social development between students. Middle school counselors focus on topics such as decision making, conflict resolution, peer pressures, sexuality, career development, and substance abuse. Voices from the Field 9.2 illustrates how important it is for middle school students to have an adult in their lives who cares about their struggles.

VOICES FROM THE FIELD 9.2   Middle School Counseling, by Corissa Fetrow

Being a middle school counselor has brought many rewards and struggles to my life. As a school counselor I have the opportunity to interact with students daily in ways that most people cannot. Every day I have the opportunity to work with amazing students and be available when they need an attentive listener: from broken hearts to failing grades, to the loss of a loved one, to simply popping in to say hello. No two days are the same for a counselor.

A school counselor is an advocate for children. The most rewarding part of my job is being there for students when they need support. During my first 2 months as a counselor, I struggled with finding the answer to a student's anxiety issues. I could not get this student to stay in school all day—each day was a challenge for him to just make it to lunchtime. One day the student walked into my office and simply handed me a card and walked out. I opened the card and it said, "Thanks for everything. It's nice to know that someone cares." Here I thought I was failing by not being able to help this child with his anxiety, and the whole time all he cared about was feeling cared for.

One thing that most people do not realize about counselors is that they do not spend the entire day talking with students. There are meetings, phone calls, scheduling, and mandated testing that are also part of being a counselor. Someone thinking of entering the field needs to remember that it all affects the student one way or another—I would not trade my job for the world!

High School Counseling

High school counselors emphasize academic advising, educational planning, and career development as they help adolescents graduate to the world of work, higher education, or the armed services. In addition, high school counselors need to be sensitive and responsive to adolescents as these teenagers create a sense of identity, which may involve students trying to understand their place in the social context and experimenting with new behaviors. A challenge for high school counselors is to be aware of students who may tend toward violent behaviors well before these students manifest these behaviors and cause a school or personal crisis. Voices from the Field 9.3 provides a picture of how the challenges in the context of high school have changed as a result of technology.

VOICES FROM THE FIELD 9.3   High School Counseling, by Eric Shellenberger

When deciding to become a school counselor, one has to be prepared to be flexible and have a positive outlook. The challenge every day of a high school counselor is helping those students who just do not care (or say that they do not care). Mental health issues and extremely dysfunctional family lives of students add to the everyday challenges for a high school counselor. Socially, we address current trends such as cyberbullying. This Internet harassment is dangerous and is jeopardizing our personal connection with people as humans. We find many students and teenagers who can't settle their differences with others socially, so they use the Internet to attack and say things to someone they would not normally say in person.

A graduate college professor once told me, "You have to believe there is a treasure in everyone; in some, you might have to dig deeper to retrieve it." I believe these are words to live by as a school counselor in today's society. One might have to dig very deep to reach the positive attribute in a student, but ultimately there is something there to resurrect. To tap into these teenagers is the ultimate reward, which I call the "Aha" effect, and it is definitely a unique reward in my job. Students who come back to visit or write thank-you notes are other verifications to me that these kids are on their way to becoming productive adults in our society.

Current Issues Affecting All School Counseling Settings

The **No Child Left Behind Act (NCLB) of 2001** (NCLB, 2001) is a federal law that specifies the creation of a national program to raise academic achievement for all students by closing the achievement gap that exists between socially or economically disadvantaged students and students with more advantages. Although school counselors are not mentioned in this educational reform, the American School Counselor Association (ASCA) responded to this movement by introducing the *ASCA National Model: A Framework for School Counseling Programs* (ASCA, 2012). The model directly involves school counseling programs in school reform by helping counselors design programs that align with the mission of the school and student achievement. Counselors using the model are able to demonstrate to the school community how school counseling programs are a vital component in students' personal, academic, and career success.

Traditionally, professional school counselors worked with students through four primary interventions: counseling (individual and group), large group guidance, consultation (with parents, teachers, and administrators), and coordination. More recently, however, the *ASCA National Model* (ASCA, 2012) called for a transformed role for professional school counselors, one that integrated delivery systems (i.e., school guidance curriculum, individual student planning, responsive services, and system support), foundations (i.e., beliefs and philosophy; mission statement; and ASCA content standards for student academic, career, and personal/social development), management system (i.e., agreements, advisory council, data, action plans, and time management), and accountability (i.e., results report, school counselor performance standards, and program audit) within the meta-interventions of advocacy, leadership, collaboration, and systemic change.

Career counseling and educational planning continue to be major components of the ASCA model across all grade levels. Complete Activity 9.1 to help you gain insight into career guidance and other activities that take place at a career technical center; it is a supplement to understanding the career counseling that occurs in elementary, middle, and high schools. Elementary counselors focus on career awareness, exposing children to the variety of career choices. Middle school counselors assist students in career exploration by introducing students to software programs that can assist them in taking interest inventories and in researching careers. High school counselors help students with the realities of planning for their upcoming careers.

ACTIVITY 9.1 SCHOOL COUNSELOR'S ROLE IN A CAREER TECHNICAL CENTER

Visit a counselor at a career technical center to gain an understanding of the counselor's role, the overall guidance program, the systemic organization and the responsibilities within it, the referral procedures and resources, and the involvement with special needs students.

The national model also calls for counselors to be accountable and to use data to show how their programs make a difference in students' lives. Although professional school counselors who did not learn about data-driven decision making in their graduate programs may be hesitant to initiate data collection as part of their overall accountability program, it is important for professional school counselors to extend their professional development by including the understanding of data and its relevance to the transformed school counselor's role. It is no longer enough for professional school counselors to list the varied tasks they perform or to log the time spent on tasks. Professional school counselors make a positive difference in their students' lives every day; however, without the benefit of capturing data in a form that can be shared with other stakeholders in the school community, these valuable data remain invisible. Collecting and reporting data about the effectiveness of the school counseling program allows counselors to be accountable to their stakeholders, to show the importance of their profession in the school community, and to assist in program evaluations and modifications.

A challenge for professional school counselors is how to serve all students. The National Office for School Counselor Advocacy's (NOSCA) 2012 report recognized that one of these challenges includes a large caseload (Peter D. Hart Research Associates, 2012). Although ASCA (2012) recommends a 1:250 school counselor to student ratio, the NOSCA national survey demonstrated that the average school counselor to student ratio is 1:367. The demographics of the school, including public versus private, developmental level, school size, and location, impact a school counselor's caseload. Public school counselors have a caseload of 386, while private schools have much smaller caseloads of 197 students. Middle school counselors have an average caseload of 415 students, which is much larger than the high school counselor to student ratio, 1:350.

The general school size affects a school counselor's caseload. Schools with over 2,000 students have an average ratio of 502 students per counselor, and institutions with 1,000–2,000 students average 411 per counselor. Schools that have under 1,000 students have a caseload ratio of one counselor to 348 students. The difference in caseload according to the school's location is as follows: Urban schools average around 401 students, suburban schools average around 402 students, and rural schools average around 362 students (Peter D. Hart Research Associates, 2012).

When counselors see students individually, they cannot meet with them for weekly, hour-long sessions over an extended time, as counselors might in community/agency or private practice settings. The use of a brief, solution-focused counseling approach has received much positive support in the schools (Garner, Baker, & Valle, 2014). Counselors appreciate its positive, direct, and empowering approach for students and generally see individual students for 10 or fewer sessions.

Professional school counselors refer students who have serious, ongoing mental health concerns to outside agencies or private practitioners for longer-term psychotherapy. A trend in schools is the appearance of counselors from mental health settings, who are employed by the school district to come directly into the school to facilitate groups and to see individual students who have ongoing issues. Although some school counselors welcome the addition of these outside counselors to assist them in their ability to serve students, others are wary that their presence could threaten their jobs.

In addition to working directly with students, professional school counselors work with all of the people who influence children's lives, including parents, teachers, staff, administrators, and the community. School counselors need to view students from a holistic approach, including how all of the environmental characteristics of a child's world and the child's own freedom of choice interact to affect the child. A school counseling position requires having a flexible approach to each school day because each day is often unpredictable. A crisis situation or an emergency meeting could change plans for the entire day. Prospective school counselors should spend time with a professional counselor before beginning their careers.

Professional school counselors and other types of counselors and professionals who work with children are **mandated reporters**, meaning that they are required by law to report suspected child abuse and neglect to the proper authorities. It is not the counselor's role to investigate the suspected maltreatment and thus substantiate the report; that is the task of the agency that is called on to conduct an investigation. However, school counselors need to be trained to identify the characteristic behaviors and physical signs that would lead a professional to suspect that child abuse or neglect is occurring. Complete Activity 9.2 to gain a working knowledge of social service agencies and to start thinking about their importance to the functions of a school counselor.

ACTIVITY 9.2 SCHOOL COUNSELORS NEED TO CONNECT WITH SOCIAL SERVICE AGENCIES

Why is it important for school counselors to have a working knowledge of social service agencies? (A version of this question is often asked of applicants in interviews for school counseling positions.) Research the functions of a minimum of five social service agencies used by professional school counselors. Be able to describe the services provided and the referral procedures. Give an example of how a school counselor may need to enlist the services of one of these agencies to assist a child in need more effectively.

Professional counselors need to be aware of the wide range of issues affecting students and be able to respond to them as part of their comprehensive developmental curriculum. Some of these issues include cyberbullying, relational aggression, disabilities, grief and loss, suicide, sexual behaviors, substance abuse, violence, poverty, and child maltreatment. For a comprehensive understanding of the great diversity of issues that professional school counselors address, refer to texts such as *Transforming the School Counseling Profession* (Erford, 2015a).

Multicultural and Social Justice Issues in Schools

In addition to the multitude of topics with which school counselors must be familiar, the idea of supporting gay, lesbian, bisexual, transgendered, and questioning (GLBTQ) students and their families is difficult for some counselors and schools to acknowledge. Counselors, teachers, and administrators may have their own personal or religious opinions about sexual orientations that are not heterosexual and gender identities that are not exclusively male or female. However, regardless of their personal or religious opinions about individuals who are GLBTQ, counselors have an ethical obligation not only to counsel these students, but also to be an active voice in the support of GLBTQ. It is a significant sign of our times that President Barack Obama was the first U.S. president to directly refer to transgender individuals in his 2015 State of the Union Address. The president's speech (Obama, 2015) included numerous statements reflecting the need for all Americans to respect one another's human dignity. He declared,

> That's why we defend free speech, and advocate for political prisoners, and condemn the persecution of women, or religious minorities, or people who are lesbian, gay, bisexual or transgender. We do these things not only because they are the right thing to do, but because ultimately they will make us safer.

Advocacy is defined by the American Counseling Association (2012) as the "promotion of the well-being of individuals and groups, and the counseling profession within systems and organizations. Advocacy seeks to remove barriers and obstacles that inhibit access, growth, and development." Advocacy is an essential responsibility of school counselors and one of the themes of the *ASCA National Model* (ASCA, 2012). GLBTQ students are a minority population that is in desperate need of counselor advocacy. Activity 9.3 helps you to think about the counselor's role in promoting a climate of support for GLBTQ youth.

ACTIVITY 9.3 PROMOTING A CLIMATE OF SUPPORT
FOR ISSUES RELATED TO GLBTQ YOUTH

School counselors need to promote a school climate of support and understanding for issues related to GLBTQ youth. Develop one strategy that you can use to support each of these areas: (1) the student who is GLBTQ, (2) the classroom curricula, and (3) the faculty and staff. What obstacles do you anticipate facing? (Internet resources include: www.outproud.org and www.youthresource.com.)

Students who are GLBTQ face adjustment problems, isolation, rejection from unsupportive family and friends, and difficulty seeking help for their concerns. Kosciw, Greytak, Palmer, and Boesen (2014) determined that this population of students is also more often the victim of hostility in many forms, including verbal harassment (e.g., homophobic remarks, threats), cyberbullying, relational aggression, property damage, and physical assault. The National Climate Survey of 2013 revealed that 55% of GLBT students do not feel safe at school because of their sexual orientation and 37.8% do not feel safe because of their gender expression. More than one third of these students change their daily routines to avoid entering gender-specific spaces (i.e., bathrooms). These negative school climates affect their everyday functioning and violate their fundamental needs, correlating to extremely unfortunate outcomes. A federal task force documented that suicide is the leading cause of death among gay and lesbian adolescents.

Professional school counselors need to promote a school climate of support and understanding for issues related to GLBTQ youth. National guidelines exist to help school counselors create this positive environment. The Office for Civil Rights (OCR) created standards and guidelines for educators under Title IX. Title IX, created in 1972, prohibits sex discrimination, but also aims to protect LGBTQ students against harassment (Stone, 2013).

In addition, the OCR protects all students against sexual harassment. The American Association of University Women (AAUW) found that of the 1,065 students surveyed in grades 7–12, 48% experienced some form of sexual harassment (Hill & Kearl, 2011). Sexual harassment, according to the OCR, can foster a negative school environment and impact the students' academic achievement. The AAUW study found that 87% of those sexually harassed experienced negative consequences. Some consequences of sexual harassment include a decrease in class participation and in ability to focus; feeling moderately to severely upset, self-conscious, or embarrassed; and having trouble sleeping. The OCR recently issued a Dear Colleague letter, which described the nature of and addressed sexual harassment and sexual violence under the Title IX guidelines (Ali, 2011). The new Title IX guidelines and the Dear Colleague letter increase the overall understanding of what constitutes sexual harassment. This enables school personnel to better identify sexual harassment and therefore protect students to the best of their ability. To deepen your understanding of issues related to sexual minorities and sexual harassment in schools, read Case Study 9.1 and answer the processing questions. Finally, complete Activity 9.4 to better grasp issues important within the school counseling profession.

CASE STUDY 9.1

Imagine that you are the school counselor in the following case study. Janet, an 11th grade English teacher, comes to you for help with a number of issues that she is currently facing related to a trans male student in her class named Marshall. Janet shares,

> I knew Marshall as a student in my class last year when she was Tracey. I really liked her as a student, and I got to know her well. And now, all of a sudden after the summer break, she's back in my class, but now *she* is a *he*, and Tracey tells me that she is now Marshall and would like to be referred to that way from now on, and that I need to use male pronouns when I refer to her, I mean *him*. So I am doing my best to deal with this situation, but I have never been around a trans individual before. Marshall is having issues with me and the classroom as well. He asks to have his seat moved all the time; he tells me that there are "things going on in class." When I ask him for a more specific reason to move his seat, he doesn't give me a better answer and just says that he's dealing with "stuff." What makes it worse is that I sometimes use the name Tracey instead of Marshall by mistake, or the wrong pronoun, and I can tell that Marshall is upset with that. I am not proud to say that on one occasion when I got so frustrated by Marshall's frequent requests to change seats, I blurted out, "Suck it up, cupcake!" I just feel like I am at the end of my rope with this situation, and I am coming to you for some expert advice on how to deal with all of my issues and also how to help Marshall be successful.

Processing questions:

- What are all of the different issues involved in this case?
- How will you respond to Janet's request for you to give her advice about how to best support Marshall?
- What is your tentative plan for providing support to both Janet and Marshall?

ACTIVITY 9.4 SEEING THE PROFESSION FROM THE INSIDE OUT

Before you enter your practicum or internship semesters, contact local school counselors and inquire whether you can volunteer to help with a special project or event. Getting involved in the activities of school counselors before you undertake your field experiences gives you the advantage of feeling more connected to the profession and more prepared to participate fully in your practicum or internship.

A professional school counselor's visibility in the school is enhanced by being seen in hallways, classrooms, meetings, the cafeteria, and the playground. Although school counselors may feel at times that they have so many issues to contend with at once they cannot adequately address them all, the career choice of a school counselor can be a gratifying one because a school counselor can develop an ongoing relationship with students and their families; observe a student's development over time; and play an active role in contributing to the student's academic, personal/social, and career success.

COLLEGE/UNIVERSITY COUNSELING AND STUDENT-LIFE SERVICES

While college counseling and student-life services are regarded as separate domains, counselors in both career choices have the opportunity to be visible in a college setting and thus play an integral role in the life of a campus community. Throughout this chapter, the term **college counseling** is used to describe college and university counseling, unless otherwise noted.

Background

College counseling centers and student-life services have evolved to meet changing cultural needs. Modern college counseling centers were established after World War II to assist returning veterans in the transition to college life and vocational choices. Counseling centers were later affected by the civil rights and the women's movements of the 1960s and 1970s, as minorities, women, and older students became more prevalent on campus. The field of student-life services also responded to the unique needs of these populations by increasing its offerings.

In the 1980s, college counseling centers began to use a variety of counseling approaches to address students' needs holistically. They took into consideration a client's interpersonal, emotional, physical, and spiritual components. In 1991, the **American College Counseling Association (ACCA)** was created as a division of the American Counseling Association (ACA). The advent of the ACCA, including the publication of the scholarly journal, *Journal of College Counseling*, allowed college counselors to demonstrate their professional identity as distinct from student-life professionals. The field of student-life services is represented by several professional organizations, including the American College Personnel Association (ACPA), the National Association of Student Personnel Administrators (NASPA), the ASCA postsecondary division, and the American Psychological Association (APA) Division 17 (Society of Counseling Psychology). Box 9.1 contains additional information on professional organizations, publications, and websites related to college counseling and student personnel services.

BOX 9.1

Professional Organizations, Publications, and Websites for College Counseling and Student-Life Services

---

American College Counseling Association (ACCA) publishes the *Journal of College Counseling*; www.collegecounseling.org

American College Personnel Association (ACPA) publishes the *Journal of College Student Development*; www.myacpa.org

American Psychological Association (APA) Division 17 (Society of Counseling Psychology); www.apa.org

American School Counselor Association (ASCA) postsecondary division; www.schoolcounselor.org

Journal of American College Health; www.acha.org
Journal of College Student Psychotherapy; www.haworthpressinc.com

National Association of Student Personnel Administrators (NASPA) publishes the *Journal of Student Affairs Research and Practice;* the *NASPA Journal About Women in Higher Education,* and the *Journal of College and Character;* www.naspa.org

New Directions for Student Services; www.jossey-bass.com

College counselors and student-life professionals need to be aware of the current demographics of today's college student population. The National Center for Education Statistics (2014b) reported that in the fall of 2013, 17.5 million students were enrolled in degree-granting higher education institutions. Of these students, 10.5 million students attended 4-year institutions and 7.0 million students attended 2-year institutions. For those undergraduate students enrolled in 4-year colleges and universities, 77% attended full time. Forty-one percent of students at 2-year universities attend full time. Of the 17.5 million, 9.8 million (56 %) students were female and 7.7 million (44%) students were male. At the post-baccalaureate level, 2.9 million students were enrolled in a master's, doctoral, law, medicine, and other degree program (National Center for Education Statistics, 2014a). As one can see, the "traditional" college student is becoming less common in the higher education field. About 74% of all 2011–2012 undergraduates had at least one nontraditional characteristic (U.S. Department of Education, 2015).

It is important for college counselors and student-life professionals to know that undergraduate binge drinking is a recent dangerous trend that is increasing nationwide. College counselors and student-life professionals are responding to this phenomenon by initiating programs and services that address awareness, prevention, and intervention. Approximately 82% of college students drink alcohol; of that number, 37% "binge drink" (U.S. Department of Health and Human Services, 2012). Binge drinking is defined for men as having five or more drinks at a time and for women as having four or more drinks at a time. Although universities present a wide variation in the number of students who binge drink, the general consensus demonstrates that drinking and binge drinking for college students is higher than peers who are of the nontraditional college age.

The American College Health Association (ACHA, 2014) surveyed 79,266 students across 140 post-secondary institutions. The survey reported the perceived and actual use of drugs and alcohol as part of its comprehensive assessment of the problems faced by college students. Within the last 30 days, 66.8% of the college students used alcohol. Interestingly enough, this total is much less than the perceived total amount of 94.9%. Believing that everyone else does it may influence some individuals to drink.

Drinking alcohol poses numerous consequences. For example, in 2012 approximately 97,000 college students were victims of alcohol-related sexual assault and date rape. Ninety-five percent of violent campus crimes involve the use of alcohol. Twenty-five percent of college students experience academic issues, such as lower grades, as a result of their drinking habits (U.S. Department of Health and Human Services, 2012). Other issues reported by the ACHA (2014) included doing "something you later regretted" (36.5%), "forgot where you were or what you did" (32.3%), "had unprotected sex" (20.4%), and physically injured themselves (14.9%).

Despite the number of students who are struggling with drinking-related issues, not nearly enough are seeking help (Lowinger, 2012). Lowinger found that students' perceptions of the severity of their own drug and alcohol problem correlated with the degree to which they sought help. This requires the college counseling center to be aware of behind the scenes issues regarding students and healthy behavior.

College and University Counseling

The role of a **college counselor** is multifaceted because college counseling centers typically offer a wide range of services. There is great variation in what a college counselor may actually do. The typical day-to-day roles depend on the type of institution and the size of the counseling staff. Counselors who work at community colleges and small college counseling centers may find that they are expected to take on noncounseling roles, such as academic advising and administration and management duties (Edwards, 2011). College counselors who work in a center with many other counselors are more likely to define a specialty area of counseling for themselves over time (e.g., a specialist in eating disorders, substance abuse, grief and loss, or anxiety and depression).

In addition, college counselors employed by an institution that has separate student-life services to handle noncounseling issues have the opportunity to focus their resources on engaging in a wide range of counseling services. Counselors employed in this type of situation are able to contribute to the mental health of the campus community in numerous ways, at the center itself and in other locations throughout the campus. They provide academic counseling to students who struggle with time management, motivation, test anxiety, test taking, and public speaking. They see students individually or as couples for personal counseling about difficulties with relationships, family problems, grief, abuse, eating disorders, self-esteem, anxiety, and depression. Activity 9.5 gives you practice in responding to students who refer other students for counseling. Because individual counseling is usually limited to approximately 10 sessions per student, professional counselors use a variety of brief counseling approaches. Students whose concerns require longer-term therapy are often referred to outside agencies.

ACTIVITY 9.5 HOW WOULD YOU RESPOND TO THIS CLIENT?

A student brings her roommate in to see you for counseling, saying that her roommate is displaying signs of an eating disorder in the residence hall. The student who is being referred admits that she does need help, but she tells you that she will work with you in counseling only if the roommate attends the counseling session as well, "for moral support." She reasons that because the two are roommates, she will tell her roommate what is happening in counseling anyway. What would you do?

College counselors periodically facilitate group experiences that relate to student needs and interests, for instance, building self-esteem or a freshman support group. They also make referrals for psychiatric consultations for students who need care outside the scope of the center. Several times a year, the center may be used as the screening site for national screening programs, such as depression screening and anxiety screening. The center may also maintain a multimedia resource room of mental health information that is available to the entire campus.

College counselors also extend their services into the larger campus community, which increases their visibility and accessibility. They consult with faculty, staff, administrators, and students who express concerns about others who are exhibiting problematic behaviors. Activity 9.6 gives you practice in responding to professors who refer students for counseling.

ACTIVITY 9.6 HOW WOULD YOU RESPOND TO THIS REFERRAL SOURCE?

A female faculty member refers a male undergraduate student from one of her classes to you, the college counselor. The student felt comfortable enough with the professor to disclose to her his personal struggles with anxiety and depression. You begin counseling with the student. The professor later sees you on campus and inquires about how the student is doing in counseling. How should you respond?

The counselors present outreach programs to student groups on eating disorders, body image, conflict resolution, sexual safety, and interpersonal relationships; present programs to faculty and staff on stress management and communication skills; and contribute to the university's wellness activities. Counselors also become more visible and involved with the life of the campus when they engage in other experiences that expand their professional development. Some of these activities include periodically teaching courses, supervising interns who are in counseling graduate programs on campus, and conducting research.

College counselors are a leading force in the crisis intervention services that are available for emergencies such as suicidal thoughts or attempts, threats, sexual assault, and severe depression. For example, the college counselors at Millersville University in Pennsylvania are members of the Emergency Counseling Team, a group of faculty and staff from all areas of the campus trained in critical incident stress debriefing (CISD). The Emergency Counseling Team is prepared to be called on at any time. Members of the team may facilitate groups of students, faculty, and staff who need to process their thoughts and feelings resulting from a crisis such as a student death, a terrorist threat or attack, or a tragic accident.

A casual observer of lively college students walking across campus to class might conclude that college students lead carefree lives; however, college counselors have a different perspective. Counselors who have been working on college campuses for much of their career share similar stories: They have noticed a marked increase in the number of students who present with intense mental health issues. The American College Health Association (2014) and Gallagher (2014) reported on problems that impacted academic performance of the students. The top issues are included in Table 9.1. Voices from the Field 9.4 offers a college counselor's reflection.

TABLE 9.1 2014 ACHA National College Health Assessment Data

Percentage of Directors	Psychological Problem
89 %	Anxiety disorders
69 %	Crises requiring immediate response
60 %	Psychiatric medication issues
58 %	Clinical depression
47 %	Learning disabilities
43 %	Sexual assault on campus
35 %	Self-injury issues
34 %	Problems related to earlier sexual abuse

**VOICES FROM THE FIELD 9.4   College Counseling,
by Joseph F. Lynch**

My friends used to give me a hard time when I would share just how great my job was working in an environment that was so exciting, rewarding, challenging, and flexible. Now I just tell them I have the greatest job in the world. I have been working as a counselor in a college or university counseling center for many years, a journey that I would not trade for anything.

In the field of counseling, there are many settings from which to choose, but there are few that allow you to work with clients who are young, articulate, motivated, and intelligent. Working in a counseling center setting has allowed me to meet and engage in counseling with clients who naturally embody the characteristics that, in my experience, foster the potential for meaningful change. After receiving my master's degree, I worked for a short period with dually diagnosed individuals with moderate to severe emotional disturbances and psychological distress. While the experience was invaluable, working with these clients often yielded results of one step forward and three steps backward. I have great admiration and respect for professionals who have chosen this route for their careers. However, this experience helped me realize how fortunate I had been to work in college counseling centers with clients whose potential for change was more likely.

My role as a counselor in a university counseling center setting has opened other doors for me at the university and within the community. I greatly enjoy the opportunities I have to provide outreach programming, supervision, and teaching as well as my work with various committees throughout the university. I really appreciate that my experiences every day are diverse. My activities and the people I meet are always changing, and I feel that adds to what makes this job so unique and enjoyable. There is a certain energy and electricity found on a college campus. Counseling with a college population has changed over the past 30-some years. We certainly see much more significant pathology, and our students face more serious issues today. Somehow, though, this has made the reward of witnessing client growth all the more fulfilling for me.

An ongoing issue on college campuses is the attention given to the topic of student retention, and college counseling centers are affected by this growing trend. Administrators are examining retention data to measure the effectiveness of counseling services. In reviewing research that correlated the influence of college counseling with student retention, Lee, Olson, Locke, Michelson, and Odes (2009) found evidence consistent with previous research: college counseling services have a positive impact on student's retention rate. However, this study demonstrated that retention rates may be more dependent on social and psychological adjustment to college as opposed to academic performance. The unique, complex part that college counselors play in students' lives cannot be measured accurately by retention data alone. Rather, counselors need to convey proactively to the administration how their comprehensive counseling services are valuable in supporting the institution's overall educational mission.

Student-Life Services

To prepare for a career in student-life services, a variety of graduate training programs are available nationwide, many of which are housed within counselor education programs. The degree programs offered may be called Student Personnel Work in Higher Education, Student Affairs, or a similar title. Depending on how the graduate program is organized, graduate students may take some of the same courses that are part of college counseling degrees, but they will likely do their field work in one or two student-life specialty areas.

On a college or university campus, the career choice of student-life services, also known as student services or student affairs, is generally regarded as a distinct setting from college counseling. The field of **student-life services** is actually a cluster of diverse specialties, which may include admissions, learning services, health and wellness services, food services, financial aid, women's center, residence life, academic advising, international students, global education, registration, and career services.

Because student-life professionals play key roles in important everyday concerns for students, this career choice offers a rich opportunity to develop meaningful relationships with students and to contribute to their academic, personal, and professional development. Student-life professionals are also at the forefront of developing activities to unite the campus community. For example, after the World Trade Center tragedy of September 11, 2001, student-life professionals from the Department of Housing and Residential Programs at Millersville University enlisted the cooperation of the entire campus in designing a visual remembrance of the tragedy. Students, faculty, staff, and administrators took part in an origami project by folding thousands of paper peace cranes, with each crane representing a life lost in the tragedy. The individual cranes were assembled into large mobiles and permanently installed on the campus.

Opinions differ as to whether career counseling should be part of a college counselor's role, or whether it should be handled by a student-life professional in an office outside the counseling center, as in a career services office. Those who favor keeping career counseling part of the college counselor's role argue that the history of college counseling is rooted in vocational counseling and that career development is a fundamental part of a student's personal growth. Those who advocate for the division of roles point to the increased mental health services that college counselors now provide as a result of the changing needs of college students.

Regardless of opinion, new college counselors and student-life professionals are likely to find that their role has already been defined for them by the particular setting. Some campuses offer career counseling in the career services office, not at the counseling center. Other campuses have a designated career counselor as a part of the counseling center. Still other campuses expect all counselors at the counseling center to engage in career counseling as part of their caseload. Activity 9.7 provides a hands-on experience in the college counseling or student-life services arena.

Student-life professionals who work in career services offices have contact with students at key points in their academic and professional development. Counselors provide career counseling when students need help deciding on a major and when they explore career possibilities. Counselors help students consider graduate school, assisting with the application process and the related graduate entry exams. Career services professionals are vital resources in preparing students to transition from college life to finding employment. They teach students how to search for jobs, design résumés, and prepare for interviews. Counselors also bring potential employers from various fields to campus for job fairs and on-campus interviews.

ACTIVITY 9.7 VOLUNTEERING AT THE COUNSELING CENTER OR A STUDENT-LIFE SERVICES OFFICE

Contact the director of your college or university's counseling center and inquire about volunteering for an upcoming event. Perhaps, as a master's level student, you can be trained to score screenings (e.g., depression and anxiety awareness day screenings that many campuses offer) or to assist in a campus workshop that the center hosts (e.g., stress management, reducing test anxiety). Or contact the student-life services office on campus. The career services office or the office of residential life will likely have programs for which you can volunteer.

Although student-life services are separate from college counseling, they share a similar niche: Both sets of professionals must be well trained to respond to the myriad developmental needs of college students. In addition, student-life professionals and college counselors can be of most help to students when they know how to interrelate. Sometimes, they simply need to know when to refer students to one another. For example, a counselor who suspects that a student is experiencing academic problems because of an undiagnosed learning disability may refer the student to learning services. A professional in residence life who notices that a new international student is having excessive anxiety making friends may refer the student to the counseling center.

At other times, student-life professionals and college counselors may join forces to amplify their effectiveness. During a **first-year experience**, which is a yearlong program to help freshmen adjust to the academic, social, and personal aspects of college life, student-life professionals and college counselors can partner to create workshops in areas such as alcohol awareness, sexual safety, and time management. Activity 9.8 provides one way to begin forming impressions about a college or university's student-life services from a distance. Activity 9.9 gives you a glimpse of a counseling center as a potential first-time visitor. Activity 9.10 gives ideas for conducting a research project on your own campus.

ACTIVITY 9.8 CRITIQUING A WEBSITE

Visit the website of your college or university's counseling center or one of its student-life services offices. What services are offered? What special events does it host or coordinate to become a visible presence on campus and to reach out to students? Discuss whether you feel the site's layout and overall presentation would be appealing to students, contains important information, and is easy to navigate.

ACTIVITY 9.9 IMPROVING YOUR COUNSELING CENTER'S ATMOSPHERE

First impressions are important when helping clients feel comfortable about a new and potentially nerve-wracking situation, such as walking into a counseling center for the first time to seek counseling. Visit the reception area of your college's or university's counseling center in person and imagine that you are a student who is considering seeking counseling there. Notice how the environment of the center feels to you, and whether it appears to be an inviting place. Pay attention to details such as the placement of the furniture, artwork, plants, lighting, and brochures and other informational materials. What are some of the positive attributes of this environment? What would you change to make it appear more welcoming?

ACTIVITY 9.10 HOW FAMILIAR IS THE CAMPUS COMMUNITY WITH THE COUNSELING CENTER AND STUDENT-LIFE SERVICES?

Conduct a brief investigative study with undergraduate and graduate students and with faculty and staff members on your campus. Develop a survey or conduct brief interviews with individuals from these groups, asking them about their familiarity with the counseling center and student-life services and the types of services that are provided. Do they know the locations of these various services and the confidentiality issues involved? Ask faculty and staff members whether they have referred students to any of these services and for what issues. Ask students if they feel that they could turn to these services for help. This study might give you a glimpse of how well informed the campus community is about the counseling center and student-life services.

Counseling College and University Students Who Have a Disability

The number of students with disabilities who attend institutions of higher education has increased almost fourfold over the last several decades (Hennessey & Koch, 2007). Raue and Lewis (2011) reported that 707,000 students enrolled in higher education in 2008 had a disability. Approximately 33% of these students had a learning disability, 18% reported ADD/ADHD, and 15% had a mental or psychiatric condition. Supporting undergraduate and graduate students who have a disability is an important consideration from the standpoints of architectural design and instructional strategies.

Universal design for instruction (UDI) is a concept that is intended to provide learners (with and without disabilities) with an "approach to teaching that uses proactive design and inclusive instructional strategies to benefit a broad range of learners in higher education" (Black, Weinberg, & Brodwin, 2015, p. 3). The intent of UDI is for all aspects of a student's experience (i.e., course materials, assignments, and activities) to be accessible. As UDI becomes a more visible component of college campuses, rehabilitation counselors may find themselves becoming more familiar with its principles, which may produce even greater opportunities for rehabilitation counselors to serve the college population.

College and university students who are not only disabled but also from a low socioeconomic status may tend to use an external locus of control, by which they feel that things happen in their lives because of outside influences such as fate or chance instead of through their own actions and choices. This external locus of control may be harmful when students use this type of thinking to decide, for example, whether to use precautions regarding HIV/AIDS (Gwandure, 2008). Rehabilitation counselors working with this population need to assess whether their clients believe that their ability to reduce their risk of contracting HIV/AIDS is out of their control and to help them become more assertive in their efforts to keep themselves protected.

Multicultural and Social Justice Issues in College Counseling and Student-Life Services

Research demonstrated that a diverse student body increases positive academic outcomes including complex thinking, openness, and a greater number of students who possess attitudes promoting equal opportunity and the desire to work with a diverse society after graduation. However, greater diversity does not always lead to accord among the members of the college campus community (Clauss-Ehlers & Parham, 2014). For example, ethnic or racially diverse students may face more stressors than their non-racially or non ethnically diverse peers. Some examples may include underrepresentation, acculturation stress, prejudice, discrimination, racism, and conflicts both between and within groups (Smith, Chesin, & Jeglic, 2014). Greater diversity also requires college counselors and student-life professionals to increase their multicultural competence to understand the needs of their students.

College counselors and student-life professionals must be attuned to the special needs of specific student populations, such as first-generation students, student athletes, and students with disabilities. Two growing populations of students—international students and reentry women—are influencing how counselors and student-life professionals deliver their services. Students from foreign countries experience the pressure of making a total life adjustment: Not only do they have to learn the culture of college life, as do native-born students, but they also have to manage the added stress of making this transition to college in a country whose culture may be vastly different from their own (Moores & Popadiuk, 2011). **Reentry women** are a subgroup of nontraditional students who return to school after a moderate or significant hiatus in their educational careers (Sweet & Moen, 2007). For example, they may have spent years raising a family or engaged in other home-making responsibilities. Although reentry women are often more academically successful than traditional students, they may struggle with issues of self-confidence and role conflict (Padula, 1994).

First-generation students may experience challenges of their own. Defined as a student whose parents did not earn a bachelor's degree, first-generation students commonly experience additional obstacles to their college education: being a nonnative English speaker or of a diverse background, holding immigrant status, living in a single parent household, having low-income status, and relying on parents for financial support (Stebelton, Soria, & Huesman, 2014). The challenges encountered by first-generation college students and barriers to success may be mediated by college counselors and student-life professionals collaborating to holistically address the needs of these students.

Additional recently developing issues related to multiculturalism and social justice include accommodating soldiers and other military members returning from the Middle East; supporting the increase of female students, examining the educational attainment gap through different cultural, racial, ethnic, and urban student groups; and reviewing the affordability of their school or university (Clauss-Ehlers & Parham, 2014).

CAREER COUNSELING ISSUES

When you see the phrase "career counseling," what do you envision: a university office with computers and counselors? A community office where specialists help clients look for jobs? A school where career needs are woven into the curriculum? Do you remember ever being asked, "What do you want to be when you grow up?" Career counseling and career development are wide-ranging terms and processes that have implications in a variety of settings and use a variety of interventions. In general, career counseling helps individuals recognize their own personal values, skills, and interests and helps connect these to meaningful work environments that meet individual needs satisfactorily. Thus, career development and career counseling issues surface at many different times across the lifespan and in many different contexts. Consider the role of career counseling and career development in these scenarios:

- A 2-year-old toddler dutifully builds a castle with blocks and finds his mother smiling broadly at his accomplishment
- A 7-year-old child happily reports to her class that her father works with computers, but he doesn't seem to play the "fun" games
- A 10-year-old child learns that her best friend's father never went to college but seems to be a happy business owner
- A 15-year-old adolescent takes her first job and realizes it just isn't as satisfying as she anticipated
- A 19-year-old college freshman considers the value of continuing to work her part-time job while taking 18 credits in the fall semester
- A 23-year-old recent college graduate finds himself unsure if he would like to seek a job in his field of study
- A 35-year-old woman learns that she is pregnant and strategizes how to balance work and family planning
- A 47-year-old woman considers returning to work after a recent divorce
- A 50-year-old man considers "going in a completely different direction" after being laid off from a job he has held for 20 years
- A 63-year-old woman reflects on her career and considers retirement, but she isn't sure what she would do with her time
- An 83-year-old man reflects on some of the most meaningful events of his life as he watches his grandchildren play in the garden

Hopefully, these brief scenarios begin to "paint the bigger picture" of career counseling and career development needs and issues. Career development is a complex process that increasingly veers away from what once may have been considered a direct, linear path or progression (Brown, 2016). Career counselors play an important role in helping individuals across the life span actualize potentials by considering personal variables, environmental variables, and the intersection of self in context. A study on the content analysis of major journals in the field of career development (Sampson et al., 2014) revealed three categories of terms and phrases: (1) those that have been consistently mentioned in the past 25 years (e.g., career theory, career assessment, gender), (2) those that have existed in the literature intermittently and still attract attention (e.g., life-career balance, self-efficacy, work life/family balance), and (3) those that have gained more attention recently (e.g., well-being, social justice, job satisfaction, social class). While a full consideration of the depth and breadth of the field of career counseling and career development is beyond the scope of this work, this broad study reveals some of the past, present, and emergent trends in the field. The following sections provide basic terms associated with the field, a brief overview of career development theories and paradigms, attention to social justice issues influencing career development, and discussion of technological tools and forces affecting the field. The popular question, "What do you want to be when you grow up?" only begins to explore these important issues. Now consider your own experiences and theoretical understanding of career development as you complete Think About It 9.1. Table 9.2 provides important terminology in the career counseling field.

THINK ABOUT IT 9.1

As you read through these scenarios and begin to develop your own theory of career development, it might be helpful to consider your own process of career development and the degree to which some of your experiences might be universal. For example, do you consider a "good" career to be the result of thoughtful, deliberate planning? Do you believe that each individual chooses his or her own career path? Do you believe that attaining a certain career of value is largely based on happenstance or chance events? How might these beliefs influence your view of the career counseling process?

Major Theories of Career Development

Career development theories, like theories in other scientific fields of inquiry, provide coherence that allows broader meaning to be made from empirical evidence as well as subjective and objective truths. In particular, theories in the field of career development allow counselors and other clinicians to consider interventions, conceptualize cases, and develop evidence bases for treatment planning. While many theories exist in the literature, they can generally be classified into four categories: trait-factor theories or person-environment congruence theories, developmental theories, theories rooted in learning theory, and constructivist or postmodern theories. Further, the expansive theoretical landscape can be more broadly organized across two major paradigms in the philosophy of science: logical positivism and postmodernism. While an exhaustive examination of this broad literature base is not the goal of this text, the reader might gain at least a nascent understanding of the role and value of these categories by examining examples in each category.

TRAIT-FACTOR/ PERSON-ENVIRONMENT CONGRUENCE THEORIES.   The field of counseling in general and career counseling in particular has its roots in the early 20th century work of Frank Parsons. In *Choosing a Vocation* (1909), Parsons advanced the idea that individuals would be able to make a career decision based on "true reasoning" after understanding their own talents and preferences for certain types of work and understanding which occupations call for these particular skills and preferences. This idea that individuals could be educated about personal variables (e.g., skills, interests, talents) and environmental variables (e.g., necessary skills, settings, etc.) and then make an informed decision connecting the two became the basis of the person-environment (P-E) relationship.

TABLE 9.2 Important Terms in Career Counseling

avocation	An activity outside work that an individual pursues usually for enjoyment and satisfaction (www.merriam-webster.com/dictionary/avocation).
career	"[T]he course of events which constitutes a life; the sequence of occupations and other life roles which combine to express one's commitment to work in his or her total pattern of self-development; the series of remunerated and nonremunerated positions occupied by a person from adolescence through retirement, of which occupation is only one" (Super, 1976, p. 4). Or stated more simply, "a series of paid or unpaid occupations or jobs that a person holds throughout his or her life" (Brown, 2016, p. 8).
career counseling	"… A specialty within the profession of counseling, one that fosters vocational development and work adjustment of individuals at each life stage by engaging them in life planning aimed at the psychosocial integration of an individual's abilities, interests, and goals with the work roles structured by the community and occupations organized by companies" (Savickas, 2003, p. 88).
career development	"[A] continuous life process through which individuals explore activities, make decisions, and assume a variety of roles. Careers are formulated by the continuous evaluation of personal goals and the perception, assessment, and decisions regarding opportunities to achieve those goals. Career development occurs as educational and vocational pursuits interact with personal goals. It continues over the life span" (National Career Development Association, 2016, p. 6).
career guidance	"… [S]ervices intended to assist people, of any age and at any point throughout their lives, to make educational, training and occupational choices and to manage their careers" (Organization for Economic Cooperation and Development, 2004, p. 10).
job	"[A] specific occupation held by an individual at any given time" (Brown & Srebalus, 2003, p. 120). Often, *job* is used synonymously with *occupation* and *vocation* (Brown, 2016).
leisure	"[P]lanned or spontaneous events, usually relatively short term in nature, aimed at enlightening, entertaining, relaxing, or stimulating the individual" (Brown & Srebalus, 2003, p. 120).
occupation	"[A] formally classified work activity that involves a group of people working in different situations" (Brown & Srebalus, 2003, p. 120).
work	"[A] paid or unpaid systematic activity aimed at producing something of value for one's self, others, or a combination thereof" (Brown & Srebalus, 2003, p. 120).

One of the most influential theories in this category, as evidenced by professional opinion (Brown, 2016), frequent attention in the scholarly literature (Sampson et al., 2014), and number of direct applications to interventions (Behrens & Nauta, 2014; Bullock-Yowell, 2015; Nauta, 2010) is Holland's theory of vocational choice (Holland, 1959). Holland proposed that individuals have a combination of six discrete personality types: Realistic, Investigative, Artistic, Social, Enterprising, and Conventional (RIASEC).

Similarly, Holland proposed that work environments can be categorized according to these six types. Thus, by categorizing work environments and having individuals complete a brief assessment, congruence might be found between personality variables of the individual and personality variables of the work environment. Holland published *The Self-Directed Search* in the early 1970s and it is now in its fifth edition (Holland & Messer, 2013). A "Holland Code" consists of the top three letters designating the person or the environment, e.g., a school counselor is SAE (Health Services Administrators, 2012). Now complete Activity 9.11 to discern your own Holland code.

ACTIVITY 9.11

Go online to www.self-directed-search.com to learn more about Holland's theory and complete your own Self-Directed Search.

DEVELOPMENTAL THEORIES. Developmental theories of career development more broadly take into account qualitative transitions across the life span, major tasks and goals of certain time periods, and various roles and functions an individual might serve at these times. Two major developmental theories have been influential in the field, as evidenced by frequent and continued citation and direct application to interventions: Super's life-span life-space theory (Super, 1990) and Gottfredson's theory of circumscription and compromise (Gottfredson, 1981).

Brown (2016) noted that it is likely that no one has written as extensively in the field of career development as Donald Super, who had authored nearly 200 articles, books, book chapters, monographs, and other publications by the time of his death in 1994. Super's theory, by his own admission, is somewhat "segmented," but operates with a number of major tenets which are too lengthy to report here (see Super, 1990 for the "final" 14 tenets). For the purposes of this writing, the theory can be understood by considering the major stages of development and major life roles.

The growth stage (birth to 14 years of age) includes the substages of fantasy, interest, and capacity. During the growth stage, individuals begin developing their self-concept as they begin to identify with significant others. The developmental tasks during this stage include gaining self-awareness of interests and abilities and obtaining an overall understanding of the world of work.

The exploration stage (14 to 24 years of age) includes the tentative substage, the transition substage, and the trial–little commitment substage. During this stage, adolescents and young adults begin testing their occupational fantasies through school, work, and leisure activities. This stage ends with individuals crystallizing their vocational interests and narrowing their vocational choices.

During the establishment stage (24 to 44 years of age), individuals seek to stabilize their career choice and advance in their chosen career. The substages include trial-commitment and stabilization. Following the establishment stage is the maintenance stage (44 to 64 years of age), which is characterized by maintaining one's current status and enjoying the security of seniority.

The final stage is the decline stage (64 years through death), in which individuals disengage from their careers and begin focusing on retirement, leisure, and avocational activities. The decline stage includes the substages of deceleration and retirement.

In addition to the career development stages, Super believed that individuals engage in various roles, such as child, student, leisurite, citizen, worker, and homemaker. These roles overlap and influence vocational development. Along with these life roles and stages, Super emphasized important constructs such as self-concept and career maturation. These constructs underscore the important dimensions of time and self-development in the career development process. Now complete Activity 9.12 to learn more about career maturity.

ACTIVITY 9.12

Visit the Vocopher website (www.vocopher.com) and take the Career Maturity Inventory. Consider the role of Career Maturity as a developmental task.

Linda Gottfredson's theory of circumscription and compromise is the second important development theory that has broad applicability to work in the field of career counseling and career development (Cochran, Wang, Stevenson, Johnson, & Crews, 2011; Ivers, Milsom, & Newsome, 2012). Gottfredson proposed that individuals form cognitive maps that are predicated on: (1) masculinity/femininity of the occupation, (2) prestige of the occupation, and (3) fields of work. She theorized that complementary processes of circumscription and compromise narrow this cognitive map into "acceptable" or "tolerable" bounds around these important variables. Gottfredson (2002) also proposed that individuals progress through four developmental stages in relation to these variables:

Ages 3 to 5 years: Orientation to size and power. Children lay the foundation for later sex-role stereotypes through play and other activities.

Ages 6 to 8 years: Orientation to sex roles. Children begin to develop perceptions of "acceptable" roles for men and women.

Ages 9 to 13 years: Orientation to social valuation. Children begin to understand that certain occupations hold more social value than others. Children begin to develop "acceptable boundaries" of tolerance for perceived high and low social value occupations.

Ages 14+ years: Choices explored. Individuals make choices based on "acceptable" boundaries of choices based first on sex-role associated with occupation, then on social status, then on perceptions of abilities.

Gottfredson's theory allows career counselors to work with their clients to directly consider a number of different practical elements. For example,

1. Does this person have alternative occupational choices, and what seems to be guiding the perception of these alternatives?
2. How are sex-roles and stereotypes being considered in occupational choices?

3. How are perceptions of "acceptable boundaries" influenced by class, race, or personal ability?
4. In what ways has this individual's career beliefs and opportunities been affected by circumscription and compromise across these developmental stages?

Now complete Think About It 9.2.

THINK ABOUT IT 9.2

How do these developmental theories relate to your own career development process? Do you recall passing through these stages? Did you recall being oriented to the variables in Gottfredson's theory? What is the value of learning and understanding these developmental theories for the client? For the student? For the counselor?

THEORIES ROOTED IN LEARNING THEORY. Learning theory has stimulated important foundational work in the field of psychology, and the value of this work has been recognized by career development theorists. In particular, Bandura's work in advancing psychological constructs such as "social learning," "modeling, and "self-efficacy" has stimulated thinking in developing two major career development theories: social learning theory of career decision making (Krumboltz, Mitchell, & Jones, 1976) and social cognitive career theory (Lent & Brown, 1996; Lent, Brown, & Hackett, 1994).

Social learning theory of career decision making (SLTCDM) generally holds that four factors influence career development: (1) genetic endowments (e.g., race, gender, talents), (2) environmental conditions (e.g., nature of job opportunities, social policies, number of training opportunities), (3) learning experiences (e.g., instrumental, associative, vicarious), and (4) task approach skills (e.g., mental sets, values, work habits). One of the chief goals of career counseling based on this theory is to advance clients' learning and insight into each of these specific areas and to help clients consider different environments that might promote learning opportunities and exploration in these areas (Turner, Conkel, Starkey, & Landgraf, 2011). Another important concept advanced by theorists in this area (Mitchell, Levin, & Krumboltz, 1999), with roots in Bandura's work in "Chance Encounters" (Bandura, 1982), is "Planned Happenstance," the notion that unexpected events happen in life, and preparing for these events can lead to broader learning through curiosity, persistence, flexibility, optimism, and risk-taking.

Social cognitive career theory (SCCT) is closely related to SLTCDM in having its roots in learning theory, but it also places more emphasis of self-regulatory cognitions, particularly self-efficacy expectations (Brown, 2016). In this way, broader attention to the role of self-efficacy emphasizes the dynamic role of the interaction between the individual (e.g., with personal agency, outcome expectations, beliefs, and goals, etc.) and the environment. Another way of organizing variables influential to the career development process according to SCCT is by considering the categories of cognitive (i.e., self-efficacy and outcome expectations), contextual (i.e., social support and career barriers), and personal (i.e., ethnic background and disability status) variables. Through techniques such as modeling, encouragement, and performance enactments, SCCT theory has many applications to assisting clients from diverse backgrounds (Ali & Menke, 2014; Gonzalez, 2012), with various developmental needs (Gibbons & Borders, 2010; Ginevra, Nota, & Ferrari, 2015;

Wright, Perrone-McGovern, Boo, & White, 2014), and presenting in various contexts with related opportunities for generalizing learning opportunities (Hoffman, 2013; Rowan-Kenyon, Perna, & Swan, 2011; Rowan-Kenyon, Swan, & Creager, 2012). Now complete Think About It 9.3 to apply career theory to your personal development.

THINK ABOUT IT 9.3

What role has learning played in your career development process? Consider jobs which helped you gained insight into your own self-efficacy, beliefs, goals, or outcome expectations. What role has happenstance played in your career development process? How have these learning opportunities and chance events influenced the way you interact with work environments?

CONSTRUCTIVIST OR POSTMODERN THEORIES.   Melding with a larger paradigm of scientific thought, postmodern theories generally share a number of important assumptions including: emphasis on subjectivity of truth, inability to determine true cause and effect relationships, nonlinearity of personal experiences and career development paths, and emphasis on narratives and stories representing legitimate contextual uniquenesses of the client. The application of postmodern thinking to the field of career development has resulted in a number of theories (Bloch, 2005; Pryor, Amundson, & Bright, 2008; Young, Marshall, & Valach, 2007), interventions (e.g., Maxwell, 2007), and case conceptualizations, (e.g., Brott, 2005; Pryor & Bright, 2008; Savickas, 2013). In this section attention will be given to two of the more developed postmodern theories of career development: contextualist theory of career (Young, Valach, & Collin, 2002) and chaos theory applications to career development (Bloch, 2003; Bright & Pryor, 2011; Pryor & Bright, 2007).

Contextualist theory of career seeks to strengthen the role of the individual in the career process as multiple contexts (e.g., school, home, work, reference groups, cultural influences) are drawn into the broader picture of a career. The contextualist view relies heavily on narratives and stories and has, at its core, a deference to and respect for the storyteller in actively constructing career goals, values, and meaning.

Two other important relevant constructs to contextualist theory are *time* and *self-construction*. Since multiple contexts exist in an individual's life, and causality is not necessarily linear, the contextualist career counselor often works to help the client understand themes of functioning in a current context and then encourages consideration of how future contexts might be influenced by or create influence on these themes. Thus, a client's perception of time and view of current life themes projected into future contexts is important to consider. The role and nature of self-construction has been explored thoroughly by Savickas (2013), who presented a tripartite view of self-construction: self as object, self as subject, and self as project. This multifaceted nature of self-construction helps the contextualist career counselor work with the client to explore how information existing in multiple times and contexts can influence the current understanding of self.

Chaos theory originates in the field of mathematics where it provides explanation for complex, multivariate, adaptive systems that are highly responsive to initial conditions. It is often used in modeling weather patterns, economic systems, and other natural systems.

The application of chaos theory to the field of career development has occurred recently and comes from two different perspectives (i.e., Bloch, 2005; Pryor et al., 2008). In general, chaos theory is undergirded by several assumptions:

- Small effects can have large reactions or impacts
- Complex, open systems such as families, world economic markets, or weather patterns are difficult to predict because initial conditions are hard to ascertain
- Open systems contain turbulence
- Feedback to individual entities in the system often makes the system more unpredictable
- Fractals are complex, recursive patterns that offer levels of interpretation in entities

In applying some of these concepts to the career development process, the reader might be able to begin to understand the expansive nature of this theory. For example, if direct, linear relationships existed in families, careers, and other dynamic systems, there would be no need to consider these more complex roles, functions, and interactions. If a train leaves a station on a defined path, there is a reasonable certainty that it will arrive at the next station sometime in the future. From what "station" does a family originate? What are the initial conditions of a marriage? How and by whom is the path or track constructed? From where and whence does a career begin? These fundamental questions and uncertainties begin to demonstrate the challenges espoused in postmodern theorizing.

An important component of chaos theory as it applies to career development is the role of attractors and phase transitions (Pryor & Bright, 2007). From this perspective, attractors can be defined "in terms of characteristic trajectories, feedback mechanisms, end states, ordered boundedness, reality visions and equilibrium and fluctuation" (p. 375). Accordingly, there are four types of attractors which can be applied to the career development process:

- *Point attractors:* provide singular points of attraction (e.g., consider the 7-year-old child who "knows" she wants to be a teacher and spends the next 2 decades of her life making this happen)
- *Pendulum attractors:* provide consistent and patterned oscillation between two points (e.g., consider the college student who wavers between choosing a major or not over the course of several years)
- *Torus attractors:* repetitious behavior that often cycles around one point, changing slightly with each new cycle (e.g., consider the disgruntled worker who feels unfulfilled in her work, decides to engage differently, enjoys a brief period of satisfaction only to find herself feeling unsatisfied again a short time later)
- *Strange attractor:* unexpected opportunities, events, or occurrences that do not repeat and may lead to emergent qualities in a dynamic system (e.g., consider the young professional who finds a mentor with connections to his hometown who sees renewed prospects in career opportunities)

Phase transitions, like changes in phases or states of matter, offer regular opportunities for transition between chaos and order. Further, phase transitions, resulting from nonlinear processes, have the ability to produce unequal sized causes and effects, for example, the butterfly effect (i.e., small initial differences can produce large later subsequent differences) (Bloch, 2005). This nonlinear, acausal process allows for clients and counselors exploring career issues to think expansively, to consider different orders or levels of change, and to see broader connections between and among themes and events in one's life (Pryor & Bright, 2008). These general features, combined with chaos theory's recent adaptation to the field of career development, have led some to suggest that theoretical advances, practical applications (particularly with regard to cultural diversity), and development of practical counseling tools and strategies, have only just begun (Pryor & Bright, 2014). Now complete Think About It 9.4 to consider your own career path more deeply.

THINK ABOUT IT 9.4

To what degree has your career development advanced along a defined, linear path? Have the signposts along the way always been in sight or were there times when you just didn't know what was next? What was the reaction to this uncertainty? Have you ever experienced attractors in your professional or personal life? If so, to what degree were they limiting vs. encouraging to your growth and development?

CASE STUDY 9.2

Thomas is a 28-year-old white, non-Latino male who has a bachelor's degree in the field of psychology and who has pursued some graduate training in the field, but has not yet completed a graduate degree. Thomas enjoys playing outdoor sports, working with technology, as well as reading classic novels and academic literature. Throughout his childhood and adolescence, Thomas was actively involved in playing sports, learning new skills, and enjoying the company of friends and family. He particularly enjoyed playing soccer, qualifying for many regional traveling teams. He was raised in a middle-class home that had, according to him, "strong family values." He reports that throughout his childhood and adolescence his "curiosity and desire to learn new things was endless" and that he "always felt successful in his pursuits" and was pleased to have supportive family members and friends.

In the senior year of his undergraduate studies (a degree which he completed in 4 years), Thomas was involved in a serious sporting accident which fractured his L1 vertebra. This resulted in an extended (i.e., 2-month) hospital stay for invasive, emergency surgery, a lengthy period of physical rehabilitation, and a slight lingering inability to initiate and maintain plantar flexion in his left foot. Despite this mild physical limitation, Thomas has attempted to stay active in sporting culture by officiating soccer games, biking, and swimming. Some of these physical challenges have proved to be too much, however, and he has noted, at times, that "it just doesn't feel the same anymore."

In the years since this accident, Thomas has completed some graduate work in the field of psychology (completing all but the thesis in his most recent program) and has worked a number of temporary and, generally, low-wage jobs. He reports wanting to find work that is meaningful, and believes in this ability to use his mind and his skills in academic and professional work. He has left a number of jobs because he feels that "they are not challenging" or because he feels he can do more than they offer.

Thomas comes to you because he is struggling to find and maintain meaningful work, has recently had a change in his living situation, and is interested in "getting back on his feet again." Thomas reports wanting to continue his education, to make meaningful contributions to his field, and generally, to gain the respect often associated with professional credentials.

Processing Questions

1. As you consider Thomas's case and career development issues, which of the theories or families of theories presented above seem(s) most applicable? Using this theory, consider narrating a brief case conceptualization. That is, how would this theory view or frame the presenting issues? What important constructs of person (e.g., self-efficacy, self-construction, interests, values), environment (e.g., type of work, engagement with environment, role of social value), or developmental context (e.g., consideration of "cognitive map" developed through time, balance of life roles) might be most salient?

2. After choosing and applying one of the career development theories, consider what you, as a counselor, might do next. Consider writing or narrating two to three goals or objectives for career counseling in Thomas's case.

3. In applying your chosen theory and explicating goals and objectives, what additional information might you like to know? What questions would you like to ask Thomas, and how would you see these questions (and resultant answers) helping the career counseling process?

VOICES FROM THE FIELD 9.5   Career Counseling in the Middle School, by Steve Sharp

The challenge of career counseling for middle school students is similar to many of the challenges faced in counseling or teaching middle school students. There is a wide range of development across dimensions for students relatively close in age to each other. Additionally, individual adolescents may experience rapid changes in both identity and maturity across a few months, let alone a school year.

Effective career counseling in middle school needs to be deliberate and comprehensive similar to the counseling programs that parent them. Most middle school counselors focus on interests, work values, abilities and or achievement. This is normally done through computer-assisted career guidance systems (CACGS), such as Bridges, Career Cruising, Naviance, or MyNext-Move. These programs can be effective to expose students to a wide range of careers. They also help teens to better understand the nature of work, training, and education required. While these programs can be time efficient, some are costly. Most important, even the best career exploration programs can't exist alone and need to be complemented by a range of other career activities.

To meet the needs of students across their rapidly changing and spanning developmental needs, we offer career-oriented field trips, career shadowing and career specific small groups to engage students in the exploration process. Students sign-up for these activities through an open invitation to the student-body, and targeted invitations based off of Holland codes, the latter promoting the most impact in career exploration.

(Continued)

We work with local community partners to connect our teens with skilled professionals, through career shadowing and small groups. The small group work is done with the community members' focus on hands-on activities to replicate aspects of specific careers or career clusters for students. While students are targeted based off of their expressed interests, traditionally under-represented students in these fields are tapped, gaining exposure while working collaboratively with peers while guided by skilled adults in the exploration.

Technology Use and Career Resources

Technological tools have fundamentally changed the way we live by allowing new and robust ways of storing information, offering new mechanisms of communication, and creating virtual environments that are immersive, engaging, and generative. Facebook, the popular social network site, cites 1.44 billion active monthly users, a group more populous than any country on earth (Stenovec, 2015). The implications for societal change amid this powerful social force are tough to ignore. In the field of career counseling and development, there has always been a desire to connect theory to practice, and this has often been through the use of emerging computer systems. As the National Career Development Association (NCDA) celebrated its 100th birthday (in 2013), a brief consideration of 50 years of development, implementation, and maintenance of computer-assisted career guidance systems (CACGS) seems applicable (Harris-Bowlsbey, 2013).

Early computer systems emerging in the 1960s were often based on the theories of Holland, Roe, and Tiedeman (Harris-Bowlsbey, 2013). These systems provided users an opportunity to sort career choices by classification type (e.g., skilled, semiskilled, professional), develop insight into one's own psychological nature in an effort to foster vocational decision making, and generally engage users with content designed to increase the world-of-work knowledge base. Throughout the 1980s and 1990s, early systems like DISCOVER, SIGI, and O*NET matured and gained widespread use in the field. While some of these systems are still in existence and being updated (e.g., SIGI, O*NET) some have been discontinued from their previous versions (e.g., DISCOVER). Regardless, modern computer systems have become more robust and immersive, offering career practitioners and seekers of career knowledge many opportunities for creating and maintaining career portfolios with rich multimedia artifacts (e.g., FOCUS-2), for engaging with content and developing personal knowledge in "gamified" ways (e.g., Career Cruising, Bridges), and for storing and sharing relevant personal information widely. See Box 9.2 for links to some of these and other career resources. Then complete Activity 9.13.

ACTIVITY 9.13

Visit the career center on your campus and see if it has access to one of these powerful tools. Explore the use of these programs for your own career decision making so that you can work better with clients and their career issues.

BOX 9.2

Professional Organizations, Publications, and Websites for Career Counseling and Development

---

National Career Development Association (www.ncda.org/aws/NCDA/pt/sp/home_page)
Journal of Counseling & Development
Journal of Counseling Psychology
Journal of Vocational Behavior
Vocational Guidance Quarterly
Career Development Quarterly
Dictionary of Occupational Titles (DOT) (www.occupationalinfo.org)

Occupational Outlook Handbook (OOH) (www.bls.gov/oco/)
*Occupational Information Network (O*NET)* (www.onetcenter.org)
Career Cruising (public.careercruising.com/en/)
Focus-2 (www.focuscareer2.com/)
Bridges Transitions, Inc. (www.bridges.com)

Social Justice Issues in Career Counseling

- In 2014, female full-time, year-round workers made 79% of what male full-time, year-round workers made (American Association of University Women, 2015).
- In the third quarter of 2015, for those workers over the age of 16 years, unemployment rates for whites were 4.5%, black or African Americans were 9.5%, and Hispanics or Latinos were 6.5% (Bureau of Labor Statistics, 2015).
- As of this writing, in the United States, no federal law prohibits discrimination of workers based on sexual orientation or gender identity, only 4 states prohibit discrimination solely on the basis of sexual orientation, while 18 states prohibit discrimination based on sexual orientation or gender identity (American Civil Liberties Union, 2015).
- In the United States, the current wealth gap between upper- and middle-income families is at the largest it has been in 30 years of data collection, with median net worth of upper-income families being 6.6 times that of middle-income families (Fry & Kochhar, 2014). Further, recent studies suggest that the wealthiest 160,000 families have as much as the poorest 145 million families (Matthews, 2014).

Mirroring most traditional theories in the field of counseling and psychology, career development theory has largely been driven by and addresses the needs of white, educated, male, heterosexual, able-bodied persons, even though the roots of social justice and meeting the needs of oppressed populations in vocational psychology date at least to Parsons' work in the early 20th century (Arthur, Collins, Marshall, & McMahon, 2013). Although diversity issues such as culture, socioeconomic status, gender, age, and sexual identity are being discussed and analyzed in the current career counseling literature (Erford & Crockett, 2012), the focus still seems to be largely conceptual as no specific multicultural theory of career development has been developed, although social justice competency categories have started to emerge (Arthur et al., 2013).

Integration of social justice issues in the field of career counseling and career development has been addressed on at least two levels: the individual level, which helps career practitioners address the unique needs of individuals who might face social barriers to success, and the societal level, which promotes the idea of addressing and targeting social policy as a means of limiting the scope and impact of oppressive social forces (Pope, Briddick, & Wilson, 2013). Interestingly, Dik, Duffy, and Steger (2012) have suggested a potential method of bridging these two levels by promoting discussions of prosocial values in counseling relationships. Regardless of how this charge for social justice is incorporated at the individual, dyadic, or societal level, addressing the needs of those who encounter social and societal barriers on the path to career development will continue to be an important call in the profession (National Career Development Association, 2016). Next complete Think About It 9.5 for a review and application of the career theories covered in this chapter.

THINK ABOUT IT 9.5

Review the career development theories discussed in this chapter. What aspects of the theories are relevant for diverse groups? What aspects are irrelevant? Consider your personal level of comfort with addressing social justice issues individually or at the societal level.

Summary

Professional school counselors work with children, parents, teachers, and others within the school community. The setting requires a flexible individual who can adjust quickly to changing demands. School counselors need to be comfortable in highly visible community situations. The job satisfaction rewards are great for counselors who can develop and maintain positive relationships with children, their families, and other school professionals.

College counselors may work in a counseling center or be integrated into student-life services. Historically, they have assisted students with career development and continue to do so, depending on the institution. Student-life professionals and college counselors help the diverse, large group of nontraditional students (students older than 22 years) with the reentry issues unique to this population. College counselors must be knowledgeable about the notable problems that undergraduate students typically present, including binge drinking, sexual risks, and eating disorders. Professional counselors who work in the college setting employ their skills in ways that build relationships with diverse students, faculty members, and administrators, depending on the size of the institution, its vision for counseling and student-life services, and its organizational frame.

Career counseling issues, in general, continue to offer a broad and deep pool of influence for counselors at the school, college, and general practitioner level. Recent theoretical developments in the field encourage practitioners to stay current while continuing to recognize the influence of seminal 20th century theorists. The continued development and maturation of technologies which affect these fields underscores the potential excitement and challenge in influencing and inspiring future generations of students.

MyCounselingLab for Introduction to Counseling

Start with the Topic 15 Assignments: *School Counseling* and then try the Topic 2 Assignments: *Career/Individual/Development Counseling.*

10 Human Development Throughout the Life Span

BRADLEY T. ERFORD*

PREVIEW

The purpose of this chapter is to describe the developmental characteristics of infancy and toddlerhood (birth through age 3 years); early childhood (ages 4 to 6 years); middle childhood (ages 6 to 11 years); early adolescence, midadolescence, and later adolescence (ages 11 to 24 years); young or early adulthood (ages 24 to 40 years); middle adulthood (ages 40 to 60 years); and later adulthood (ages 60 years and older). The information in these approximate age categories serves as a basis for examples of interventions that helping professionals can use to facilitate development at several of these stages. Because the focus is on the practical application of development theory, readers are encouraged to consult human-development books referred to in this chapter for more in-depth information.

COUNSELING AND HUMAN DEVELOPMENT: A LIFE SPAN PERSPECTIVE

The knowledge contained within this chapter and a subsequent life span development course that counselors in training will take is essential to counseling practice. Knowledge of what is developmentally appropriate provides the context for abnormal development and helps clients and counselors set appropriate therapeutic goals and objectives. In the larger picture, human development informs counseling practice. Therefore, as you proceed through this chapter, think about how you can apply this knowledge to your own life, and the lives of loved ones, and current and future clients. Readers will likely participate in an entire class or two related to life span development issues and have ample opportunities to practice developmental skills and use developmental knowledge in experiential classes.

The information contained in this chapter was derived from decades of empirical study. While much of the information will make sense as you relate it to your own life, consider that others you encounter will have differing worldviews and life experiences. This body of empirical study applies to diverse human experiences, so don't be too quick to accept some evidence and reject other evidence. Clients' lived experiences may be very different from yours.

*Many thanks to Dr. Ann Vernon for her outstanding contributions to previous versions of this chapter.

Life is a journey, with each developmental stage posing a new set of challenges and opportunities, as Robert Munsch (1995) beautifully portrays in his children's book *Love You Forever*. In this poignant story that describes a mother's unconditional love for her child at each stage of development, Munsch also reminds us that life is a circle; toward the end of our journey, we are once again dependent, as we were in infancy. As professional counselors, we are in the unique position of not only experiencing our own growth and development, but also of facilitating our clients' journeys.

According to Erford (2017), the **life span perspective** includes the belief that development is lifelong, multidimensional, multidisciplinary and contextual, multidirectional, and plastic. Development does not end with early adulthood, as the traditional approach emphasizes; instead, there are various changes at every stage. There is some debate about how much capacity for change people retain as they age, because some characteristics might become more stable and less plastic. However, there are many different components within the biological, socioemotional, and cognitive dimensions of development that continue to change and develop over time (Santrock, 2013). Now complete Think About It 10.1.

THINK ABOUT IT 10.1

What are some things that immediately come to mind when you think about human development throughout the life span and the changes that might occur over time? How might these issues and changes have implications for counseling?

Life span development is complex, and the field continues to evolve, placing greater emphasis on cross-cultural perspectives, including feminism (Gielen & Roopnarine, 2004; Miller & Scholnick, 2000). Erford (2017) noted that life span developmental theory provides an organizational framework for understanding how the different stages of life are linked together and how the three adaptive processes of growth, maintenance, and regulation of loss are a part of the developmental journey from infancy through old age. This theory helps people resolve normal and abnormal conflicts to attain and maintain a healthy lifestyle throughout the life span.

There are numerous developmental issues that are essential for counselors to know, and you will encounter many of these during a life span development course and experiential application courses. For now, consider several of these important issues to whet your appetite (Erford, 2017). If you have ever taken an introductory psychology course you no doubt are aware of the **nature versus nurture** controversy: Is human (and other organismic) development the product of a tightly controlled, genetic unfolding of characteristics and behaviors, or does environmental context influence human characteristics and behaviors? While some human characteristics are very highly heritable (e.g., some genetic disorders), most developmental phenomena are influenced substantively by both genetics and environment, what developmental researchers call epigenetics. Thus, human DNA has a lot to say about human development, especially early on in one's life cycle, but how genes are expressed is strongly influenced by environmental context. This is good news for counselors and clients: Precious little in life is predetermined. So, even though a client is depressed or anxious, or has a long family history of depression or anxiety, and even though depression and anxiety are highly hereditable (influenced strongly by parents through genetics), a client is not doomed to be forever severely depressed or anxious. Counseling and medicine can help clients alter their environmental context, exposure, and behaviors, thus alleviating many of the challenges and consequences that depression and anxiety present.

Our understanding of human development also changes in response to changing research evidence and sociocultural influences. For example, a century ago, the concept of an adolescent life stage did not even exist (Erford, 2017). Children were viewed as little adults and went from childhood to adulthood around the ages of 12–14 years. Sociocultural influences over the 20th century (e.g., education, increased standard of living) created a new stage of development (i.e., adolescence) defined as from the onset of puberty to the end of the high school (teenage) years. Now the push for higher and higher levels of education among school-aged youth has led some developmental theorists and researchers to expand adolescence into what was formerly "young adulthood" territory in the mid-20s. So now it is more common to hear of early adolescence, midadolescence, and late adolescence, with many youth not entering young adulthood until well into their 20s.

Likewise, David Elkind first wrote *The Hurried Child: Growing Up Too Fast Too Soon* in the 1970s to draw attention to the phenomenon that, as a society, we are pushing our children to accomplish and achieve more and more at earlier and earlier ages. As you fast forward to today, look at how early children have their own smart phone or other tech savvy device, play organized sports, date, and have sex. What was not normal a generation earlier becomes normative very quickly. We rely on the use of empirical studies to support our knowledge of life span development because our understanding of human development alters with new empirical evidence and in response to sociocultural influences and changes.

Still, a great deal of the accumulated evidence over the past century continues to inform our practice as counselors. As one example, Erikson (1950) identified the following stages of psychosocial development, which are reflected throughout the chapter in the specific discussions about life span development:

1. **Basic trust versus mistrust** *(birth to 1 year):* In this stage, infants gain trust from a warm, responsive environment, in contrast to mistrust if they are mistreated or ignored.
2. **Autonomy versus shame and doubt** *(1 to 3 years):* In this stage, autonomy is nurtured when children can use their skills to make their own decisions.
3. **Initiative versus guilt** *(3 to 6 years):* Children experiment with who they can become through imaginative play. If parents do not support their ambitions and experimentation and expect too much self-control, children might feel guilty.
4. **Industry versus inferiority** *(6 to 11 years):* As they become more involved in school, children develop the ability to work with others. If they have negative experiences with peers or in the home or school setting, they might experience feelings of inferiority.
5. **Identity versus role confusion** *(adolescence):* Developing an identity is a key issue during this stage but can result in a negative outcome if there is confusion about future adult roles.
6. **Intimacy versus isolation** *(young adulthood):* Establishing intimate ties with others is a major task at this stage. Individuals who are unable to do this remain isolated.

7. **Generativity versus stagnation** *(middle adulthood):* Giving to the next generation is the essence of this stage, and individuals who fail to do this feel stagnated without this meaningful sense of accomplishment.

8. **Ego integrity versus despair** *(old age):* During this time of self-reflection, individuals who have lived satisfying lives develop a feeling of integrity, whereas individuals who perceive they have not lived satisfying lives experience dissatisfaction and fear death.

Interestingly, the left sides of Erikson's stage continua are viewed as pro-developmental, and therefore they build upon each other in a positive manner (i.e., trust leads to autonomy which leads to initiative, etc.). Likewise, the right side of each continuum also tends to build on itself, but in a more developmentally problematic manner (e.g., mistrust leads to shame, which leads to guilt, etc.). Importantly, Erikson, a neo-Freudian, believed people could revisit and overcome negative events with a counselor's help.

INFANCY AND TODDLERHOOD

The first 24 months of life constitute **infancy** (Newman & Newman, 2014), when major changes in all areas of development occur at an astonishing pace. During this fascinating, almost magical time, the personality of an infant begins to evolve as the infant begins to establish a presence in this world. Toddlers also make their presence felt by their high energy and "unpredictable, startling thoughts and actions that keep adults in a state of puzzled amazement" (p. 182). During **toddlerhood** (ages 2 to 3 years), remarkable changes, particularly in locomotion and language development, significantly contribute to the young child's growing autonomy. While there are many developmental accomplishments during this period, the following major ones are described: gross and fine motor development, emotional development, and cognitive/language development.

Motor Development in Infancy and Toddlerhood

Gross and fine motor development is essential during infancy. Erford (2017) noted that new motor skills are dramatic during the first year of life. By age 3 months to 4 months, infants begin to roll over; they can typically sit without support at 6 months; and by 7 months to 8 months, they can crawl and stand without support. Infants can generally walk without assistance by 13 months (Feldman, 2014; Santrock, 2013). There can be a 4-month variation as to when these milestones occur, but the sequence of the accomplishments typically does not vary. Between ages 2 and 3 years, locomotion becomes a key factor; leg muscles are stronger, and children walk, run, and jump several inches from the floor. They seem to be in constant motion and enjoy what their bodies can do.

Fine motor skills, which are almost nonexistent at birth, include reaching and grasping. At about 3 months, infants have more control over their heads and shoulders, which increases their ability to reach and grasp (Berk, 2013). Fine motor skills follow a gradual progression. Between 6 months and 12 months, infants can focus on small objects and reach out to grasp them. Scribbling and turning pages of a book occur between 12 months and 18 months.

Fine motor skills continue to develop as toddlers begin to build high block towers and put puzzles together. Their drawings also advance. An 18-month-old can scribble;

these scribbles start to become pictures. And toddlers use lines to represent the boundaries of objects by age 3 years (Berk, 2013).

As Feldman (2014) stressed, these norms are based primarily on white Americans, and there are differences in the timing of development relative to cultural, racial, and social groups. African American infants exhibit more accelerated motor development than whites. Also, variations in the timing of gross or fine motor skills might be affected by malnutrition, which is not only a problem in underdeveloped countries, but also in countries where there is significant poverty.

Emotional Development in Infancy and Toddlerhood

Newman and Newman (2014) identified age-related changes in **emotional differentiation**. In particular, they distinguished between joy and pleasure, weakness and fear, and rage and anger. Infants at 3 months can smile and display rage or anger when they experience physical discomfort. From 6 months to 12 months, they are more aware of situations, and their joy, anger, and fear are related to their environments. At 1 year of age, infants not only display elation, but also anxiety, fear, and anger. At age 2 years, they begin to respond to others' emotions and can show love by giving hugs and kisses. A more nonspecific anxiety is also more prevalent during this second year of life, in contrast to the fear of strangers that emerges at about 6 months and the separation anxiety at 9–12 months (Feldman, 2014).

According to Santrock (2013), toddlers are able to express their feelings verbally. They can say, "feel bad" or "dog scare." Toddlerhood is also characterized by the **terrible twos**; if their attempts to achieve greater autonomy are thwarted, anger and its expression through tantrums are common.

Cognitive/Language Development in Infancy and Toddlerhood

What intellectual abilities do infants and toddlers have, and how do these develop over time? **Piaget's cognitive-developmental theory** contributes in part to our knowledge about cognitive development. Because a detailed discussion of cognitive theorist Piaget's contributions and those of other theorists is beyond the scope of this text, the reader is encouraged to do further research about this important area of development.

Piaget's theory is based on the premise that children discover or construct their knowledge through their own activity and that they move through four stages of development, including sensorimotor, preoperational, concrete operational, and formal operational. The **sensorimotor stage,** which pertains to the period from birth to age 2 years, is divided into six substages, following a progression of development from cause and effect to simple trial-and-error problem solving to a level of cognitive development that results in some degree of mental representation (Berk, 2013).

Children move from Piaget's sensorimotor stage to the **preoperational stage** (ages 2 to 7). During this period, mental representation increases dramatically (Berk, 2013), along with make-believe play. Children younger than 2 years of age can engage in some make-believe play, such as talking into a toy telephone, but after age 2 years, children pretend with less realistic toys. Toddlers are also less self-centered than infants, and their make-believe play is more complex.

With regard to language development, infants cry and coo and then begin to babble (Santrock, 2013). Infants typically speak their first words at 10 months to 15 months, with rapid progression after that. The average 18-month-old has a 50-word vocabulary, which increases to 200 words by age 2 years. Language development continues to increase rapidly during toddlerhood. By age 3 years, a toddler's typical vocabulary is 1,000 words, and a toddler's communication is generally understood.

EARLY CHILDHOOD

Curiosity, questioning, and new socialization experiences through exposure to preschool and kindergarten characterize the stage of **early childhood development**. The intriguing changes continue as young children increasingly become more independent and their world broadens. Significant accomplishments in emotional, social, and cognitive development are briefly highlighted.

Social Development in Early Childhood

Play serves an important role for children in their own skill development and in relation to others. **Associative play**, in which children interact and share but do not seem to be playing the same game, characterizes 4-year-olds. By age 5 years, children begin to be more cooperative, take turns, and create games (Berk, 2013).

Although children in this age group still engage in make-believe play, they also participate in more structured games that are based more on reality (Newman & Newman, 2014). By the time they are in school and begin spending more time with other children, they learn to share, deal with conflict, and be a follower or a leader (Rathus, 2010).

Children at this age prefer same-gender playmates, not only in the United States, but also in other cultures (Newman & Newman, 2014). In addition, they show noticeable gender differences in play behavior: Boys tend to be more involved in rough and tumble play (Rathus, 2010), whereas girls are more inclined to engage in nurturing activities. Also, girls are more cooperative, whereas boys are more aggressive and competitive (Feldman, 2014).

Emotional Development in Early Childhood

Throughout this period, children become increasingly adept at understanding their emotions (Erford, 2017). Not only are they able to talk about their feelings, but they can also incorporate them into pretend play, which gives them a better understanding of their feelings and how to express feelings in acceptable ways. Although they gradually develop a better understanding of others' emotions, initially they are quite literal and confuse overt emotional expression with what someone might be feeling. According to Berk (2013), children at this age have difficulty understanding that they can experience different emotions about a situation simultaneously, even though they can understand the idea of experiencing different emotions at different times.

Although they will have made progress managing their emotions, this progress might be very uneven. Their emotional vocabularies are expanding, and they are beginning to understand which emotions are appropriate to specific situations (Lewis, Haviland-Jones, & Barrett, 2010). However, because they often lack the ability to verbalize their feelings accurately, young children tend to express them directly through action. Complete Activity 10.1 to help you understand more about how children express their emotions.

ACTIVITY 10.1 EMOTIONAL EXPRESSION IN EARLY CHILDHOOD

If you have access to a child between the ages of 4 and 6, ask him or her to speak with you for a few minutes and describe a time recently when he or she got into an argument with a friend or sibling. Ask the child to tell you about the argument and what feelings he or she had at the time. Then ask the child to draw a picture of the feelings. Afterward, address the following questions:

- How well did the child orally explain his or her feelings?
- What convergence or discrepancy between the child's drawing and oral description did you observe?
- What limitations, if any, did you note in the way the child identified his or her feelings?
- Comparing your observations with the literature, how typical or atypical is this child's emotional expression?

Cognitive Development in Early Childhood

Preoperational thought patterns characterize the cognitive development of 4-, 5-, and 6-year-olds (Berk, 2013; McDevitt & Ormrod, 2012). Because children are able to represent objects and events mentally, they can think and act more flexibly than during the sensorimotor stage. The fact that they can recall past events and envision future events allows them to connect experiences, and thus results, forming more complex understandings.

Although children at this age become increasingly more adept at relating symbols to each other in meaningful ways, there are some definite limitations. First, they have preoperational **egocentrism**, which is the inability to see things from another perspective. Also characteristic of their cognitive style is what Piaget described as **centration**, or centering (Erford, 2017), which refers to the tendency to focus on one aspect of a situation rather than on a broader view. As a result, they understand things in terms of an either/or framework and have difficulty exercising flexibility or grasping multiple details and solutions. Piaget's concept of adaptation was composed of two primary vehicles: **assimilation**, or making sense of new information in terms of some existing knowledge structure; and **accommodation**, or making sense of new information by reorganizing one's knowledge structure. A 3- or 4-year-old who encounters any dog will refer to the dog as a dog: assimilation. However, by later childhood most children have learned that there are different breeds of dogs, so refer to this dog as a golden retriever, and that dog as a beagle. They reorganized the structure by which they classify and understand "dogness": accommodation.

Language progresses rapidly during this period of growth, but children's vocabularies reflect their concrete stages of development. By age 5 years, children can understand almost anything explained to them in context if the examples are specific (Bjorklund, 2011), but they might have difficulty with concepts such as time and space. Imaginative play and vivid fantasies characterize this period of development, particularly for preschoolers. At age 4 years, they often have imaginary friends and engage in pretend play by themselves and with others, assuming different roles as they act out familiar routines, such as going to the store or to the doctor. Activity 10.2 facilitates understanding about imaginative play.

ACTIVITY 10.2 IMAGINARY PLAY

If you have access to several preschool children, observe these children in play to see if they engage in pretend play and, if so, how they assume different roles. Reflect on the similarities and differences the children displayed in terms of how they engaged in pretend play. Based on what you observed, what did you learn about imaginary play at this stage of development?

Developmental Interventions in Early Childhood

EMOTIONAL DEVELOPMENT IN EARLY CHILDHOOD   Because young children have a limited emotional vocabulary, teaching preschoolers to identify and describe feelings is helpful. A simple strategy is to draw a happy face, sad face, mad face, and worried face on four different paper plates. Secure these plates to the wall and put a different colored dot under each face (yellow for happy, blue for sad, red for mad, and green for worried). Then randomly place several of each of the colored dots in a square around the four faces. After explaining what each feeling is, take turns rolling a die and moving a marker along the dots in accordance with the number on the die. Both the child and the professional counselor then share a situation associated with the feeling on which they landed.

SOCIAL DEVELOPMENT IN EARLY CHILDHOOD   As children begin spending time with other children in preschool, they have increased opportunities to share and cooperate. Facilitating social development is best done in a small group of three to four children. After discussing what sharing means, indicate to the children that they are going to make a snowman (or another object) using the materials in a paper sack (e.g., cotton balls, one pair of safety scissors, one tube of glue or roll of tape, buttons of different shapes and sizes, pieces of colored construction paper, and five different colored crayons). If possible, record the children as they work so you can later review the footage and look for examples of cooperation and sharing. If it is not possible to record their efforts, you can stop at various points throughout the construction of the project to ask for examples of sharing and cooperation. Now read Voices from the Field 10.1 For an interesting perspective on working with young children.

VOICES FROM THE FIELD 10.1   Working with Young Children: Generalization from One Context to Another, by Nicole Bradley

Having worked with children and adolescents for the majority of my professional career, I have had a variety of interesting experiences and learned a lot from my clients. One 5-year-old client reminded me of the importance of being specific and being certain that clients are able to apply information learned in sessions to their regular lives. I had been meeting with the 5-year-old for a few weeks. Because he had witnessed domestic violence on multiple occasions, I had been focusing on safety planning, or helping him understand how to be safe should another violent situation emerge. We had worked on what to do if there was "an emergency" and what an emergency was in the context of safety and domestic violence. He had the safety plan down pat; he could explain to me different situations that constituted an emergency and what he needed to do.

After creating a safety plan, the next issue that arose for this boy was having enuresis, or bladder accidents, at school. This was his first year of all-day school, so his parent and teacher thought that the problem was due to adjustment associated with managing a full day away from home. One session, when I was exploring with the boy what was occurring on the days he had accidents, he explained that his teacher told the class that students could only use the restroom when it was "an emergency." It was then that I realized he had generalized the concept of emergency from safety planning to restroom breaks. We then discussed different types of emergencies in different situations and how to respond to each type. Once he understood that "really having to go" was one type of emergency, he began asking for permission to use the restroom at school, and the accidents stopped. From this experience, I learned the importance of considering how children, and clients in general, might apply what we work on in sessions to other contexts of their lives and the importance of thoroughly processing these issues.

MIDDLE CHILDHOOD

Middle childhood is a stage of development filled with growth and change. Although their physical rates of growth have stabilized, 6- to 11-year-olds mature remarkably during these school-age years. Key characteristics relative to social, emotional, and cognitive development are described.

Social Development in Middle Childhood

When they begin formal schooling, children increasingly encounter peers who are different from them with regard to accomplishments, personality, religion, and ethnicity, which enhances their perspective-taking abilities. Consequently, they are better able to communicate with their peers and are more prosocial.

Socialization in the context of a peer group becomes a central issue for children in this age range. Acceptance in a group and a "best friend" contribute significantly to a child's sense of competence (Berger, 2012). Friendships serve important functions; children learn to cooperate and compromise, negotiate, and assume roles as leaders and followers. They also learn how to deal with peer-group pressure and rejection.

Throughout this period, friendships become increasingly intense and intimate, particularly for girls. They generally choose friends who are of the same age, gender, and ethnicity and who have similar interests (Siegler, DeLoache, & Eisenberg, 2011). As opposed to early childhood, when children are more egocentric and do not need friends as much, children in middle childhood are becoming more dependent on friends for help in academic and social situations and for companionship and self-validation (Berger, 2012; Siegler et al., 2011). Team play is a new dimension of social development.

Emotional Development in Middle Childhood

A school-age child's understanding of emotions is more complex than a preschooler's. In general, the school-age child is more sensitive, empathic, and better able to recognize and communicate his or her feelings to others (McDevitt & Ormrod, 2012). Berk (2013) pointed out that sociable, assertive, and good emotional regulators are most likely to be empathic and helpful to others.

At this age, children now understand that a person can have two conflicting emotions simultaneously, which extends to self-conscious emotions. In addition, these children have learned that feelings can change and that they are not the cause of another person's emotional discomfort (Erford, 2017).

During middle childhood, fears and anxieties are related to real life, as opposed to imaginary issues. For example, some children become less concerned about ghosts but become more worried about tests and grades or being harmed by someone. Happiness is often related to peer acceptance and achieving goals (Siegler et al., 2011).

Cognitive Development in Middle Childhood

During middle childhood, vast differences occur in cognitive development. Piaget (1967) proposed that a transitional period between preoperational and **concrete operational** thought occurs between the ages of 5 and 7 years, but by ages 7 or 8 years, most children are definitely concrete operational thinkers. Berk (2013) noted that this is a major turning point because when children are in the concrete operational stage, their thinking is more like that of adults. Concrete operational thinkers are able to understand logical operations, such as identity, reversibility, reciprocity, seriation, and classification and can apply them in different contexts, such as friendships, rules in games, or team play. Because play is such an integral part of early and middle childhood, Activity 10.3 is a reflection on this aspect of development.

ACTIVITY 10.3 PLAY IN MIDDLE CHILDHOOD

Think back to when you were a child, or think of a child or children you have seen engage in play activities. First, think of early childhood. What types of games did you play with others? Next, think of games you played as you and friends transitioned through middle childhood. Frequently, children in early childhood participate in make-believe and then structured games based on reality (e.g., playing "house" or "school"). Children in middle childhood frequently participate in more team play and games that have rules (e.g., board games, kickball, other sports that require teams). Based on what you recall about your play, in what ways were you (or children you observed) typical according to developmental stereotypes?

School-age children's thinking is more flexible and rational than that of children in early childhood, and, for the most part, school-age children have better problem-solving abilities and organizational skills. They learn best by questioning, exploring, and doing, and they use language in more sophisticated ways. Despite the growth in cognitive development, there are limitations. Although they can reason more logically than when they were younger, children in this age group still have difficulty with abstract concepts; they do not readily think about things they cannot see (Erford, 2017). Because they focus on what they can see, their problem-solving abilities are sometimes limited because they do not consider other possible solutions (Siegler et al., 2011). Children operate from assumptions, mistaking their assumptions for facts and jumping to conclusions. All of these factors affect how children respond to events in their lives.

Developmental Interventions in Middle Childhood

EMOTIONAL DEVELOPMENT   To facilitate emotional development during middle childhood and to help children learn that feelings vary in intensity, professional counselors can engage them in the activity How Strong (Vernon, 2006). After discussing how feelings can vary in intensity and sharing several examples, give the child three cans, labeled *strong, mild*, and *weak.* Then give the child a list of situations on individual notecards, such as *someone calls you a name, someone steals your new bike,* and *your best friend moves away.* Ask the child to read each situation, write how he or she would feel in each case, and put each card in one of the cans to signify the degree of intensity of that particular feeling. Discuss why feelings often vary in intensity and how to decrease the intensity of strong negative emotions.

SOCIAL DEVELOPMENT   Social skills become increasingly important during middle childhood. One classroom guidance intervention to facilitate social development is to play a game similar to musical chairs. The children move around the circle of chairs and sit when the music stops; the child left standing draws a friendship strip from an envelope and reads it aloud. The child is asked to decide if the message gives an example of a good or bad friendship behavior. After discussing the reasons for his or her answer, the child puts the strip of paper in the appropriately labeled (good or bad) friendship box. The game continues until there are no chairs left. Examples of behaviors for the friendship behavior strips include *compliments you, calls you names, refuses to share, invites you to play, spreads rumors about you,* and *turns friends against you.*

ADOLESCENCE

The relative stability of middle childhood can vanish overnight as children enter puberty, signifying the beginning of early adolescence (ages 11 to 14 years), which is followed by midadolescence (ages 15 to 18 years) and late adolescence (ages 19 to 24 years), often referred to as emerging young adulthood. In particular, the first few years of early **adolescence** can be difficult because of the rapid physical changes and the significant cognitive and emotional maturation (Newman & Newman, 2014). Despite some turmoil, however, adolescence can be an exciting time as young people develop more complex social and intimate relationships, gain more autonomy and mastery, and experience many new things.

Early Adolescence

Except during infancy, physical changes occur more rapidly during early adolescence than at any other point in the life span (Erford, 2017), affecting the young adolescent in numerous ways. For more specific development that occurs during puberty, the reader is encouraged to consult sources referred to in this chapter.

SOCIAL DEVELOPMENT IN EARLY ADOLESCENCE   As early adolescents become more socially distant from their families, peers play a dominant role and are a vital part of the growing-up process, although, in some cultures, this is not as pronounced (McDevitt & Ormrod, 2012). Peers are important because they are socialization agents, helping adolescents try out and grow comfortable with new adult-like roles. In one-on-one interactions, peers help adolescents search introspectively for potential future roles and lifestyles. Peers also provide a safe space for testing out new beliefs and behaviors, but at the same time, adolescents are very vulnerable to peer ridicule and rejection. Because they have a strong need to belong and to be accepted and they fear being judged or put down, young adolescents tend to conform to peer norms and expectations.

As they get older, friendships become increasingly more intimate, and adolescents confide in their peers more than in their parents. Adolescent friendships are more emotionally bonded and stable than childhood friendships. Adolescents want psychological closeness, loyalty, and mutual understanding, and they typically choose friends who are like themselves (Berk, 2013).

EMOTIONAL DEVELOPMENT IN EARLY ADOLESCENCE   Heightened emotionality and rapid mood fluctuations characterize this period, with the adolescent capable of shifting from intense sadness to anger to excitement to depression in a brief time. In addition to the unpredictable moodiness that is often accompanied by emotional outbursts, negative and painful emotional states are experienced more frequently (Siegler et al., 2011), along with troublesome emotions, including anxiety, shame, depression, embarrassment, guilt, and loneliness (Vernon, 2010).

Young adolescents are more aware of others' feelings and thoughts. Consequently, they are more sensitive to the ups and downs associated with social interactions, often overreacting to who said what about whom. Although their more advanced cognitive abilities help them interpret unpleasant emotional experiences, this often results in an increase in self-consciousness and self-criticism (Erford, 2017).

There are cultural and gender differences related to the acceptability and expression of feelings. In some cultures, emotional openness is not valued (Saarni, Campos, Camras, & Witherington, 2006). Respect for these cultural differences is essential, as is an understanding of gender differences. For example, girls are often more emotionally expressive and more sensitive to the emotional states of others than boys are. Girls frequently also experience more anxiety, shame, guilt, and depression (Garber, Kelley, & Martin, 2002; Meece & Daniels, 2008). Girls, more so than boys, are depressed by problems in their peer relationships (Nolen-Hoeksema, 2001) and by their appearances and body images (Garber et al., 2002).

The increased intensity of emotions permeates all aspects of early adolescents' lives; they feel confused and anxious about the roller coaster of emotions they might be experiencing (Vernon, 2010). Their negative emotions can be overwhelming, resulting in increased vulnerability. Case Study 10.1 invites you to apply developmental theory to a short case study about a young adolescent.

CASE STUDY 10.1

A Seventh-grade Girl

The parents of a girl in early adolescence bring her to counseling. She is in seventh grade. According to her parents, she has recently become very quiet and does not spend as much time with them. She stays in her room most of the time and is more withdrawn than usual. She often says she hates school and does not want to go. Her grades have also declined.

1. With what types of developmental issues might this adolescent be struggling?
2. Which aspects would you focus on as her professional counselor?

COGNITIVE DEVELOPMENT IN EARLY ADOLESCENCE   The cognitive changes that gradually occur during adolescence profoundly affect the young person's social relations and psychological development (Steinberg, 2014) and constitute the most dramatic change in cognition that occurs in anyone's life. Erford (2017) noted that **formal operational-stage** thinking begins at about age 11 years but is not consistently attained until at least ages 15 to 20 years. As early adolescents move into this realm, they begin to think more abstractly and hypothetically, often engaging in idealization and then comparing themselves and others with these ideal standards. Steinberg (2014) emphasized that the changes in cognition allow adolescents to think about possibilities, which has a positive impact on their problem-solving abilities. In addition, they become better arguers and do not accept others' viewpoints without questioning them.

With the development of abstract thinking comes an ability to think more logically and hypothesize about the logical sequence of events. Although they are better able to predict consequences of actions, adolescents inconsistently apply these skills to themselves (Erford, 2017). Adolescents might see discrepancies between what is and what is supposed to occur conceptually at this period of development. Considerable variability exists in the way early adolescents think. Although thinking continues to improve throughout adolescence, even by the end of middle school, most young adolescents have not attained formal-operational thinking. Cultural expectations and experiences also influence the development of formal-operational thinking, so it is important to consider the cultural context with regard to how thinking skills develop.

Developmental Interventions in Early Adolescence

Emotional Development.   The emotional volatility of early adolescence is often confusing and disturbing. The intervention described below, intended for small-group or classroom guidance, helps adolescents learn to distinguish between helpful and unhelpful ways to manage their moods. Introduce the lesson by discussing how hormonal changes during puberty contribute to mood swings, and engage students in a discussion about how adolescents often feel overwhelmed and confused when they experience these. In small groups, have students discuss what they do to manage their moods and record their ideas on newsprint. After each group has shared ideas, give each group a sorting board (a sheet labeled *very helpful, somewhat helpful, not at all helpful, not helpful/negative consequences*, and *could be either helpful or unhelpful*). Give each group a set of cards that name coping strategies, such as *listen to music, write poetry, attempt suicide, get drunk, talk to a parent, talk to a friend, punch something or someone, binge eat, stop eating, journal, talk to a counselor, leave the scene,* and *cut yourself*. Have groups sort the cards onto their sorting boards. When finished, process the activity by asking students to share which strategies they have used or would like to use to help manage their moods (Vernon, 1998b).

Cognitive Development.   Young adolescents' emotions commonly overshadow their ability to think clearly, which affects their problem-solving ability. The following intervention, which can be done with an individual or within a small-group or classroom guidance situation, helps students think more rationally.

Introduce the idea of rational thinking by handing a pair of dark sunglasses and a pair of glasses with clear lenses to the adolescent. Ask the adolescent to first put on the dark "doom-and-gloom" glasses and imagine going to a party with these glasses on. Ask, *What will the party be like?* Then have the adolescent put on the clear glasses; things will look different. Ask: *What will the party be like?* Discuss the idea that the way we look at situations or think about situations affects how we feel about them. Introduce the following concepts, explaining with examples that pertain to adolescence: tunnel vision (i.e., seeing only a small part of the issue), overgeneralizing and *awfulizing* (i.e., blowing the situation out of proportion and assuming the worst), self-downing (i.e., putting yourself down or assuming you are not good), and mind reading (i.e., assuming you know what someone is thinking without checking it out). Discuss how these negative thinking patterns apply to issues in the adolescent's life, and help identify ways to counteract them by checking out assumptions, not jumping to conclusions, looking at things from multiple perspectives, and looking for other possibilities (Vernon, 1998a).

Midadolescence

Midadolescence is frequently described as a period when teenagers try out adult roles (Erford, 2017), discover who they are and are not, and establish new beliefs and behaviors. Depending on when they entered puberty and when they attained formal-operational thinking, midadolescence is often a calmer, more predictable stage of development.

SOCIAL DEVELOPMENT IN MIDADOLESCENCE   The importance of peer relationships continues into midadolescence. The increased time spent with peers serves various functions for teenagers, including to try out various roles, to learn to tolerate individual differences as they come in contact with people who have different values and lifestyles, and to prepare themselves for adult interactions as they begin to form more intimate relationships (Erford, 2017).

For an adolescent who has attained formal-operational thinking, relationships take on a new dimension. Because these adolescents are more self-confident and less egocentric than younger children, they are not as dependent on peers for identity and emotional support (Erford, 2017). They are also more willing to express their uniqueness and are less likely to conform to peers. Peers continue to be a source of support, however, and play an important role in adolescents' development as friendships become more stable and less exclusive.

Intimate friendships with people of the same gender and opposite gender increase during midadolescence (Newman & Newman, 2014), with girls seeking these intimate relationships sooner than boys. Teenagers begin to experience casual sexual contact through participation in group activities before actual dating begins (Erford, 2017), typically after age 15 or 16 years (Steinberg, 2014). Sexual experimentation generally increases during this period. Now complete Think About It 10.2.

THINK ABOUT IT 10.2

Think back to when you were in high school. How important were peer relationships to you, and how did these relationships differ from those of early adolescence? Peer relationships serve a variety of functions. How can you apply this statement to your personal experiences? If you could do it over, what, if anything, would you change about your peer relationships during adolescence?

EMOTIONAL DEVELOPMENT IN MIDADOLESCENCE In contrast to the emotional upheaval characteristic of early adolescence, more emotional stability comes in midadolescence (Erford, 2017) because teens are not as vulnerable and are not as likely to be overwhelmed by their emotions. Increased emotional complexity occurs during this period and adolescents are able to identify, understand, and express more emotions and be more empathic. Although these adolescents are typically more emotionally stable, there is great variability in how they deal with emotionally charged issues, which depends on their level of cognitive maturation, accounting for the wide variation in how adolescents manage emotions. More emotionally mature adolescents have better coping skills and are less likely to behave impulsively or act out behaviorally.

A compounding factor in adolescents' emotional development is depression, which was not well addressed in adolescents until the 1990s because it was discounted as adolescent turmoil. However, Newman and Newman (2014) reported that about 35% of adolescents experience periods of sadness and depressed feelings regularly.

COGNITIVE DEVELOPMENT IN MIDADOLESCENCE During midadolescence, formal-operational thinking continues to develop, although many adolescents and even adults do not reach this level of thinking. Steinberg (2014) stressed that advanced reasoning capabilities develop gradually, that these advanced skills are employed by some adolescents more often than by other adolescents, and that when they apply the advanced skills could depend on the situation. As formal-operational thinking develops, adolescents begin to think and behave in qualitatively different ways. According to Newman and Newman (2014), they can also hypothesize, think about the future, be introspective, and detect inconsistency in statements. Their thought processes are more flexible; they are less likely to think in either/or terms, which has a positive effect on how they problem solve (Erford, 2017). Although their cognitive abilities have improved considerably since early adolescence, 15- to 18-year-olds are still likely to be inconsistent in their thinking and behavior. Some days teens may appear wise and mature far beyond their years; other days teens may appear to have regressed in wisdom and maturity.

Developmental Interventions in Midadolescence

Social Development. Although the emotional stability of midadolescence generally affects social relationships in a positive way, adolescents continue to have issues related to rumors, gossip, and unfounded assumptions that can result in interpersonal relationship difficulties. The intervention (Vernon, 1998b) discussed below helps adolescents learn to stop the negative cycle of rumors and assumptions. It is most effective in a classroom or small-group setting.

Introduce the intervention by asking for several volunteers. Whisper a complicated message about a relationship issue to the first volunteer, who passes it on to the second volunteer, who passes it to the third volunteer. The last person states the message out loud, which stimulates discussion about distorted communication. Next, ask the adolescents to each identify in writing a time when they have been the object of a rumor or gossip, how they felt, and a consequence of the situation. After sharing responses with partners, encourage discussion on how to stop this negative cycle by checking out assumptions; considering whether what someone said about them is true, and if not, not reacting personally; and not participating in this type of behavior.

Cognitive Development.   Although many adolescents still live in the here and now, midadolescence is a period in which they need to begin making decisions about the future. The following intervention can facilitate that decision-making process.

After initiating a discussion with the adolescent about plans after high school, give him or her a set of *what's next* cards (Vernon, 2002) that list potential opportunities, such as *full-time job away from the community, part-time job in the community, 2-year college part time, 2-year college full time, getting married, trade or technical school, 4-year college full time,* and *joining a branch of the U.S. Armed Services.* The adolescent sorts these onto a sheet of paper labeled *very likely, somewhat likely,* and *not at all likely.* After the sorting is complete, debrief by discussing viable options, obstacles the adolescent might have to overcome, and feelings about these next steps.

Late Adolescence (Emerging Adulthood)

As adolescents transition into adulthood, they experience new freedoms and responsibilities (Santrock, 2013). As young people search for meaning and direction in their lives, identity development becomes a primary focus (Newman & Newman, 2014). Accompanying this search is increasing anxiety and uncertainty about what they want to do with their lives and whether they will be successful.

SOCIAL DEVELOPMENT IN LATE ADOLESCENCE (EMERGING ADULTHOOD)   During this emerging-adulthood period, young people are beginning to see themselves as adults and as contributing members of society (Arnett, 2000). They become less dependent on parents, gradually achieving a psychological sense of autonomy in which adolescents are still connected to their parents, while adolescents and parents accept each other's individuality (Broderick & Blewitt, 2014). The degree of autonomy depends on culture.

Feldman (2014) noted that there is a basic need for belongingness, which results in young people's establishment of close relationships with others. Ultimately, a close relationship might become a loving one, although romantic, passionate love is not the norm in every culture. However, for many young adults, choosing a lifelong partner is a major task at this stage of development.

COGNITIVE DEVELOPMENT IN LATE ADOLESCENCE (EMERGING ADULTHOOD)   In contrast to Piaget's theory, which implied that formal-operational thinking was the final stage of cognitive development, theorist Gisela Labouvie-Vief suggested that there are several cognitive changes that go beyond this stage, including confronting societal paradoxes, using analogies to make comparisons, and reasoning subjectively. Because thinking is more flexible, interpretation and understanding subtleties are more prevalent. Labouvie-Vief labeled this type of thinking as *postformal thought* (Erford, 2017), which also includes dialectical thinking (i.e., arguing, debating, and realizing that issues are not always absolutely right or clear) and the realization that problem resolution involves drawing on past experiences.

Erford (2017) also discussed theorist K. Warner Schaie's stages of cognitive development, indicating that applications of intelligence in late adolescence and emerging adulthood are more specifically directed toward attainment of long-term career and family goals, and possible societal contributions. This stage is called the achieving stage, during which the decisions they make have lifelong implications, specifically in terms of job and marriage.

Broderick and Blewitt (2014) noted that cognitive functioning during this stage is characterized by acquiring knowledge and becoming more expert in particular areas. A shift to using knowledge to achieve long-term goals also occurs at this time (Feldman, 2014). The reader is encouraged to learn about William Perry's theory of intellectual and ethical development in the college years, in which he described changes in young adults' knowledge and assumptions of the world. Theorist Karen Strohm Kitchener's model of reflective judgment also describes the different stages of thinking relative to this period of development (Broderick & Blewitt, 2014). Activity 10.4 encourages reflection about your own intellectual and ethical development.

ACTIVITY 10.4

Research Perry's theory of intellectual and ethical development in the college years. What connections can you make to your own life at this stage? Reflect on any significant changes of worldviews and assumptions, recalling whether or not you became more interested in world news or any world topics. What implications does Perry's theory have for professional counselors seeing adult clients?

SELF-DEVELOPMENT IN LATE ADOLESCENCE (EMERGING ADULTHOOD) Several important tasks must be assumed by young adults. First, they need to each formulate their gender identity. Although role expectations in this culture and some others are more flexible, there are still expectations and choices that young people need to consider (Newman & Newman, 2014). In addition, as they move out into the world, they encounter other adult role models aside from their parents and are faced with the challenge of analyzing beliefs and values they had assumed as children and reevaluating those beliefs and values based on their young-adult perspectives. Now complete Think About It 10.3 to deepen your thinking about the importance of beliefs and values.

THINK ABOUT IT 10.3

What changes in beliefs and values frequently take place during emerging adulthood? Reflect on your own beliefs and values; how (if at all) were they altered during emerging adulthood? In what ways are your values different from those of your parents or guardians, and how does this affect your relationship with them?

In addition to integrating gender identity and clarifying their personal vision of themselves (Newman & Newman, 2014), people in late adolescence are more aware of their bodies and clarify their sexual orientation within the context of intimate relationships.

Developmental Interventions in Late Adolescence (Emerging Adulthood)

Social Development. Choosing a life partner or becoming involved in a serious romantic relationship often occurs during late adolescence. Sometimes, young adults operate with tunnel vision, seeing only the good aspects of their relationships. So when problems occur, they are often blindsided and devastated. The following intervention is designed to help them look realistically at romantic relationships. Give the individual a sheet of paper featuring a smaller square surrounded by a larger square. In the inside square, have the young adult list all the positive traits about the relationship and the individual with whom he or she is involved. In the outside square, he or she should list all the negative realities represented by the relationship. Process this by discussing the positive and negative aspects of the relationship and the significance and consequences of what he or she has identified. This process helps a young adult clarify the areas of concern and strengths (Vernon, 2002).

Self-Development.   As young people question their values and continue to define their own roles, an intervention such as the following can provide clarification. First, have the young adult brainstorm a list of strong beliefs and values (i.e., what *matters*). After the list is complete, invite the emerging adult to code these values and beliefs as follows: IM (important to me but not to others close to me), IF (important to me and to my immediate family), IP (important to me and to my partner and/or closest friends), PA (can publicly affirm), A (alienates me from others), E (evident in my behavior, such as work or volunteer activities), TM (takes money), P (proud of), and C (contributes to society, or to the greater good). After coding, ask the emerging adult to discuss what insights resulted from completing the intervention and what the insights tell him or her about who he or she is. Encourage dialogue about changes in priorities or actions he or she wishes to make as a result of the insights gained.

EARLY ADULTHOOD

Although **early adulthood** is typically identified as beginning at age 24 years, the tasks associated with this phase could have begun during emerging adulthood, depending on the individual. However, during this stage, three roles evolve: the worker, the committed partner, and the parent (Erford, 2017). With each of these significant roles come multiple challenges and adjustments.

The Worker in Early Adulthood

Through work, an adult develops his or her personal identity, values, and social status (Newman & Newman, 2014). In the **early career stage**, the worker questions his or her competence and degree of commitment. How to advance, relate to colleagues and supervisors, and balance work and family are salient issues. Concerns of this nature can create stress as the young worker seeks a fulfilling career and assumes major responsibility for earning a living and navigating the dynamics of the work environment.

As the role of a worker evolves, challenges emerge, including dealing with the demands and expectations of the job and negotiating the hierarchy of authority. As young adults take on new responsibilities or discover their own limitations, they might experience anxiety, coupled with the worry about being financially self-sufficient.

The Partner in Early Adulthood

Developing an intimate relationship might have happened during late adolescence. With the average age of marriage being delayed, it is likely that committing to an intimate relationship that could involve marriage might not occur until early adulthood, depending on culture. Newman and Newman (2014) identified stages of a committed relationship, beginning with the original attraction and moving to deeper attraction as self-disclosure occurs and partners discover ways in which they are similar. Values and other background characteristics help determine compatibility. The more self-aware young people are, the greater the likelihood that they can select partners for intimate relationships based on similarities and differences.

If the relationship progresses, the next phase occurs as the couple takes new risks in discovering more about each other. At this point, they might experience role compatibility and empathy that strengthens the relationship, find out their self-disclosure creates barriers that could lead to a breakup if they discover they are incompatible, or that there are significant undesirable differences. If the relationship endures, intense caring, sexual desire, and euphoria characterize this stage, which might culminate in marriage or an exclusive partnership.

If the couple decides to marry or cohabitate, there are many adjustments. Compromise and flexibility are crucial as couples come to agreement about such issues as spending and saving money, work schedules and habits, relationships with friends and in-laws, alone time versus couple time, eating and sleeping patterns, and other daily living matters. All of these topics are potential sources of tension, so it is imperative that couples have good communication and conflict-management skills to successfully navigate this important task during early adulthood.

The Parent in Early Adulthood

Although not all couples choose to or are able to have children, those who become parents typically do so during this stage of life. According to Newman and Newman (2014), the decision about parenthood is one of the major commitments of early adulthood. These decisions are considered within the context of culture, religious beliefs, family expectations, career aspirations, and personal and family goals.

Feldman (2014) noted that "The birth of a child brings about a dramatic shift in the roles spouses must play . . . and these new positions may overwhelm their ability to respond in their older, although continuing, roles of 'wife' and 'husband'" (p. 507). This shift might be quite stressful given that each parent could adapt to the transition differently. Although having children is a major responsibility that can be overwhelming as well as rewarding, having children led to greater marital satisfaction for couples who were already satisfied with their relationships. In contrast, couples who had significant conflict before becoming parents had increased difficulties after the birth of a child (Newman & Newman, 2014). Now complete Think About It 10.4.

THINK ABOUT IT 10.4

What implications do the roles of worker, partner, and parent have for professional counselors trying to help adult clients? What types of issues related to these three roles might be presented to a professional counselor?

Developmental Interventions in Early Adulthood

Given the many transitions that occur during the early adult stage, interventions such as the ones discussed below can help individuals identify changes in roles, responsibilities, routines, and relationships as partners, parents, and workers. Awareness of these changes is the first step in identifying how to deal more effectively with the challenges associated with assuming more responsibility as young adults.

Give the individual a sheet of paper with the words *roles, relationships, routines,* and *responsibilities* written across the top. Under each heading, have the individual list three to four changes associated with one or more of the roles *partner, parent,* and *worker.* After discussing the changes, work with the individual to minimize the stress associated with the various roles and identify healthy coping strategies.

Another intervention that addresses the stress and overload that can occur for the young worker, parent, or partner is to give the individual a circle representing a 24-hour day. Ask the individual to divide that circle into sections representing how that time period is currently spent. Then give the individual another circle and have him or her divide it into sections representing how the individual would ideally like the time to be spent. Compare the two circles, and discuss what gets in the way of the ideal circle being the reality. Discuss identifying priorities, establishing realistic goals, and other ways to achieve balance.

MIDDLE ADULTHOOD

According to Broderick and Blewitt (2014), many developmental theorists see the 40s as a time of life-structure reassessment. People often question occurrences from the past and realize that life is finite, sometimes resulting in a midlife crisis. Feldman (2014) stressed that most people make the transition to midlife with little difficulty. Childrearing is typically easier, many adults have been successful in their careers, and, for the most part, they are more content with life.

Cognitive and physical changes occur during this period. But because of the increased life span and the fact that individuals are healthier at older ages, middle-age boundaries often are pushed upward (Santrock, 2013). Aging is different for every individual and varies according to culture, but there are general trends that occur at some point during this developmental stage.

Physical Changes in Middle Adulthood

Although the changes that occur are not as dramatic as during adolescence, by **middle adulthood**, most people experience some change in physical appearance (Santrock, 2013). Skin begins to wrinkle and sag, hair becomes thinner or grayer, and muscle strength decreases while bone loss increases. Vision and hearing can also start to decline, while occurrences of arthritis and hypertension increase. Typically in the late 40s or early 50s, women go through menopause; men also experience some hormonal changes, including a decrease in testosterone and sperm count.

Cognitive Changes in Middle Adulthood

Memory loss is something middle-aged adults joke about but at the same time still worry about. In reality, sensory and short-term memory do not decline during this period. Although there is some long-term memory loss for some people, Feldman (2014) pointed to relatively minor memory declines in middle age. Whether or not intelligence declines with age is controversial. A very gradual decline starting at age 25 years is noted in inductive reasoning, spatial orientation, verbal memory, and perceptual speed, but verbal ability increases until about age 40 years and then remains steady throughout the remainder of life.

Key Developmental Tasks in Middle Adulthood

The middle adulthood years can be challenging as adults juggle job, children, parent, and partner responsibilities. Key developmental tasks of midlife include continuation of intimacy and other primary relationships, work productivity, and generativity (Feldman, 2014).

INTIMACY AND RELATIONSHIPS   If they have children, middle-aged adults could (depending on their ages during pregnancy) be dealing with raising teenagers, launching them into the world, and dealing with the empty-nest syndrome (Newman & Newman, 2014). Family roles change as children become adults and parents need to find other areas of focus. Middle-aged adults might become caretakers for aging parents, which can be a significant challenge (Feldman, 2014). During this period, some parents might also become grandparents, which is another symbol of aging.

WORK   According to Feldman (2014), middle-aged workers are more concerned with pay, working conditions, and policies as opposed to opportunities for advancement and recognition, which were young-adulthood concerns. Many might experience this time as one of high productivity, success, and earning power. However, while some older workers experience more job satisfaction than younger workers, burnout also occurs during this period. During the first half of middle adulthood, time spent working and work intensity increase. As adults reach the peak of their careers, the energy spent at work might decline and time with friends and family might increase.

GENERATIVITY   **Generativity**, which refers to the contributions an individual makes to family, community, work, and society, is a concept that was developed by theorist Erik Erikson. According to this perspective, adults in midlife play an important role in mentoring and focus efforts on continuing their own lives by guiding and encouraging future generations (Feldman, 2014). **Stagnation**, which is equivalent to lack of growth, can occur if people feel they have not made significant contributions. This could serve as motivation to find more fulfilling, challenging careers or other ways to find meaning in their lives, or it might result in increased rigidity, isolation, and depression if individuals do not have a sense of accomplishment or feel as if they have nothing to contribute to society (Newman & Newman, 2014). Activity 10.5 helps the reader identify issues of middle adulthood.

ACTIVITY 10.5 ROLES IN MIDDLE ADULTHOOD

Place a check mark in all the following spaces that correctly describe the issues of middle adulthood (key at end of the chapter):

_____1. Reassessment of life structure
_____2. Some long-term memory loss
_____3. Emergence of three roles
_____4. Gradual decline in verbal memory and inductive reasoning
_____5. Decisions about parenthood
_____6. Intelligence is applied to specific situations involving long-term goals
_____7. Hormonal changes

Developmental Interventions in Middle Adulthood

Midlife can be a time when adults experience some dissatisfaction in life and need to find new challenges and opportunities. The following goal-setting intervention is an effective strategy for helping individuals assess their lives and set new goals.

Ask the individual to list 8 to 10 things that are going well in his or her life and then separately list things he or she would like to change. Categorize the things to change into topics, such as *social, financial, career, family,* and *spiritual,* depending on what was on the list. Then ask the adult to select one item from each category that he or she most wants to change and write these on a separate piece of paper. Next, ask the adult to identify three doable goals for each selected item that would lead to greater life satisfaction. After discussing the benefits and barriers related to each goal, have the adult identify at least one specific strategy to achieve each of the identified goals and create a time line for their completion.

Another intervention that helps middle-aged adults evaluate how they feel about their lives at this stage is to complete unfinished sentences that stimulate discussion about various aspects of life. Consider the following sentence stems:

My greatest accomplishment thus far is . . .

What I would still like to achieve is . . .

As I grow older, I feel . . .

If I could have done things differently, I would have . . .

The best thing about being this age is . . .

The worst thing about being this age is . . .

What I most regret is . . .

My family life is . . .

My relationships are . . .

After discussion, invite the middle-aged adult to identify an action plan and goals for the changes he or she wishes to make at this point in life.

LATER ADULTHOOD

In the early 1930s, Carl Jung studied older-adult development, concluding that this was a creative period of life as opposed to the prevailing notion that it was characterized by decline and deterioration. For the most part, his theory was ignored. It was not until more recently that theorists such as Paul Baltes, John C. Cavanaugh, Brian P. O'Connor and Robert J. Vallerand, and K. Warner Schaie revisited this period of life, finding that older adults develop capacities that are noticeably different.

During the final 30 years of life, from age 60 on, a period of reinvention occurs. In contrast to the negative stereotypical views about older adulthood, this period of development is characterized by a search for personal meaning as individuals are faced with the opportunity to "invent solutions to their changing conditions . . . [T]hey apply the wealth of their life experiences, their perspective on time, and their adaptation to life crises to construct personally satisfying answers to the questions of life's meaning" (Newman & Newman, 2014, p. 470).

This period of reinvention is tempered by the degree to which individuals are able to minimize loss and confront challenges successfully during the later years. However, as

Erford (2017) emphasized, despite loss and physical decline, most people follow a normal trajectory. Major developmental tasks during this developmental period involve accepting one's life and achieving satisfaction, redirecting energy to new roles and activities dealing with physical and cognitive changes, and dealing with loss.

Accepting Life in Later Adulthood

Older adults face two tasks related to accepting life and achieving satisfaction. First, they need to reflect on the past and accept the reality of their lives, incorporating disappointments, failures, achievements, and successes into an integrated view of self. Second, they need to establish new goals and challenges to maintain optimal functioning (Erford, 2017). In contrast to the traditional idea that things wind down in later adulthood, older adults fare better if they can achieve a balance between goal achievement and adjustments that might be necessitated by physical limitations or serious stressors.

Redirecting Energy to New Roles and Activities in Later Adulthood

Later adulthood is characterized by many role changes brought about by retirement: death of a spouse, parent, or friends; birth of grandchildren; and assuming new positions as community leaders or volunteers. Each of these changes necessitates adaptation and presents new challenges and opportunities. Older adults cope successfully with these role changes by becoming involved with new activities and developing new interests (Newman & Newman, 2014). Creatively searching for ways to enhance new roles and compensating for one kind of loss by finding another way also contribute to successful aging (Broderick & Blewitt, 2014). Activity 10.6 relates to developmental issues during later adulthood.

ACTIVITY 10.6 DEVELOPMENTAL ISSUES IN LATER ADULTHOOD

Consider the developmental issues that commonly occur in later adulthood and reflect on the following questions:

- What are some negative stereotypes about later adulthood, and how does more recent research differ from these earlier notions?
- If you were a counselor working with a person in later adulthood, what developmental issues would you expect this client to present?
- What types of role changes are necessary during this stage of development?

Physical Changes in Later Adulthood

As people age, health concerns increase. Decreased sensory abilities, such as changes in vision and hearing, can have a significant impact on older adults' lives. Arthritis and osteoarthritis constitute another major decline for many older adults and can result in a continuum of physical limitations. The quality of life during this period is affected not only by these two changes, but also by other chronic illnesses. As health declines, dependence on others increases, which can cause difficult role adjustments for the person receiving care and the caregiver. This is a period when the body begins to break down, and as this occurs, stress, frustration, and anxiety affect everyone involved with an individual whose health is declining.

Cognitive Changes in Later Adulthood

Cognitive changes do occur in older adulthood. However, because cognition is complex, some facets of cognition might decline while others might remain quite stable or even improve (Santrock, 2013). There is a definite decline in the speed of processing information in later adulthood, but also a great deal of individual variation in this ability. Changes in attention generally occur at this stage as well, and while older adults have less selective attention than younger adults, age-related differences are minimal if older adults have sufficient practice. Santrock noted nonexistent age-related differences in the area of divided attention when the tasks were simple, but if the tasks were more complex, older adults did not divide their attention as effectively as younger adults. Regarding sustained attention, which is often referred to as vigilance, older adults performed as well as middle-aged and younger adults.

Memory changes also occur during aging, but not all aspects of memory decline. Specifically, Santrock (2013) noted that episodic and working memory decline, but not semantic memory, which is knowledge about the world and people's fields of expertise. According to Santrock, good health is associated with less memory decline, and education and socioeconomic status can affect performance on memory tasks. Although cognitive functioning declines in old age, the negative effects of memory loss can be mitigated if older adults read, do crossword puzzles, and attend lectures; disuse might cause the atrophy of cognitive skills.

Dealing with Loss in Later Adulthood

It goes without saying that aging adults must adapt to and cope with increasing losses in multiple areas: loss of relationships as people close to them die or suffer from debilitating illnesses, loss of abilities (e.g., physical, cognitive), and loss of income. Another type of loss that may involve a significant loss is meaning, or existential loss. They may ask: Did my life matter? What difference did I make? Did I spend my time properly? What do I mean to other people?

Newman and Newman (2014) proposed that there are three key processes that help older adults cope with increasing loss. The first is selection, which helps individuals narrow goals and limit areas in which energy is expended. The second is optimization, or finding ways to maximize the achievement of remaining goals. The third is compensation, or finding ways to achieve a means to an end when a loss occurs. Broderick and Blewitt (2014) noted that successful coping relates to how well older adults are able to maintain some degree of competence and connectedness to others.

Coming to terms with death is another task for the older adult. Newman and Newman (2014) emphasized that the issue of death becomes more of a reality during this stage of life, not only as it pertains to others, but to themselves as well. With regard to their own deaths, individuals who accept death as a natural part of the life cycle and appreciate the contributions they have made to society could develop a greater appreciation for life and be more optimistic and enthusiastic about their remaining years.

Developmental Interventions in Later Adulthood

An intervention that helps adults in the later stages of life deal with the concept of reinventing themselves is to have them make Twenty Things I Want To Do lists. Once an older adult completes the list, ask him or her to rank the entries and then code each with one or more of the following symbols: $ (requires money), P (involves physical stamina),

M (involves mental challenge, stimulation), I (involves others), V (volunteer activity), S (spiritual), and D (doable). This intervention should stimulate thinking and discussion about how the individual wishes to spend time as these later years evolve without as many family and work obligations. Goal setting can be included as a part of this intervention.

A second intervention involves dealing with the multiple losses that can occur during this developmental period. A simple but very cathartic strategy is to have the individual write a letter to the loss, which could be an activity, person (e.g., parent, spouse, child, friend), ability, disease, home or location, work or volunteer activities, or other losses. Encouraging the individual to continue to write these letters facilitates the expression of grief and helps the individual deal more effectively with the loss.

Given the fact that people are living longer than ever before, there is a pressing need for gerontological counseling. Multiple issues arise at this stage of development that differ considerably from those at earlier stages, and counselors need to be well versed in how best to address the needs of this population. Now read Voices from the Field 10.2 and then complete Case Study 10.2.

VOICES FROM THE FIELD 10.2   Go Developmental, by Brad Erford

Counseling is so challenging because all individuals are embedded in systems, including families, classrooms, peer groups and cliques, schools, workplaces, and communities. So when you counsel an individual, you must consider the challenges that individual brings into a counselling session as also embedded in, stemming from, or a reaction to relational issues between the client and the various systems into which he or she is embedded. When I get confused with a client, unsure of what is up or which way to proceed, I "go developmental" and get as much context and background about the individual as possible. When I start to understand the developmental and relational challenges of my client, I am better able to generate and test hypotheses and understand the contextual richness of their struggles. This also helps me to think systemically rather than linearly, consider sources of client support and resilience, and provide a richer, more meaningful approach to intervention. Start by trying on "frames" of developmental theories: What would Erikson, Adler, Rogers, Glasser, Ellis, and various SFBC, feminist, constructivist, systemic-family, cognitive-behavioral, and other theorists say is going on with this individual within the individual's multiple systems contexts? At the very least, this mental checklist gives me a rich list of generative hypotheses to validate or disconfirm, but usually it helps me to frame the challenges in a positive developmental light, and pursue a viable resolution.

CASE STUDY 10.2

Is Individual Counseling Ever Really Individual Counseling?

Wayne is a third-grade student whose grades, motivation, and attitude have been in decline for the past few weeks. When seen by the professional counselor and asked what he thinks is happening, Wayne bursts into tears and it all spurts out, "My dad left us and we had to move in with gram (grandmother) so mom could pick up more work and

(Continued)

pay the bills. I have been helping with my little brother and sister because gram is so sick and needs a walker or wheelchair. I think she has the cancer! We haven't seen dad in more than a month; mom said he moved away with some new friend. I don't know what to do. I have so many feelings bottled up inside of me. . ."

- What are the multiple contexts and system elements at play in Wayne's situation?
- Wayne certainly has some concerns with which he is struggling, but what are the likely developmental concerns with which others in his multisystemic context are dealing?
- Thinking developmentally and systemically, how can you help Wayne?

As we end our whirlwind tour through the life span, here are some final thoughts about applying the life span perspective to counseling. There is no perfect counseling technique or approach to use with clients at different life stages, so it is important to keep shifting frames and reframing the issues in developmental terms, then using resiliency, social support, and wellness approaches to help maintain therapeutic gains. The therapeutic alliance is key to counseling outcomes, regardless of a client's age, and regardless of whether you adopt a pre-modern, modern, or postmodern approach to application of empirical research. Just as clients grow and change over time, so do counselors. Enjoy the journey.

Summary

Knowledge of human development is essential for helping professionals in terms of assessment and intervention. Without this awareness, problems can easily be misdiagnosed and interventions might be less effective because they are not geared to the appropriate developmental level. Looking through the lens of human development also helps professional counselors clarify what is normal, which then helps clients put their problems into perspective and anticipate challenges as they navigate their journeys through life.

In working with developmental issues, it is crucial to remember how cultural and diversity factors affect the developmental process. For example, during adolescence, the need to belong is very important. Students from families with low socioeconomic status might not be as readily accepted because they cannot live up to the standards of the *in* group. Professional counselors working with clients across the life span must be cognizant about how low socioeconomic status, oppression, racism, and prejudice might limit opportunities and result in depression or anxiety. It is important to deal with these issues within the context of culture.

There are developmental tasks to master at each stage in the life cycle. Professional counselors can facilitate development in numerous ways, including through individual, family, and small-group counseling and classroom guidance. Classroom lessons can facilitate children's and adolescents' understanding of social, emotional, cognitive, and physical development and self-development. Readers are encouraged to read more in depth about each stage of development covered in this chapter and to apply the information as they design interventions to facilitate clients' development through the life span.

Answer Key

Activity 10.5   Check marks should be placed by items 1, 2, 3, 4, 7.

11 Multicultural Counseling

GENEVA M. GRAY*

PREVIEW

As U.S. demographics change to reflect greater diversity, professional counselors are charged with becoming more competent in working with diverse populations. This chapter defines and presents the various dimensions of multicultural counseling, including cultural identity developmental processes and culturally specific information and intervention strategies across the cultural dimensions of socioeconomic status, race, ethnicity, gender, sexual orientation, spirituality, ability level, and age.

MULTICULTURALLY COMPETENT COUNSELING

Multicultural counseling, *cross-cultural counseling*, and *diversity awareness* are terms used to discuss counseling that occurs with individuals from diverse cultural backgrounds. **Multicultural counseling** is a method of counseling that takes into consideration the backgrounds and environmental experiences of diverse clients and how special needs might be identified and met through the resources of the helping professions (Hays & Erford, 2018). It involves assessing an individual's needs and values (i.e., individualism) within the context of community value systems (i.e., collectivism). Key terms related to multicultural counseling are presented in Table 11.1; other important concepts are presented throughout the chapter. Activity 11.1 allows you to consider the terms presented in Table 11.1 in concrete and specific ways.

ACTIVITY 11.1

Develop examples for each term in the following table and write them under the 'Examples' column. Use the definitions provided in Table 11.1.

Key Terms	Examples
Culture	
Diversity	
Multiculturalism	
Cultural encapsulation	
Cultural pluralism	
Worldview	

(Continued)

---

*Special thanks to Danica G. Hays for her outstanding contributions to the first two editions of this chapter.

Key Terms	Examples
Social Justice	
Advocacy	
Discrimination	
Race	
Ethnicity	

TABLE 11.1 Key Terms in Multicultural Counseling

Key Terms	Definition
Culture	The totality of socially transmitted behavior patterns, arts, beliefs, institutions, and all other products of human work and thought. This could be a particular society at a particular time and place or a symbolic system of meanings, attitudes, feelings, values, and behaviors that are shared by a group of people, a particular society, or population and is communicated from one generation to the next via language and observation. Culture regulates and organizes what its group members feel, think, and do and could be expressed individually in a variety of ways.
Diversity	Ethnic, gender, racial, and socioeconomic variety in a situation, institution, or group; the coexistence of different ethnic, gender, racial, and socioeconomic groups within one social unit.
Multiculturalism	The preservation of different cultures or cultural identities within a unified society, as a state or nation; a condition in which many cultures coexist within a society and maintain their cultural differences.
Cultural encapsulation	State in which a professional counselor is the culture of origin, is unaware of mutual influences between self and sociocultural context, and holds onto an ethnocentric, monocultural view.
Cultural pluralism	A condition in which minority groups participate fully in the dominant society yet maintain their cultural differences.
Worldview	The overall perspective from which one sees and interprets the world; a collection of beliefs about life and the universe held by an individual or a group.
Advocacy	The act of pleading or arguing in favor of something, such as a cause, idea, or policy; active support for marginalized individuals or groups.
Discrimination	Treatment or consideration of, or making a distinction in favor of or against, a person or thing based on the group, class, or category to which that person or thing belongs rather than on individual merit.
Race	An arbitrary classification based on any or a combination of various physical characteristics, such as skin color, facial form, or eye shape. Race is related to **racism**, or the belief or doctrine that inherent differences among the various human races determine cultural or individual achievement, usually involving the idea that one's own race is superior and has the right to rule others. Racism includes hatred or intolerance of another race or other races.
Ethnicity	Characteristic of a people or a group (**ethnic group**) sharing a common and distinctive culture, religion, or language.
Social Justice	The active promotion of a fair and just society while challenging injustice, advocating for others, and valuing diversity.

Over the years, the ideas regarding multicultural counseling have changed almost as much as U.S. demographics. The U.S. Census Bureau (2011a) reported that foreign-born individuals constituted more than 11% of the population. Of this group, 53.3% were born in Latin America, 25% were born in Asia, 13.7% were born in Europe, and 8% were born in other regions of the world. The Pew Research Center (2012) projected the foreign-born sector's growth will increase to 19% of the population by 2050. In addition to changes in the immigrant population, other aspects of the cultural composition of the United States are shifting. For example, the baby boomer generation began to turn 65 years old in 2011, which marks a shift in the percentage of the elderly population. Baby boomers currently make up about 40% of the U.S. population. The U.S. population is also becoming more racially and ethnically diverse, with approximately 30% of Americans currently belonging to a racial/ethnic minority group. By 2050, the United States is likely to see a total population of 438 million, with a significant decrease in the overall population percentage of white/non-Hispanics (47%), a stable percentage of those of black/African descent (13%), and increases for those of Hispanic/Latin descent (29%) and Asian descent (9%).

Based on these changes, professional counselors must be prepared to provide multicultural counseling services to diverse populations. Since the early 1990s, the counseling profession has expected professional counselors to be multiculturally competent. At that time, the American Counseling Association (ACA) adopted the AMCD Multicultural Counseling Competencies to set guidelines for professional counselors to increase their awareness, knowledge, and skills related to multicultural counseling. These 31 standards (Sue, Arredondo, & McDavis, 1992) were designed to ensure professional counselors are self-aware, examine their beliefs and attitudes regarding other cultures, understand how various forms of oppression influence counseling, appreciate other cultural norms and value systems, and intervene in a culturally appropriate manner. Ratts, Singh, Nassar-McMillan, Butler, and McCullough (2015) recently revised these standards in the document *Multicultural and Social Justice Counseling Competencies*.

Specifically, culturally competent counselors are competent in three primary ways. First, counselors are aware of their own values and biases. Counselors appreciate and value their clients' and own cultural makeup. To this end, counselors are knowledgeable (or seek out new knowledge) about the relationship between cultural membership and oppression experiences that influence mental health. Second, counselors are aware of their clients' worldviews and whenever possible immerse themselves in diverse experiences. Professional counselors regularly seek information about their clients' backgrounds and experiences within counseling, family, and other systems. Finally, counselors engage in culturally appropriate interventions, respecting indigenous methods of healing and being sensitive to preferred interventions.

Thus, a culturally competent counselor has self-awareness of values and biases, understands client worldviews, and intervenes in a culturally appropriate manner. Professional counselors understand the importance of within-group differences as they become more culturally competent because these within-group differences are usually more variable than the between-racial-group differences. Increasing one's multicultural competency is a lifelong process and involves competency in social advocacy. The *Multicultural and Social Justice Counseling Competencies* (Ratts et al., 2015) presented in Chapter 15, provide a framework for addressing oppression and inequity across various client systems. Counselors equipped with multicultural counseling knowledge, awareness, and skills (i.e., are multiculturally competent) can advocate for their clients. In becoming culturally competent, professional counselors should reflect on the key issues in multicultural counseling in the following section that affect how the profession of counseling considers culture and promotes appropriate multicultural counseling practice.

KEY ISSUES IN MULTICULTURAL COUNSELING

Etic versus Emic Debate

A key issue involves the degree to which an individual's culture should be incorporated into counseling. This is often described as the etic versus emic debate: Should multicultural counseling use more general interventions based in Western values that propose to have universal applications to most individuals (etic approach), or should counseling incorporate more culturally specific aspects (emic approaches)? Activity 11.2 presents an example to consider from etic and emic approaches.

ACTIVITY 11.2

In the following example, discuss how the professional counselor could work with this client from an etic or emic approach or a combination of both. The client, a Middle Eastern woman, is having difficulty with her role within the family as a woman. She wants to decrease her feelings of discomfort and feel more independent without violating the traditional gender roles within her family.

Professional counselors who subscribe to the **etic** perspective suggest that counseling should involve techniques related to the sameness among human beings to create a better understanding of general psychological processes for more systematic and consistent approaches among various professional counselors. **Emic** approaches allow for the professional counselor to conceptualize the client as an individual and attend to cultural variations and culturally specific interventions. Individuals who promote the emic approach assert that lack of specialized assessment and treatment in a culturally sensitive manner fails to address how cultural values and environmental stressors affect the presentation of symptoms or the idioms of distress. Many professional counselors struggle, however, with the degree to which each should be incorporated in multicultural counseling.

How Much of Counseling Is Multicultural?

An issue related to the etic versus emic debate is the definition of multicultural counseling itself. Specifically, which cultural identities get included in the definition of multicultural counseling? Should multicultural counseling be defined narrowly to include select cultural groups, such as race and ethnicity, or expanded more broadly to include other identities, such as gender, sexual orientation, socioeconomic status, age, and spirituality? As our understanding of multicultural counseling increases, more and more multicultural theorists are using a broader definition of *multicultural*. A general benefit of expanding this definition is that there is an increased understanding of how various cultural identities influence how counseling issues are presented and addressed in counseling. Also, professional counselors might be more willing to acknowledge how individuals' cultural identities intersect in unique ways to create unique constructions and presentations of symptoms, available resources, and general value systems.

One major critique of having an expanded view of multicultural counseling is that the more cultural identities that get included in the definition, the less *distinct* the definition of multicultural counseling becomes. In a sense, the questions then become: If professional counselors consider most (if not all) of a client's personal and social identities as cultural, then isn't all counseling multicultural? And what is the difference then between general counseling and multicultural counseling? Many who prefer a more limited definition of multicultural counseling argue that it allows for more appreciation of major cultural identities (e.g., race, ethnicity) to help generalize to subgroups in more definitive ways and avoid individualizing counseling practice so much that common interventions lose their value. Activity 11.3 presents questions for you to reflect on in your definition of multicultural counseling.

ACTIVITY 11.3

How do you define multicultural counseling? Which cultural groups are included in that definition? Why? What are the strengths and challenges of applying your definition?

Assessment and Treatment

Another issue involves the dominance of counseling theories based on European/North American cultural values (Orr, 2018). Counseling theories practiced in Western cultures often are constructed based on white cultural values and beliefs that are not always applicable to clients from diverse cultural traditions. Some of the dominant Western values are individualism, action-oriented approaches to problem solving, work ethics, scientific methods, and emphasis on rigid time schedules. These values are present in most counseling theories today and might not be congruent for clients of various racial and ethnic backgrounds.

Neukrug (2012) suggested that because of this emphasis on individualism and expression of feelings and a lack of awareness of how diverse cultures influence and drive behaviors, counseling might not be effective for most clients. Professional counselors could be implementing techniques and interventions that might conflict with client values and worldviews, leading clients to terminate counseling prematurely and creating psychological harm for the client. Activity 11.4 presents some key questions to reflect on how your values might affect your counseling experience.

ACTIVITY 11.4

Consider some values and norms of your own culture. Would you find it offensive or ineffective if a professional counselor did not take these into consideration when helping you with a social or emotional issue? How do you think it would affect the counseling process?

Related to the biased nature of counseling theories are the Western views of mental illness. Abnormality according to the U.S. culture might be normal and appropriate in other cultures. Most Western theories that relate to working with couples and families pathologize high interdependency as *enmeshment*. Many individuals who do not identify with white cultural values, such as individuals belonging to racial/ethnic minority groups, might highly value connections with family and community. Professional counselors could view these individuals as having suboptimal mental health. Another example relates to culturally accepted behaviors and attitudes among various racial/ethnic groups that might be viewed as pathological by Eurocentric counselors. For example, Latino men could demonstrate high masculinity, which is gender appropriate in Latin culture, yet might be viewed as pathological on personality tests in the United States (Erford, 2013). Professional counselors with limited knowledge of multicultural issues might lack the understanding of diverse expressions of symptoms and misdiagnose and fail to appropriately treat client problems. These key issues should be considered as professional counselors gain an understanding of cultural identity in general.

Evidence-Based Practices in Multicultural Counseling

Evidence-based practice (EBP) is "an attempt to balance external validity and internal validity in the promotion of treatment to inform clinical practice, as well as to base science on both deductive and inductive reasoning strategies" (Whaley & Davis, 2007, p. 568). In multicultural counseling, evidence-based practice guides the counseling process to insure the best level of client care. It is the most effective method of advancing the knowledge of culturally competent mental health services.

Bernal and Saez-Santiago (2006) developed a cultural adaptation framework for implementing evidence-based and culturally competent practice that included: (1) *language:* language transmits culture and emotional experience; therefore, providing treatments in the native language of the target population is essential to integrating culture into the counseling relationship; (2) *metaphors:* awareness and demonstration of culturally based symbols and concepts in the therapeutic environment; (3) *persons:* engaging in culturally centered counseling through the consideration and open discussion of ethnic and racial similarities and differences in the client–counselor relationship; (4) *content:* working knowledge of the values, customs, and traditions of various racial and ethnically diverse groups; (5) *concepts:* the method in which a client's presenting problems is conceptualized based on ethnic and cultural background; (6) *goals:* designed treatment goals are culturally based and agreed upon by the client and counselor; (7) *methods:* the process by which treatment is facilitated is based on the client's cultural background; and (8) *content:* acknowledgement of the client's social, economic, and political context (e.g., acculturation, immigration, coming out process, and slavery). Additionally, implementing culturally appropriate evidence-based practices requires the inclusion of ethnically and racially diverse participants in efficacy-based research studies. It also involves an adaptation of counselor service delivery and increased "inclusion of cultural knowledge, attitudes, and behaviors to make empirically supported treatment more culturally appropriate" (Whaley & Davis, 2007, p. 570).

CULTURAL IDENTITY DEVELOPMENT AND MULTICULTURAL COUNSELING

Engaging in multicultural counseling involves understanding cultural makeup of clients and counselors and how cultural identities change and develop over time. The personal identity model (Figure 11.1) was developed to describe the basic premises that we are all

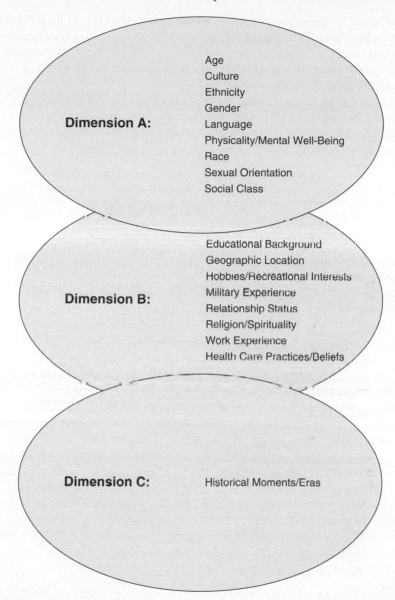

Dimension A:

Age
Culture
Ethnicity
Gender
Language
Physicality/Mental Well-Being
Race
Sexual Orientation
Social Class

Dimension B:

Educational Background
Geographic Location
Hobbies/Recreational Interests
Military Experience
Relationship Status
Religion/Spirituality
Work Experience
Health Care Practices/Beliefs

Dimension C:

Historical Moments/Eras

FIGURE 11.1 Personal identity model.

multicultural beings with unique compositions of identities, influenced by sociocultural, environmental, political, and historical events (Arredondo & Glauner, 1992). It serves as a framework for understanding the complexities of all individuals and considers individuals to be unique despite assigned social and cultural categories.

Personal identity is described in the model as involving three dimensions. Dimension A consists of characteristics that are universal for all people. These are characteristics that are predetermined, such as race, gender, ethnicity, language, culture, and sexual orientation. Dimension B consists of characteristics that are not as observable as those in

Dimension A. These are personal characteristics that might be selected by the individual, such as educational background, geographic location, hobbies, military experience, relationship status, work experience, and health care practices. Dimension C is a composite of positive and negative individual experiences influenced by events in society in which individuals might have little control.

According to the model, the characteristics of Dimension B are often dictated by Dimensions A and C. An individual's predetermined characteristics and societal experiences are instrumental in shaping his or her experiences of the characteristics in Dimension B. Complete Activity 11.5 to identify your personal identity.

ACTIVITY 11.5

Fill out the following tables with your own information.

Dimension A:
Age:
Culture:
Ethnicity:
Gender:
Language:
Physical/Mental Well-Being:
Race:
Sexual Orientation:
Social Class:

Dimension B:
Educational Background:
Geographic Location:
Hobbies/Recreational Interests:
Military Experience:
Relationship Status:
Religion/Spirituality:
Work Experience:
Health Care Practices/Beliefs:

Dimension C:
Historical Moments/Eras:

Which of these aspects of your life help to determine who you are? Explain how.

Cultural Identity Development Models

Cultural identity development models refer to descriptions of processes by which individuals make meaning of multiple cultural identities described in the personal identity model, including race, ethnicity, gender, sexual orientation, and spirituality. The degree to which individuals identify with various cultural groups changes with new experiences; cultural identity development is contextual. Professional counselors have different intrapersonal and interpersonal experiences based on how their identity statuses interact with their clients' statuses (see Activity 11.6). Most of these models are based on individuals negotiating their cultural group memberships in the context of oppression experiences.

ACTIVITY 11.6

After reading about the models of identity development that follow, consider the listed paired identity development statuses within multicultural counseling relationships:

a. *Contact* counselor and *internalization* client
b. *Embeddedness–emanation* counselor and *passive acceptance* client
c. *Encounter* counselor and *disintegration* client
d. *Identity synthesis* counselor and *identity acceptance* client
e. *Achievement* counselor and *moratorium* client

What cognitions, emotions, and behaviors might be associated with each pairing?

The purpose of these models is to help explain ways by which individuals come to know themselves culturally and engage in relationships with others from a variety of cultural memberships. Having a strong cultural identity could protect and facilitate mental health and might be helpful in cross-cultural counseling relationships (Hays & Erford, 2018). Although the models outline developmental issues for cultural identities independently, professional counselors need to consider that cultural identities intersect to create complexities in identity development. In addition, these models are presented linearly, but identity development is a circular process in which individuals move back and forth among statuses while often being characterized by multiple statuses within an identity development model. Thus, there are themes common in developing various cultural identities (Table 11.2).

Racial and Ethnic Identity Development

Racial identity refers to the psychosocial orientation toward membership in a racial group based partly on attitudes and actions toward other racial groups. **Ethnic identity** refers to individuals' sense of belonging to an ethnic group, often influenced by the degree to which an ethnic group conforms to the values of the dominant culture, a process referred to as **acculturation**. Because race and ethnicity are closely related, racial identity development models often describe processes by which individuals retreat, identify, or deny aspects of their ethnicity. Implicit in racial identity development models is the idea that self-identification with a racial group involves dealing with racism and integrating other aspects of self. Prominent models include models for white (Hardiman, 1982; Helms, 1995), persons of color (Helms, 1995), and biracial identity development (Poston, 1990).

WHITE RACIAL IDENTITY DEVELOPMENT   Hardiman's (1982) and Helms's (1995) models of white racial identity development (WRID) describe movement from a lack of awareness of one's racial self toward increased awareness and capacity to relinquish privileges associated with whiteness (e.g., skin tone, values, European descent). The general developmental issues for whites include the abandonment of entitlement (Helms, 1995) and an integration of their whiteness with other components of their cultural identities (Hardiman, 1982).

TABLE 11.2 Common Themes of Cultural Identity Development

Themes	Identity Stages/Statuses
Unawareness/denial	Naiveté, contact (WRID)
	Pre-encounter (POCRID)
	Personal identity (BID)
	Passive acceptance (FID)
	Pre-awareness, diffusion (SPID)
Conflict/anxiety	Resistance, disintegration, reintegration, pseudoindependence (WRID)
	Encounter (POCRID)
	Choice of group categorization, enmeshment/denial (BID)
	Revelation (FID)
	Identity confusion, identity tolerance, awareness, initial confusion (SID)
	Awakening, foreclosure (SPID)
Retreat into own group/interact cautiously	Redefinition, immersion/emersion (WRID)
	Immersion, emersion (POCRID)
	Embeddedness–emanation (FID)
	Identity acceptance, identity pride, exploration, deepening commitment, finding and applying the label of bisexuality (SID)
	Moratorium (SPID)
Integrate cultural identity with other identities and other factors	Internalization (WRID)
	Internalization (POCRID)
	Appreciation, integration (BID)
	Synthesis (FID)
	Identity synthesis, identity integration, settling into the identity (SID)
	Recognition, integration, achievement (SPID)
Advocacy	Autonomy (WRID)
	Integrative awareness (POCRID)
	Active commitment (FID)

Note: BID, biracial identity development (Poston, 1990); FID, feminist identity development (Downing & Roush, 1985); POCRID, people of color racial identity development (Helms, 1995); SID, sexual identity development (Cass, 1979; MaCarn & Fessinger, 1996; Weinberg, Williams, & Pryor, 1995); SPID, spiritual identity development (Griffith & Griggs, 2001; Poll & Smith, 2003); WRID, white racial identity development (Hardiman, 1982; Helms, 1995)

Hardiman constructed a five-stage model: *naiveté, acceptance, resistance, redefinition,* and *internalization.* Whites in the *naiveté* stage early on categorize people by race and receive and transmit messages concerning the amount of power or privilege a particular racial group has. For individuals who move into the *acceptance* stage, there is a belief that there is equal opportunity for all racial groups with whites serving as the ideal reference group for success. During the *resistance* stage, whites experience anxiety as they engage in meaningful cross-racial interactions that could challenge earlier meanings assigned to racial groups. With the *redefinition* stage, whites engage in active self-reflection and attempt to gain self-understanding of ethnic identities independent of attitudes toward other racial/ethnic groups. The final stage, *internalization*, involves whites defining themselves without the resistance and anxiety characteristics of the other stages.

Helms (1995) portrayed white racial identity development as a six-status model: *contact, disintegration, reintegration, pseudoindependence, immersion–emersion*, and *autonomy*. Individuals in the *contact* status are oblivious to racism and deny that race plays a role in their social interactions. In the *disintegration* status, whites experience anxiety, guilt, and anger when they encounter events that challenge the idea of racial superiority. To lessen anxiety and other feelings, individuals in the *reintegration* status exhibit intolerance and dislike for individuals of other racial groups. Whites in the *pseudoindependence* status strive to address racism at a superficial level; however, there are discrepancies between attitudes and actual interactions with people of color. For some whites there are increased efforts to address racism and redefine what it means to be white, known as the *immersion–emersion* status. For the last status, *autonomy*, whites become social advocates and attempt to relinquish some of the advantages they have experienced.

PEOPLE OF COLOR RACIAL IDENTITY DEVELOPMENT Helms (1995) adapted an earlier model of black identity development (Cross, 1971) to apply broadly to any racial minority, or person of color. There are six statuses associated with this model: *pre-encounter, encounter, immersion, emersion, internalization*, and *integrative awareness*. During the *pre-encounter* status, there is a strong preference for dominant cultural values either because individuals are unaware of racism or because they minimize the role race plays. People of color in the *encounter* status experience a crisis or conflict that increases their awareness that racism exists. They might begin to see that there are positive aspects of their racial group membership and become distrustful of dominant-group members. During the *immersion* and *emersion* statuses, people of color actively reject white culture, have increased racial pride, and retreat into their racial communities. *Internalization* then occurs for people of color as they negotiate self-concept and racial group membership. During this status, they might seek out other groups that have experienced oppression. For the final status, *integrative awareness*, people of color develop more complex and relative views of all racial groups and actively commit to eliminating all forms of oppression.

BIRACIAL IDENTITY DEVELOPMENT As the United States becomes increasingly diverse, individuals of multiracial descent increase in number. Poston (1990) developed a model to examine the identity development processes of biracial individuals, which may be applied to individuals of more than two races. The model contains five stages: *personal identity, choice of group categorization, enmeshment/denial, appreciation*, and *integration*. Individuals typically experience the *personal identity* stage at a young age, when race/ ethnicity is not salient. In the *choice of group categorization* stage, biracial individuals experience anxiety and guilt as they select one racial group over another. During the *enmeshment/denial* stage, negative feelings increase because individuals cannot fully express their racial and ethnic backgrounds. In the *appreciation* stage, biracial individuals begin to value their multiple identities. However, some might continue to identify primarily with one reference group. In the final stage, *integration*, biracial individuals increasingly recognize and infuse all aspects of their racial and ethnic heritage into their cultural presentation.

Feminist Identity Development

Downing and Roush's (1985) model of **feminist identity development** is widely used to understand the process by which women come to know themselves in a gendered world. The model assumes that women experience sexism and enhance their identity as female by addressing sexism. Five stages are proposed in the model: *passive acceptance, revelation, embeddedness–emanation, synthesis,* and *active commitment. Passive acceptance* refers to women adhering to traditional gender roles without awareness of how sexism might perpetuate these roles and create and maintain negative, limiting experiences for them. In the *revelation* stage, women might experience an event that calls into question an earlier notion of men as superior to women and highlights how sexism exists and hinders development. As a result of such an experience, women could feel anger and guilt regarding their oppression experiences and engage in dualistic thinking related to gender and sex (i.e., all men are bad and all women are good). Women characterized by the *embeddedness–emanation* stage develop close, supportive relationships with other women to help assist with negative feelings associated with the *revelation* stage. Through this process, they gradually engage with men and consider gender relatively. In the *synthesis* stage, women develop positive feminist identities by considering that external events may be influenced by sexism as well as other causes. With the final stage, *active commitment,* women seek to advocate for other women and work to eradicate sexism.

Sexual Identity Development

Considering the increasing number of models that seek to describe **sexual identity development** for sexual minorities, presented here are historically classic models outlining gay (Cass, 1979), lesbian (McCarn & Fessinger, 1996), and bisexual identity development (Weinberg, Williams, & Pryor, 1995). Cass's (1979) model is widely cited and applied to counseling sexual minorities. It involves the following six stages:

1. *Identity confusion:* Individuals feel *different* and experience inner conflict.
2. *Identity comparison:* Conflict leads to three possible responses, including passing as heterosexual while recognizing gay identity, rejecting common portrayal of public gay identity while accepting gay identity, or rejecting gay identity and seeking to be heterosexual.
3. *Identity tolerance:* There is a desire to connect with other sexual minorities and alienate from heterosexuals.
4. *Identity acceptance:* There is increased contact with the gay community with movement away from simple tolerance of gay identity.
5. *Identity pride:* Gay individuals increase self-disclosure and immersion into gay community with some social activism.
6. *Identity synthesis:* Gay identity is integrated into self-concept.

McCarn and Fessinger (1996) developed a model for lesbian identity development, adapted from Cass's (1979) model. Their four-stage model examined the simultaneous development of individual and group sexual identity development:

1. *Awareness:* There is an acknowledgment at individual and group levels that there are other sexual orientations besides heterosexuality.
2. *Exploration:* Individuals begin to experience intimate feelings toward other women and concurrently seek to obtain information about lesbians in the community to assess their degree of belonging.

3. *Deepening commitment:* Individuals solidify their commitment to their sexuality as lesbians. They are actively committed to lesbian group identity and culture and might reject some heterosexual norms.
4. *Identity integration:* Individuals integrate their sexual identity with other aspects of their self-concept and engage fully and securely in their lesbian identity across settings.

Weinberg et al. (1995) outlined three stages of bisexual identity development, a process they saw as occurring for some individuals with an already developed heterosexual identity. In the *initial confusion* stage, individuals experience attraction to both sexes with some discomfort with having to fit into one sexual orientation. When *finding and applying the label of bisexuality,* individuals acknowledge feelings for both sexes and select the label of bisexuality. The final stage, *settling into the identity,* is characterized by self-identification as bisexual with increased self-acceptance.

Spiritual Identity Development

Spiritual identity relates to the degree of connection to individuals' ideas of what or who their god is. The models discussed below examine spirituality and religiosity. One describes increased awareness of self as a spiritual being (Poll & Smith, 2003), and the other highlights the process by which individuals infuse religiosity into their lives (Griffith & Griggs, 2001).

Poll and Smith (2003) outlined a four-stage model whereby individuals become increasingly personally connected to their god. The first phase, *pre-awareness,* involves individuals who do not view themselves as spiritual beings. After a conflict or spiritual learning has occurred, individuals begin to become aware of themselves as spiritual beings in the *awakening* phase. During the *recognition* phase, individuals generalize new spiritual learning across settings until they have integrated their spiritual selves into their self-concepts and interact authentically with others (i.e., the *integration* phase).

The second model (Griffith & Griggs, 2001) is a four-status approach that describes ways individuals experience their faith:

1. *Diffusion:* This status involves a lack of interest in religiosity or participation in religious activities that is largely guided by external motivation.
2. *Foreclosure:* Individuals conform to ideas and practices of religious communities, which creates a crisis because religious identity might be significantly based on personal needs for social approval.
3. *Moratorium:* This status involves active self-reflection and spiritual exploration as individuals confront the anxiety characteristic of the *foreclosure* status.
4. *Achievement:* Core religious values become integrated into all aspects of the individuals' lives, and spiritual inquiry becomes internally motivated.

An important component of spiritual identity development is the role of **spiritual differentiation**. In this process individuals may identify as spiritual but not religious, religious but not spiritual, religious and spiritual, or neither. Individuals who identify as spiritual often search for meaning, wholeness, and connections with others through a spiritual experience. However, religious-but-not-spiritual people often participate in organized religious rituals, maintain theistic beliefs, and institutionalize moral values. The spiritual and religious person holds characteristics of both while the neither spiritual nor religious person holds few if any of these characteristics (Blando, 2006).

With this introductory framework for understanding key issues in multicultural counseling and cultural identity development as a reference, the remainder of this chapter focuses on counseling culturally diverse individuals and clinical implications. As culturally diverse groups categorized by socioeconomic status, race and ethnicity, gender, sexual orientation, spirituality, disability, and age are introduced, consider how culture is presented in U.S. society (see Activity 11.7).

ACTIVITY 11.7

Peruse several magazines and consider the role of culture in the articles, pictures, and advertisements. Discuss in dyads how race, gender, and sexual orientation are portrayed in various popular magazines. What are the direct and indirect messages in advertisements and articles? How do these messages influence the way we think about ourselves and individuals with other cultural identities?

COUNSELING CULTURALLY DIVERSE INDIVIDUALS

Clients present complex cultural identities that involve aspects such as socioeconomic status, race, ethnicity, gender, sexual identity, spiritual affiliation, ability status, and age. To further complicate matters, these identities intersect to create unique cultural experiences for clients that warrant special considerations in counseling.

Socioeconomic Status and Poverty

Socioeconomic status (SES) relates to individuals' relative positions in cultural groups based on social and economic factors. It is typically indicated by household income, education level, occupational status, use of public assistance, and access to health care. SES is difficult to define, and household income is often used as the primary indicator of status. Clients with a low SES require special attention in counseling because of the inaccessibility of basic resources that affect their physical and psychological well-being. Although there is lack of consensus on what constitutes *low SES*, for 2015 the U.S. poverty threshold has been defined as an annual income of $20,090 for a family of three and $24,250 for a family of four (U.S. Department of Health and Human Services, 2015).

In 2014, approximately 14.5% of all U.S. residents reported annual household incomes below the poverty line (U.S. Department of Health and Human Services, 2015). When looking closer at statistics, poverty disproportionately affects individuals of racial/ethnic minority statuses. White/non-Hispanics experienced a 9% poverty rate; meanwhile, 26% of African Americans, 25% of Hispanics, 12% of Asian Americans, and 31% of Native Americans live below the poverty threshold. In addition, approximately 33% of women who are head of household live in poverty. Because poverty is often experienced by clients of oppressed statuses (e.g., racial/ethnic minorities, women), its influence in counseling cannot be ignored.

Because it is closely related to factors such as low education levels, inadequate housing, malnutrition, and exposure to violence and trauma, poverty often prevents access to mental health services and increases clients' sense of vulnerability to mental illness. Research shows that counseling issues such as depression, suicide, post-traumatic stress disorder, behavioral problems, and substance abuse are often associated with poverty and related environmental conditions (World Health Organization, 2013). Children living in poverty have an increased risk for lower academic and intellectual achievement, developmental delays, health problems, and dysfunction in social interactions (World Health Organization, 2011). Individuals in low SES groups are significantly more likely to exhibit criteria for mental illnesses and live in neighborhoods characterized by crime, high unemployment, substandard housing or homelessness, schools with inadequate resources, and substance abuse (Albrecht & Albrecht, 2007; World Health Organization, 2013). Individuals with mental illness are overrepresented in these neighborhoods, which often lack available social, psychological, and economic resources. Poverty becomes a vicious cycle for many clients, as aspects of economic depression, underemployment, and low educational attainment become self-perpetuating and transcend generations. Within this cycle, individuals' mental health is negatively affected as they try to cope with related issues. Poverty perpetuates mental illness, and vice versa.

When working with clients with a low SES, professional counselors should attend to the connection between SES and environmental factors and evaluate their own biases related to SES. Some areas of exploration could include the following:

- What role does SES play in my client's immediate surroundings (e.g., school, neighborhood, community)?
- What types of resources are available to my client in his or her community? Are some of these resources determined by the financial status of that community?
- Do my client's socioeconomic resources affect his or her mental and physical health?
- What have been my experiences with SES? What material, educational, and social resources have been available (or limited) to me?
- How do I view individuals of SES groups different from mine?

In addition, professional counselors are charged with advocating for groups with low SES. Some ways that professional counselors can work to minimize the impact of poverty in clients' lives include the following:

- Provide psychoeducation to individuals in impoverished neighborhoods about mental health concerns and the role of counseling in addressing these concerns.
- Provide information through community agencies about accessible resources they may use for a host of issues related to having limited financial resources (e.g., mental health issues, physical health issues, transportation, housing, limited food).
- Because individuals who lack financial resources and transportation often have limited access to counseling services, consider different strategies beyond counseling in your office for 50 minutes. Some alternatives could include providing in-home counseling to individuals and their families; collaborating with churches or other community organizations to connect to individuals in need of mental health services; and providing counseling to particularly vulnerable groups, such as children, elderly individuals, and racial/ethnic minorities.
- Educate people who are not experiencing socioeconomic concerns, such as poverty, about the role of SES on an individual's mental and physical health. This could include school personnel, other counselors in your mental health agency, or government leaders.

Voices from the Field 11.1 provides additional strategies for working with clients with low SES.

VOICES FROM THE FIELD 11.1   Working with Clients from Diverse SES Backgrounds, by Nicole Adamson

As a neophyte counseling graduate, I accepted a position as a behavioral consultant for an urban school district. The school district was poorly funded and had been listed as being on academic emergency for the preceding two years. Most of the students were living in poverty and navigating multiple chronic stressors, which translated into emotional and behavioral difficulties in the school environment. To meaningfully influence the students' lives, it was necessary to involve the students' families in my efforts.

Significant cultural differences related to race and socioeconomic status contributed to parents' hesitation in allowing me to counsel their children. Because of the cultural stigma surrounding counseling and the daily stressors that prevented parents from committing precious time for this extra service, it was difficult to engage parents, to say the least. Through trial and error, I found a way to connect with parents and encourage their involvement.

Whenever I received a referral for a student who had mental health needs, I called the student's parents and spoke with them casually. It was important that I de-emphasize differences in dialect and use universal language with which they could relate (e.g., saying "having some trouble" instead of "experiencing difficulty"). It was also helpful to provide positive feedback about the student's progress before mentioning any areas of concern. Demonstrating that I was not judging them or their child and taking a down-to-earth approach helped them to feel more comfortable with me.

After a phone introduction, I also found it was most effective to connect with parents by visiting their homes. Fortunately, my agency's policy allowed for in-home counseling. This solved many practical and logistical problems, such as a client's lack of transportation; allowed me to understand the environment in which the child and family lived; and showed the parents that I accepted them. Many of my colleagues felt uncomfortable visiting students' homes due to safety or hygiene concerns, but I believed this was necessary for effective engagement. I truly enjoyed the experiences and the connections with the students and their parents.

In working with clients from cultures different from my own, I found that I must first understand the clients before I can help them. I also found that I needed to give them time and space to trust me. Visiting the students' homes was a simple, easy way to understand the dynamics of their cultures and to build trust with their parents.

Racial and Ethnic Diversity

In this section, the five major racial and ethnic groups are presented along with a discussion of multiracial individuals.

EUROPEAN AMERICANS   **European Americans** make up most (63.7%) of the U.S. population and consist of various non-Hispanic backgrounds (U.S. Census Bureau, 2011a). During the past decade, the growth rate of this population has slowed, and projections suggest that by 2050, European Americans will comprise 47% of the U.S. population. However, their numbers are increasing among older age groups, especially the elderly population. There are approximately 50 categories of European Americans, including people from England, Italy, Russia, Austria, and France. This group has experienced the most ethnic blending of any other cultural group (McMahon, Paisley, & Skudrzyk, 2018). European Americans typically include individuals whose families have three or more generations in the United States and whose immigration experiences vary.

European American values include individualism, autonomy, status and power, direct communication, linear time orientation, rationality, emphasis on the scientific method, and a nuclear family structure. European Americans might undervalue a group or collectivistic orientation. Judeo-Christian beliefs are predominant for group members, and many uphold Protestant values that include individual direction, self-fulfillment through direction, mastery over one's nature, and dedication to moral living (McMahon et al., 2018). Many counseling theories are based on Western views of individualism and self-determination, and European Americans tend to respond well to counseling theories that stress these common values (Orr, 2018).

European Americans have a long and dominant history in the United States. As a group, they possess the most power in the United States and have had a significant influence on the values and standards of the general U.S. society. Because of these factors, many European Americans are faced with difficulty defining their ethnicities and get placed in a larger category of *whiteness* (McMahon et al., 2018). Being white affords many special, unearned advantages in U.S. society, known as **white privilege**. European Americans are just as much victims of societal forces as other cultural groups because of the indoctrination of racism, privilege, and discrimination passed through generations (Branscombe, Schmitt, & Schiffhauer, 2007; Hays & Erford, 2018; Knowles & Lowery, 2012). As a result, professional counselors should be aware of the role of white privilege and white guilt in the lives of many European Americans and work to strengthen clients' understanding of clients' ethnicities. Activity 11.8 highlights a reading that allows for deeper reflection on the issue of white privilege.

ACTIVITY 11.8

Review McIntosh's (1988) article on white privilege and male privilege. Identify items that cause reactions, either positive or negative, for you. Prepare a journal entry describing your reactions to at least five items.

HISPANIC AMERICANS **Hispanic Americans** constitute approximately 16.3% of the U.S. population; 50.4 million individuals identify as Hispanic alone (U.S. Census Bureau, 2011a). Hispanic Americans comprise the largest and fastest growing ethnic minority group. Of this group, 60% are Mexican, 10% are Puerto Rican, 3.5% are Cuban, and 28% are from other Latin American countries. Projections suggest that by 2050, Hispanic Americans will comprise 29% of the U.S. population. It is difficult to estimate accurately the number of Hispanic Americans in the United States because there are numerous undocumented individuals (an estimated 12 million) currently living and working in the United States. Several different terms are used to describe individuals of Hispanic descent, such as *Latino/Latina*, *Hispanic*, and *Chicano/Chicana*. The term *Hispanic American* is used here to refer to individuals from Mexico, Puerto Rico, Cuba, El Salvador, Dominican Republic, and other Central and Latin American countries.

Familism is a central theme in the Hispanic culture; this term refers to family unity, loyalty, and respect. Interpersonal relationships within the family and overall community are highly valued and nurtured, and households are often composed of an extended kinship network. The family structure is usually hierarchical, with emphasis placed on elderly parents and men, structured gender roles, and child care of younger siblings by older children. In addition, spirituality and religion, particularly Roman Catholicism, has a major influence on this culture, emphasizing prayer, salvation, and charity. Professional counselors should pay close attention to the client's relationship with the family and spirituality and be willing to include community spiritual leaders as sources of support.

There are several differences among Hispanic American individuals based on immigration status, SES, education level, and acculturation level. Hispanic Americans are currently experiencing difficulty with immigration and establishing citizenship. This struggle has contributed to feelings of distrust and frustration with government and state officials, including social services. Many have fallen victim to disproportionate rates of poverty, unemployment, and substandard living. Because of various oppression experiences, some Hispanic Americans also experience problems with alcoholism and substance abuse. As a result, professional counselors must be aware of the roles of racism and discrimination in the lives of many of these clients.

Acculturation conflicts can be a source of stress for many Hispanic American clients. They might struggle with rejection or acceptance of values of the U.S. culture. Adolescents and older adults might differ over bicultural values and assimilation. Professional counselors should be prepared to discuss how individuals can negotiate conflict between mainstream values and ethnic group values.

Hispanic Americans might be more likely to seek assistance for mental health issues from community and religious leaders before searching for public assistance because of the barriers discussed above. In general, they are more likely to wait longer to seek mental health assistance. Counselors should be aware of potential referral sources for bilingual counseling services. Consider Case Study 11.1 and answer the guided questions.

CASE STUDY 11.1

Jesus is a 42-year-old Puerto Rican male living in the southeast region of the United States. He and his wife have lived in the United States for approximately 7 years. The couple has two young children, ages 6 and 4 years, who were born in the United States. Jesus works 45–50 hours per week as a freelance construction worker. Two years ago, he arrived home from work and began to experience headaches, loss of control of his body, and described being attacked by "spirits." His wife transported him to the local emergency room for a medical evaluation.

When they arrived at the hospital, there were no Spanish-speaking medical professionals available. A local translator from Mexico soon arrived to assist the family. The translator met with the family and the ER doctor to describe Jesus's symptoms. Based on the evaluation, it was determined that Jesus should receive further evaluation from the "on-call" psychiatrist. The translator remained with the family and facilitated the evaluation with the psychiatrist. It was determined that Jesus was experiencing hallucinations.

Later, Jesus was referred to a local mental health agency for evaluation and treatment. Based on the ER evaluation, he was prescribed medication for the treatment of hallucinations. He attended monthly appointments with the psychiatrist and the agency translator reported Jesus' continued complications with "spirits" taking over his body. One day, the regular translator was unavailable to assist with Jesus' appointment with the psychiatrist. As a result, a Spanish-speaking master's level intern from Puerto

Rico was asked to translate Jesus' session with the psychiatrist. During the visit, Jesus reported no decrease in his symptoms as the intern listened to Jesus and realized that his description of the "spirits" were actually described in a dialect that is explained as seizures. The intern quickly explained to the psychiatrist that to Jesus the "spirits" are actually a culturally based method of describing seizures and not auditory or visual hallucinations.

- What can the psychiatrist and overall treatment facility learn from this experience with Jesus?
- Although the master's level intern is in training, what opportunities does she have to advocate for Jesus to obtain appropriate treatment?
- How do you think this experience may have impacted Jesus' perception of the helping profession?

AFRICAN AMERICANS **African Americans** make up approximately 12.6% of the U.S. population; many reside in the southern United States, where they constitute 19% of the population. Projections suggest that by 2050, African Americans will comprise 13% of the U.S. population (U.S. Census Bureau, 2011a). Much of the research has focused on low SES groups, masking a great diversity among African Americans. African Americans comprise a heterogeneous group in relation to background, heritage, traditions, and skin pigmentation. However, ancestors of many African Americans were brought to the United States as slaves. African Americans have a tumultuous history that has been characterized by racism, poverty, oppression, and discrimination.

African American strength lies in the relationship bonds that extend beyond the biological family. Because about 70% of African American households are led by single women, collaboration among extended family members, neighbors, and community leaders is often the norm in the African American culture (Bounds, Washington, & Henfield, 2018). African Americans have elastic family boundaries, and children are readily accepted into the family regardless of the marital status of their parents. Men within the family are more accepting of female work and sharing household responsibilities than men without families. Spirituality plays an important role in many African American families and is often used as a comfort regarding oppression and economic struggles. Professional counselors should work with spiritual leaders to support the family and address client problems.

Because of oppression experiences and resulting socioeconomic issues, physical and mental health, substance abuse issues, and exposure to and involvement in criminal activity might be factors to consider when working with African American clients. Some issues cited in research (Bounds et al., 2018) include decreased physical health, such as cardiovascular problems and HIV/AIDS; problems in academic performance among boys (**disidentification**); disproportionate poverty rates among this population; and unequal numbers of incarcerated African American men as compared to other ethnic groups.

Professional counselors must be aware of the possible feelings of powerlessness and rage regarding the environmental factors related to discrimination. Professional counselors should also be aware of the cultural mistrust and lack of trust for social service agencies and medical staff (So, Gilbert, & Romero, 2005; Washington, Bickel-Swenson, & Stephens, 2008). This mistrust often results in an unwillingness to seek help and negative responses to health care systems. It is important to examine an African American client's response to an adverse situation because he or she might have unique, limited, or reflexive problem-solving skills (Sue & Sue, 2013).

ASIAN AMERICANS   **Asian Americans** comprise about 4.8% of the U.S. population, and most are immigrants from China, India, Vietnam, Korea, Philippines, and Japan. Despite the many misconceptions within U.S. society, Asian Americans comprise a very diverse group that is experiencing rapid growth in the United States. Estimates suggest that this group will make up 9% of the population by 2050. According to the U.S. Census Bureau (2011a), 25% of the foreign-born population is Asian American, and 63% of Asian Americans living in this country are foreign born. Professional counselors need to gain knowledge of within-group diversity and be careful not to make assumptions about individuals' origins and nationalities.

Asian Americans tend to have a collectivist orientation and place emphasis on family and community (Lu, Inman, & Alvarez, 2018). There is also a strong emphasis on older adults as opposed to individualism. The family is usually hierarchical and patriarchal in structure, giving men and older adults higher statuses. Parenting is authoritarian and directive in nature, and shame might be used to reinforce appropriate behaviors within the family and the community. Children are expected to strive for family goals and engage in behaviors that honor the family (i.e., to save face).

Other key concepts in understanding Asian Americans could be related to expression of emotions, views on the mind–body connection, and familial conflict related to levels of acculturation (Lu et al., 2018). For instance, the open display of emotions could be considered immature or out of control in the Asian American culture. Adhering to traditional gender roles, fathers provide for most of the economic and physical needs of the family, whereas mothers are primarily responsible for meeting the emotional needs of the children. Within the Asian American community, much emphasis is placed on the mind–body connection, and emotional difficulties could be expressed through somatic symptoms. Physical problems cause emotional disturbances; professional counselors should treat somatic complaints as real problems.

Asian American children could experience acculturation conflicts with their parents and other family members. This is generally the case when the children's parents are first-generation immigrants. Children are exposed to different cultural standards that often contribute to the conflict with parents who have held to traditional values. An inability to resolve these differences often leads to identity issues and conflict within the family. Professional counselors should be aware of the possible existence of this struggle and make efforts to inquire about the impact that family might have on the decisions of Asian Americans who are involved in individual counseling.

Similar to many other ethnic minority groups, Asian Americans have experienced racism, discrimination, and stereotypes. They have also struggled with being labeled as the **model minority** because of examples of individuals from this group being seen as financially successful, intelligent, and nonaggressive. Many Asian Americans experience stress from these stereotypes because of struggles they face on a daily basis. Many issues within the Asian American community, such as discrepancies between education and income, lack of job skills, unemployment, poverty, language barriers, health problems, and juvenile delinquency, might be hidden because of the underuse of community mental health services.

NATIVE AMERICANS   **Native Americans** comprise the smallest ethnic minority group and include Native American Indians, Alaskan Natives, and Native Hawaiians. There are currently 3.1 million Native Americans living in the United States (U.S. Census Bureau, 2011b). About 39% of the Native American population is younger than age 29 years. There are currently 512 Native American tribes in the United States, and about 54% of Native Americans live on reservations (Garrett et al., 2018).

Native Americans value harmony with nature, cooperation, and holism and have strong feelings about the loss of their ancestral lands (Garrett et al., 2018). Other key themes in Native American culture are sharing, noninterference, time orientation, spirituality, nonverbal communication, and extended family network. Native Americans have experienced a difficult history in the United States since the arrival of European Americans. It is a history of betrayal by and conflict with local, state, or federal governmental officials. Native Americans have a poverty rate three times higher than that of European Americans and are less likely to have a high school diploma. In addition, Native Americans experience difficulty with survival because of the high rates of unemployment and poverty. Alcoholism and domestic violence are also major concerns in the Native American community.

This tension with the dominant culture might have a negative impact on Native Americans' perceptions of mental health services. Garrett et al. (2018) suggested that this has been due partly to the lack of understanding of Native American traditions, values, and worldviews. Native Americans primarily view mental health and wellness as harmony within mind, body, and spirit. Disharmony among these three dimensions creates illness and is often ameliorated by the community. Native Americans might be unlikely to seek assistance from professional counselors owing to a lack of inclusion of spiritual beliefs in counseling, lack of outreach to Native American communities, and unwillingness by counselors to address contextual factors that could influence the lives of this cultural group.

MULTIRACIAL INDIVIDUALS   In 1967, the United States overturned the law against interracial marriage. Before this formal and legal recognition, most individuals who were **multiracial** in the United States were the products of sexual relations between slaves and slave owners or Native Americans and white Americans. After 1967, the United States experienced a biracial baby boom, and the U.S. Census began devising methods for counting members of this growing group.

Currently, 2% of marriages in the United States are interracial (U.S. Census Bureau, 2011a). Societal stereotypes regarding interracial partnerships still exist and could contribute to the identity problems of children who are multiracial. Individuals who are multiracial often do not have the same level of familial or societal support as their monoracial parents and sometimes experience racial and ethnic ambiguity that might lead to feelings of isolation. It is common for many individuals who are multiracial to accept the racial/ethnic identity assigned to them by society. Because of the growing number of multiracial individuals, professional counselors should be aware of their unique needs and concerns. Also, professional counselors should not assume that a client is a member of a particular race based on the characteristics of one particular group.

RACISM   **Racism** is the classification of groups of individuals based on physical characteristics, such as skin color, eye shape, and hair texture, and inappropriately ascribing intellectual, physical, and psychological traits to them. Subsequently, prejudice and discrimination have created negative experiences for certain groups (i.e., racial and ethnic minorities). Professional counselors have a responsibility to attend to racism in their clients' lives as well as to how they might perpetuate racism themselves:

- Explore your own feelings toward particular racial and ethnic groups with others. How might your views and experiences differ from others'?
- Immerse yourself continually in communities composed of racial and ethnic groups that differ from your own. Reflect on your attitudes and behaviors regarding various experiences. Note any changes in your attitudes and behaviors based on the types of experiences, and discuss these changes with others you trust.
- Discuss race and ethnicity with your clients. How has a client's race and ethnicity affected his or her daily experiences? How does your race and ethnicity affect various counseling relationships?
- Educate others in your personal and professional community about concrete instances of racism.

Gender

Messages about gender and gender roles are present in clients' daily lives. Appropriate ways in which men and women should think, behave, and feel are present in media, social interactions, career and education arenas, and family systems. **Gender** is a concept that involves attitudes, behaviors, and relationships associated with being male and female; this concept includes, but is not limited to, biological sex (i.e., chromosomal makeup, hormonal and physical expression of genetic material). Gender roles are roles men and women engage in based on their biological sex (Singh & Mingo, 2018).

From an early age, girls are socialized to be caregivers with traits such as nurturance, dependence, agreeableness, emotionality, and submissiveness. Boys are socialized to be rational, autonomous, aggressive, competitive, nonemotional, and powerful. In addition, boys and men receive more negative consequences for embracing feminine characteristics. Bem (1993) coined the term *androcentricism* to describe masculinity as the ideal trait for which humans strive that has associated privileges of greater wealth and power in relationships. In addition, masculinity as an ideal often serves as a basis for most theories of human development. Activity 11.9 provides an opportunity for you to consider how your gender has influenced your opportunities and assumptions.

ACTIVITY 11.9 GENDER EXPLORATION EXERCISE

- Think about your earliest memories of when you realized you were a member of your gender. Describe the situation and any feelings and behaviors associated with prescribed roles and expectations.
- In general, what messages did you receive about your gender in your family of origin?
- What opportunities have been available to you because of your gender? What barriers have been present?
- Which gender roles do you still adhere to as an adult?
- How has your gender and related opportunities and barriers affected your physical and psychological well-being?
- How do you think your life would be different if you had been born a member of the opposite gender?
- How do you think your gender might be helpful as a counselor? Challenging?

Following the women's movement in the 1960s, greater attention was paid to the role of gender in human development and counseling. In a landmark study exploring gender stereotypes among therapists, Broverman, Broverman, Clarkson, Rosenkrantz, and Vogel (1970) identified that therapists held gender stereotypes and devalued femininity as a healthy characteristic of adults. In this study, healthy adults were described as having predominantly masculine traits. Women were viewed as psychologically less healthy because they were primarily "feminine."

With gender biases present among helping professionals, Chodorow (1978) and Gilligan (1993) proposed in classic works that adult development is different for men and women and that differences should be equally respected. They provided evidence showing that traditional models of human development favor masculine traits as indicators of mental health. Chodorow discovered that women's sense of self emerges within relationships, as opposed to popular assumptions that healthy development emerges from increased independence. To develop as a healthy man means to reject femininity. Gilligan expanded Chodorow's research to show that gender differences exist in moral development. Specifically, as a result of gender socialization and early developmental experiences, females and males generally make decisions and find safety in relationships and in autonomy respectively.

Sparse research is available that looks at the intersection of gender, race/ethnicity, and the influence of social status (i.e., degree of privilege and power in cross-cultural situations). In general, social status seems to have a negative effect on men. Specifically, men in low social statuses tend to behave in ways typically stereotyped as feminine. Because traditional gender role socialization is so salient (i.e., men as masculine and women as feminine), men experience distress because they are often unable to meet the expectations of being fully masculine.

Two groups for which there is some research involve Mexican American and African American families, specifically heterosexual family relationships (Villalba, 2018). *Machismo* and *marianismo* are terms typically identified in Mexican American culture to describe traditional gender role socialization. **Machismo** refers to extreme masculinity, with avoidance of caretaking roles and dominance over other men and women. **Marianismo**, derived from the concept of the Virgin Mary in Roman Catholicism, involves extreme femininity (i.e., passivity, submission to the needs of the family, and belief in male superiority). *Marianismo* is considered an ideal gender role in that women in Latino culture are described as spiritually superior to men and hold special status in the family when they bear children.

Gender roles are less traditional for African American men and women. This could partly be due to the experiences of racism and the restricted power and social status of African American men in society. Although traditional gender roles were present in Africa, slavery diminished men's sense of power within their families because they could no longer protect women, demystifying the myth that men were superior. As a result, women have almost always been in the position of caretaking and working outside the home, while men have been denied social access, leaving them unable to fulfill masculine roles of provider and protector. African American families have been stereotyped as matriarchal, with the female role described as one of strength and resourcefulness.

SEXISM **Sexism**, defined as negative beliefs and behaviors about the ways in which women should be treated based on the notion that femininity is of low value and less healthy than masculinity, is closely associated with the concept of androcentricism. The belief in male superiority and the idea that masculinity is considered healthier for male adults created the assumption women were inferior and deserved negative treatment. Sexism is potentially more harmful for women of color because of the additional experiences of racism and poverty. Some examples of sexism toward women include the glass-ceiling effect (i.e., invisible barrier to occupational and economic advancement); sexual victimization; physical violence; and the entertainment industry's promotion of violence against women, submissiveness, and extreme female thinness as an ideal.

Women and men could experience negative psychological consequences based on strict conformity to gender roles and failure to meet societal standards. Women's problems with gender roles occur when they accept and conform to a low status as designated by society. Likewise, when women resist conforming to what is deemed appropriate behavior for women, they experience negative reactions from others. Women often are not allowed to be aggressive and as a consequence use indirect and unhealthy coping methods. Despite the women's movement, women might still feel marginalized, disempowered, and isolated. These experiences often lead to issues related to human development; lack of power and control over their lives; lack of self-confidence; and feelings of anger, guilt, and shame. As a result of their experiences with sexism, more women than men grapple with depression, anxiety, and eating disorders. Women's symptoms could be a result of inequitable power relationships and related social, economic, and political conditions.

Men's problems often result from failing to attain a high status of dominance as prescribed in masculine roles; men could have a low self-image and cope in destructive ways. In a groundbreaking book, Harris (1995) identified key messages men hear about appropriate ways to express their gender: "Be self-sufficient and don't depend on others." "Don't admit weakness." "Don't show emotions." "Men pursue power and success." "Men are courageous." Masculinity denies mental and physical illness, and men are less likely to seek professional help than are women. In attempts to fulfill these expectations, men experience many physical and psychological issues, including ulcers, heart attacks, completed suicides, hypertension, depression, addiction, problems with intimacy, and stress. Men are more likely than women to engage in violence (e.g., crimes, domestic violence, assaults) partly because of traditional gender role socialization.

TRANSGENDER INDIVIDUALS   Because most of the focus in counseling has been on men and women as they relate to existing gender categories for their biological sexes, there is little known about transgender individuals and their needs in counseling. **Transgender** is a term used to identify individuals who permanently or periodically do not identify with the gender assigned to their biological sex at birth. A related term is *transsexual*, which describes individuals who strongly disidentify with their birth sex and seek sex reassignment and hormonal therapy. *Trans individuals*, an umbrella term for individuals who have evolving gender identities, may possess any sexual orientation (Reicherzer, 2008; Singh & Mingo, 2018).

The increased focus on trans individuals in counseling calls attention to the ways gender and sex have been traditionally considered. Professional counselors can play an important advocacy role by accepting trans individuals' experiences and serving as allies to educate the community and profession on trans individuals' needs, assisting them to connect to support systems and appropriate occupational opportunities, and identifying strengths trans individuals possess as they deal with societal discrimination. The key to working with this population involves changing the context in which they live, not changing the client (Singh, Hays, & Watson, 2011). The ACA endorsed guidelines for counseling transgender clients, the ACA Competencies for Counseling with Transgender Clients (ALGBTIC Transgender Committee, 2010).

GENDER-SENSITIVE COUNSELING PRACTICES Professional associations such as the ACA have attempted to promote gender-sensitive counseling practices through the development of guidelines. Professional counselors are strongly encouraged to review various guidelines for attending to gender in professional practice. Themes of various guidelines include the following (American Psychological Association, 2007; ALGBTIC Transgender Committee, 2010):

- Attend to sexist assumptions found in counseling theories, interventions, and assessments.
- Focus on counselor biases regarding the influence of gender on mental health and continued evaluation of attitudes toward men and women.
- Increase knowledge about the unique needs of men and women.
- Increase knowledge about the intersection of sexism and other forms of oppression (e.g., racism, heterosexism).
- Use nonsexist language and gender-sensitive skills in counseling.
- Facilitate client knowledge of how gender, gender-role stereotyping, and sexism affect physical and psychological health.

Sexual Minorities

Although more than 3% of the U.S. population identifies with a sexual orientation other than heterosexual, little attention has been paid to the mental health needs of sexual minorities. *Sexual diversity* refers to differences in sexual orientation. This section focuses on sexual minorities whose members identify as gay, lesbian, and bisexual (GLB).

Part of the lack of focus relates to the attitudes and biases of professional counselors. Although homosexuality as a form of mental illness was removed from the *Diagnostic and Statistical Manual of Mental Disorders* in 1973, negative stereotypes and limited understanding of the experiences of individuals who do not identify as heterosexual continue to exist. Chen-Hayes (1997) identified 18 stereotypes that affect GLB clients. Professional counselors are encouraged to review this seminal article and reflect on which stereotypes they may hold.

Some GLB individuals experience depression, stress and anxiety, substance abuse, eating disorders, high-risk sexual behaviors, suicide, harassment, and violence. Often, professional counselors identify any mental health concerns in sexually diverse individuals as caused by their sexual orientation rather than because of the societal discrimination they face. Societal stressors can worsen an existing mental illness for GLB individuals (Chaney & Brubaker, 2018).

Because sexually diverse clients experience these stereotypes in their daily lives with resulting mental health considerations, the process of self-identifying as GLB (i.e., the **coming out process**) is complex and difficult. The coming out process is the basis of sexual identity development, which was discussed earlier in this chapter. Heterosexism, internalized homophobia, and sexual identity management are three concepts that heavily influence an individual's coming out process. Heterosexism refers to the belief that heterosexuality is the normative model for healthy romantic and sexual relationships. Heterosexist individuals often have an irrational fear or hatred of sexual minorities, known as **homophobia**.

Many individuals who are GLB experience these negative attitudes and may believe their sexual orientation is morally or socially wrong, resulting in internalized homophobia.

As they come to identify their sexual orientation and deal with heterosexism, homophobia, and internalized homophobia, individuals who are GLB engage in sexual identity management strategies. Some of these strategies include passing as heterosexual or covering or minimizing their true orientation to avoid discrimination and displaying pride for their sexual minority status (Szymanski & Owens, 2008). The identity development process for sexual minorities is often complex because of valid safety concerns.

Although the coming out process is an important part of the psychological development of individuals who are GLB, professional counselors should be careful to not assume this is the primary reason clients with diverse sexual orientations are seeking counseling. Clients who are GLB might consider counseling for daily issues that are likely affected by others' attitudes regarding their sexual orientation. Some issues that might affect sexually diverse individuals include variations on general concerns of career development, parenting, and relationship status. Examples of these issues include assessing level of safety, job security, and sense of belonging regarding various career options; experiencing legal battles related to custody of children from a previous relationship or barriers to adoption; and, in many states, not being able to file joint tax returns or receive insurance benefits for their partners.

COUNSELING IMPLICATIONS   To address the specific needs of clients who are GLB or identify as transgender, the Association for Lesbian, Gay, Bisexual, and Transgender Issues in Counseling (ALGBTIC) developed competencies that correspond to CACREP core areas. Professional counselors should strive to increase their competence for working with this population by examining the ALGBTIC (2013) competencies. In addition to the ALGBTIC competencies above, consider the following guidelines (Chaney & Brubaker, 2018):

- Use gender-neutral language if clients do not specify a gender when referring to their partners.
- Use clients' language when describing their sexual orientation; avoid using the term *homosexual*.
- Do not assume client problems are related to sexual orientation.
- Do not ignore the possible impact of sexual orientation on client problems.
- Focus on sexual orientation to the same extent a client focuses on it.

Now read Case Study 10.2 and answer the processing questions.

CASE STUDY 10.2

Ahmed is a 17-year-old male from Pakistan but living in the northeast region of the United States. He and his family (father, mother, and two sisters) have lived in the United States for 5 years. For Ahmed, the transition to the Western culture has been a difficult process. He has struggled to make social connections with his peers and reports feeling isolated and disconnected most of the time. Overall, his family has adjusted to the new environment by establishing relationships with other individuals from Pakistan who live in the local neighborhood.

The family has a strong religious connection and reports practicing as Muslim. Ahmed reports that he has a strong faith and connection with his religion. However, he often struggles with balancing his religious beliefs with Western cultural norms. At school, Ahmed is often observed by his teachers as being isolated. He has a low academic performance and doesn't appear to be motivated to engage in any social or extra-curricular activities. School administrators have recognized that he spends most of his time alone at lunch and other times during the school day. Out of increasing concern, Ahmed's math teacher makes a referral to the school counselor.

Initially, Ahmed was resistant to meet with the school counselor; however, he reluctantly consented to a meeting. After several sessions with the school counselor, Ahmed admitted to feeling depressed and unhappy. He informed the school counselor that he has struggled with dealing with his sexual attraction toward other males. He states that these feelings began before his family moved to the United States and he feels ashamed and alone. He informs the school counselor that homosexuality is unaccept-able in his culture and religion. He also reported that in some instances of disclosure of homosexual orientation can lead to isolation from the family and community and can even be life-threatening. He refuses to discuss his sexual orientation with his family or anyone in his cultural environment, thus further perpetuating his feelings of depres-sion, loneliness, and isolation.

- What are your initial thoughts about Ahmed's struggle with reconciling his sexual orientation and his cultural/religious beliefs?
- How can the counselor support Ahmed in the school environment while respect-ing his wishes of non-disclosure?
- What are the potential opportunities to engage in advocacy and support for Ahmed?

Spirituality

The counseling profession is increasingly addressing spirituality in the counseling relation-ship. **Spirituality** has several dimensions, including the search for meaning and purpose; connection to something larger and a sense that one is part of a greater whole; drive for creativity, love, relationships, and personal growth; and value in developing a relationship with a transcendent life force. **Religiosity**, one framework for organizing one's spirituality, refers to construction of and adherence to a belief system of faith, traditions, and commu-nity worship (Cashwell & Giordano, 2018). While spirituality and religiosity are related, it is important to assess the degree to which clients identify as spiritual, religious, or both.

Because spirituality is a broad concept that deals with themes of relationships and self-development, many counseling issues could be considered spiritual issues. Clients might present with concerns of isolation, meaninglessness, difficulty connecting with oth-ers, and loss of values. Clients' religious beliefs might or might not influence their ways of coping with these issues. Ceasar and Miranti (2005, p. 250) offer the following reflections for integrating spirituality in counseling:

- How important are spiritual practices in the client's life?
- What is the client's spiritual or religious orientation? To what degree does the client identify with this orientation?
- How does the client view his or her spirituality in relation to the presenting problem (e.g., potential source of strength, cause of current problem, decreasing as a result of current problem)?

- Does the client view the presenting problem as a spiritual issue?
- Is the client willing to explore any spiritual needs?
- From where or whom does the client seek strength and comfort?
- How does the client make meaning in his or her life?

Professional counselors have an ethical responsibility to address diversity issues and promote client growth and development in the counseling process. This responsibility includes addressing spiritual concerns as appropriate. Although addressing spirituality seems to be congruent with the purposes of multicultural counseling, professional counselors might fear imposing their values or could have had negative personal experiences with spirituality and religiosity. Also, professional counselors might lack knowledge of various religious belief systems. Professional counselors are encouraged to review literature describing major religions and their belief systems as they prepare to work with diverse clients.

Professional counselors must be aware of their attitudes, beliefs, knowledge, and experiences related to spirituality and its integration into counseling. The Association for Spiritual, Ethical, and Religious Values in Counseling (ASERVIC) developed the Competencies for Integrating Spirituality into Counseling (ASERVIC, 2016, pp. 1–2). They include the following preamble and 13 competencies:

Preamble: The Competencies for Addressing Spiritual and Religious Issues in Counseling are guidelines that complement, not supersede, the values and standards espoused in the *ACA Code of Ethics*. Consistent with the *ACA Code of Ethics* (2014), the purpose of the ASERVIC Competencies is to "recognize diversity and embrace a cross-cultural approach in support of the worth, dignity, potential, and uniqueness of people within their social and cultural contexts" (p. 3). These Competencies are intended to be used in conjunction with counseling approaches that are evidence-based and that align with best practices in counseling.

Culture and Worldview

1. The professional counselor can describe the similarities and differences between spirituality and religion, including the basic beliefs of various spiritual systems, major world religions, agnosticism, and atheism.
2. The professional counselor recognizes that the client's beliefs (or absence of beliefs) about spirituality and/or religion are central to his or her worldview and can influence psychosocial functioning.
3. The professional counselor actively explores his or her own attitudes, beliefs, and values about spirituality and/or religion.
4. The professional counselor continuously evaluates the influence of his or her own spiritual and/or religious beliefs and values on the client and the counseling process.
5. The professional counselor can identify the limits of his or her understanding of the client's spiritual and/or religious perspective and is acquainted with religious and spiritual resources and leaders who can be avenues for consultation and to whom the counselor can refer.
6. The professional counselor can describe and apply various models of spiritual and/or religious development and their relationship to human development.
7. The professional counselor responds to client communications about spirituality and/or religion with acceptance and sensitivity.
8. The professional counselor uses spiritual and/or religious concepts that are consistent with the client's spiritual and/or religious perspectives and are acceptable to the client. The professional counselor can recognize spiritual and/or religious themes in client communication and is able to address these with the client when they are therapeutically relevant.
9. During the intake and assessment processes, the professional counselor strives to understand a client's spiritual and/or religious perspective by gathering information from the client and/or other sources.

10. When making a diagnosis, the professional counselor recognizes that the client's spiritual and/or religious perspectives can a) enhance well-being; b) contribute to client problems; and/or c) exacerbate symptoms.

11. The professional counselor sets goals with the client that are consistent with the client's spiritual and/or religious perspectives.

12. The professional counselor is able to a) modify therapeutic techniques to include a client's spiritual and/or religious perspectives, and b) utilize spiritual and/or religious practices as techniques when appropriate and acceptable to a client's viewpoint.

13. The professional counselor can therapeutically apply theory and current research supporting the inclusion of a client's spiritual and/or religious perspectives and practices.

In the spirit of professional collaboration, ASERVIC endorses the counseling competencies that have been established by the Association for Multicultural Counseling and Development (AMCD) and the Association for Lesbian, Gay, Bisexual and Transgender Issues in Counseling (ALGBTIC). In so doing, these three divisions seek to enhance the counseling of clients and the training of students by intentionally focusing on honoring the many facets of diversity.

Source: Association for Spiritual, Ethical, and Religious Values in Counseling. (2016). *Competencies for integrating spirituality into counseling.* Retrieved from http://www.aservic.org/wp-content/uploads/2010/04/Spiritual-Competencies-Printer-friendly1.pdf. Reprinted with permission. Further reproduction prohibited.

Now read Voices from the Field 11.2.

VOICES FROM THE FIELD 11.2   My Experience with Multicultural Counseling, by Nicholette Leanza

Societal labels or membership in particular groups can shade people's perceptions of the world and their interactions with others. I carry this point of view with me in my work as a counselor in a large urban school district that understands how poverty can devastate a community. My clients cover the spectrum of cultural diversity, including students who are African American, Hispanic, Caucasian, biracial, and gay or lesbian. As a self-described middle-aged, White lady from the suburbs, I work hard to understand my clients' points of reference in regard to how societal labels can be an added stress on their psychological well-being. My cultural competency generally serves me well; however, there was one client who challenged my confidence in this area.

She was born in Puerto Rico, and her family moved to the United States when she was very young. As a bilingual high school student on track for college, she was referred for counseling due to depressive symptoms and strained family dynamics. During a phone call with her mother to set up the intake appointment, I struggled to communicate effectively because her mother only spoke Spanish and the Spanish I took in high school/college did not render me proficient enough to speak to her fluently. To remedy this issue, her mother signed a consent form to allow the school's Spanish teacher to serve as an interpreter. I quickly learned during the intake that the client struggled with anger originating from her father abruptly deserting the family for another woman. She also wrestled with severe trust issues. In my first therapy session with her, the client declared, "Why would I talk to a total stranger about my problems?" She spent the remainder of the time refusing all my attempts to build rapport.

Resistance to counseling is not a surprise when an adolescent feels he or she is being forced by a parent or guardian. Therefore, I did my best to enable my client to feel some control over the situation, but she continued her resistance and adamantly stated during our second session, "Why

(Continued)

would I talk to a counselor when I could just pray to God about my problems?" It was during this session that I really paid attention to her strong spiritual beliefs. She identified as a devout Pentecostal Christian, and this seemed to color her perception of the world. I was eager to develop the therapeutic relationship, and so I attempted to engage her in a conversation about her specific spiritual beliefs. This strategy outraged her as she uttered in an indignant tone, "If you do not understand the Pentecostal religion, then you are not able to help me."

Before the third session, I did some research and found that Pentecostal Christians are taught to seek guidance and healing *only* from God and that could be why the client did not want to be in counseling. Once again, I attempted to engage her in a dialogue about her beliefs, but she still was not a willing participant. At one point during the session, as the air between us was thick with a tense silence, she snidely remarked, "Stop staring at me. You're creeping me out!" Flustered and slightly insulted, I quickly darted my eyes around the office to avoid any eye contact with her. After that uncomfortable session, I took some time to explore my frustration and further pondered how to connect with this client.

One important point I had to acknowledge was my bias regarding conservative Christian ideologies. My spiritual beliefs reflect a tendency toward Eastern cultural traditions like Buddhism, so I genuinely grapple with what I perceive as the constraints of traditional Christian religion. I had to consider whether some of my frustration stemmed from my liberal religious beliefs. To get a second opinion, I consulted a trusted colleague to see if she could offer any further guidance. She was empathetic to my insight and wondered if the client would benefit from "getting out of the office and going out for a walk," in the hopes that the client would not feel so pressured by the office environment. I thought it was a good suggestion, but the client quickly informed me that she "didn't want anyone" to see her with me.

Now I questioned whether this was a cultural issue, religious issue, personal resistance, or all of the above. My guess was that it was most likely a combination of all of them. I continued to plan ways to gain her trust and engage her in counseling. During the next several sessions, I tailored my therapeutic activities and discussion to encompass her spiritual belief system. She participated half-heartedly and would often roll her eyes as she figured out my strategy. I proposed during the eighth session that she might feel more comfortable with a pastoral counselor whose specialty lies in spiritual matters and recommended that we set up a meeting with her mother to discuss this option. This seemed to soften her, and she apologized for being so difficult. That said, she remained insistent that "only God can help me" and "I will continue to pray for healing," but she still did not want to be in any type of counseling.

I scheduled the next session with her mother, and my client served as the interpreter. Before I offered my recommendation, the client's mother complimented me on her daughter's progress in counseling and how much "happier" she was at home and at school. Of course, I was rather shocked to hear this news. I even briefly wondered whether my client was truly interpreting what her mother was actually saying. I soon dismissed this thought as her mother's eyes genuinely reflected gratitude as she smiled brightly at me. It was decided that the client would continue counseling with me.

With continued persistence, the client slowly opened up and became more sincerely engaged in the counseling process. Using her fervent belief in God and her church as a foundation, she was able to confront some of the root causes of her depression. I also found that my frustration dissolved as well as my initial bias regarding her established religious beliefs. Although it was definitely a challenge to establish the therapeutic relationship with her, I eventually recognized that the foundation of her spiritual beliefs and mine were not that different. Ultimately, she helped me to further my cultural competence by breaking a perceived stereotype I had about conservative Christian ideologies. I am grateful that this client was such a challenge, because this therapeutic relationship enabled me to stretch outside my comfort zone and expand my own perceptions of spirituality.

Counseling Individuals with Disabilities

According to the Americans with Disabilities Act (ADA, 2008), Americans with disabilities should be protected against discrimination. ADA defines **disability** as physical or mental impairment that substantially limits a major life activity. The determination of whether a particular condition is a disability is made on a case-by-case basis. Examples of physical disabilities include vision loss, deafness or significant hearing loss, speech impediments, and physical impairment (e.g., arthritis, limited or no use of limbs, wheelchair bound). Examples of mental disabilities include major depression, bipolar disorder, and schizophrenia. In addition to protection against discrimination, ADA mandates that businesses make adjustments and accommodations to facilities to make them accessible and appropriate for individuals with disabilities.

Individuals with disabilities have faced several challenges in society related to discrimination that have created social, vocational, educational, and economic segregation. Individuals with disabilities also have been characterized by many myths and stereotypes. For example, many people believe disabilities are visible, and that physical disabilities create the most barriers for this population (Smart & Smart, 2011). Similar to the general public, professional counselors often struggle with feelings of guilt and pity toward disabled clients. To assist this population effectively, professional counselors are encouraged to:

- explore their own personal views of disabilities and challenge any prejudicial assumptions;
- not make the disability the only focus of counseling, because many individuals with disabilities struggle with other life problems, such as sexuality, divorce, or depression, which might not be directly related to their disabilities;
- identify environmental factors and issues related to negative stereotypes;
- ask about the disability but not succumb to the *spread phenomenon*, or the belief that the disability affects unrelated aspects of the individual's life;
- explore damage related to the individual opportunities for accountability and self-reliance;
- incorporate family counseling as appropriate;
- focus on improving the quality of life in rehabilitation, which can be accomplished through community involvement, physical adjustments, and psychosocial adjustments; and
- gain knowledge about various disabilities and resources available to clients.

Activity 11.10 provides a method for increasing your knowledge about disability services at your college or university.

ACTIVITY 11.10

Visit the office that provides disability services at your college or university. Interview an employee of that office, and gather information on the types of students who typically visit the office, what services are most sought, and any mental health concerns with which these students present. Explore the individual ways by which professional counselors may better meet the needs of individuals with disabilities.

Counseling the Elderly

In 1935, the Social Security Act deemed 65 years as the appropriate age for retirement and eligibility for federal retirement funds. According to the U.S. Census Bureau (2011a), adults age 65 years and older are 12% of the population. Estimates suggest that the elderly population (adults age 65 years and older) will substantially increase during the years 2010–2030. The elderly population currently comprises mostly the baby boomer generation. Baby boomers are individuals born between the years 1945 and 1965, a period when the United States experienced its largest population growth. The first baby boomers turned 65 years old in 2011, and by 2030, the total elderly population is expected to double from that of 2000. With an increase in the number of elderly adults, professional counselors are more likely to be employed in community-based facilities, such as nursing homes, hospices, retirement communities, and day treatment centers.

Some elderly adults face major roadblocks to functioning, such as poor economic and physical health, mental health issues, dementia, substance abuse, physical abuse, neglect, and depression (Berens & Erford, 2018). In addition, many elderly adults are affected by **ageism**, which is defined as negative attitudes related to the process of aging or elderly people. The elderly have been viewed erroneously as having rigid thought processes and little interest in sexual activity (Berens & Erford, 2018). Maples and Abney (2006) suggest there are several challenges related to ageism specific to baby boomers. Baby boomers are more likely than older adults to be affected by anticipated declines in Social Security and by financial insecurity, age discrimination owing to change of demographics in the work environment, and relationship and divorce issues.

In response to the need for appropriate guidelines for working with elderly adults, gerontological competencies were developed in 1973 and provide professional counselors with 16 essential competencies of gerontological counseling. Some of these address end-of-life concerns, social and cultural aspects of aging, importance of family involvement, and roles of professional counselors. The competencies also mandate that all professional counselors be familiar with a variety of service providers in the community who specialize in gerontological care. This community care might consist of day treatment, senior centers, residential/long-term care, and wellness programs (Maples & Abney, 2006).

As professional counselors become more culturally competent, they must recognize that the elderly are not a homogeneous group and should be treated based on individual needs. According to Maples and Abney (2006), professional counselors are encouraged to assist elderly clients to identify the positive aspects of aging by incorporating creativity, positivism, and wellness into the counseling relationship. It is also important to help promote self-empowerment through helping elderly clients recognize that aging is a natural part of development and helping clients envision a healthy lifestyle until the end of life.

SOCIAL JUSTICE IN COUNSELING

Understanding the role of social justice in counseling is an important aspect of the role of the counselor. It is about advocacy and activism in addressing the issues of inequity and other sociopolitical and economic injustices that encumber individuals. Therefore counselors must recognize that human development is not merely based on affective, behavioral, or cognitive problems, but rather a more expansive perspective that considers issues of racism, oppression, and discrimination as environmental barriers. Establishing social justice in counseling is both a goal and a process (Adams, Bell, & Grifffin, 2007). The goal is to help each individual achieve his or her highest potential. The counseling process should be collaborative in nature where the client maintains an active role in the focus and direction of his or her treatment. Therefore the counseling relationship is empowering rather than an oppressive experience for the client. Crethar and Ratts (2008) suggest the use of four guiding principles in this process:

- *Equity:* equal allocation of resources, rights, and responsibilities to every individual in society.
- *Access:* ". . . includes notions of fairness for both the individual and the common good based on the ability of all people to access the resources, services, power, information and understanding crucial to realizing a standard of living that allows for self-determination and human development" (p. 24).
- *Participation:* Each individual has the right to participate in the decision-making process on issues that impact their lives and the lives of other individuals within the cultural context or system.
- *Harmony:* Promotion of an overall societal adjustment where the actions of an individual or group are in the best interests of the overall system or entire community.

The incorporation of social justice perspectives into the counseling process is beneficial to the overall helping professions. It provides a comprehensive approach to conceptualizing client problems, changes the role and identity of the counselor, and lends itself to increasingly advanced approaches to counseling (Ratts, 2009).

MULTICULTURAL ORGANIZATIONAL DEVELOPMENT: CREATING A CULTURALLY SENSITIVE ENVIRONMENT

Professional counselors might find in their work settings that they are one of only a few trained in multicultural sensitivity. Clients ideally enter the professional counselor's office, whether in a school or agency, feeling as though the counselor is sensitive to their cultural identities and privy to salient cultural issues that affect their daily lives. The good news is that information presented in this chapter can assist professional counselors in a school or agency setting. Having self-awareness, knowledge, and skills for working with culturally diverse individuals is a good foundation for creating a culturally sensitive organization. To increase multicultural sensitivity within the workplace and create a positive, therapeutic experience for clients, employ the following additional strategies:

- Evaluate collaboratively with other staff in the school or agency the demographics of the setting, what demographics are not being served well, what mental health resources are typically used, and if the purpose of the setting is fulfilling the mental health needs of current and potential clientele.
- Whether clients are waiting in a lobby or sitting in the office in a counseling session, the surrounding environment should be affirming to a variety of cultural identities. Include resources and magazines that represent the experiences of as many cultural groups as possible. Ensure that one cultural group is not overrepresented so as to not create a sense among particular clients that they do not belong or in general that counseling is not for them.
- Ensure that policies and procedures of the school or agency do not systematically discriminate against certain groups. For example, having a Spanish version of important

documents for clients ensures that Latino individuals who speak Spanish as a first language understand their rights and roles as clients.

- Educate staff and other stakeholders in an organization about cultural groups and cultural issues that affect clients. Provide workshops or printed materials for individuals who might not have received training in multicultural sensitivity. Encourage an active, positive dialogue with colleagues about cultural issues.
- Engage in program evaluation to improve the cultural climate of an organization whereby staff and client needs with respect to multicultural sensitivity are assessed and their experiences with counseling are explored.
- Collaborate with others in the organization to apply for local and federal grants to expand counseling services to individuals who have limited access to services.
- Take on leadership roles in the local community and find ways to serve as an agent for social change.
- Serve as an ally and join with other community leaders and assist in improving interpersonal relationships within the community, provide trainings in specific areas of need, or conduct research that will inform change in the community.

These are just a few activities that can foster a culturally sensitive environment. For each of these strategies, examine through the lens of the various cultural identities presented in this chapter how each strategy can be implemented in concrete ways. Activity 11.11 is helpful in identifying positive and negative cultural stereotypes.

ACTIVITY 11.11

Identify positive and negative stereotypes (i.e., what others would say about members of that cultural group) as well as advantages and disadvantages (i.e., your personal views on privileges and challenges) for each cultural identity listed in the first column of this activity's table. After independently working on the activity, discuss in dyads and small groups, to the extent you are comfortable, your cultural group memberships. Note any surprising findings or challenges with identifying some of the stereotypes, advantages, or disadvantages for particular cultural groups.

Cultural identity	Positive stereotypes	Negative stereotypes	Advantages	Disadvantages
Age				
Gender				
Race				
Ethnicity				
Ability (e.g., physical, cognitive, emotional)				
Spiritual affiliation				
Sexual orientation				
Socioeconomic status				

Summary

Multicultural counseling involves increasing professional counselors' awareness, knowledge, and skills in working with clients who might be diverse with respect to race, ethnicity, SES, gender, sexual orientation, spiritual affiliation, disability, and age. To attend to cultural factors affecting clients, a professional counselor should consider her or his own personal views on cultural group memberships. In addition, the following are key points to consider as one counsels individuals and families in an increasingly diverse society:

- Attend to the role of culture in counseling by increasing your knowledge of clients' cultural identities. This may be accomplished by discussing with clients how they identify culturally, reviewing the latest research in multicultural counseling, and engaging in self-exploration to identify personal biases and behaviors.
- Increase your knowledge of available resources to help clients develop stronger support networks within communities.
- Pay attention to how SES, especially poverty, plays a role in client mental health.
- Consider new ways to provide counseling services to clients who might not have access to or interest in individual counseling.
- Develop a referral resource network to consult on multicultural issues as they arise in counseling.
- Determine ways in which your unique cultural makeup grants you privileges but might oppress you. How can you advocate for others to experience some of the privileges you have? How can you advocate in counseling to end oppression for yourself or other groups?
- Participate in activities that create opportunities to interact with individuals of different races and ethnicities. In these immersion experiences, attend to how your cultural makeup influences the way others respond to you.

- Be cognizant of how differences between and within racial and ethnic groups might be a result of cultural values for a particular group, oppression experiences, or both.
- While there are unique aspects of being of a particular racial/ethnic makeup, consider overarching themes related to being a member of a racial/ethnic minority group compared with that of the dominant racial/ethnic group (e.g., white).
- Increase your understanding of the unique needs of men and women. For both genders, it might be helpful to explore the family-of-origin messages received about gender. Reflect on the benefits and challenges of gender roles as they relate to presenting mental health issues.
- When working with women, assist them to express anger and frustration with sexism and other forms of oppression, empower them by allowing space for their voices, and provide assertiveness and other skills training as needed.
- Consider using holistic counseling approaches that, particularly when used in group counseling, might be suitable for men; these include stress-management and relaxation training, nutrition education, exploration of emotions, and assistance with relationship difficulties.
- Assess the degree to which a client's sexual orientation affects his or her mental health status. Consider how sexual identity intersects with spiritual beliefs, gender roles, and race/ethnicity.
- If you are heterosexual, reflect on any privileges in social, educational, and occupational settings you receive based on your heterosexual identity.
- Some spiritual issues presented in counseling might not be associated with religious beliefs. Keep a broad perspective of spirituality as it applies to a client's presenting situation.

- Consider interventions such as journaling, guided imagery, mindfulness exercises, and meditation and other relaxation techniques when addressing spiritual concerns within a counseling session.
- Acknowledge that many disabilities are not visible in a client's appearance. Assess any disabilities and a client's experiences without automatically assuming that ability status plays an important role in the presenting problem.
- Familiarize yourself with the ADA of 2008 and other legislation to assist clients with disabilities in dealing with social, academic, and occupational challenges.
- Reflect on your own thoughts about aging and death and how these thoughts might influence your present attitudes about counseling elderly people.

MyCounselingLab for Introduction to Counseling

Try the Topic 12 Assignments: *Multicultural Considerations.*

---

12 Assessment, Case Conceptualization, Diagnosis, and Treatment Planning

BRADLEY T. ERFORD*

PREVIEW

This chapter reviews assessment, case conceptualization, diagnosis, and treatment planning in counseling. Assessment is the systematic gathering of information to effectively address a client's presenting concerns. A case conceptualization reflects how the professional counselor understands the nature of the presenting problems and includes a diagnostic formulation. Treatment plans outline counseling outcome expectations and interventions to meet these expectations.

A COMPREHENSIVE APPROACH TO UNDERSTANDING CLIENT ISSUES AND DESIGNING PLANS TO HELP

Effective counseling requires many skills. The abilities to gather and interpret information, apply counseling theories and diagnostic frameworks to develop case conceptualizations, and engage in collaborative treatment planning are all important parts of the counseling process. Attending to developmental and cultural considerations in the application of these skills is essential to the practice of professional counseling.

Assessment is a broad term that includes many structured and unstructured processes for gathering information to understand the issues that bring people to counseling. Case conceptualization refers to how professional counselors understand the nature of clients' concerns, how and why the problems have developed, and the types of counseling interventions that might be helpful. Diagnosis is the identification of a problem that becomes the target of the counseling intervention. Treatment planning provides a road map for the counseling process. Treatment plans identify what the professional counselor and the client have agreed to work on together, and what strategies are to be used to achieve these goals. Each of the above concepts is discussed in detail in the following sections.

*Special thanks to Gail Mears and Jodi Bartley for their outstanding contribution to the previous edition of this chapter.

ASSESSMENT

Assessment is the process of gathering information in a systematic way to evaluate concerns or questions that a client brings to counseling. It is a broad umbrella term that includes intake interviews, tests and inventories, behavioral observations, and relevant information gathered from other sources (Erford, 2013). The types of information and gathering methods used depend on many factors, including answers to the following questions:

- What is the presenting question or concern?
- What types of information are commonly used in the field to evaluate this concern?
- Where is counseling taking place (e.g., school, clinic, hospital)?
- What does the client want out of counseling?
- Is the client an accurate reporter regarding the presenting concern? Ordinarily, this depends on the developmental level, motivation, and level of insight and judgment of the client.
- What is the client's cultural background?
- Who is asking for the assessment?
- Why is the question being asked at this time?
- What assessment skills and expertise does the professional counselor have?

The assessment process informs case conceptualization, diagnostic formulation, and the resulting counseling plans, and helps to identify resources that could allow the client to cope better with the presenting concern. Determining what information to gather is an important assessment skill. Use the cases found in Activity 12.1 to practice identifying important assessment information.

ACTIVITY 12.1

In small groups, discuss the types of information you think would be useful to gather for each of the following clients. Why do you think this information would be useful?

- Hugo, age 12 years, is brought to the local mental health center because of an escalation in conduct problems. Hugo is referred by the court and is brought to the center by his mother. Hugo's father left the family and moved out of state 6 months ago. Hugo has had very limited phone contact with his father for the past few months. Recently, he was brought to the police station after breaking several windows in an abandoned house. Hugo reports lack of interest in counseling. His mother reports concern about Hugo's behavior and about his emotional state.
- Susan is a 35-year-old married woman who recently gave birth to her first child. She comes to the center at her husband's request because of feelings of sadness, intrusive thoughts about hurting her baby, irritability, fatigue, and emerging suicidal thoughts. She is fearful of letting the professional counselor know how she feels and is ashamed that she could feel this way about her child.
- Jamal is a 19-year-old second-year college student. He is referred to the college counseling center because of his worry over not being able to decide on a major. He reports guilty feelings that he is wasting his parents' money and feels increased pressure to choose a major. Jamal reports vague ideas about wanting to work in the recreational field, but he does not have any clear ideas about what types of jobs are available in this field. He reports no idea about what courses and majors would be consistent with his interests.

Testing and the Counseling Profession

The terms *testing* and *assessment* are often used interchangeably; however, testing is only one type of assessment tool. A **test** is any instrument or device that evaluates a person's performance or behavior. Testing has been an integral part of the counseling profession for a century, with roots in vocational guidance. The counseling field has a long history of using tests and inventories to assist with career planning. However, the field is also rooted in a philosophy of wellness and personal growth. This philosophy has resulted in ambivalence around the use of tests. Despite concerns about testing, counselors are expected to possess the knowledge and ability to administer various forms of tests and assessments.

An entire section of the ACA (2014a) *Code of Ethics* is dedicated to assessment and diagnosis issues. Counselors need to be sensitive to the appropriate use of tests and the need to be vigilant about discriminatory practices in testing. Professional counselors need to be attentive to cultural biases in tests and to use only those tests with norms developed on a sample that is representative of the test taker. Professional counselors should also be sensitive to an overinterpretation of test results, understanding that a test provides a limited sample of behavior. Counselors also need to ensure that test results are not used to put the test taker at a disadvantage.

Access to some tests is regulated by test makers, and the purchase of these regulated tests requires advanced levels of education and training. Tests are often categorized by publishers using a system akin to level A, B, or C (Erford, 2013). Generally, level A tests require no special training to purchase and administer; level B tests require a master's degree, relevant coursework in testing, and supervision in the use of the test; level C tests require a doctorate or a license with a scope of practice to interpret these tests and also require training and supervision in the use of the instrument. State licensing boards regulate what types of assessments are within a licensed professional counselor's scope of practice, and ethical standards help counselors determine if they have the requisite education, training, and supervision to administer a given test. Professional counselors should use only tests for which they have specialized training and for which they understand the testing theory, the concepts of test construction, and statistics. Professional counselors must understand the cultural, legal, and ethical issues relevant to testing (American Counseling Association, 2014a).

Despite an earlier history of collaboration among the American Psychological Association, the American Educational Research Association, the National Council on Measurement in Education, the American Speech and Language Hearing Association, and the American Counseling Association, psychologists in some states have tried to limit the use of some standardized tests by counselors and other professionals. The Fair Access Coalition on Testing (FACT) was formed to advocate for the testing rights of qualified individuals, including counselors (National Board for Certified Counselors, 2017). Activity 12.2 encourages a review of websites to help you better understand the history, standards, and advocacy efforts related to testing and assessment.

ACTIVITY 12.2

Go to the website for the *Association for Assessment and Research in Counseling* (**AARC**; a division of the American Counseling Association) at aarc-counseling.org/. Review the history and mission statement of the association. Also review the testing standards,

(Continued)

multicultural assessment competencies, test reviews, and other posted information. Next, go the website for the **Fair Access Coalition on Testing (FACT)** www.fairaccess.org/home.html. Review the FACT document *Model Testing Practices* (www.fairaccess.org/model.html) and other information on the website.

Why Should Professional Counselors Know About Testing?

Most professional counselors have some involvement with tests during their careers. Professional school counselors are often in charge of achievement testing, and in many schools, they are considered the experts in testing. They are called on to explain test results to parents and use testing evaluations to develop school-based intervention plans. Mental health and rehabilitation counselors administer tests or interpret testing results to help with diagnosis and treatment planning. Career counselors frequently rely on interest inventories, such as the *Strong Interest Inventory*, to help guide the career exploration process. Foster's (2005) review of the literature includes the following uses of tests by professional counselors: (1) preliminary problem exploration and diagnosis, (2) selection and screening, (3) placement and planning, (4) facilitation of self-understanding, and (5) licensure or certification.

The Council for Accreditation of Counseling and Related Educational Programs (CACREP), in its 2016 assessment standards, requires that CACREP-accredited programs provide students with instruction regarding testing and the relevant statistical concepts; strategies for selecting, administering, and interpreting tests; diversity considerations in testing; and legal and ethical issues. The following discussion examines the different types of tests and the important concepts associated with testing. First complete Activity 12.3 to demonstrate your understanding of what professional counselors need to know about testing.

ACTIVITY 12.3

Create a two- to three-page letter to a colleague that explains (a) why professional counselors need to know about testing, (b) why they should be concerned about practice rights, and (c) what a professional counselor needs to know to use tests competently. Break into small groups, and share your letters.

Categories of Tests

Tests are often categorized as standardized or nonstandardized depending on the latitude given to examiners to vary the procedures of administration and scoring. Tests are also categorized as norm-referenced or criterion-referenced depending on whether the examiner wants to compare a client's results with the results of individuals with similar characteristics, or with some established performance standard.

STANDARDIZED TESTS   Standardized tests have defined protocols for administration and scoring. This means that the test is administered in the same way, under similar conditions, whenever it is administered. The methods used for scoring the test are predetermined and are followed consistently. Scores from a standardized test are interpreted in relationship to a norm group (i.e., a group of people who are similar to the test takers along dimensions such as age, gender, race/ethnicity, and grade) or are measured against some performance criteria. Norms and criteria used for scoring standardized tests are developed through extensive test administrations and statistical analyses. The SAT Reasoning Test (SAT-I) and the Wechsler Adult Intelligence Scale (WAIS-IV; Wechsler, 2008) are examples of standardized tests.

NONSTANDARDIZED TESTS **Nonstandardized tests** do not have defined administration protocols and have not been extensively studied to create norms or criterion-related scoring protocols. If your instructor gives you a test on the material in this chapter, you may be taking a nonstandardized test, depending on how tightly controlled the administration conditions are (e.g., open book, take home, untimed, etc.).

NORM-REFERENCED TESTS When scores on a test are compared with the scores of a group of people with similar characteristics to the examinee who took the same test, the test is a **norm-referenced test**. The Wechsler Intelligence Scale for Children: Fifth Edition (WISC-5; Wechsler, 2014) is an example of a norm-referenced, standardized test. The test is administered in the same way whenever it is offered, and an individual's raw scores are compared with the scores of a norm group. This comparison yields a derived score (standardized score or percentile rank) that places individual scores in relationship to the test norms.

CRITERION-REFERENCED TESTS When you take a test and the score is based on performance criteria, you are taking a **criterion-referenced test**. If you are given a test while taking this class, it is likely that the instructor will be looking for some indication that you have mastered the material in the course. Your score will likely reflect the number of items answered correctly, and some criterion, such as a grade or percentage score, and this score will be compared to some criterion or standard of performance, such as a grading scale. You will be taking a criterion-referenced test.

Types of Tests

Tests are frequently categorized as cognitive or affective tests depending on whether they measure thinking and reasoning skills or personality, interests, and behavioral symptoms.

COGNITIVE TESTS Ordinarily, cognitive tests include intelligence tests, other aptitude tests, and achievement tests.

   Intelligence Tests. **Intelligence tests** are designed as broad measures of cognitive ability. The Wechsler Intelligence Scale for Children, Fifth Edition (WISC-5; Wechsler, 2014), and the Wechsler Adult Intelligence Scale, Fourth Edition (WAIS-IV; Wechsler, 2008), are examples of intelligence tests used to evaluate intellectual functioning in educational and clinical settings. Although there is ongoing controversy regarding the validity of the constructs that underlie intelligence tests (e.g., is general intelligence a useful concept?), it is essential that professional counselors be familiar with these tests. Use of individual intelligence tests sometimes requires training beyond a master's program, but professional counselors are often called on to consider the implications of these test results in educational and clinical planning. Group intelligence tests are frequently administered by professional counselors. Examples of group intelligence tests include the Otis-Lennon School Ability Test (OLSAT) and the Cognitive Abilities Test (CogAT). These tests are highly correlated with academic achievement and are often used to make educational planning or screening decisions.

Aptitude Tests.   Intelligence tests are considered to be one type of aptitude test. However, **aptitude tests** also measure a broad range of more specific cognitive abilities or the ability to master particular skill sets in the future. The O*Net Ability Profiler (O*Net), developed and used by the U.S. Department of Labor, is an example of a multiscale aptitude test and measures verbal abilities, arithmetic reasoning, computation, spatial ability, form perception, clerical perception, motor coordination, finger dexterity, and manual dexterity. These types of tests aim to predict a person's ability to master some skill set in the future.

Achievement Tests.   **Achievement tests** are typically used in educational settings and are designed to measure student learning. Examples of achievement tests used by elementary and secondary schools include the Iowa Tests of Basic Skills (ITBS), Terra Nova, and Stanford Achievement Test. Professional school counselors are often in charge of or involved in a school's group achievement testing program. Individual achievement tests that measure specific areas of achievement (e.g., reading or math) are used diagnostically by learning disability specialists and school psychologists. Individual diagnostic tests of achievement (e.g., Woodcock-Johnson Tests of Achievement, Fourth Edition [WJ-IV; Woodcock, Schrenk, Mather, & McGrew, 2014], Wechsler Individual Achievement Test, Third Edition [WIAT-III; Wechsler, 2009]) in specific domains are compared against broader measures of intelligence to determine the presence of a learning disability. The diagnosis of a learning disability requires a discrepancy between the measures of general intelligence and achievement in specific areas.

AFFECTIVE TESTS   Affective tests include personality inventories, interest inventories, and symptom checklists used for the screening and diagnosis of clinical issues.

Personality Tests and Inventories.   **Personality tests and personality inventories** are designed to measure personality traits, temperament, and levels of pathology. These tests are categorized as objective or projective. **Objective personality tests** are paper-and-pencil (or computer-administered) tests that require examinees to answer questions in specific ways (e.g., multiple choice) and can be easily scored. The Minnesota Multiphasic Personality Inventory–2 (MMPI-2), the Millon Clinical Multiaxial Inventory–III (MCMI-III), and the Myers Briggs Type Indicator (MBTI) are examples of objective personality tests.

Projective Personality Tests.   **Projective personality tests** provide examinees with ambiguous tasks, and examinees' answers can be quite varied. An example of this type of test is the Rorschach Inkblot Test (Exner, 2003). Examinees are presented with cards that contain symmetrical inkblots and asked to tell the examiner what they see in the inkblot. Another example of a projective test is the Thematic Apperception Test (Rotter, 1946). Examinees are shown pictures and instructed to tell a story about the picture. These tests originated from psychoanalytic ideas and assume that examinees project their psychic conflicts into their answers. The use of these projective tests often involves specialized training.

Interest Inventories.   **Interest inventories** are an essential tool for career counseling. They are used to help individuals identify their areas of interest and to aid in the process of matching individual preferences to recreational and work contexts. Examples of interest inventories include the Strong Interest Inventory (SII) and Holland's Self-Directed Search (SDS).

Symptom Checklists. **Symptom checklists** measure the presence and intensity of symptoms associated with various problems or disorders. While a diagnosis should not be made solely on endorsed items in a symptom checklist, they are valuable assessment tools. They are also used to monitor the effect of treatment on symptom reduction. Common symptom checklists used in mental health settings to aid in diagnosis and treatment planning include the Beck Depression Inventory, Second Edition (BDI-II) (Beck, Steer, & Brown, 1996); Symptom Checklist-90-Revised (SCL-90-R) (Derogatis, 1990); the Child Behavior Checklist (Achenbach & Rescorla, 2001); and the Connors 3 Rating Scales (Connors, 2008).

Qualities to Consider When Evaluating Tests

Several qualities help professional counselors decide if a test is a useful tool to administer and how much consideration to give to a test score, including accessibility, psychometric acceptability, clinical utility, and appropriateness (Erford, 2013). Other important factors in test selection include the professional counselor's training and the cultural fairness of the selected test.

If a professional counselor wants to know how depressed a client is and gives the client the Beck Depression Inventory–II, it would be important for the professional counselor to know the reliability and validity of scores derived by this inventory. **Validity** refers to how well a test measures what it is intended to measure, and **reliability** refers to the consistency of scores the test provides.

TYPES OF VALIDITY In the classic test theory, score validity is frequently described as three types: content validity, criterion-related validity, and construct validity.

Content Validity. **Content validity** refers to how well test questions represent the domain being tested (Erford, 2013). Have you ever taken a test during one of your courses and been surprised that the test focused on only part of the material you were asked to study (perhaps the material you studied less!) and did not represent all of the material you were asked to study? This test probably had low content validity. Suppose you want to determine if someone was depressed. As part of your assessment, you administer a depression inventory that asks only about sleep, energy, and appetite. How helpful would this inventory be in evaluating depression? Such an inventory would lack content validity because it did not sample the full range of symptoms associated with depression. Poor sleep, lack of appetite, and fatigue are symptoms associated with depression, but other important symptoms, such as sad mood, hopelessness, and helplessness, have been overlooked. Content validity is frequently determined by experts in the content areas covered by the test. In other words, would these experts agree that the subject matter was sampled in a representative way?

Criterion-Related Validity. **Criterion-related validity** refers to the correlation between a test or inventory and another measure (the criterion) that is closely associated with what the test is intended to measure. An intelligence test with an acceptable level of criterion-related validity would be associated with academic achievement, and a test of mechanical aptitude that has an acceptable level of criterion-related validity would be associated with mechanical skill. There are two types of criterion-related validity: concurrent validity and predictive validity. Criterion-related validity is **concurrent** when both measures (i.e., the test and the criterion) are taken at the same point in time. It is **predictive** when the closely associated measure (i.e., the criterion) will be available in the future (Erford, 2013). Do people who are skilled auto mechanics score well on the mechanical aptitude test (concurrent validity)? What is the correlation between GRE scores taken before beginning graduate school and success later in graduate school (predictive validity)?

Construct Validity.   **Construct validity** refers to how effectively a test measures the construct (e.g., intelligence, depression, anxiety) that it is intended to measure. Construct validity is determined by multiple methods, including expert judgment, correlation with other measures of this construct, and scale structure analysis. **Convergent validity** refers to the correlation between a test and other measures of a similar construct. **Divergent validity** is the lack of significant correlation between test scores and measures of constructs that are unrelated to the test construct. A test of spatial ability should have a significant, positive correlation with other measures of spatial relations (convergent validity). The same scores should not be strongly related, however, to measures of verbal reasoning (divergent validity). It is important in test construction to evaluate whether there is a relationship between measures of similar constructs. For the relationship between similar constructs to be meaningful, however, there needs to be an absence of correlation between the test and measures of unrelated concepts (Erford, 2013).

RELIABILITY   Reliability refers to the consistency of testing scores. Test scores cannot be valid unless they are reliable; however, test scores could be reliable and not be valid. The purpose of reliability measures is to determine the degree to which test scores are free from errors that would cause test scores to vary for random reasons. Multiple forms of reliability address the consistency of scores. Reliability can be the correlation between test scores when the test is administered at different times (test-retest reliability), the correlation between scores on two similar versions of a test (alternate forms reliability), and the correlation between items within the test itself (split-half reliability or internal consistency) (Erford, 2013).

Table 12.1 provides a brief summary of these various methods for determining score reliability. Activity 12.4 asks you to apply your understanding of the important concepts in testing by reviewing a test manual of your choice.

TABLE 12.1 Various Types of Reliability

Test-retest (temporal stability)	Correlation between scores on two administrations of the same test within a given time period. This reliability measure would be inappropriate when there is a prediction that scores may change over time.
Parallel forms (alternate forms, equivalent forms)	Alternate forms (e.g., A & B) of a test are administered, and the scores are correlated with each other.
Split-half reliability	A test is divided into two halves in such a way that there is an assumption that each half is similar. The internal consistency of the test is determined by the correlation between the two sets of scores.
Internal consistency (KR-20, coefficient α)	Computer software uses formulas to compute average correlations among items on a scale from a single administration of a test.

ACTIVITY 12.4

In consultation with your course instructor, choose a test that a professional counselor in your area of specialization is likely to use. Review the test and the test manual, and answer the following questions.

1. Who is qualified to give this test?
2. For whom is this test appropriate?
3. Does the test manual detail validity and reliability information? What types of validity and reliability were measured?
4. Under what circumstances would you use this test?

Cultural Fairness

Professional counselors need to consider whether a test is a fair measure to use with a client. Were test norms developed using participants who were representative of the client to be tested? Might language or other barriers affect performance? It is essential for professional counselors to remember that a test may accurately predict differences between majority and minority groups but that these differences may be a result of environmental disadvantage and not innate qualities. Counselors should be familiar with the assessment standards and statements set forth by the Association for Assessment and Research in Counseling (AARC, 2017) regarding fair testing, ethics in assessment, responsibilities of test users, test takers' rights and responsibilities, and standards for multicultural assessment. It is also important that counselors read and abide by the Joint Committee on Testing Practices' Code of Fair Testing Practices in Education (Joint Committee on Testing Practice). This document provides guidelines for test developers and test takers with respect to diversity in four key areas: developing and selecting appropriate tests, administering and scoring tests, reporting and interpreting test results, and informing test takers.

Technology and Testing

The use of computers greatly expands professional counselors' testing resources, and computers may provide significant testing benefits. Using computers to administer tests is advantageous: Computer-administered tests are often cost friendly, may be more efficient in scoring and reporting results than hand methods, often allow for testing accommodations, can be easily revised, can be administered in remote areas around the world, and can be structured to be more interactive (Erford, 2013). However, there are also disadvantages to using computer-based tests. Computer-based tests do not provide observational assessment of test takers, they may not be subject to the same technical rigor, and results are more difficult to keep confidential and secure. It is important that counselors be aware of these advantages and disadvantages before engaging in computer-based testing procedures.

Ethical Considerations

The American Counseling Association (2014a) *Code of Ethics* is based on the underlying principles of autonomy, beneficence, nonmalificence, justice, fidelity, and veracity. When selecting, using, and interpreting tests, it is important to consider the following questions: What does the client want (autonomy)? How will a test or test battery be helpful to a client (beneficence)? How could the testing process be harmful to the client (nonmalificence)? Is the test a fair measurement tool for the client (justice)? Are you working in the client's best interest when you use tests in counseling (fidelity)? Are you responding truthfully to clients, caregivers, and colleagues (veracity)?

In addition to the underlying ethical principles, it is critical that counselors be aware of the American Counseling Association's 2003 Standards for Qualifications for Test Users. This document asserts that test users must have the following: (1) skill and practice in knowledge and theory relevant to the testing context and type of counseling specialty; (2) a thorough understanding of testing theory, techniques of test construction, and test reliability and validity; (3) a working knowledge of sampling techniques, norms, and descriptive, correlational, and predictive statistics; (4) ability to review, select, and administer tests appropriate for clients or students and the context of the counseling practice; (5) skill in administration of tests and interpretation of test scores; (6) knowledge of the impact of diversity on testing accuracy, including age, gender, ethnicity, race, disability, and linguistic differences; and (7) knowledge and skill in the professionally responsible use of assessment and evaluation practice (American Counseling Association, 2003). It is essential that counselors be mindful of these standards in order to ensure ethical use of testing and assessment. To read the full document, go to aarc-counseling.org/resources

Testing Resources

The *Eighteenth Mental Measurement Yearbook* (Carlson, Geisinger, & Jonson, 2014) and *Tests in Print (VIII)* (Murphy, Geisinger, Carlson, & Spies, 2011) are the primary sources of test information (see the website for the Buros Institute in the following list for more information on these volumes). The Internet, publication manuals, assessment texts, and information from experts in the testing field are also important sources of information. The following websites are useful resources for professional counselors involved in testing:

- American Counseling Association: www.counseling.org
- Association for Assessment and Research in Counseling: aarc-counseling.org/
- Fair Access Coalition on Testing: www.fairaccess.org
- Buros Institute of Mental Measurements: www.unl.edu/buros
- American Educational Research Association: www.aera.net
- ERIC Clearinghouse on Assessment and Evaluation: www.ericae.net

Intake Interviews

The counseling interview is a hallmark of the counseling process. The formality and the content of the intake interview are determined by the context in which the interview occurs. Professional school counselors do not typically conduct formal intake interviews, and they are typically not developing diagnostic formulations. However, they do use counseling interviews to gather information about students' problems and concerns, and they use this information to develop appropriate counseling plans. Mental health counselors often conduct formal intake interviews, write and develop diagnostic formulations based on their clinical assessments, and develop intervention plans that direct treatment. The **intake interview** has three prime objectives:

1. Identifying, evaluating, and exploring the client's chief complaint and the associated therapy goals
2. Obtaining data related to the client's interpersonal style, interpersonal skills, and personal history
3. Evaluating the client's current life situation and functioning (Sommers-Flanagan & Sommers-Flanagan, 2009, p. 177)

The intake interview, in conjunction with any other types of gathered information, leads to a diagnosis. Erford's (2013) Appendix I includes a comprehensive intake assessment for clinical use. In clinical mental health settings, the following types of information are typically gathered during the intake interview:

- Identifying information, such as name, date of birth, relationship status, and ethnicity
- Presenting problem (why the person is seeking counseling) and what symptoms are occurring
- Current functioning, including living arrangements; family, social, academic, vocational, and military status; recreational interests; spiritual practices; and resources
- Past history, including physical/medical, family, social, academic, vocational, legal, substance use, and psychiatric history
- Mental status
- Assessment of suicide and exploration of intent to harm others
- Strengths and resources
- Roadblocks to counseling
- Client's goals for coming to counseling

What Is a Mental Status Examination?

A **mental status examination** (MSE) ordinarily is an integral part of the intake interview and is a general assessment of primary mental systems, serving in a similar capacity to how a physician's general medical examination covers the major body physical systems. The mental status section of the clinical intake requires the professional counselor to solicit specific information and make observations about a number of areas of client functioning (Erford, 2013; see Erford's Appendix K for a semistructured MSE). Interestingly, there is no standardized or agreed upon way to conduct an MSE, as some clinicians use brief procedures and others lengthier or more comprehensive procedures. Here is a sampling of the types of mental status categories that counselors and other mental health practitioners might assess.

- *Appearance and Behavior:* What does the professional counselor observe regarding the client's dress, posture, motor activity, and behavior toward the counselor during the meeting?
- *Speech Patterns:* Is it easy to follow the meaning of the client's sentences? Is speech particularly rapid or slow?
- *Thought Process:* What is the content of the client's thoughts (e.g., obsessions)? Does the client's thinking seem disorganized (as represented by speech that is tangential, hard to follow, or lacks meaning)? Does the client report psychotic symptoms, such as delusions or hallucinations?

- *Mood and Affect:* How does the client report his or her emotional state (mood)? What are the counselor's observations of the client's emotional state (affect)? A client may report that he or she has felt sad for some time (mood), and the counselor might notice tears and hunched body posture during the interview (affect); in this case, the client's affect would be appropriate to mood.
- *Intellectual Functioning:* What is the professional counselor's estimate of the client's intellectual functioning? This is based on the counselor's observation of the client's level of comprehension and complexity of thinking and speech.
- *Sensorium:* Is the client oriented to his or her surroundings? Is the client aware of where he or she is, what day it is, who he or she is, and who the counselor is?
- *Judgment:* Does the client seem to make decisions that apparently are helpful rather than harmful to him- or herself?
- *Insight:* Does the client have an understanding of his or her problems and the ways in which these problems interfere with his or her life?
- *Reliability:* Is the client a credible reporter? (Is he or she old enough to relay information in an accurate manner? Is the client psychologically well enough to represent information important for the professional counselor to know?)

What Are the Elements of a Suicide Assessment and an Exploration of Intent to Harm Others?

This section is a brief extension of the comprehensive information in Chapter 7 as it pertains to clinical interviewing. A **suicide assessment**, also an important part of the intake interview, helps to determine if a person is a danger to him- or herself and includes questions intended to gauge the client's level of risk. It is important for professional counselors to know what specific types of questions are useful in assessing suicide risk. These questions center on thoughts of suicide (suicidal ideation), suicidal plans and means, history of attempted suicide, and family history of attempted suicide (Sommers-Flanagan & Sommers-Flanagan, 2009). Additional risk factors of suicide include giving away prized possessions, verbalizing feelings of being trapped, and maintaining a hopeless outlook for the future.

According to a "Suicide Intent Checklist" developed by Lee and Bartlett (2005, p. 865), four critical questions about suicide, when answered in the affirmative, indicate client hospitalization: "1) Does the client express suicidal ideation? 2) Does the client have a plan? 3) Has the client identified a means? and 4) Does the client have access to the means?" Other questions in this checklist that could be used to assess for suicidal risk include a client's use of substances, any prior suicidal attempts, recent losses in the client's life, and/ or evidence of hallucinations and disorganized thought processes.

In addition to asking about suicide, it is also important to ask about thoughts of harming others. This can be done by asking questions specifically related to thoughts about harming others, plans about harming others, history of harming others, and issues with substance abuse and/or impulse control problems. When dealing with a client who indicates a threat to another person, it is important to consult with supervisors, to know the state laws regarding responsibilities to inform the potential target of violence and/or the police, and to consult with legal counsel if indicated.

Many tools attempt to help professional counselors remember important aspects of suicidal assessment. These tools include "IS PATH WARM," developed by the American

Association for Suicidology; "SAD PERSONS," developed by Patterson, Dohn, Bird, and Patterson (1983); and "SAFE-T," developed by the National Suicide Prevention Lifeline. To read about these tools and find more information about suicidal assessment and response, see Chapter 7 and visit www.mcf.gov.bc.ca/suicide_prevention/practical_tools.htm?WT. svl=LeftNav Case Study 12.1 provides a chance to practice assessing for suicidal risk and responding accordingly.

CASE STUDY 12.1

Ralpheo, a 60-year-old man, comes into your office looking dirty and disheveled. He states that he doesn't know why he is living anymore. His wife recently left him, and his children have all moved out of the house and rarely call him. Ralpheo reports that he recently lost his job due to his excessive drinking habits. Currently, he spends his days sitting alone in his apartment, drinking, and watching TV. He says that he has no reason for living and doesn't ever believe that his situation will improve. He recently gave his favorite coin collection away to a neighbor, and he reports having access to a large collection of knives, spending increasing amounts of time sharpening them, and imagining slitting his wrists.

- What questions would you ask to assess Ralpheo's risk?
- What actions would you consider taking to ensure his safety?

Intake interviewing is a difficult counseling skill. Counselors need to balance gathering information and developing a supportive relationship. In some clinical settings, the intake interview is a separate process from the counseling itself and is sometimes done by someone other than the counselor to whom the client will be assigned. Even in these instances, however, helping people feel comfortable and letting them know that someone is listening to their concerns is vital. Learning how to conduct effective intake interviews takes practice. Activity 12.5 gives a chance to practice conducting intake interviews.

ACTIVITY 12.5

Break into groups of three. Rotate among the roles of professional counselor, client, and observer. Each person chooses one of the following scenarios and develops a character based on this role (feel free to create an alternative role if you prefer):

- A 40-year-old married woman comes to counseling because she found out that her husband had an affair. Although the affair is over and the couple continues to live together, she continues to feel sad and angry. She has difficulty sleeping and eating, and does not like to leave the house.
- A 35-year-old man recently was laid off from the brokerage firm he has worked in for the past 8 years. As a result of injuries sustained in a car accident 15 years ago, he has difficulty walking, and he relies on a cane to get around. He reports feeling demoralized by the loss of his job. He also finds himself thinking a lot about the accident, and about the activities he can no longer participate in.

(Continued)

- A 17-year-old high school student was recently arrested for shoplifting. The hearing is pending, and the student is very worried about the consequences. This student does not have a history of legal involvement and is beginning the process of applying to colleges.
- A 15-year-old high school sophomore finds herself attracted to another female. She has been bullied much of her school life and does not imagine it will ever get any better. She comes to counseling expressing suicidal ideation with a vague suicidal plan.

Practice conducting an intake interview (40 minutes per interview). Use the intake format provided in the previous section to guide your questions. Each person takes a turn being the professional counselor, the client, and the observer. Discuss what each experience is like. Give each other feedback on your interviewing techniques. Were you able to gather information while also developing rapport and demonstrating listening skills? If you struggled with this exercise, remember that you will have a lot of instruction and practice in interviewing throughout your program.

Behavioral Observation

Behavioral observations can provide important information not readily available through interviewing or testing. **Behavioral observations** are done in a natural setting in which the client is experiencing the difficulties that precipitated counseling. The purpose of the behavioral observation is to note the frequency of behaviors that are the focus of concern, to notice what precedes these behaviors, and to identify what consequences follow these behaviors (Barlow & Durand, 2014). A professional school counselor might be asked to observe a student with disruptive behavior in the student's classroom. The counselor would want to have a clear understanding of the behaviors that are of concern (target behaviors). The counselor would then observe what behaviors of the child, the teacher, and other classmates directly preceded the target behaviors (i.e., antecedent behaviors), and how the student, teacher, and classmates responded to the target behaviors (i.e., consequences). This type of observation helps the counselor identify the chain of events that leads to the target behaviors and understand how these behaviors might be reinforced in the classroom. When the chain of events is understood, the counselor can consult with the teacher and the student to interrupt the chain of events that leads to unwanted behaviors and eliminate reinforcement for these behaviors.

While mental health counselors may not always have opportunities to directly observe their clients outside the counseling session, they can document their clients' behaviors and use this to establish goals. For example, if a client has difficulty controlling his or her binge eating, the counselor might ask the client to record what was happening immediately before the binge eating (i.e., antecedents) and then record what happened immediately after the behavior (i.e., consequences). This type of behavioral analysis might encourage clients to become observant of their own behaviors; they could use this new awareness to promote change.

Environmental Assessment

An **environmental assessment** involves a holistic evaluation of the client within his or her environment, focusing on how the environment affects the client, family, or group, rather than on the client as "the problem." Physical space, organization and supervision of space, materials, peer environment, organization and scheduling, safety, and responsiveness are important environmental factors to consider. Personality; learning, parenting, and teaching styles; school, work, and home environments; and group relationship characteristics are the prospective dimensions of an environmental assessment. The procedures used for these assessments include observation, diagrams, checklists, and rating scales. Environmental dimensions chosen for evaluation and how these dimensions are evaluated depend on the referral or presenting concern. Now read Voices from the Field 12.1 to deepen your understanding of the importance of environmental and contextual factors in assessment.

VOICES FROM THE FIELD 12.1 Considering Client Contextual Factors in Assessment, by Amanda C. Healey

---

After I completed my master's degree in marriage and family counseling, I started working with children and adolescents in foster care. We did a variety of assessments throughout clients' time with us to track their progress as we worked toward reunifying them with family members (when possible). One of the most difficult things about conducting the assessments was finding times when the clients could usefully engage in the process. The children and adolescents placed in care were under a lot of stress. They were separated from their families, from the life they knew. They had experienced a variety of traumatic events, the results of which they dealt with emotionally on a daily basis. Therefore, it became very important for everyone involved in the care of these clients to understand how environment and context influenced assessment. The need for this type of consideration was highlighted for me on one specific occasion during which one of my clients was placed into a group home for long-term care.

My client did not want to be in this group home (for good reason) and many of us involved in the client's treatment did not agree with the placement; therefore, the controversy of the decision led to further distress. During the first 3 days on campus the client was administered a battery of inventories and assessments to gauge emotional state, symptomology, achievement levels, and intelligence. I remember distinctly a situation in which a supervisor, after reading the subsequent report, stated that she felt this client "couldn't be helped" because the client's resulting IQ score was a 96. A previous report 2 years earlier had concluded that the client had an IQ of 138. Now, I had a lot of problems with this supervisor's statement. First, IQ doesn't mean a client is untreatable. Second, short of head trauma, a 40-point drop in IQ should signify that perhaps the testing conditions were not optimal to gauge intellectual potential. The picture painted by the other assessments attested to this possibility. She was ready to write this client off based on the value she put into one test score and, unfortunately, in my experience during my time as a clinician, this mistaken perspective was not uncommon. This situation taught me how essential it is for client advocacy to understand all of the factors that influence assessment. Having the baseline knowledge necessary to understand how to interpret and use assessments in treatment is critical to client empowerment and successful outcomes.

Developmental Considerations

During the assessment process, it is important that professional counselors consider the role of development as it relates to the client's issues. Attention should be paid to stages of development, developmental tasks that are being negotiated, and perceptions of normal development in the client's culture. For example, difficulty separating from parents when entering school is normal for a 6-year-old child; however, it is of more concern when these same behaviors are observed in a 16-year-old adolescent. You are encouraged to reread the chapter on human development through the life span (see Chapter 10) and apply this knowledge to your understanding of assessment, diagnosis, and treatment planning.

Assessment is an important counseling task. The professional counselor, keeping an overall plan in mind, collects and reviews information to address the concerns of the client while developing a supportive relationship. The types of information the counselor requests depend on the client, the client's developmental stage in life, the presenting concern, the context in which counseling occurs, and the skills of the counselor.

Overall, *assessment* is a broad term covering many areas and methods such as tests, intake interviews (including mental status exams and suicide assessments), and behavioral and environmental observations. The effective use of appropriate assessment strategies allows professional counselors to develop useful case conceptualizations, diagnoses, and treatment plans, to which we now turn our attention. But first, complete Case Study 12.2 Then read Voices from the Field 12.2.

CASE STUDY 12.2

Eric is a 10-year-old boy who is brought to your center by his maternal grandmother, who is currently Eric's legal guardian. She is concerned about Eric's recent irritability and increased difficulties in school. Eric came to live with his grandmother last year after his parents divorced, and his father moved out of state. Eric's mother felt unable to care for Eric and asked the grandmother to do so. Eric has a younger sister who remains in his mother's care. Eric has always had difficulty in school. He is very active, not particularly interested in classroom work, and often gets into trouble for being inattentive or disrupting the class. He loves skateboarding and is quite good at it. He also makes friends easily and, despite his often impulsive behavior, he is well liked by the other children. More recently, though, he has gotten into several fights, an unusual behavior for Eric, and he is no longer interested in skateboarding.

1. List the methods of assessment you would recommend and why you would recommend them.
2. What skills would the professional counselor need?
3. How does client development affect assessment?
4. How could the identified assessment methods be used effectively and ethically?

VOICES FROM THE FIELD 12.2   A Case of Mistaken Identity, by Meghan Brown

During my first 2 years as a clinical counselor, I worked as a counselor in an adolescent, residential, drug and alcohol treatment center. Many of our clients were referred for residential treatment through the juvenile court system. As a result of this referral relationship, I would often go to juvenile detention centers throughout our state to assess young men for admission into the program. These assessments, as well as the travel associated with them, took up nearly 30% of my time in the field. Due to the need to meet with as many clients as possible, and to be a productive counselor, I would try to do as many assessments as I possibly could fit into one trip to each center.

I got into the habit of scheduling anywhere from two to five assessments in each trip to a specific detention center. Because the clients were in detention, there was little chance of a "no show." I carried on this practice for about 3 months before I realized, for several reasons, that this was not in the best interest of the clients or my clinical skill development.

I developed a good rapport with the staff at the detention centers and they would take my list of clients the moment I walked in the door. I would wait patiently while they lined my clients up in holding cells and, one by one, I brought the clients into the "interview room," which was merely another holding cell, *sans* writing on the wall and the concrete blocks for a seat. In meeting with the clients, I would note that I received permission from their parents to meet with them, provide informed consent, and discuss my role as a counselor and what it meant for them to participate in the assessment. Usually the client would be either very agreeable or totally refuse to participate. In the latter instances, I would do all that I could to engage the recalcitrant client in the assessment, and if that did not work, I would let them know that it is their right to refuse and allow them to leave.

One day, I was meeting with the fifth young man in the line of potential clients. I had been in the "interview room" for more than four hours at this point and was certainly ready to call it a day. However, I put my best counselor face on and attempted to engage the young man in the assessment. He repeatedly and adamantly denied that he had a drug problem, but felt that he would get in trouble if the judge heard he refused the assessment. I tried to explain to the young man that he was under no obligation to engage, but that I was here to help and would be happy to do so if he was okay with meeting. He continued to note that he never used a drug in his life. After approximately 45 minutes of meeting, I felt that there was something very genuine about this client's insistence that he did not have a drug problem and that he did not need treatment for drug use. I asked the client his name and birth date again, to which he replied with what I had on paper. I then noted that his mom and dad, who I identified by name, agreed that he had a problem with alcohol and other drugs. The client then stated, "Those aren't my parents." I realized in that moment that I had never noted his parent's names when I covered informed consent with him and that the juvenile detention staff had brought me a client with the right name and the right birth date, but didn't take notice that there were two clients with the same name and birth date in detention. I immediately apologized to the young man, who was very relieved at the mix-up. I was very embarrassed. The response of the juvenile staff was, "That's not the first time this has happened." I chose to not assess the actual client and rescheduled him for another trip. Before leaving, I asked the juvenile staff to have the parents of the client I erroneously assessed call me at my office as soon as possible.

Upon returning to my workplace, I immediately informed my supervisor of this event. I then spoke with the parents of the young man that I had actually attempted to assess and did as much "damage control" as possible. Though this "event" turned out all right in the end, I could not help but notice how complacent I had become in the practice of assessments so early on in my career.

As a result of this incident, I took a step back and evaluated my clinical practice. I was given the independence to establish a method of doing assessments in a way that would "get the job done." Unfortunately, I lost the view that our clients are people who deserve to not be lined up like cattle so that I can be more productive. In trying to be as productive as possible, I lost sight of all the factors needing to be done to confirm a client's identity when they are incarcerated (e.g., birth date, full name, names of parents/guardians). Though I was able to concentrate on assessing the client's appropriate level of care, I unnecessarily exposed a young man to counseling interventions aimed at helping him to gain insight into a drug problem he never actually had. I now use this incident as a teaching tool with students/supervisees and as a reminder to myself to never, ever become more focused on my needs or the needs of my agency before those of the client sitting in front of me.

CASE CONCEPTUALIZATION

Case conceptualization refers to the way that professional counselors make meaning out of the information they have gathered, how the client's presenting concerns are embedded in some theoretical and practical context. The case conceptualization integrates the information gathered during the assessment with counseling and developmental theory, as well as diversity and social justice issues, and leads to a diagnosis and effective treatment planning.

Formulating a case conceptualization involves organizing the information gathered in the assessment phase in a meaningful way to identify: (1) the client's major concerns, (2) the reason that the client is experiencing these concerns at this time, (3) the dynamics that work to maintain the problem, (4) the resources the client can draw on to address the concerns, (5) the desired counseling outcomes, and (6) the strategies that are likely to be most effective. In essence, the case conceptualization forms a bridge between assessment and treatment planning. A useful case conceptualization includes attention to counseling theories, developmental theories, cultural considerations, and the client's level of motivation.

Professional counselors typically conceptualize cases through their own theoretical orientation (Sommers-Flanagan & Sommers-Flanagan, 2009). Theories provide views of what promotes emotional well-being, distress, and change. Cognitive theories focus on how clients think and make meaning out of situations, humanistic theories focus on core conditions needed for growth, psychodynamic theories focus on past experience and unconscious dynamics, behavioral theories focus on learning and actions, and systems theories focus on the interrelationships between or among people. Developmental theories focus on the process of growth and development over the life span—including specific developmental tasks. These life tasks and the client's ability to navigate these tasks effectively need to be accounted for in case conceptualization.

Multicultural considerations and attention to social justice are vital to case conceptualization. Professional counselors need to consider how intersections of race, ethnicity, religious beliefs, socioeconomic status, family structure, trauma, and sexual and gender orientation relate to clients' presenting concerns and affect subsequent interventions.

As mentioned in Chapter 4, clients come to counseling with varying levels of motivation to engage in the counseling process. Norcross, Krebs, and Prochaska (2011) reviewed the Stages of Change (part of the transtheoretical model). An understanding of these stages can be helpful when trying to develop a case conceptualization and ultimately a treatment plan. According to this model, there are five stages of readiness for change: (1) precontemplation, (2) contemplation, (3) preparation, (4) action, and (5) maintenance. As a review, sometimes clients come to counseling because other people say they need to make a change, but they do not intend to change, or they lack awareness that a problem exists. This is the **precontemplation stage**. Clients who are aware that a problem exists and have begun thinking about the benefits of change are in the **contemplation stage**. However, clients in this stage are not yet committed to make a change. Once clients have made a commitment to change in the very near future and have begun making minor behavioral changes, they are in the **preparation stage**. Clients who are in the process of practicing the desired changes are in the **action stage**. Norcross et al. (2011) state that individuals in the action stage have successfully altered their behavior for 1 to 6 months. After 6 months of maintaining behavioral change successfully, clients are said to be in the **maintenance stage**. At this time, clients work to integrate new behaviors into their lives and at the same time prevent relapse. Professional counselors need to evaluate a client's readiness for change and integrate this information into their case conceptualizations and treatment plans. Successful counselors use counseling strategies consistent with the client's readiness for change. At lower levels of motivation, counseling strategies that focus on consciousness raising and exploring the pros and cons of changing are recommended. Clients with higher levels of motivation are more likely to benefit from counseling strategies that are more action-oriented.

Consider the following example. Ted, a first-year college student, comes to counseling concerned about his level of alcohol consumption. He was recently cited for having beer in his room and is awaiting disciplinary procedures. He is aware that there is a problem but is ambivalent about whether he wants to reduce his level of drinking. Ted is in the contemplation stage of this model. This means that he will likely benefit from opportunities to consider the pros and cons of his drinking behaviors and to explore what it would mean to him to reduce his drinking.

Once Ted has determined that he stands to benefit from reducing his drinking and has made some effort to do so, he has moved into the preparation for change stage. At this stage, Ted will likely benefit from counseling strategies that help him develop and monitor a plan to reduce drinking, identify substitute activities for drinking, and create a social network that encourages and supports his desire to reduce his drinking.

Overall, a case conceptualization integrates client information into meaningful themes that take into account development, culture, and motivation and helps counselors decide on appropriate counseling interventions informed by the professional counselor's theoretical perspective. Case Study 12.3 provides practice in applying concepts in case conceptualization.

CASE STUDY 12.3

Maria is a first-year college student. She has always been a good student and describes herself as "always trying to do the right thing." She comes from a Latino family reported to be quite conservative in their views. She reports that she and her parents are close, but that when Maria does something that they disapprove of, the consequences are harsh and have ranged from being spanked as a child to long periods of grounding in adolescence. Maria finds herself attracted to another young woman on campus. She is terrified that she may be a lesbian, and that, if this is true, she will disgrace her family. Maria comes to the counseling center reporting disrupted sleep, constant worry about her sexual orientation, and excessive exercising to distract herself from her concerns. She reports that she has been crying daily for the past month, is tired most of the time, and has experienced some suicidal thoughts. Maria reports that it is helpful to know that she can come and talk to her professional counselor about anything and not be judged. She is not interested in talking with her parents at this point regarding her current romantic interest or about her distress over instances when she felt judged by them.

A. A case conceptualization should integrate the information that is gathered into categories.
- What do you know about Maria's relationship to her family?
- What do you know about her academic achievement?
- What do you know about her symptoms?
- What do you know about her social relationships?
- What do you know of Maria's cultural background?

(Continued)

B. From the above categories of information, the professional counselor can look at patterns and themes.
- Do you see any patterns or themes emerging from the information?
- How does approval of Maria's family (as perceived by Maria) influence her thoughts, feelings, and behavior?
- What are some developmental issues you would expect given her age and life stage?

C. Counseling theories address human nature, causes of emotional distress and well-being, and promotion of change. Bridging theory and case conceptualization requires professional counselors to apply these theoretical dimensions to the case at hand.
- Consider Maria's case from a client-centered perspective; apply this model's ideas of human nature (self-actualizing), emotional distress and well-being (congruence of self and ideal self, conditions or worth), and what promotes change (unconditional positive regard, genuineness, and empathy) to Maria's case.
- Apply a cognitive or behavioral model of your choice to Maria's case.
- Apply other counseling theories or models of your choice.
- In Maria's case, what words would you attach to the symptoms she reports, and how are these symptoms affecting her ability to perform her expected tasks?

D. It is important to consider issues of culture, diversity, and social justice.
- What issues need to be considered in this case?

E. Evaluating motivation is an important step.
- Is Maria motivated to engage in counseling?
- What do you think Maria would like to get out of counseling?
- What is Maria motivated to do at this time?
- What types of strategies would help her attain her goals?
- What model or models of counseling are most consistent with these strategies?

A case conceptualization is your best interpretation of the client's presenting concerns based on the information you have. Professional counselors need to be prepared to adjust their case conceptualizations when new information demands a change in perspective. Excellent supervisors help developing counselors master the case conceptualization process (see Chapter 13) and emphasize the flexible use of diverse theoretical frameworks. In addition, counselors often are expected to give clear and efficient case conceptualizations at staff meetings in agencies with a balance of breadth and depth in order to facilitate an interdisciplinary treatment approach. Voices from the Field 12.3 offers a perspective on case management and assessment.

VOICES FROM THE FIELD 12.3   Case Management and Assessment in the Schools, by Bella Bikowsky and Christopher Sink

---

Over the past several years serving as a high school counselor, case management and related assessment duties are some of my most time-consuming and challenging responsibilities. Key to these roles is my ability to understand and implement effective strategies and techniques based on the needs of my student caseload, including their developmental levels, and the teachers' needs and concerns. In addition, I must support the students' families in these roles as well as ethically consult with the various staff and faculty in the building (e.g., school psychologist, nurse, special education) and external resources (e.g., mental health therapist).

More specifically, there are many aspects to a high school counselor's job connected to assessment and case conceptualization processes that are complicated and require excellent interpersonal skills. For example, as indicated above, there are many different individuals that I interact with on a daily basis, each often with his or her agenda. When there is a request or concern from a teacher, building administrator, or caregiver over a student's behavior, academic achievement, social development, or emotional well-being, I am generally the first person called for support. Thus it is vital for me to respond proactively in order to meet the needs of all parties involved, while respecting the process at the same time. The following experience illustrates how I work with the high school students and their significant others through the steps of case conceptualization, management, and appraisal

Lucy was a 14-year-old young woman who had previously attended a private K–8 school and recently transitioned to the ninth grade at a parochial high school. At the private school, Lucy had the same teacher for grades 6 to 8 and moved with the same small cohort of fellow students. Upon starting her freshman year, Lucy was finding the transition to the new high school quite difficult. There was a great deal to take in and process. For instance, Lucy now was attending much larger classes, in a much larger school with approximately 1,500 students, grades 9 through 12. Even with the care and support of a community-based psychiatrist, Lucy still had to manage her notable level of anxiety in a "scary" school. Moreover, Lucy had taken the Independent School Entrance Exam as part of the transfer process from private to parochial school. Lucy's transition to the new school did not go well. Lucy's parents had concerns about her anxiety, cognitive abilities, and self-confidence. They came to me requesting that a 504 plan be established for their daughter.

I knew in my mind that this case was going to require some significant work. I would not only be writing a 504 plan for Lucy's academic needs, but I would need to carefully and sensitively address Lucy's social-emotional needs as well. Lucy self-reported that she didn't want to "look like a freak" if she was given some extra support. In an effort to respect Lucy's parents' concerns, as well as remain sensitive to Lucy's apprehensions, I cautiously began the assessment process. In the summer leading up to the ninth grade, Lucy had completed a battery of assessments with an outside psychologist. Based on the eight norm-referenced assessments administered, it was noted that Lucy's profile indicated average overall cognitive and academic abilities, with some relative challenges in the sub-dimensions of speed of processing complex information, particularly for nonverbal, visual-motor, and spatial processing tasks. Lucy also had some difficulty on the math and writing fluency areas of the assessment, although her performance was still in the average range. The most remarkable issue arising from the assessment process was her self-reported and observed anxiety. From a counselor's stance, I knew that this was an area I needed to advocate for and address with Lucy, particularly if she was to have a successful year. Reviewing this information and deciding what findings were the most pertinent to share with the staff was my first step.

Now that I had a good idea of the academic and psychosocial support that Lucy was going to need, I could move to more "hands on" assessments and pre-intervention planning (e.g., interviews, observations, behavior planning). I was able to interview both of Lucy's parents, who identified several of Lucy's strengths. Taking a strengths-based approach was a starting point to help positively structure Lucy's day. I also talked with Lucy to obtain a better sense of how she was feeling. She identified very well with scaling questions, rating her anxiety level on a 1- to 10-point scale for different activities that happen through her day. From her responses, I was able to gauge where her anxiety was heightened most at school. In the meantime, I was able to consult with several of her middle school teachers as well as all of her new high school teachers to get an idea

(Continued)

of their experiences with her. I was also able to observe Lucy in a few of the classes that she had rated as a seven or higher on the anxiety scale. This entire assessment process required about a week and a half of my time. Following this data-collecting phase, Lucy's 504 team (Lucy, counselor, teachers, parents, outside support) was able to meet and provide a comprehensive plan that included the following elements. Lucy would:

- stay after school to get extra math help several days a week when she felt that she was falling behind.
- have extended time on tests, including standardized tests.
- continue with outside individual counseling that focused on cognitive-behavioral therapy for her diagnosed anxiety disorder.
- carry a small laminated ticket in her backpack. When her anxiety level was at a seven or higher, she would take the ticket out, put it on the corner of her desk, and she would then be free to go to the counseling office. This was a safe place for her to practice the strategies and techniques that she had identified as helpful from her cognitive-behavioral therapy groups.
- meet weekly with the school counselor for a regular check-in to see how things were going and to fill out an overall anxiety rating form. From this, the counselor would keep an Excel spreadsheet to track the data and Lucy's progress. This was helpful in assessing if there were certain areas that needed more focus. If so, we were able to re-evaluate, re-strategize, and implement different interventions.
- continue to practice self-advocacy if her needs were not being met.
- consistently check the school's online class webpage in an effort to closely monitor assignments, tests, etc. Her parents would also check on the online materials.

Finally, Lucy's outside mental health counselor and school counselor were in weekly contact via e-mail about the different strategies that were being practiced outside school in an effort to replicate those strategies when Lucy needed the support.

DIAGNOSIS

Diagnosis is the identification of a disease, disorder, problem, or syndrome based on some form of systematic assessment. The word *diagnosis* can be used more generally as counselors in nonclinical settings (i.e., school counselors) attempt to identify issues. In the counseling field, however, the word *diagnosis* is usually known for identifying disorders of clinical significance (e.g., post-traumatic stress disorder, major depressive disorder) as published in diagnostic systems manuals. The two common diagnostic systems that professional counselors encounter in the United States are the DSM-5 (American Psychiatric Association, 2013) and the *International Classification of Diseases, Tenth Revision, with Clinical Modification* (ICD-10 CM; World Health Organization, 2016). The *International Statistical Classification of Diseases, Eleventh Edition* (ICD-11; World Health Organization, 2017) is used internationally.

The DSM-5 is typically used in clinical mental health settings and is the manual most professional counselors encounter and use. This manual is essentially a long list of diagnoses classified and organized by their presenting symptoms. (In other words, diagnoses with symptoms of anxiety are grouped together.) The ICD-10 CM and ICD-11 are typically used more frequently in international medical settings. The DSM-5 co-lists psychiatric diagnoses with ICD codes. States regulate who can make a clinical diagnosis, and licensed professional counselors are allowed to provide diagnostic assessments in most states.

Whether licensed or not, it is necessary for professional counselors to be familiar with DSM diagnostic codes and to consider the implications of a client's diagnosis during the counseling process. Accurate diagnosis is important to treatment planning.

To qualify as a clinical disorder a person must exhibit the type and number of symptoms required to meet diagnostic criteria for the syndrome under question. The symptoms must be present for a designated time period, and they must cause a significant level of psychological distress and/or interfere with the client's ability to function effectively. The following are some examples of disorders and problems: anxiety disorders, mood disorders, psychotic disorders (e.g., schizophrenia), substance use disorders, and impulse control disorders. **Personality disorders** refer to long-standing patterns of relational and functional impairment. Examples of personality disorders include borderline, antisocial, and narcissistic.

A diagnosis is not synonymous with a mental disorder. **V codes** are used for problems that are the focus of treatment but are not a mental disorder. These V codes help inform the focus of treatment, but they do not, in and of themselves, meet the criteria for a mental illness. A client may come into counseling because of conflict with a partner. The client is upset, but not more than would be expected given the reported relational distress. The client is not having difficulty with work, school, self-care, or other expected tasks. This person would be diagnosed with a V code: V61.10 Relationship Distress with Spouse or Intimate Partner.

The DSM-5 also includes an appendix of cultural formulation explaining aspects of culture to consider in formulating diagnoses, including the client's cultural identity, the cultural explanation of the client's symptoms, cultural factors related to the psychosocial stress a client experiences, the cultures of the client and the clinician, and the culture's influence on case conceptualization and treatment planning. Case Study 12.4 outlines a DSM-5 diagnostic formulation.

CASE STUDY 12.4

DSM Diagnosis

Anya comes to counseling because she has been experiencing episodes of intense anxiety that come over her "out of the blue." During these times, she feels like she is "going crazy," and experiences heart palpitations. The episodes last about 2 hours and have been occurring for the past 2 months. Anya reports being constantly worried about when the next attack might occur. Anya is a first-year college student from India and is studying biology. She has always been a good student, but she is finding it difficult to keep up with her coursework. In addition to her classes, she works 20 hours per week in a local restaurant. Anya continues to work and go to classes, but she reports that keeping up with these activities is becoming harder and harder. Anya reports that she has always been a bit "high-strung," but she has never experienced anything like these episodes.

She denies any history of other emotional problems and reports being physically healthy. She denies any substance abuse. Anya's parents recently divorced, and Anya has been worried about both of them and is trying to stay in frequent contact with them. She is worried about the financial implications of the divorce, and she is sad over the way her family life has changed. Anya's DSM-5 diagnosis might look like this: 300.01 (F41.0) Panic disorder without agoraphobia (F41.0 is the ICD-10-CM code).

Regardless of the concerns about diagnosis and specific concerns about the DSM-5 (American Psychiatric Association, 2013), it is important that counselors become aware of diagnostic processes and procedures. The scenarios presented in Activity 12.6 will help you explore the importance of diagnosis to counseling.

ACTIVITY 12.6

In small groups, discuss why considering a diagnosis might be important in the following scenarios:

- You are a professional counselor assigned to work with a fourth-grade boy. He has great difficulty completing his work and is falling behind academically. He is unable to complete his written work perfectly and ends up tearing up all of his attempts. He has become more irritable in the past few months and cries easily.
- You are a career counselor working with a second-year female college student. She was recently hospitalized for an episode during which she did not sleep for many days, had sex with men indiscriminately without using any form of protection, and got in a serious car accident attributed to her reckless driving. She reports that she has a history of severe depression, but that this is the first time she has experienced this type of mania.

Social Justice Counseling and Assessment, Diagnosis, and Treatment

Historically, the counseling profession has been ambivalent about the use of diagnosis. The humanistic roots of counseling, with its emphasis on development and growth, can seem inconsistent with the use of diagnostic labels. However, with the advent of licensure for mental health counselors and the workplace requirement for developing DSM diagnostic formulations, diagnosis is now accepted as an important knowledge base for counselors.

Professional counselors need to be diligent regarding the use of diagnosis. It is an ethical requirement that counselors are competent to make accurate diagnostic formulations (American Counseling Association, 2014a). Professional counselors also need to be sensitive to multicultural and social justice issues and ensure that the process of diagnosing does not label issues of difference and the normal reactions to social oppression as pathology. The concept of normality is a cultural construction, and what is considered pathological in one culture may be seen as normal in another. In 1851, a southern physician, Samuel Cartwright, tried to promote a new disease, drapetomania, characterized by a slave's desire to run away (Bynum, 2000). Until 1973, homosexuality was a diagnosable DSM mental illness (Rubinstein, 1995). Counselors often have mixed reactions to the use of diagnosis and must use assessment, diagnosis and treatment of clients to promote social justice ideals, rather than marginalize and oppress clients, which historically has been a professional concern (Hays & Erford, 2018). The cases presented in Case Studies 12.5 and 12.6 give you practice in thinking diagnostically.

CASE STUDY 12.5

Chao is a 25-year-old single man who comes to counseling at the request of his mother. Chao is currently unemployed and has no history of successful sustained employment. He periodically picks up short-term jobs for some money to spend. He was an average student in high school and has taken some college courses, although he has not identified an area of major interest. He has no close social relationships and seems to be satisfied spending most of his time alone playing computer games. He is not sure why he was referred for counseling. He reports no distress and says that he is quite comfortable with his current life. He has no current reported medical conditions.

- What do you think should be the focus of counseling? Explain.
- Is there evidence of long-standing interpersonal dysfunction? Explain.
- Is there a reported medical condition that is relevant to the presenting concern? Explain.
- What psychosocial/environmental stressors are important in understanding the concerns? Explain.
- What levels of symptom distress and functional impairments are reported? Explain.
- What cultural implications may need to be considered? Explain.
- How helpful do you think counseling would be?

CASE STUDY 12.6

Raven is a 16-year-old high school junior who is referred by her parents. Raven reports that she has been very sad since her boyfriend of 6 months ended their dating relationship. She notes that she cries every day, is not interested in her usual activities, is not sleeping well, and cannot stop wondering what she "did wrong." She has always been a good student and to date has been able to keep up with her schoolwork, but she reports that it is getting too hard to "keep it together during school." She has stopped spending time with her friends and spends most of her time after school in her bedroom.

- What do you think should be the focus of counseling? Explain.
- Is there evidence of long-standing interpersonal dysfunction? Explain.
- Is there a reported medical condition that is relevant to the presenting concern? Explain.
- What psychosocial/environmental stressors are important in understanding the concerns? Explain.
- What levels of symptom distress and functional impairments are reported? Explain.
- What cultural implications may need to be considered? Explain.
- How helpful do you think counseling would be?

Benefits of Diagnosis

Both benefits and drawbacks are associated with diagnosis. The benefits of diagnosis include the provision of a common language for professionals and clients to describe disorders or problems, a framework that aids in treatment planning and facilitates insurance reimbursement for services, a classification system that facilitates clinical research and helps to determine what treatments are most effective with what types of problems, a framework to help clients understand the problems that they bring to counseling (clients are sometimes relieved to discover a name for the symptoms they have been struggling with), and a classification system that helps clients find support networks with people sharing similar problems (Christensen, 2013).

Drawbacks of Diagnosis

The problems associated with diagnosis include identifying clients by their diagnosis as opposed to focusing on their unique situations and experiences, which can lead to limiting counseling to address only pathology; misdiagnosis; biases that tend to pathologize minority clients; and stigmatization that can impede a client's ability to get disability insurance and may interfere with the possibilities of some types of employment (Seligman & Reichenberg, 2012). David Satcher, former surgeon general of the United States, in his groundbreaking *Mental Health Report* (Satcher, 1996), noted that the public sees a stronger correlation between mental illness and violent behavior now than it did in the 1950s. He also noted that because of the stigma attached to mental illness, most people in need of mental health services did not seek these services.

According to Welfel and Patterson (2005), professional counselors are likely to make three mistakes in the assessment and diagnostic process. The first mistake occurs when the professional counselor attributes problems to psychological or social issues when there may be an underlying medical condition. The second mistake occurs when the professional counselor considers that there is only one diagnosis that fits a client's condition. Professional counselors need to explore all areas in which a client is experiencing difficulty. The third mistake occurs when a professional counselor relates to a diagnosis as if it is an absolute reality. Counseling is a dynamic process, and areas of concern and focus may shift.

Our knowledge about mental illness is continually evolving, and the DSM has benefits and limitations. Regardless of your counseling specialty area, you need to become familiar with the DSM. If you plan to be a licensed professional counselor, you are required to develop the skills necessary to be a competent and ethical diagnostician. It is vital that professional counselors follow ethical practice in the use of diagnosis. Complete Think About It 12.1.

THINK ABOUT IT 12.1

Go to the website for the American Counseling Association (www.counseling.org). Find the 2014 American Counseling Association Code of Ethics. Read the sections relevant to diagnosis. In small groups, discuss the ethical considerations when making diagnoses in counseling. How do you feel about diagnosis as a function of counseling? Consider the potential benefits and disadvantages of diagnosis.

TREATMENT PLANNING

What are you and the client agreeing to work on together? What strategies will you use? How will you know if treatment is working? Treatment planning is an essential part of the counseling process and is designed to answer these questions. Without a treatment plan, the professional counselor and the client lack a roadmap of where they hope to go and how to get there. A good **treatment plan** requires an assessment appropriate to the client's presenting concerns and a case conceptualization that includes an understanding of what the problem is, how it developed, and how to deal with it. Attention should be paid to a client's subjective experience (e.g., feelings, thoughts), behaviors, and the cultural context in which the client lives. The influence of biology on emotional distress needs to be considered and may require consultations with other health care providers. The client's level of motivation needs to be considered. How ready is the client to engage in the change process?

The formality of a treatment plan and the actual form that it takes vary from setting to setting. Professional school counselors help students identify the ways in which the student would like to change, determine with the student the goals of their work together, and identify activities that might help meet these goals. Professional school counselors may not, however, formally detail this in a written treatment plan. A counselor working in a community mental health center typically needs to develop a written document that is signed by the counselor and the client. This document needs to be periodically reviewed and revised. Regardless of setting, it is important that goals are identified and mutually agreed upon, and the strategies to reach these goals are identified. A counselor should always be able to answer the question, "What are you trying to accomplish?"

Treatment Plans

The format of a treatment plan depends on the setting in which you work. All treatment plans begin with an understanding of the presenting concerns, followed by a goal setting model. For this discussion, a three-tiered system is outlined including goals, objectives, and interventions or strategies.

Goals are broad statements of desired outcome, as follows:

- Viktor will experience positive mood.
- Sophie will be an effective manager of stress.
- Joseph will develop effective social skills.

Objectives are statements of observable or measurable outcome targets, as follows:

- Viktor will report an absence of suicidal ideation.
- Sophie will learn and apply two time management strategies.
- Joseph will engage in two after-school activities at least two days per week.

Interventions are counseling strategies designed to meet the objectives, as follows:

- Viktor will learn skills to tolerate distress effectively.
- Sophie will learn how to use a day planner.
- Joseph will engage in social skills training.

For each counseling goal, objectives are identified to help the client reach the goal. For each objective, interventions are identified to help the client reach the objective. Below is an example of the relationship among a counseling goal, a supporting objective, and interventions targeted to help the client meet the counseling objective. It should be noted that some goals will have multiple objectives, and each objective needs to have interventions: activities that the counselor and client will engage in to meet the objective.

Here is an example goal with objective and interventions:

Goal: Susan will be an effective communicator.

Objective 1: Susan will control angry outbursts.

> *Intervention 1:* Susan will identify situations that trigger anger.
>
> *Intervention 2:* Susan will learn strategies to deescalate when angry.
>
> *Intervention 3:* Susan will participate in assertiveness training.

This system provides a road map of the counseling process. Sometimes the road map seems clear, while at other times it merely provides a basic starting point that is built upon as the case unfolds. Treatment plans should address the major concerns the client brings to counseling; be consistent with the diagnostic formulation; be culturally relevant; and consider interventions that target thoughts, feelings, behaviors, and social relationships, when appropriate. The interventions often reflect the theoretical framework of the counselor. For example, a professional counselor who ascribes to humanistic/existential models may be more inclined to identify interventions that create an environment that facilitates growth, provides opportunities for clients to tell their stories and understand their emotions as related to their stories, and helps clients consider how the personal meaning of their stories enhances or detracts from their sense of well-being. Professional counselors who subscribe to a cognitive theoretical framework are likely to identify counseling interventions that help clients identify cognitive lenses that influence behaviors and emotion. The goal is to help clients become more aware of their thoughts and learn strategies to influence their thinking styles. In this theoretical model, thoughts, behaviors, and emotions are intertwined systems, each influencing the other.

When developing treatment plans, it is essential to consider the client's level of motivation. Sometimes clients are motivated to come to counseling and truly want to feel better, but they may be less committed to some of the behavior changes that would lead to reduced distress. It is important to evaluate not only your clients' desired goals, but also their commitment to the change process. The work of Norcross et al. (2011) helps one to understand a client's readiness to engage in the change process. It is important to match counseling goals, objectives, and interventions to a client's level of readiness for change. Many clients come to counseling not yet ready to engage in actual behavior change. Professional counselors who are able to approach these clients in a supportive, nonjudgmental manner and who have realistic counseling expectations are more successful in developing a therapeutic alliance than counselors who cannot.

It is important that professional counselors be aware of the role that psychopharmacology plays in treatment planning. According to Preston, O'Neal, and Talaga (2013), psychiatrists and physicians are responsible for writing prescriptions for psychotropic medications, while mental health professionals (such as professional counselors) are typically responsible for mental health counseling services. Therefore, it is critical that professional counselors become familiar with the basic tenets of psychopharmacology and how various medications can complement therapeutic approaches. CACREP (2016) includes specialty standards indicating that counselors should understand the basics of psychopharmacological medications to facilitate appropriate referrals and treatment.

There are many different types of medications—each with its own unique pharmacological properties and associated side effects. However, the major classes of medication that professional counselors should be aware of are antidepressant, antipsychotic, anti-anxiety, and bipolar medications. Each of these classes of psychopharmacological treatment is designed to target chemical imbalances in the brain and facilitate recovery on a biological level. Professional counselors are encouraged to research the various medications prescribed to their clients, help their clients manage these medications, and provide therapeutic services that capitalize on the medication's desired effects.

Before developing treatment plans, professional counselors need to consider the role that counseling can play in effectively helping clients deal with the issues they bring. Sometimes another service (e.g., vocational services, legal services, medical services) might be more helpful. In these instances, counseling might play an adjunctive role, but it is important to help clients identify the resources that will be most useful. Clients may bring issues that are beyond the counselor's scope of competence and/or are not offered at the organization in which the counselor is employed. Professional counselors need to evaluate their own areas of competence and what types of services can be delivered effectively in their practice setting. A referral should be made when the client's counseling needs are beyond the professional counselor's scope of competence (i.e., prescribing medications) or when the required services are unavailable at the facility where the professional counselor is practicing. Case Study 12.7 provides an opportunity to practice treatment planning, and Activity 12.7 provides an opportunity for personal reflection.

CASE STUDY 12.7

Jennifer, a 40-year-old mother of three, comes to counseling because she is feeling "blue," tired, and upset with her appearance. Her friends are encouraging her to take more time for herself and perhaps to join an exercise program. She thinks exercise is a good idea, but she does not see how she can fit it into her life because she works 20 hours per week and has many demands with her school-age children. She reports that she feels responsible for child care and housework when she is not at her job. Jennifer thinks that exercise would reduce her fatigue, probably raise her spirits, and help with her concerns about her appearance. She realizes that other issues are involved in her mood and self-dissatisfaction, and that finding the time for exercise will require that she delegate some of her current responsibilities. She worries that it would be selfish to take this time for herself, and she is not sure what kind of support she would get from her husband and children.

- How ready is Jennifer to take time for herself or join an exercise program?
- What kinds of interventions would help Jennifer decide if she wants to begin taking time for herself or join an exercise program?
- What would Jennifer need to be able to do to take time for activities such as joining an exercise program?

After answering these questions write the following:

- A goal (*Hint*: This is a broad statement about desired change.)
- An objective that would support the goal (*Hint*: This is a short-term, measurable, or observable goal, and Jennifer needs to be motivated to achieve this objective.)
- Interventions that would help Jennifer accomplish her objective (*Hint*: Jennifer is not yet ready to take time for herself or to join the exercise program. What strategies would be consistent with helping Jennifer move in this direction?)

ACTIVITY 12.7

Identify some change that you are considering making in your life. Develop a goal (remember, this is a broad aspirational statement). Next, develop an objective aligned with your goal. (What is it that you plan to accomplish in the next few months?) Now identify interventions that will help you achieve that objective. How committed to change do you think you are? What kinds of interventions would be helpful to you (remember, action-based interventions work best when motivation levels are high)? What kinds of interventions would not be helpful to you? To the extent that you are comfortable, share your goal, objective, and interventions in small groups. Discuss why you chose the interventions you did and provide feedback to others regarding the alignment between classmates' level of motivation and the objectives and interventions indicated.

Comprehensive Models of Assessment and Treatment Planning

Two models of assessment and treatment planning helpful to professional counselors are Lazarus's BASIC ID Model (Lazarus & Beutler, 1993) and Seligman's DO A CLIENT MAP model (Seligman, 2004).

BASIC ID   The **BASIC ID** model (Sommers-Flanagan & Sommers-Flanagan, 2009) is an assessment model that looks at multiple client domains: **B**ehavior, **A**ffect, **S**ensation, **I**magery, **C**ognition, **I**nterpersonal, and **D**rugs/biology. The professional counselor evaluates what problems, if any, exist in each of these domains, and treatment objectives are developed from this holistic assessment. Table 12.2 provides an overview of this model. The BASIC ID model can be very helpful in developing a case conceptualization, and it can help the client and professional counselor better understand the ways in which the client's

TABLE 12.2 Using the BASIC ID Model

Behavior	What does the client do that may be problematic (e.g., isolates self in room, gets into physical fights)?
Affect	What distressing feelings is the client experiencing (e.g., sadness, anger, guilt, shame)?
Sensation	What unwanted physical sensations is the client experiencing (e.g., dizziness, tingling in limbs, headache)?
Imagery	What distressing mental pictures, memories, or dreams is the client experiencing (e.g., images of death, past trauma, failure situations)?
Cognition	What difficult thoughts is the client having about self, others, or situation (e.g., "I am worthless," "This is unfair," "I deserve better")?
Interpersonal	What problems does the client have in her or his relationships with others (e.g., estranged from family, few friends, abusive relationship)?
Drugs/biology	What types of substances and what quantity does the client use (e.g., caffeine, medication, illegal drugs, alcohol)? Are there medical/biological issues (e.g., diabetes, thyroid, cancer)?

presenting problems disrupt multiple aspects of the client's life. This approach helps clients and professional counselors determine what areas to focus on, and it informs treatment planning.

DO A CLIENT MAP   The **DO A CLIENT MAP** model (Seligman, 2004) includes assessment, case conceptualization, and treatment planning issues. This comprehensive system ensures that counselors consider a broad range of factors in their counseling interventions and can be quite helpful in developing a treatment plan. Table 12.3 provides a sample of this model. Remember, the format of your treatment plans will vary depending on your area of specialization and where you work. Using the BASIC ID and DO A CLIENT MAP models, as well as developing a three-tiered treatment plan in collaboration with your client, will help ensure that you consider a broad range of variables. It will also help in the development of interventions targeted to the client's wants, needs, and motivation level. Case Study 12.8

TABLE 12.3 Sample Client Map

Diagnosis	What is the DSM diagnosis?
Objectives	What are you and the client hoping to accomplish? Objectives are short-term behavior targets for treatment.
Assessment	What do you know about the client and the problem? What information have you gathered that will be helpful to treatment planning?
Clinician-counselor characteristics that would be helpful to the client's progress	What counselor characteristics would facilitate counseling? These characteristics might include age, gender, or ethnicity.
Location of treatment	What level of treatment setting will be needed for the client to engage safely and effectively in counseling? Locations could include outpatient settings, inpatient settings, or day treatment programs.
Interventions based on the literature	What treatment models are likely to be most effective? The specific interventions would be drawn from these selected models.
Emphasis	Will the emphasis of counseling be on the past, present, or future? Will counseling be supportive, confrontational, or insight-oriented? Will counseling be client-centered or directive?
Number of people in treatment	Who should be involved in the treatment? Will treatment be individual, family, or group (or some combination of these)? This would be determined by the nature of the problem, the client's resources, and the client's desires.
Timing	How frequently and for how long should this client be seen for counseling? Consideration needs to be given to the level of emergency that exists and the client's ability to work on issues outside sessions.
Medication	Should the client be referred to a physician or psychiatrist for medication management?
Adjunct services	What services other than counseling will be helpful for the client to achieve the desired change?
Prognosis	What are the reasonable outcome expectations?

provides practice in applying the DO A CLIENT MAP and the BASIC ID models of assessment and treatment planning.

CASE STUDY 12.8

Benjamin

Benjamin is a 30-year-old single man referred to counseling because of distress he is experiencing after witnessing a fatal car accident. He reports that he is reexperiencing the distressing images associated with the accident, he is feeling very anxious and irritable, he is unable to sleep, and he is experiencing an increased sense that life is not worth living. Benjamin has a history of recurrent depression. He has been treated episodically with a variety of antidepressant medications. At the time of the accident, he was in a period of wellness that had lasted approximately 6 months.

Benjamin works in a local discount retail store. Because of his history of depression, he has an erratic work history, but he has been at this job for 2 years. He is finding it difficult to continue working at this time because of his anxiety, flashbacks, and lack of sleep. He had been dating a woman for 1 year, but this relationship ended just before the accident at his initiation. He has few friends, but he has a supportive immediate family (i.e., parents and an older sister).

Benjamin has a history of substance abuse. He drinks about four nights a week and recently this has escalated to every night. He typically drinks about eight beers per night. He smoked marijuana regularly but was able to give it up 3 years ago. However, he has begun smoking marijuana again on a daily basis since the accident.

He has a history of multiple hospitalizations because of the suicidal ideation that often accompanies his depressive episodes. Currently, he denies any active suicidal ideation and plan, but the idea that "life is not worth living" intrudes on his thinking.

- Using Tables 12.2 and 12.3, apply the BASIC ID and the DO A CLIENT MAP models to Benjamin.
- Develop a case conceptualization and treatment plan using the three-tiered model for this case.
- Discuss your experience of applying the BASIC ID and DO A CLIENT MAP models.
- In what ways did using these specific models facilitate case conceptualization and treatment planning?
- What was difficult?

Summary

This chapter reviewed the major concepts involved in assessment, case conceptualization, diagnosis, and treatment planning. Assessment includes many processes: testing, clinical interviewing, analyzing behavior, and collecting information from collateral sources when indicated.

This process would need to be done with the client's consent and knowledge, and the counselor should consider how this process would benefit or potentially harm the client.

Case conceptualization refers to the meaning counselors make of the information they gather. A case conceptualization includes looking for themes and patterns and applying counseling and developmental theory. Issues of diversity and social justice, and an evaluation of clients' motivation for counseling and for change need to be considered.

Diagnosis refers to the framework used for identifying problems that are the target of intervention. The DSM is the diagnostic system with which most counselors need to be familiar. Whether a professional counselor provides a DSM diagnosis depends on competency, scope of practice as regulated by state law, and practice setting. Understanding the implication of a diagnosis on the client and the counseling relationship is something that all professional counselors ought to consider.

The counseling profession has generally been ambivalent about the use of diagnosis, and professional counselors need to consider the pros and cons of this process. A diagnosis provides a common language for clinicians, a way of talking about and understanding problems for clients, and a direction for treatment. The problems associated with diagnosis include focusing on the diagnosis rather than the person; labeling normal reactions to prejudice and discrimination as pathological; limiting the scope of counseling to address only the problems captured in the diagnosis; and potentially misdiagnosing clients, which can lead to ineffective treatment and possible stigma.

Treatment planning is the process of developing mutually agreeable counseling goals, identifying short-term objectives related to each goal that are observable and measurable, and determining treatment interventions that facilitate accomplishing these objectives. Professional counselors need to be careful not to move into problem solving until it is clear what the client wants to address in counseling, and what type of change the client is hoping for. Effective treatment plans are consistent with the client's desires, consider the objectives and interventions that match the client's level of motivation for change, and are within the counselor's scope of competence.

The practice of counseling requires attention to multiple factors. It is an intentional process that demands counseling skills; knowledge of counseling, developmental theory, and diagnostic frameworks; attention to the requirements of ethical practice; and the desire to engage and collaborate with clients to develop treatment plans that reflect the counseling goals of the client. Becoming a competent counselor requires dedication, but the journey is rewarding.

MyCounselingLab for Introduction to Counseling

Start with the Topic 1 Assignments: *Assessment and Diagnosis* and then try the Topic 16 Assignments: *Substance Abuse*.

13 Supervision and Consultation

MARK A. YOUNG AND ALAN BASHAM

PREVIEW

This chapter examines the important activities of supervision and consultation, both of which enable experienced counselors to expand their constructive influence beyond their own clients. Presented are the models, techniques, types of activities, and important skills used to fulfill the role of supervisor or consultant.

USE OF SUPERVISION AND CONSULTATION IN COUNSELING

Not all counseling activity involves working directly with individual clients or groups of clients. This chapter presents two important additional roles for the professional counselor. Many experienced counselors use their expertise and advanced skills to train new and emerging counselors, assuming responsibility for and clinical authority over their work with clients. This is called supervision. Other accomplished counselors often respond to requests from individuals, groups, and organizations to help solve problems when the resources or knowledge at hand are inadequate. This is called consultation.

Here is an analogy to help you grasp the essential similarities and differences in these two counselor roles. Imagine that you want to backpack into the wilderness to an alpine lake nestled high in a mountain range. You are determined to go, but you have a serious deficit of knowledge and skill for traveling and surviving in the wilderness. Until this adventurous idea struck, your idea of roughing it was a hotel without room service. If you want to become highly skilled at exploring the wild places of nature on your own, you will need an expert in wilderness survival who can supervise your training. This expert *supervisor* will take you through a course of personal growth and skills development until you are capable of safely exploring the mountains alone. This requires that you learn to trust your wilderness training supervisor and assume the open-minded and open-hearted stance of a learner. The supervisor will undoubtedly ask you to clarify your own motives for seeking such training. He or she will probably praise you for getting it right and correct you when you head down the wrong trail. You will be taught to pay attention to yourself, including your strengths and limitations, and to remember the unforgiving demands of the high country. This is necessary, both for your own survival and to ensure that you have a positive, not destructive, effect on the environment. Only when the supervisor believes that you are ready will you be encouraged to explore the wilderness on your own.

Perhaps you want an experienced wilderness guide who will go with you; provide you with gear; help you get to the lake and back; prevent any damage you might inadvertently cause to the environment; perhaps teach you some things about wilderness survival;

and make it possible to have a great trip without getting lost, being eaten, or freezing to death. For this scenario, what you need is a wilderness *consultant* who will help you accomplish this particular trip with her or his guidance. Activity 13.1 helps you explore your relevant talents, abilities, and skills.

ACTIVITY 13.1

Make a list of your talents, abilities, and skills. For example, are you musically talented? Are you an experienced athlete and team player? Do you know how to obedience-train a dog? Be creative in forming your list. Then get together with two or three other students to brainstorm about how your (and their) unique constellation of abilities might be the doorway to effective consultation practice early in your career. For example, if you know how to lead a process group and you understand music, would you be qualified to lead team-building and interpersonal process meetings for an orchestra? Remember, not every counseling consultation is provided for other counselors.

Get the difference? Consider the following definitions of the two terms. **Supervision** is "an intensive, *interpersonally* focused, individual or *group relationship* in which a more experienced *helping professional* is designated to *facilitate* the development of therapeutic competence in less experienced professionals" (Gladding, 2013, p. 150). Corey, Corey, Corey, and Callanan (2014) described supervision as follows:

> [A] process that involves a supervisor overseeing the professional work of a trainee with four major goals: (1) to promote supervisee growth and development, (2) to protect the welfare of the client, (3) to monitor supervisee performance and to serve as a gatekeeper for the profession, and (4) to empower the supervisee to self-supervise and carry out these goals as an independent professional. (p. 366)

In contrast, **consultation** is "a voluntary *relationship* between a professional helper and an individual or *group* that needs help. In such a relationship, the *consultant* provides assistance by *helping* to define and resolve a *problem* or potential problem of the *client*" (Gladding, 2013, p. 38). Dougherty (2014) described consultation as "an indirect process in which a human services professional assists a consultee with a work-related (or caretaking-related) problem with a client system, with the goal of helping both the consultee and the client system in some specified way" (p. 8).

Supervision and consultation are similar in some ways and different in others. The first and most obvious similarity is that both activities rely on the competence and expertise of an advanced professional. Supervisors and consultants are able to create constructive change because of what they know or can do better than others know or do less well. Second, supervision and consultation are triadic in nature (Gladding, 2013). Because counseling involves the interaction between counselor and client (or group of clients), it is dyadic in nature. However, both supervision and consultation involve three participants, including potentially the client system. Dougherty (2014) described the tripartite relationship of consultation as one involving the three parties of the consultant, a consultee, and the consultee's client system. A consultant interacts with the consultee, who then affects his or her staff, clients, or organization. A counseling supervisor is also engaged in activity that affects both the supervisee and the client. One of the major purposes of supervision is to help the counselor become more effective, which also affects the client. Third, supervision and consultation have some ethical considerations in common. For example, supervisors and consultants (similar to professional counselors) should avoid dual relationships, should refrain from practicing outside the limits of their abilities and training, and should seek positive outcomes for supervisees and their clients or for consultees and their clients or client systems.

How are supervision and consultation different from each other? First, supervision tends to be authoritative, whereas consultation tends to be collaborative (Dougherty, 2014). While consultant and consultee can work together as equals to solve problems, supervisors carry a higher level of singular responsibility for what their supervisees do in their interactions with clients (Corey et al., 2014). Supervisees may reject the directions given by a professional supervisor and still maintain the supervisory relationship, but there can be professional consequences for such refusal. However, consultees are free to reject the suggestions of a consultant if they disagree. A second distinction is that supervision is usually imposed by educational, organizational, or credentialing standards, whereas consultation is typically voluntarily sought by the consultee. Third, ongoing performance evaluation is one of the defining attributes of supervision, whereas there is no professional evaluation role implied in consultation because of its collaborative nature (Dougherty, 2014). Fourth, supervision is most often an ongoing relationship between professionals that requires time to develop its full potential, whereas consultation is usually a temporary, task-specific relationship.

Individuals qualified to supervise counselors and counselors in training are themselves in the counseling field. However, individuals in the consultation relationship are often not of the same professional discipline. It is not unusual for educators or business professionals to call on professional counselors for consultation assistance. With this understanding of supervision and consultation as context, the remainder of this chapter describes the important models and techniques of supervision and consultation. Now read Voices from the Field 13.1.

VOICES FROM THE FIELD 13.1   A Consultant's Cunundrum, by Alan Basham

The following events are relevant to both consultation and supervision. A religious leader contacted me seeking assistance to help set up a paraprofessional counseling support group to assist the clergy with the high volume of marriage and family counseling needs in the faith community. The plan proposed by the clergy was to have a professional counselor educator familiar with marriage and family counseling issues and the beliefs of the community train hand-selected members to assist the clergy with counseling skills. This request led to a number of important questions regarding professional and ethical practice. Should I provide beginning training in counseling skills without knowing who, if anyone, would provide ongoing professional supervision? What criteria would be used to select the paraprofessionals who would be trained? Because of the separation of government authority and religious freedom in the United States, to what degree should I expect this program and its leaders to abide by the *ACA Code of Ethics* (2014a) or current state law? Who on site would be responsible for crisis intervention? What happens when best practices in counseling conflict with religious ideology? While I initially perceived this as an excellent opportunity to help, should I contribute to the perception, however unintentionally, that effective counseling can be accomplished by those without adequate, formal, professional training?

SUPERVISION

Supervision is the process by which a helping professional with appropriate training and experience mentors and teaches another individual. It is a process of professional and personal development in which the supervisor challenges, stimulates, and encourages a professional counselor to reach higher levels of competence (Ladany & Bradley, 2011). Bernard and Goodyear (2013) defined **supervision** as follows:

> [A]n intervention provided by a more senior member of a profession to a more junior member or members of that same profession. This relationship is evaluative, extends over time, and has the simultaneous purposes of enhancing the professional functioning of the more junior person(s), monitoring the quality of professional services offered to the client(s) she, he, or they see(s), and serving as a gatekeeper of those who are to enter the particular profession. (p. 6)

Aspects of supervision overlap with consultation in several ways, and for some professionals, supervision often evolves into consultation. Experienced counselors may meet informally with other professionals to discuss ideas about how to work with specific clients or to gain different perspectives, a practice often called **peer supervision**.

Counselor supervision has many purposes, and its focus may change depending on the developmental level of the supervisee. The main purposes of supervision include protecting client welfare, promoting and monitoring the growth of the supervisees initially as a gatekeeper, and empowering the supervisee to self-supervise (Corey et al., 2014). To accomplish the purposes of supervision, the supervisor assumes several different roles, including mentor, advocate, teacher, case consultant, and collaborator, in exploring supervisee countertransference issues. Through each of these roles, the supervisor engages in specific activities, which may include support, interpersonal and intrapersonal exploration of the supervisee, training, instruction, and evaluation.

Supervisors should also pay attention to diversity issues in supervision (Bernard & Goodyear, 2013). As in the counseling relationship, the potential effect of diversity issues on which supervisor and supervisee differ should be explored openly and honestly as part of the learning experience for both. In addition, supervisors should assist supervisees in exploring the diversity issues of the clients being served and the communities in which they live and work. Appropriate topics for consideration include differences in belief systems; communication and learning styles; and cultural, racial, and social justice issues.

The Association for Counselor Education and Supervision (ACES) has worked to establish standards, expectations, and guidelines to be followed regardless of work setting. *Best Practices in Clinical Supervision* (Association for Counselor Education and Supervision, 2011) provides supervisors with directives on how to initiate supervision, set goals, give feedback, conduct supervision, monitor the supervision relationship, address diversity and advocacy considerations, address ethical concerns, and maintain supervision preparedness. Think About It 13.1 helps you explore previous experiences with supervision.

THINK ABOUT IT 13.1

Before beginning discussion of the models, formats, and interventions of supervision, reflect on previous experiences when you have engaged in supervision, either as the supervisor or supervisee. Can you identify the specific purpose of the supervision? What roles did you (as the supervisee) or the supervisor assume? List the qualities of the supervisor that helped in the process. What qualities did you display that helped the process? Were there any unhelpful qualities displayed? What made the experience meaningful or effective?

Models of Supervision

Supervisors employ numerous models, including theory-based models, developmental approaches, and models developed specifically for supervision. A supervision theory or model allows a supervisor to organize, conceptualize, and integrate into practice various pieces of information relevant to the supervision process (Palmer-Olsen, Gold, & Woolley, 2011). Once a model of supervision has been formulated, the supervisor can then attend selectively to those aspects of the supervision that are most important, depending on the specific needs of the supervisee.

THEORY-BASED MODELS   One group of supervision models is based on counseling theories and can best be described as a direct extension of the particular counseling theory. Supervisors who work from a theory-based supervision model engage with supervisees in a manner that is consistent with their counseling philosophy. At least some of the content, focus, and process of supervision is grounded in the supervisor's counseling model.

Examples of theory-based models include psychodynamic, person-centered, cognitive-behavioral, experiential, and systemic supervision. Person-centered supervision assumes that the facilitative conditions (e.g., genuineness, empathy, warmth) necessary for counseling apply to the supervisory relationship as well. A successful person-centered supervisor must have a profound trust that the supervisee has the ability and motivation to grow and to explore the therapy situation and the self. A major goal of person-centered supervision is to help the counselor grow in self-confidence, in self-understanding, and in understanding the therapeutic process (Bernard & Goodyear, 2013).

When the cognitive-behavioral model is used, the purpose of supervision is to teach appropriate counselor behaviors and to extinguish inappropriate behaviors. Training and supervision should also assist the supervisee in developing specific skills and in applying and refining them. In cognitive-behavioral supervision, counseling skills are behaviorally defined, and supervision employs the principles of learning theory within its procedures (Bernard & Goodyear, 2013). New theory-based approaches to supervision are being developed with each new counseling theory, where each approach infuses concepts into the supervision process that are key components of the counseling theory to both encourage professional and clinical development in the supervisee and to model how to use the same skills with clients (Cummings, Ballantyne, & Scallion, 2015).

DEVELOPMENTAL MODELS   Developmental supervision approaches focus on how supervisees change as they gain training and supervised experience. Developmental approaches focus on the development of the supervisee and on how the supervisor might work with the supervisee at different developmental levels. Developmental approaches to supervision are based on the assumption that, in the process of moving toward competence, supervisees move through a series of stages that are qualitatively different from one another. Awareness of developmental stages assists supervisors to develop different supervision strategies for growth based on the supervisee's developmental stage (Stoltenberg & McNeill, 2012).

One of the best-known developmental approaches to supervision is the integrated developmental model (IDM) (Stoltenberg & McNeill, 2010), which focuses on issues supervisees face throughout their development. According to this model, supervisees pass through three levels of development in three main areas during their training: awareness of self and others, motivation, and autonomy. As supervisees deal with each of their issues, they might be at one of the three stages or in transition between stages. In this model, the supervisor's role is to assess each supervisee for each issue and to help the supervisee move to the next stage of development. Apply the supervision models discussed here to the case of Nicole in Case Study 13.1.

CASE STUDY 13.1

Nicole was in her first experience of practicum supervision. During her first session, she was asked to be prepared to show video segments of her counseling sessions during each supervision session. At one of her sessions she told her supervisor that she forgot her video at home and asked to discuss the client without the video. A few sessions later, Nicole again arrived for supervision without a video, stating that the video camera failed to record her sessions.

- What developmental issues may Nicole be dealing with?
- What stage or stages of development is she in?
- If you were Nicole, how would you want the supervisor to address your concerns and help you move to the next stage of development?

INTEGRATIVE MODELS   In addition to theory-based and developmental approaches to supervision, numerous approaches have been developed or modified specifically for supervision. One prominent model is the **discrimination model** (Bernard & Goodyear, 2013), which attends to three separate areas of focus in supervision and assumes three supervisor roles. In the discrimination model, supervisors focus on the following skills of supervisees:

- **Intervention skills**, or what the supervisee is doing in session that is observable by the supervisor.
- **Conceptualization skills**, or how the supervisee understands what is occurring in the session, identifies patterns, or chooses interventions.
- **Personalization skills**, or the supervisee's personal style.

In addition to the three areas of focus, the supervisor chooses one of three roles to accomplish the supervision goals. The roles of the supervisor are as follows:

- *Teacher:* The supervisor teaches specific concepts and techniques and may assign reading to assist the supervisee.
- *Counselor:* The supervisor may help the supervisee focus on personal issues such as discomfort or abilities, and help the supervisee confront personal issues that may affect the counseling sessions.
- *Consultant:* The supervisor may work with the supervisee to identify different interventions, may discuss several models for the supervisee to consider, or may address issues related to specific client populations.

Depending on the chosen role, the supervisor's interactions differ as they work with any of the three focus areas.

Supervisors may employ a theory-based model, a developmental model, or an integrative model that focuses on their social role. Some supervisors may develop an eclectic or integrated approach to supervision (Bernard & Goodyear, 2013). When supervisors develop an integrated approach, they customize their supervision to the needs and differences of the individual or group of supervisees. To explore these differences, see Activity 13.2.

ACTIVITY 13.2

Contact some of the community agencies or schools in your area to learn what supervision they offer to interns and to employees. What models, formats, and interventions do they employ? What type of training did the supervisors receive and how do they build the supervisory working alliance? Ask if all employees receive supervision or how they determine who receives it and how often.

Supervision Formats

Counselor supervision is conducted through many different formats, each presenting benefits and drawbacks. Individual supervision is the most widely used form of supervision and is what most people think of when they think of supervision. Group supervision and triadic supervision are also commonly used formats.

Individual supervision, often considered the cornerstone of professional development, is exactly what the term indicates, an individual supervisee meeting with one supervisor. Although supervisees may experience some form of group or live supervision, almost all will engage in individual supervision during their professional development (Bernard & Goodyear, 2013). Supervisors may employ a variety of models or interventions when working one-on-one with a supervisee. Across models and interventions, supervisors need to adhere to professional standards and create plans that are structured, purposeful, and meet the goals of the supervisee (Borders, 2014).

Session goals are generally anchored to the respective roles of supervisor and supervisee and constructed in a manner that is realistic, measureable, and attainable (Borders, 2014). Session goals also tie into assessments, evaluations, areas for growth, and interventions or techniques as each of these relate to the current clinical work of the supervisee. Supervision goals may also be set according to the model used by the supervisor, which may focus on personal insight or growth of the supervisee, better conceptualization of client concerns, or a review of strengths that have been observed to reinforce what is working and what the supervisee is doing well. During individual supervision, the supervisor may employ specific interventions to aid in the process. Some of those interventions will be discussed in a later section of this chapter.

In many ways, supervision conducted in a group is similar to individual supervision, except that it is conducted in a group format. The supervisor uses many of the skills, models, and professional values that characterize individual supervision. Group supervision complements individual supervision and provides another forum in which to implement the roles, learning objectives, and responsibilities agreed to in the supervisory contract. Many university training programs use group supervision at one point or another during practicum and internship in conjunction with individual supervision. Bernard and Goodyear (2013) defined **group supervision** as follows:

> [A] regular meeting of a group of supervisees with a designated supervisor, for the purpose of furthering their understanding of themselves as clinicians, of the clients with whom they work, or of services delivery in general, and who are aided in this endeavor by their interaction with each other in the context of group process. (p. 111)

Group supervision can be conducted in several different formats, the choice of which may influence the focus and the goals of the supervision sessions. One sort of group in the clinical setting is organized around basic administrative or organizational issues and is often presumed to focus on the agency's needs. This group is often called a staff meeting, or agency-based supervision, and the structure of the group is typically organized around an agenda that communicates information about policies and procedures, service delivery, productivity, coverage, and record keeping (Cohen, 2004).

A second form of group supervision is a training group, which may include didactic seminars centering on specific clinical matters or issue-oriented sessions and tutorials of interest to the staff. In training groups, members may also review cases or other service delivery issues. These meetings are usually set by the group supervisor and are structured in a way that employs educational principles to enhance learning (Borders, 2014).

A third form of group supervision is group clinical supervision, with its major emphasis on facilitating professional growth. Supervisors focus on supervisee development, but they must also understand and manage group process and all the dynamics that can be present in any group format. Group clinical supervision focuses on many of the same issues covered under individual supervision, with the added advantages that can be found only in the group format.

Advantages of group supervision include minimized supervisee dependence; opportunities for vicarious learning; exposure to a broader range of clients; and economies of time, money, and expertise. Group supervision also allows for greater quantity and diversity and possibly greater quality of feedback for the supervisee (Bernard & Goodyear, 2013). Given increased pressure to maintain services with limited or reduced resources, group supervision provides a means for multiple people to be supervised at one time and by one supervisor.

Despite the numerous advantages of group supervision, the group format has some drawbacks. The group format may not allow individuals to get what they need, and certain group dynamics can impede learning. Confidentiality may be a greater concern for some in group supervision. Some group members may spend too much time on issues not of particular relevance to or interest for the other group members (Bernard & Goodyear, 2013).

Triadic supervision attempts to combine the benefits of individual and group supervision by bringing two supervisees together with one supervisor (Stinchfield, Hill, & Kleist, 2010). This format allows enrichment and expansion of conversation, and may encourage multiple perspective-taking within the supervisees. Now engage in Think About It 13.2.

THINK ABOUT IT 13.2

After reviewing the different supervision formats, picture yourself in individual, group, and triadic formats.

- *List three possible pros and three possible cons of each supervision format.*
- *In what format would you feel most comfortable? In what format would you feel most anxious? Discuss your answers, and highlight which elements of each format would affect your comfort level and your anxiety.*
- *If you were engaged in group supervision, what characteristics do you have that would help the group process? What role might you have in the group? What techniques do you hope your supervisor would employ to help maximize the group supervision process? What characteristics in the participants would impede the group process?*

Supervision Interventions

Within the varied supervision formats, supervisors can employ numerous supervision interventions to enhance supervisee experience and learning. These interventions include self-report, process notes, digital recording, co-therapy, and live supervision. Each intervention can be used in individual, triadic, or group supervision, and some interventions are more commonly used in certain formats. Before proceeding, consider the supervision needs of diverse professional groups by engaging in Think About It 13.3.

THINK ABOUT IT 13.3

As we begin to explore supervision interventions, think about other professionals, such as surgeons, dentists, or ophthalmologists. If you were a patient and one of these professionals performed a specific procedure on you, what type of supervision would you hope they had received in order to provide their respective service?

Self-report is seen as an intense tutorial relationship in which the supervisee fine-tunes case conceptualization ability and knowledge of self as each relates to counselor–client relationships. Self-report is commonly used for postgraduate supervision; it is generally viewed as inappropriate for novice supervisees (Bernard & Goodyear, 2013). Even with its apparent limitations of the amount or accuracy of information provided during the supervision session, it remains a very common form of supervision (Amerikaner & Rose, 2012).

In order to accurately accomplish the goals of supervision, supervisors need to have firsthand knowledge of their supervisees' work based on some form of direct observation (Amerikaner & Rose, 2012). Rogers was one of the first to use audio recordings in supervision, which brought about a dramatic shift in the supervision process (Bernard & Goodyear, 2013). The review of audiotaped segments can allow the supervision to focus on specific therapy techniques, help the supervisee see the relationship between process and content, focus on how points are made in session, and help the supervisee differentiate between a conversational tone and a therapeutic tone. Audiotape review also allows supervisees to receive feedback about specific points in a session when they may be struggling personally with their own issues or interpersonally with the client. Many supervisors now digitally record, encrypt, and archive professional interactions with clients (Byrne & Hartley, 2010). **Digital recording review** allows for the same advantages as audiotape, with an additional opportunity to focus on details such as nonverbal communication, incongruence in the client, or lack of synchrony between the client and the supervisee.

With digital recording in supervision, professionals' knowledge base and experiential alternatives have increased greatly. Supervisors can better see themselves in the role of the helper, allowing them to be a more complete observer of the work than is possible with just an audiotape (Bernard & Goodyear, 2013). Supervisees can review their sessions privately at their own pace, play selected parts for the supervisor, and come prepared with questions and observations of their own. Supervisors also have the option of picking out particular interactions and focusing on them to share observations about supervisee implementation of specific interventions and evaluate the impact of these interventions (Byrne & Hartley, 2010).

Live supervision is used in many training programs and is becoming more accessible with advances in technology. Live supervision combines direct observation of the counseling session with a method that enables the supervisor to communicate with the supervisee using one or multiple interventions such as co-therapy, bug-in-the-ear, bug-in-the-eye, or telephone (Kolodinsky et al., 2011). All these techniques are similar, because they enable the supervisor to monitor the session as it occurs. Counseling sessions are observed either through a one-way mirror or monitor. Each live supervision technique can be modified to fit individual, triadic, and group formats.

During **co-therapy**, or **direct observation**, the supervisor is present in the room with the supervisee, making interventions and comments when appropriate. This intervention permits the supervisor to observe the supervisee while modeling counseling skills in session. When co-therapy is used, most supervisory feedback is given following the session.

Bug-in-the-ear and telephone interventions are the two most popular forms of live supervision. The bug-in-the-ear method uses an ear bud placed in the ear of the supervisee to transmit communications from a supervisor watching behind a one-way mirror or monitor. This intervention has several advantages, including the fact that it allows the supervisor to make minor adjustments or to reinforce the supervisee briefly without interrupting the flow of the counseling session. Bug-in-the-ear also protects the counseling relationship more fully than other live supervision interventions because clients are unaware which counselor interventions are the direct suggestions of the supervisor and which originate from the professional counselor (Bernard & Goodyear, 2013). A more recent alternative to bug-in-the-ear is **bug-in-the-eye**, in which supervisors type suggestions from a keyboard in the observation room to be read on a monitor placed behind the client in the therapy room. One possible advantage to bug-in-the-eye is that the supervisee can choose when to receive the communication from the supervisor and does not have to receive two forms of communication at the same moment (from supervisor and client) (Young, Lindsey, & Kolodinsky, 2010).

Similar to the bug-in-ear/eye methods, supervisors may employ telephone interventions to monitor counseling sessions and to offer feedback to the supervisee during a counseling session. In contrast to bug-in-the-ear, where the flow of the session is not interrupted, a telephone intervention does disrupt the flow, but it can offer the supervisee an opportunity to clarify or discuss the supervisory message. Telephone interventions and bug-in-the-ear/eye methods are the optimal live supervision methods used for communicating brief, uncomplicated, and action-oriented messages, rather than addressing more complicated process issues. When the supervisee needs more clarification than can be provided with a phone directive, the supervisee should leave the session temporarily for a consultation break.

Supervisory consultation breaks can be used as the sole live supervision intervention or in addition to one of the several types of interventions. This supervisory consultation break should not be confused with the professional counselor's multiple consultation roles described earlier. When supervisory consultation breaks are used, the supervisee leaves the counseling session to receive more in-depth feedback, to discuss the client process, or to address personal concerns. When a supervisee uses a consultation break, the supervisee must consider how long he or she is out of the room, the impact on the momentum and flow of the session, and the time needed to process the suggestions. Some professional counselors take a break during a session even when there is no one to consult. A temporary break during a session can allow a professional counselor to reflect on an issue, gather thoughts, or regroup before proceeding.

In addition to or in place of phone-in interventions, some supervisors may choose simply to observe the counseling session, make no interventions during the counseling session, and provide all feedback after the session. When monitoring live sessions, another type of intervention is called **in vivo**, in which the supervisor consults with the supervisee in view of the client. The conversation between the supervisor and the supervisee can be seen as an intervention to heighten the client's awareness of particular dynamics that are present in the session. Another intervention that is similar to in vivo is called a walk-in. The supervisor literally walks into the counseling room to consult directly with the supervisee in view of the client, or to interact with the supervisee and the client. The walk-in does not imply an emergency, and it does not imply the kind of collegiality that is evident with in vivo supervision. A walk-in can be used to redirect the session and to establish certain dynamics between the supervisor and the client or the supervisee and the client. All three interventions involve the supervisor's being present behind a one-way mirror or video monitor and choosing how and when to enter the therapy room. These modes of supervision intrude more on the counseling process than do the methods of phone-in interventions.

When live supervision is used, pre-session planning and postsession debriefing are vital parts of the process. The goal of pre-session planning is to prepare the supervisee for the upcoming counseling session. The supervisor may help the supervisee plan for the upcoming session and focus on the specific learning goals. It is important for the supervisor and the supervisee to complete the pre-session planning with some clarity about their roles for the counseling session (Bernard & Goodyear, 2013).

A postsession debriefing allows the supervisor and the supervisee to discuss what transpired in the counseling session. This is a time to share perceptions, review the effectiveness of interventions, offer feedback, address any remaining concerns, and begin planning for the next session. Postsession debriefing is an optimal time for conceptual growth for the supervisee, so the supervisor should allow a proper amount of time for in-depth processing and discussion.

When conducting live supervision, supervisors may use the various interventions in individual, triadic, and group formats. When using triadic and group formats, supervisors can use the observation rooms as key learning laboratories for the other supervisees. Group members may be asked to watch for specific interventions and work to enhance their conceptualization skills without having the pressure to engage with the client. In the presession and postsession planning, group members can offer additional support, alternative perceptions, and constructive feedback.

When supervisees receive direct observation and coaching through live supervision, there is a greater likelihood that the counseling session will go well and that the supervisee will learn more efficiently and profoundly as a result of these successful counseling sessions (Bernard & Goodyear, 2013). Because live supervision provides more safety for client welfare than other forms of supervision, the presence of the supervisor allows supervisees to work with more challenging cases. Another advantage of live supervision is that the supervisee's view of the process of counseling is positively affected because counseling unfolds far more systematically as a result of input from the supervisor. As technology continues to advance, costs and equipment will become more affordable and accessible, which will address a common barrier to its implementation (Kolodinsky et al., 2011).

The most noted disadvantages of live supervision are the time it demands of supervisors, the cost of facilities, the problem of scheduling cases to accommodate all the individuals involved, and the potential negative reactions from clients (Bernard & Goodyear, 2013). Another disadvantage or potential risk is the danger of the supervisor dominating counseling through live supervision or of supervisee dependence on the supervisor's interventions.

Regardless of the supervision intervention or format, supervisors must adhere to ethical and legal guidelines (Borders, 2014). Each intervention, format, and model must be reviewed for its effectiveness, the experience of the supervisee, and the agreed upon goals of the supervision. To help consolidate your understanding of supervision interventions, complete Activity 13.3 and Think About It 13.4. Then read Voices from the Field 13.2.

ACTIVITY 13.3

Under the direction of the class instructor, divide into small groups and set up role-plays to practice as many of the different kinds of supervision interventions as possible.

- How do the interventions change depending on the specific model of intervention (e.g., phone-in, bug-in-the-ear/eye, walk-in, consultation break)?
- What is the role of the observers? How can your peers best assist your learning?
- When did you feel anxious? How did you respond?

When using live supervision, make sure you allow time for a pre-session and postsession meeting.

THINK ABOUT IT 13.4

After reviewing each of the supervision interventions, reflect on the question about which type of supervision you would want your surgeon, dentist, or ophthalmologist to have received during training or while performing your procedure. Rank each of the interventions discussed in this section from most effective to least effective in training the health professional to be competent in performing the particular procedure. Now reflect on your role as a counselor. Does your training effectiveness list change? How can this experience influence how you approach different supervision interventions?

VOICES FROM THE FIELD 13.2   Using Live Supervision, by Mark Young

I have used some form of live supervision as part of my training ever since I was on the receiving end of live supervision. Now I offer what is called bug-in-the-eye supervision by typing suggestions to my supervisees on a computer monitor during session. Supervisees work with their clients while I observe from another room and watch on my computer. To offer supervision, I send in theory-based suggestions throughout each session. Students have shared a number of positive responses to the experience. Some of the feedback includes statements like these:

- The greatest impact for me with live supervision was it allowed me to stretch myself by trying to incorporate feedback within the session.
- I saw, by changing an aspect of my approach, given to me by immediate feedback, that I could assist the client toward deeper work.
- Watching a live supervision and being able to discuss it and give feedback was a great way to learn a theory and also to view immediately how a client responds to a different approach.
- It was energizing to be the audience and discuss what is going on within the sessions and other interventions one could use.
- When you get feedback after [the session], you are never in that moment again, so it is more difficult to implement it.
- When you get the suggestions immediately, it is easier to connect the result and see it if worked in the way you were hoping.
- I was able to give and receive feedback that could be used and experienced immediately.
- I think live supervision promoted a depth to my counseling development that I would not have experienced otherwise.

I have also used bug-in-the-eye supervision as a form of course instruction. Students engage in live demonstrations in another room while receiving prompts from the instructor. The remaining members of the class observe the session and the written prompts on a video monitor. They are able to reflect in the moment on what is occurring in session, the impact of the prompt or feedback, and what they may do differently if they were in the counseling demonstration.

Supervisory Relationship

Any form of supervision can cause anxiety for the supervisee. Specific efforts should be made to develop a working supervisory relationship that provides a safe and trusting learning environment (Borders, 2014). Supervisors should receive training on supervision models, formats, interventions, and issues specific to supervisee development. Just as a positive and productive relationship is critical to successful counseling, it is also critical for successful supervision. More and more literature supports the importance of a strong working alliance between supervisor and supervisee and that the outcomes and experience of supervisees are tied to the quality of the relationship (Ellis et al., 2014; Goodyear, 2014). Supervisors need to continually focus on diversity and cultural factors, pay attention to power differentials in the supervisory relationship, and avoid or manage dual relationships (ACES, 2011).

A strong supervisory relationship based on trust and respect is vital to the supervisee's exploration of personal and professional issues while in supervision. Similar to the conditions required to develop a strong relationship between the professional counselor and the client, the supervision literature suggests that several elements are necessary to establish an effective supervisory relationship, including empathic understanding, genuineness, respect, and concreteness. In a positive working relationship, the supervisee's mistakes are not seen as failures; rather, the supervisor works to create an environment of experimentation that allows for supervisee risk taking (Ladany & Bradley, 2011).

The supervisor and supervisee must be clear about specific interventions being observed and the therapeutic goals. The supervisor must provide specific supportive and corrective feedback to supervisees. Part of establishing and maintaining a strong supervisory relationship is establishing clear expectations for supervision and addressing the power within the supervisory relationship throughout the supervisory process. The supervisor must also be aware of and responsive to supervisees' personal and professional histories (Palmer-Olsen, Gold, & Woolley, 2011).

Given the nature and purpose of supervision, supervisees often experience anxiety because they are continuously being scrutinized and evaluated by themselves and their supervisors. Within the context of a strong supervisory relationship, however, supervisees can feel that they have a safe space in which to learn to cope with and to tolerate their anxiety. Supervisors should provide supervisees with support, encouragement, and openness in their presence and in the manner in which feedback is delivered (Goodyear, 2014). Supervisors should also pay attention to differences in belief systems; learning styles; and cultural, racial, legal/ethical issues, and gender issues in supervision (Borders, 2014). Supervisors should provide a learning environment in which the supervisor and the supervisee can readily address potential conflicts and concerns. Supervisors must be aware that the quality of the supervisory working alliance influences how supervisees disclose in supervision, how satisfied they are with the experience (Goodyear, 2014), and how key the relationship can be to the effectiveness of supervision (ACES, 2011).

Supervisors build and monitor a strong working alliance and employ interventions and models of supervision that allow them to adequately and accurately monitor the progress and development of the supervisee. Supervisors and supervisees are expected to adhere to best practice and the appropriate ethical codes (ACA, 2014a; ACES, 2014). Supervisors continually monitor diversity and advocacy competencies, ethical guidelines, ongoing performance assessment, and evaluation (Borders, 2014). The supervisor intentionally addresses cultural competencies and encourages supervisees to infuse diversity and advocacy considerations in their work with clients (ACES, 2011).

Not all professional counselors are capable of being supervisors. First, supervising requires advanced levels of expertise that not all counselors possess. Second, evaluative scrutiny and honest reflection about another's counseling skills requires a deft balance of support and confrontation that necessitates special skills to maintain. Third, supervision works only when the relationship between the supervisor and the supervisee consists of trust and mutual respect, especially when the supervisee's own issues are being discussed. Finally, very few professional counselors have received training in supervision skills. Some states are beginning to require a certain level of training in supervision in order to be considered an approved supervisor and to supervise counselors-in-training seeking to be licensed. Supervisors must be competent in a number of areas and abide by national and state requirements for supervisor credentialing and licensing (ACES, 2011).Years of counseling experience and an accumulation of academic credits should not be viewed as sufficient qualifications for supervisors (Ladany & Bradley, 2011). Novice supervisors should be trained in specific skills related to supervision before their work with supervisees (Bernard & Goodyear, 2013); such training is considered essential for best practice (ACES, 2011). To further your thoughts on the issues relevant to supervision, complete Activity 13.4. Then read Voices from the Field 13.3.

ACTIVITY 13.4

Develop a list of questions regarding the ethical, legal, and client issues surrounding supervision. Interview counseling supervisors from community agencies, private practice, and schools and ask them your list of questions. Discuss with the supervisors how they address these issues.

VOICES FROM THE FIELD 13.3   The Essential Role of a Counselor Supervisor, by Melanie Morlan

In my case, four years of post-graduate professional supervision have had a positive impact on every aspect of my life. My supervisor had a career spanning five decades, across multiple disciplines. As a supervisee, my supervisor's lifetime achievements and skills as a professor, nurse practitioner, writer and clinician presented vast opportunities for a rich and multi-faceted supervision experience. Most importantly, she mentored a rich and meaningful life beyond retirement; her commitment to the profession was actively maintained through lifestyle choices and a deeply compassionate way of living. At the foundational core of our relationship was great respect and admiration for her as a person. She had concern for my well-being as a new professional and human being in equal measure. She was always willing and deeply engaged in the process of our supervision sessions, providing education, community networking and regularly advocating for me as a new professional within our state and local communities. She was always accessible, responsive, and willing to share her opinions and ideas from a place of strength and compassion. Our interactions, even when discussing a difficult case, were foundationally comforting and my growing competence was recognized, encouraged, and affirmed. I absorbed, admired, and grew wholeheartedly as a person and professional along the journey of our supervision time together and will thankfully carry her positive influence with me for the rest of my professional career.

SELECTING A SUPERVISOR   Supervision is often offered by a supervisor or administrator within a school or agency as part of the professional agreement to practice. If a supervisor is not available through the place of employment, counselors seeking licensure are required to find a supervisor to provide supervision hours. Whether the supervision is sought out or part of employment, all supervisors should meet the requirements for best practice guidelines published by relevant professional organizations and credentialing bodies (ACES, 2011). Supervisees should inquire about the amount and focus of training received by potential supervisors and the professional approach each applies to the supervision process. Supervisees should consider the personal philosophy, relevant professional training (beyond supervision training), and the scope of professional experience of each supervisor. Supervisees should consider their own expectations and goals for supervision and the type of relationship they hope to establish with a supervisor. Because of the importance of the supervision relationship, finding someone who can develop and maintain this alliance is an important, ongoing part of the supervisory experience (Palmer-Olsen et al., 2011). Now read Voices from the Field 13.4.

VOICES FROM THE FIELD 13.4   The Importance of Continued Field Supervision, by Mark Young

---

Many states require postgraduate supervised experience before one can become licensed. A few years ago I was approached by an individual looking for supervision as she worked toward licensure. She had taken a position in a rural agency and soon realized that the agency lacked an approved supervisor who could provide the needed supervision toward state licensure. We developed a contract regarding informed consent and a release of information so that the supervisee could share content from her sessions with me in supervision. We met weekly to discuss her transition to her new position, staff her cases, and work to expand her conceptual and theoretical knowledge. Through proper consent, the supervisee brought in segments of her sessions to supervision so we could discuss her clients and her own counseling process. She continued to receive supervision until she found employment where an approved supervisor was on-site.

SUPERVISORY DISCLOSURE   In addition to the important task of developing a strong alliance with the supervisee, supervisors have the responsibility to properly clarify specific interventions and goals within the supervisory relationship. *Best Practices in Clinical Supervision* (ACES, 2011) recommends that supervisors develop and use informed consent *and* develop a written contract that outlines expectations, goals, and methods for evaluation. Similar to the informed consent process between a counselor and client, supervisors provide supervisees with a professional disclosure statement regarding training and experience as both a counselor and a supervisor. Supervisors inform supervisees of their supervisory style, the limits of confidentiality, and clear parameters for conducting supervision. Supervisors draw on the best practices in supervision, including establishing the relationship and providing disclosure statements, goals, and roles to maximize collaboration in the context of accountability (Borders, 2014). A template of a supervision disclosure statement is included in Figure 13.1.

Within the informed consent, supervisors should work to clarify how evaluation works within the supervisory relationship. Based on the type of supervision used, the nature and format of the evaluation will vary. Supervisors may employ a number of formal or informal tools that provide structure for the supervision process. The evaluation process should be both formative and summative, and supervisors must decide when and

Name and Credentials_____

This document is designed to inform you, the supervisee, of my educational and professional experience in the supervision and counseling fields, the scope of the supervisory relationship, and interventions used during supervision.

SUPERVISEE
Business Address and Contact Information
Name: _____
Street: _____
City: _____ ST: _____ Zip Code: _____
Telephone: Work: _____ Cell: _____ Home: _____
Email address: _____

SUPERVISOR
Business Address and Contact Information
Name: _____
Street: _____
City: _____ ST: _____ Zip Code: _____
Telephone: Work: _____ Cell: _____ Home: _____
Email address: _____

Background
Credentials
Member of the following organizations:

Education
Brief description of degrees, universities attended, and specialized training in supervision.

Licensure
List of each license, state, and number.

Experience
Brief description of professional experiences in both counseling and supervision.

Process and Interventions of Supervision
Brief description of the process of supervision, including goals and evaluation procedures.

Limits and Scope of Confidentiality in the Supervisory Relationship
Ethical and legal limitations to the supervisory relationship.

Fee Schedule
Complete description of fees and payment process.

FIGURE 13.1   Template for Supervision Disclosure Statement.

how to use specific instruments within the evaluation process (Bernard & Goodyear, 2013). Supervisors work to balance their roles as supervisor and evaluator, while focusing on the clinical needs of the supervisee's clients. Goal setting, specific evaluation instruments, and professional disclosure statements serve as support to both the supervisor and supervisee in this process. Supervisors must understand that evaluation is fundamental to supervision and accept the responsibilities of this aspect of the supervision relationship (ACES, 2011). Supervisees should also have the opportunity to evaluate the effectiveness of their supervisor, and this process can be either formal or informal and supervisors should receive supervision of their work by another supervisor or professional. Now read Voices from the Field 13.5 for a school counselor's view of consultation and supervision.

VOICES FROM THE FIELD 13.5   Consultation and Supervision, by Kami Wagner

---

One of the most important resources counselors have in their work is consultation. There is so much about working with people that is hard to anticipate and for which to prepare. When a situation arises that may not have been encountered previously, consulting with a colleague is invaluable. Also, since other counselors and staff members are usually held to the same standards of confidentiality as we are, consultation is a great way to problem-solve, using the resources of others' knowledge to our advantage.

A critical time to consult with a colleague occurs when an issue of safety comes up. For example, in a recent incident with a student expressing suicidal ideation, it was helpful and essential for me to consult with other colleagues. As a school counselor, it is important to know who else in the building or at my disposal has had the same training as I have. In my current position, there is another school counselor in my building and a resource psychologist who often provides training on suicide interventions to other counselors and psychologists in the county. When we learned of the student who had expressed some suicidal thoughts, both the other counselor and I met with the student. This is an important piece in our school system's suicide intervention procedures. Because of the sensitive and very serious nature of this topic with students, having at least two trained professionals working together is a way to protect ourselves and come up with the best options for the student. Because the other school counselor was in her first year of professional practice, it was helpful for us to work together in order to process and problem-solve the best ways to help support this student.

I am located at a satellite school that some students attend for a partial day and then return to their home schools. Because of the timing and location of the incident, the other counselor and I were unsure of the best course of action to support the student and ensure his safety, so the resource psychologist helped us brainstorm a few things that we may not have thought of in this unique situation without his expertise and experience. In addition, the parent requested some information in writing regarding the incident that he wanted to share with the student's outside counselor. To further protect the student, we worked with the psychologist to make sure what we were putting in writing would ensure the student's confidentiality while providing vital facts to the family for future use.

Because many counseling departments are diverse in their background knowledge and prior experience, in unique or difficult situations tapping into what others may have to offer can be critical to helping students or clients. In a situation such as this, when the safety of a student is in question, having another person to hear the problem and be an additional witness to actions that are taken can also be a safeguard and puts the counselor in a defensible position, should that ever become necessary.

CONSULTATION

Consultation can be understood by examining the types or models of consultation, the various roles assumed by the consultant, the skills required of an effective consultant, and the variety of professional arenas in which consultation takes place. Although these are described differently by different authors, there are some common themes to the published descriptions of the consultation field. To learn about consultation firsthand from an experienced consultant, complete Activity 13.5.

ACTIVITY 13.5

Interview an experienced professional counselor in your area who provides some form of consultation service. What training and experience were necessary for the consultant to become effective? In what techniques or types of consultation is the counselor most skilled? How did the counselor expand from being a professional counselor into the practice of consultation? What important tips can the counselor provide to help you understand consultation better? Discuss your findings with classmates.

Models of Consultation

Models of consultation have evolved over time, beginning in the 1940s. Early pioneers in the field include Caplan (1970), Schein (1978, 1991), and Gallessich (1982), from whom came some of our earliest models. Caplan focused on types of consultation in the mental health field. Schein emphasized the interpersonal process aspects of consultation. Gallesich identified several models of consultation practice that vary according to the problems faced by the consultee and the intervention techniques used by the consultant, including education and training, case consultation, and clinical models.

Gladding (2016) provided a helpful synthesis of several of the most comprehensive models of consultation. He described four categories that reflect many of those presented by earlier scholars. In the **expert** or **provision model**, the consultant functions as one who has the knowledge and skill to resolve problems that other professionals either cannot or do not have time to deal with. The consultant assumes responsibility for effecting change. For example, a consultant might be hired to provide staff training in conflict resolution because no one else in the organization has the background or ability to do the training.

In the **doctor–patient** or **prescription model**, the consultant functions (as the analogy indicates) by diagnosing the problem and prescribing what the consultee should do about it. This is different from the expert model in that the responsibility for the application of the prescribed action and final "cure" lies with the consultee, not the consultant. The consultant operating from the prescription or doctor–patient model identifies the sources of interpersonal conflict in an organization and presents a list of actions that the management team could carry out to resolve the conflict.

The **mediation model** calls for the consultant to unify the activities and processes of different people who are trying to provide services to the same population. A mediating consultant could bring together the directors of several human services agencies to reduce territoriality and to negotiate a cooperative plan for referral.

In the **process consultation** or **collaboration model**, the consultant facilitates the problem-solving process rather than providing the actual solution. The consultant's efforts are aimed at improving consultees' communication and helping them to work together more effectively as they resolve their mutual problems.

Another way to conceptualize types of consultation is to consider the emphasis placed on one of two categories: consultant-centered consultation and system-centered consultation (Neukrug, 2012). Consultant-centered consultation has three subtypes: expert, prescriptive, and trainer/educator. In the **expert consultation model** the consultant is asked to help an organization solve specific problems based on her or his expertise. For example, a consultant highly skilled in needs assessment may assist a human services agency by conducting research to identify the counseling needs of the community the agency serves. The **prescriptive consultation model** (another name for the doctor–patient model) requires the consultant to collect information, correctly identify the nature of the problem, and provide recommendations for its resolution. In this case, a counselor serving as a consultant may tackle the question of why so many clients are not keeping their scheduled counseling appointments at a given agency. The consultant would work to discover why this is happening and to formulate suggestions for the staff to improve session attendance. In the **trainer/educator consultation model**, the consultant is contracted to provide educational and training opportunities for staff members. For example, one of the authors conducted a staff training workshop on the use of sand play techniques with traumatized children.

As the name indicates, **system-centered consultation** is focused on the organizational dynamics of the working team or agency (Neukrug, 2012). It has three major approaches. **Collaborative consultation** relies on the shared expertise of consultant and consultee, who work as partners to identify problems, consider solutions, and implement joint decisions. For example, a counseling consultant could work with an agency director to identify together the most important qualifications to be sought in hiring new employees for the agency. In **facilitative consultation** the consultant helps persons who work within a given system to communicate more effectively with each other and to understand each other. This form of systemic intervention is intended to maximize the effectiveness of a group of employees by helping them to improve and sustain a constructive relational dynamic. A **process-oriented consultant** believes that the most effective resolution of systemic conflict is that which emerges from among the system members themselves. Such a consultant helps to create a trusting environment in which the group dynamic can improve, empowering the group to solve its own problems. For example, a counselor skilled in conflict resolution and team building could be asked to conduct group process meetings for an interpersonally conflicted working group. The purpose of the consultation would be to identify the history and sources of conflict among the staff members and to use group process meetings to improve their communication and working relationships. Activity 13.6 helps you apply what you have learned about consultation models.

ACTIVITY 13.6 CONSULTATION CASES

The following consultation cases are based on actual situations in which one of the authors served as an external consultant. Determine which model or models of consultation would best apply for each and explain why.

Case 1

The management team of a family-owned manufacturing business is experiencing difficulty with a transition of leadership. The founder of the company is turning it over to her four adult children, but she is having difficulty letting go. She still wants to influence the direction of the company, making sure it does not falter. In addition, the new management team of four siblings wants to establish their leadership by involving all the other managing employees in a team-building process to maximize efficiency and employee satisfaction. Their intention is to empower the broader management team while communicating that they are now in charge of the company. One of the siblings calls you to ask what kind of help they need, if any.

(Continued)

Case 2

A small, rural town had no social services agencies or counseling centers available to help the few hundred people who live there. Some of the citizens called the nearest university to ask if students or faculty members could provide community awareness workshops on mental illness, especially to help the families of persons diagnosed with schizophrenia, bipolar disorder, or depression.

Case 3

A professional counselor in a college counseling center is very skilled at helping undergraduate students with typical career, relational, and developmental counseling issues but has no experience with clinical mental health counseling. She has a new client whom she thinks fits the diagnosis of borderline personality disorder, but she is unsure. In addition, she feels unable to provide helpful counseling to this client. At the suggestion of her administrative supervisor, she calls a local psychiatrist for assistance.

Case 4

A school principal calls a professional counselor for problem-solving assistance in dealing with intense interpersonal conflict among the teaching staff members. Apparently, long-standing grievances exist among some of the teachers, along with the gossip, mistrust, hostility, and resistance to change that frequently accompany such problems. The principal is unsure about solutions to the problem and calls the professional counselor for assistance in resolving the conflict.

Case 5

The director of a community counseling agency wants to know whether the programs currently being implemented at her agency are the best or even a reasonable expenditure of the limited funds available. Not knowing how to conduct program evaluation or action research, she calls on the director of another agency for help with her lack of evaluative expertise.

Consultant Roles

Because consultation is a multifaceted activity, consultants must fulfill many different roles to be effective. Different consultation situations call for different consultation roles, several of which may be synthesized into the professional presence of a single consultant. Following are descriptions of the most common roles assumed by consultants (Dougherty, 2014; Scott, Royal, & Kissinger, 2014).

EXPERT   Individuals receiving assistance from a consultant can reasonably and justifiably expect the consultant to know more about the problem or its potential solutions than they do. A consultant often serves as a source of expertise, in knowledge and in skill, which the consultee does not have. In part because of this expertise and because it is easier for them to be objective observers of the problem situation, consultants can suggest ideas or courses of action that have yet to be considered by the consultee. Supportive guidance in the right direction often provides the solution needed by the consultee who is seeking assistance.

RESEARCHER   Often, consultants function as fact finders, collecting data for use in program evaluation, to aid in decisions about organizational change, or to develop awareness of community and social trends. Sometimes the consultant is asked specifically to conduct research as the major task for an organization; sometimes research is one of the many tasks initiated by the consultant to reach a broader set of objectives.

PROGRAM EVALUATOR   Continued funding for human services or educational programs is increasingly contingent on the demonstrated effectiveness of the program. Consultants are often called on to document program outcomes or to make recommendations for program improvement when the program staff members do not have the time or the ability to conduct such an evaluation themselves.

TEACHER/TRAINER/EDUCATOR   Sometimes the major problem facing a human services professional or organization can be resolved by learning new information or acquiring new skills. In this case, the consultant develops curricula if needed, presents instructional materials, and facilitates learning experiences germane to the subject area.

ADVOCATE   Consultants can advocate for a person or position. Advocacy for a person occurs when the consultant champions the rights of an individual or group in the face of injustice or disadvantage. Advocacy for a position occurs when the consultant attempts to persuade others to accept a particular answer or make a certain decision about an issue.

PROCESS SPECIALIST   In this role, the consultant focuses more on the interactive process itself than on the content of the problem. The consultant facilitates constructive interaction among participants to help resolve the problem at hand and enhance their understanding of the interpersonal dynamics at work in their setting. Process skills are especially important in cases of conflict resolution among coworkers and in effective team building among working groups.

COLLABORATOR   The consultant and consultee share a mutual contribution to problem identification and solution development. They function as equal and interdependent sources of information and judgment, working as partners to create an effective resolution to the issue. Now apply what you have learned about consultant roles by completing Activity 13.7. Then read Voices from the Field 13.6.

ACTIVITY 13.7 CONSULTATION ROLES

Consider again the consultation cases presented in Activity 13.6. Determine which consultant role best fits the needs of each situation and explain why.

VOICES FROM THE FIELD 13.6   Reaching Out to the Community through Consultation, by Alan Basham

I created an opportunity for graduate students in counselor education to apply consultation principles firsthand while still in training. As part of their consultation course, the instructor connected students in the class with staff members at an outreach program whose purpose was to help meet

(Continued)

the physical and emotional needs of homeless persons in the community. One of the difficulties faced by the staff members was that few of them had any formal education beyond high school and none had any training or supervision in basic counseling skills. Several of the staff members were volunteers. Because they were attempting to help a population marked by high need and often limited interpersonal skills, the staff communicated that they frequently felt "in over their heads" and at a loss about how to help those who came for assistance. This was especially true when dealing with angry people. At the request of the agency director, the counselor educator brought three teams of three students each to help with staff training at the agency. They prepared and presented three interactive workshops on basic communication microskills, what to say and do when interacting with someone who is angry, and principles of self-care relevant to those in the helping professions. The agency staff members were uniformly pleased and appreciative, not just because of the information and skills they acquired, but also because the university and its students cared about their mission and well-being in the first place. This turned out to be a very beneficial exercise for students, who learned, among other things, that you do not have to be a recognized, advanced professional in your field to accomplish important tasks in the role of consultant. In many cases, you just need to know more about the subject or task than the consultee.

Consultation Skills

As evidenced by the types of consultation described earlier, professional counselors who choose to serve as consultants need a variety of skills (Dougherty, 2014; Scott et al., 2014). Although some of those skills are likely to be possessed by any effective counselor, others are personal characteristics and areas of expertise that are different from counseling skills per se.

Of course, for case consultation the consultant must have advanced *knowledge* about the diagnosis and treatment of any psychological disorder under consideration. The counselor being consulted about the characteristics, etiology, and best practice treatment of a mental disorder can be of assistance only if the counselor can reasonably and ethically assume the role of expert for the consultee.

An effective consultant must have strong *interpersonal skills*. There is no substitute for effective communication and a positive, accepting attitude toward others. Communication skills include the willingness and ability to listen, which every competent counselor can do.

To communicate well with groups and organizations, consultants also need skills in *professional writing* and in *public speaking*. For example, advocating publicly for a particular decision requires the ability to talk comfortably with a group or audience; the ability to speak comfortably to audiences is invaluable. In addition, most consultation activity includes a written report of findings, outcomes, or an established plan; the ability to write clearly and accurately is essential.

Because most of the problems encountered by professional counselors who serve as consultants emerge from the human nature of consultees and their clients, it is also important to understand people, their motives, needs, shortcomings, and strengths. Consultants should be able to identify problems and have *problem-solving skills*. It helps to have some background in organizational development, which enables the consultant to understand the environmental setting of some consultations or the nature of an organization that needs help. Consultants also need skills in group process and team-building. Understanding the typical reasons why working groups are conflicted can enable a consultant to identify problems quickly and act to resolve the problems of an ineffective team (Basham, Appleton, & Dykeman, 2000).

Because of the heterogeneous nature of society and the importance of treating all individuals with respect, consultants should be aware, inclusive, and considerate of racial and cultural diversity issues in the consultation process. Ideally, consultants should have interpersonal experience with and be respectful of ethnic, economic, and other sources of diversity among consultees and their clients.

Consultants must maintain the same level of professional ethics expected of the professional counselor, including appropriate privacy, informed consent, and practicing only within one's level of competence. Consultants must be objective in their efforts to understand and to help resolve consultee problems, especially when contracted by an administrative supervisor to interact with subordinates. Now use your understanding of the various consultation skills to complete Activity 13.8. Then read Voices from the Field 13.7.

ACTIVITY 13.8 CONSULTATION SKILLS

Consider again the consultation cases presented in Activity 13.6. Determine which consultant skills you think would be needed or most effective in each situation and explain why.

VOICES FROM THE FIELD 13.7   A Systemic High School Consultation, by Alan Basham

I was asked to assist a teacher at an alternative high school by providing a creative way to expand student awareness of each student's personal identity. The teacher's project involved students' consideration of their own self-image and way of relating with others. I created a three-session module in which students helped each other make a mask of their own face using gauze and flour water. After the masks dried, students decorated their own masks to represent how they related with the world around them and, by contrast, what was true within that they rarely disclosed to others. During the third session I discussed with the students what led them to decorate the inside and outside of their masks in the way they did. What were they trying to say to themselves and to others? What did they think the choice of decoration meant about themselves? I was struck by how many of these troubled students colored the outer surface of their masks mostly black and angry in appearance, but tended to put the colors and symbols of nature, children, and hope on the inside. As you think about this real-life consultation experience, what were the skills and applied knowledge presented by the consultant? What type of consultation was this?

Consultation Settings

Consultation performed by professional counselors usually occurs in one of three settings: human services agencies; schools; and a broad category of business, government, and other organizations. Consultant activity among practitioners in mental health and other human services agencies often involves **case consultation** about a specific client, staff training for an agency, or organizational problem solving such as team building and conflict resolution. Whether the consultant chooses a client-focused, system-focused, or consultee-focused approach to case consultation depends on the nature of the problem and the expressed needs of the persons seeking consultation assistance. Rimehaug and Helmersberg (2010) denote this flexible approach as *situational* consultation.

Much of this activity is **external consultation**; the consultant is often assisting those outside her or his own agency. This means that the consultant must spend some time getting to know the consultee's practice, professional competencies, and presented problems. Although the professional counselor's consultation activities are often focused on the consultee's clients, staff training, or resolution of interpersonal dynamics, at times the external consultant's focus is on the nature of the consultee's organizational system, seeking to facilitate systemic change in the organization itself (Moe & Perera-Diltz, 2009).

There is a growing trend toward consultation and collaboration between mental health professionals and medical professionals (Fredheim, Danbolt, Haavet, Kjonsberg, & Lien, 2011). In addition, increased communication and networking between family practitioners and marriage and family counselors can enhance physicians' ability to provide effective treatment for their patients (Clark, Linville, & Rosen, 2009). Child care agencies and early childhood education centers also benefit from the assistance provided by mental health counselors, especially regarding staff development and management of emotional/behavioral problems that appear in children (Alkon, Ramler, & Maclennan, 2003; Green, Everhart, Gordon, & Gettman, 2006; Heller et al., 2011). Rehabilitation counselors routinely act as consultants to the medical community and to employers of their clients, a part of their role that is increasingly important to the success of their counseling endeavors (Zanskas & Leahy, 2008).

Consultation in the educational setting is a complex process through which school counselors emerge as advocates, collaborators, and leaders at their schools (Baker et al., 2009). The professional school counselor functions primarily as an **internal consultant**, fulfilling the role of expert resource for a variety of individuals connected to the educational setting (Dougherty, 2014; Erford, 2013), including parents, teachers, principals, and sometimes students themselves. School counselors consult with teachers regarding the needs of specific students (Clemens, 2007; Erford, 2015a), collaborate with teachers to provide support in the classroom setting (Clark & Breman, 2009), and frequently consult with parents (Holcomb-McCoy & Bryan, 2010). The professional school counselor can also have a substantial role as a systems change agent, using team-building, conflict resolution, and group dynamics skills to help create a more constructive learning and working environment at the school. Because the counselor is contributing to a familiar system, less time is needed to become acquainted with the setting or the consultee than in external consultation. Professional school counselors who are skilled in applied research techniques can assist other educators in program evaluation to improve the quality of educational and counseling services provided.

In addition to the expanding role of the professional school counselor as a systems change agent, consultant activity in the educational setting from other professionals in the community has increased (Conwill, 2003). The role of schools has changed over the years because they have become centers of intervention for problems such as youth violence, teen pregnancy, substance abuse, and child abuse and neglect. Outside consultants to the education system, including mental health counselors, have been instrumental in helping educators and school counselors provide on-site assistance to children, adolescents, and their families. A key factor in the success of this collaboration between school counselors and mental health counselors is the establishment and maintenance of strong working relationships across professional disciplines (Lemberger, Wachter-Morris, Clemens, & Smith, 2010).

Many counseling professionals serve as consultants to organizations that are unrelated to the human services or educational fields. The primary purpose of most organizational consultation is to strengthen the effectiveness of the organization (Dougherty, 2014). Businesses, government agencies, and nonprofits frequently seek the assistance of professional counselors because the problems faced by the organization are rooted in the interpersonal and group process components of working together. Because professional counselors are supposed to be experts in understanding people, many organizations seek the consultation assistance of a professional counselor to help resolve interpersonal conflicts, train managers to be more effective leaders, create appropriate professional development workshops for employees, help employees manage a changing work environment, and in other ways assist the organization through an applied understanding of human nature. Activity 13.9 helps you to further consider your own potential as a consultant. Then read Voices from the Field 13.8.

ACTIVITY 13.9 PERSONAL APPLICATION

Which types of consultation activities would you most like to provide? Which of the consultation skills listed previously do you already possess? Which skills represent lines of growth (not weaknesses) to pursue in your professional development?

VOICES FROM THE FIELD 13.8   Consultation Is Essential to Effective Practice, by Megan Kidron

Consultation is of the utmost importance in making ethical and legal decisions. Rarely is there one right way to do something in the counseling profession. Every setting has its own protocols and specific client populations (e.g., children, adolescents, adults, the elderly) and every client and situation is unique. Thus, it is difficult to know the right course of action for every possible scenario.

Consultation with colleagues involves getting the opinions of other professionals about the best course of action to take in problem situations. It can take many different forms, such as consulting with a supervisor, peers, or specific agencies. Consultation may be with one person or include working with and seeking the opinions of many different individuals or groups.

Depending on what setting you work in and for how long, you will be encouraged or required to discuss complex cases with your supervisor to problem-solve. You will discuss specifics of the case, legal and ethical guidelines that pertain to that specific case, and possible courses of action. Supervisors can often provide alternative ways of looking at things and bring in their knowledge and expertise to help you with your case. In my opinion, having a good supervisor is a great resource and makes you a more effective and knowledgeable counselor.

(Continued)

While there is no foolproof way to protect yourself from lawsuits or ethical quandaries, consulting with other professional counselors is one way to make sure you are doing everything you can to help the client, follow ethical and legal guidelines, and protect yourself. While there is no set number of people you have to consult with, consulting with about three other professional counselors about a challenging case is a good number to strive for. Keep in mind that when consulting with other counselors, client confidentiality needs to be maintained. You should document each consultation: the date, time, person, and what was discussed. It is important to also document what you decide to do and why you made that particular choice.

One agency that I used to consult with frequently was Child Protective Services (CPS). As a professional counselor, you are a mandated reporter, meaning you must report any suspicions or indicators of abuse or neglect. Many times as a counselor, you are unsure if the information you have or the specific situation should be reported. Calling an agency like CPS and asking to consult with them about your specific case helps to make sure you are following the correct legal procedures. Again, remember that, unless you are making an actual report to CPS, you should maintain client confidentiality when consulting with the agency.

There are also other reasons you might want to consult with different agencies on behalf of clients. You may want to find out if a client qualifies for a program at the agency, how the agency could help the client, and what the client needs to do to become involved with the agency.

Without consultation, professional counselors would be left on their own to make decisions that they hope are legal and ethical. In the first few years of practice, these kinds of decisions can be very scary for a lot of counselors, but because we, as counselors, can consult with many other professionals, we can have confidence that we are making the best decisions possible when working with our clients.

Summary

The roles of supervisor and consultant enable highly skilled and professionally advanced counselors to contribute to the professional development and accomplishment of others, within and outside the counseling profession. Supervisors are essential to the training of new counselors, guiding neophytes in the development of their counseling skills while ensuring the well-being of the clients of inexperienced helpers. Supervisors help emerging professional counselors achieve their potential and provide ever more competent counseling services to the population. Consultants engage with and assist more persons than they ever could by working only with their own counseling clients, as important as that is. Skilled consultants positively affect not only their individual consultees, but also the consultees' clients or client systems, thus multiplying their constructive influence on society. Consultants can use their expertise to modify organizational systems, solve interpersonal conflicts, and empower others through training. Thus, both supervisors and consultants perform an expansive role as professional counselors, bringing their advanced knowledge and skill to bear on empowering the work of others. This is what is meant by the triadic nature of both supervision and consultation.

There are some differences between the two roles. Supervision is authoritative, while consultation is collaborative. Supervision is often mandated by training programs or state law, while consultation is a voluntary relationship. Ongoing performance evaluation is a central part of supervision, while in consultation it is not. The supervisory relationship tends to be ongoing until training and licensure are completed, while consultation is typically a temporary relationship focused on a particular task or problem.

Supervisors assume a variety of roles in their work, including mentor, advocate, teacher, case consultant, and collaborator. Supervisor activity includes support, teaching, and evaluation. An understanding of diversity is essential for supervisors, both for building a positive working relationship with the supervisee and to enhance the supervisee's understanding of diversity in the lives of clients.

There are several different models of supervision. Theory-based models are each grounded in a particular approach to counseling, such as person-centered and cognitive-behavioral theories. Developmental models consider the gradual personal and professional changes that occur in the new counselor over time, enhancing that development by contributing to the supervisee's motivation, awareness of self and others, and autonomy. Integrative models include the discrimination model, in which the supervisor attends to the intervention skills, conceptualization skills, and personalization skills of the new counselor.

Supervision of counselors also occurs in a variety of formats, including individual, group, and triadic supervision. Each format has particular advantages and disadvantages. For example, triadic supervision allows for vicarious learning, as does group supervision, although both reduce the amount of privacy and supervisor attention provided by individual supervision. A limitation of individual supervision is the lack of collaborative learning from and with other supervisees.

Supervisors can employ a variety of interventions, that is, means of learning about or observing the supervisee's work with clients. These interventions include self-report, audio-recorded review, and video-recorded review. The counseling session is reported by one of these three methods, and the supervisor responds sometime after the session occurs. Other types of supervisor interventions are more immediate, taking place as the counseling session is conducted. Among these interventions are walk-ins, consultation breaks, live or in vivo supervision, and co-therapy or direct observation of the session. Bug-in-the-ear and bug-in-the-eye are two innovative types of live supervisory interventions in which technology is used to enable the supervisor to communicate with the counselor during the session without unnecessarily interrupting it.

Selecting a supervisor to assist in one's training is a very important consideration. In most counselor education programs, the supervisor is assigned to students. Counselors who have graduated and are seeking supervision to meet licensure requirements have more latitude in this decision. Some agencies assign the supervisor, but typically more than one person on staff is available to supervise recent graduates. Frequently, counselors seeking licensure are able to contract with a supervisor they have chosen. However the relationship begins, it is very important that a trust-based alliance be developed with the supervisor and that the supervisor possesses advanced skill in client conceptualization and treatment.

Models of consultation include the expert, doctor–patient, mediation, and process consultation. Another way to consider the types of consultation is to see them as either consultant-centered or system-centered. Expert, prescriptive, and trainer/educator consultants are engaged in consultant-centered activities. System-centered consultation also has three major approaches: collaborative, facilitative, and process-oriented. The skilled consultant identifies and implements the model of consultation most suited to the needs of the consultee or client system.

Consultants function in one or more roles to accomplish the needs of the consultee. Among these roles are the expert, researcher, program evaluator, process specialist, teacher/trainer/educator, and collaborator. Depending on the nature of the problems presented when he or she is contacted for assistance, the consultant selects which role or synthesis of roles would be most appropriate for the resolution of the presented problems. Each of these roles has different techniques and ways of conceptualizing the tasks, enabling the consultant to formulate a plan of intervention that is most effective for the specific setting and needs of those being assisted.

Consultants need a variety of skills in order to function in a variety of settings. Strong interpersonal skills and the ability to communicate in a positive, accepting manner are essential. It is also important to understand people and the organizational environment in which they work. Case consultation, for example, requires a sophisticated understanding of human nature, the etiology of psychopathology, and appropriate therapeutic techniques for various disorders. Throughout, consultants must be mindful of diversity in all its forms, maintaining and communicating respect for the individuality of persons. Whether teaching/ training, engaging in conflict resolution through group process, or helping clinicians with specific clients, consultants contribute to educational settings, business and government organizations, medical practitioners, and the work of human services agencies.

MyCounselingLab for Introduction to Counseling

Try the Topic 13 Assignments: *Supervision.*

---

14   Advocating for the Counseling Profession

AMY MILSOM

PREVIEW

Little has been written about the concept of professional advocacy in counseling. What does it mean to advocate for the counseling profession? Why is professional advocacy important? In what ways can professional counselors advocate for the profession? The concept of professional advocacy is explored throughout this chapter, and the answers to these questions will become clear.

DEFINING ADVOCACY

According to Gladding (2013), **advocacy** means "actively working for, supporting, or espousing a cause . . . counselors advocate for the welfare of their clients and the profession of counseling" (p. 5). Although advocacy for both clients and the profession are important, the focus of this chapter is advocating for professional counselors, or the profession of counseling. Chapter 15 focuses on counselors advocating on behalf of clients.

Synonyms of advocacy include words such as "encouragement," "justification," "promotion," and "recommendation" (*Roget's New Millennium Thesaurus*, 2018). By focusing on the synonyms, one can understand better what advocating for the profession might look like. For example, professional counselors might *encourage* someone to seek counseling as opposed to psychotherapy, or they might provide *justification* for various organizations to hire or retain counselors instead of social workers or psychologists. In addition, professional counselors could *promote* their services or *recommend* that legislators earmark funding for the training of professional counselors.

A simplistic way of thinking about advocating for the counseling profession is to consider a main emphasis on increasing public awareness. The information that professional counselors want people to be more aware of and the outcomes of their public awareness efforts would be unique. Consider the first two examples presented in the preceding paragraph. By sharing information about the potential benefits of counseling, professional counselors might be able to convince someone to seek counseling services for the first time. In addition, information shared by a group of professional counselors with their employer regarding the increase in profits generated by clients during the past year might serve as justification for the employer to support each of the staff counselor positions for at least one more year. Now consider professional advocacy a bit deeper as you complete Think About It 14.1.

THINK ABOUT IT 14.1

What other ways can you think of to advocate for the counseling profession? What might be the outcomes of those efforts? After you have brainstormed a few ideas, go to www.stephanietburns.com/SLCA/loai.html to review an extensive list of ideas for how to advocate for the profession.

BRIEF HISTORY OF COUNSELORS ADVOCATING FOR THE PROFESSION

Professional advocacy can be an individual endeavor or a group effort. Many professional counseling organizations and individual counselors have engaged in formal advocacy efforts at the local, state, and national levels. Myers, Sweeney, and White (2002) and Sweeney (2012) provided comprehensive summaries of how counselors came to advocate for themselves and their clients and identified the mid-1900s as the origin of those efforts. That period marked the emergence of counseling specialty areas and the evolution of professional counseling organizations at the national level. By formally joining together, counselors could promote their specialized skills and knowledge to the public and identify how they differed from other related professionals. Counseling organizations were also able to increase the public's awareness of different types of counselors and to recommend that the government recognize the importance of their efforts. For example, counselors advocated for federal legislation to provide funding to support the training of school counselors in the 1960s and rehabilitation counselors in the 1970s.

Myers et al. (2002) also identified the establishment of state counselor licensure boards and national accrediting associations (e.g., CACREP, CORE) in the 1970s and 1980s as examples of counselor efforts to advocate for the profession. By creating and maintaining strict standards for training and practice, the counseling profession communicates to the public that entry into the profession is a rigorous process.

In the 1990s, the counseling profession started placing greater emphasis on advocacy. For example, in *Counseling Futures*, Walz, Gazda, and Shertzer (1991) identified the need to increase the visibility of the counseling profession and to help counselors develop advocacy skills. Then, the Counselor Advocacy Leadership conferences held in 1998 and attended by representatives of numerous professional counseling organizations resulted in discussion of how to advance advocacy in counseling (Kaplan & Gladding, 2011). These initiatives informed the advocacy concepts that are reflected in *20/20 Principles for Unifying and Strengthening the Profession*.

This increased emphasis on advocacy is reflected in current counseling accreditation standards and ethical codes. The Council for Accreditation of Counseling and Related Educational Programs (CACREP, 2016) includes content related to professional advocacy in its curricular requirements for both entry-level and doctoral-level counseling students. Specifically, entry-level counselors must learn about "the role and process of the professional counselor advocating on behalf of the profession" (Standard 2.F.1.d) and doctoral students must learn the "role of counselors and counselor educator advocating on behalf of the profession and professional identity" (Standard 6.B.5.i). Further, the American Counseling Association (ACA, 2014a) delineates advocacy as an appropriate and ethical counselor role in relation to promoting "changes at the individual, group, institutional, and societal level that improve the quality of life for individuals and groups and remove potential barriers to the provision or access of appropriate services being offered (p. 8).

CURRENT COUNSELING ADVOCACY AGENDAS

Counseling organizations and individual counselors have been and are currently actively advocating for the profession. For example, ACA, the National Board for Certified Counselors (NBCC), and CACREP have been very involved in advocating for legislation and regulations that recognize professional counselors as legitimate and important mental health providers. Many of their efforts have strong implications for clients, and these issues are discussed in Chapter 15. The following paragraphs overview just a few recent advocacy agendas, with an emphasis on implications for the counseling profession.

One of the main advocacy agendas of numerous counseling organizations and individual counselors has been to have state and federal governments recognize licensed professional counselors (LPCs) as just as qualified as other professionals (e.g., psychologists, social workers) to provide mental health services. This agenda plays out in relation to the ability of licensed mental health counselors to be included in the list of providers that insurance companies reimburse for services. For example, for many years ACA has encouraged its membership to contact legislators to convey the message that licensed mental health counselors and marriage and family therapists should be eligible to deliver services to Medicare beneficiaries, provided they are legally authorized to perform those services under their state's licensure law (ACA, 2013). Recognition that these professionals are *not* lesser qualified mental health professionals is an important message inherent in these advocacy efforts; professional counselors deserve to be reimbursed at the same rates and under the same conditions as social workers.

Another current counseling advocacy agenda addresses a lack of appreciation for the specialized training and supervision needs of professional counselors. In the past, the Department of Defense's TRICARE Health Services Program forced military personnel to obtain referrals from their physicians before they could receive mental health counseling services from licensed professional counselors. The program also stipulated that the referring physician must supervise the mental health treatment, while other mental health professionals were permitted to practice independently (NBCC, 2015a). Among other concerns, the implied message that a physician is qualified to supervise a professional counselor reflects a lack of information or awareness about counseling as a specialized profession. As a result of this advocacy initiative, through the National Defense Authorization Act, the Department of Defense now must allow individuals who meet provider eligibility requirements for the *TRICARE certified mental health counselor* to practice independently.

A similar advocacy agenda relates to LPCs providing services through the Department of Veterans Affairs (VA). In 2006, LPCs and marriage and family counselors were recognized as mental health specialists within all programs operated by the VA. In an update provided on its website in March 2013, the ACA (2013) reported that although the VA is establishing qualified licensed professional mental health counselors with the same level of pay and responsibility as clinical social workers, the VA is advertising very few positions for which these individuals would be eligible. The ACA reported little support from the VA regarding its requests to better promote the hiring of counselors, and continues to encourage counselors to advocate directly with their local VA facilities as well as congressional offices.

In relation to the progress made with the Department of Defense and the VA, individual states have started advocating for licensure requirements that would ensure all LPCs in that state would meet TRICARE certified mental health counselor requirements. For example, individual counselors and numerous counseling organizations recently advocated that individuals must graduate from a CACREP-accredited, clinically focused counseling program in order to be eligible for the LPC credential in Virginia (G. Lawson, personal communication, July 27, 2015). Arguments for the recommendation included (a) the large number of military personnel living in Virginia, (b) the confusion that would be created if only some LPCs would be eligible to provide services to military personnel and veterans, and (c) the importance of establishing a uniform set of educational requirements (i.e., CACREP) across all states in the hope of moving toward greater licensure portability.

Another ongoing advocacy agenda relates to communicating the important role counselors play in schools. Both ACA and the American School Counselor Association (ASCA) have consistently focused on emphasizing the importance of having adequate numbers of counselors in schools and having time to engage in counseling versus administrative work. They have supported legislation over the years related to increased federal funding for school-based professional counselors and efforts to reduce counselor–student ratios in schools. These same kinds of efforts often occur at the local level. Now read Voices from the Field 14.1.

VOICES FROM THE FIELD 14.1   Advocating for Counselors in School, by Rob Rhodes

As Director of School Counseling Services for a very large district, I formally requested an increase in school counselors to provide for one full-time counselor in each elementary school in our district, regardless of the size of the school. At the time, we had 11 schools that only qualified for 0.5 counselors based on their student enrollment. To qualify for a full-time counselor, a school was required to have a minimum of 500 students. We approached this by emphasizing that students in these schools were without access to a counselor for half of their school experience. In this situation, it was virtually impossible for a counselor to split between two schools and establish a presence, develop a program or form substantial relationships with his or her students. Consequently, our staffing formula was changed to provide a full-time school counselor at all elementary schools, regardless of size. Also, our school board supported an increase in school counselors at the middle and high level as well, resulting in a ratio decrease from 350:1 to 325:1 at these two building levels. Regarding school-based mental health counselors, I advocated to the district administration for the addition of these counselors in more schools for the major purpose of increasing access to mental health services and the need to have that level of tiered intervention available to students. We have doubled the number of schools with school-based mental health counselors over the past three years. Additionally, our model has worked well, allowing us to provide more services via referrals to these counselors for students experiencing mental health issues.

In addition to national and local advocacy efforts, the counseling profession also targets its efforts internationally. The NBCC has been engaging in advocacy efforts internationally to help increase awareness of and access to counseling throughout the world. Most recently it has been working to expand national counseling certification in Mexico and

Argentina and supporting efforts to grow the counseling profession in Malawi and Malaysia. NBCC also continues to collaborate with the European Board for Certified Counselors to promote and expand counseling throughout Europe (NBCC, 2014).

Similarly, through its subsidiary, the International Registry of Counsellor Education Programs (IRCEP), CACREP has helped to promote counseling throughout the world. IRCEP's vision is to

> promote the ongoing development and recognition of the counselling profession worldwide through the creation of a registry of approved counsellor education programs that use common professional requirements essential to the education and training of counsellors regardless of culture, country, region, work setting, or educational system. (CACREP, 2015)

Among their core values are emphases on educating the public as well as ensuring quality counselor preparation that takes into consideration the uniqueness of cultures. At the time of publication, IRCEP had counselor education programs from Argentina, Canada, India, Mexico, Singapore, South Africa, and the United States in its registry.

The issues discussed above are only a few of the many agendas being addressed by counseling organizations and individuals. Advocacy agendas change as societal issues change, and you are encouraged to explore the types of issues to which national- and state-level counseling organizations currently are dedicating time and resources for advocacy. The ACA's Government Affairs link (www.counseling.org/government-affairs/public-policy) is a good place to find current national initiatives as well as resources and suggestions for action. Chi Sigma Iota shares interviews with numerous *Advocacy Heroes and Heroines* at www.csi-net.org/?page=Interviews_Advocacy. Now complete Activity 14.1.

ACTIVITY 14.1

Search the websites of organizations such as the ACA (www.counseling.org), ACA divisions, Chi Sigma Iota (www.csi-net.org), and the National Board for Certified Counselors (www.nbcc.org) to find out what those organizations are saying about current advocacy initiatives. You also might search Google, YouTube, or other popular news sites to see what you can find regarding advocating for the counseling profession.

- What information did you find regarding the advocacy efforts supported and/or initiated by counseling organizations and/or individuals?
- What types of long-term advocacy efforts are they engaged in?
- What opportunities and resources do the counseling organizations provide for members who are interested in becoming involved in professional advocacy?
- Who are the individuals recognized for their advocacy efforts?

WHY ADVOCATE?

Understanding what advocacy means is essential. With an awareness of why advocacy is important, professional counselors can be purposeful in their efforts. Simply put, Eriksen (1999) stated that "advocacy efforts are critical to the future of the counseling profession.

Only through persistent advocacy have counselors become respected professionals, able to practice without too many constraints what they are trained to do" (p. 33). In essence, professional counselors are encouraged to advocate to retain their unique status among helping professionals and to engage in activities deemed important by the profession. Now read Voices from the Field 14.2.

**VOICES FROM THE FIELD 14.2   Why I Advocate,
by Stephanie Burns**

My passion for professional advocacy began early in my Master's program when I realized that there would be no counseling services for the clients I wanted to serve unless I also advocated for the professional rights of counselors. Currently, I advocate in three different roles, that of a mental health counselor, as a counselor educator, and as a researcher. I enjoy all three of these roles for different reasons. As a researcher I am advocating for better understanding of our profession and our clients. As a counselor educator, I am advocating for resources to better train counselors to fulfill their scope of practice upon graduation. As a mental health counselor I am advocating for my ability to receive reimbursement for the counseling services I provide to a wide range of clients, receive equal recognition from my fellow mental health colleagues and the public, and perform counseling services as provided in my scope of practice and through my training.

Although the focus of this chapter is advocating for the counseling profession, clients often indirectly benefit from counselors' professional advocacy efforts. Counselors might advocate for themselves because they know that doing so also benefits the general public. By continually advocating for federal funding to train counselors (i.e., Rehabilitation Services Administration training grants), rehabilitation counselors have consistently been able to produce graduates. Clients benefit by having access to rehabilitation counseling services. By increasing awareness of their backgrounds and the services they can provide, counselors offer information that helps the general public make informed decisions about who might best meet their needs. Finally, by promoting themselves through the development of standards and credentials that encourage self-reflection and regulation, counselors ensure clients receive services from qualified professionals. Think About It 14.2 challenges you to consider your advocacy passions.

THINK ABOUT IT 14.2

Based on what you have learned about the profession of counseling so far, what challenges do you anticipate having to face as a counselor in your specialty area? Which of those challenges are ones you envision feeling passionate enough about to engage in advocacy activities?

Aside from a general interest in increasing awareness about the counseling profession, professional counselors might have very specific agendas driving their advocacy efforts. Personal experiences related to things such as job cuts, professional roles, or training standards often spark counselors' desires to take action via advocacy. Activity 14.2

helps you to explore why counselors in your area advocate for themselves and the counseling profession.

ACTIVITY 14.2

What prompts professional counselors in your local area or state to engage in professional advocacy efforts? Interview some professional counselors, counselor educators, or leaders of counseling organizations in your area, and ask them to share times when they felt it necessary to advocate for the counseling profession.

- Ask them to explain what prompted them to engage in advocacy activities and what advocacy activities they engaged in.
- Inquire about how their advocacy efforts paid off.
- Compare the information you gathered with that of other classmates, and discuss commonalities and differences.
- What main themes arise in their stories?

To examine other reasons professional counselors might engage in professional advocacy efforts, consider the following Case Studies, and respond to the questions that follow. Case Studies 14.1, 14.2, and 14.3 are intended to help you understand some of the current issues different types of counselors are facing and why advocating for themselves and the profession is crucial. The questions in Activity 14.3 encourage you to consider how others view the role of counselors and to brainstorm specific ways the counselors might respond to their situations.

CASE STUDY 14.1

Hiring Paraprofessional Counselors

Since graduating with your master's degree in counseling 10 years ago, you have worked at a mental health counseling agency where your daily responsibilities include providing individual and group counseling, providing case management services, leading community-based workshops, and, recently, supervising junior staff members. You enjoy opportunities to provide direct services to clients the most. Over time, you have seen the staff in your agency increase in size from three to eight, based on the growing needs in your community.

Your state recently passed legislation permitting the hiring of bachelor's-level counseling paraprofessionals whose responsibilities can include counseling and case management. These individuals cannot provide diagnoses or bill for their services, and their work must be supervised at all times. Because these individuals can be hired at a cheaper rate than master's-level counselors, your agency has decided to downsize the number of full-time licensed professional counselors (LPCs) and replace them with these paraprofessionals. The organization decided it would retain four LPCs whose main responsibilities would be to provide diagnoses, develop treatment plans, co-lead groups, and supervise the paraprofessionals. Your job is not at stake because you have more experience than most of the other LPCs on staff; however, you are not sure you want to continue working at this agency given these changes.

CASE STUDY 14.2

Social Workers Replacing Professional School Counselors

You have worked as an elementary school counselor in a school in your hometown for the past 4 years. You were thrilled to be able to find employment near your family and have enjoyed working with the students, even though your caseload of 400 is far too large. You have a pretty good relationship with your principal. He has allowed you to initiate a rotating schedule of small-group interventions and cut back on classroom guidance. Parents and teachers have been very appreciative of your efforts.

Nevertheless, the large school district in which you work has decided to eliminate elementary school counselors. It has prioritized a greater emphasis on school–family collaborations and has decided to hire school social workers because its leaders believe the social workers are better qualified to coordinate those types of collaborative efforts. You have no interest in, and you do not feel qualified to work in, a middle or high school, and the closest school district that still hires elementary school counselors is an hour's drive from your home. Someone suggests you should pursue the school social work degree.

CASE STUDY 14.3

Licensed Counselor versus Licensed Psychologist

Your degree in college counseling has served you well for the past 20 years in your position in the Office of Student Support Services on a college campus. Your main responsibilities have been to provide services to students with disabilities and students in need of general academic support. You are currently serving on a search committee whose charge is to review applications to fill a new clinical staff member position at the campus counseling center.

This center currently functions as the only option for students needing campus-based counseling services. It historically has been staffed by clinical and counseling psychologists and student interns from those programs. You feel strongly that having a licensed counselor on staff is important. In addition, given the existing counselor education program on campus, the addition of an LPC could open up the possibility of using that site for counseling student internships. Your efforts are futile, however, and the committee ends up hiring another counseling psychologist.

ACTIVITY 14.3

The three scenarios just described have important implications for clients that are worth exploring. When you read the next chapter, you might want to revisit these scenarios. For now, though, consider the counseling profession as a whole. For the case studies described, ask yourself the following questions:

- Based on their unique experiences, what specific goals might these professional counselors have regarding advocating for the profession?
- What are the potential implications of these hiring decisions on the counseling profession as a whole?

- How are the roles of existing professional counselors in these organizations affected by the hiring decisions?
- What factors do you think led the decision makers in these scenarios (i.e., head of the agency or school administrator) to replace or simply not hire professional counselors?
- What, if anything, could the professional counselors have done proactively to prevent the outcomes described in the scenarios?
- What types of information do you think would have been beneficial for the decision makers to know regarding professional counselors that might have led them to different outcomes?
- What, if anything, could the professional counselors in the situations described do *now* to advocate for the counseling profession?

The above-described cases are reflective of situations that occur throughout the United States. Counselors, psychologists, social workers—aren't they all the same? You already have read about the history of the counseling profession and by now have a basic awareness of issues related to training and licensure. You probably understand more than you did before starting your graduate program about how professional counselors differ from other mental health professionals. To the general public, however, these differences are not so clear. Often, members of the general public serve on advisory boards or hiring committees and are responsible for decisions, such as those in the above described cases, that affect the counseling profession.

Without knowledge related to differences in training requirements, scope of practice, and credentials among mental health professionals, employers might assume one professional could be easily replaced with another. Without an appreciation for the unique contributions professional counselors can offer, employers might underuse them. In talking with professional counselors, you might hear them complain about having to engage in **administrative tasks**, such as coordinating client files, which could easily be completed by office personnel. You might also hear them express frustration related to the agencies that employ them contracting out to other mental health professionals for services the professional counselors themselves would be qualified to perform. Although numerous factors might cause employers to use professional counselors in those ways, it is likely that employers' misunderstandings of professional counselors' skills and abilities influence their decisions regarding counselor roles and responsibilities.

Proactive advocacy might not prevent people or policy makers from questioning various aspects of the counseling profession. Nevertheless, as with the benefits of any type of preventive strategy, proactive advocacy efforts might help to decrease the frequency or delay the onset of concerns from various stakeholders. Consider the suggestion by Crouch and Walz (1992) that advocacy efforts should focus on showing and explaining what professional counselors do, what roles are appropriate for them based on their training, and what the potential benefits are of hiring them. To advocate proactively in this manner, counselors might use existing materials, such as those available in the Government Affairs section of the American Counseling Association's website. For example, the two-page brochure titled *Who are LPCs?* (ACA, 2011) could be used to convey general information about counselor training and qualifications as well as populations counselors serve. This kind of information could be shared during Counseling Awareness Month (April) as a general public relations activity. Furthermore, individual counselors or groups could convene to present this type of information in person to an agency or institutional advisory board to clarify issues and address questions prior to hiring decisions being made.

Historically, Gilchrist and Stringer (1992) discussed the importance of advocates being able to communicate to stakeholders what works, consistent with the current expectation that professional counselors provide data to show their effectiveness. More recently, Hays, Wood, and Smith (2012) indicated that identifying best practices in counseling is critical to professional advocacy via informing counselor preparation and validating what counselors do.

Questions such as: *What do professional counselors do? What makes professional counselors different from other mental health professionals? Why should I seek counseling? What are the benefits of counseling?* can serve as guides for the types of information that could be shared proactively in counselors' efforts to advocate for the profession. Complete Activity 14.4 to demonstrate your ability to plan, implement, and evaluate a proactive effort to advocate for the counseling profession.

ACTIVITY 14.4

Revisit the questions in Activity 14.3 and your reaction to Think About It 14.2. Generate a list of things you could do to advocate proactively for the counseling profession. Think specifically about your specialty area and some of the advocacy needs for that particular group of counselors. After answering the questions below, choose one of your ideas and implement it.

- Who would be your target audience?
- What would you want them to know about counseling?
- Why do you believe that information would be important to share?
- How would you share the information?
- How would you assess the effectiveness of your efforts?

PREREQUISITES TO EFFECTIVE ADVOCACY

What is required to become an effective advocate for the counseling profession? First, Eriksen (1999) argued that specific skills are important, and that **advocacy skills** are not that different from counseling skills. She specifically identified basic counseling skills and data-gathering skills as crucial to effective advocacy. Listening and questioning skills are important for understanding concerns expressed by various stakeholders, as are skills in clarifying and summarizing. Oral and written communication skills are valuable for disseminating information accurately, concisely, and clearly. To assess the needs of the counseling profession, data-gathering skills, such as knowing how to conduct needs assessments and how to gather and summarize descriptive information, are crucial.

Hof, Dinsmore, Barber, Suhr, and Scofield (2009) proposed four main categories of professional advocacy interventions that can be used to group the types of activities and initiatives discussed throughout this chapter. They also identified a number of competencies relevant to each category. For example, for the first category, *Promoting Professional Identity*, they listed competencies to promote pride in the counseling profession and support for professional counseling organizations, just to name a couple. *Increasing the Public Image of Counseling* included competencies such as increasing the public's knowledge of counseling as well as the impact of counselors. Promoting professional accountability and collaboration with other mental health professionals are examples of competencies related to the third category, *Developing Interprofessional/Intraprofessional Collaboration*. Finally, *Promoting Legislative/Policy Initiatives* included competencies such as identifying legislation that causes barriers to counseling practice and promoting licensure reciprocity across states.

As reflected in the categories outlined by Hof et al. (2009), Eriksen (1999) emphasized possessing a clear **professional identity** is necessary before engaging in advocacy efforts for the profession. Similarly, Myers and Sweeney (2004) suggested that professional advocacy efforts require coordinated efforts among counseling organizations. Lack of consistency or coordination within or among various professional counseling organizations can result in unclear messages being sent to the public. In many ways, sharing inconsistent information can potentially be more detrimental to the counseling profession than sharing no information at all. The case in Activity 14.5 helps you to think more clearly about the potential effect of counselors presenting inconsistent identities.

ACTIVITY 14.5

Think back to the case example of social workers replacing elementary school counselors (Case Study 14.2). Suppose lawmakers in your state are debating whether to replace all elementary school counseling positions in the state with social worker positions or to redefine the role of elementary school counselors. School counselors in the state differ in their opinions about this issue. On one side, the state school counseling organization is lobbying to retain elementary school counselors with an emphasis on those individuals mainly providing preventive and responsive services (e.g., direct contact via individual, group, and classroom interventions). A small subset of elementary school counselors whose job responsibilities for the past 5 years have involved teaching classroom guidance lessons, assisting with the design and monitoring of behavioral modification plans, and coordinating testing services is not interested in leading groups or providing individual counseling. This group's counselors believe the classroom-based services and coordination services are not only important, but also allow them to address the needs of all students. This group of professional school counselors presents a different agenda to legislators.

- If you were one of the state legislators, what would you do with the different information shared by these constituents? How would their perspectives inform your decision?
- Would you favor one group's perspective? If so, which one and why?
- Would your decision be easier if the groups had the same agenda or a unified message?
- What messages would you leave with regarding how elementary school counselors view their roles?

Differing agendas have plagued the counseling profession for years, and because professional counselors are unique individuals, there are bound to be differences in their thoughts and actions. Regarding advocating for the profession, counselors must realize that sometimes it is important to put the needs of the profession as a whole before their own needs. Legislators and other important stakeholders might have a hard time taking a profession seriously if its members cannot agree on the messages they are sending.

Eriksen (1999) indicated that conflicts within professional counseling organizations often are major barriers to their professional advocacy efforts. Current threats to a consistent professional identity among counselors include (1) professional counselors identifying first by their specialty areas rather than as professional counselors who work in different settings (e.g., a marriage, couples, and family counselor versus a professional counselor who works with couples and families); (2) professional counselors identifying with other complementary professions before identifying as counselors (e.g., student affairs and college counselors overlapping with higher education personnel, or school counselors describing themselves as educators first); (3) counseling divisions becoming organizations that function independently from the ACA; (4) inconsistent counselor licensure requirements from state to state; (5) inconsistent training requirements (e.g., counselor education programs that do not have to be accredited); (6) counselor education programs hiring psychologists or individuals with doctoral degrees in other professional areas to teach counseling courses; and (7) placing counseling interns at sites where they are supervised by licensed psychologists or social workers rather than by counselors. Complete Activity 14.6 to explore the professional identities of counselors in your local area.

ACTIVITY 14.6

With your classmates, identify professional counselors in your area who represent a variety of specialty areas. Try to interview a few from each area. Consider the issues numbered 1–4 in the preceding paragraph as you interview them.

- How do these individuals describe their professional identities?
- What consistencies are there in their descriptions?
- What differences are there in their descriptions?
- If they were to speak as a whole on behalf of the counseling profession, what consistent message could be shared?

A final prerequisite for effective advocacy involves resources. The amount of money and time required varies depending on the types of advocacy activities in which professional counselors plan to engage (Myers & Sweeney, 2004). Even when their desire to advocate is strong and motivation is high, inadequate financial resources and time constraints might prevent some professional counselors from engaging in advocacy efforts or might restrict the scope of their efforts. Professional counselors must be creative in finding inexpensive and efficient ways to advocate for the profession (examples are provided later in this chapter), or they must be prepared to use time and energy securing enough resources in the form of personnel or money to ensure their efforts do not have to be halted partway through.

PROCESS OF ADVOCACY

According to Eriksen (1997), advocating for the profession requires counselors to progress through numerous steps: (1) identify the problem, (2) assess the availability of resources, (3) engage in strategic planning activities, (4) train professional counselors to advocate, (5) implement a plan of action, and (6) celebrate accomplishments.

Identify the Problem

A crucial first step in advocacy involves deciding when something is worth advocating for. The last thing counselors want is to be perceived as taking issue with everything that does not exactly work for them or for their clients. The phrase *choose your battles wisely* comes to mind. Quoting one of the participants in her study, Eriksen (1997) stated, "'I think that may be the most challenging part of advocacy . . . coming to some agreement among ourselves' as to what problems should receive priority attention" (p. 23). Eriksen suggested that problems deemed as greater threats tend to receive priority, as do problems whose solutions seem feasible. Prioritizing concerns might be simple for individual professional counselors. For groups, however, consensus on which problems are more significant might be more difficult to obtain.

Even when problems are identified, Eriksen (1997) suggested that "problem definition involves using language to frame the problem so that decision-makers and the wider public will be motivated to take action" (p. 23). In other words, professional counselors who are unable to explain their concerns to important stakeholders in terms of outcomes that will be meaningful to those individuals are likely to be unsuccessful in securing public or legislative support for their efforts. Activity 14.7 helps you to understand what factors might motivate a counselor to feel strongly about advocating for the counseling profession.

ACTIVITY 14.7

Earlier in this chapter, you were encouraged to ask a local professional counselor to identify a time when he or she felt a need to advocate for the profession. Now find another professional counselor and ask him or her to identify any issues regarding the counseling profession as a whole that are currently affecting him or her. Ask him or her the following questions:

- What are the issues, and how are you being affected?
- How much of a concern, on a scale of 1 (low) to 10 (high), are the issues?
- Based on your ratings, which concerns warrant action?
- What do you believe might happen if the concerns are not addressed?
- How motivated are you to take action?

Assess the Availability of Resources

As mentioned previously, availability of time and money are important considerations in developing advocacy plans. Factors such as personnel, expertise, and motivation must also be considered before advocacy plans are finalized. For example, groups that want to affect change in legislation ideally need the involvement of someone who possesses knowledge of the legislative system, including timing of advocacy efforts and effective methods and procedures for contacting legislators (e.g., letter-writing campaigns versus lobbying in person). Most state counseling organizations have a board member who is responsible for overseeing legislative and lobbying initiatives. That individual keeps local counselors informed about federal and state issues as well as opportunities to get involved in legislative advocacy efforts. In addition, the ACA has on its website a very useful document, *Effective Advocacy with Members of Congress*, that state counseling organizations often share with members interested in engaging in lobbying efforts. This document offers specific guidance regarding which advocacy methods tend to be the most effective (i.e., meet in person or send individualized letters rather than form letters), how much to say (i.e., be brief and focus on one issue at a time), and how specific to be in your message (i.e., reference a specific bill or law). Furthermore, in its Call to Action section in the Public Policy link of its website, the ACA also provides detailed information about current initiatives that need support as well as information regarding who to contact, how to contact them, and sample messages to send.

Level of outside support is another key resource area to assess. Outside support might include individuals outside the counseling profession who would support professional counselors' efforts and individuals in key positions who could help professional counselors to access important stakeholders. Professional counselors might enlist support from former clients, from agencies with which they have partnerships, or from local organizations that benefit from their work. Personal stories or anecdotes that illustrate how helpful a particular counseling agency was or how critical a specific counselor was to someone's progress can go a long way to enlist support. Depending on their advocacy agendas, professional counselors might also target influential community members who might be able to help them communicate their agendas to local government officials or funding agencies or connect them to local media sources. Sometimes a connection is what is lacking, and finding an *in* to convey the message can be very important. By asking around, professional counselors might easily identify people who know people who can make introductions. In any event, by determining the amount and types of outside support they have, professional counselors can plan advocacy activities accordingly. Complete Activity 14.8 to explore further the resources that might be available in your community.

ACTIVITY 14.8

Consider possible sources of outside support you might be able to enlist in your community to help your advocacy efforts. Consider the following:

- Which individuals or groups outside the counseling profession might be willing to be involved in this effort? Are there former clients who might be willing to share stories?
- How would you decide which outside individuals would be the most influential in advocating for the profession?
- Consider some ways you could contact community support figures or local media sources. Who do you know who might be able to connect you to them?

Engage in Strategic Planning Activities

This next step essentially focuses on professional counselors developing ideas for addressing their concerns by designing advocacy plans. Eriksen (1999) indicated that individual advocacy efforts can be implemented more easily than group efforts. For groups of professional counselors involved in advocating for the profession, Eriksen suggested they use a planning process that involves the creation of a small, representative group of professional counselors. This small planning group would take on the responsibility for developing long-term plans and short-term goals that reflect the larger group's concerns. The planning group would also develop a list of the activities in which the larger group would engage and disseminate any materials, documentation, and information to stakeholders. To ensure all group members are thinking about the issue in the same way, the following questions can be helpful to review during this step:

- What is our main concern?
- Who is our target audience?
- What do we want that audience to know?
- What is a realistic time frame for addressing our concern?
- How can we best go about addressing our concern?

As discussed earlier in this chapter, a lot of advocacy efforts really boil down to educating the public about who counselors are, what they do, how they differ from other mental health professionals, and what the benefits are of working with counselors. As professional counselors plan their advocacy efforts, they could tap resources about generating public awareness that the ACA and other counseling organizations have compiled (e.g., *Public Awareness Ideas and Strategies for Professional Counselors*, ACA, 2012). Activities such as submitting press releases to announce the opening of a private practice can help increase a professional counselor's exposure. At the same time, such press releases can share other information to help clarify who counselors are (e.g., training and credentials) and the benefits of counseling.

Train Professional Counselors to Advocate

If groups are to advocate effectively, they must have involvement from more than one individual who possesses the knowledge and skills to do so. Eriksen (1999) believed that training members of an organization for advocacy would help to motivate those members to become involved. Doing so could also result in the group having increased resources in the form of more qualified personnel to carry out advocacy tasks. Eriksen suggested that training should occur in the form of workshops or conferences, and many professional counseling organizations hold sessions related to advocacy. The advocacy-knowledge needs of professional counselors before participating in training might include how to approach legislators, kinds of information to share, and what not to do. Many of the ACA resources discussed in this chapter could be used as training materials. Skills related to things such as assertiveness, public speaking, and communicating effectively in writing could also be addressed via various training opportunities. Graduate students or practitioners seeking to grow in this area might seek out individuals in state counseling organizations who serve in board positions related to government relations and public relations/awareness. Now complete Activity 14.9.

ACTIVITY 14.9

Use the following questions to assess your own readiness to engage in professional advocacy activities:

- How confident are you in your ability to speak effectively and clearly in public?
- Do you know how to express your concerns to legislators?
- Can you identify local counseling organizations that might be willing to partner with you in your efforts?
- Are you able to identify effective formats for sharing information?

Implement a Plan of Action

Implementing an advocacy plan might seem like a straightforward step. Nevertheless, many factors are crucial to the success of that implementation. First, a clear, organized strategic plan sets the stage for successful plan implementation. Second, ensuring group members are aware of and able to perform their assigned task is crucial to the success of the group's advocacy efforts. Third, monitoring the implementation process and assessing any concerns or needs along the way allow professional counselors to make modifications as needed. The core planning team might need to reconvene to revise plans, provide training for other members, or reallocate their resources. In many instances, the time frame for implementing the advocacy plan might limit opportunities to implement modifications.

Finally, as all good professional counselors learn, assessing the effectiveness of one's efforts is necessary to inform future actions. Assessment is an important component of implementation. Professional counselors engaged in professional advocacy efforts can use short-term goals to engage in ongoing assessment, or, depending on their time frames, simply assess final outcomes. Having clear, measurable goals in mind from the start should make assessing those goals manageable. Practice developing potential outcome measures by completing Activity 14.10 and use Activity 14.11 to discuss further how you might collect outcome data from those measures. Then read Voices from the Field 14.3.

ACTIVITY 14.10

Consider the following **advocacy goals**, and develop outcome measures that could be used to assess whether your advocacy efforts were successful:

1. Community members will know how to access counseling services through your agency.
2. Administrators will recognize how your efforts affected students academically.
3. Legislators will possess a clear understanding of the unique training that professional counselors receive.

ACTIVITY 14.11

Determine one way to collect outcome data from Activity 14.10 from stakeholders to meet your advocacy goals.

VOICES FROM THE FIELD 14.3   Persistence in Advocacy, by Stephanie Burns

Counselors need to be mindful that professional advocacy is a marathon and not a sprint. I believe that counselors need to redirect dismissals to focus on the issues at hand and not be intimidated. If intimidation gets you to remove yourself from the conversation and stop advocating for your profession, you have lost your power. Even if you are being dismissed, stay in the conversation.

Eventually you can make a principled case and can make improvements to the situation. However, it may take some time. Just because you hear 'no' in the present doesn't mean it won't change in the future. Advocacy is a process, a conversation you are having on multiple fronts; it could be with legislators, insurance companies, or other mental health providers. You must stay in the conversation or other people will write the ending for you and in a way that you may not desire. Each professional advocacy victory helps to positively impact counselor professional identity.

Celebrate Accomplishments

A final step in advocacy is to celebrate. Professional counselors know that it is important to celebrate the little things. It is also important to celebrate the big things. Not only is reflecting on the amount of time and effort invested by the individuals involved important, but also communicating successes to others can be helpful toward future advocacy efforts. Eriksen (1999) suggested that professional counselors consider documenting and disseminating information about their successes via newsletters or press releases. She also recommended thanking important stakeholders as a way to increase potential support from them over time.

WAYS TO ADVOCATE

By now you should understand why advocacy is important, and you probably have some understanding of how to begin the process of advocating for the profession. Examples of activities that could be used as part of advocacy efforts should help to complete the picture. Professional counselors can advocate for the profession in countless ways. The ACA (2012) and other counseling organizations have developed resource guides that can be helpful to members during the strategic planning step. The questions mentioned earlier in this chapter regarding who professional counselors are, what professional counselors do, and how professional counselors can make a difference can be addressed through advocacy activities. The general goal of advocacy is to share information and increase **public awareness**, with potential outcomes of those efforts ranging from changing public policy to securing funding to keep a job to increasing the number of clients who seek counseling services. The following ideas represent only some of the ways professional counselors can advocate for the profession. An extensive list of ideas for how to advocate for the counseling profession can be found at www.stephanietburns.com/SLCA/loai.html. Further, a compilation of links to resources to help you better understand how to advocate for the counseling profession is available at www.stephanietburns.com/SLCA/ar.html.

Identifying Yourself as a Professional Counselor

One simple way to advocate for the profession is for professional counselors to identify themselves as professional counselors whenever possible (ACA, 2012). This can be as simple as listing **credentials** on letterhead and publications, mentioning involvement in professional counseling organizations, or displaying a counseling license prominently in the office. Some people feel uncomfortable listing numerous professional credentials next to their names, indicating that doing so feels pretentious. Others express a desire to be cautious about alienating clients who might be intimidated by someone whom they perceive to be very well educated. Explore how you and other people react to counselor credentials by completing Activities 14.12 and 14.13.

ACTIVITY 14.12

Test this concern. Obtain some business cards from professional counselors in your area, and ask some of your friends and family members to share their reaction to the information on those cards. Try to find a range of professional counselors—some who list many credentials and others who list only one.

- How often did your friends and family members comment on the credentials?
- Were their reactions more positive or negative?

ACTIVITY 14.13

Think back to a time when you became familiar with a professional's credentials (e.g., a professor, mental health professional, physician of any kind). How did you react to this information? Did it change your perception of the professional or influence your decision to work with or see the professional?

Eriksen (1999) discussed the importance of taking opportunities to clarify the uniqueness of the counseling profession, particularly when professional counselors are mistakenly referred to as other helping professionals. One might argue that it is simply a matter of semantics to the general public—that by referring to professional counselors as psychologists they mean no harm. It seems likely that most people simply have not differentiated among the professions. This is important to keep in mind, and professional counselors must be careful not to appear defensive about the counseling profession in their efforts to educate the public. Now complete Think About It 14.3.

THINK ABOUT IT 14.3

Have you ever seen a group of people wearing matching shirts to reflect their workplace while out in the community engaging in some sort of project? What do you usually think of the people or organization involved in these organized community service efforts?

Serve Your Community

Professional counselors can clarify their professional identities not only through displaying their credentials, but also through engaging in activities as a group. The ACA (2012) suggested professional counselors consider working in groups to provide services in their local communities. They could host blood drives, gather supplies for local charitable organizations, or find other creative ways to support or raise money for local causes. An important aspect of these efforts is to publicize the events. Some professional counselors feel uncomfortable doing this because they want their efforts to be viewed as altruistic rather than self-serving. By publicizing their efforts, however, professional counselors can potentially increase awareness about their roles and services. Individuals with whom they interact during the events could be engaged in brief discussions about the counseling services available in their communities. However, public knowledge of the events might also increase awareness of the communities' needs, and professional counselors can be very intentional about taking opportunities to balance their efforts to advocate for themselves with opportunities to advocate for others, a concept that is addressed in more detail in Chapter 15.

Another way professional counselors can become involved in their communities, securing local support for services, is to provide professional services outside their typical day-to-day work. Professional counselors might consider the benefits of donating their time to lead informational workshops through local libraries or to speak to parents at PTA meetings. Topics could include coping with elderly parents, enhancing relationships, and becoming more assertive. Through direct contact with professional counselors, various stakeholders might gain better understandings of the profession and the importance of the profession.

Similarly, the ACA (2012) suggested that professional counselors consider participating in the various National Screening Day initiatives related to depression, eating disorders, alcohol, and anxiety disorders. The purposes of these initiatives are to educate the general public about issues, conduct screenings, and help people identify places where they can receive help. Through involvement in these events, professional counselors can demonstrate their expertise and explain their services. Complete Activity 14.14 to examine the ways counselors in your local area have been involved in the community. Then complete Activity 14.15 to consider your expertise and ways that you might become involved.

ACTIVITY 14.14

Peruse the local newspaper and bulletin boards throughout this semester.

- With what types of community organizations have local professional counselors been involved?
- How have they, individually or in groups, given back to the community?
- What types of free, public workshops have they offered?
- How effective were their efforts in terms of advocating for the profession?

ACTIVITY 14.15

Identify ways you can provide a service to your local school or community while simultaneously advocating for the counseling profession.

- What types of services do you think are needed?
- How difficult would they be to organize?
- What types of resources would you need?

Choose one of your ideas and implement it.

Use the Media

Disseminating information for advocacy can be done through a variety of media. The ACA (2012) suggested that professional counselors develop **media kits** that individually address either a specific issue on which professional counselors are focusing or counseling services specific to professional counselors' workplaces or areas of expertise. They recommended that professional counselors develop and include items such as brochures, flyers, fact sheets, press releases, photographs, summaries of recent events, role statements, frequently asked questions, and biographical information. Professional counselors can be very creative with the formats in which they share information.

The ACA (2012) advised that with media kits in place, professional counselors would be prepared to respond to spur-of-the-moment questions, and they would have comprehensive information available in various formats to accommodate their needs at any given time. Information in media kits should be updated regularly; for professional counselors working in agencies, perhaps someone could assume the responsibility for compiling information on a regular basis to update the kits. In addition, professional counselors might consider having information available in formats designed for different target audiences (e.g., informational brochures designed for potential clients would look different from ones designed for local policy makers or funding agencies).

Newspapers, radio, Internet, and television also serve as useful outlets for professional counseling advocacy efforts. The ACA (2012) provided examples of press releases and radio spots that professional counselors could use to disseminate information about the profession. Via newspapers, professional counselors can submit letters to the editor in which they attempt to educate the public about important public policy issues affecting professional counselors, make the public aware of services or special events, or thank the public for their support. Radio spots played during special events could help professional counselors promote awareness of the profession and their services. The ACA suggested that Counseling Awareness Month is a good time to flood the market with messages about the counseling profession. Complete Activity 14.16 and discuss the types of public relations activities that would best fit different situations.

ACTIVITY 14.16

List as many avenues as you can for disseminating information.

- Discuss the types and amounts of resources (e.g., money, time, personnel) that would be needed for each approach.
- Which would you recommend for individuals who have small budgets?
- Which would you recommend for individuals who have limited time?

Technology

Finally, not much has been written about the use of websites, blogs, or social media to advertise events or launch advocacy petitions, but with an increasing number of people using the Internet and social media in general, technology-based advocacy efforts seem very timely. Regarding websites, Milsom and Bryant (2006) discussed the importance of disseminating information via websites to clarify counselor roles, while also emphasizing being intentional about what information is and is not posted in order to ensure that the information accurately portrays their competencies and the scope of their work. An additional consideration might be to use websites to disseminate outcome data; counselors could share (as appropriate) information related to the outcomes of their specific services or to the effectiveness of counseling in general.

In addition to developing and maintaining a website containing information related to services specific to the agencies in which they work, professional counselors should consider the benefits of using social media to disseminate information about the counseling profession in general. More and more counselors are using Facebook to promote their services or post information about counseling. Other counselors and counseling organizations use blogs to disseminate information about how counseling can make a difference and to promote a professional counseling identity. There is no limit to the ways in which professional counselors could use technology to advocate for the profession. Counselors should identify whatever outlet makes sense for them and take time to examine what others counselors have done. Now complete Activity 14.17 and then read Voices from the Field 14.4.

ACTIVITY 14.17

1. Look up the website for a counseling agency or school counseling office, or try to locate counselors who have Facebook sites.
   - What type of information do they share?
   - What impression of counseling do you get after reviewing their information?
2. Now, design a website or social media page either for your counseling program or for a local counseling agency.
   - What types of information do you want to share via the website?
   - Who is your target audience?
   - How will you promote the website?

VOICES FROM THE FIELD 14.4　Targeting Legislators, by Stephen Kennedy

When I was serving as Government Relations Chair for the North Carolina School Counselor Association (NCSCA) in 2013, our lobbyist and members encouraged state lawmakers to pass North Carolina's "Duties of School Counselors" law. The law defines appropriate duties for school counselors, specifies that school counselors should be allowed to spend at least 80% of their time in direct service to students, and prohibits school counselors from being placed in the time-intensive role of test coordinator. Although the NCSCA advocated for this law for many years, they were finally able to gather enough support when legislators were seeking to pass school safety measures following the tragic school shooting at Sandy Hook Elementary School in Connecticut. Educating our legislators about the many ways that school counselors keep students safe helped them to understand that passing the law would support their legislative efforts. Other common legislative priorities related to school counseling include career and college readiness and dropout prevention. By identifying areas of common interest, professional counselors will have more success in encouraging legislators to pass beneficial legislation.

Target Policy Makers

One final way to advocate for the counseling profession is to communicate with **policy makers** at the local, state, and national levels. The idea of participating in lobbying efforts was discussed previously, and many counseling organizations offer opportunities for interested members to talk as a group with state or national legislators. Additionally, the ACA provides information on its website regarding current legislation affecting the counseling profession. It also provides sample letters that can be sent by individuals to legislators to express concerns and recommend public policy changes. A more comprehensive perspective on impacting policy is provided by Eriksen (1997) in her book *Making an Impact: A Handbook for Counselor Advocacy*. Eriksen walks professional counselors through various ways to effect change on a systemic level through legislation or the courts. Use Activity 14.18 to plan your own advocacy efforts aimed at policy makers.

ACTIVITY 14.18

Develop an advocacy plan to be implemented during Counseling Awareness Month. Use the steps described previously to identify a goal, target audience, and resources needed to develop and implement your plan.

Summary

Advocating for the counseling profession requires that professional counselors possess knowledge and understanding of what it means to advocate, why advocacy is important, steps involved in advocacy, and ways to advocate. These issues were addressed in this chapter on a very basic level, and references were made to resources that could be useful in your future advocacy efforts.

Examining the advocacy activities of professional counseling organizations is a good starting point. Professional counselors can seek guidance from professional organizations such as the ACA regarding types of issues to focus on and ways to approach advocacy. By examining what types of advocacy efforts have been effective for others, professional counselors can potentially save time and money and be more effective in their efforts.

To advocate effectively for the profession, professional counselors can expect to engage in many steps. Before developing plans to advocate for the profession, professional counselors must determine what issues are

worth advocating for. When they have specific agendas in mind, they must generate clear messages they can consistently communicate. Next, after determining the availability of resources, professional counselors can work with other professional counselors to develop and implement their advocacy plans. They should assess their plans' effectiveness along the way, if possible, and upon completion at a minimum. Finally, professional counselors are encouraged to share their advocacy successes with others and particularly with the public.

There are myriad ways to advocate for the profession, and professional counselors are limited only by their own lack of knowledge and the resources available to them. Common methods for advocating include sharing credentials, talking about the counseling profession, and being present in the community. Professional counselors can also use various types of media, including print, broadcast, and Internet. Finally, professional counselors might take political action by interacting with policy makers.

With some knowledge of the advocacy process, a desire to fight for their profession, and minimal resources, professional counselors can potentially make a great impact on the future of the counseling profession. Professional counselors are encouraged to make connections with and gather resources from their local and state counseling organizations. From that point, there are a wide variety of resources available to help guide professional counselors in their individual advocacy efforts.

MyCounselingLab for Introduction to Counseling

Try the Topic 6 Assignments: *Current Trends in Counseling.*

15 Advocacy Counseling: Being an Effective Agent of Change for Clients

Donna M. Gibson

PREVIEW

Addressing external barriers that interfere with human development is the core purpose of advocacy. Although this purpose can be met by advocating for the profession of counseling, it is often met by advocating at the individual client level. Through an examination of the counseling and advocacy interventions specified in the Multicultural and Social Justice Counseling Competencies of the Association for Multicultural Counseling and Development (Ratts, Singh, Nassar-McMillan, Butler, & McCullough, 2015), specific guidelines are provided on how to increase clients' empowerment and to be a successful advocacy counselor.

ADVOCACY COUNSELING

Advocacy in counseling has traditionally been known as the efforts of professional counselors to support clients based on clients' needs or some social cause. Advocacy has a rich tradition in the fields of social work and education. Over the past decade, there has been a movement within the counseling profession to focus on factors external to clients that adversely affect the emotional and physical well-being of clients. Advocacy in counseling has become known as advocacy counseling with an emphasis on social action and justice (Ratts & Hutchins, 2009; Smith, Reynolds, & Rovnak, 2009).

Advocacy counseling not only includes the actions of professional counselors on behalf of clients, but also includes professional counselors intervening with systems and organizations relevant to clients. In considering the "world" (e.g., family, educational, social, political, religious systems) of clients, the context for understanding the problems of clients begins to take shape. However, this conceptualization also includes consideration of the **barriers** inherent in these systems (e.g., prejudice, social class) encountered by clients. Professional counselors take on the role of advocate when employing social action to confront these issues on behalf of clients, which may result in social justice to confront injustice and inequality in society (Ratts & Hutchins, 2009; Smith et al., 2009). This type of advocacy counseling was defined as social justice counseling, which "includes empowerment of the individual as well as active confrontation of injustice and inequality in society as they impact clientele as well as those in their systemic contexts" (Counselors for Social Justice, 2017). Within this definition is recognition of the advocacy process and the sought-after product (justice) that affects the counselor, client, and the system/community

(Crethar & Winterowd, 2012). It involves an analysis of personal and professional values and being open to change interpersonally and effecting change professionally. Now complete Activity 15.1 to explore some potential advocacy situations.

ACTIVITY 15.1

Consider some possible advocacy situations for which clients may need your assistance as a professional counselor. Some examples follow:

- A middle-class client who has no medical insurance but is presenting with mental health issues that require medication.
- A student who recently moved to the area and started school. His teacher has not had time to pay special attention to him, and he is struggling academically and socially. His teacher thinks he is simply a low-achieving student.

What are some issues intrinsic to working with these clients? Think of other clients or scenarios you may have to advocate for in the future.

Much of the past literature on advocacy counseling focused on strategies employed by professional counselors to address clients' needs through social action or interventions specific to oppressed groups (Myers, Sweeney, & White, 2002). This work has spanned the disciplines of counseling, psychology, social work, sociology, and religion. However, systematic training guidelines and practices of advocacy counseling have historically not been in place for professional counselors. Although advocacy counseling is a professional and ethical responsibility of professional counselors, only recently has attention been given to outlining advocacy competencies for professional counselors.

In this chapter, guidelines for recognizing when advocacy counseling is needed are discussed. In addition, **counseling advocacy competencies** provided by the Association for Multicultural Counseling and Development (Ratts et al., 2015) are outlined. For each of the competency areas, case examples or applications are provided to illustrate the connection of each case to the competency and the appropriate methods to use as advocacy counselors in working with clients in all types of counseling settings.

When to Advocate

It is essential for professional counselors to integrate the role of advocate into their professional identity. Just as when learning how to apply various theoretical approaches to case conceptualization and treatment planning, professional counselors should identify characteristics within themselves that would make them successful advocates for clients. Values, personalities, and skills taught in counseling programs are necessary to the development of successful professional counselors and are strong contributors to the development of successful advocates.

In one study, participants reported that an educational approach, relationship building, and good communication are necessary to successful advocacy (Eriksen, 1999). In addition to these characteristics, a clear sense of professional identity is essential. Professional counselors need knowledge of what and whom they represent and what they are promoting in the role of advocate. Other essential elements are also required for successful advocacy. Leadership, organizational strength and unity, perseverance, maintaining an advocacy focus at all times, and education and training are components included in successful advocacy counseling. Activity 15.2 helps you to reflect on your own identity as a professional counselor.

ACTIVITY 15.2

How do you identify yourself? To be effective as a helping professional who attends to issues related to age, gender, race, sexual orientation, or social class, it is necessary to develop an awareness of your own perceptions and experiences related to these issues. Reflect on the following questions to begin this process or to start it anew because you may have a change in perspective that can inform your practice:

1. What does _____ (e.g., ageism, racism, sexism, classism) mean to you? Has it had the same meaning for you during your entire life? If not, what were your previous definitions? What made it change?
2. Have you been marginalized based on characteristics rightly or wrongly attributed to a particular group? If so, describe your thoughts and feelings at the time. Did you create a plan to change how you were treated? If so, what was it and did you act on it?
3. Have you treated anyone differently based on his or her age, race, sex, sexual orientation, or social class? If so, describe your thoughts and feelings at the time. Would you react differently now? Why or why not?

Learning to identify when to advocate has been a focus of educating and training advocates. In an effort to provide structure and training standards, the Association for Multicultural Counseling and Development has identified advocacy competencies and interventions for professional counselors and counselor educators engaged in these activities (Ratts et al., 2015). Using competencies encourages counselors to use strategies and interventions at multiple levels in their advocacy efforts (Rubel & Ratts, 2010). According to the AMCD Multicultural and Social Justice Competencies, there are multiple layers, identities, and dynamics that lead to competence in these areas (see Figure 15.1), including counselor self-awareness (represented by the first inner layer surrounding the core of multicultural and social justice praxis), client worldview (second inner layer), counseling relationship (third inner layer), and counseling and advocacy interventions (represented by outer layer). The three inner layer domains include the attitudes, beliefs, knowledge, skills and action important to multicultural competence and set the foundation for a framework of individual counseling and social justice advocacy. Now complete Activity 15.3.

ACTIVITY 15.3

Activity 15.1 described a middle-class person without insurance who needs medication.

- Think of a way you, as a professional counselor, can work with the client to overcome these issues.
- What possible community resources could you help him or her to research?
- Think of a way you can work on behalf of this client to deal with these issues. What additional issues may need to be considered or addressed?

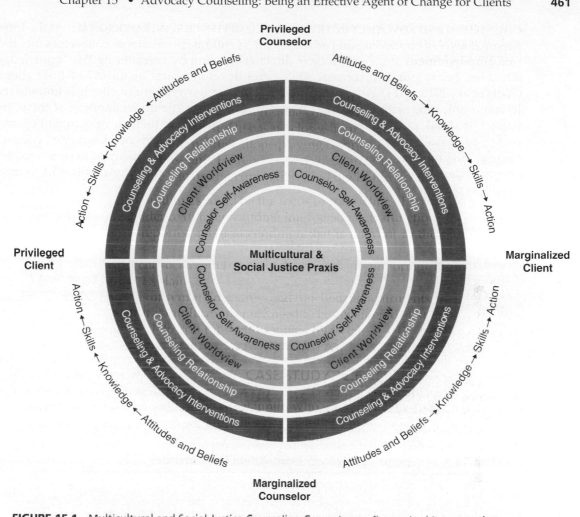

FIGURE 15.1 Multicultural and Social Justice Counseling Competences Conceptual Framework.

Source: Ratts, M. J., Singh, A. A., Nassar-McMillan, S., Butler, S. K., & McCullough, J. R. (2015). *Multicultural and social justice counseling competencies*. Retrieved from www.multiculturalcounseling.org/index.php?option–com_content&view=article&id=205:amcd-endorses-multicultural-and-social-justice-counseling-competencies&catid=1:latest&Itemid=123. Reprinted with permission.

Advocacy Counseling and Intervention Competencies

In Figure 15.1, advocacy counseling and interventions include the intrapersonal, interpersonal, institutional, community, public policy, and international/global levels of advocacy. In this chapter, the discussion focuses on working with clients in counseling versus graduate students in counseling programs, although the process is similar. In working with clients, it is important to remember basic fundamental counseling skills, which include good communication with clients. Professional counselors understand the importance of empathy and of establishing positive, trusting relationships with clients to make advocating effective (see Chapters 5–6). Assertive behavior is promoted through empathic understanding and good communication, which is a component of feeling empowered.

COUNSELING AND ADVOCACY INTERVENTION COMPETENCIES: INTRAPERSONAL   At the intrapersonal level of counseling and advocacy interventions, professional counselors incorporate **empowerment** strategies in their direct counseling by considering the "knowledge, attitudes, behaviour, self-concept, skills, and developmental histories" of their clients (Ratts et al., 2015, p. 11). A large component of the empowerment of clients is knowledge. In communicating with clients and developing an empathic understanding of them, the impact of social, political, economic, and cultural factors on their development becomes part of professional counselors' awareness. Part of the role of advocacy-oriented counselors is to integrate this awareness into the direct counseling relationship with clients to help clients understand their own lives in these contexts. Now complete Activity 15.4 to more deeply explore oppressions.

ACTIVITY 15.4

In Activity 15.2, you identified if and when you have been marginalized. Reflect on those experiences now. Where or whom did those oppressions (barriers) come from? From a specific group or culture of people? An organization? Part of the system? Have those barriers changed now? Why or why not?

Table 15.1 outlines specific intrapersonal counseling and advocacy intervention competencies of the Multicultural and Social Justice Counseling Competencies (Ratts et al. 2015). In providing direct interventions that help to empower clients, professional counselors can help clients learn to **self-advocate** (Adams, Bell, & Griffin, 2007). A key counseling skill involved in self-advocacy is assessment, as can be seen in several of the competencies in Table 15.1.

TABLE 15.1 Intrapersonal Advocacy Intervention Competencies

Multicultural and social justice competent counselors:

1. Take action by initiating conversations to determine how the worldviews, values, beliefs and biases held by privileged and marginalized counselors and clients influence the counseling relationship.

2. Take action by collaborating with clients to identify the ways that privileged and marginalized counselor and client identity development influence the counseling relationship.

3. Take action by exploring how counselor and clients' privileged and marginalized statuses influence the counseling relationship.

4. Take action by inviting conversations about how culture, stereotypes, prejudice, discrimination, power, privilege, and oppression influence the counseling relationship with privileged and marginalized clients.

5. Take action by collaborating with clients to determine whether individual counseling or systems advocacy is needed with privileged and marginalized clients.

6. Take action by using cross-communication skills to connect with privileged and marginalized clients.

From Ratts, M. J., Singh, A. A., Nassar-McMillan, S., Butler, S. K., & McCullough, J. R. (2015). *Multicultural and social justice counseling competencies.* Retrieved from www.multiculturalcounseling.org/index.php?option=com_content&view=article&id=205:amcd-endorses-multicultural-and-social-justice-counseling-competencies&catid=1:latest&Itemid=123. Reprinted with permission.

Specifically, **problem assessment** is essentially required to discern the need for advocacy. In advocacy models, problem assessment is usually one of the first steps. In problem assessment, professional counselors should identify the etiology of the problem. In other words, where did the problem come from? By systemically examining the problem, professional counselors can assess if problems arise from clients, their families, their work or school environments, the client-family characteristics, other environments in which clients interact, or the interactions among the environments. Professional counselors quickly discover that when examining problems systemically, the worldviews of clients are not the only worldviews of importance. The worldviews of the different systems and environments are also important in creating interventions that help to empower clients. In discovering the worldviews of clients and the worldviews from these systemic environments, clients may begin to identify external barriers that affect their development.

A second part of problem assessment is for professional counselors to recognize clients' behaviors and concerns that are responses to systemic or internalized **oppression**, which occurs when another entity imposes an object, label, role, experience, or set of living conditions that is unwanted, is painful, and detracts from the physical and psychological well-being of the client (Hays & Erford, 2018). Carefully confronting those behaviors or concerns may help clients gain knowledge about oppression and become more assertive in their efforts to combat it.

In helping clients gain a sense of empowerment, professional counselors need to be reminded that empowerment is an ongoing process. An empowerment-centered philosophy for promoting positive counseling emphasizes that everyone has the ability to shape events in life, rather than being powerless and helpless. Empowered individuals participate in active and meaningful ways in making decisions that affect their lives. In addition, empowerment becomes essential and necessary for clients to self-advocate. Case Study 15.1 presents an application of intrapersonal advocacy intervention competencies. Then read Voices from the Field 15.1.

CASE STUDY 15.1

Application of Intrapersonal Advocacy Intervention Competencies

Mark is a graduate student who has been attending counseling for one semester at the university counseling center. He identifies himself as gay and has been "out" since the start of his graduate studies, approximately 1.5 years ago. His family lives in a large city in the southwest. Mark describes his family as religiously and politically conservative. He has not discussed his sexual orientation with his family members because of their conservative beliefs and values. He reports that they primarily have been concerned about his career choice of student affairs in higher education influencing him to be more liberal in his values, beliefs, and behaviors.

His reason for coming to counseling was initially to deal with some feelings of anxiety about returning to school at the beginning of the semester. However, the counseling sessions have focused more and more on how his anger is growing toward his family members as they continue to make disparaging remarks, not only about homosexuals but also other minority groups. He sometimes avoids their phone calls and

(Continued)

makes only a few visits home. After a recent holiday visit home, he decided to delay coming out to them. He is also committed to his religious beliefs and attends religious study groups. Mark reports that he has found peace in his relationship with God as a gay man. Recently, a friend from the group confronted Mark about his sexual orientation and ended their friendship after learning that he is gay.

Questions for Consideration:

1. What could be some strengths and resources for Mark?
2. What are the social, political, economic, and cultural factors affecting Mark?
3. What are some of the signs that the professional counselor has recognized in Mark that may be a reflection of his response to systemic or internalized oppression?
4. What are some self-advocacy skills that you could teach Mark to apply to his situation?
5. How would you help Mark carry out his self-advocacy action plan?

In Mark's case, the research indicates that several factors must be considered in promoting empowerment and self-advocacy. Being a gay man, Mark is considered to be part of a marginalized population that is frequently overwhelmed by a sense of powerlessness (Savage, Harley, & Nowak, 2005). Powerlessness manifests itself in the form of oppression through language, **heterosexism**, simultaneous support and curtailment of civil rights, and hate crimes (Hays & Erford, 2018). Mark seems to be experiencing oppression through the language used by his family. His family members and the religious group member also inflicted oppression through their prejudiced beliefs and values, which they voiced to him. More specific to Mark's family, it seems that he may be experiencing heterosexism, which is the ideology that denies, denigrates, and stigmatizes any nonheterosexual form of behavior, identity, relationship, or community. This form of prejudice can make individuals who are gay or lesbian feel like second-class citizens, promoting feelings of powerlessness and worthlessness.

To increase Mark's self-advocacy, his feelings of empowerment need to be cultivated. To do this, he needs to form coalitions with other marginalized groups in every system that he incorporates into his "world," including his family system. In answering the question about Mark's resources, the answers may help to create an action plan that helps him form these coalitions. For example, Mark may identify other family members who have experienced some level of marginalization within the family. Reaching out to them may be a step in finding support within his family. In the area of religion, the college counselor may know of on-campus religious leaders who are open to homosexual individuals and are willing to have discussions with Mark about his religious concerns. A second goal is to help Mark develop an accurate representation of the lives and identities of gay men because he has recently come out to his work and school environments. How can this be accomplished? Through the identification of Mark's responses and behaviors related to oppression, counseling can offer Mark an outlet to express his emotions about the challenge of being a gay man in a heteropatriarchical society. A third component of Mark's action plan to self-advocate is to focus on Mark learning self-acceptance and acceptance by others. In the midst of oppression, Mark can develop a positive self-identity that can be a source of strength and empowerment. Finally, Mark should be encouraged to put into practice in the "real world" the action steps he has been developing in counseling. Once he identifies family members, friends, and community resources, he can prioritize these areas in his plan of action. Only when he demonstrates these actions himself can empowerment be fully realized.

VOICES FROM THE FIELD 15.1   Empowering Young Clients to Self-Advocate, by Danielle L. Geigle

---

Growing up as a younger sibling in a very small family provided me with little experience and opportunity to be around children. When I decided to enter into training as a community mental health counselor, I was one of the exclusive few who did *not* have any intention of working with the young people. In fact, throughout my academic program, I successfully managed to avoid nearly all of the play therapy and counseling children courses. When it came time for internship, my plan quickly and inevitably failed.

My internship experience involved working for a private agency in the heart of Appalachia, one of the most poverty-stricken areas in the country secondary to few job opportunities, a lack of resources, and the ensuing elevated drug and alcohol abuse. As a practicing counselor I was responsible for managing a caseload that, as an intern, felt overwhelming! I stayed busy learning how to navigate the public health care system and its ever-changing policies, maintaining tedious paperwork, and performing what seemed to be endless diagnostic assessments. As with all things in life, as I gained more experience and consulted with fellow colleagues, I became skilled in each of these areas. What proved most challenging was counseling the 20 or so children who had been assigned as my clients. I quickly learned that I *needed* to do something to develop my competency in this area and ultimately assist these children who so desperately needed my attention.

In preparation, I gathered various play-therapy resources, including several books that provided useful interventions and a wide variety of toys that I thought could have multiple uses. My toolbox helped me to effectively work with a variety of children, but mostly those who were younger and experiencing minor familial, academic, and communication issues. It was not until one 13-year-old girl with several emotional and behavioral issues stepped into my office that I learned none of these interventions would likely be of any assistance. In addition to violent anger outbursts and symptoms of mania, this young girl had to deal with being taunted at school because of severe obesity, which was a side effect of the numerous medications that she had been taking for several years.

Like many children today in rural Appalachia, Samantha was prescribed nearly a dozen different types of high-dosage medications, including mood stabilizers, antipsychotics, and antidepressants. Yet her behavior showed little consistent improvement over time. In addition, Samantha's monthly visits with the psychiatrist always resulted in an adjustment to her medication regimen. Samantha reported that the medication made her feel "tired and lazy" and even her mother stated that she had seen little overall improvement. Nearly every consultation I had with Samantha's mother consisted of her voicing complaints about the psychiatrist and the lack of attention that he was giving to Samantha. Samantha's mother also expressed feelings of uncertainty regarding the purposes and advantages of the multiple prescribed medications.

As counselors, we are not permitted to provide any medicinal or pharmaceutical advice to our clients; this is outside the scope of practice of counselors and goes beyond our training and competence. Although I had some training on psychotropic medications and wanted to answer some of the mother's questions, I had to navigate carefully in order to ensure that I was remaining ethical. I first suggested that she and Samantha both become more familiar with the prescribed

(Continued)

medications by reading the drug information inserts and talking with the registered nurse within our agency. Next, I helped Samantha and her mother define, articulate, and document the exact symptoms and side effects that Samantha experienced. I then suggested that Samantha and her mother ask questions and express their concerns to the psychiatrist. Not a single counselor before me had suggested that Samantha or her mother ask the psychiatrist questions throughout their tenure as clients at the agency. Nor had any counselors assisted them in developing a list of symptoms and side effects that could be clearly communicated to the psychiatrist.

With increased encouragement, Samantha and her mother finally gained the strength to speak to the psychiatrist, which resulted in the gradual reduction of some of Samantha's medications. In counseling, I ensured that Samantha was always part of my consultation with her mother so that Samantha could become better aware of her role as an important player in her treatment process. I can happily say that with ongoing therapeutic treatment, Samantha's emotional stability improved and her behavioral issues subsided. She also lost a substantial amount of weight, which allowed her to feel more confident and experience less ridicule from her peers at school. Today Samantha is preoccupied with boys and the latest romance film, and she is on her way to becoming a happy and healthy teenage girl. The most rewarding part of Samantha's case for me was receiving the heartfelt thank you for empowering her and her mother to take control of their situation.

COUNSELING AND ADVOCACY INTERVENTION COMPETENCIES: INTERPERSONAL As relationships between professional counselors and clients grow, counselors gain awareness of the external factors that act as barriers to clients' development that often includes the interpersonal relationships that provide clients with identity and support. These relationships are often found in the clients' family and among peers, colleagues, and friends. During this time, professional counselors may discover that clients do not have adequate awareness and/or skills to self-advocate with family, friends, or peers who may not be supportive. In addition to teaching clients skills, professional counselors have a decision to make about how they will act as advocates. The previous section addressed how helping clients gain a sense of empowerment may lead to clients' self-advocacy. However, professional counselors may decide to choose to be clients' advocates, especially when clients lack access to needed services. Table 15.2 outlines interpersonal advocacy intervention competencies.

In advocating for clients, professional counselors are acting for clients and not only with them, as in the previous discussion on client empowerment. Similar to the process of client empowerment and self-advocacy, a problem assessment has to be conducted to determine if client advocacy is warranted and what needs to be included in the plan of action for the advocacy. In the client advocacy counselor competencies, assessing and using available resources is essential to an effective action plan. In a study of counselor advocates, the study participants encouraged advocates to plan advocacy efforts to match their available resources (Eriksen, 1999). Assessing the systems that are part of clients' realities helps professional counselors identify any barriers to the well-being of clients and identify resources for clients. Identification of human resources helps in making a plan to include these allies of clients in confronting present and future barriers.

Because counselors are trained to understand life span development and possess technology and research skills, they are usually in the best position to advocate (Ratts & Hutchins, 2009). As client advocates, professional counselors have to be able and willing to use the "power" inherent in the role of counselor. This means that professional counselors

TABLE 15.2 Interpersonal Advocacy Intervention Competencies

Multicultural and social justice competent counselors:

1. Employ advocacy to address the historical events and persons that shape and influence privileged and marginalized client's developmental history.

2. Examine the relationships privileged and marginalized clients have with family, friends, and peers that may be sources of support or non-support.

3. Assist privileged and marginalized clients to understand that the relationships they have with others may be influenced by their privileged and marginalized status.

4. Assist privileged and marginalized clients with fostering relationships with family, friends, and peers from the same privileged and marginalized group.

5. Reach out to collaborate with family, friends, and peers who will be a source of support for privileged and marginalized clients.

6. Assist privileged and marginalized clients in developing communication skills to discuss issues of power, privilege, and oppression with family, friends, peers, and colleagues.

7. Employ evidenced-based interventions that align with the cultural background and worldview of privileged and marginalized clients.

Source: Ratts, M. J., Singh, A. A., Nassar-McMillan, S., Butler, S. K., & McCullough, J. R. (2015). *Multicultural and social justice counseling competencies.* Retrieved from www.multiculturalcounseling.org/index.php?option=com_content&view=article&id=205:amcd-endorses-multicultural-and-social-justice-counseling-competencies&catid=1:latest&Itemid=123. Reprinted with permission.

may have certain privileges that accompany their positions and that would facilitate clients' access to information. This "influential power" may be required to negotiate with outside agencies and institutions to provide better services for clients. Professional counselors may also need to act as mediators between clients and institutions, specifically to resolve impasses. Now complete Think About It 15.1 to more deeply explore the role of power in your role.

THINK ABOUT IT 15.1

What "power" will be inherent in your role as a professional counselor that clients do not possess?

Professional counselors need to be careful not to seem overzealous, because it may work against clients. Counselors should remember several classic strategies proposed long ago by Ponzo (1974) as they advocate for clients. First, professional counselors should be flexible and demonstrate the willingness to compromise with others. Second, professional counselors should have some perspective on their own personalities and the impact of their personalities on others. Professional counselors may need to adjust their style to be effective client advocates. Third, professional counselors should understand not only their clients, but also others in various systems, such as agencies and institutions. By employing basic counseling skills (e.g., empathy, warmth, concreteness), professional counselors can gain the trust of the contacts in these various systems. Fourth, professional counselors should learn from the different systems to create advocacy plans that would work in these systems to create change. Finally, professional counselors and clients should set realistic goals. Remembering to work with the resources that are available and to delineate short-term versus long-term goals makes advocacy plans and interventions successful. Case Study 15.2 illustrates the application of client advocacy counselor competencies.

CASE STUDY 15.2

Application of Interpersonal Advocacy Intervention Competencies

Julie is a 25-year-old woman recovering from a crack cocaine addiction. She has been drug-free for 1 year. Julie gave birth to a daughter approximately 5 years ago and relinquished custody to her parents immediately after the birth of her daughter. She has recently experienced more frequent visits with her parents and daughter, but the visits with her daughter continue to be supervised. Currently, Julie continues to live with her boyfriend of 4 years, who chronically abuses alcohol. She reported that he is verbally and emotionally abusive, and she wishes to move out of the house and end the relationship. Julie's current professional counselor has been helping her with her recovery and dealing with the emotional issues that are inherent to her environmental and family systems. The professional counselor referred Julie to a Narcotics Anonymous (NA) group, which Julie attends every day. Julie's sponsor agreed to have Julie move in with her until Julie is able to arrange new living arrangements. Julie expressed a desire to continue her sobriety and was inspired about the developing relationship between herself and her daughter. However, she is frustrated by the supervised visits with her daughter and her own lack of employment.

Questions for Consideration:

- What are the relevant services and education systems that may need to be negotiated by the professional counselor on Julie's behalf?
- How can the professional counselor help Julie gain access to needed resources? What are those resources?
- What are the barriers to Julie's well-being?
- What is an initial plan for confronting the barriers to Julie's well-being? What are some short-term goals?
- Who are some of Julie's allies in confronting those barriers?

In the case of Julie, the professional counselor is helping with drug addiction recovery. With Julie and with many clients, however, advocacy may be required to address other aspects of the client's experience beside the initial reason for counseling (i.e., recovering from a crack cocaine addiction). Professional counselors who work with clients dealing with drug addiction may consider advocacy activities on behalf of clients such as obtaining direct services, obtaining practical help for the client, securing support from the client's employer or school, and obtaining information for the client. For Julie, the professional counselor may want to consider acting as a mediator between Julie and her parents with regard to planning unsupervised visits with her daughter. This may also include obtaining information from the department of social services to consider a plan for future custody and living arrangements. In assessing Julie's resources, it is important for the professional counselor to consider the role of Julie's NA sponsor. A meeting to include Julie, her sponsor, and her professional counselor may be warranted to create a plan for Julie to move away from her boyfriend and take steps to gain some form of employment. The NA sponsor may be willing to help Julie put her plan into action. Inherent in all of these steps is helping Julie acknowledge the barriers in this process. For Julie, her drug addiction and possible relapse can act as an internal barrier, family relationships in scheduling visitation with her child can act as a family systems barrier, and she may face possible legal barriers with the department of social services. Now read Voices from the Field 15.2.

VOICES FROM THE FIELD 15.2   Listening to Your Inside Advocacy Voice, by Donna Gibson

As a licensed professional counselor, I often have internal debates about my role as advocate with and for my clients. How do I determine when a client can self-advocate and when I need to advocate for them? I follow the same guidelines as outlined in this first section on client advocacy. It comes down to how I assess my client's ability to self-advocate and what his or her barriers are in the situation. Logically, I am able to better assess those things the longer I have been working with the client. If I have been working with them for some time, they have usually acquired some context for their barriers and skills on how to begin to address these barriers. Hence, clients are usually able to self-advocate. However, I have noticed that the social class of clients is a strong determinant in willingness, not necessarily ability, to self-advocate. From my experience, our private and public organizational systems (e.g., medical, educational) marginalize individuals systematically through policies and access requirements. This is something to consider when you assume that these organizations have readily available access points for all people.

Counseling and Advocacy Intervention Competencies: Community

Professional counselors work in various settings, including public and private K–12 schools, colleges and universities, mental health settings, medical settings, private and public businesses, and rehabilitation settings. Part of the role of the professional counselor is to be attuned to the communities that are being served in those settings. In working with the clients in these communities, professional counselors gain an awareness of recurring themes in the community that are based on "spoken and unspoken norms, values, and regulations that are embedded in society that can be empowering or oppressive to human growth and development" (Ratts et al., 2015, p. 13). Professional counselors may be the first to become aware of specific issues in a community that can impede the development of those individuals within it.

Part of the identity of an advocate is to address problems that are brought into awareness. Professional counselors can choose to share recurring problematic themes with other groups in the community that may also be aware of these issues and are attempting to address them. Ethical standards help guide professional counselors on how to share this information and interact with these communities. For example, counselors who live and work in small rural communities are often at risk ethically for violating issues related to competence, multiple relationships, and confidentiality (ACA, 2014a; Bradley, Werth, & Hastings, 2012). In this type of community, the consequences of social justice advocacy within the community system may have an impact on the entire community and not only a subset of individuals. Hence, Toporek and Williams (2006) suggest that counselors engaging in this type of advocacy take reasonable steps to avoid harm. Now read Think About It 15.2.

THINK ABOUT IT 15.2

Think of some "themes" or problem situations that you are already aware of within your community. Where would you find information about problem situations: news media, government, educational institutions? How could these themes affect your clients?

At this level, counselors are not only acting as allies to other organizations in addressing issues of concern in the community; they are also often assuming a role of leadership (Lopez-Baez & Paylo, 2009). Specifically, professional counselors can offer particular skills, such as communication, training, interpersonal relations, assessment, and research, to collaborate with other interested groups to address these issues. Table 15.3 outlines community advocacy intervention competencies.

As mentioned in the previous sections, problem assessment is always a key component of advocacy. At this particular level of advocacy, assessment of the problem begins with the recognition of the themes that professional counselors hear from clients. However, problem assessment does not begin and end with listening to clients. Professional counselors continue this process as alliances with other community groups are created and expanded. Learning from these other groups about their own perspectives on these thematic issues helps to delineate the specific components of the issues. It is essential for professional counselors to know which community groups are aware of or could be affected by these issues. Thus, part of this advocacy process is to identify groups that could be part of the process of finding solutions to address the issues. Sometimes, the specific community groups that are common to the issue are obvious. For example, in public K–12 schools, common community groups could be mental health groups, law enforcement, and school boards. However, it may not be obvious because of the specificity of the issue, and counselors have to consider potential appropriate groups. Now complete Think About It 15.3.

TABLE 15.3 Community Advocacy Intervention Competencies

Multicultural and social justice competent counselors:

1. Take the initiative to explore with privileged and marginalized clients how community norms, values, and regulations embedded in society hinder and contribute to their growth and development.

2. Conduct qualitative and quantitative research to evaluate the degree to which community norms, values, and regulations influence privileged and marginalized clients.

3. Employ social advocacy to address community norms, values, and regulations embedded in society that hinder the growth and development of privileged and marginalized clients.

4. Utilize the norms, values and regulations of the marginalized client to shape the community norms, values, and regulations of the privileged client.

Source: Ratts, M. J., Singh, A. A., Nassar-McMillan, S., Butler, S. K., & McCullough, J. R. (2015). *Multicultural and social justice counseling competencies.* Retrieved from www.multiculturalcounseling.org/index.php?option=com_content&view=article&id=205:amcd-endorses-multicultural-and-social-justice-counseling-competencies&catid=1:latest&Itemid=123. Reprinted with permission.

THINK ABOUT IT 15.3

How will you use your skills as a professional counselor to build alliances with community groups? Can you think of specific community groups that will be pertinent to your profession? How might you first contact these groups to begin a collaborative relationship?

Once alliances are formed with community groups, the ability to listen effectively becomes paramount. The professional counselor is at least one member of the alliance trained in effective communication, a skill needed in assessing, planning, and implementing interventions to address the issue in the community. Using communication skills, professional counselors can help alliances identify the strengths and resources of community group entities to implement those into the intervention plan. In addition, professional counselors can offer their own specific skills to help this process. Case Study 15.3 illustrates community collaboration competencies for advocacy.

CASE STUDY 15.3

Application of Community Advocacy Intervention Competencies

At a recent case staffing at a midsize college counseling center, professional counselor Joan reported that she has worked with at least five individuals with issues of self-injury in the past month. The other seven professional counselors reported that they had also worked with at least an average of five individuals each on similar issues. After discussing the cases in more depth, the professional counselors concluded that most of the clients reporting these behaviors were freshmen and sophomore young women who lived on campus. Therefore, the counselors were able to determine that on-campus living may be an environmental factor that was affecting the students' development. Additional factors, such as familial support, on-campus network of friends, college major and requirements, and residence hall support, were also assessed.

Joan and another professional counselor worked together to determine which other community groups within the college system would be effective in helping to plan interventions. They decided to meet with representative staff members from student-life, residence hall, and undergraduate academics. When meeting with these individuals, it became obvious that self-injury had become an issue for all of these groups. Interventions were designed, and implementation was coordinated through Joan at the counseling center.

Questions for Consideration:

- Why do you think those three college community groups were identified with this issue?
- What do you think became the main goal of this alliance group?
- What are some of the skills the professional counselors can offer in this situation?
- How would you assess the effectiveness of the professional counselor's interaction within this community?

One of the great strengths of working with college groups is the ability to use education as a tool in providing effective intervention. In Case Study 15.3, three separate groups were identified to assess, plan, and implement strategies for clients in three separate areas of their lives on campus: student life (i.e., social environments on campus); residence life (i.e., living environments on campus); and undergraduate academics (i.e., learning environments on campus). Other groups on campus might be included in this collaborative effort.

Education about self-injury can act as a method of preventing the stigma associated with it. Self-injury needs to be demystified, not only for students on campus but also for college staff and faculty members who are working with students who self-injure. The college counseling center can lead this effort by posting information on the counseling center website and by creating and disseminating brochures about self-injury and how to receive help with this issue.

In educating campus groups, an additional group to consider is one that handles judicial affairs. Many campuses have mandatory withdrawal policies for students who engage in disruptive behaviors and suicide attempts (Hodges, 2001). Because self-injury is often erroneously equated with attempted suicide, professional counselors can help these groups understand the differences between suicide and self-injury. Part of the collaboration may help enact new policies that clarify discipline guidelines for students who self-injure.

It is important to consider how effective the professional counselor is in these collaborative efforts. A variety of formal and informal methods can be used in this process. Asking for feedback from the community groups that are working collaboratively with the professional counselor can be done through a formal written process or informally by gauging the interactions within meetings and other types of communication. If the professional counselor is involved in providing outreach education sessions to students or staff and faculty members, a preevaluation and a postevaluation of the education session can be used. Finally, the counseling center may want to employ a confidential method for students who are either engaging in or contemplating self-injury to self-report their concerns. No matter the method, assessing the professional counselor's effectiveness provides information that would be helpful in planning future collaborative activities with community groups. Now complete Activity 15.5. Then read Voices from the Field 15.3.

ACTIVITY 15.5

Create a written evaluation to send to community groups that have collaborated with you in a recent community effort against self-injury. Determine how citizens considering self-injury could confidentially refer themselves to your agency or school for mental health services.

VOICES FROM THE FIELD 15.3   Student and Community Advocacy: A View from the Schools, by Lacey Wallace

During my first year as a school counselor, I faced a number of duties I did not anticipate. Throughout graduate school we discussed the importance of communicating my school counseling program to all stakeholders but, most important, to administrators. At the start of the school year,

I held a conference with my administrators to convey the integral role I hoped to have at the school. I left the conference feeling that I was an important member of the school team, but I also started to see some of the limitations I was going to combat throughout the year. My principal asked that I recognize the importance of students being in the classroom for instruction and that I see the students only during lunch or recess. Although I agree with this philosophy, as a mental health professional I also realize that, at times, there is a need for a student to miss class in order to receive the help needed to mature socially, emotionally, and academically.

When the duty schedule was distributed, I began to feel a bit discouraged. I was scheduled to have morning and afternoon duties, along with lunch duty every day for second and fourth grade. It took me some time to get the words and courage together to approach my administrators, but with help from my colleagues I was able to. I asked my principal if I would be able to take second- and fourth-graders out of class because of the difficulty I would have servicing all of the students during lunch and recess if I was on duty. She told me instruction was the priority so unless the child is disruptive, she would rather me go into the classrooms and try to work with students there. I asked her if she would be willing to support me if parents began to complain that I wasn't able to work with their children because of my scheduling conflicts. She looked at the duty schedule and took me off lunch duty for three days for second grade and two days for fourth grade.

I was happy to have this success, but I also felt that I didn't want to start the year off on a bad note, especially during my first year of employment in the school system. I told my principal that I wasn't trying to be difficult, but that I wanted to make sure I had enough time for direct service hours with students. Although she did not seem completely pleased, I left feeling as if I had taken a step in the right direction and felt a bit more confident about the remainder of the school year.

Many requests were made for me to attend meetings that were intended for administrators, to act as the administrator in charge and discipline students when they were out of the building, and to attend trainings for state testing coordination. I had to reiterate the same message in order to stand strong and do what was in the best interest of the students. I tried to say that these types of responsibilities would take direct services away from children. It was important to share that research has shown that our work as professional school counselors increases student achievement.

COUNSELING AND ADVOCACY INTERVENTION COMPETENCIES: INSTITUTIONAL In order to address inequities at the institutional level, it is necessary to understand how social institutions or systems work. Early in this chapter, we discussed clients' systems to examine how these systems affect clients and how empowerment and advocacy can address systemic issues. Systems can include social institutions within a community or organization, such as schools, churches, and community organizations. When professional counselors identify systemic factors that are acting as barriers to clients' development, they may wish to change the environment to prevent some of the problems that are occurring because of these barriers being in place within the system. Although clients' experiences are the basis for this institution-level intervention, clients are not necessarily involved in this form of advocacy (Toporek, Lewis, & Crethar, 2009). In this case, advocacy means the counselor is attempting to change the system.

Regardless of the type of system change, professional counselors engage in processes that help effect change (Ratts et al., 2015). These processes require professional counselors to have a vision of change; to be persistent; to provide leadership; to engage in collaboration; to provide systems analysis; and to collect, analyze, and disseminate accurate data.

TABLE 15.4 Institutional Advocacy Intervention Competencies

Multicultural and social justice competent counselors:

1. Explore with privileged and marginalized clients the extent to which social institutions are supportive.

2. Connect privileged and marginalized clients with supportive individuals within social institutions (e.g., schools, businesses, church, etc.) who are able to help alter inequities influencing marginalized clients.

3. Collaborate with social institutions to address issues of power, privilege, and oppression impacting privileged and marginalized clients.

4. Employ social advocacy to remove systemic barriers experienced by marginalized clients within social institutions.

5. Employ social advocacy to remove systemic barriers that promote privilege and that benefit privileged clients.

6. Balance individual counseling with systems level social advocacy to address inequities that social institutions create that impede human growth and development.

7. Conduct multicultural and social justice based research to highlight the inequities that social institutions have on marginalized clients and that benefit privileged clients.

Source: Ratts, M. J., Singh, A. A., Nassar-McMillan, S., Butler, S. K., & McCullough, J. R. (2015). *Multicultural and social justice counseling competencies*. Retrieved from www.multiculturalcounseling.org/index.php?option=com_content&view=article&id=205:amcd-endorses-multicultural-and-social-justice-counseling-competencies&catid=1:latest&Itemid=123. Reprinted with permission.

The training that professional counselors receive provides the requisite knowledge and skills required in these processes, in effect, helping counselors to act as systems-change leaders. Table 15.4 outlines the competencies for institutional advocacy interventions.

In order to be an agent of change within an organization, counselors need to examine their own personal and professional obstacles. Experiencing personal fear and discomfort, being labeled as a troublemaker, coping through apathy, responding ineffectively due to anger, having a false sense of powerlessness, and feeling guilty are personal considerations that discourage many counselors from implementing any social advocacy strategies and organizational changes (Bemak & Chung, 2008). Professional barriers can include being overwhelmed by needed changes that results in inaction, being discounted in taking action by others within the organization if action is perceived as outside the scope of the counselor's role, being occupied with administrative-directed activities, fearing job insecurity through advocacy actions, and experiencing personal and professional character assassination. In order to mediate these barriers, Bemak and Chung encourage counselors to "routinely collaborate with like-minded colleagues in the field" (p. 376) to give and receive support and encouragement. Advocacy strategies that are created from data are difficult to doubt when implementing for institutional and systems change. To make a case for change, evidence for the *need* to change has to be provided. Similar to other advocacy competencies, the problem has to be assessed, but the second step is to collect data on how this issue is a problem.

In the case study about self-injury (Case Study 15.3), the college judicial policy may be to have the student withdraw for any type of injurious behavior. To present this policy as a problem in the system, professional counselors may need to analyze data to determine which students were attempting suicide versus engaging in nonsuicidal self-injury. In addition, outcome data may need to be presented on individuals who received treatment for self-injury and those who did not to determine if intervention plans can be put in place for students who self-injure but are not asked to withdraw from school. Activity 15.6 explores some issues in data collection.

ACTIVITY 15.6

What are your strongest data collection skills? What are the areas that need improvement? How will you address your strengths and weaknesses in this area? Create a method for collecting data in the case of self-injury.

This level of advocacy continues the collaborative efforts between professional counselors and community groups that are affected by the identified issues. However, the collaboration among the individuals moves to create a vision for change by analyzing the sources of political power and social influence within the system. Groups need to create an **action plan** that outlines clear and specific goals in a step-by-step method for implementing change that also shows how to use resources effectively and anticipate difficulties (Trusty & Brown, 2005). The action plan includes methods on how to handle anticipated responses to change, including resistance. Finally, professional counselors need to use their assessment and research skills to evaluate advocacy initiatives. Case Study 15.4 illustrates the application of institutional advocacy competencies.

CASE STUDY 15.4
Application of Institutional Advocacy Competencies

In a large public school system, one of the roles of professional school counselors at every high school includes testing. Every counselor at each high school in Testemall School District was required to coordinate and help in the administration of specific tests at the high school level. After some time, the directors of school counseling at these schools identified the theme of testing as being an activity that interfered with the ability of the professional school counselors to perform other roles and duties. At a district-wide school counseling director meeting, one of the school counseling directors brought this issue to the meeting for discussion. The directors decided that this issue was one that could be changed only at the district level (i.e., identifying environmental factors affecting development). They created a plan to collect and analyze data about how the activities of the professional school counselors within the district compared with the activities recommended by the American School Counselor Association (ASCA, 2012) *National Model for School Counseling Programs*. In addition, they collected data on how much time and effort was devoted to testing responsibilities compared with the recommended activities by the ASCA. After these data were collected and analyzed, all high school counseling directors met with the district superintendent to present the information and ask for the testing duties to be eliminated from the duties required of high school counselors. The superintendent took the issue to his administration team, agreed that the issue had merit, and a testing director position was created for each high school.

Questions for Consideration:

- What other data could have been considered by the counseling directors?
- What do you think were the school counseling directors' political and social power within the system? Who held this power? How could this power have been better used?
- How could the directors handle a refusal from the superintendent to their request?

Public schools have many subsystems (e.g., students, teachers, parents, departments, staff, administrators). In Case Study 15.4, it seems that the professional school counselors may have thought they were not fulfilling their counseling duties to many of these subsystems. For these professional school counselors, being in charge of school testing was an ineffective use of their time. They also believed it was not consistent with the *National Model for School Counseling Programs* (ASCA, 2012). Being able to advocate for systemic change, these school counseling directors were also engaging in leadership activities. This was an example of not only school reform, but also of systemic change. To transform school counseling practices, effective leadership by professional school counselors is required (Erford, 2015a).

In Case Study 15.4, the school counseling directors were able to present data about the immediate need for change within the smaller systems of the individual high schools and the larger system of the district. Other components needed to be considered, however. It is unclear who or what was identified as political resources and social power for this group. Did the professional school counselors consider their constituent groups (e.g., teachers, students, parents, school administrators) as resources for making change? Who at the district level (beyond the superintendent) could have acted as a political resource? This may have been the district-wide assessment coordinator. In addition, this person could have supplied them with additional data to present and act as an ally in the presentation process. Finally, in assessing and evaluating the effectiveness of the advocacy efforts of the professional school counselors, it is easy to note what could have been conducted differently. However, it is equally important to identify actions and steps that were effective so that they can be employed in future systemic advocacy efforts. Although the system-level change occurred during the first efforts of the counseling directors, it may not occur on first efforts in other instances. Counselors may need to document and/or collect data for lengthy periods before any level of change occurs. Change may occur at a building level (e.g., one high school) before it occurs systemically, or the counselor may consider the building level to be the system. The counselors may also meet resistance to any form of change that they present. In this example, other individuals in the schools may think that they will have to add assessment duties to their already existing responsibilities, and they may feel threatened by the school counselors' call for change. Resistance is a normal response to change (Lopez-Baez & Paylo, 2009). If it is encountered in advocating for systemic change, counselors need to inquire about it and address these concerns. Finally, counselors need to evaluate their own efforts at advocating for change. Did it work? If so, how well? If not, what factors interfered with its success? Who and what is needed to make it successful in future attempts? Counselors need to remember that all efforts in advocating are worth the time and energy. Now read Voices from the Field 15.4.

VOICES FROM THE FIELD 15.4 Leadership in Advocacy, by Donna Gibson

From my perspective as both a counselor educator and counselor, it is easy to doubt my leadership skills when trying to advocate at a community and/or systems level. Will I be "heard" on these issues that I am advocating for or against? When I change my perspective from thinking about my own skills and power to thinking of what the students, program, or clients need, I am able to think in terms of action and creating a plan. As a counselor, you will have the skills and abilities to lead in advocating systemically. However, there have been times when the resistance I ran into was irrational. For example, an administrator I worked for in my organization simply did not like counseling. He did not see the need for it and for training counselors in providing services to the public. Instead of capitulating on this opinion, I continued with a strong message (and data) of the need for counselor training, and the program continues to this date. It is difficult for people to maintain irrational resistance in the face of consistent and logical data.

Counseling and Advocacy Interventions Competencies: Public Policy

Instead of examining oppression and barriers in systems and subsystems, professional counselors advocate at a macrosystemic level for issues regarding human dignity (Ratts et al., 2015). In doing so, counselors take stands on social and political issues and work at eradicating "systems and ideologies that perpetuate discrimination and disregard human rights" (Lee & Rodgers, 2009, p. 284). Providing **public information** is one method of encouraging the public to become aware of environmental factors that act as barriers to all individuals' human development. Professional counselors employ political advocacy as direct methods to bring about change in a much larger arena than at the systems level. Utilizing both public information and political advocacy interventions address the public policy advocacy competencies listed in Table 15.5.

Chapter 14 addressed advocating for the profession of counseling and outlined methods that professional counselors can use in actively advocating for the profession. Ratts et al. (2015) outlined several techniques for using the media to advocate for the profession. These techniques are also applicable to advocating for clients. In essence, when professional counselors advocate for the profession, they are also advocating for clients and against environmental barriers to human development. However, many professional counselors who are beginning advocacy efforts may not feel confident in preparing materials to be used in the media.

In addressing this concern, Ratts et al. (2015) provide several guidelines for beginning these efforts. First, professional counselors need to examine ongoing issues that are important concerns to members of counselors' schools, institutions, or communities. In addition, professional counselors need to determine if these same issues are appearing in local newspapers and other media. Today, technology is the advocate's primary tool for disseminating information and eliciting support for change. Social networking sites (e.g., Facebook) are online communities that allow individuals to customize the page and interact with others. Organized advocacy events and event details can be advertised with unlimited space to post the information (Thackeray & Hunter, 2010). Additionally, Real Simple Syndication (RSS) is a web feed that notifies subscribers automatically of new content on webpages. Twitter is similar to RSS but information is directed by organizations, businesses, and individuals and can be sent and retrieved by mobile devices (e.g., cell or

---

TABLE 15.5 Institutional Advocacy Intervention Competencies

Multicultural and social justice competent counselors:

1. Initiate discussions with privileged and marginalized clients to determine how they shape and are shaped by local, state, and federal laws and policies.

2. Conduct research to examine how local, state, and federal laws and policies contribute to or hinder the growth and development of privileged and marginalized clients.

3. Engage in social action to alter the local, state, and federal laws and policies that benefit privileged clients at the expense of marginalized clients.

4. Employ social advocacy to ensure that local, state, and federal laws and policies are equitable toward privileged and marginalized clients.

5. Employ social advocacy outside the office setting to address local, state, and federal laws and policies that hinder equitable access to employment, healthcare, and education for privileged and marginalized clients.

6. Assist with creating local, state, and federal laws and policies that promote multiculturalism and social justice.

7. Seek out opportunities to collaborate with privileged and marginalized clients to shape local, state, and federal laws and policies.

Source: Ratts, M. J., Singh, A. A., Nassar-McMillan, S., Butler, S. K., & McCullough, J. R. (2015). *Multicultural and social justice counseling competencies.* Retrieved from www.multiculturalcounseling.org/index.php?option=com_content&view=article&id=205:amcd-endorses-multicultural-and-social-justice-counseling-competencies&catid=1:latest&Itemid=123. Reprinted with permission.

smart phones) as well as web-enabled devices (i.e., computers, tablets). Blogs, individual online journals, and podcasts (audio or video files distributed over the Internet) are also forms of technology-based information sources. Last but not least, cell phones can receive much of the information from these information sources and can also send text and multimedia messages to others. For counselors, this technology can help them gauge the issues and provide an outlet for public information to effect change. These tools promote communication and discussion about important issues that may get overlooked if not publicized. The convenience and affordability of technology also allows for more immediate responses to these needs. Now complete Think About It 15.4 to deepen your understanding of the interplay between technology and the legalities of counseling practice.

THINK ABOUT IT 15.4

Although technology is convenient and affordable, there may be some ethical and legal considerations to using it for advocacy. Which 2014 ACA Ethical Code provisions would apply to advocacy activities conducted through the use of technology?

Second, professional counselors need to determine if their skills and expertise can be used to address these issues. Third, professional counselors need to assess and determine the resources (e.g., human, monetary, services) they have to carry out public information activities. Finally, professional counselors need to determine how much time they can devote to these activities. Professional counselors can participate in a variety of activities that can address these issues. Examples of public interventions are listed in Table 15.6. Next, complete Activity 15.7.

TABLE 15.6 Public Policy Intervention Competencies

Public Policy Interventions: Privileged and marginalized counselors address public policy issues that impede on client development with, and on behalf of clients. Multicultural and social justice competent counselors:

- Initiate discussions with privileged and marginalized clients about how they shape and are shaped by local, state, and federal laws and policies.
- Conduct research to examine how local, state, and federal laws and policies contribute to or hinder the growth and development of privileged and marginalized clients.
- Engage in social action to alter the local, state, and federal laws and policies that benefit privileged clients at the expense of marginalized clients.
- Employ social advocacy to ensure that local, state, and federal laws and policies are equitable toward privileged and marginalized clients.
- Employ social advocacy outside the office setting to address local, state, and federal laws and policies that hinder equitable access to employment, healthcare, and education for privileged and marginalized clients.
- Assist with creating local, state, and federal laws and policies that promote multiculturalism and social justice.
- Seek out opportunities to collaborate with privileged and marginalized clients to shape local, state, and federal laws and policies.

ACTIVITY 15.7 APPLICATION OF PUBLIC POLICY COMPETENCIES

Using the competencies and public information activities listed in Table 15.6, answer the following questions:

1. What issues at a macrosystemic level are you interested in currently? How can you identify these issues? Through what sources?
2. How can you advocate for one or more of these issues using the activities listed in Table 15.6 and through the use of technology?
3. Who are some other professionals that you could involve in disseminating public information on these issues?
4. What resources do you need to disseminate information to the public?
5. How will you assess your efforts in using public information to advocate for these issues?

Utilizing political advocacy, you can reach a larger and broader arena to address concerns and issues for clients and other individuals who have faced barriers to their human development (American Counseling Association, 2016). At this macrosystemic level of advocacy, counselors illustrate their ethical obligation to assume an advocacy role that can affect public opinion, public policy, and legislation (ACA, 2014a). By learning how to use counseling skills and knowledge through public information outlets as a tool to advocate, professional counselors are prepared to carry out political advocacy.

Lee and Rodgers (2009) noted that political advocacy operates at a personal level for counselors. A self-exploration of personal experiences encourages counselors to recognize their own values and beliefs, which are the foundation for promoting access and equity. Exploring self-development of racial identity, social class, gender, and other relevant identities allows for recognition of beliefs about maintaining the status quo with its systemic marginalization and oppression. By working to achieve these personal insights, counselors become more effective in helping clients and in becoming leaders who offer a vision for social/political change.

Becoming active as leader and advocate often necessitates taking both professional and personal risks (Lee & Rodgers, 2009). Counselors who speak publicly and take a stand on certain issues may experience some form of harassment. Coworkers, professional associates, or friends may decide to sever relationships based on these verbalized beliefs. At the same time, counselors may experience the benefit of obtaining new professional associations based on these same beliefs. New relationships, based on congruent values and beliefs, may counteract any losses incurred from advocating publicly, a positive consequence that will also encourage counselors to act.

Once counselors explore the personal level of this form of advocating, their vision for change has to be clearly articulated (Lee & Rodgers, 2009). The vision entails the political challenge, including how the challenge will be resolved. Ultimately, the vision will act as the rallying cry for all the stakeholders to take action, so creating it will not be an overnight process. Consideration should be given to the history of the political challenge: how long it has been in existence, how it was created, and how it has been maintained. Consideration must also be given to why it is resistant to change, and how changing it will be good for all individuals and not only for select groups. Combining this information with data that "break old myths; eliminate denial; and challenge existing behavior, funding patterns, programs, and policies" (Lee & Rodgers, 2009, p. 286) will help create the "urgency for change," which should incite policy makers and agents of power to make change occur.

More and more individuals are becoming comfortable with this level of advocacy. With more politicians active within social media, they are often perceived as more approachable. In addition to emailing, calling, or tweeting state and/or national legislators, counselors may determine that a personal visit to the legislator's office is needed. Table 15.7 includes suggestions for planning a visit to a state or national capitol office (Congress.org, 2018), and Activity 15.8 presents a second application of public policy advocacy competencies. Then read Voices from the Field 15.5, 15.6, and 15.7.

ACTIVITY 15.8 APPLICATION OF PUBLIC POLICY ADVOCACY COMPETENCIES

1. Who are the local, state, and national politicians you could approach to present or discuss an issue?
2. What is one local issue that you believe could be a national issue in addressing barriers to human development?
3. Who are two professional counseling organization officials who could act as resources for this issue?
4. What is another organization that you could approach to be an ally in advocating for this issue?
5. Find a blog or website that could provide you more information about this issue and organizations that are advocating for this issue.

TABLE 15.7 Tips on Visiting a State or National Legislator

1. Identify your state district representative or state representative/senator.

2. Determine the issue you wish to discuss and plan your presentation carefully. Most of the time, you will not have a lot of time with the state or national legislator and a 5-minute presentation should be planned. If it is related to a specific bill being proposed, learn the bill number or identification to correlate with the issue you will be discussing.

3. Prepare some written materials to accompany your presentation, including factual information that supports your position on the issue. Information and examples of the benefits of your position should be included and highlighted in your meeting.

4. Make an appointment with the legislator by contacting the appointment secretary/scheduler. You will need to explain your purpose and who you represent (if applicable).

5. Be prompt for your appointment but also expect to wait due to the busy schedule and sometimes unexpected subcommittee meetings being held that pre empt the legislator's time.

6. In the meeting, remember you are a constituent and represent many other constituents. Present your information but also explain how you can be of assistance to him on this matter. Ask the legislator for a commitment on the issue.

7. Wrapping it up! Be prepared to answer questions in your meeting and then follow up the meeting with a thank you that reiterates the points covered in the meeting. Additional materials can be included with this follow-up.

VOICES FROM THE FIELD 15.5   Responding to the Call, by Donna Gibson

Do you ever receive emails or notices through other forms of social networking sites that ask you to join the cause or to forward the email or notice to others? What do you do? I take these fairly seriously because most that I receive involve issues related to advocating for groups that either represent who I am or that I serve as a counselor. I am typically thrown into an examination of my personal beliefs and what I believe in connection to those issues. Although I can argue that every level of the advocacy competencies makes you examine your personal beliefs and values, the public exposure connected with this level is significant for me. I point this out because it speaks to the developmental nature of advocacy and multicultural identity development. They go hand in hand, and advocacy comes a lot easier when your multicultural identity development is congruent with your willingness to act on your beliefs and actions.

VOICES FROM THE FIELD 15.6   Data-Driven Decision Making: How Your Voice Can Influence Change, by Tracy Macdonald

Professional counselors have a natural tendency to keep things peaceful. Sometimes, however, it is important to step outside the comfort zone and "shake things up a bit" in order to advocate for change. School counselors who work for school systems can find themselves in situations where they become aware of injustices behind closed doors, and they must display the courage to open the door and confront situations on behalf of students in order for change to occur. Advocacy is an essential component of student support services in public education.

(Continued)

During one particular school year, I noticed that 62 students, including 10 minority students, were overlooked and not recommended for advanced classes. The teachers relied upon one major test score as their criterion for determining these students' eligibility for advanced classes rather than considering other pertinent data points. Using an isolated test score to determine eligibility had been the practice for several years. I reviewed various forms of data, including multiple test scores, quarterly grades, attendance, and personal observations of the students' academic attitude, and I concluded that the students should be invited into advanced courses. I determined that the current system and practice of using one major test score to determine eligibility for advanced placement was acting as a barrier to accessing a rigorous academic program for these 62 students. I voiced my concerns to the principal and talked with the teachers. The teachers reconsidered a few of their recommendations based on the data I presented. But I was not able to convince them to recommend the majority of the 62 students, even though many of these students were straight-A students and, in my data-driven judgment, deserved the opportunity.

My principal authorized me to have a dialogue with the families of these students and empower the families to request in writing that the students be placed in advanced courses. I explained to the families that the data supported their children as appropriate candidates for advanced classes. Having this conversation with these families and encouraging them to make these requests would cause some teachers to become resentful of the violation of the system in place, the challenge to the status quo. However, I was willing to take this risk. It was needed in order to remove barriers to achievement for selected groups of students.

Professional counselors need to have the skills to deal with resistance. I learned that I needed to be comfortable with being uncomfortable from time to time in order to advocate and be a voice for my students. I am happy to say that 100% of the students successfully passed the advanced courses at the end of the year, which led to further academic opportunities. But it all started with assessment and data-driven advocacy and decision making.

VOICES FROM THE FIELD 15.7   Using Data: Campus Advocacy for Students Who Self-Injure, by Victoria E. Kress

During the time I worked as a college counselor, the campus community was just starting to see an increase in students who self-injured (e.g., cutting, burning, embedding). It came to my attention that students who self-injured were being threatened with removal from the dorms and university. In order to assess the views of the student life staff and campus administrators toward managing this population, I developed and sent out a campus-wide survey.

The results were surprising: Most of the people who responded expressed negative views toward those who self-injure, and their thoughts on strategies for addressing the behaviors were punitive. For example, one responder stated: "In our office, our job is to address the cutting as 'disruptive behavior' and sanction accordingly." Another administrator stated: "I think we should set criteria for students to be able to return to the university only if they receive appropriate treatment and refuse to engage in self-mutilating behavior." Another student life staff member stated: "I wonder what a student who self-injures is telling us about their ability to be on a campus and a successful student." In the college counseling center we realized that there was lack of understanding of self-injury and how to manage the behavior, and we felt a responsibility to advocate for this population.

To remedy this situation, we put together self-injury trainings for student life staff and administrators. The trainings were intended to educate the staff about the etiology and function of self-injury, and to ultimately empower staff to develop proactive, productive approaches to addressing the behaviors. We worked to dispel myths and break down stereotypes regarding self-injury. We found that framing self-injury as a coping skill one uses to manage overwhelming feelings and regulate negative moods helped the staff to approach the behavior in a more adaptive way. The college's health care staff was also provided with training and psychoeducation so that they would not overreact (i.e., misinterpret the self-injury as a suicide attempt), or underreact (i.e., view the self-injury as "attention seeking").

By going into the dorms and educating students on how to help students manage situations where they knew or believed another student was self-injuring, we were also able to engage in early intervention efforts. Pamphlets and handouts on self-injury were also developed and distributed to students and staff to help them understand self-injury and identify students who may be at risk for the behavior.

Self-injury can have a contagion effect by which others imitate the behavior, so prevention was also an important aspect of our advocacy efforts. We worked with the staff to develop a policy that would limit the potential impacts of contagion, thus theoretically preventing some students from beginning to self-injure. We also helped staff develop a global policy on self-injury that was respectful of people who self-injure. But assessment and empathic understanding were the key to systemic change.

Counseling and Advocacy Intervention Competencies: International and Global Affairs

Due to high immigration rates in the United States, Canada, and Europe, resulting demographic changes have created populations that are different in culture, ethnicity, and religions (Moodley, Lengyell, Wu, & Gielen, 2015). Recent court decisions have endorsed legal unions between same-sex couples, and personal and group acts of violence have affected worldviews, belief systems, values, customs, lifestyles, and how mental health is presented and perceived. Hence, international or global advocacy does not occur only when visiting/traveling/working in a different country of origin.

According to Nassar-McMillan (2014), a framework for social justice and advocacy in the context of global multiculturalism includes the counselor's attitudes, beliefs, knowledge, and skills related to self-awareness and other-awareness. The complexity of the interaction of cultural beliefs, values, and the impact of worldwide political events on public perception creates a need for advocacy interventions that reflect the needs of a global society. These competencies are outlined in Table 15.8.

With the amount of social media and news exposure we have today, it would be very difficult not to be aware of current events. There are multiple methods of how news is delivered, often occurring in real time. As professional counselors, it is a responsibility to be aware of how current events may be affecting our clients. The challenge today is to expand knowledge-seeking to include international news. It can be easy to perceive international news beyond business as not important to life and work. However, it can be important to clients and may have an impact on their emotional well-being and development. Now, complete Activity 15.9, and then read Voices from the Field 15.8.

TABLE 15.8 International and Global Affairs Advocacy Intervention Competencies

Multicultural and social justice competent counselors:

1. Stay current on international and world politics and events.

2. Seek out professional development to learn about how privileged and marginalized clients influence, and are influenced by, international and global affairs.

3. Acquire knowledge of historical and current international and global affairs that are supportive and unsupportive of privileged and marginalized clients.

4. Learn about the global politics, policies, laws, and theories that influence privileged and marginalized clients.

5. Utilize technology to interact and collaborate with international and global leaders on issues influencing privileged and marginalized clients.

6. Take initiative to address international and global affairs to promote multicultural and social justice issues.

7. Utilize research to examine how international and global affairs impact privileged and marginalized clients.

Source: Ratts, M. J., Singh, A. A., Nassar-McMillan, S., Butler, S. K., & McCullough, J. R. (2015). *Multicultural and social justice counseling competencies.* Retrieved from www.multiculturalcounseling.org/index.php?option=com_content&view=article&id=205:amcd-endorses-multicultural-and-social-justice-counseling-competencies&catid=1:latest&Itemid=123. Reprinted with permission.

ACTIVITY 15.9 APPLICATION OF INTERNATIONAL AND GLOBAL ADVOCACY COMPETENCIES

How knowledgeable are you about world events? Where do you get your news? How much time do you think about how world events affect individuals in the country you are living in? If these questions are difficult to answer, do the following:

1. List all news sources that you attend to currently. How much global news is reported from these sources? What is the quality of this news and is it analyzed by the reporters in any systematic way?

2. What is the historical context for this news? What will this mean for individuals in your country who may be affected directly (i.e., family or friends are still in the other country or have been part of the news)?

3. How do you help clients whose development is affected by these events?

At the core of this type of advocacy, as with all other types of advocacy, is the concept of humanism. We are all humans, with feelings, thoughts, and relationships. As counselors, we need to embrace this for ourselves. In discussing social class and counseling, West-Olatunji and Gibson (2012) proposed three specific advocacy steps to become more fully human in regard to social class that could be expanded to include a focus on our global society:

1. Move away from our single stories about social class or international events and cultures.

2. Expand our circle of influence by seeking interactions with those individuals who are outside of our social class and/or cultural groups.

3. Challenge false assumptions made by others. (p. 10)

These ideas can be extrapolated to global issues and international clients. Instead of trying to maintain a premise of objectivity in the counseling relationship by ignoring socio-political and geopolitical forces that affect their lives on a daily basis, we should actively seek this information and acknowledge its existence in our clients' lives. Making it "real" and being "human" does not mean losing objectivity. Instead, it means building a relationship with clients where trust can bridge cultural differences and highlight similarities.

VOICES FROM THE FIELD 15.8   The Intersection of Public Policy and Global Action, by Donna Gibson

Several years ago I attended a national counseling conference in which the director of the National Board of Certified Counselors (NBCC) was describing the NBCC's efforts in expanding licensure internationally. The director reported that he called and was granted an appointment with a high-ranking official, an important decision maker with the World Health Organization (WHO), to discuss why licensed professional counseling was essential in different countries. The NBCC director reported his amazement in gaining this appointment. Hearing this story reminded me of the role of the professional counselor as advocate. Do not be afraid to *ask* for help or simply to present a cause. Meet with people who can make a difference. By educating the individuals who can affect change about harmful conditions to human development, change can be made. These individuals may be local, state, federal or international government officials. They may include other officials who work for human health organizations and need to be given data to "make the case" for change for budgetary reasons. Professional counselors may start with local representatives to learn how lobbying and legislatures work in their communities. Counselors also need to determine what issues need this level of advocacy and the appropriate method of achieving this goal. For example, counselors can contact the American Counseling Association to obtain more information on current lobbying efforts on specific issues. Information from other states may be applicable to the issue presenting in the counselor's state. Finally, professional counselors can use failed attempts to learn how to design and implement social/political advocacy efforts that will succeed.

Summary

Advocacy is a core component of the identity of the professional counselor. Over time, advocacy has changed from professional counselors helping clients achieve a sense of empowerment to professional counselors engaging in social action activities or social justice advocacy on behalf of clients, systems, and communities to bring justice to individuals who are experiencing barriers to their development.

In this chapter, the Multicultural and Social Justice Counseling Competencies (Ratts et al., 2015) were explained by discussing the various counseling and advocacy intervention competencies: intrapersonal, interpersonal, community, institutional, public policy, and international and global affairs. This model illustrates the levels of need for advocacy. In addition, it depicts professional counselors as individuals who can work *with* clients and communities to break down barriers and advocate *for* clients and community systems when required.

To know when to advocate, professional counselors need to engage in problem assessment. By using assessment strategies, professional counselors can examine the systems that are interacting with clients and communities to determine if barriers are evident within these systems and preventing the growth of clients and/or communities. Assessment of these systems also allows professional counselors to determine what resources are available to clients and communities to include in advocacy action plans. These plans can include a range of activities: from practicing assertiveness skills in counseling sessions or encouraging a feeling of empowerment by clients, to promoting awareness by providing public information about it through various types of media and technology.

Opportunities to engage in counseling advocacy are abundant in most environments in which professional counselors interact on a daily basis. From an ethical standpoint, professional counselors have an obligation to empower clients and community systems and advocate for those who cannot self-advocate. If professional counselors do not engage in advocacy counseling, in essence, they are part of the barriers to human development and growth.

MyCounselingLab for Introduction to Counseling

Try the Topic 12 Assignments: *Multicultural Considerations.*

The Effectiveness of Counseling

Section Four, "The Effectiveness of Counseling," addresses the crucial issues of accountability and outcomes in counseling. The future of the counseling profession lies in the ability of counselors to show that counseling practices are effective in helping clients reach their stated goals. Counselors-in-training need to learn to conduct needs assessments, outcomes studies, and program evaluation to determine what services are needed, and the effects of those services. Chapter 16, "Accountability in Counseling," proposes that accountability is a central responsibility of all professional counselors. At its core, accountability shows the effect that a professional counselor has in producing changes in clients and program stakeholders. The conduct of outcomes studies is approached from traditional research methods perspectives and more contemporary perspectives, including action research and single-subject research designs.

Counselors also need to realize that a great wealth of extant literature exists to inform their daily counseling practice with clients. This literature is reviewed in Chapter 17, "Outcome Research in Counseling," to bolster the students' knowledge of what does and does not work in counseling, and so counselors can use effective counseling interventions. Professional counselors have an ethical responsibility to use counseling methods grounded in theory and empirically validated through research. It is now known that counseling is effective in many forms and for many client conditions. Chapter 17 reviews research on the effectiveness of counseling in several areas: client–counselor characteristics, individual approaches, group approaches, career intervention, and school-based student interventions. This body of information should be used by professional counselors to inform their practice and increase treatment efficacy.

16 Accountability in Counseling

BRADLEY T. ERFORD

PREVIEW

Accountability is a central responsibility of all professional counselors. However, accountability is not just tallying the number of clients seen or how much time has been spent providing various types of services. At its core, accountability demonstrates the effect that a professional counselor has in producing changes in clients and program stakeholders. This chapter presents models and methods for how professional counselors can demonstrate accountability through implementing effective needs assessment, program evaluation, service assessment, and outcome studies. Outcome studies are approached from traditional research methods perspectives and from more contemporary and site-based perspectives, including action research and single-subject research designs.

ACCOUNTABILITY

Research has established that counseling is an effective treatment delivery system (see Chapter 17). However, this knowledge alone does not satisfy the public's justified need for continued accountability in counseling services, particularly for individual clients seeking counseling services. Professional counselors need to provide evidence of effectiveness to multiple stakeholder groups, including clients, third-party payers (e.g., insurance companies), and school administrators. For counseling to remain valued by the public and paid for by third-party payers, taxpayers, and clients, professional counselors must provide evidence showing that their work is worthwhile and produces results. Lack of accountability can lead to the elimination of counseling positions, specific counseling practices, and entire delivery systems. Being accountable and providing effective services is the best way counselors can advocate for their profession. This is a profession-wide imperative, not limited to schools, universities, clinics or private practices. Counselors who make positive differences in peoples' lives demonstrate effective services which promote the best interests of the public and the counseling profession.

A new era of educational reform and a lack of accountability in the school counseling profession have caused some positions to be eliminated from school districts across the United States (Martin, 2015). Likewise, third-party insurance payers have made increasing demands for the demonstration of effectiveness of mental health services with clients. Professional counselors who demonstrate effectiveness may receive more referrals and develop a reputation for skill and efficiency.

Accountability in counseling answers the question, "How are clients different as a result of the services provided by professional counselors?" Use of assessment techniques to measure outcome allows counselors to provide accountability to clients, funding sources, administrators, and other stakeholders, and demonstrate how their program is affecting client outcome, development, and achievement. Accountability requires responsibility for professional actions. According to various authors (e.g., Erford, 2015c; Loesch & Ritchie, 2004), **accountability** ordinarily involves the following:

- Identifying and collaborating with stakeholder groups (e.g., advisory committees, clients, parents, teachers, students)
- Collecting data and assessing the needs of clients, staff, and community
- Setting goals and establishing objectives based on data and determined needs
- Implementing effective interventions to address the goals and objectives
- Measuring the outcomes or results of these interventions
- Using these results for program improvement
- Sharing results with major stakeholder groups (e.g., clients, administrators, teachers and staff members, parents and guardians, students, school boards, community and business leaders, professional counselors, and supervisors)

Conducting accountability studies has both advantages and challenges, although the challenges are often easily overcome by collaborating with colleagues with some accountability expertise. These advantages and challenges are outlined in Table 16.1. It is the professional and ethical responsibility of counselors to ensure that the services offered to stakeholders are truly effective. This chapter focuses on the wide-ranging accountability functions of the professional counselor, including needs assessment, program evaluation,

---

TABLE 16.1 Advantages and Challenges of Accountability Studies

Advantages

1. Data are almost always better than perception when it comes to guiding decision making about programs, practices, and interventions.
2. Accountability studies help show the necessity, efficiency, and effectiveness of counseling services.
3. Accountability studies can help identify professional development and staff development needs.
4. Professional counselors can network to share program results, spreading the word about effective practices.
5. Conducting accountability studies is a professional responsibility and demonstrates commitment to personal and professional improvement.
6. Accountability results can serve a public relations function by informing clients and the public of a counseling program's accomplishments.

Challenges

1. Outcome measures and surveys require some training and skill to develop (sometimes including consultation with experts).
2. It requires time and resources to do quality outcome research and evaluation, time and resources that could be dedicated to additional service delivery.
3. Many do not understand the nature and purpose of accountability because of misperceptions or previous bad experiences.
4. Data are sometimes overinterpreted or given undue meaning (e.g., the facts may not support the conclusion). All studies have limitations that must be considered when arriving at conclusions.

service assessment, and outcome research. This information allows professional counselors to speak the language of decision makers; promote social and academic advocacy for clients with diverse needs; and overcome systemic barriers to academic, career, or personal/social success. Every professional counselor should be constantly asking and gathering information to answer the question, "Is what I'm doing working with clients?" Comprehensive evaluations are seldom conducted. More often, bits and pieces of evaluative information are collected, and the big picture is often incomplete.

USING A COUNSELING PROGRAM ADVISORY COMMITTEE

A counseling program **advisory committee** serves as a sounding board and steering committee. These committees are commonly used in school, university community, or agency counseling environments. The most important factor to consider when composing a counseling program advisory committee is influence. The professional counselor must seek to include individuals who can influence and hold the confidence of program decision makers. In schools, decision makers may include the principal and central office administrators, while in community agencies, decision makers may include program administrators or directors of funding sources. Including influential members on the committee eases the way for necessary programmatic changes and resource attainment.

From a personnel perspective in agencies, it is essential for the program administrator or the representatives from important funding sources to be part of the advisory committee. In this way, the directors can hear firsthand the ideas and planning that go into recommendations for improvement and the rationale behind why increased funding may be needed. In addition to the professional counselor, at least several influential stakeholders (e.g., community leaders, activists, politicians, business leaders, parents) should be included. The members can inform the advisory committee of various constituencies' concerns and provide information to the constituencies regarding actions recommended by the committee.

It is essential for the lead administrator to be a member of an advisory committee. In this way, the administrator can hear firsthand the ideas and planning that go into recommendations for improvement and the rationale behind why additional funding may be needed. In addition to the professional counselor(s), at least several influential past clients and community members should be included. In schools, several teachers and parents should be included. Political linkages to parent-teacher organizations often play to the advantage of a professional school counselor because these members can serve as conduits to and from the organizations. The members can inform the advisory committee of various constituencies' concerns and provide information to the constituencies regarding actions recommended by the committee.

To round out the committee, an influential resource person and community organization or business leader should be included. Individuals from the community and businesses are useful for providing an external perspective and partnership, as well as external funding and resources.

The advisory committee should convene at least twice annually, and more frequently if the program is new or undergoing major changes. The primary role of the advisory committee is to review the results of the needs assessment, make recommendations for program development, review accountability data and outcome research generated by staff members, and locate internal and external funding sources for program development.

Locating funding sources often requires the cooperation of administrators; this is where it pays off to include directors or administrators and other influential individuals in the committee. The advisory committee can serve practical and political functions, making it a top priority on the professional counselor's agenda. One of the most important roles of the advisory committee is to help professional counselors determine constituent needs and program goals. Activity 16.1 provides an opportunity to think about and apply this information on forming an advisory committee.

ACTIVITY 16.1

Imagine that you are tasked to form a counseling program advisory committee for your school or agency. Who would you invite to participate in the committee? Why would you include these particular individuals and/or groups?

CONDUCTING A NEEDS ASSESSMENT

At least two primary purposes underlie the use of a needs assessment in counseling programs. First, **needs assessment** helps professional counselors understand the needs of various subpopulations of a community. These subpopulations may include clients, congregations, neighborhoods, teachers, parents, students, administrators, community organizations, or local businesspeople. Subpopulations within schools also may include subgroups of students experiencing achievement gaps or differential access to rigorous academic programming. Each of these groups holds a stake in the success of the total educational enterprise; they are called **stakeholder** groups. Second, needs assessment helps establish the priorities that guide the construction of a counseling program and the continuous quality improvement of the program. A needs assessment emphasizes what currently exists compared with identified goals and objectives. Assessing the needs of a community or community population provides a trajectory for addressing what the community values and desires to pursue. Needs assessments can be classified as data-driven needs assessments and perceptions-based needs assessments.

Data-Driven Needs Assessment

Data-driven decision making deals with demonstrated needs and impact, not perceived needs. Data-driven needs assessment is most frequently used in school systems because standardized assessment is systematically collected, primarily due to local, state, and federal initiatives. However, this process can also be applied just as easily to community-based agencies.

    Data-driven needs assessment begins with an analysis of school-based or community-based performance data. Given the prominence of high-stakes testing and large-scale testing programs, schools are frequently provided with aggregated and disaggregated achievement performance results. **Aggregated** means that all student results are lumped together to show total grade level or school-wide (average) results. Aggregated data are helpful in understanding how the average students perform in a given class, grade, or school, but they tell very little about the diversity of learner performance or needs, and nothing about how various subgroups or subpopulations performed. In Table 16.2, the

TABLE 16.2 Aggregated and Disaggregated Results of a Typical Large-Scale Math Achievement Test for a Total School Fifth-Grade Level*

	n	NPR	% in Quartile			
			Q_1	Q_2	Q_3	Q_4
Total grade	**100**	**50**	**19**	**31**	**26**	**24**
Male	48	45	22	34	26	18
Female	52	56	10	31	31	28
Asian	8	72	0	25	38	38
Black	31	37	29	52	13	6
Hispanic	8	43	25	50	25	0
White	52	58	9	30	33	28
Other	1	44	0	100	0	0
Low SES	48	31	36	38	23	3
Non–low SES	52	71	5	24	36	35
English (second language)	3	43	0	67	33	0
English (primary language)	97	51	19	30	27	24
Special education	10	25	60	20	20	0
Non–special education	90	58	11	31	32	26

*Note: % in Quartile (Q) = percentage of the sample that actually performed in a given quartile; n = number of students in sample; NPR = national percentile rank; SES = socioeconomic status.

aggregated results are represented by the "Total grade" line near the top for a school with 100 fifth graders.

To understand fully how to use performance data, professional counselors must become proficient in understanding norm-referenced and criterion-referenced score interpretation. A comprehensive explanation of score interpretation is beyond the scope of this chapter, and the topic is typically encountered by counselors in an assessment or testing course. What follows can be considered a primer on the interpretation of norm-referenced scores. For a more advanced understanding of interpreting standardized test score data, see Erford (2013).

In the example in Table 16.2, the mean (average) national percentile rank was 50. A **percentile rank** is most easily understood if one visualizes a lineup of 100 individuals, all with certain characteristics in common; in this case, they are all fifth-grade math students. When interpreting percentile ranks, the first student on the line is the lowest performing student, whereas the 100th student is the highest performing student. A student's place indicates the relative standing compared with other fifth grade math students across the United States (thus the term *national percentile rank*). For example, a student scoring at the 79th percentile performed better than 79% of the fifth graders in the national norm group, or was the 79th student standing in the line. Likewise, a student performing at the 5th percentile would be standing in the fifth place in line and has outperformed only 5% of the fifth graders in the nationwide norm group.

A **quartile** is a commonly used interpretive statistic that divides the percentile rank distribution into four population segments, with 25% of the population within each segment. The first quartile includes percentile ranks ranging from less than 1 to 25, the lowest quarter of a distribution and designated as Q_1. The second quartile (Q_2) includes percentile ranks ranging from 26 to 50. The third quartile (Q_3) includes percentile ranks ranging from 51 to 75. The fourth quartile (Q_4) includes percentile ranks ranging from 76 to greater than 99, the highest quarter of the distribution.

Some test publishers also use an interpretive statistic known as stanines. Stanines, short for "standard nine," divide a normal distribution into nine segments, albeit in a manner quite different from quartiles. Stanines actually represent one-half standard deviation units. So while each quartile represents 25% of the population, stanines may be composed of varying percentages of the population. The first stanine represents the lowest level of performance, while the ninth stanine represents the highest level of performance, each composing only 4% of the population. In contrast, the fifth stanine represents the middle of the distribution and is composed of 20% of the population.

Clients, students, parents, and teachers understand performance easiest and most accurately when using percentile ranks or quartiles, although quartiles are less precise than percentile ranks. Other standardized scores can require some sophistication and may lead to errors in interpretation. Figure 16.1 provides a graphic of the normal curve and commonly used standardized scores that the professional counselor may encounter. Because

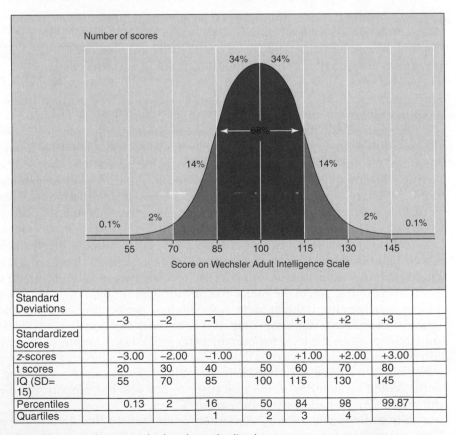

Standard Deviations								
		−3	−2	−1	0	+1	+2	+3	
Standardized Scores								
z-scores		−3.00	−2.00	−1.00	0	+1.00	+2.00	+3.00	
t scores		20	30	40	50	60	70	80	
IQ (SD= 15)		55	70	85	100	115	130	145	
Percentiles			0.13	2	16	50	84	98	99.87	
Quartiles					1	2	3	4	

FIGURE 16.1   The normal curve and related standardized scores.

all are based on the normal curve, each of these types of standardized scores can be converted into percentile ranks for easy explanation to clients, students, parents, and teachers.

Disaggregated means that the data have been broken down by subpopulations so that performance differences between or among groups can be analyzed. Usually, this analysis involves intergroup differences (e.g., male versus female, race, ethnicity, special education status versus regular education status). Most test publishers can provide this information upon request, broken down by school, grade level, and even individual classes. Differences can be determined using statistical methods or by informal comparison. Seeing differences in disaggregated data helps provide hard evidence of gaps in student performance and avoids reliance on perceptions. It also provides direction for the types of strategies and interventions needed to close these gaps. Case Studies 16.1 and 16.2 provide explanations of how to implement a data-driven needs assessment in school and agency venues, respectively.

CASE STUDY 16.1

Looking at the data provided in Table 16.2, one can see several noticeable gaps in achievement. First, students from the low socioeconomic status (SES) grouping performed at the 31st percentile rank, on average, whereas students from the non–low SES group (e.g., middle-class and upper-middle-class in this example) performed at the 71st percentile rank, on average. Second, there is a noticeable difference between the average math performance for black and Hispanic students (37th and 43rd percentile ranks, respectively) compared with Asian and white students (72nd and 58th percentile ranks, respectively). Third, girls outperformed boys, on average (56th and 45th percentile ranks, respectively). From these comparisons of disaggregated data, discussions can commence and strategies can be developed to reduce the math performance gap. However, it all starts with the data—hence the term *data-driven*. In this way, data provide the impetus and drive behind school improvement plans and responsive counseling programs.

1. How could you use the disaggregated data in Table 16.2 to develop an action plan to enhance the academic performance of these students?
2. What additional data would you need?
3. What areas for improvement would you identify?
4. What strategies and interventions would you recommend or implement?

CASE STUDY 16.2

For an example from clinical practice, see Table 16.3. The table provides treatment change data from the Beck Anxiety Inventory (BAI) (Beck & Steer, 1993) for a group of 50 clients seen for a group counseling treatment regimen with no concurrent medication treatment. Analyzing the aggregated data, one would conclude that the 50 clients began with an average BAI raw score of 30 (moderate to severe levels of anxiety symptoms) and finished the group counseling treatment regimen with an average BAI raw score of 20 (mild to moderate levels of anxiety), an average raw score decline of 10 points. On

(Continued)

TABLE 16.3 Aggregated and Disaggregated Data for 50 Clients Treated for Anxiety with a 24-Week Group Counseling Regimen on the BAI (Raw Score)

	n	BAI Baseline (A)	BAI (24 sessions) (B)	BAI Change (A–B)
Total sample	**50**	**30**	**20**	**10**
Males	20	26	17.2	8.8
Females	30	32.7	21.9	10.8
White	36	33.3	20.8	12.5
Black	14	21.5	18	3.5
Low SES	20	25.5	22.4	3.1
Non–low SES	30	33	18.4	14.6

the surface, and on average, these data show that the group treatment was successful in reducing average symptoms of anxiety for the group. However, conscientious professional counselors are interested in determining whether the treatment differentially affected members with various characteristics (e.g., gender, race, SES).

When the total sample data in Table 16.3 is disaggregated, notice that some differences do appear to exist regarding the effectiveness of the treatment on certain subgroups. For example, low SES participants experienced only a 3-point raw score improvement after treatment, whereas non–low SES participants experienced more than four times that level of symptom relief (i.e., a change of 14.6 raw score points for non–low SES versus a change of only 3 points for low SES participants). Likewise, African American clients reported average BAI raw score declines of only 3.5 points, whereas white participants reported a decline of 12.5 raw score points.

On the surface, one may reach a tentative conclusion that the group counseling treatment was more effective for white and non–low SES participants. Disaggregated data can help professional counselors make decisions about treatment efficacy for prospective clients and make program improvements to help future clients benefit equitably from an otherwise effective approach or program. Data-driven approaches to needs assessment use existing data, or easy-to-collect data, to determine client population needs and treatment equity.

These differences can be determined through more advanced statistical procedures or by less sophisticated procedures, such as simply reviewing the data to note gaps in performance. Identified gaps provide objective (not perception-based) evidence of differential results, identifying needs to be addressed. When such needs are identified, professional counselors can begin the process of addressing these needs through well-written objectives, interventions, and programmatic initiatives. (See the section called Converting Needs to Program Goals and Objectives.)

1. How could you use the disaggregated data in Table 16.3 to develop an action plan to enhance the treatment of these clients?
2. What additional data would you need?
3. What areas for improvement would you identify?
4. What strategies and interventions would you recommend or implement?

Perceptions-Based Needs Assessment

In contrast to a data-driven needs assessment, a traditional perceptions-based needs assessment process is more content-driven and subjective. Professional counselors are often interested in what clients, community leaders, citizens, teachers, parents, and students perceive as primary needs to be addressed. Before undertaking a **perceptions-based needs assessment**, professional counselors are wise to consider issues of how often to conduct a needs assessment, which stakeholder groups to assess, and how to design an efficient needs assessment.

FREQUENCY OF CONDUCTING A NEEDS ASSESSMENT Although it may seem tempting to design and conduct a global needs assessment on an annual basis, such an endeavor would be a massive administrative undertaking. It is probably best to follow a multiyear continuous cycle of assessing programmatic needs. This approach allows ample time for program development and improvements over the course of the cycle. The timing of needs assessments varies for community and school venues. In schools, the American School Counselor Association (ASCA) *National Model* (American School Counselor Association, 2012) designates the areas of academic, career, and personal–social development as the cornerstones of a comprehensive developmental school counseling program; it makes sense that school community needs be assessed according to those components on a rotating basis.

For a new program or one undergoing major renovations, years 1 and 2 of a 6-year cycle can be spent conducting needs assessment and implementing programmatic changes to address horizontal articulation (within grade level) and vertical articulation (across grade levels) issues surrounding student academic development. Years 3 and 4 can be spent on student career development needs, and years 5 and 6 can focus on student personal–social issues. The 6-year cycle also could rotate among the three domains, addressing half of the domain issues every 3 years (i.e., year 1, academic; year 2, career; year 3, personal–social; year 4, academic; year 5, career; year 6, personal–social). An established school counseling program that is in good condition and requires only fine-tuning may be put on a 3-year continuous improvement cycle.

Community-based mental health counseling programs may require a comprehensive needs assessment only every 3 to 5 years, or when societal or political changes deem it essential to maintaining quality service levels within the community. The main point here is that assessing needs is part of a much bigger endeavor: that of implementing programmatic changes to continuously improve the counseling program. Implementing changes can be time-intensive and simply a waste of time if not guided by accurate needs assessments and program outcome research. An effective program uses this information to fine-tune its decision-making efforts.

POPULATIONS TO BE ASSESSED In the broadest sense, any stakeholder group can provide helpful information about the needs of a population or community. However, it is most practical and efficient to seek out individuals who are informed and likely to respond. Community leaders, teachers, administrators, clients, students, and parents are the most likely to be informed of community and school issues and needs, and under most circumstances they are the primary stakeholder groups surveyed during a needs assessment. Valuable information can also be garnered from community organizations, local businesses, and the general citizenry. It is more difficult to obtain a large response sampling from these groups.

Information from these stakeholders is probably best obtained through personal contacts and interviews.

Return rate is another factor in the needs assessment process. **Return rate** is the percentage of returned surveys out of those distributed. As in any research sampling procedure, the higher the return rate, the lower the sampling error; a higher return rate leads to greater confidence in the accuracy of the results. Return rate is generally maximized when the participants are a "captured audience." For example, if a social skills needs assessment of fourth grade students is conducted in the classroom, the response rate should be nearly 100%. If a needs assessment for parents is sent home, the professional school counselor may be lucky to have 25% to 50% of the surveys returned. The return rate probably would be even lower if mailed to community stakeholders. Whenever possible, surveys should be distributed and collected immediately during client gatherings, community gatherings, faculty meetings, class meetings, and parent gatherings.

Triangulation of needs across populations should be attempted when possible; that is, the highest priority needs should be those agreed to by all or most populations assessed. This ensures that the community's needs, not an individual's agenda, drive the counseling program. For instance, in a community agency, directors can be powerful influences, and their agendas for the agency may constrict services from being applied where and how they are most needed. Determining different needs and priorities confirmed by multiple stakeholder groups can provide strong evidence that the director's agenda is off course. Likewise, if a principal of a school has decided to place a high priority on social skills, but teachers, parents, and students indicate this is a low priority, far below other issues such as school safety, substance abuse, and study skills, the triangulated responses of the teachers, parents, and students can provide compelling evidence to guide the program's focus.

DESIGNING AN EFFICIENT NEEDS ASSESSMENT   Designing an efficient needs assessment is essential to meaningful results. While some experts advocate for a comprehensive needs assessment simultaneously assessing all goals and topics associated with a comprehensive counseling program, others have found it more helpful to focus the assessment on specifically defined topics or issues that are being updated or altered. This chapter focuses on the latter method.

Many methods exist for determining needs, including questionnaires, surveys, and inventories; interviews; use of outside consultants; analysis of records; and existing evaluation and outcome study results. Perhaps what is most important is that the needs assessment uses objective methods for data gathering and analysis. It is essential to understand that different questions can be addressed by different methods. Although all of these methods are important and useful, questionnaires (formal or informal surveys) are most commonly used and are the focus here. Open-ended questionnaires or surveys are generally easier to design and yield rich and diverse information, but such questionnaires or surveys can be more difficult to interpret and translate into goals and objectives.

From a return rate perspective, it is good practice to design a needs assessment that is only one to two pages in length (the maximum of two pages is a good rule to observe) and can be completed in less than 5 minutes. The content of the needs assessment should be topical (e.g., social skills, changing families, substance abuse, college application procedures) rather than service-related (e.g., individual counseling, group counseling, consultation). Services are definitely important, but professional counselors must keep in mind that services are simply methods for meeting needs, not needs in themselves. The topics should be related to the program goals (e.g., agency standards or mission statement, the ASCA Mindsets and Behaviors local or state standards) so that priority status can be placed on addressing the most pressing needs in comparison to these standards. A good needs assessment directly translates into program development.

In general, the following steps form the basis of an efficient needs assessment:

1. Decide what you need to know.
2. Decide on the best approach to derive what you need to know.
3. Determine or develop the needs assessment instrument or method.
4. Enlist the support of colleagues and a few individuals from the target groups to review and try out items for understanding (i.e., pilot test).
5. Implement the final version on the target groups.
6. Tabulate, analyze, and interpret the results.
7. Translate the results into programmatic goals and objectives.

The design of the scale itself warrants mention. The client survey should ask for the name of the individual completing the form (unless the form is to be completed anonymously). Teacher surveys may ask for the grade level, the number of students in class, or other pertinent information. Parent surveys should ask for the names of the parent's children in case their response to the survey requires contact by the professional counselor. Student surveys should ask for the student's grade and homeroom teacher's name. Questions or response items should be short, to the point, and easy to understand. The reading level of the items should also be appropriate for the target audience. Figure 16.2 provides an example of a topic-focused needs assessment for students/clients.

Substantial consideration should also be given to the response format. If the purpose of the survey is to determine the importance or frequency of a potential problem, it is generally best to use a multipoint scale with four to seven choices. For example, Figure 16.2 asks about the frequency of stressors, so the response choices "Almost Never," "Sometimes,"

Name: _____

Place a check mark (✓) in the appropriate space below to indicate how well you handle each issue.

	Almost Never	Some-times	Often	Almost Always	I Need Help with This Yes	No
1. I am able to focus my thoughts when I need to.						
2. I have a good workout schedule.						
3. I have good time management skills.						
4. I can control my breathing when I am upset.						
5. I can control my level of stress.						
6. I have good organizational skills.						
7. My muscles are relaxed.						
8. I have good nutritional habits.						
9. I think positive thoughts about myself.						
10. I can readily identify stressors in my life.						

FIGURE 16.2   A topic-focused stress management needs assessment.

"Often," and "Almost Always" are appropriate. The response choices "Never" and "Always" do not appear. It is rare that behaviors never or always occur; to include these descriptors may force responses to the center of the distribution and truncate the range of possible results. Also notice how each category has a descriptor. Hopefully, gone are the days in survey construction when a survey lists the response categories of 0, "Almost never" and 3, "Almost always," and then provides the center points of 1 and 2 with no accompanying descriptor. The reliability problems of such a scale are obvious: Would all respondents agree on what an unlabeled 1 and 2 represent? All choice categories must be accompanied by a verbal descriptor.

Another important response component of a needs assessment is a frequency count. Suppose a professional counselor wants not only to assess the importance of an issue, but also to determine how many clients were likely in need of services to address the problems stemming from the issue. When possible, the needs assessment should include an indication of whether the respondent should be targeted for intervention. In Figure 16.2, notice how the far right-hand column asks for a yes or no answer to the statement, "I need help with this." An affirmative response targets the client for future assessment or intervention to address a self-perceived weakness.

Tallying, or computing the information from a needs assessment, is simple. Tallying involves counting the number of clients who may benefit from intervention. Computing the results of a needs assessment is probably best accomplished by assigning a number value to each response category and averaging all responses for a given item. In Figure 16.2, assume that the response categories are assigned the following values: Almost never = 0, Sometimes = 1, Often = 2, and Almost always = 3. For item 1, "I am able to focus my thoughts when I need to," simply add all client response values and divide by the number of responses.

Review the data in Table 16.4. If 50 clients completed the needs assessment, and 10 clients marked "Almost never" ($10 \times 0 = 0$) for item 1, 12 clients marked "Sometimes" ($12 \times 1 = 12$), 21 clients marked "Often" ($21 \times 2 = 42$), and 7 clients marked "Almost always" ($7 \times 3 = 21$), simply sum the points ($0 + 12 + 42 + 21 = 75$) and divide by the number of client responses (sum of 75 divided by 50 students = 1.50) to compute the average frequency rating (1.50). Although this assumes a ratio scale and is nebulous from a statistical interpretation perspective (i.e., what does a 1.50 really mean?), it does offer a reasonable estimate of the average frequency of a behavior, or of the importance of one issue compared with the other issues under study. For example, when viewing the mean computations of the 10 items in Table 16.4, the professional counselor gets a good idea about the importance of item 1 compared with the other nine items in the needs assessment. It was ranked as the ninth highest need, so quite low in importance compared with many higher need items. Now complete Activity 16.2.

ACTIVITY 16.2

As a class or as individuals, choose a counseling topic or goal and design a brief perceptions-based needs assessment to determine the needs of a client group. As a class, complete the needs assessment, tally the responses, conduct descriptive statistics, and prioritize objectives for an intervention program to address group needs.

TABLE 16.4 Data from the Stress Management Needs Assessment ($n = 50$)

	AN (0)	S (1)	O (2)	AA (3)	Yes	No	Average (rank)
1. I am able to focus my thoughts when I need to.	10 (0)	12 (12)	21 (42)	7 (21)	21	29	1.50 (9)
2. I have a good workout schedule.	22 (0)	17 (17)	7 (14)	4 (12)	33	17	0.86 (3)
3. I have good time management skills.	15 (0)	12 (12)	14 (28)	9 (27)	22	28	1.34 (6)
4. I can control my breathing when I am upset.	29 (0)	12 (12)	7 (14)	2 (6)	42	8	0.64 (1)
5. I can control my level of stress.	24 (0)	9 (9)	10 (20)	7 (21)	33	17	1.00 (4)
6. I have good organizational skills.	14 (0)	9 (9)	17 (34)	10 (30)	19	31	1.46 (8)
7. My muscles are relaxed.	28 (0)	8 (8)	8 (16)	6 (18)	35	15	0.84 (2)
8. I have good nutritional habits.	19 (0)	15 (15)	7 (14)	9 (27)	35	15	1.12 (5)
9. I think positive thoughts about myself.	17 (0)	12 (12)	7 (14)	14 (42)	23	27	1.36 (7)
10. I can readily identify stressors in my life.	6 (0)	9 (9)	10 (20)	25 (75)	4	36	2.08 (10)

Note. Almost never (AN) = 0; Sometimes (S) = 1; Often (O) = 2, Almost always (AA) = 3. The tally (number of clients responding) is entered in each column first followed by the product of the tally and response value; for example, item 1 under the AA (3) column reads 7 (21), meaning that seven clients responded "Almost always," and this tally was multiplied by 3 to obtain the product of 21. The rank indicates the order of greatest need, with the lower average scores indicating the greater degrees of need.

HELPFUL TIPS FOR DEVELOPING A NEEDS ASSESSMENT   A helpful set of commonsense guidelines for questionnaire or survey development was provided by Fitzpatrick, Sanders, and Worthen (2011, pp. 355–356):

1. Sequencing questions
   a. Are later responses biased by early questions?
   b. Does the questionnaire begin with easy, unthreatening, but pertinent questions?
   c. Are leading questions avoided (ones that "lead" to a certain response)?
   d. Is there a logical, efficient sequencing of questions (e.g., from general to specific questions; use of filter questions when appropriate)?
   e. Are closed-ended or open-ended questions appropriate? If closed, are the categories exhaustive and mutually exclusive? Do responses result in the desired scale of data for analysis (i.e., nominal, ordinal, interval)?
   f. Are the major issues covered thoroughly while minor issues passed over quickly?
   g. Are questions with similar content grouped logically?
2. Wording questions
   a. Are questions stated precisely (who, what, when, where, why, how)?
   b. Does the questionnaire avoid assuming too much knowledge on the part of the respondent?
   c. Does each item ask only one question?

d. Is the respondent in a position to answer the question, or must he or she make guesses? If so, are you interested in his or her guesses?

e. Are definitions clear?

f. Are emotionally tinged words avoided?

g. Is the vocabulary at the reading level of the audience? If any technical terminology, jargon, or slang is used, is it the most appropriate way to communicate with this audience?

h. Are the methods for responding appropriate, clear, and consistent?

i. Are the questions appropriately brief and uncomplicated?

3. Establishing and keeping rapport and eliciting cooperation

a. Is the questionnaire easy to answer? (Questions are not overly long or cumbersome.)

b. Is the time required to respond reasonable?

c. Does the instrument look attractive (i.e., layout, quality of paper)?

d. Is there a "respondent orientation"? (Does it motivate the respondent?)

e. Does the cover letter provide an explanation of purpose, sponsorship, method of respondent selection, and anonymity?

f. Is appropriate incentive provided for the respondent's cooperation?

4. Giving instructions

a. Is the respondent clearly told how to record responses?

b. Are instructions for return clear? Is a stamped, self-addressed return envelope provided?

Professional counselors conducting needs assessments must choose an appropriate response format, ordinarily: yes or no (or yes, sometimes, no), multiscale formats (e.g., almost never, sometimes, frequently, almost always), Likert-type scales (e.g., very dissatisfied, dissatisfied, satisfied, very satisfied), true/false formats, or multiple choice formats. Note the wording of items, scaling method, and single-page format of the needs assessment presented in Figure 16.2.

CONVERTING NEEDS TO PROGRAM GOALS AND OBJECTIVES   If the needs assessment was designed correctly, translating the results into goals and learning objectives is easy. The first step is to prioritize the needs in the order of importance and their relationship to existing components of the program. Prioritization can be accomplished most easily by the use of the tallying, computing, and triangulation strategies mentioned earlier. Next, the needs must be matched with, or translated into, goals aligned with the program mission and standards. Finally, the goals are operationalized through the development of learning objectives. Erford (2015c, 2016) provides an excellent nuts-and-bolts discussion of how to write learning objectives using the **ABCD model**: **a**udience, **b**ehavior, **c**onditions, and **d**escription of the expected performance criterion.

A reasonable goal stemming from the needs assessment shown in Figure 16.2 would be "To increase clients' abilities to manage stress and anxiety." Notice how the wording of a goal is nebulous and not amenable to measurement as stated. In developing learning objectives related to goals, particular emphasis is given to specific actions that are measurable. For example, a possible objective stemming from this goal could be: "After participating in a group counseling program and learning thought stopping procedures, 80% of the clients will experience a 50% reduction in obsessive thinking over a 1-week period." Another possible objective might be: "After participating in a 6-week program on the importance of exercise with follow-up goal setting monitoring, 80% of members will engage in at least 20 minutes of aerobic exercise at least three times per week." Notice how the objectives designate the audience, the stated behavior, measurement of the behavior, and the level of expected performance (Erford, 2015c, 2016). Gain some more familiarity with the ABCD model by completing Activity 16.3. Then read Voices from the Field 16.1.

ACTIVITY 16.3

Write the following statements into measurable behavioral objectives using the ABCD model:

1. Group members will increase verbal interactions.
2. Class members will engage in more appropriate social skills with each other during classroom activities.
3. The client will become less depressed after participating in individual counseling sessions.

VOICES FROM THE FIELD 16.1   Accountability in Counseling, by Annette Bohannon

Having spent the majority of my career as a counselor in the K–12 public school setting, I have concluded that accountability is talked about a lot, policies and guidelines are written, but very few adhere to the accountability "on the books." What I have experienced is accountability used as a measuring stick for the individual, rather than for the system. Many times I have seen the efforts of school counselors to be accountable go unappreciated by the administration.

While no accountability system is perfect, flaws are particularly evident when comments are made from education administrators (i.e., school, central office, and state department) to not worry about accountability because "no one is going to check." Those attitudes are disheartening when the school counselor is making every effort to comply with the accountability guidelines, is looking to improve a program, or is looking for leadership from the people making decisions.

This leads me to where I am today. I have my school plan, my calendar of activities, and yet I am held accountable for things like data entry, cumulative file folder filing, state testing, and "other duties as assigned." It saddens me that in my long career, no administrator, not even a counseling supervisor, has ever asked me, "How many students have you helped today?" or even "How have you helped a student today?" Instead, I have worked to advocate for my role as an integral part of the school culture and curriculum. At times I have gotten administrators to listen, but more often than not, no action resulted.

For example, with test coordinator duties, most have asked, "If not you, then who?" When they did not have a counselor, an assistant administrator or a teacher was assigned the test coordinator duty. The teacher was given scheduling time to plan, so the teacher was not at the school until the wee hours of the night and weekends to get the task done. The assistant administrator assigned duties to other clerical staff or teachers to assist in test coordination. Even after I requested such clerical assistance, no administrator has ever granted that request while I was the test coordinator.

(Continued)

Why the wee hours of the night? I was responsible for 600 to 1,250 students at any given test session, and without assistance. I have always operated from a counseling philosophy of "people first and paper second," so both people and paper had to get done. This can lead to burnout for some professional school counselors. However, I work on myself all the time and tell myself that what I am doing is in some way going to help students in the long run. Without reframing the situation, my passion for helping students could be weakened. It is also my firm belief that accountability is the responsibility of the individual counselor, whether working in schools, agencies or communities. No written document or administrator is going to make a counselor accountable. It is the responsibility of the professional counselor.

Do you remember the following saying about character: "Who are you when no one else is looking?" Professional counselors must strive to demonstrate and document accountability—whether or not anyone will ever check—because how the clients or students are different as a result of your interventions is what being a professional counselor is all about.

EVALUATING PROGRAMS

In this age of accountability, program evaluation is more important than ever. Traditionally, however, professional counselors—for many reasons—have failed to hold their programs and services accountable or to provide evidence that activities undertaken achieved intended results. Some professional counselors complained that the nature of what counselors do is so abstract and complicated that it renders the services and results unmeasurable. Other professional counselors are so busy attempting to meet the needs of clients that they shift time that should be spent in evaluation to responsive interventions. Some lack an understanding of how to implement the methods and procedures of accountability studies. Still others may be unsure of the effectiveness of the services provided and thus shy away from accountability unless forced to do so by supervisors.

Whatever the reason, the end result is a lack of accountability, which poses dangers for the future of the profession. Each instance contributes to a shirking of professional and ethical responsibility for ensuring that the services provided to clients are of high quality and are effective in meeting intended needs and goals. Think about it from a business perspective. How long would a business last if it continued to engage in indiscernible or ineffective activities, the value of which were unknown to the business's consumers, managers, or employees? Such businesses usually fall victim to competitive market conditions. Now extend that thought to the counseling profession. Without accountability data to back up service provision, counseling services are often among the first services to go during budget cutbacks. Evaluation of counseling services must become and remain a top priority.

In the context of counseling, professional counselors must be concerned with three areas of accountability: (1) process evaluation, (2) service assessment, and (3) results or outcome evaluation. All three are important facets of program evaluation. **Evaluation** is the measurement of worth and indicates that a judgment will be made regarding the effectiveness of a program. In an evaluation process, it is essential to be very specific about what you are measuring and how you are measuring it. This is made clear in the writing of specific learning objectives. Too often, professional counselors are not specific about what they are trying to accomplish, and they become frustrated when they fail to measure what they may or may not have achieved. If a person does not know where he or she is heading, the person must either get specific directions (write a specific, measurable objective) or be satisfied with wherever he or she ends up (perhaps with an ineffective program).

PROGRAM EVALUATION **Program evaluation** (also sometimes called **process evaluation** or **program audit**) is akin to the measurement concept of content validity, which is a systematic examination of a test's (in this case, program's) content. Program evaluation asks whether the counseling entity (e.g., agency, school system) has a written program and whether the written program is being fully implemented by the entity (Gysbers & Henderson, 2012). In short, the audit or evaluation of a program involves determining whether there is written program documentation and whether the program is being implemented appropriately. A program audit frequently provides an analysis of each facet of the comprehensive counseling program.

For school counselors, the ASCA *National Model* (American School Counselor Association, 2005) provided a sample program audit aligning with model components. Sample criteria included "a statement of philosophy has been written for the school counseling program" and "addresses every student's right to a school counseling program" (p. 66). The ASCA suggested that program criteria be evaluated on the following response choices: "None: meaning not in place; In progress: perhaps begun, but not completed; Completed: but perhaps not implemented; Implemented: fully implemented; Not Applicable: for situations where the criteria does not apply" (p. 66). In practice, a program audit should be conducted near the end of each academic year. Reports derived from the audit should address program strengths, areas in need of improvement, and long-term and short-term improvement goals. These goals drive program development procedures and activities during subsequent years.

Service Assessment

Service assessments are sometimes requested by agency directors, counselor supervisors, superintendents, and school boards to document how counselors are spending their time. Two types of service assessments are commonly used: event-topic counts and time logs. **Event-topic counts** involve the professional counselor documenting each time an individual is contacted or provided with a counseling service and the nature of the topic addressed. In this way, professional counselors can keep a weekly or monthly tally of the number of clients seen not only for global individual counseling, but specifically for individual counseling for depression, anxiety, behavior, family issues, social skills, anger management, or conflict resolution issues. Such data are quite impressive when aggregated and presented to a supervisor to indicate that, for example, 961 individual counseling sessions were held with clients last year.

A **time log** is sometimes kept by professional counselors to document the amount of time spent in various counseling and non-counseling-related activities. Some administrators may wish to know the percentage of time that counselors actually spend doing group counseling or consultation. Time logs require professional counselors to document and categorize their activities for every minute of the workday. In states with mandates for providing direct service activities (e.g., elementary professional counselors must spend at least 50% of their time in the direct service activities of individual counseling, group counseling, and group guidance), time logs may be necessary to document compliance for funding purposes.

While service assessments are helpful for telling what or how much a professional counselor is doing, such assessments give no information about the quality or effectiveness of counselor interventions. The important question becomes "What good things happen as a result of professional counselors choosing to use their time this way?" After all, what do professional counselors really accomplish if they spend 80% of their time doing group and individual counseling, but they have ineffective counseling skills? For this kind of information, we must conduct results or outcome studies. Now complete Activity 16.4.

ACTIVITY 16.4

Keep a time log of all activities you participate in for the next week. Include everything you do, from the time that you wake up until you go to sleep. Tabulate and analyze the results. How could you use these data to improve your efficiency as an employee, student, or parent?

OUTCOME OR RESULTS EVALUATION

Outcome evaluation (also called **results evaluation**) answers the important question, "How are clients or students different as a result of the intervention?" Evaluation is an ongoing, cyclical process represented by the assessment loop shown in Figure 16.3. Many people view accountability or assessment as a discrete component, but it is actually an integrated part of a continuous process for program improvement. All accountability procedures must have the organization's mission in mind because institutional values and needs determine the focus of study. Questions of worth and effectiveness are derived from a confluence of values, needs, goals, and mission, and these questions lead to the determination of what evidence must be collected.

Evidence may exist in many places, but typically it is derived using preplanned measures or from the performances or products clients produce during program activities. After information has been gathered, it must be interpreted and conclusions must be drawn from it regarding the program's or activity's worth, strengths, and weaknesses. Finally, the interpretations and conclusions must be used to change the program or parts of the program to improve it.

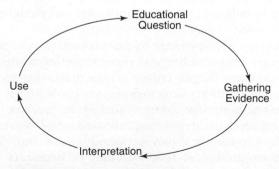

FIGURE 16.3   The assessment cycle.

Notice how the loop in Figure 16.3 never stops; it represents a continuous process in which assessment results are interpreted and fed back into the improvement process. As assessment information is used to prompt programmatic changes, goal setting and the posing of new questions about the revised program keep the cycle going. Many professional counselors gather evidence and then stop, believing that the program has been evaluated and the job finished. But why spend valuable time collecting evidence and not use it to improve what you are doing?

Important Assessment Terms

Many terms associated with research and evaluation are important to understand. **Evidence** is any data that help make judgments or decisions and can be quantitatively or qualitatively derived. **Formative evaluation** is evaluative feedback that occurs during the implementation of a program, and **summative evaluation** is feedback collected at a specified end point in an evaluation process. Although summative evaluation is conducted most frequently, formative evaluation has the advantage of allowing corrective action to occur if an implemented program is shown to be off course. This makes sense when you consider that some programs are expensive to implement in terms of time and money. If you know, after one-third of the program has been implemented, that desired results are not occurring, midcourse corrections can be made to tailor the program to the audience and the desired outcome.

A **stakeholder** is anyone involved in or potentially benefiting from the counseling program. Stakeholders may include clients, parents, teachers, professional counselors, administrators, community organizations, and local businesses. A **baseline** is data gathered to establish a starting point. It is essential to know where clients are at the beginning of an evaluation so that you can tailor interventions to help facilitate their development. **Inputs** are any resources (e.g., personnel, material) that go into a program; **outcomes** are what stakeholders can do as a result of the program.

A **pretest** is a measure administered before a program is implemented (often to establish a baseline), while a **posttest** is a measure administered after the program or intervention has been completed. If a study calls for a pretest and a posttest, usually there is tremendous overlap in their content because the goal is to determine changes in the individual or group as a result of participating in the program. Any changes that occur in the examinee between administration of the pretest and posttest are usually attributed to the program activities.

Value-added assessment generally uses a pretest–posttest design, but the question posed is "How much value has been added to the client's performance as a result of participating in the program?" This is an interesting question to ask because it focuses attention on the timing of interventions and the final yield of an intervention. If 80% of the targeted clients have already met a given criterion, why introduce the concept to the entire group at this time? Would it have been more appropriate to introduce it earlier in the vertically articulated curriculum (earlier in the year or in a previous year)? Value-added assessments also focus on the improvements (yield) of the products of a program. For example, elite schools are famous for their desire to produce creative thinkers and problem solvers, but if students entering the school are selected because of their higher levels of intelligence, achievement, creative thinking, and problem-solving capacities, what improvements are these schools really making? Value-added assessment seeks to answer that question by establishing a baseline and evaluating the students' progress over time.

SOURCES OF EVIDENCE   Both people and products merit discussion as potential sources of accountability evidence. Almost anyone can serve as a helpful source of evidence: clients, members, students, teachers, staff members, administrators, parents, employers, graduates, and community resource people. Numerous products from data-collection methods can also be used. A short list includes portfolios, performances, use of ratings from external judges or examiners, observations, local tests, purchased tests, self-assessments, surveys, interviews, focus groups, and client/student work. Each of these sources or products can produce helpful evaluative data, but what is collected must result from the specific question to be answered. Some of these sources of evidence are explained in more detail later in this chapter.

Practical Program Evaluation Considerations

To be of practical value, assessment must be connected to real program concerns and the core values of the program. Avoid overwhelming the data collectors, participants, and stakeholders; focus on only one or several important questions at a time; and always select measures that yield reliable and valid scores for the purposes under study. Often, ineffective program outcome stems from poor or inappropriate measurement rather than faulty programming. Be sure to involve the relevant stakeholders and use a variety of approaches. Perhaps most important, do not reinvent the wheel; use what you are already doing to generate useful data about program effectiveness. Also, consult with outside experts about the development and evaluation of a program.

It is good advice to start small and build on what is found to work; the methods and goals of individual programs that are successful can be shared across programs. This often leads to a cross-pollination effect that yields diversity of approach and homogeneity of results. In other words, professional counselors can learn from each other what works, and they can implement these strategies with their own populations after necessary refinements based on the needs of a differing client population. Different can still be effective!

Aggregated Outcomes

As mentioned earlier, aggregation is the combining of results to provide a more global or generalized picture of group performance. Although such a practice may deemphasize subgroup or individual performance, aggregation can be a valuable tool when it comes to evaluating how well counseling programs meet higher-level standards or goals. Because of their more abstract or generalized wording, **standards** (sometimes called **goals**) are difficult, if not impossible, to measure directly. This is why curriculum development begins with a statement of standards (goals), which are then described further through a series of outcomes (sometimes called **competencies**).

These outcomes, while more specific and well-defined, are still not amenable ordinarily to direct measurement in the classic sense. Instead, we rely on specific objectives (such as those discussed in the earlier section called Converting Needs to Program Goals and Objectives). Objectives are written in such specific, measurable terms that everyone (e.g., clients, professional counselors, teachers, parents, administrators, significant others) can tell when an objective has been met. The use of objectives, outcomes, and goals composes an **aggregated hierarchical model**, which is an important way for professional counselors to demonstrate the effectiveness of a counseling program. Figure 16.4 provides an example of an aggregated hierarchical model.

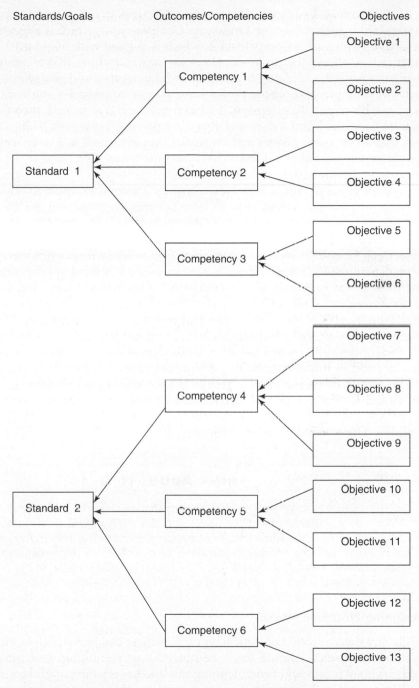

FIGURE 16.4 Aggregated hierarchical model for evaluating the effectiveness of a counseling program.

In Figure 16.4, note the alignment of objectives to outcomes/competencies and then to standards/goals. Objective 1 measures Competency 1, which is aligned with Standard 1. Objective 13 measures Competency 6, which is aligned with Standard 2. Such a hierarchical structure allows the professional counselor to conclude that meeting the lower-order objectives provides evidence that higher-order outcomes and goals have been successfully met. For example, assume the professional counselor provides evidence that Objectives 1 to 6 have been met. By extension, if Objectives 1 and 2 were met, then Competency 1 was met. If Objectives 3 and 4 were met, then Competency 2 was met. If Objectives 5 and 6 were met, then Competency 3 was met. Because Competencies 1 to 3 were met, the professional counselor has provided evidence that Standard 1 was met. Success! In addition, areas of programmatic strength have been identified.

Refer again to Figure 16.4. Now consider a second example in which Objectives 7 to 10 were met, but Objectives 11 to 13 were not met. By extension, if Objectives 7 to 9 were met, then Competency 4 was met. If Objective 10 was met, but Objective 11 was not met, then Competency 5 either was not met or, more accurately, was met only partially. If Objectives 12 and 13 were not met, then Competency 6 was not met. Because of some inconsistent results, interpretation is a bit cloudier. It is most appropriate to conclude that Standard 2 was only partially met because Competency 4 was met, Competency 5 was partially met, and Competency 6 was not met. Given the inconsistency of the outcomes, it would be inappropriate to conclude that Standard 2 had been met; it would be equally inappropriate to conclude that Standard 2 had not been met. A conclusion of "partially met" identifies the hierarchical set of goals, outcomes, and objectives as a programmatic area in need of improvement, or perhaps the criteria for establishing successful performance should be revised. From these examples, one can see that an aggregated hierarchical model can be a valuable curriculum evaluation method. It also underscores the importance of a measurable objective as the building block of an effective program. Now complete Think About It 16.1.

THINK ABOUT IT 16.1

Consult Figure 16.4. What would be the conclusion regarding standards attained if each of the odd-numbered objectives were met, but each of the even-numbered objectives were not met? As a professional counselor administering this psychoeducational program, what adjustments would you need to make before implementing the program a second time?

Designing Outcome Studies

While any data collected on counselor effectiveness can be helpful, in most instances, professional counselors should measure outcome or results by designing a research-type study. A bit of forethought and planning can lead to very meaningful conclusions. Research studies are typically empirical in nature and involve providing some control over how students are assigned to counseling interventions, and the timing and circumstances under which data are collected. Campbell and Stanley (1963) discussed helpful, easy-to-implement designs, and several of these designs that may be particularly useful to professional school counselors have been included in Table 16.5.

TABLE 16.5 Common Designs Used for Outcome Research

Nonexperimental Designs	
1. Pretest–posttest single-group design	O I O
2. Case study	I O
3. Static-group comparison	
group 1	O
group 2	I O
Quasiexperimental Designs	
4. Two-sample pretest–posttest design	R O
	R I O
5. Nonequivalent control group design	O I O
	O O
6. Time series design	O O O I O O O
True Experimental Designs	
7. Randomized pretest–posttest control group design	R O I O
	R O O
8. Randomized posttest only control group design	R I O
	R O

Note: R = participants are randomly assigned to groups; I = intervention (implemented treatment or program); O = observation or other data collection method.

A comprehensive treatise of research methodology is beyond the scope of this text; what follows are some of the relevant points professional counselors should consider when designing outcome studies. Counselors generally receive an entire course in research, which can be useful in this context. The interested reader should consult Erford (2015c) for helpful resources on the research methodology and statistical analysis written specifically for professional counselors.

Answering several questions can help the professional counselor determine which research design to use.

1. *Has the treatment already been implemented?* So much for planning ahead! If the intervention has not already occurred, one has many possible options. If the intervention has already occurred, one is relegated to a nonexperimental design, probably a case study or static-group comparison design. It is critical to think about outcome assessment in the early stages of planning for an intervention and certainly before the intervention has begun.

2. *Can I randomly assign participants to treatment conditions?* If the answer is yes—outstanding! Control over the random assignment of participants is crucial to implementing true experimental designs. If one does not have control over assignment of participants, the professional counselor must choose a quasiexperimental or nonexperimental design.

3. *Can I conduct (one or several) pretests, posttests, or both?* Usually, measuring the dependent variable before (pretest) and after (posttest) (and at a follow-up point) is desirable, although not always essential.

The answers to these questions help the professional counselor choose the most useful and powerful design. For example, if the answers to the three questions are no, yes, and yes, the professional counselor may opt for an experimental design (i.e., designs 7 or 8 in Table 16.5). If the answers are yes, no, and posttest only, one is relegated to a nonexperimental design (designs 2 or 3 in Table 16.5). As one can no doubt surmise, outcome studies require some level of planning early in program development.

Nearly all true experimental designs involve random assignment of participants, which also randomizes various sources of error allowing for the control of numerous threats to validity. True experimental designs allow causative conclusions to be reached. This is a big advantage when the professional counselor wants to know conclusively if his or her interventions resulted in significant improvements in clients. For example, if a professional counselor wants to know if a group intervention designed to improve study skills and academic performance was effective, he or she could use the randomized pretest–posttest control group design (design 7 in Table 16.5). The counselor would begin by randomly assigning clients into two groups of optimal size (designated control and treatment) and determining a data-collection method (e.g., test, survey, observation) to measure an outcome of interest (e.g., depression, stress management skills, anger management skills, social skills). The counselor would begin by administering the test (called the pretest) to all participants in the control and treatment groups. Next, the counselor would implement the intervention (e.g., group counseling experience) to the treatment group but not to the control group.

The **control group** would either experience nothing (i.e., wait-list control), undergo a placebo group counseling experience for some issue other than the purpose of the group, or receive a treatment-as-usual condition (i.e., what the participants would normally receive if they sought counseling [case management, supportive therapy]). Upon conclusion of the treatment program or intervention, the professional counselor would again administer the test (this time called the posttest) to participants in both groups. It would be expected that no change in the control group participants' scores would be observed (i.e., no statistically significant difference between pretest and posttest scores). However, if the counseling intervention was successful, it would be expected that a significant change would be observed in the treatment group (e.g., posttest scores are higher than pretest scores, grades at the end of group are higher than at the beginning). The other designs in Table 16.5 could also be used with this or other examples. However, quasiexperimental and nonexperimental designs do not allow the professional counselor to conclude that the treatment was the cause of the changes noted in the participants. In many ways, results or outcomes from studies with experimental designs are more valuable and powerful.

A lot of thought must be given to the design of the outcome measure used. Often, nonsignificant results are not due to the counseling intervention but are due instead to the selection of an outcome measure not sensitive enough to show the effect of the treatment. Some outcome measures can be easily obtained because they are a matter of record (e.g., grade point average, percentage grade in math class, number of days absent, number of homework assignments completed), or they already exist in published form (e.g., Achenbach System of Empirically Based Assessment [ASEBA], Beck Depression Inventory [BDI-II], Children's Depression Inventory–Second Edition [CDI-II]). The number of available outcome measures is vast. Still, professional counselors sometimes need to design an outcome measure with sufficient sensitivity and direct applicability to the issue being studied (e.g., adjustment to a divorce, body image, social skills, math self-efficacy). When professional counselors need to develop an outcome measure from scratch, the basics of scale development covered earlier in the discussion of needs assessments can be helpful. In addition, Weiss (1998, pp. 140–142) provided a dozen principles the assessor should consider:

1. Use simple language.
2. Ask only about things that the respondent can be expected to know.
3. Make the question specific.
4. Define terms that are in any way unclear.
5. Avoid yes-no questions.
6. Avoid double negatives.
7. Do not ask double-barreled questions (i.e., two questions in one).
8. Use wording that has been adopted in the field.
9. Include enough information to jog people's memories or to make them aware of features of a phenomenon they might otherwise overlook.
10. Look for secondhand opinions or ratings only when firsthand information is unavailable.
11. Be sensitive to cultural differences.
12. Learn how to deal with difficult respondent groups.

These principles apply to most types of data-collection procedures. Professional counselors can use a wide range of procedures, each with advantages and disadvantages. Table 16.6 presents descriptions of several of the most common methods of data collection used by professional school counselors. Complete Activity 16.5.

ACTIVITY 16.5

Use the research designs in Table 16.5 and the data collection methods in Table 16.6 to design a simple outcome study using a treatment method, sample, and outcome measure of your choice. Describe how you could implement the study in a clinical setting. What would be the challenges or barriers to conducting the study? What would be the potential benefits? How could you use the results to improve counseling practice?

Single-Subject Research Design

Professional counselors do not always have access to groups of clients who can be randomly assigned to various experimental conditions. Most professional counselors need to document the effectiveness of services one client at a time and for widely varying presenting problems. An interesting form of experimental research design used by practicing professional counselors is the **single-subject research design (SSRD)** (or **single case research design**). SSRD involves an intensive study of a single individual or sometimes of a single group. This type of study examines client changes over a period of time before and after exposure to some treatment or intervention. The pressure for accountability and managed care within all fields of the counseling profession makes SSRDs particularly helpful to professional counselors as they strive to document outcome.

TABLE 16.6 Common Data Collection Methods

1. *Interviews* of the professional counselors, key personnel, or members of stakeholder groups can provide valuable data. Interviews can be structured, semistructured, or unstructured. **Structured interviews** present a formal sequence of questions to interviewees with no variation in administration, generating clear evidence of strengths and weaknesses. **Unstructured interviews** allow for follow-up and deeper exploration and are commonly used in qualitative studies. **Semistructured interviews** combine the facets of unstructured and structured approaches. Usually, multiple respondents are required for patterns and conclusions to emerge. Face-to-face interviews are generally better than phone interviews, although they are usually more costly and inconvenient. Careful consideration must be given to question development, and interviewers must guard against introducing bias.

2. *Observations* can be classified as informal or formal. **Informal observations** tend to yield anecdotal data through a "look-and-see" approach. **Formal observations** (or structured observations) usually involve a protocol and predetermined procedures for collecting specific types of data during a specified time period. Structured procedures tend to minimize bias. As an example of observation, professional counselors can be observed implementing a group counseling session by a supervisor or peer.

3. *Written questionnaires, surveys, and rating scales* are usually paper-and-pencil instruments asking a broad range of open-ended or closed-ended questions. Questionnaires and rating scales typically ask for factual responses, whereas surveys generally solicit participant perceptions. The greatest weakness of this data-collection method is that many surveyed participants do not complete or return the instrument (i.e., low return rate). It also requires a certain level of literacy. Few respondents take the time to write lengthy responses, so usually it is best to keep open-ended questions simple or even closed-ended with the opportunity for participants to expand upon a response if needed. Multiscaled response formats (e.g., Likert-type scales) often provide more helpful results than yes or no questions. Emailed or online versions of these instruments are becoming more common.

4. *Program records and schedules* are a naturally occurring and helpful source of evaluation data. If stored on a computer in a database format, this kind of data is particularly accessible, and a professional counselor is well advised to consider this ahead of time when determining how best to maintain electronic records and schedules. Archives should also be kept in good order to facilitate record searches. In particular, professional counselors should keep previous program improvement documents and outcome study reports.

5. *Standardized and counselor-made tests* provide objective sources of measurable client outcomes. Individual, classroom, and school-wide tests can be extremely helpful and powerful measures. Tests exist that measure academic achievement, depression, anxiety, substance use, distraction, career indecision, and myriad other client behaviors. Professional counselors can design and develop tests to measure client behaviors and characteristics, much as teachers design tests to measure academic achievement.

6. *Academic performance indicators* may include a student's grade point average (GPA) or classroom grade, as well as include daily work behaviors and habits (e.g., attendance, homework completion, disruptions) and attitudes (e.g., academic self-efficacy, attitude toward school). *Products and portfolios* are real-life examples of performance. A **product** is anything created by a client (or the professional counselor) that stemmed from a program standard (e.g., artwork, composition, poster). A **portfolio** is a collection of exemplar products that can be evaluated to determine the quality of an individual's performance.

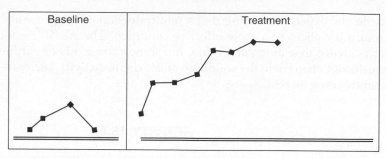

FIGURE 16.5 AB design.

SSRDs start by measuring the state of the individual before the intervention begins. This is called a **baseline** (no treatment) and is designated by *A*. The intervention is designated *B*. Ordinarily, the condition of the client is observed or measured several times during the baseline phase (*A*) and several times during the intervention phase (*B*). A line graph is usually used to display the client's behavioral changes over time. Line graphs are interpreted visually, rather than statistically, and so are popular among mental health professionals and health maintenance organization workers. The behavior being observed or tracked (i.e., the **dependent variable**) is displayed on the vertical axis. Scores on a behavior rating scale, number of times a client gets out of his or her seat without permission, scores on a depression scale, or number of negative self-talk statements are some examples of these observed or tracked behaviors that clients may be trying to change. The horizontal axis usually indicates the observation session (i.e., passage of time). Client observations may occur each hour, day, or session, as determined by the professional counselor. **Data points** indicate the client's score at each time of collection throughout the study, and the slope of the **condition lines** indicates whether a client's condition has changed over time. Figure 16.5 provides a diagram of a commonly used SSRD, the AB design.

There are numerous types of SSRDs, including the AB design, ABA design, ABAB design, BAB design, ABCB design, and multiple-baseline design. The two most commonly used designs by professional counselors (AB and ABAB) are discussed here; the interested reader should see Erford (2015c) for an expanded discussion of SSRDs.

The most common SSRD, the **AB design**, introduces an intervention to the client after a baseline period during which the client acts as his or her own control. In the AB design, the client is observed or measured for several sessions (i.e., the pretreatment baseline phase, *A*), the intervention is implemented, and the client is observed or measured for several more sessions (the treatment phase, *B*). The general rule of thumb regarding the number of sessions to measure is to keep measuring until a stable pattern emerges, whether the pattern shows the treatment to be effective or ineffective.

A disadvantage of using the AB design is that it does not control for extraneous or confounding variables. The **ABAB design** may minimize this problem because it includes two baseline periods interspersed with two intervention periods. Initially, the baseline (*A*) is established, and then treatment (*B*) is introduced. When the treatment is shown to have the desired effect, the intervention is withdrawn to collect a second baseline (*A*). If the client's scores on the dependent variable return to a level of diminished effectiveness, the counselor has provided evidence that the intervention was responsible for the changes the client exhibited during the *B* phase. At that point, the treatment is reintroduced (*B*), and more observations are made, the expectation being that a reintroduction of the previously effective treatment will return the client to a more effective condition. The ABAB response pattern provides strong evidence that the intervention, not some extraneous or confounding variable, was responsible for changes in the condition of the client. Activity 16.6 asks you to create an outcome study using an SSRD.

ACTIVITY 16.6

Use an SSRD to create an outcome study of a client issue, treatment method, and outcome measure of your choice. Describe how you could implement the study in a clinical setting. What would be the challenges or barriers to conducting the study? What would be the potential benefits? How could you use the results to improve counseling practice?

Action Research

Action research allows professional counselors to focus on changing social, ecological, or client conditions in particular situations or settings by creating a study and intervention to explore and solve a particular problem, usually in the client's environment. Designed and conducted by practitioners or researchers, action research involves the analysis of data to improve practice and solve practical problems. Action research presents the professional counselor with many advantages over traditional experimental research procedures because action research requires minimal training; helps develop effective, practice-based solutions for practical problems; and creates a collaborative atmosphere where professionals work together to address and improve conditions affecting clients. The steps ordinarily considered when developing an action research plan include: (1) Identify and clarify the research question, (2) gather data, (3) analyze and interpret data, (4) create an action plan, and (5) evaluate and reflect. A more lengthy discussion and some case examples of action research can be found in Erford (2015c). Now complete Think About It 16.2.

THINK ABOUT IT 16.2

Describe how you could implement an action research study in a clinical setting. What would be the challenges or barriers to conducting the study? What would be the potential benefits? How could you use the results to improve counseling practice?

REPORTING RESULTS

Although professional counselors, or perhaps an outside consultant, may write most of an accountability report, the counseling program advisory committee should be involved during every step of the process. A comprehensive report may be helpful for analysis purposes by the advisory committee; however, a one- to two-page executive summary should also be prepared for release to administrators, the community, and other stakeholders and decision makers. Dissemination of counseling program results could occur through a written report, verbal presentation, multimedia presentation, journal article, webpage, television, video, poster, email, newspaper article, or other viable modality.

Technological innovations allow for multiple modes of dissemination simultaneously and inexpensively.

Regardless of the vehicle for dissemination, the results of the program outcome should be released to relevant stakeholder groups at regular intervals after the results have been reviewed by the advisory committee, professional counselors, and administrators. Results must be circulated for accountability to occur.

As mentioned previously, the results of the outcome studies are used to make substantive program improvements, which then prompt more questions to be studied. And the process cycles again and again. This cycle is essential to the transformation and continuous quality improvement of any counseling program. Read Voices from the Field 16.2.

VOICES FROM THE FIELD 16.2   Accountability for What I Do, by Carol Kulbeck and Christopher Sink

As a counselor for elementary-age children for many years, I [Carol Kulbeck] remain committed to accountability, not only because my profession's ethical codes (e.g., ASCA, ACA) require me to do so, but also for the simple reason that accountability makes me a better counselor, informs practice, and improves student outcomes. For example, assessments have been developed by Washington state educators that are designed to measure learning for selected components of the Health and Fitness Essential Academic Learning Requirements (EALRs). The classroom-based assessments (CBAs) provide immediate information to educators regarding how well students in grades 5 and 8 and high school have acquired the knowledge and skills for health and fitness expectations. The assessment booklets include directions for administration, student response activity, scoring rubrics and notes, and glossaries. One of the assessment booklets, entitled *New Kid on the Block* for children, helps me be accountable for student learning in this developmental area.

During the assessment process, fifth-grade students are required to identify reasons for, and emotional effects of, bullying, and write a skit to demonstrate negative and positive choices, and possible outcomes that could be responses to bullying. A scene is given to the children, and it is their task to create two versions of the "final act," one with a positive ending and one with a negative ending. The skit needs to also include reasons why people bully and how the bullying affects the target and bystander to get the full points.

Enumclaw School District's elementary counselors met during one Professional Learning Community (PLC) early release session to plan and implement the *New Kid on the Block* CBA. The counselors concurred that antibullying lessons had been taught since kindergarten. Therefore, a common lesson was developed district-wide to review types of bullying, the roles played during the situation, the emotional effects experienced by each person in the situation, negative choices that would be regarded as hurtful, and positive choices that would be regarded as helpful in a bullying situation.

After the lesson to the children was presented by the school counselors in all schools, the CBA was administered. The counselors jointly scored the CBAs using the provided state rubric during one of the PLC early release meetings. Then a spreadsheet was developed to record student names, teachers, CBA scores, and performance levels. The confidential results were shared with building principals and district administrators. A few accountability questions came up. Is this CBA an accurate indicator of student bullying knowledge and skill usage? And if so, how should the school counselors follow up on the students that did not pass the CBA? How would that data direct follow-up small group counseling experiences? I set about this year in collaboration with my district-wide counseling team to provide some answers.

Accountability and Social Justice Counseling

A historical criticism of health and mental health services has been there use to patholo-gize, marginalize, and oppress culturally diverse individuals. To undo centuries of mis-trust, accountability and outcome research are needed to show equity and effectiveness of counseling for individuals across diverse backgrounds. If counseling approaches are not as effective with some cultural groups, professional counselors must find out and alter the approach to maximally benefit all citizens. Identification of such differential outcomes using data-driven procedures can also be used to alter systemic barriers based on gender, race, and socioeconomics. When counselors are accountable, they consistently provide evi-dence that counseling works effectively with diverse clientele.

Accountability and Technology

Technological innovations facilitate the ease and accuracy of counseling assessment and accountability. As mentioned in Chapter 12, computerized assessment can be more timely, efficient, and accurate, although it presents additional security challenges. Perhaps most importantly, professional counselors should be proficient with data analysis to demon-strate accountability, and in today's world this can all be accomplished with easy to use computers applications like Windows-based SPSS, R-stat, and even Excel spreadsheets. Particularly exciting is the use of technology to monitor short-term and long-term effec-tiveness (outcome) to follow-up with clients who have undergone termination to check on continuing progress and prevent recidivism. A timely email, text, or phone call can help prolong treatment gains and enhance a client's quality of life.

Summary

Accountability involves the demonstration of responsibility for professional actions. Profes-sional counselors demonstrate accountability by providing evidence that answers several pri-mary questions. First, what are the needs of the client and stakeholder populations? A needs assessment can be implemented using one of two primary methods: data-driven and percep-tions-based. A data-driven needs assessment evaluates real needs demonstrated through derived information. Aggregated results are broken down (disaggregated) so that they can be examined at the subgroup level. Such analy-sis is crucial to demonstrate whether all clients are benefiting from the counseling program and services. A perceptions-based needs assess-ment determines what primary stakeholder groups (e.g., clients, directors, teachers, par-ents) perceive as needs. These perceptions can be gathered through various methods, but some form of quantifiable result is preferred so that various perceived needs can be compared and prioritized.

The second question is particularly rele-vant to school counselors: Is a comprehensive, standards-based program in place? A program evaluation (or audit) should be conducted annually near the end of the school year to determine whether a written counseling pro-gram is being fully implemented.

Third, what services were implemented to address the identified needs and standards? A service assessment provides an accounting of who did what, how much, and for how long. This type of evidence is helpful in demonstrat-ing that professional counselors are using their time to provide valuable (or even not so valu-able) services, and is often requested by admin-istrators. Service assessment is more of a process evaluation (i.e., how one spends one's time) rather than an outcome evaluation (i.e., what valuable result has occurred by spending one's time that way). In other words, time is a process variable. Results stem from the actions one performs given the precious commodity of time.

What was the result of the implemented services? Some would argue that this question is the most important; they believe that results or outcome studies are the most valuable facet of accountability. The assessment loop shows that the purpose of evaluation is continuous quality improvement. Data are collected to evaluate actions and interventions so that judgments can be made on the worth or value of services and programs. Often, traditional research designs can yield the most helpful and authoritative information about program or event quality, but single subject research designs and action research are making useful and powerful contributions to quality client and program services. Because of the wide-ranging nature of goals and outcomes, professional counselors attempting to demonstrate the effectiveness of developmental or psychoeducational interventions may want to use an aggregated hierarchical model in which evidence is collected at the objectives level to demonstrate whether higher-order outcomes and goals have been met.

Accountability applies to every facet of a counseling program. Professional counselors must be prepared to engage in accountability activities, continuously collect evidence, and report on program performance. Being responsible for one's actions and the quality of services provided is an important ethical and professional responsibility.

MyCounselingLab for Introduction to Counseling

Try the Topic 14 Assignments: *Research and Evaluation.*

---

17 Outcome Research in Counseling

BRADLEY T. ERFORD

PREVIEW

Outcome research is intended to answer the question of counseling effectiveness. The outcome of a counseling intervention, occurring in response to the therapeutic process, is measured through outcome research, resulting in knowledge about what is and is not effective. Professional counselors have an ethical responsibility to use counseling methods grounded in theory and empirically validated through research. It is now known that counseling is effective in many forms and for many client conditions. This chapter reviews best practice and evidence-based counseling research on the effectiveness of counseling in several areas: client–counselor characteristics, individual approaches, group approaches, career intervention, and school-based student interventions. This body of information should be used by professional counselors to inform their practice and increase treatment efficacy. While the focus of this chapter is on the counselor as a consumer of research, a basic understanding of how research is conducted is essential in the training of all counselors for counselors to understand and evaluate the meaningfulness of the research consumed.

HOW RESEARCH ASSISTS COUNSELORS: THE IMPORTANCE OF AND BARRIERS TO CONDUCTING OUTCOME RESEARCH

As should have been surmised from the previous chapter, the current practice of counseling is one that is being increasingly dominated by **accountability**. Accountability is now a component of professional practice (American Counseling Association, 2014a) and more important than theory congruence or philosophical allegiance. Some have viewed this as a negative shift for the field, one that stifles creative independence and instinct, while absorbing time better used in treatment. Instead, it can be viewed as an opportunity to transition from a profession historically based on theory and intuition to one that now combines theory, intuition, and science. Because of the inclusion of science, research and its focus on outcomes is now a major component of the profession of counseling that has the ability to transform the effectiveness of practice. As such, it is necessary for professional counselors to understand the importance of outcome research and attend closely to what we know works in counseling.

The ethical imperative of **nonmaleficence** (i.e., do no harm) is of paramount concern when using counseling interventions. One of the most important means of achieving this end is to use empirically validated or evidence-based research and treatment approaches. To do so, professional counselors must stay abreast of and trained in the most current, empirically supported treatments for the populations they serve. Despite this importance, training in evidence-based treatment is often a neglected aspect of the counseling professional's identity for a variety of reasons. It is not always easy to be a good consumer of outcome research. Outcome research is published in such a wide variety of journals that it is often difficult for counselors to keep up with relevant findings. In addition, it is sometimes difficult to decipher results and identify valid and reliable findings that are pertinent to counseling practice. This chapter is designed to assist counselors by summarizing recent outcome research related to professional counseling activities and to help decipher the results and findings.

Counselors in training are entering the counseling profession at an exciting and dynamic period in history, when the need for counseling services is at an all-time high. According to the National Institute of Mental Health (2018), mental illness is the leading cause of disability in the United States. Approximately one in four individuals age 15 to 44 years experiences a diagnosable mental disorder in any given year, an increase compared with the 20% reported almost 3 decades ago (Rice, Kelman, Miller, & Dunmeyer, 1990). In addition, nearly half of the individuals currently diagnosed also meet the criteria for two or more mental disorders.

While the need for mental health treatment continues to soar, only one in five individuals who need mental health services actually seeks treatment (NIMH, 2018). A host of factors contribute to this low rate of help-seeking behaviors, including geographical restrictions, transportation issues, financial constraints, lack of service knowledge, and stigma. Because of these factors, it is even more important for professional counselors to be adequately prepared to address effectively the innumerable concerns of the individuals who do seek services.

Such effectiveness and preparedness are not only helpful in improving client outcomes, but also an ethical responsibility. Knowledge and use of empirically validated treatment shown to be effective in counseling outcomes is an obligation of every professional counselor (American Counseling Association, 2014a). Ethical counseling is not possible without a thorough understanding of the current and relevant outcome research. Professional counselors have an obligation to keep current on and use empirically validated research and treatment approaches not only to avoid treatment approaches proven to be harmful, but also to use the approaches proven most helpful, thus maximizing effectiveness. Now complete Think About It 17.1.

THINK ABOUT IT 17.1

If a counselor means well, and has a kind and caring disposition, is that enough to prevent doing harm? Is a counselor doing harm by not using evidence-based practices and interventions?

Outcome research is vital to the well-being of the client, to the ethical obligations of the counselor, and to the advancement of the field. For the counseling profession itself to continue, it must prove itself effective. To be effective, treatment must be empirically validated by research. If the profession and practice of counseling cannot show improved outcomes for clients, it cannot continue to move forward and receive support. It is crucial for each professional counselor to be knowledgeable of the research base, to understand how to use the therapy modalities and treatment approaches validated, and to select and tailor interventions based on best practices.

Despite the existence of overwhelming support for the superiority of systematic, research-based decision-making models (Erford, 2015c), professional counselors in clinical practice typically do not conduct research (Byrd, Crockett, & Erford, 2012a, 2012b; Crockett, Byrd, Erford, & Hays, 2010, 2014; Erford, Crockett, Giguere, & Darrow, 2011; Erford, Gugiere, Glenn, & Schein, 2015; Erford, Miller, Duncan, & Erford, 2010; Erford, Miller, Schein et al., 2011). In addition, many professional counselors do not read current research or use research to shape their therapeutic knowledge, skill, or practice (Erford, 2015c). In 1983, Norcross and Prochaska (1983) found that selecting a counseling intervention based on outcomes research ranked 10th out of 14 reasons for approach selection. Nearly two decades later, Norcross (2000) stated there was little evidence to believe that trend had improved. In 2011, Berke, Rozell, Hogan, Norcross, and Korpiak found that familiarity and use of evidence-based practices differed according to theoretical orientation. These authors also found that clinicians ascribing to the cognitive-behavioral orientation were more likely to be familiar with evidence-based practices than those using humanistic or existential approaches. In addition, years of clinical experience was also found to influence familiarity with evidence-based practice. Those with the least experience were more familiar with evidence-based practices than those with the most clinical experience.

Although the need for outcome research and the subsequent use of it are so necessary, outcome research is underused. Despite the necessity for empirically supported treatment, outcome research remains under-produced for several reasons. In general, the practitioners who have access to the populations in need of study typically have not been adequately trained in research methods. Additionally, practitioners trained in research methods often have difficulty gaining access to the population in need of study (Erford, 2015c). The resources of time and money also become issues because practitioners are often pressured to engage in billable time, and research is often seen as time away from that purpose.

Not only is outcome research under-produced, but what is produced is understudied and underused. Often, practitioners prefer to continue using the approaches they are most comfortable with, regardless of their effectiveness. Sexton, Whiston, Bleuer, and Walz (1997) identified seven myths, or misconceived criticisms, used by practitioners in an effort to disregard relevant research findings. Several of these are combined and presented here (pp. 10–15):

1. Research results cannot be trusted and are not useful in practice.
2. Findings are irrelevant to the practitioner because studies examine minute details, not clinical problems.
3. Outcome research looks at groups and evaluates theory, while practitioners are more concerned with individuals and specific techniques.
4. Practitioners are not concerned with statistical significance, only with practical differences.

Other reasons that professional counselors often resist the idea of assessing their own outcomes include a fear that their services are ineffective, reluctance to use time set aside for counseling, and a belief that effectiveness cannot be quantifiably measured. Although some of these criticisms may have held merit in the past, they have largely been discarded by today's professionals as outcome research becomes incorporated into practice. Regardless, they are evidence of the large divide between research and practice that, while narrowing, still seems to exist. Such a research/practice split can also be veiled as a split between individuals advocating the art of counseling versus the science of counseling. Put another way, differences in philosophical ideals and theoretical orientations can become the basis for individuals who believe in clinical intuition and individuals who rely on the scientific method. But this type of practice can integrate evidence with clinical judgment, not replace it, as some fear. The true scientist–practitioner incorporates the best available research evidence, in addition to client preferences, with clinical judgment. If researchers engage in practice, and practitioners in research, it would be possible to bridge the subjective experiences of therapy with the objective evidence of science to make research and practice more meaningful and efficacious (Erford, 2015c). Activity 17.1 invites you to consider the gap between research and practice in professional counseling.

ACTIVITY 17.1

As a group, discuss the following issues. As a future practitioner, how might you both stay current in and contribute to evidence-based practice research? Of all the many reasons that contribute to the gap between research and practice, what might be some of the most difficult to overcome? What ideas can you think of that could help reduce this problem?

As stated earlier, the chasm between research and practice has begun to close substantially over the years as practitioners have realized the need for more relevant outcomes research, and counseling researchers have made the effort to produce more relevant outcome research. The establishment and rapid growth of managed care also forced the issue. Today, professional counselors must convince third-party payers that they are providing effective services. To practice competitively counselors must provide proof that interventions used are research-based, empirically sound, and capable of producing desired outcomes (Crane & McArthur, 2002). And if professional counselors want to continue receiving referrals, they must provide evidence of treatment efficacy to mental healthcare panels and companies.

I advocate for a model that trains practitioners to be researchers by combining clinical and research training, and valuing both equally. This **scientist–practitioner model** teaches professional counselors to view all counseling as a formal research project. By taking a scientific approach to problem identification and using empirical evidence to design treatment interventions, monitor symptoms, and evaluate outcomes, practitioners ideally should become both consumers and producers of research (Crane & McArthur, 2002).

Sexton et al. (1997) proposed an integrated process for practitioners and researchers to collaborate and thus increase the relevance and applicability of outcomes research. Within the proposed model, practitioners and educators devise relevant and critical questions that can be further conceptualized and researched, leading to more relevant graduate training and applicable empirical information. Findings are disseminated to clinicians who can integrate them into clinical practice. For this process to be successful, practitioners must be abreast of the current literature to know what information is lacking. They must also digest information produced as a result of their inquiries. Similarly, researchers must understand the difference between clinical efficacy and effectiveness studies for practitioners to view findings as relevant and for them to view making contributions feasible.

The classic and most scientifically sound approach to outcome research involves **clinical efficacy studies**, which are tightly controlled experiments designed to test a particular intervention. Because of the conditions of random assignment, control groups, standardized measures, and use of practice manuals, these studies are able to show causation. However, these same advantages are often impossible to carry out in naturalistic settings such as community mental health centers, schools, or homes. The second approach, **effectiveness research**, is most concerned with the use of interventions and techniques with a broad population across multiple settings. These studies test the utility of what works in practical circumstances.

As emphasized earlier, professional counselors have an ethical responsibility to use effective techniques and processes when working with clients and students (American Counseling Association, 2014a; Herlihy & Corey, 2015). Professional counselors must become familiar with the current extant literature on counseling effectiveness, commonly known as **outcome research**, and the procedures for establishing one's own effectiveness, commonly known as accountability (see Chapter 16).

Typically, outcome research involves three separate types of methodology: clinical trials, qualitative reviews, and meta-analytic reviews. Clinical trial studies are common in the existing literature; they usually consist of a single study of a specific type of treatment or approach. Such studies, or **clinical trials**, are important because they use comparison groups (e.g., placebo, wait-list control, treatment-as-usual), outcome measures, and standardized treatment protocols (Erford, 2015c), which, when used collectively, tremendously enhance the replicability of results. However useful, clinical trials are limited as well because they offer only a single result from a single study, and a subsequent study with a different methodology is likely to yield inconsistent or even contradictory results for reasons that may be difficult to determine.

Problems with clinical trials are frequently seen in the media when a new study is reported that contradicts a previous study, which is often the case on dietary and health issues. Inconsistencies such as these create confusion in the public and lead to decreased faith in the reliability of research. It is often wiser for professional counselors to use accumulations and summarizations of numerous research results to inform their counseling practice, rather than rely on the potentially unreliable results of a select few. Activity 17.2 invites you to consider how bias influences the interpretation of research of professional counseling practice.

ACTIVITY 17.2

What examples in the media can you think of where studies have claimed a finding only to later be contradicted? When you consume research, are you aware and mindful of potential bias and subjective conclusions that may be stated?

Instead of relying on individual studies to guide practice, many studies can be identified and collapsed into summaries using quantitative and qualitative methodologies. Advantages and disadvantages accompany each of these approaches. **Qualitative analysis** is a commonly used approach in which researchers examine and summarize robust trends and findings across studies, clients, and contexts. Similar to all experimental methods, qualitative reviews can sometimes result in biased or subjective conclusions, so procedures and criteria must be put into place by researchers to ensure that the information is processed systematically and that conclusions are replicable and robust (Erford, 2015c; Erford, Miller et al., 2010).

Meta-analysis is a specific quantitative technique that amasses and summarizes the results of numerous studies using a meaningful quantitative index, commonly known as an **effect size (ES)**. Generally, an ES conveys the magnitude of difference detected as a result of treatment. In other words, when a difference can be detected easily with a relatively small sample, the ES is large. Conversely, a small ES indicates difficulty in finding even a small difference.

To compute an ES, one simple and commonly used method is to subtract the mean of the control group from the mean of the experimental group, then divide the difference by the standard deviation of the control group $[M_e - M_c]/SD_c$, or the pooled variance of the experimental and control groups $[M_e - M_c]/SD_p$. There are several benefits to using ES. First, the ES from various comparable studies can be combined and averaged to yield a result across several studies. Second, this index can be weighted according to the sample size and variance so that larger, more stable samples are given greater weight than smaller, less stable samples. Several options exist for determining the strength of an ES, including the popular ES range developed by Cohen (1988): ES = 0, no treatment effect; ES = 0.20, small treatment effect; ES = 0.50, medium treatment effect; and ES = 0.80 or more, large effect. Lipsey and Wilson (2001) presented an alternative interpretive strategy that was empirically derived: ES = 0, no treatment effect; ES = 0.20, small treatment effect; ES = 0.50, medium treatment effect; and ES = 0.67 or more, large effect.

An ES, using the formula $[M_e - M_c]/SD_c$ (or pooled variance) is basically a z-score. Thus, another way to interpret ES is in terms of the number of standard deviations above or below the control group mean that a given treatment group score lies. For example, an ES of 0 means that the treatment and control group means were equal, and there was no difference, which in turn means that the average client in the treatment group performed neither better nor worse than the average participant in the control group. In other words, the treatment had no effect, and the average treatment group participant scored at about the 50th percentile of the control group. If ES = 0.50, this indicates that the treatment mean was one-half standard deviation above the mean of the control group. The "medium effect" associated with an ES = 0.50 can also be expressed in terms of percentage outcome; that is, an ES = 0.50 indicates that the average client in the treatment group attained a better outcome than 69% of the control group participants (0.50 standard deviations above the mean is a percentile rank of about 69). Likewise, an ES = 2.00 is not only a large effect (i.e., an ES > 0.80), but also indicates that the average treatment group participant performed better than 98% of control group participants (i.e., 2.0 standard deviations above the mean is the 98th percentile rank). When an empirical study is correlational (usually involving the computation of a Pearson r), Cohen (1988) suggested interpreting ES according to the following criterion-referenced interpretive range: $r = 0$ (no effect); $r = 0.10$ (small effect); $r = 0.30$ (medium effect); and $r = 0.50$ (large effect).

Many additional formulas exist for estimating ES, but the reader of outcome research is likely to encounter the two types mentioned above most frequently in the extant research. While meta-analysis has been commonly used in counseling and psychological research, it is by no means free of criticism, some of which concludes that combining numerous studies into a single result simply spreads errors from less well-designed studies onto better designed studies. At the very least, readers should view meta-analysis as a potentially helpful procedure for analyzing robust trends across studies, but they should view results with some caution, as should be common practice with any research findings. Now read Voices from the Field 17.1.

VOICES FROM THE FIELD 17.1   Outcome Research in Counseling, by Annie Carmona and Christopher Sink

Over the past several years serving as a counselor, I've [Annie Carmona] needed to understand and implement useful techniques and interventions based on the requirements of my caseload, client developmental levels, and the expectations of administrators. Although I finished my graduate studies with a solid knowledge base about school-based counseling theory and practice, I quickly realized while "in the trenches" that my learning had to be extended.

My workload and activities vary each day. One situation may involve counseling a student through a challenging friendship issue, and the next may include reviewing pertinent data for appropriate math class placement. Some days I'm not on top of my game with each situation I encounter. It's on those days, while doing some self-reflection on my way home, that I realize my knowledge is still lacking to successfully care for all my clients, their families, and the school system. It's those days when I need to return to appropriate counseling sources to better guide my practice. Peer consultation, journal articles, Internet searches, textbooks, local and national organization materials (e.g., ACA [American Counseling Association], ASCA [American School Counselor Association], AMHCA [American Mental Health Counselor Association]), and community agencies, are just a few sources I find time to review.

Specifically, it is not uncommon that I am called on to implement effective counseling techniques to assist students who experience tragedies that I have not handled before. In these situations, I tend to ask myself, "What does the research say about how to better serve students with this issue?" For example, during my first year as a high school counselor, a situation called for me to support a young woman whose mother had been murdered. Just a few weeks later, a young man learned of his father's suicide. This year, as a middle school counselor, I am assisting a girl whose single mother ended her life. Although I have a reasonably adequate understanding of the grief process, with these challenging cases I also needed to deepen my grasp of how to effectively support the students and families not only through the crisis itself, but in the days, weeks, and months following the tragedy.

How do I support these drastically changed families in their journey toward some semblance of recovery? To gather further information, I started my research with a simple Google search attempting to locate any reputable sites that could provide insight to best practices for counselors. From my online search, I found a document from a reliable organization that provided some language to use when I e-mail my students' teachers about a tragedy. That same document also offered books and other resources for caregivers and children who are grieving or traumatized.

The next phase of my research included finding helpful and relevant literature. I located several journal articles related to best practices for caring for a student experiencing a tragedy at home. I obtained several ideas from these articles, such as communicating with the staff and outside community, caring for other students who may have been affected by the tragedy, and using bibliotherapy as an individual counseling intervention. Along with reviewing Internet resources and relevant literature, I also found it necessary to collaborate with my peers since they may have additional resources I had not identified, such as useful books, small group curricula, or individual counseling exercises that they have used successfully. After securing some additional ideas and new action steps, I will be able to try new strategies in supporting my current families who have experienced a tragedy and will feel prepared for similar situations in the future as they arise.

HOW EFFECTIVE IS COUNSELING?

Over the past 50 years, the effectiveness of counseling has been explored through numerous studies to reach continually the overwhelming conclusion that counseling is effective. Regardless of the methodology employed to examine the extant literature, counseling is shown to produce more favorable outcomes than placebo and other control groups (Table 17.1). Most studies indicate little or no difference in the effectiveness of counseling regardless of the counseling modality used or the population studied. Individual and group counseling both are shown to be effective, although some specific conditions may be more amenable to individual counseling approaches.

Because counseling has superior outcomes compared with **placebo treatments** and **control groups**, there is evidence to support that factors due to counseling are responsible for improvements made. It cannot be ignored, however, that occasionally factors outside the counseling relationship and independent of the treatment provided may account for improvement in client symptoms. In a classic study, Lambert, Masters, and Ogles (1991) reported that factors outside counseling may account for about 43% of client improvement. This is reinforced by studies indicating that 90% of clients seem to improve on their

TABLE 17.1 Selected Meta-Analytic Studies from the Extant Literature

Source	Outcome Explored	Effect Size
Client/Counselor Characteristics		
Sharf, Primavera, & Diener (2010)	Therapeutic alliance and dropout	Medium
Horvath, Del Re, Fluckiger, & Symonds (2011)	Therapeutic alliance and outcome	Small to medium
Effectiveness of Counseling Adults		
Town, Diener, Abbass, Leichsenring, Driessen, & Rabung, (2012)	Pschodynamic approach	Large
Erford, Gunther et al. (2015)	PTSD	Medium to Large
Erford, Richards et al. (2013)	Bulimia	Medium
Mitte (2005)	CBT for anxiety	Large
	CBT for depression	Medium to large
Career and Educational Planning		
Whiston, Tai, Rahardja, & Eder, (2010)	Educational planning	Small
Youth and School-Based Interventions		
Erford, Paul, Oncken, Kress, & Erford (2014)	Oppositional behavior	Medium
Erford, Bardhoshi, Ross, Gunther, & Duncan (2016)	Conduct disorder	Medium
Bratton, Ray, Rhine, and Jones (2005)	Play therapy	Large
Erford, Erford, Lattanzi et al. (2011)	Depression	Medium to large
Erford, Kress, Giguere, Cieri, & Erford (2015)	Anxiety	Medium to large
Rongione, Erford, & Broglie (2010)	Substance use	Small to medium
Whiston et al. (2010)	School counseling program	Small to medium

own over time regardless of professional assistance. Now complete Activity 17.3 to deepen your understanding of remission.

ACTIVITY 17.3

In small groups, discuss the following issues. Why do you think spontaneous remission (i.e., an unanticipated reemergence of the symptoms or condition after a period when serious displays of the condition were absent) occurs? Have you ever experienced spontaneous remission from a physical or mental health concern? If some clients do get worse after entering counseling, might there be times when this is not considered a negative outcome? Explain.

Sexton et al. (1997) concluded that during counseling some clients actually get worse. However, it is important to consider that, while it is true that some individuals do regress, such instances should not be attributed to counseling alone. Numerous factors may contribute to Sexton and colleagues' conclusion, including the acknowledgment that some counselors lack the appropriate level of skills. Also, therapeutic relationships or alliances may be of poor quality. Inappropriately prescribed treatments are sometimes to blame as well. Often, issues outside counseling can contribute to worsening of client symptoms, just as factors outside counseling can contribute to improvements. Finally, the process of counseling itself is often difficult because it brings to the surface uncomfortable emotions and awareness, and if counseling is prematurely terminated before these issues can be resolved, the client condition may be described as worse.

Facets of Counseling That Contribute to Outcomes

With few exceptions, counseling is useful and valuable. Its use and value are consistent across settings and counselors, regardless of theoretical approaches (Erford, 2015c). Despite differences among theoretical approaches, therapeutic variations seem to have similarly equivalent effectiveness (Cuijpers, van Straten, Andersson, & van Oppen, 2008; Sexton et al., 1997). For this reason, it is important to focus on the specific facets of counseling that contribute to successful treatment outcomes. In other words, there must be common denominators within the process of counseling, and such commonalities must be considered. While research does support the increased efficacy of certain theoretical approaches with specific mental health conditions, it is generally accepted that counseling is effective regardless of the theory used.

Putting theoretical orientation aside, many other factors related to counseling effectiveness have been studied, including the length of treatment and the counseling relationship or therapeutic alliance. Treatment length is often connected to therapeutic outcome, with some practitioners concluding that more sessions are more beneficial, whereas other researchers find that most change occurs early in treatment. In their classic study, Howard, Kopta, Krause, and Orlinsky (1986) concluded that about 50% of improvement occurred by the eighth session, 75% by the sixth month, and 85% by the end of the first year of counseling. These results support the philosophy of brief, solution-focused counselors who indicate that a good deal of change occurs by the eighth session, if it is going to occur at all (Sklare, 2014). In general, however, it is accepted that clients who display more severe symptoms and disturbance at the start of counseling and clients with diagnosable personality disorders (Paris, 2002) have more to gain from a longer course of treatment and may require longer treatment to show improvements. With a similar rationale, clients who display milder impairment at the outset of counseling seem to make sufficient progress in fewer sessions.

While research does support the effectiveness of shorter-term treatment for clients with milder impairment, terminating treatment after the first several sessions does not produce substantial or long-lasting improvements. Clients who drop out of counseling, known as **premature termination**, are problematic in counseling, regardless of the setting, presenting problems, or therapeutic approaches. Some clients never show up for the initial session after referral or setting an appointment. Nearly 49% never arrive for the first session. Of those who do follow through with counseling, many terminate counseling by the eighth session (Garfield, 1994). Approximately one-third of those who begin counseling return for a second appointment, and 40% to 60% of those drop out prematurely (Owen, Imel, Adelson, & Rodolfa, 2012).

While many factors contribute to premature termination, personal client variables have been found to correlate with these rates (Erford, 2015c). Income, education, and race seem to be related to dropout rates; clients with lower incomes, a lower educational level, and an African American racial heritage are more likely to terminate counseling prematurely. Premature dropout rates do not seem to be related to sex, age, or diagnosis.

While factors related to education, income, and race cannot typically be altered in an effort to improve counseling commitment or engagement, other factors related to the counseling relationship can. Relationship building or developing a strong therapeutic alliance can reduce dropout rates and can be improved through attention to initial impressions and purposeful counseling activities (Horvath et al., 2011; Sharf et al., 2010). The outcome literature indicates that clients are less likely to end counseling prematurely if professional counselors (a) administer complete psychological evaluations; (b) are perceived as trustworthy and competent; (c) are perceived as skillful; (d) convey respect, directness, and a strong alliance; and (e) establish mutually agreed upon goals and expectations (Erford, 2015c). Now complete Activity 17.4.

ACTIVITY 17.4

In small groups, discuss the following issues. *Other than severity of symptoms, can you think of other factors that may contribute to variations in timing of improvement? What ethical concerns might you have related to premature termination?* Why do you think a good match between the professional counselor and the client is so important in determining counseling outcome?

All of the above-mentioned counseling characteristics contribute to the occurrence of a strong match between the client and the professional counselor and are crucial to rapport, therapeutic commitment, and initial outcome. The term **patient–therapist match** is used to refer to the fit experienced by the client and the counselor. This perceived fit determines whether the counselor can resonate with the client, and if the client perceives the counselor as capable of doing so. Match has less to do with matching similarities between client and counselor, and more to do with the client finding the counselor to be agreeable, likable, and possessing characteristics the client wishes to emulate. In general, a good match will reduce the likelihood of premature dropout and increase initial gains made in counseling. In his classic study, Beutler (1989) estimated that the therapeutic alliance as shown through the client–counselor match may contribute 63% of treatment outcome variance, far outweighing the effect of the theoretical approaches used, which accounted for only 10% of the outcome variance. Beutler's estimate has been criticized on methodological grounds as too high, and a much lower, but still very robust estimate was provided in another classic study by Lambert (1991). Lambert showed that a counselor's theoretical orientation or approach accounts for about 15% of the outcome while 15% of therapeutic outcome is due to client expectations, 40% is due to factors outside the counseling setting, and 30% is due to core conditions, or what is today referred to as the therapeutic alliance.

Therapeutic alliance is similar to match. Several meta-analyses (Horvath et al., 2011; Sharf et al., 2010) have explored the therapeutic alliance as a factor in determining treatment outcome and SAMHSA's National Registry for Evidence-Based Programs and Practices (NREPP, 2018) provides helpful information about strengthening the therapeutic alliance and repairing relational ruptures (Safran, Muran, & Eubanks-Carter, 2011). The APA Presidential Task Force on Evidence-Based Practice (2006) also studied this issue and made recommendations. Considered one of the four primary determinants of treatment outcome, **therapeutic alliance** is defined as a collaborative relationship between the client and the professional counselor in which an affective bond has been established (Martin, Garske, & Davis, 2000). Although match is crucial in reducing premature termination and in initial gains made in counseling, therapeutic alliance continues to be influential in determining eventual outcome. Table 17.2 provides some specific facets of counseling and reported ES. Interested readers are referred to Sexton et al. (1997) for an outstanding comprehensive review of factors that seem to influence counseling effectiveness.

TABLE 17.2 Selected Effect Sizes for Specific Facets of Counseling Effectiveness

Study	Characteristic	Effect Size
Hoag and Burlingame (1997)	Group counseling for disruptive behavior	Medium
	Group counseling for anxiety/fear	Medium
	Group counseling for adjustment to divorce	Medium
	Group counseling for social skills	Medium
	Group counseling for depression	Small
Mitte (2005)	Cognitive-behavioral therapy for anxiety	Large
	Cognitive-behavioral therapy for depression	Medium
	Cognitive-behavioral therapy for quality of life	Large
Erford, Richards et al. (2013)	Diverse treatments for bulimia	Medium
Erford, Erford, Lattanzi et al. (2011)	Diverse treatments for depression	Medium
Rongione et al. (2010)	Diverse treatments for substance use	Small

WHICH CLIENT AND PROFESSIONAL COUNSELOR FACTORS CONTRIBUTE TO SUCCESSFUL OUTCOMES?

Because premature termination can be detrimental for the client, it is especially important to understand as much as we can about the factors found to contribute to successful outcomes. Although some client and professional counselor factors are important in predicting treatment outcomes, their effects are still small. Sexton et al. (1997, p. 81) concluded, "there is no single counselor or client characteristic, no single theory, or no technique that can account for the success of good counseling." For this reason, researchers have begun to look at the various interactions among the many aspects of counseling.

Counseling is effective in producing positive change despite theoretical application. In response to this, researchers have spent much time identifying client and professional counselor characteristics common across therapeutic approaches that influence or create successful therapeutic outcomes. While such characteristics do show a relationship to outcomes, the ES of these client and counselor characteristics on treatment outcome appear small (see Table 17.1). As a result, researchers have instead explored the interaction among these factors, including treatment approach, client concern, client characteristics, and professional counselor characteristics (Sexton et al., 1997). In other words, if it is known that cognitive-behavioral therapy is effective for a client with depression (matching client concern with treatment approach), is it possible to match certain client characteristics with specific counselor characteristics to improve treatment effectiveness? This is an important question that warrants much future attention from practitioners, researchers, and counselor educators because the answer is currently unknown. The remainder of this section explores what is known about the relationship between client and professional counselor factors and treatment outcomes. Now complete Think About It 17.2.

THINK ABOUT IT 17.2

Do you think it is important to match certain client characteristics with specific counselor traits? If so, which traits might be important to consider when matching? What evidence exists to support your beliefs?

The demographic traits of professional counselors have been well studied using correlational procedures. Variables of counselor sex, age, and race have yielded mixed results, however, generally as a result of unsound methodology and the correlational nature of the research (Sexton et al., 1997). Typically, while clients tend to prefer professional counselors they perceive to be similar to themselves, thereby increasing fit and reducing premature termination, these similarities have little effect on eventual counseling effectiveness (Whiston & Sexton, 1993).

Results of meta-analyses also show little relationship between treatment outcomes and discipline, training, or experience (Erford, Gunther et al., 2013; Erford, Kress et al., 2015; Erford, Erford, Lattanzi et al., 2011; Erford, Richards et al., 2013; Rongione et al., 2010), although Stein and Lambert (1995) proposed that experience became an especially salient factor when treating more severely disturbed clients. On the other hand, Svartberg and Stiles (1991) concluded through meta-analytic review that counselor effectiveness actually decreases with experience. This observation has led many to consider counseling *skill* as the determining factor in outcomes, rather than training and experience.

The perception of skill as a critical determinant of counseling outcome has resulted in the introduction and validation of **treatment manuals** into professional practice (Erford, 2015c). Such treatment manuals standardize the treatment of certain conditions by providing an empirically validated protocol for professional counselors to follow. Managed care providers encourage the use of such manuals even though early studies on their use have resulted in mixed findings (Robinson, Berman, & Neimeyer, 1990). Henry, Strupp, Butler, Schacht, and Binder (1993) indicated that the use of such treatment manuals may result in poorer outcomes, especially if the structured protocols affect counselor–client relationship and perceived supportiveness. In other words, manuals may increase technical proficiency, while decreasing factors pertinent to the therapeutic alliance. According to Staudt and Williams-Hayes (2011), counseling professionals may be open to the use of the treatment manuals if they feel they have been adequately trained and supervised in the approach and if it generalizes to everyday settings. This is an area of counseling that is currently progressing and thus pertinent for the counselor-in-training to consider. Complete Think About It 17.3 and then read Voices from the Field 17.2.

THINK ABOUT IT 17.3

If you had access to empirically supported treatment protocols for the various conditions and populations you serve, would you use them? What would be the advantages and disadvantages of this approach?

VOICES FROM THE FIELD 17.2   Secondary Benefits of Outcome Assessment, by Nicole Adamson

As a clinical behavioral consultant, it was important to demonstrate that my work was necessary and effective. However, my co-workers and I grumbled when our supervisor informed us that we would be using five new assessments in order to measure the efficacy of our counseling interventions. Part of my apprehension came from a place of insecurity and I worried that my outcome data would be poor. I was also disappointed by the addition of another regulation, as we were already consumed with a great deal of paperwork. However, the implementation of these assessments turned out to be invaluable for us and our clients.

A second-grade boy was referred to me for classroom behavioral difficulties. After completing an intake with the student and his mother, I administered the five initial assessments (which were surprisingly quick and simple). I noticed that his depression assessment score was significant. Based upon my knowledge of childhood depression and the way it is typically expressed in males, I concluded that the client's treatment should primarily focus on decreasing the depression. My decision was supported by the assessment results, which actually made my job more manageable as it provided a direction in which to head.

After working with this client for a few weeks, his classroom behavior drastically improved. The client became more compliant in the classroom, made new friends, and completed his assignments more consistently; a re-administration of the assessments showed a significantly decreased depression score. Although I was initially skeptical of the implementation of outcome assessment research in my agency, it resulted in confirmation of effective counseling practices and enhanced our ability to accurately diagnose, treat, and support our clients. Clients benefitted from the outcome assessments, my work as a counselor was improved, and my agency was able to concretely display that our interventions were worthwhile.

THE EFFECTIVENESS OF INDIVIDUAL COUNSELING

Although it was not statistically significant because of the small number of studies, Weisz, Weiss, Alicke, and Klotz (1987) found a larger ES for individual therapy than for group therapy, with ES = 1.04 for individual therapy and ES = 0.62 for group therapy. While this difference was smaller in a subsequent meta-analysis conducted by Weisz, Weiss, Han, Granger, & Morton (1995), there was still a slight difference, with individual counseling (ES = 0.63) producing greater results than group counseling (ES = 0.50) in the follow-up study.

Several diverse meta-analytic studies have been conducted in mental health clinics, schools, and research laboratories, all of which explore the general effects of individual counseling with children and adolescents. Kazdin, Bass, Ayers, and Rodgers (1990) reported an ES = 0.88; Weisz et al. (1995) reported an ES = 0.71. Erford, Erford, Lattanzi et al. (2011), Erford, Erford, Broglie, and Erford (2013), Erford, Paul et al. (2014), Erford, Kress et al. (2015), Erford, Bardhoshi et al. (2016), and Rongione et al. (2010) all reported significant, medium overall effects and no difference in treatment outcome across diverse settings. Taken together, these meta-analyses indicate the effects of individual counseling to be medium to large.

In another example of the effectiveness of individual counseling interventions, an individual dropout prevention program, comprising tutoring and counseling, significantly improved academic success, confidence, and behavior (Edmondson & White, 1998). In this example, individual counseling was deemed effective without being long in duration. It has been found that brief, individual counseling can be just as effective as long-term counseling. Three approaches to brief counseling designed to address the emotional adjustment of high school students were implemented by Littrell, Malia, and Vanderwood (1995). Participants in each of the three brief interventions reduced anxiety and increased motivation necessary to move them closer to their goals. This is important to recognize and continue to study because increasing numbers of insurance companies limit the number of visits of clients seeking counseling services. Similarly, Gingerich and Eisengart (2000) reviewed 15 outcome studies examining the efficacy of solution-focused brief therapy (SFBT) for depression, anxiety, parenting skills, psychosocial adjustment, antisocial behaviors, criminal recidivism, alcohol use, and family conflict. Five of the studies were tightly controlled, and each of these found SFBT to be significantly better than no treatment. However, because these studies were unable to use a control group and did not compare SFBT with another intervention, it was impossible to conclude that outcomes were due to SFBT and not to counseling alone. Taken collectively, the results of all 15 studies supported the effectiveness of SFBT.

Ray, Armstrong, Balkin, and Jayne (2015) conducted a meta-analysis of play therapy interventions and reported small effect sizes for externalizing problems ($d = 0.34$) and internalizing problems ($d = 0.21$). LeBlanc and Ritchie (2001) reported an ES of 0.66 after conducting a meta-analysis of play therapy outcomes with children. Specifically, they found a strong relationship between treatment effectiveness and the inclusion of parents in counseling with the child, especially when parents were taught therapeutic play behaviors. Parents acting as counselors increased the ES by 0.33 standard deviations. In addition, the length of treatment was shown to be related to outcomes, with the greatest positive effect occurring after 30 treatment sessions. In other words, the ES associated with play therapy continually increased until reaching its maximum ES at about 30 sessions. Finally, play therapy interventions with children were shown to be equally effective as verbal therapies with adults and nonplay therapies with children experiencing emotional difficulties.

Although the effectiveness of specific individual counseling interventions such as play therapy and solution-focused therapy have been stated, even more positive effect sizes (ESs) have been noted specifically for cognitive-behavioral counseling interventions (Ewing, Monsen, Thompson, Cartwright-Hatton, & Field, 2015; Lenz & Hollenbaugh, 2015; Ma, Zhang, Zhang, & Li, 2014; Özabacı, 2011; Park, Park, & Hwang, 2015; Sukhodolsky, Bloch, Panza, & Reichow, 2013) and family therapy (Baldwin, Christian, & Berkeljon, 2012; Karver, Handelsman, Fields, & Bickman, 2006; Wampler, Reifman, & Serovich, 2005). These studies did not differentiate among youth who were counseled in schools, agencies, or private practice, or by the level of counselor experience, but they did find cognitive-behavioral interventions similarly effective across a wide array of populations, settings, and mental health concerns and issues. Similarly, behavioral approaches in individual counseling were found to be most effective when addressing aggressive behavior (Wilson, Lipsey, & Derzon, 2003).

In addition to examining the specific types of interventions common to individual counseling, several meta-analyses have been conducted examining the effectiveness of individual counseling with specific problems and disorders. Erford, Gunther et al. (2015) and Van Etten and Taylor (1998) studied psychotherapeutic treatments for post-traumatic stress disorder and found significant ESs for individual counseling interventions, both of which reported medium-to-large ESs for the use of counseling in reducing symptoms. Solomon and Johnson (2002) found similarities in treatment procedures for post-traumatic stress disorder. According to their qualitative review of the literature, most therapies include components to address the meaning of the traumatic events, provide exposure to and reintegration of the trauma, and provide support and coping skills. When these components are included in treatment, the experiencing of post-traumatic stress disorder symptoms was shortened from more than five years to less than three years.

Outcome research has also been conducted to examine the effectiveness of individual counseling for survivors of abuse, with the overall results showing that individual counseling does lead to improvements for this population. When analyzed separately according to the type of abuse (e.g., sexual, physical, emotional, neglect), the strongest and most compelling evidence stems from studies analyzing the effectiveness of individual counseling for sexual abuse. The literature on the other forms of abuse is too limited to draw sound conclusions, although preliminary findings are suggestive of its benefits. Taken together, outcome research in this area is limited by small sample sizes, nonrandom sampling, inconsistent definitions of abuse, use of measures yielding less reliable scores, and failure to discern the types of abuse (James & Mennen, 2001). Now complete Case Study 17.1

CASE STUDY 17.1

Dennis works for a multidisciplinary medical and mental health clinic in the inner city that was just bought out by a multinational conglomerate corporation famous for streamlining services and cutting costs. A meeting with the new corporate management representatives is scheduled for next Monday morning and Dennis was asked to represent and present on counseling services.

- When asked if counseling was effective, if the counseling profession was of use, how might Dennis answer?
- Could Dennis support his response with scientific evidence from the outcome research literature? Explain.
- Is there cost- or time-effectiveness evidence to support counseling if management starts asking about the differential effectiveness of counseling, psychology, social work and psychiatry services?

THE EFFECTIVENESS OF GROUP COUNSELING

Frequently debated is the question of whether group or individual counseling is more effective. McRoberts et al. (1998) found no significant differences between the two interventions when therapist characteristics related to gender, training, and experience were taken into account. In general, group treatment is as effective as individual treatment for most conditions, as long as the group is specific to the focus of treatment (Erford, Erford, Lattanzi et al., 2011; Erford, Erford et al., 2013; Erford, Paul et al., 2014; Erford, Kress et al., 2015; Erford, Bardhoshi et al., 2016; Fuhriman & Burlingame, 1994; Rongione et al., 2010). Not only are individual counseling and group counseling equally effective under most circumstances, but also they sometimes can be combined for optimal treatment gains.

The effectiveness of group work is a consistent theme in the literature and is found to be useful for children and adults. Bachar (1998) reported that the results of meta-analyses of group counseling outcome studies ordinarily yield medium ESs. There is general agreement that group treatment is outcome-effective and cost efficient (Yalom & Leszcz, 2005). Table 17.3 provides a summary of some available meta-analyses that are referred to throughout the remainder of this section.

Process Issues in Group Outcome Research

The process variables in group work can be difficult to decipher and analyze because of the nature of human interaction. Ordinarily, group process variables include factors such as

TABLE 17.3 Effectiveness of Group Work

Source	Outcome Explored	Effect Size
Burlingame, Fuhriman, and Mosier (2003)	Group counseling	Medium
Hoag and Burlingame (1997)	Group counseling	Medium
McDermit, Miller, and Brown (2001)	Group counseling for depression	Large
Whiston et al. (2010)	Group counseling	Small

(1) group planning characteristics, (2) group structure, (3) pregroup training, (4) therapeutic factors, and (5) leader characteristics.

To begin, some of the issues inherent to the **group planning** phase are related to treatment outcomes. McRoberts, Burlingame, and Hoag (1998), in a fascinating, complex, and comprehensive meta-analysis, reported that group work was more effective than individual counseling when ten or fewer sessions were conducted, confirming the use of group work as a short-term treatment alternative. However, McRoberts and colleagues found no significant differences based on group size (fewer than nine versus nine or more participants), group type (psychoeducational versus process), or group membership (open versus closed).

Regarding **group structure** and its relationship to outcomes, unstructured groups, where the leader is less directive, tend to be related to client difficulties with interpersonal fears, cognitive distortion, subjective distress, and premature termination (Rhode & Stockton, 1994). Structure is especially imperative in the early stages of the group to define boundaries and build trust and cohesion (Erford, 2016; Keene & Erford, 2007). However, Lee and Bednar (1977) found that increased structure can lead to lower group cohesion, probably mediated by certain member personality characteristics. Structured group approaches should be used strategically and always matched with member personalities to enhance effectiveness.

Leader characteristics are often explored in the group counseling literature to determine their effect on client outcome. Effective leaders have been shown to nurture a sense of hope in group members (Erford, 2016) and to display encouraging personal characteristics, including a positive attitude and emotionally supportive behaviors. Group leaders with certain personality traits, including absence of genuineness, coldness, excessive need to make people change, excessive unconscious hostility, greed, lack of interest or warmth, lack of self-awareness, narcissism, pessimism, obsessiveness, sadism, and seductiveness, could be harmful to clients. Group leaders who seek advanced group coursework and quality supervision are better able to increase skills and identify ineffective and harmful personal behavior.

Group Counseling with Children

Group work with children and adolescents is effective and as effective as individual counseling (Erford, 2016). Some studies have pointed to interesting differential effects. For example, Tillitsky (1990) indicated that adolescents reported better outcomes when treated with group counseling rather than with individual counseling, whereas children reported the opposite effect, benefiting more from individual treatment than group work. It is important to note that these were self-perception studies, not clinical outcome studies.

Most of the counseling research studies involving children explored the effectiveness of group approaches (Prout & Prout, 1998; Whiston et al., 2010), although the overall quality and sophistication of these studies was inferior to group outcome studies for adults (Hoag & Burlingame, 1997). Whiston et al. (2010) concluded that group approaches with school-age children were very effective in addressing social skills, discipline, and family adjustment problems. Hoag and Burlingame (1997) reported a large ES for depression; medium ES for behavioral disorders, learning disorders, and children of divorce; and small ES for social problems when using group therapy as the primary treatment modality. Various other recent meta-analysis support group work with children and adolescents (Erford, Erford, Lattanzi et al., 2011; Erford, Erford et al., 2013; Erford, Paul et al., 2014; Erford, Kress et al., 2015; Erford, Bardhoshi et al., 2016; Rongione et al., 2010).

Regarding depression in adolescents, Beeferman and Orvaschel (1994) reported that group counseling is a very effective treatment, with the most promising results stemming from a combination of supportive group processes and cognitive-behavioral interventions, combined with behavioral skills training and homework. Bauer, Sapp, and Johnson (2000) support the use of cognitive-behavioral approaches and relaxation because the combination seems to be particularly effective with high school students.

Group approaches were also shown to produce short-term (Pedro-Carroll & Alpert-Gillis, 1997) and long-term (Pedro-Carroll, Sutton, & Wyman, 1999) positive outcomes for children of divorce. Generally, Whiston, Feldwisch, and James (2015) suggested that group approaches with children have ample support in the outcome research literature, whereas group work effectiveness with high school students needs further study. This conclusion is of interest because of the general perception that adolescents learn and process best in peer group interactions. Given that group work is effective with children and adults, it is reasonable to conclude that it is also likely to be effective with adolescents; however, group leaders and researchers must collaborate to promote research with this population of students.

EFFECTIVENESS OF GROUP WORK WITH ADULTS   The outcomes research on adults is far more compelling and convincing than that available for children and adolescents. Group treatment of depression and of bipolar disorder in adults is quite effective (Erford, 2015c). Group interventions for these mood disorders seem to be helpful in assisting members to access interpersonal support, learn effective coping skills, and understand the nature and course of the conditions. In the treatment of adults with eating disorders, group interventions seem to be very effective as well (Erford, Richards et al., 2013), and even more effective when coupled with individual counseling. In a meta-analysis of more than 100 studies of bulimia, Erford and colleagues concluded that nearly every study resulted in treatment gains, such as reduced binging and purging, and improved body image. Similar effectiveness results were likewise attained in a meta-analysis of PTSD (Erford, Gunther et al., 2015).

Group therapy with adults was highly effective (ES > 0.80) in the treatment of depression, eating disorders, personality disorders, substance abuse, and anxiety disorders, and moderately effective (0.50 < ES < 0.80) for adults with thought disorders, criminal behavior, stress, or neuroticism, or who were sexually abused. While this may be partially due to treatment modality, it should also be considered a potential reflection of differences in responsiveness of some disorders in general. No significant relationships were found with the degree of patient diagnosis, group size, pregroup training, membership (open versus closed), therapist experience, or client gender or age (Burlingame et al., 2003).

Differences in outcome can be seen according to different group compositions and warrant mentioning. Members of heterogeneous groups attained an overall ES of only 0.25, whereas members of homogeneous groups attained a significantly higher level of improvement (ES = 0.56) (Burlingame et al., 2003). Group interventions that aimed more directly at underlying, common difficulties that are the focus of the group seem more effective rather than those that take a less targeted approach.

Outpatient groups (ES = 0.55) reported more improvement than inpatient groups (ES = 0.20), although this is likely explained by the severity of members' conditions and the current level of crisis prevalent (Burlingame et al., 2003). Mixed-gender adult groups were more efficacious (ES = 0.66) overall than all-male (ES = 0.41) or all-female groups (ES = 0.39). Perhaps the diverse perspectives and interpersonal learning opportunities available in mixed-gender groups accounted for this difference.

THE EFFECTIVENESS OF SCHOOL-BASED INTERVENTIONS FOR CHILDREN AND ADOLESCENTS

The Centers for Disease Control and Prevention (2018) reported that approximately 2.7 million children experience intense, severe emotional or behavioral problems, interfering with family relations, peer relationships, and academics. In total, about 20% of school-aged students have diagnosable psychiatric disorders requiring intervention; while behavior and attention problems may be most common in primary school settings, depression and suicidal behaviors are more typical of secondary school populations.

As with any area of counseling service, it is critical for professional school counselors to be informed about outcomes research and know which interventions are supported. **Professional school counselors** are employed by schools and provide direct and indirect counseling services at the school sites. In contrast to the traditional individual and group counseling services typically offered by professional counselors in agencies, the services offered by professional school counselors are more diverse and complex and include increased consultation and collaboration with teachers and administrators, educational planning services, developmental classroom guidance lessons, peer mediation, and comprehensive school counseling programs.

Numerous studies have explored the effectiveness of this broader range of interventions, and Table 17.4 contains results from meta-analyses, several of which warrant mentioning. In a review of 117 studies published since 1980, Whiston et al. (2010) yielded an overall unweighted ES = 0.46. Other meta-analyses focused more on the specific aspects of school counseling programs. Sink and Stroh (2003) indicated that elementary students who attended schools with a comprehensive school counseling program had slightly higher achievement scores. Prout and Prout (1998) conducted a meta-analysis of school-based individual counseling and documented a large ES for counseling services in schools.

Several qualitative reviews of the literature have been conducted as well. Whiston and Sexton (1993) indicated that positive changes in students generally resulted from the broad range of services offered by professional school counselors. The conclusion of an earlier qualitative review by Borders and Drury (1992) was even more favorable. After examining studies published between 1960 and 1990, they concluded that significant student improvements in academic performance, attitudes, and behaviors resulted from school-based counseling services, leading to a substantial impact on student development.

The availability of outcome research in the area of school counseling effectiveness continues to lag compared with the areas of counseling pertaining to career and individual interventions (Whiston et al., 2015). In addition, the outcome research in school counseling that is available is replete with methodological limitations. Such limitations are partly due to the complexity of assessing highly variable, multifaceted, and wide-ranging programs. Conclusions about the effectiveness of school counseling interventions should be viewed with caution.

TABLE 17.4 Effectiveness of the Specific Facets of Counseling for Youth and School-Based Interventions

Study	Characteristic	Effect Size
Wilson, Gottfredson, and Najaka (2001)	Prevention programs for problem behaviors	None
	For delinquency	None
	For alcohol/drug use	None
	For dropout/attendance	None
Bratton, Ray, Rhine, and Jones (2005)	Nondirective play therapy	Large
	Directive play therapy	Medium
	Group play therapy	Medium
	Individual play therapy	Medium
	Parent-led filial trained play therapy	Large
	Play therapy for behavior problems	Large
	Play therapy for social adjustment	Large
	Play therapy for family relationships	Large
Whiston et al. (2010)	School counseling program effectiveness	Small
	Group guidance curricular activities	Small
	Responsive services	Small
	Peer mediation	Small
Erford, Bardhoshi et al. (2016)	Conduct disorder	Small to Medium
Erford, Erford, Lattanzi et al. (2011)	Depression	Medium
Erford, Kress et al. (2015)	Anxiety	Medium
Erford, Paul et al. (2014)	Oppositional behavior	Medium

Specific Types of School-Based Interventions

It is important to consider outcome research within each type of intervention offered because school-based services are multifaceted and may result in different effectiveness rates. Outcome research that focused on the specific types of school-based interventions is considered. First, Whiston and colleagues (2010) conducted a meta-analysis to evaluate **developmental classroom guidance** activities. Such activities are used to promote healthy social and emotional development and are typically taught through a variety of methods, including activities, music, drawing, stories, games, worksheets, role playing, puppets, and videos. Whiston and colleagues concluded that this intervention had primarily small ESs across the K–12 curriculum; this may be because many professional school counselors are using materials that have not been studied for their effectiveness (Carey & Dimmitt, 2012; Rowley, Stroh, & Sink, 2005). Although an effect was detected, an even greater effect may result if the materials used were empirically validated.

Regardless, other studies found classroom guidance to be quite effective in addressing personal/affective issues (Rowley et al., 2005), school attitude and behavior (Schlossberg, Morris, & Lieberman, 2001), and self-management skills (Brigman & Campbell, 2003;

Campbell & Brigman, 2005). In general, the evaluation of materials used for the purposes of classroom developmental guidance is an area of research needing increased attention from empirically oriented practitioners and researchers (see www.umass.edu/schoolcounseling/).

Another type of service specific to school-based counseling is that of **responsive services**. In general, responsive services are aimed at immediate attention and intervention in response to problematic issues that might arise in the school setting but typically result from personal situations.

While the literature does not always agree on which method is more effective, individual and group counseling responsive services are found to be effective in the remediation of problems displayed by children and adolescents. In a meta-analysis of 58 studies, Whiston and colleagues (2010) assessed the effectiveness of group counseling interventions and reported an overall ES = 0.35. Group counseling was also determined to be effective for a wide range of school-based behaviors, including discipline problems, social skills training, adjustment to divorce, and relaxation (Whiston et al., 2015). Additional studies conducted by Littrell and colleagues (1995) concluded that brief, solution-focused approaches to individual counseling were effective with adolescents, indicating lengthier treatment is unnecessary. Thompson and Littrell (1998) reached a similar conclusion when counseling students with learning disabilities.

Research on conflict resolution and peer mediation programs in schools continues to be scarce. With the increase in school violence and bullying behaviors on campus, more attention is being focused on the implementation and effectiveness of such programs. In 2010, Whiston and colleagues completed a study of peer mediation programs that showed a small effect (ES = 0.39) for improving student knowledge of how to address conflict and potentially problematic situations. While this study did provide evidence of increased knowledge, little is known about the effects of such programs on actual student behaviors and conflict.

One study that was aimed at examining the effectiveness of peer mediation, conducted by Wilson et al. (2003), found little improvement in aggressive behaviors. However, Lewis and Lewis (1996) noted that findings such as this could be more indicative of the training level of the individuals operating such programs rather than a result of the program itself. Program implementation was often conducted by noncounselors who lacked the necessary skills. Regardless, Gerber and Terry-Day (1999) concluded that insufficient empirical support exists to say with confidence that the programs are theoretically sound and result in desirable effects. Thus, there is insufficient cause to warrant the widespread use of peer mediation and conflict resolution programs in schools without more study.

Some outcome research has focused on specific problem areas, such as disruptive behavior, delinquent behavior, substance use, truancy, moral education, and coping skills. Regarding disruptive classroom behavior, studies show behavior modification techniques to be generally effective. Stage and Quiroz (1997) (see Table 17.4) reported an ES = 0.78, indicating that 78% of treatment group participants receiving behavior modification fared better than the average control group participant. Such effects were noted regardless of the type of behavior modification technique used (i.e., token economies, response cost procedures, or time-out procedures using contingency delay) (Erford, 1999; Erford, Bardhoshi et al., 2016; Erford, Paul et al., 2014; Stage & Quiroz, 1997). Now complete Activity 17.5.

ACTIVITY 17.5

With the increase in behavior problems, AD/HD, and bullying, in combination with a concentration on testing outcomes in the schools, consider how the role of the school counselor and mental health counselor has changed. How can outcome research be helpful in improving interventions, advocacy, and social justice?

Research on school-based prevention programs for problem behaviors yielded mixed results. Wilson et al. (2001) concluded that ESs were either not significant or extremely small when studying the effectiveness of primary prevention programs. In addition, they found that prevention programs aimed at reducing attendance-related problems were most effective at the high school level (ES = 0.14) compared with elementary (ES = 0.05) or middle schools (ES = 0.09) (see Table 17.4). ES for prevention programs for delinquency (ES = 0.04) or alcohol/drug use (ES = 0.05) were generally not significant. When examined alone, however, a substantial number of these studies were effective for the prevention of drug use (Caria, Faggiano, Bellocco, & Galanti, 2011; Chhabra et al., 2010; Lipp, 2011; Newton, Vogl, Teesson, & Andrews, 2009; Teesson, Newton, & Barrett, 2012) and delinquency, aggression, and bullying (Bernbaum, 2014; Hall & Bacon, 2005; Musci et al., 2014; Neft, 2005).

As Tobler and Stratton (1997) and Wilson and Williams (2005) noted, the student's level of involvement and how the program is delivered contribute substantially to a program's effectiveness. As is true for many areas of counseling research, the research in this area is not vast or of high methodological quality (Shi & Erford, 2016). Increased consistency in methodology is required to improve the outcome research in this area.

CAREER INTERVENTIONS Career interventions are implemented with students and adults and typically involve interventions aimed at helping individuals define and understand their career interests and abilities, culminating in a plan of action to achieve vocational direction and success. Not only are career interventions helpful in the initial steps of determining aptitude and interests, but they are also helpful in gaining the skills necessary to seek work, transition to work, cope with work-related stress, and perhaps change areas of work in adulthood. A wealth of outcome research exists to document the effectiveness of counseling interventions aimed at career development. Oliver and Spokane (1988) reviewed 58 studies (7,311 total participants) conducted between 1950 and 1982 focusing on career counseling interventions. In 1998, Whiston and colleagues continued Oliver and Spokane's intention through a replication study designed to analyze the results of an additional 47 studies conducted between 1983 and 1995 (4,660 total participants). Such meta-analytic reviews have supported the effectiveness of career counseling with large ESs (0.85 and 0.82) (Oliver & Spokane, 1988; Spokane & Oliver, 1983). In general, outcome research has supported the effectiveness of career interventions, especially individual career counseling and classroom guidance using individual planning services, which coordinates continuous activities designed to assist in the establishment of personal goals and future plans (American School Counselor Association, 2012; Oliver & Spokane, 1988; Whiston et al., 1998).

Evans and Burck (1992) conducted a meta-analysis of 67 studies on the impact of career interventions aimed at providing education in an effort to improve the academic achievement of more than 82,000 primary and secondary school students. Small positive effects (ES = 0.22, unweighted) were found, with the greatest improvements resulting when the program was in its second year with the same students. Overall, providing career education interventions was more beneficial to academic achievement than no education or alternative interventions.

Students benefited from parent consultation about career development and career services, including students considered ethnic minorities, academically gifted, and as having disabilities (Sexton et al., 1997). Programs lacking a professional counselor and instead relying on computer-based programs were not as effective (Whiston et al., 2003). However, the use of such computerized guidance was helpful when used as a supplemental activity, in addition to counselor-directed activities. Student age has also been examined and is found to be a factor contributing to career counseling success (Sexton et al., 1997). Career-focused interventions are least effective for elementary-age students, who are developmentally unprepared to consider vocational interests and choices. As would be expected, Oliver and Spokane (1988) concluded that career counseling was most effective for junior high and high school students.

Regarding the length of treatment, longer treatment seems more effective and of more benefit than shorter treatment (Sexton et al., 1997). In addition, directive interventions are found to be more efficacious than person-centered interventions with regard to career counseling. Because length of treatment and therapy modality are considered important variables in determining the effectiveness of career counseling interventions, Sexton and colleagues suggested the development and use of standardized and empirically validated treatment manuals to increase the effectiveness and consistency of counseling.

Table 17.5 summarizes effect sizes for the outcomes measured in the meta-analyses conducted by Oliver and Spokane (1988) and Whiston et al. (1998). Overall, 83% of the studies of career intervention reported at least some positive effects (Sexton et al., 1997).

IMPLICATIONS FOR THE FUTURE OF PROFESSIONAL COUNSELING

While much helpful outcome research has accumulated over the years, much is still needed to help professional counselors skillfully implement therapeutic interventions. As future professionals in the field, consider ways that you can add to what is known about best practices. Generally, professional counselors can help in three primary ways: (1) collaborate with researchers, (2) advocate for outcomes research funding, and (3) increase knowledge and use of outcome literature.

Collaborate with Researchers

Students and practitioners alike should make every effort to collaborate with researchers whenever possible. Many forego such opportunities, however, because it is often viewed as costly, complex, time-consuming, and remote. However, for current counseling students, graduating with the ability to evaluate their own effectiveness will provide a distinct advantage in their ability to gain employment, as much as possessing basic counseling skills and theoretical knowledge.

While in training, counseling students can develop skills necessary to consume, incorporate, and produce outcome research. Counseling students should work alongside professors in an effort to assist with research projects. Although research can be a long and intense process, often taking several years to complete, students can provide valuable aid

TABLE 17.5 Effectiveness of Career Interventions as Determined by Oliver and Spokane (1988) and Whiston, Sexton, and Lasoff (1998)

Oliver and Spokane (1988) ES	Whiston et al. (1998) ES	Characteristic
Overall Effect		
0.82	0.45	All studies combined and unweighted
Length of Treatment		
0.31	0.61	Single session intervention
1.01	0.53	Two to seven sessions intervention
0.65	0.74	More than eight sessions intervention
Age of Client		
−0.01	0.04	Elementary school students
1.28	0.42	Middle school students
1.02	0.31	High school students
0.85	0.59	College students
0.82	0.54	Adults
Experience of Counselor		
0.72	0.51	Experienced counselor
0.83	0.81	Counselor-in-training
0.31	0.29	Counselor-free
0.38	0.60	Other (usually facilitator or group leader)
Treatment Types		
0.74	1.08	Individual counseling
0.62	0.73	Group counseling
0.76	0.36	Group test interpretation
0.75	0.36	Workshop
2.05	0.54	Class
0.59	0.45	Computer intervention
0.10	0.12	Counselor-free
Specific Treatment Outcomes		
2.45	1.40	Accuracy of self-knowledge
0.97	0.73	Securing job or probability of hire
0.40	0.38	Certainty/decidedness
0.88	0.88	Career-related knowledge
1.30	1.03	Skills (interview, writing, and problem solving)
1.05	0.55	Career maturity

in conducting portions of studies and thus contribute to the final product. Not only are students of great help during this process, but they also learn valuable research and evaluation skills that prove useful as future practitioners. Students who become active in research studies begin to understand the research process and are more likely to stay active in research after becoming a professional counselor in the field.

Just as counseling students must assist with research, practitioners too can collaborate with professors, researchers, and other practitioners to conduct site-based action research and program evaluation with clients. Engaging in outcome research does not have to be an impossible task. Simple measures of functioning can be used to measure the effectiveness of treatment and incorporated into routine paperwork obligations. While the results found by one practitioner may seem too small to matter, when combined with the results found by other practitioners, they can lead to meaningful outcomes. Such efforts by practitioners would be invaluable to researchers because researchers frequently attempt to coordinate such studies but struggle for lack of access to necessary populations or samples. Not only can practitioners conduct their own research and collaborate with other counseling professionals, but they should also consider making their worksite available to researchers. Simply making your worksite or willing clients available as a pool of potential participants can lead to a wealth of information when combined with others. The large populations served by professional counselors in schools and community agencies can be particularly useful for outcomes research. Providing access to participants and helping to collect data are the two components of outcomes research with which practitioners can be of greatest aid. Most important, becoming active in research studies as a student to understand the process and then staying active once you have become a professional counselor in the field are crucial to the future of outcome research.

Advocate for Outcome Research Funding

In addition to engaging in collaborative research efforts with colleagues and researchers, professional counselors must also advocate for increased funding for outcome research. Ordinarily, funding for research can be obtained from government agencies, private foundations, universities, and professional organizations (Erford, 2015c). Advocating for research funding by these sources is a professional responsibility that generates new practice-improving findings—findings that will help professional counselors understand how to help their clients meet their goals, help researchers communicate this information to professional counselors, and conduct basic research meant to inform counseling practice. But all this hinges on your advocacy efforts.

Increase Knowledge and Use of Outcome Literature

Because research has shown that some practices are more effective than others, and some client problems are helped most by specific counseling models (Sexton, 1999), professional counselors can greatly improve their effectiveness and ethical practice by reading and using knowledge gained from an understanding of the outcome research. Membership and involvement in national, regional, and state counseling organizations ensures access to the literature through journals and other scholarly publications. Professional counselors should read and use such information to shape their practice. In addition, such information should be passed along to other colleagues so they too may keep informed on the most recent, relevant, and rigorous information.

Reynolds (2000) introduced a five-step model for practicing professional counselors to use in an effort to increase the use of empirically based treatment:

1. The professional counselor determines the specific clinical question pertinent to the client's progress.
2. The professional counselor seeks out the empirical literature to answer the clinical question.
3. The professional counselor evaluates the evidence found in the literature for its usefulness.
4. The results are used to shape treatment and are integrated into counseling interventions.
5. The outcome of the intervention is evaluated.

To move through these steps, the professional counselor must first be aware of what research is available, be able to assess it, have the ability to identify the implications of it, and possess the knowledge and skill to integrate the findings into her or his practice. Through a systematic process, professional counselors can be encouraged to approach client care more scientifically, not in an effort to dehumanize the experience, but rather in an effort to increase the efficacy of interventions. For counselors to be unconcerned about the outcomes of their interventions is unethical. To maximize effectiveness, professional counselors must combine their professional experience, intuition, and knowledge of theory with the external evidence.

Having stressed the importance of consuming research, it is also important to recall that, in reality, most of what works is determined by factors other than the specific counseling technique or intervention chosen. Research shows that this accounts for only 15% of the outcome (Lambert, 2013). The remaining 85% of client outcome is heavily determined by other facets of effective helping. Lambert concluded that 15% of therapeutic outcome is due to client expectations, 40% is due to factors outside the counseling setting, and 30% is due to therapeutic alliance. The point is that, although many counselors are oblivious to the current research, others may rush through it to find a solution or the newest technique available for a particular client situation, failing to focus on the importance of establishing an effective counseling relationship. Instead, it is known that a counselor's level of skillfulness, capacity to conceptualize, and ability to match relationally with the client is also important to outcomes (Sexton, 1999). Now complete Case Study 17.2 to explore your potential future role in counseling research.

CASE STUDY 17.2

With a few counseling courses behind you, you are beginning to learn a bit about not only what is known about counseling, but also what is yet unknown. During an informal chat with your professor, you are convinced that you want to collaborate on a research project to help document the effectiveness of counseling services. Give some thought to the following questions:

1. What important research questions emerge about the effectiveness of counseling that might warrant further study?
2. Would you rather pursue an outcome study or an action research project at a field placement?

(Continued)

3. From the perspective of a researcher, how would you gain access to the client population of interest?
4. From a practitioner's perspective, how would you conduct a research study to examine your own effectiveness, while simultaneously adding to the outcome research?
5. How can research be used to promote social justice with clients and client systems?

Putting It All Together: Working for the Future

The current accountability movements in schools and clinical practice point to the need for practitioners to focus on process and outcome evaluation. It is more essential than ever that students, practitioners, and researchers work together to establish effective practices. In the past, practitioners have often viewed research as artificial, even as a necessary evil. Such a view is counterproductive. Instead, students, practitioners, and researchers must work together—quite literally—to become collaborators in research and consumers of research. Such collaboration would significantly improve our understanding of efficient and effective counseling interventions and improve personal practice and client outcomes.

The research available on the outcomes of the counseling process has grown substantially and is considered a reliable and valid source of knowledge. Earlier research was in many ways irrelevant to practice; however, that trend has shifted, and a growing body of evidence has evolved that is directly applicable to the specific problems and populations seen daily in practice. Research now shows stable trends supporting the usefulness of some counseling practices over others, the increased value of certain aspects of counseling over others, and the effectiveness of specific models paired with specific problems. The production, proliferation, dissemination, and incorporation of outcomes research has the ability to continue moving the profession of counseling forward, to shape a practice that is not merely one of theory and instinct, but of sound science.

While hundreds of studies have explored the effectiveness of the various facets of counseling, much remains unknown. The extant literature on counseling outcome research to date gives a general idea of what is and is not effective as it relates to work with adults, adolescents, and children, with a multitude of issues, across various counseling settings. As stated previously, no theoretical approach to counseling has shown superiority over another, although some approaches show more promise with specific issues and under certain conditions. This observation has led some researchers to conclude that a great deal of counseling effectiveness is due to core therapeutic conditions common to most counseling approaches. If outcome research continues to proliferate and flourish, with increasingly more knowledge gained regarding the effectiveness of particular methods, and if this information is used in conjunction with the core conditions of counseling, imagine how much more effective counseling could become. With increased focus on accountability, this is no longer an ideal vision of the future of counseling, but a necessary direction.

Outcome research is vital to the well-being of the client, the ethical obligations of the counselor, and the advancement of the field. For the counseling profession to remain competitive, it must show effectiveness. To do so, treatment must be empirically validated by research, and improved outcomes must be shown. It is crucial for each individual professional counselor, at a minimum, to be knowledgeable of the research base, to understand how to use the counseling modalities and treatment approaches that are evidence-based, and to select and tailor interventions based on best practices. Even more so, professional counselors must shift to become producers, in addition to consumers, of outcome research in an effort not only to increase the effectiveness of research, but also to add substantially to the profession of counseling.

Summary

Simply put, outcome research is intended to answer questions about counseling effectiveness. The need for counseling services is at an all-time high, so we must continue to prove the effectiveness of our treatments to gain reimbursement for counseling services and advance the reputation of the counseling profession. However, not only do practicing counselors tend to refrain from conducting outcome research, they also sometimes fail to keep informed of the current outcome research and newest empirically validated treatments. Not only is outcome research underproduced, but what is produced is understudied and underused.

As stated earlier, the chasm between research and practice has begun to close substantially over the years as practitioners have realized the need for more relevant outcome research and counseling researchers have realized the need for more pertinent and applicable research studies. The scientist–practitioner model has been advocated in training future researchers and practitioners to make everyone effective at research and practice.

Meta-analysis is used to combine statistically the results from different studies examining the same variables to analyze across studies the effectiveness of interventions. For each study, an ES is usually calculated, resulting in a numerical index showing if participants receiving the intervention improved beyond participants who did not.

Eysenck (1952) initially claimed that psychotherapy was not only ineffective, but also potentially harmful to clients. Since then, hundreds of studies have instead supported the effectiveness of such interventions. While a very small percentage of individuals do not improve with counseling, and may worsen for a variety of reasons (many of which are unrelated to the counseling itself), outcome research points to the overwhelming conclusion that counseling is helpful for a wide array of populations, presenting with various concerns, in a host of settings. In addition, it is generally accepted today that such positive outcomes are obtained regardless of the theoretical approach. However, it is also known that particular interventions typically are better with certain disorders. Even more important are the interactions of the various facets of the counseling process that are also known to contribute independently. These interactions are now the focal point of much research.

While still often debated, it is generally accepted that individual counseling and group counseling are about equally effective, although each may be slightly more appropriate or helpful at particular times and in particular conditions. It has also been documented that the combination of the two yields especially promising results. Comprehensive school-based programs seem effective in improving student academic performance, social skills, and behavior, although they are less effective when the focus is on prevention programs related to substance use and delinquency. Nearly all career counseling interventions seem effective when implemented by a professional counselor, whereas interventions by untrained individuals are ineffective, if not harmful.

Several implications and suggestions for how professional counselors can help bridge the research–practice gap and tap into a wealth of continuing outcome research are offered. Professional counselors should collaborate with researchers, evaluate their own effectiveness, and advocate for increased funding for counseling research. Professional counselors should read, summarize, and disseminate research on effective counseling practice to other practitioners.

The importance of establishing a collaborative relationship with clients cannot be underestimated. While many counselors are unmindful of the current research, others may focus only on current research findings regarding treatment protocols and techniques.

Instead, as a professional counselor, strive for a balance between emphasizing the core conditions of counseling, and being knowledgeable of the current outcome literature and examining your own effectiveness.

MyCounselingLab for Introduction to Counseling

Try the Topic 14 Assignments: *Research and Evaluation.*

REFERENCES

Achenbach, T. M., & Rescorla, L. A. (2001). *Manual for the Achenbach System of Empirically Based Assessment* (ASEBA). Burlington, VT: University of Vermont Department of Psychiatry.

Adams, M., Bell, L. A., & Griffin, P. (Eds.). (2007). *Teaching for diversity and social justice* (2nd ed.). New York, NY: Routledge.

Administration on Aging. (2014). *What is elder abuse.* Retrieved from http://www.aoa.gov/AoA_programs/elder_rights/EA_prevention/whatisEA.aspx

Alabama Suicide Prevention & Resources Coalition. (2014). *Comprehensive suicide prevention resource directory.* Retrieved from www.legacy.montevallo.edu/asparc

Albrecht, D. E., & Albrecht, S. G. (2007). The benefits and costs of inequality for the advantaged and the disadvantaged. *Social Science Quarterly, 88,* 382–403.

Alcoholics Anonymous. (2016). *World services.* Retrieved from http://www.alcoholics-anonymous.org

Ali, R. (2011, April 4th). *The dear colleague letter.* Washington, DC: United States Department of Education Office for Civil Rights.

Ali, S. R., & Menke, K. A. (2014). Rural Latino youth career development: An application of social cognitive career theory. *Career Development Quarterly, 62,* 175–186. doi:10.1002/j.2161-0045.2014.00078.x

Alkon, A., Ramler, M., & MacLennan, K. (2003). Evaluation of mental health consultation in child care centers. *Early Childhood Education Journal, 31*(2), 91–99. doi:10.1023/B:ECEJ.0000005307.00142.3c

American Association for Marriage and Family Therapy. (2012). *American Association for Marriage and Family Therapy code of ethics.* Washington, DC: Author.

American Association of Pastoral Counselors. (2017). *About pastoral counseling.* Retrieved from http://www.aapc.org/about-us/pastoral-counseling-today/

American Association of State Counseling Boards. (2017). *Welcome to AASCB.* Retrieved from http://www.aascb.org/aws/AASCB/pt/sp/home_page

American Association of Suicidology. (2006). *IS PATH WARM.* Washington, DC: Author.

American Association of Suicidology. (2015). *USA suicide: 2013 official final data.* Retrieved from http://www.suicidology.org/Portals/14/docs/Resources/FactSheets/2013datapgsv3.pdf

American Association of Suicidology (2016). *Suicidal behavior among lesbian, gay, bisexual, and transgender youth fact sheet.* Retrieved from http://www.suicidology.org/Portals/14/docs/Resources/LGBT%20Resources/SuicidalBehaviorAmongLGBTYouthFacts.pdf

American Association of Suicidology. (AAS). (2018). *Know the warning signs of suicide.* Retrieved from http://www.suicidology.org/resources/warning-signs

American Association of University Women. (2015). *The simple truth about the gender pay gap.* Retrieved from http://www.aauw.org/research/the-simple-truth-about-the-gender-pay-gap/

American Civil Liberties Union. (2015). *Non-discrimination laws: State by state information.* Retrieved from https://www.aclu.org/map/non-discrimination-laws-state-state-information-map

American College Counseling Association. (2018). *Who we are.* Retrieved from http://www.collegecounseling.org/who-we-are

American College Health Association. (2014, Spring). *American College Health Association-National College Health Assessment II: Reference group executive summary.* Hanover, MD: Author.

American Counseling Association. (2003). *Advocacy competencies.* Alexandria, VA, Author.

American Counseling Association. (2011). *Who Are LPCs?* Retrieved from http://www.counseling.org/docs/public-policy-resources-reports/whoarelpcs.pdf?sfvrsn=2

American Counseling Association. (2012). *Public awareness ideas and strategies for professional counselors.* Alexandria, VA: Author.

American Counseling Association. (2013). *Medicare coverage of licensed professional counselors.* Retrieved from http://www.counseling.org/government-affairs/current-issues/position-papers/2013/03/19/medicare-coverage-of-licensed-professional-counselors-bill-introduced-in-113th-congress

American Counseling Association. (2014a). *ACA code of ethics*. Retrieved from http://www.counseling.org/resources/aca-code-of-ethics.pdf

American Counseling Association. (2014b). *Licensure requirements for professional counselors*. Alexandria, VA: Author.

American Counseling Association. (2015). *ACA's Taskforce on Counselor Wellness and Impairment: Definitions-counselor impairment*. Retrieved from http://www.counseling.org/knowledge-center/counselor-wellness/definitions

American Counseling Association. (2016). *ACA mission*. Retrieved from http://www.counseling.org/about-us/about-aca/our-mission

American Counseling Association. (2017). *20/20: A vision for the future of counseling. Consensus definition of counseling*. Retrieved from http://www.counseling.org/knowledge-center/20-20-a-vision-for-the-future-of-counseling

American Counseling Association. (2018a). *ACA divisions, regions and branches*. Retrieved from http://www.counseling.org/about-us/divisions-regions-and-branches

American Counseling Association. (2018b). *Disaster mental health*. Retrieved from http://www.counseling.org/knowledge-center/trauma-disaster

American Mental Health Counselors Association. (2010). *American Mental Health Counselors Association code of ethics*. Alexandria, VA: Author.

American Mental Health Counselors Association. (2015). *Standards for the practice of clinical mental health counseling*. Alexandria, VA: Author.

American Mental Health Counselors Association. (2018). *About us*. Retrieved from http://www.amhca.org/?page=facts

American Psychiatric Association. (2013). *Diagnostic and statistical manual of mental disorders* (5th ed.). Washington, DC: Author.

American Psychological Association. (2007). Guidelines for psychological practice with girls and women., *American Psychologist, 62*, 949–979. doi:10.1037/0003-066X.62.9.949

American Psychological Association. (2015). *The road to resilience*. Retrieved from http://www.apa.org/helpcenter/road-resilience.aspx

American Psychological Association (APA) Presidential Task Force on Evidence-Based Practice. (2006). Evidence-based practice in psychology. *American Psychologist, 61*, 271–285. doi:10.1037/0003-066X.61.4.271

American School Counselor Association. (2005). *The ASCA national model: A framework for school counseling programs* (2nd ed.). Alexandria, VA: Author.

American School Counselor Association. (2010). *Ethical standards for school counselors*. Alexandria, VA: Author.

American School Counselor Association. (2012). *The ASCA national model: A framework for school counseling programs* (3rd ed.). Alexandria, VA: Author.

American School Counselor Association. (2013). *The school counselor and safe schools and crisis response*. Retrieved from https://www.schoolcounselor.org/asca/media/asca/PositionStatements/PS_SafeSchools.pdf

American School Counselor Association. (ASCA). (2014). *Mindsets and behaviors for student success*. Retrieved from https://schoolcounselor.org/asca/media/asca/home/MindsetsBehaviors.pdf

Americans with Disabilities Act. (2008). *Americans with Disabilities Act of 1990, as amended*. Retrieved from http://www.ada.gov/pubs/adastatute08.pdf

Amerikaner, M., & Rose, T. (2012). Direct observation of psychology supervisees' clinical work: A snapshot of current practice. *Clinical Supervisor, 31*, 61–80. doi:10.1080/07325223.2012.671721

Arnett, J. J. (2000). Emerging adulthood: A theory of development from the late teens through the twenties. *American Psychologist, 55*, 469–480.

Arredondo, P., & Glauner, T. (1992). *Personal dimensions of identity model*. Tucson, AZ: Empowerment Workshops.

Arthur, N., Collins, S., Marshall, C., & McMahon, M. (2013). Social justice competencies and career development practices. *Canadian Journal of Counselling and Psychotherapy, 47*, 136–154.

Association for Adult Development and Aging. (2017). *Association of Adult Development and Aging*. Retrieved from http://www.aadaweb.org/

Association for Assessment and Research in Counseling. (2017). *Assessment and testing documents*. Retrieved from http://aarc-counseling.org/resources

Association for Counselor Education and Supervision. (2011). *Best practices in clinical supervision*. Retrieved from http://www.acesonline.net/sites/default/files/ACES-Best-Practices-in-clinical-supervision-document-FINAL.pdf

Association for Creativity in Counseling. (2018). *About us*. Retrieved from http://www.creativecounselor.org/

Association for Humanistic Counseling. (2018). *Above all, we are counselors.* Retrieved from http://afhc.camp9.org/Who-Are-We

Association for Lesbian, Gay, Bisexual and Transgender Issues in Counseling (ALGBTIC) Transgender Committee. (2010). American Counseling Association Competencies for Counseling with Transgender Clients. *Journal of LGBT Issues in Counseling, 4,* 135–159. doi:10.1080/15538605.2010.524839

Association for Lesbian, Gay, Bisexual, and Transgender Issues in Counseling (ALGBTIC) LGBQQIA Competencies Taskforce. (2013). ALGBTIC competencies for counseling with lesbian, gay, bisexual, queer, questioning, intersex and ally individuals. *Journal of LGBT Issues in Counseling, 7,* 2–43. doi:10.1080/15538605.2013.755444

Association for Multicultural Counseling and Development. (2018). *Home.* Retrieved from http://www.multiculturalcounseling.org/

Association for Specialists in Group Work. (2007). *Best practice guidelines.* Retrieved from http://static1.squarespace.com/static/55cea634e4b083e448c3dd50/t/55d3f792e4b08c827e15cb79/1439954834126/ASGW_Best_Practices.pdf

Association for Spiritual, Ethical, and Religious Values in Counseling. (2016). *Competencies for integrating spirituality into counseling.* Retrieved from http://www.aservic.org/wp-content/uploads/2010/04/Spiritual-Competencies-Printer-friendly1.pdf

Association for Spiritual, Ethical and Religious Values in Counseling. (2018). *Home.* Retrieved from http://www.aservic.org/

Bachar, E. (1998). Psychotherapy—an active agent: Assessing the effectiveness of psychotherapy and its curative factors. *Israel Journal of Psychiatry and Related Sciences, 35,* 128–135.

Baker, S. B., Robichaud, T. A., Westforth Dietrich, V. C., Wells, S. C., & Schreck, R. E. (2009). School counselor consultation: A pathway to advocacy, collaboration, and leadership. *Professional School Counseling, 12,* 200–212. doi:10.5330/PSC.n.2010-12.200

Baldwin, S. A., Christian, S., & Berkeljon, A. (2012). The effects of family therapies for adolescent delinquency and substance abuse: A meta-analysis. *Journal of Marital and Family Therapy, 38,* 281–304.

Bandura, A. (1982). The psychology of chance encounters. *American Psychologist, 37,* 747–755.

Barclay, J. R., Brown, B. M., Gladding, S. T., Goodyear, R. K., Hays, D. G., Hohenshil, T. H., Smith, D., & Barclay, J. R. (1981). Counseling and the future: Some views of editorial board members. *Personnel and Guidance Journal, 60*(3), 131–134. doi:10.1002/j.2164-4918.1981.tb00763.x

Bardhoshi, G., Schweinle, A., & Duncan, K. (2014). Understanding the impact of school factors on school counselor burnout: A mixed-methods study. *Professional Counselor, 4,* 426–443. doi:10.15241/gb.4.5.426

Barlow, D. H., & Durand, V. M. (2014). *Abnormal psychology: An integrative approach* (7th ed.). Belmont, CA: Cengage Learning.

Barrett, R. (2015). *Distance counseling approved training.* Retrieved from http://distancecounselingtraining.edubrite.com/oltpublish/site/coursePlayer.do?dispatch=show&courseSessionId=a28ca0dc-f775-11e4-9e53-002590f9ff98

Bartholomew, C. (2003). *Gender-sensitive therapy: Principles and practices.* Prospect Heights, IL: Waveland Press.

Basham, A., Appleton, V., & Dykeman, C. (2000). *Team-building in education: A how-to guidebook.* Denver, CO: Love Publishing.

Bauer, S. R., Sapp, M., & Johnson, D. (2000). Group counseling strategies for rural at-risk high school students. *High School Journal, 83,* 41–50.

Beck, A. T., & Steer, R. A. (1993). *Manual for the Beck Anxiety Inventory.* San Antonio, TX: Psychological Corporation.

Beck, A. T., Steer, R. A., & Brown, G. K. (1996). *Beck Depression Inventory* (2nd ed.). San Antonio, TX: Psychological Corporation.

Bedi, R. P. (2006). Concept mapping the client's perspective on counseling alliance formation. *Journal of Counseling Psychology, 53,* 26–35. doi:10.1037/0022-0167.53.1.26

Beeferman, D., & Orvaschel, H. (1994). Group psychotherapy for depressed adolescents: A critical review. *International Journal of Group Psychotherapy, 44,* 463–475.

Beers, C. W. (1908). *A mind that found itself.* New York, NY: Longmans, Green.

Behrens, E. L., & Nauta, M. M. (2014). The self-directed search as a stand-alone intervention with college students. *Career Development Quarterly, 62,* 224–238. doi:10.1002/j.2161-0045.2014.00081.x

Bem, S. L. (1981). *Bem Sex-Role Inventory: Professional manual.* Palo Alto, CA: Consulting Psychologists Press.

Bem, S. L. (1993). *The lenses of gender: Transforming the debate on sexuality inequality.* New Haven, CT: Yale University Press.

Bemak, F., & Chung, C. (2008). New professional roles and advocacy strategies for school counselors: A multicultural/social justice perspective to move beyond the nice counselor syndrome. *Journal of Counseling & Development, 86,* 372–382. doi:10.1002/j.1556-6678.2008.tb00522.x

Berens, D. E. (2018). Disability, ableism, and ageism. In D. G. Hays & B. T. Erford (Eds.), *Developing multicultural counseling competence: A systems approach* (3rd ed., pp. 166–191). Boston, MA: Pearson.

Berg, I. K., & Miller, S. (1992). *Working with the problem drinker.* New York, NY: Norton.

Berger, B., & Newman, S. (2011). *Money talks: In therapy, society, and life.* New York, NY: Routledge.

Berger, K. S. (2012). *The developing person through childhood and adolescence* (9th ed.). New York, NY: Worth Publishers.

Berk, L. E. (2013). *Child development* (9th ed.). Boston, MA: Pearson.

Berke, D., Rozell, C., Hogan, T., Norcross, J., & Karpiak, C. (2011). What clinical psychologists know about evidence-based practice: Familiarity with online resources and research methods. *Journal of Clinical Psychology, 67,* 329–339. doi:10.1002/jclp.20775

Bernal, G., & Saez-Santiago, E. (2006). Cultural centered psychosocial interventions. *Journal of Community Psychology, 34*(2), 121–132. doi:10.1002/jcop.20096

Bernard, J., & Goodyear, R. (2013). *Fundamentals of clinical supervision* (5th ed.). Upper Saddle River, NJ: Pearson.

Bernbaum, E. L. (2014). Internet bullying in female middle school adolescents: A comprehensive school-based prevention program. *Dissertation Abstracts International: Section B: The Sciences and Engineering, 74*(9-B)(E).

Beutler, L. E. (1989). Differential treatment selection: The role of diagnosis in psychotherapy. *Psychotherapy, 26,* 271–281. doi:10.1037/h0085436

Bjorklund, D. F. (2011). *Children's thinking: Cognitive development and individual differences* (5th ed.). Florence, KY: Cengage Learning.

Black, R. D., Weinberg, L. A., & Brodwin, M. G. (2015). Universal design for learning and instruction: Perspectives on students with disabilities in higher education. *Exceptionality Education International, 25,*1–16.

Blando, J. (2006). Spirituality, religion, and counseling. *Counseling and Human Development, 39*(2), 1.

Blevins, J. (2009). Changing (dis)course: Psychology and theology in light of social construction. *Sacred Spaces: e-Journal of the American Association for Pastoral Counselors, 1,* 35–53.

Bloch, D. P. (2003). *The living career: Complexity, chaos, connections and career.* Retrieved from http://eric.ed.gov/?id=ED480520

Bloch, D. P. (2005). Complexity, chaos, and nonlinear dynamics: A new perspective on career development theory. *Career Development Quarterly, 53,* 194–207. doi:10.1002/j.2161-0045.2005.tb00990.x

Blouin, M., & Vallejo Echeverri, L. E. (2012). Rehabilitation. In J. H. Stone & M. Blouin (Eds.). *International encyclopedia of rehabilitation.* Retrieved from http://cirrie.buffalo.edu/encyclopedia/en/article/304/

Borders, L. D. (2014). Best practices in clinical supervision: Another step in delineating effective supervision practice. *American Journal of Psychotherapy, 68,* 151–162.

Borders, L. D., & Drury, S. M. (1992). Comprehensive school counseling programs: A review for policymakers and practitioners. *Journal of Counseling and Development, 70,* 487–498. doi:10.1002/j.1556-6676.1992.tb01643.x

Boss, P. G. (2002). *Family stress management: A contextual approach* (2nd ed.). Thousand Oaks, CA: Sage.

Bounds, P. S., Washington, M. R., & Henfield, M. S. (2018). Individuals and families of African descent. In D. G. Hays & B. T. Erford (Eds.), *Developing multicultural counseling competence: A systems approach* (3rd ed., pp. 220–244). Columbus, OH: Pearson.

Bowen, M. (1966). The use of family theory in clinical practice. *Comprehensive Psychiatry, 7,* 345–374. doi:10.1016/S0010-440X(66)80065-2

Bowen, M. (1976). Theory in the practice of psychotherapy. In P. J. Guerin (Ed.), *Family therapy: Theory and practice.* New York, NY: Gardner Press.

Bradley, J. M., Werth, J. L., & Hastings, S. L. (2012). Social justice advocacy in rural communities: Practical issues and implications. *Counseling Psychologist, 40,* 363–384. doi:10.1177/0011000011415697

Bradley, N., Whisenhunt, J., Adamson, N., & Kress, V. E. (2013). Creative approaches for promoting counselor self-care. *Journal of Creativity in Mental Health, 8,* 456–469. doi:10.1080/15401383.2013. 844656

Bradley, P. D., Bergen, L. P., Ginter, E. J., Williams, L. M., & Scalise, J. J. (2010). A survey of North American marriage and family therapy practitioners: A role delineation study. *American Journal of Family Therapy, 38,* 281–291. doi:10.1080/01926 187.2010.493119

Branscombe, N. R., Schmitt, M. T., & Schiffhauer, K. (2007). Racial attitudes in response to thoughts of White privilege. *European Journal of Social Psychology, 37,* 203–215. doi:10.1002/ejsp.348

Bratton, S. C., Ray, D., Rhine, T., & Jones, L. (2005). The efficacy of play therapy with children: A meta-analytic review of treatment outcomes. *Professional Psychology: Research and Practice, 36,* 376–390. doi:10.1037/0735-7028.36.4.376

Bright, J. E., & Pryor, R. G. (2011). The chaos theory of careers. *Journal of Employment Counseling, 48,* 163–166. doi:10.1002/j.2161-1920.2011.tb01104.x

Brigman, G., & Campbell, C. (2003). Helping students improve academic achievement and school success behavior. *Professional School Counseling, 7,* 91–98.

Brock, S. E. (2013). Preparing for the school crisis response. In Sandoval, J. (Ed.). *Crisis counseling, intervention and prevention in the schools* (3rd ed., pp. 19–30). New York, NY: Routledge.

Broderick, P. C., & Blewitt, P. (2014). *The life span: Human development for helping professionals* (4th ed.). Upper Saddle River, NJ: Pearson Education.

Brodwin, M. G., Boland, E. A., Lane, F. J., & Siu, F. W. (2012). Technology in rehabilitation counseling. In R. M. Parker & J. B. Patterson (Eds.), *Rehabilitation counseling: Basics & beyond* (pp. 333–367). Austin, TX: Pro-ed.

Brott, P. (2005). A constructivist look at life roles. *Career Development Quarterly, 54,* 138–149. doi:10.1002/j.2161-0045.2005.tb00146.x

Broverman, I., Broverman, D., Clarkson, F., Rosenkrantz, P., & Vogel, S. (1970). Sex role stereotypes and clinical judgments of mental health. *Journal of Consulting and Clinical Psychology, 34,* 1–7. doi:10.1037/h0028797

Brown, D. (2016). *Career information, career counseling, and career development* (11th ed.). Upper Saddle River, NJ: Pearson.

Brown, D., & Srebalus, D. J. (2003). *Introduction to the counseling profession* (3rd ed.). Boston, MA: Allyn & Bacon.

Bullock-Yowell, E. M. (2015). Using the self-directed search in practice. *Career Planning and Adult Development Journal* (Winter 2014–2015), 113–126.

Burck, A. M., Bruneau, L. B., Baker, L., & Ellison, L. (2014). Emerging counselors' perception of wellness: Implication for counselor development. *Counseling Outcome Research and Evaluation, 5,* 39–51. doi:10.1177/2150137813518554

Bureau of Labor Statistics. (2015). *Labor force statistics from current population survey.* Retrieved from http://www.bls.gov/web/empsit/cpsee_e16. htm

Burlingame, G. M., Fuhriman, A., & Mosier, J. (2003). The differential effectiveness of group psychotherapy: A meta-analytic perspective. *Group Dynamics: Theory, Research, and Practice, 7,* 3–12. doi:10.1037/1089-2699.7.1.3

Burrow-Sanchez, J. J. (2006). Understanding adolescent substance abuse: Prevalence, risk factors, and clinical implications. *Journal of Counseling & Development, 84,* 283–290.

Bynum, B. (2000). Discarded diagnosis. *Lancet, 356* (9241), 1615. doi:10.1016/S0140-6736(05)74468-8

Byrd, R., Crockett, S. A., & Erford, B. T. (2012a). *Journal for Specialists in Group Work* (JSGW) publication pattern review: A meta-study of author and article characteristics from 1981-2010. *Journal for Specialists in Group Work, 37,* 56–70. doi:10.108 0/01933922.2011.632812

Byrd, R., Crockett, S. A., & Erford, B. T. (2012b). A meta-study of *Journal of College Counseling* (JCC) author and article publication characteristics from 1998 to 2009. *Journal of College Counseling, 15,* 172–185. doi:10.1002/j.2161-1882.2012.00014.x

Byrne, A. M., & Hartley, M. T. (2010). Digital technology in the 21st century: Considerations for clinical supervision in rehabilitation education. *Rehabilitation Education, 24*(1–2), 57–68. doi:10.1891/088970110805029912

Campbell, C. A., & Brigman, G. (2005). Closing the achievement gap: A structured approach to group counseling. *Journal for Specialists in Group Work, 30,* 67–82. doi:10.1080/01933920590908705

Campbell, C. A., & Dahir, C. A. (1997). *Sharing the vision: The national standards for school counseling programs.* Alexandria, VA: American School Counselor Association.

Campbell, D. T., & Stanley, J. C. (1963). *Experimental and quasi-experimental designs for research*. Boston, MA: Houghton Mifflin.

Caplan, G. (1970). *The theory and practice of mental health consultation*. New York, NY: Basic Books.

Capuzzi, D., & Gross, D. (Eds.). (2013). *Introduction to the counseling profession* (6th ed.). Boston, MA: Allyn & Bacon.

Carey, J., & Dimmitt, C. (2012). School counselling and student outcomes: Summary of six statewide studies. *Professional School Counseling, 16,* 146–153.

Caria, M. P., Faggiano, F., Bellocco, R., & Galanti, M. R. (2011). Effects of a school-based prevention program on European adolescents' patterns of alcohol use. *Journal of Adolescent Health, 48,* 182–188.

Carlson, J., Geisenger, K. F., & Jonson, J. L. (Eds.). (2014). *The nineteenth mental measurements yearbook*. Lincoln: University of Nebraska Press.

Cartwright, B. Y., & Fleming, C. L. (2010). Multicultural and diversity considerations in the new code of professional ethics for rehabilitation counselors. *Journal of Applied Rehabilitation Counseling, 41*(2), 20–24. doi:10.1177/0034355210368564

Cashwell, C. A., & Giordano, A. L. (2018). Spirituality diversity. In D. G. Hays & B. T. Erford (Eds.), *Developing multicultural counseling competence: A systems approach* (3rd ed., pp. 320–344). Columbus, OH: Pearson.

Cass, V. (1979). Homosexual identity formation: Testing a theoretical model. *Journal of Homosexuality, 4,* 219–235. doi:10.1080/00224498409551214

Ceasar, P. T., & Miranti, J. G. (2005). Counseling and spirituality. In D. Capuzzi & D. Gross (Eds.), *Introduction to the counseling profession* (4th ed., pp. 240–255). Boston, MA: Pearson Allyn & Bacon.

Center for Substance Abuse Treatment. (2009). *Addressing suicidal thoughts and behaviors in substance abuse treatment. Treatment Improvement Protocol (TIP) Series 50. HHS Publication No. (SMA) 09-4381.* Rockville, MD: Substance Abuse and Mental Health Services Administration.

Centers for Disease Control and Prevention. (2014). Youth risk behavior surveillance: United States 2009. *Morbidity and Mortality Weekly Report, 2013, 63*(4), 1–172. Retrieved from http://www.cdc.gov/mmwr/pdf/ss/ss6304.pdf

Centers for Disease Control and Prevention. (2015a). *Child maltreatment prevention*. Retrieved from http://www.cdc.gov/violenceprevention/childmaltreatment/

Centers for Disease Control and Prevention. (2015b). *Intimate partner violence and surveillance*. Retrieved from http://www.cdc.gov/violenceprevention/pdf/intimatepartnerviolence.pdf

Centers for Disease Control and Prevention. (2017). *Suicide fact sheet*. Retrieved from http://www.cdc.gov/violenceprevention/pdf/suicide_factsheet-a.pdf

Centers for Disease Control and Prevention. (2018). *Coping with stress*. Retrieved from http://www.cdc.gov/violenceprevention/pub/coping_with_stress_tips.html

Chaney, M. P., & Brubaker, M. (2018). Sexual orientation and heterosexism. In D. G. Hays & B. T. Erford (Eds.), *Developing multicultural counseling competence: A systems approach* (3rd ed., pp. 113–141). Columbus, OH: Pearson Merrill.

Chen, J., Chen, T., Vertinsky, I., Yumagulov, L. & Park, C. (2013). Public-private partnerships for the development of disaster resilient communities. *Journal of Contingencies and Crisis Management, 21*(3), 130–143. doi:10.1111/1468-5973.12021

Chen-Hayes, S. F. (1997). Counseling, lesbian, bisexual, and gay persons in couple and family relationships: Overcoming the stereotypes. *Family Journal, 5,* 236–240. doi:10.1177/1066480797053008

Chester, A., & Bretherton, D. (2001). What makes feminist counselling feminist? *Feminism & Psychology, 11,* 527–545. doi:10.1177/0959353501011004006

Chhabra, R., Springer, C., Leu, C-S., Ghosh, S., Sharma, S. K., & Rapkin, B. (2010). Adaptation of an alcohol and HIV school-based prevention program for teens. *AIDS and Behavior, 14*(Suppl 1), S177–S184.

Chodorow, N. (1978). *The reproduction of mothering*. Berkeley, CA: University of California Press.

Christensen, E. (2013). Diagnosis and treatment planning. In D. Capuzzi, & D. R. Gross (Eds.), *Introduction to the counseling profession* (6th ed., pp. 313–336). New York, NY: Routledge.

Clark, M. A., & Breman, J. C. (2009). School counselor inclusion: A collaborative model to provide academic and social-emotional support in the classroom setting. *Journal of Counseling & Development, 87*(1), 6–11. doi:10.1002/j.1556-6678.2009.tb00543.x

Clark, R. E., Linville, D., & Rosen, K. H. (2009). A national survey of family physicians: Perspectives on collaboration with marriage and family therapists. *Journal of Marital and Family Therapy, 35,* 220–230. doi:10.1111/j.1752-0606.2009.00107.x

Clauss-Ehlers, C. S., & Parham, W. D. (2014, April). Landscape of diversity in higher education: Linking demographic shifts to contemporary university and college counseling center practices. *Journal of Multicultural Counseling and Development, 42,* 69–76. doi:10.1002/j.2161-1912.2014.00045.x

Clemens, E. (2007). Developmental counseling and therapy as a model for school counselor consultation with teachers. *Professional School Counselor, 10,* 352–359. doi:10.5330/prsc.10.4.t1420l0klu723434

Cochran, D. B., Wang, E. W., Stevenson, S. J., Johnson, L. E., & Crews, C. (2011). Adolescent occupational aspirations: Test of Gottfredson's theory of circumscription and compromise. *Career Development Quarterly, 59,* 412–427. doi:10.1002/j.2161-0045.2011.tb00968.x

Cochran, J. L., & Cochran, N. H. (2006). *The heart of counseling: A guide to developing therapeutic relationships.* Belmont, CA: Thomson Brooks/Cole.

Cohen, J. (1988). *Statistical power analysis for the behavioral sciences* (2nd ed.). Hillsdale, NJ: Erlbaum.

Cohen, R. (2004). *Clinical supervision: What to do and how to do it.* Belmont, CA: Brooks/Cole.

Colburn, A. A. N. (2013). Endless possibilities: Diversifying service options in private practice. *Journal of Mental Health Counseling, 35,* 198–210. doi:10.17744/mehc.35.3.8870230745378517

Cole, R., Hayes, B., Jones, D., & Shah, S. (2013). Coping strategies used by school staff after a crisis: A research note. *Journal of Loss and Trauma, 18,* 472–481. doi:10.1080/15325024.2012.719335

Commission on Rehabilitation Counselor Certification. (2010). *Code of professional ethics for rehabilitation counselors.* Retrieved from http://www.crccertification.com/filebin/pdf/CRCCodeOfEthics.pdf

Commission on Rehabilitation Counselor Certification. (2017). *Scope of practice for rehabilitation counseling.* Retrieved from http://www.crccertification.com/pages/crc_ccrc_scope_of_practice/43.php

Commission on Rehabilitation Counselor Certification. (2018). *About us.* Retrieved from http://www.crccertification.com

Congress.org. (2018). *Visiting Capitol Hill.* Retrieved from http://www.congress.org/advocacy-101/visiting-capitol-hill/

Connors, C. K. (2008). *Manual for the Conners 3.* North Tonawanda, NY: MHS.

Conwill, C. (2003). Consultation and collaboration: An action research model for the full-service school. *Consulting Psychology Journal: Practice and Research, 55,* 239–248. doi:10.1037/1061-4087.55.4.239

Corey, G. (2012). *Theory and practice of counseling and psychotherapy* (9th ed.). Belmont, CA: Wadsworth/Thomson Learning.

Corey, G., Corey, M., Corey, C., & Callanan, P. (2014). *Issues & ethics in the helping professions* (9th ed.). Pacific Grove, CA: Brooks/Cole.

Corey, M. S., & Corey, G. (2016). *Becoming a helper* (7th ed.). Boston, MA: Cengage.

Cottone, R. R., & Tarvydas, V. M. (2007). *Counseling ethics and decision making* (3rd ed.). Upper Saddle River, NJ: Pearson Education.

Council for Accreditation of Counseling and Related Educational Programs. (CACREP). (2015). *IRCEP vision, mission, and core values.* Retrieved from http://www.ircep.org/ircep/template/page.cfm?id=93

Council for Accreditation in Counseling and Related Educational Programs. (CACREP). (2016). *2016 CACREP standards.* Retrieved from http://www.cacrep.org/wp-content/uploads/2015/05/2016-CACREP-Standards.pdf

Counselors for Social Justice. (2017). *What is social justice in counselling?* Retrieved from http://www.counseling-csj.org/

Counselors for Social Justice. (2018). *About us.* Retrieved from http://counseling-csj.org

Crane, D. R., & McArthur, H. (2002). Meeting the needs of evidence-based practice in family therapy: Developing the scientist-practitioner model. *Journal of Family Therapy, 24,* 113–124. doi:10.1111/1467-6427.00206

Crethar, H. C., & Ratts, M. (2008, June). Why social justice is a counseling concern. *Counseling Today,* 24–25.

Crethar, H. C., & Winterowd, C. L. (2012). Values and social justice in counseling. *Counseling & Values, 57,* 3-9. doi:10.1002/j.2161-007X.2012.00001.x

Crockett, S. A., Byrd, R. J., & Erford, B. T. (2012). The *Journal of Mental Health Counseling* publication pattern review: A meta-study of author and article characteristics, 1994–2009. *Journal of Mental Health Counseling, 34,* 82–94. doi:10.17744/mehc.34.1.50l68v2635223144

Crockett, S. A., Byrd, R. J., & Erford, B. T. (2014). *Career Development Quarterly:* A 22-year publication pattern meta-study. *Career Development Quarterly, 62,* 327–339. doi:10.1002/j.2161-0045.2014.00086.x

Crockett, S. A., Byrd, R. J., Erford, B. T., & Hays, D. G. (2010). Golden Anniversary publication pattern review: Author and article characteristics from 1985–2009. *Counselor Education & Supervision, 50,* 5–20.

Crosby, A. E., Ortega, L., & Melanson, C. (2011). *Self-directed violence surveillance: Uniform definitions and recommended data elements version 1.0.* Atlanta, GA: Centers for Disease Control and Prevention, National Center for Injury Prevention and Control.

Cross, W. E., Jr. (1971). The Negro-to-Black conversion experience: Toward a psychology of Black liberation. *Black World, 20,* 13–27.

Crouch, T., & Walz, G. (1992). *CHDF-partner in professionalism.* ERIC Document (ED347471).

Cuijpers, P., van Straten, A., Andersson, G., & van Oppen, P. (2008). Psychotherapy for depression in adults: A meta-analysis of comparative outcome studies. *Journal of Consulting and Clinical Psychology, 76,* 909–922. doi:10.1037/a0013075

Cummings, J. A., Ballantyne, E. C., & Scallion, L. M. (2015). Essential processes for cognitive behavioral clinical supervision: Agenda setting, problem-solving, and formative feedback. *Psychotherapy, 52,* 158–163. doi:10.1037/a0038712

Curran, L. A. (2010). *Trauma competency: A clinician's guide.* Eau Claire, WI: PESI.

Curran, L. A. (2013). *101 Trauma-informed interventions.* Eau Claire, WI: PESI.

Cutts, L. (2011). Integration in counselling psychology: To what purpose? *Counselling Psychology Review, 26*(2), 38–48.

Daughhetee, C., Jackson, J., & Parker, L. (2018). Safety issues and concerns in crisis situations. In L. R. Jackson-Cherry & B. T. Erford (Eds.), *Crisis assessment, intervention and prevention* (3rd ed., pp. 27–36). Columbus, OH: Pearson Merrill.

Davis, T. E. (2015). *Exploring school counseling* (2nd ed.). Stamford CT: Cengage.

Derogatis, L. R. (1990). *SCL-90-R (Symptom Checklist-90-Revised).* Minneapolis, MN: NCS Pearson Assessments.

de Shazer, S. (1988). *Clues: Investigating solutions in brief therapy.* New York, NY: Norton.

de Shazer, S. (1991). *Putting difference to work.* New York, NY: Norton.

Despenser, S. (2007). Risk assessment: The personal safety of the counselor. *Therapy Today, 18*(2), 12–17.

DiCaccavo, A. (2002). Investigating individuals' motivations to become counselling psychologists:

The influence of early caretaking roles within the family. *Psychology and Psychotherapy: Theory, Research and Practice, 75,* 463–472. doi:10.1348/147608302321151943

Dik, B. J., Duffy, R. D., & Steger, M. F. (2012). Enhancing social justice by promoting prosocial values in career development interventions. *Counseling & Values, 57*(1), 31–37. doi:10.1002/j.2161-007X.2012.00005.x

Doering, C. (2009). Theological accountability: The hallmark of pastoral counseling. *Sacred Spaces: The e-Journal of the American Association of Pastoral Counselors, 1,* 4–34.

Dougherty, A. (2014). *Psychological consultation and collaboration in school and community settings* (6th ed.). Belmont, CA: Brooks/Cole.

Downing, N. E., & Roush, K. L. (1985). From passive-acceptance to active commitment: A model of feminist identity development for women. *Counseling Psychologist, 13,* 695–709.

Drapeau, C. W., & McIntosh, J. L. (for the American Association of Suicidology). (2015). *USA suicide 2013: Official final data.* Retrieved from http://www.floridasuicideprevention.org/PDF/2013%20US%20Suicide%20Official%20Final%20Data%20AAS.pdf

Dyregrov, A. & Regel, S. (2012). Early interventions following exposure to traumatic events: Implications for practice from recent research. *Journal of Loss and Trauma, 17,* 271–291. doi:10.1080/15325024.2011.616832

Edmondson, J. H., & White, J. (1998). A tutorial and counseling program: Helping students at risk of dropping out of school. *Professional School Counseling, 1,* 43–47.

Edwards, J. (2011, Spring). *Community College Task Force: Survey of community/2 year college counseling services.* Retrieved from http://www.collegecounseling.org/docs/ACCA-CCTF-SurveyFlyer.pdf

Egan, G. (2013). *The skilled helper: A problem-management and opportunity-development approach to helping* (10th ed.). Pacific Grove, CA: Brooks/Cole.

Eisel v. Board of Education, 597 A.2d 447 (Md. Ct. App. 1991).

Elkind, D. (2001).[0] *The hurried child: Growing up too fast too soon.* Jackson, TN: Perseus Publishing.

Ellis, M. V., Berger, L., Hanus, A. E., Ayala, E. E., Swords, B. A., & Siembor, M. (2014). Inadequate and harmful clinical supervision: Testing a framework and assessing occurrence. *Counseling*

Psychologist, 42, 434–472. doi:10.1177/0011000013508656

Erford, B. T. (1999). A modified time-out procedure for children with noncompliant or defiant behaviors. *Professional School Counseling, 2,* 205–210.

Erford, B. T. (Ed.). (2011). *Group work: Process and applications.* Columbus, OH: Pearson Merrill Prentice Hall.

Erford, B. T. (2013). *Assessment for counselors* (2nd ed.). Boston, MA: Cengage Learning.

Erford, B. T. (Ed.). (2015a). *Transforming the school counseling profession* (4th ed.). Columbus, OH: Pearson.

Erford, B. T. (2015b). *40 techniques every counselor should know.* Columbus, OH: Pearson.

Erford, B. T. (2015c). *Research and evaluation in counseling* (2nd ed.). Boston, MA: Cengage Learning.

Erford, B. T. (Ed.). (2016). *Groupwork in the schools* (2nd ed.). New York, NY: Routledge.

Erford, B. T. (Ed.). (2017). *The odyssey: An advanced life span adventure for counseling professionals.* Boston, MA: Cengage Learning.

Erford, B. (2018). Emergency preparedness and response in schools and universities. In L. R. Jackson-Cherry & B. T. Erford (Eds.), *Crisis assessment, intervention and prevention* (3rd ed., pp. 267–291). Columbus, OH: Pearson Merrill.

Erford, B. T., Bardhoshi, G., Ross, M., Gunther, C., & Duncan, K. (2016). Meta-analysis of counseling outcomes for youth with conduct disorders. *Journal of Counseling & Development, 94* (1), 13–30.

Erford, B. T., Clark, K. H., & Erford, B. M. (2011). *Adultspan* publication patterns: Author and article characteristics from 1999–2009. *Adultspan, 10,* 52–62. doi:10.1002/j.2161-0029.2011.tb00006.x

Erford, B. T., & Crockett, S. A. (2012). Annual review: Practice and research in career counseling and development–2011. *Career Development Quarterly, 60,* 290–332. doi:10.1002/j.2161-0045.2012.00024.x

Erford, B. T., Crockett, S., Giguere, M., & Darrow, J. (2011). A meta-study of *Journal of Employment Counseling* publication patterns from 1994 through 2009. *Journal of Employment Counseling, 48,* 81–92. doi:10.1002/j.2161-1920.2011.tb00117.x

Erford, B. T., Erford, B. M., & Broglie, C. (2012). *Journal of Humanistic Counseling, Education and Development* (JHCEAD) publication patterns from 1994–2009. *Journal of Humanistic Counseling, Education and Development, 51,* 21–32. doi:10.1002/j.2161-1939.2012.00003.x

Erford, B. T., Erford, B. M., Broglie, C., & Erford, M. R. (2013). *Counseling & Values* (C&V) publication patterns from 1990–2009. *Counseling & Values, 58*(1).

Erford, B. T., Erford, B. M., Lattanzi, G., Weller, J., Schein, H., Wolf, E., Hughes, M., Darrow, J., Savin-Murphy, J., & Peacock, E. R. (2011). Counseling outcomes for school-aged youth with depression from 1990–2008: A meta-analysis. *Journal of Counseling & Development, 89,* 439–458. doi:10.1002/j.1556-6676.2011.tb02841.x

Erford, B. T., Gugiere, M., Glenn, K., & Schein, H. (2015). *Professional School Counseling* (PSC) publication pattern review: A meta-study of author and article characteristics from the first 15 years. *Professional School Counseling, 18,* 61–70.

Erford, B. T., Gunther, C., Duncan, K., Bardhoshi, G., Dummett, B., Kraft, J., Deferio, K., Falco, M., & Ross, M. (2016). Meta-analysis of counseling outcomes for the treatment of PTSD. *Journal of Counseling & Development, 94*(1), 13–30. doi:10.1002/jcad.12058

Erford, B. T., Kress, V. E., Giguere, M., Cieri, D., & Erford, B. M. (2015). Meta-analysis: Counseling outcomes for youth with anxiety disorders. *Journal of Mental Health Counseling, 37*(1), 63–94. doi:10.17744/mehc.37.1.mgj66326868u33g2

Erford, B. T., Miller, E. M., Duncan, K., & Erford, B. M. (2010). Submission patterns: *Measurement and Evaluation in Counseling and Development* author and article characteristics from 1990–2009. *Measurement and Evaluation in Counseling and Development, 42,* 296–307. doi:10.1177/0748175609354619

Erford, B. T., Miller, E. M., Schein, H., McDonald, A., Ludwig, L., & Leishear, K. (2011). *Journal of Counseling & Development* publication patterns: Author and article characteristics from 1994–2009. *Journal of Counseling & Development, 89,* 73–80. doi:10.1177/0748175609354619

Erford, B. T., Paul, L. E., Oncken, C., Kress, V. E., & Erford, M. R. (2014). Counseling outcomes for youth with oppositional behavior: A meta-analysis. *Journal of Counseling & Development, 92,* 13–24. doi:10.1002/j.1556-6676.2014.00125.x

Erford, B. T., Richards, T., Peacock, E. R., Voith, K., McGair, H., Muller, B., Duncan, K., & Chang, C. Y. (2013). Counseling and guided self-help outcomes for clients with bulimia nervosa: A meta-analysis of clinical trials from 1980–2010. *Journal of Counseling & Development, 91,* 152–172. doi:10.1002/j.1556-6676.2013.00083.x

Erickson, W., Lee, C., & von Schrader, S. (2012). *2011 disability status report: United States.* Ithaca, NY: Cornell University Employment and Disability Institute (EDI).

Eriksen, K. P. (1997). *Making an impact: A handbook for counselor advocacy.* Muncie, IN: Accelerated Development.

Eriksen, K. (1999). Counselor advocacy: A qualitative analysis of leaders' perceptions, organizational activities, and advocacy documents. *Journal of Mental Health Counseling, 21,* 33–49.

Erikson, E. (1950). *Childhood and society.* New York, NY: Norton.

Evans, D. R., Hearn, M. T., Uhlemann, M. R., & Ivey, A. E. (2011). *Essential interviewing: A programmed approach to effective communication* (8th ed.). Belmont, CA: Cengage.

Evans, J. H., & Burck, H. D. (1992). The effects of career education interventions on academic achievement: A meta-analysis. *Journal of Counseling & Development, 71,* 63–68. doi:10.1002/j.1556-6676.1992.tb02173.x

Ewing, D. L., Monsen, J. J., Thompson, E. J., Cartwright-Hatton, S., & Field, A. (2015). A meta-analysis of transdiagnostic cognitive behavioural therapy in the treatment of child and young person anxiety disorders. *Behavioural & Cognitive Psychotherapy, 43,* 562–577. doi:10.1017/S1352465813001094

Exner, J. E., Jr. (2003). *The Rorschach: A comprehensive system* (4th ed.). New York, NY: Wiley.

Eysenck, H. J. (1952). The effects of psychotherapy: An evaluation. *Journal of Consulting Psychology, 16,* 319–324. doi:10.1037/h0063633

Family Educational Rights and Privacy Act. (2008). *Family Educational Rights and Privacy Act; Final Rule.* Retrieved from http://www.ed.gov/legislation/FedRegister/finrule/2008-4/120908a.pdf

Feldman, R. S. (2014). *Development across the lifespan* (7th ed.). Upper Saddle River, NJ: Pearson.

Feldman, S. (2013, November 8). *Re: Insurance companies must now cover mental health benefits at parity with medical benefits.* Retrieved from http:www.whitehouse.gov/blog/2013/11/08/ensuring-access-mental-health-services

Figley, C. R., & McCubbin, H. I. (1983). *Stress and the family volume II: Coping with catastrophe.* Levittown, PA: Brunner/Mazel.

Fitzpatrick, J. L., Sanders, J. R., & Worthen, B. B. (2011). *Program evaluation: Alternative approaches and practical guidelines* (4th ed.). Boston, MA: Allyn & Bacon.

Foltran, F., Gregori, D., Franchin, L., Verduci, E., & Giovannini, M. (2011). Effect of alcohol consumption in prenatal life, childhood, and adolescence on child development. *Nutritional Reviews, 69,* 642–659. doi:10.1111/j.1753-4887.2011.00417.x

Forester-Miller, H., & Davis, T. (1996). *A practitioner's guide to ethical decision making.* Retrieved from http://www.counseling.org/docs/default-source/ethics/practioner's-guide-to-ethical-decision-making.pdf?sfvrsn=0

Foster, L. H. (2005). Assessment practices in counseling. In D. Capuzzi, & D. R. Gross (Eds.), *Introduction to the counseling profession* (6th ed., pp. 291–312). New York, NY: Routledge.

Frankel, Z. F., & Levitt, H. M. (2008). Clients' experiences of disengaged moments in psychotherapy: A grounded theory analysis. *Journal of Contemporary Psychotherapy, 39,* 171–186. doi:10.1007/s10879-008-9087-z

Frankl, V. (2006). *Man's search for meaning.* Boston, MA: Beacon.

Franko, D., Becker, A., Thomas, J., & Herzog, D. (2007). Cross ethnic differences in eating disorder symptoms and related distress. *International Journal of Eating Disorders, 40,* 156–164. doi:10.1002/eat.20341

Fredheim, T., Danbolt, L. J., Haavet, O. R., Kjonsberg, K., & Lien, L. (2011). Collaboration between general practitioners and mental health care professionals: A qualitative study. *International Journal of Mental Health Systems, 5,* 1–7. doi:10.1186/1752-4458-5-13

Friedlander, M. L., Lambert, J. E., & de la Peña, C. M. (2008). A step toward disentangling the alliance/improvement cycle in family therapy. *Journal of Counseling Psychology, 55*(1), 118. doi:10.1037/0022-0167.55.1.118

Fry, R., & Kochhar, R. (2014). *America's wealth gap between middle-income and upper-income families is widest on record.* Retrieved from http://www.pewresearch.org/fact-tank/2014/12/17/wealth-gap-upper-middle-income/

Fuhriman, A., & Burlingame, G. M. (1994). Group psychotherapy: Research and practice. In A. Fuhriman & G. M. Burlingame (Eds.), *Handbook of group psychotherapy* (pp. 3–40). New York, NY: Wiley.

Gallagher, R. P. (2014). *National survey of counseling center directors.* Alexandra, VA: International Association of Counseling Services.

Gallessich, J. (1982). *The profession and practice of consultation.* San Francisco, CA: Jossey-Bass.

Garber, J., Kelley, M. K., & Martin, N. C. (2002). Developmental trajectories of adolescents' depressive symptoms: Predictors of change. *Journal of Consulting and Clinical Psychology, 70,* 79–95. doi:10.1037/0022-006X.70.1.79

Garfield, S. L. (1994). Research on client variables in psychotherapy. In A. E. Bergin & S. L. Garfield (Eds.), *Handbook of psychotherapy and behavior change* (3rd ed., pp. 190–228). New York, NY: Wiley.

Garner, N. E., Baker, J., & Valle, J. P. (2014). The practice of career counseling through a solution-focused lens. In G. Eliason, T. Eliason, J. Samide, & J. Patrick (Eds.), *Career development across the lifespan: Counseling for community, schools, higher education, and beyond* (pp. 313–347). Charlotte, NC: Information Age Publishing.

Garrett, M. T., Garrett, J. T., Portman, T. A. A., Grayshield, L., Rivera, E. T., Williams, C., ... Kawulich, B. (2018). Counseling Native Americans. In D. G. Hays & B. T. Erford (Eds.), *Developing multicultural counseling competence: A systems approach* (3rd ed.) (pp. 301–332). Columbus, OH: Pearson.

Gaubatz, M. D., & Vera, E. M. (2002). Do formalized gatekeeping procedures increase programs' follow-up with deficient trainees? *Counselor Education & Supervision, 41,* 294–306. doi:10.1002/j.1556-6978.2002.tb01292.x

Gerber, S., & Terry-Day, B. (1999). Does peer mediation really work? *Professional School Counseling, 2,* 169–171.

Gibbons, M. M., & Borders, L. D. (2010). Prospective first-generation college students: A social cognitive perspective. *Career Development Quarterly, 58,* 194–208. doi:10.1002/j.2161-0045.2010.tb00186.x

Gielen, U. P., & Roopnarine, J. (2004). *Childhood and adolescence: Cross-cultural perspectives and applications.* London, UK: Praeger.

Gilbert, L. A. (2010). *Gender and sex in counseling and psychotherapy.* Eugene, OR: Wipf & Stock Publishers.

Gilchrist, L. A., & Stringer, M. (1992). Marketing counseling: Guidelines for training and practice. *Counselor Education & Supervision, 31,* 154–162. doi:10.1002/j.1556-6978.1992.tb00156.x

Gilligan, C. (1993). *In a different voice.* Cambridge, MA: Harvard University Press.

Ginevra, M. C., Nota, L., & Ferrari, L. (2015). Parental support in adolescents' career development: Parents' and children's perceptions. *Career Development Quarterly, 63,* 2–15. doi:10.1002/j.2161-0045.2015.00091.x

Gingerich, W. J., & Eisengart, S. (2000). Solution focused brief therapy: A review of the outcome research. *Family Process, 39,* 477–498. doi:10.1111/j.1545-5300.2000.39408.x

Gladding, S. T. (1996). Bandits: A lesson in identity and direction. *Counselor Education & Supervision, 36,* 99–104. doi:10.1002/j.1556-6978.1996.tb00375.x

Gladding, S. (2013). *The counseling dictionary: Concise definitions of frequently used terms* (3rd ed.). Upper Saddle River, NJ: Pearson Education.

Gladding, S. T. (2016). *Counseling: A comprehensive profession* (8th ed.). Upper Saddle River, NJ: Pearson.

Glasser, W. (2000). *Counseling with choice theory.* New York, NY: HarperCollins.

Glosoff, H. L., & Schwarz-Whittaker, J. E. (2013). The counseling profession: Historical perspectives and current issues and trends. In D. Capuzzi & D. R. Gross (Eds.), *Introduction to the counseling profession* (6th ed.). New York, NY: Routledge.

Gonzalez, L. M. (2012). College-level choice of Latino high school students: A social-cognitive approach. *Journal of Multicultural Counseling & Development, 40,* 144–155. doi:10.1002/j.2161-1912.2012.00014.x

Goodyear, R. K. (2014). Supervision as pedagogy: Attending to its essential instructional and learning process. *Clinical Supervisor, 33,* 82–99. doi:10.1080/07325223.2014.918914

Gottfredson, L. (1981). Circumscription and compromise: A developmental theory of occupational aspirations. *Journal of Counseling Psychology, 2,* 545–579. doi:10.1037/0022-0167.28.6.545

Gottfredson, L. (2002). Gottfredson's theory of circumscription and compromise. In A. D. Brown (Ed.), *Career choice and development* (4th ed., pp. 85–148). San Francisco, CA: Jossey-Bass.

Green, B. L., Everhart, M., Gordon, L., & Gettman, M. G. (2006). Characteristics of effective mental health consultation in early childhood settings: Multilevel analysis of a national survey. *Topics in Early Childhood Special Education, 26*(3), 142–152. doi:10.1177/02711214060260030201

Greenberg, L. S., & Pascual-Leone, A. (2006). Emotion in psychotherapy: A practice friendly review. *Journal of Clinical Psychology: In Session, 62,* 611–630. doi:10.1002/jclp.20252

Griffith, B. A., & Griggs, J. C. (2001). Religious identity status as a model to understand, assess, and interact with client spirituality. *Counseling and Values, 46,* 14–25. doi:10.1002/j.2161-007X.2001.tb00203.x

Guillot-Miller, L., & Partin, P. W. (2003). Web-based resources for legal and ethical issues in school counseling. *Professional School Counseling, 7,* 52–60.

Guttmacher Institute. (2015). *An overview of minor's consent law.* Retrieved from http://www.guttmacher.org/statecenter/spibs/spib_OMCL.pdf

Gwandure, C. (2008). Disability, locus of control and HIV and AIDS prevention and control. *International Journal of Disability, Community and Rehabilitation, 7*(1). Retrieved from http://www.ijdcr.ca/VOL07_01_CAN/articles/gwandure.shtml

Gysbers, N. C., & Henderson, P. (2012). *Developing and managing your school counseling program* (5th ed.). Alexandria, VA: American Counseling Association.

Hackney, H., & Cormier, S. (2012). *The professional counselor: A process guide to helping* (7th ed.). Upper Saddle River, NJ: Pearson.

Halbur, D. A., & Halbur, K. V. (2014). *Developing your theoretical orientation in counseling and psychotherapy* (3rd ed.). Boston, MA: Pearson.

Hall, B. W., & Bacon, T. P. (2005). Building a foundation against violence: Impact of a school-based prevention program on elementary students. *Journal of School Violence, 4,* 63–83. doi:10.1300/J202v04n04_05

Hambrick, E., Rubens, S. L., Vernberg, E. M., Jacobs, A. K., & Kanine, R. M. (2014). Towards successful dissemination of psychological first aid: A study of provider training preferences. *Journal of Behavioral Health Services & Research, 41,* 203–215.

Hansen, J. C., Stevic, R. R., & Warner, R. W. (1986). *Counseling: Theory and process* (4th ed.). Boston, MA: Allyn & Bacon.

Hansen, J. T. (2006a). Counseling theories within a postmodern epistemology: New roles for theories in counseling practice. *Journal of Counseling & Development, 84,* 291–297. doi:10.1002/j.1556-6678.2006.tb00408.x

Hansen, J. T. (2006b). Humanism as moral imperative: Comments on the role of knowing in the helping encounter. *Journal of Humanistic Counseling, Education, and Development, 45,* 115–125. doi:10.1002/j.2161-1939.2006.tb00011.x

Hardiman, R. (1982). *White identity development: A process-oriented model for describing the racial consciousness of white Americans.* Doctoral dissertation, University of Massachusetts.

Haring-Hidore, M., & Vacc, N. A. (1988). The scientist-practitioner model in training entry-level counselors. *Journal of Counseling & Development, 66,* 286–288. doi:10.1002/j.1556-6676.1988.tb00870.x

Harrington, J. A. (2013a). *Understanding suicide prevention.* Alexandria, VA: American Mental Health Counselors Association.

Harrington, J. A. (2013b). Contemporary issues in private practice: Spotlight on the self-employed mental health counselor. *Journal of Mental Health Counseling, 35,* 189–197. doi:10.17744/mehc.35.3.8742717176154187

Harrington, J. A., & Daughhetee, C. (2018). Suicide and homicide. In L. R. Jackson-Cherry & B. T. Erford (Eds.), *Crisis assessment, intervention and prevention* (3rd ed., pp. 135–159). Columbus, OH: Pearson Merrill.

Harris, J. R. (1995). Where is the child's environment? A group socialization theory of development. *Psychological Review, 102,* 458–489. doi:10.1177/0010002030004008

Harris-Bowlsbey, J. (2013). Computer-assisted career guidance systems: A part of NCDA history. *Career Development Quarterly, 61,* 181–185. doi:10.1002/j.2161-0045.2013.00047.x

Hasin, D., Hatzenbuehler, M. L., Keyes, K., & Ogburn, E. (2006). Substance use disorders: *Diagnostic and Statistical Manual of Mental Disorders*, fourth edition (*DSM-IV*) and *International Classification of Diseases*, tenth edition (ICD-10). *Addiction Supplement, 101,* 59–75. doi:10.1111/j.1360-0443.2006.01584.x

Hawley, L., & Calley, N. (2009). Professional identity of counseling. *Michigan Journal of Counseling: Research, Theory, and Practice, 36*(1), 1–12.

Hays, D. G., & Erford, B. T. (Eds.). (2018). *Developing multicultural competence: A system's approach* (3rd ed.). Columbus, OH: Pearson.

Hays, D. G., Wood, C., & Smith, J. E. (2012). Advocacy and leadership through research best practices. In C. Y. Chang, C. A. Barrio Minton, A. L. Dixon, J. E. Myers, & T. J. Sweeney (Eds.), *Professional counseling excellence through leadership and advocacy* (pp. 227–242). New York, NY: Routledge.

Health Services Administrators. (2012). *Brief 145.* Moravia, NY: Chronicle Guidance Publications, Inc.

Heller, S. S., Boothe, A., Keyes, A., Nagle, G., Sidell, M., & Rice, J. (2011). Implementation of a mental health consultation model and its impact on early childhood teachers' efficiency and competence. *Infant Mental Health Journal, 32,* 143–164. doi:10.1002/imhj.20289

Helms, J. E. (1995). An update of Helms' white and people of color racial identity. In J. G. Ponterotto, J. M. Casas, & C. M. Alexander (Eds.), *Handbook of multicultural counseling* (pp. 181–198). Thousand Oaks, CA: Sage.

Hennessey, M. L., & Koch, L. (2007). Universal design for instruction in rehabilitation counselor education. *Rehabilitation Education, 21,* 187–194.

Henry, W. P., Strupp, H. H., Butler, S. F., Schacht, T. E., & Binder, J. L. (1993). The effects of training in time-limited dynamic psychotherapy: Changes in therapist behavior. *Journal of Consulting and Clinical Psychology, 61,* 434–440. doi:10.1037/0022-006X.61.3.434

Heppner, P. P., Kivlighan, Jr., D. M., Wright, G. E., Pledge, D. S., Brossart, D. F., Bellatin, A. M., … Krull, L. A. (1995). Teaching the history of counseling: Training the next generation. *Journal of Counseling & Development, 73,* 337–341. doi:10.1002/j.1556-6676.1995.tb01760.x

Herlihy, B., & Corey, G. (2015). *ACA ethical standards casebook* (7th ed.). Alexandria, VA: American Counseling Association.

Hershenson, D. B., Power, P. W., & Waldo, M. (2003). *Community counseling: Contemporary theory and practice.* Long Grove, IL: Waveland Press.

Hill, C., & Kearl, H. (2011). *Crossing the line: Sexual harassment at school.* Washington, DC: American Association of University Women.

Hill, N. R. (2007). Wilderness therapy as a treatment modality for at-risk youth: A primer for mental health counselors. *Journal of Mental Health Counseling, 29,* 338–349. doi:10.17744/mehc.29.4.c6121j162j143178

Hoag, M. J., & Burlingame, G. M. (1997). Evaluating the effectiveness of child and adolescent group treatment: A meta-analytic review. *Journal of Clinical Child Psychology, 26,* 234–246. doi:10.1207/s15374424jccp2603_2

Hodges, S. (2001). University counseling centers at the twenty-first century: Looking forward, looking back. *Journal of College Counseling, 4,* 161–174.

Hof, D. D., Dinsmore, J. D., Barber, S., Suhr, R., & Scofield, T. R. (2009). Advocacy: The TRAINER model. *Journal of Social Action in Counseling and Psychology, 2*(1), 15–28.

Hofelich, A. J., & Preston, S. D. (2012). The meaning in empathy: Distinguishing conceptual encoding from facial mimicry, trait empathy, and attention to emotion. *Cognition & Emotion, 26*(1), 119–128. doi:10.1080/02699931.2011.559192

Hoffman, R. M. (2001). The measurement of masculinity and femininity: Historical perspectives and implications for counseling. *Journal of Counseling & Development, 79,* 472–485. doi:10.1002/j.1556-6676.2001.tb01995.x

Hoffman, T. D. (2013). Project HOPE: A career education program for rural middle school students. PhD thesis. University of Iowa.

Holcomb-McCoy, C., & Bryan, J. (2010). Advocacy and empowerment in parent consultation: Implications for theory and practice. *Journal of Counseling & Development, 88,* 259–268. doi:10.1002/j.1556-6678.2010.tb00021.x

Holland, J. L. (1959). A theory of vocational choice. *Journal of Counseling Psychology, 6,* 35–45. doi:10.1037/h0040767

Holland, J. L., & Messer, M. A. (2013). *The Self-Directed Search professional manual.* Lutz, FL: Psychological Assessment Resources.

Horvath, A., Del Re, A. C., Fluckiger, C., & Symonds, D. (2011). Alliance in individual psychotherapy. *Psychotherapy, 48,* 9–16. doi:10.1037/a0022186

Howard, K. I., Kopta, S. M., Krause, M. S., & Orlinsky, D. E. (1986). The dose-effect relationship in psychotherapy. *American Psychologist, 41,* 159–164. doi:10.1037/0003-066X.41.2.159

Hudson, J. I., Hiripi, E., Pope, H. G., & Kessler, R. C. (2007). The prevalence and correlates of eating disorders in the National Comorbidity Survey Replication. *Biological Psychiatry, 61,* 348–358. doi:10.1016/j.biopsych.2006.03.040

Humane Society of the United States. (2011). *Animal cruelty and human violence.* Retrieved from http://www.humanesociety.org/issues/abuse_neglect/qa/cruelty_violence_connection_faq.html

Hummel, T. J., & Lichtenberg, J. W. (2001). *Predicting categories of improvement among counseling center clients.* Retrieved from http://eric.ed.gov/?id=ED451434

Hunt, H. T. (2012). A collective unconscious reconsidered: Jung's archetypal imagination in the light of contemporary psychology and social science. *Journal of Analytical Psychology, 57*(1), 76–98. doi:10.1111/j.1468-5922.2011.01952.x

Individuals with Disabilities Education Improvement Act. (2004). *IDEA 2004 Resources.* Retrieved from http://www.ed.gov/policy/speced/guid/idea/idea2004.html

International Association of Addictions and Offender Counselors. (IAAOC). (2018). *Home.* Retrieved from http://www.iaaoc.org/

International Association of Marriage and Family Counselors. (IAMFC). (2018). *Home.* Retrieved from http://www.iamfconline.org/

Ito, K. L., & Maramba, G. G. (2002). Therapeutic beliefs of Asian American therapists: Views from an ethnic-specific clinic. *Transcultural Psychiatry, 39*(1), 33–73. doi:10.1177/136346150203900102

Ivers, N. N., Milsom, A., & Newsome, D. W. (2012). Using Gottfredson's theory of circumscription and compromise to improve Latino students' school success. *Career Development Quarterly, 60,* 231–242. doi:10.1002/j.2161-0045.2012.00019.x

Ivey, A. E., Ivey, M. B., & Zalaquett, C. P. (2013). *Intentional interviewing and counseling: Facilitating client development in a multicultural society* (8th ed.). Belmont, CA: Brooks/Cole.

Jackson-Cherry, L. R., & Erford, B. T. (Eds.), *Crisis assessment, intervention and prevention* (3rd ed., pp. 245–265). Columbus, OH: Pearson Merrill.

James, R. K., & Gilliland, B. E. (2012). *Crisis intervention strategies* (7th ed.). Boston, MA: Cengage Learning.

James, S., & Mennen, F. (2001). Treatment outcome research: How effective are treatments for abused children? *Child and Adolescent Social Work Journal, 18*(2), 73–95.

Jobes, D. A. (2006). *Managing suicidal risk: A collaborative approach.* New York, NY: Guilford Press.

Jourard, S. M. (1971). *The transparent self.* New York, NY: Van Nostrand Reinhold.

Juhnke, G. A., Granello, P. F., & Lebrón-Striker, M.A. (2007). *IS PATH WARM? A suicide assessment mnemonic for counselors (ACAPCD-03).* Alexandria, VA: American Counseling Association.

Kaplan, D. M., & Gladding, S. T. (2011). A vision for the future of counseling: The 20/20 principles for unifying and strengthening the profession. *Journal of Counseling & Development, 89,* 367–372.

Kaplan, D. M., Tarvydas, V. M., & Gladding, S. T. (2014). 20/20: A vision for the future of counseling: The new consensus definition of counseling. *Journal of Counseling & Development, 92,* 366–372. doi:10.1002/j.1556-6676.2014.00164.x

Karver, M. S., Handelsman, J. B., Fields, S., & Bickman, L. (2006). Meta-analysis of therapeutic relationship variables in youth and family therapy: The evidence for different relationship variables in the child and adolescent treatment outcome literature. *Clinical Psychology Review, 26,* 50–65. doi:10.1016/j.cpr.2005.09.001

Kazdin, A. E., Bass, D., Ayers, W. A., & Rodgers, A. (1990). Empirical and clinical focus of child and adolescent psychotherapy research. *Journal of Consulting and Clinical Psychology, 58,* 729–740. doi:10.1037/0022-006X.58.6.729

Keene, M., & Erford, B. T. (2007). *Group activities: Firing up for performance.* Columbus, OH: Pearson Merrill Prentice Hall.

Keeping Children and Families Safe Act. (2003). 42 U.S.C.S. §5101.

Kelly, G. A. (2013). *A theory of personality: The psychology of personal constructs.* New York, NY: Norton.

Kleespies, P. M. (Ed.). (2000). *Emergencies in mental health practice: Evaluation and management.* Washington, DC: American Psychological Association.

Kleespies, P. M. (Ed.). (2009). *Behavioral emergencies: An evidence-based resource for evaluating and managing risk of suicide, violence, and victimization.* Washington, DC: American Psychological Association.

Kleespies, P. M. (2014). *Decision making in behavioral emergencies.* Washington, DC: American Psychological Association.

Klott, J., & Jongsma, A. E. (2015). *The suicide and homicide risk assessment and prevention treatment planner, with DSM-5 updates.* Hoboken, NJ: Wiley.

Knowles, E. D., & Lowery, B. S. (2012). Meritocracy, self-concerns, and Whites' denial of racial inequity. *Self & Identity, 11,* 202–222. doi:10.1080/15298868.2010.542015

Kohl, H., Saunders, B., & Blumenthal, R. (2012). Elder abuse: What is the federal role? Retrieved from http://www.asaging.org/blog/elder-abuse-what-federal-role%20

Kolodinsky, P., Lindsey, C. Young, M., Lund, N., Edgerly, B., & Zlatev, M. (2011). An analysis of supervision modalities utilized in CACREP on-campus clinical training. *Professional Issues in Counseling,* Spring, 2011. Retrieved from http://www.shsu.edu/~piic/AnAnalysisofSupervisionModalitiesUtilizedinCACREPOnCam pusClinicalTraining.htm

Kosciw, J. G., Greytak, E. A., Palmer, N. E., & Boesen, M. J. (2014). *The 2013 national school climate survey: The experiences of lesbian, gay, bisexual and transgender youth in our nation's schools*. New York, NY: GLSEN.

Kottler, J. A. (2010). *On being a therapist* (4th ed.). San Francisco, CA: Jossey Bass.

Krumboltz, J. D., Mitchell, A. M., & Jones, G. B. (1976). A social learning theory of career selection. *Counseling Psychologist, 6*(1), 71–81. doi:10.1177/001100007600600117

Ladany, L., & Bradley, L. J. (2011). *Counselor supervision* (4th ed.). Philadelphia, PA: Brunner-Routledge.

Lambert, M. J. (1991). Introduction to psychotherapy research. In L. F. Beutler & M. Crago (Eds.), *Psychotherapy research: An international review of programmatic studies* (pp. 1–23). Washington, DC: American Psychological Association.

Lambert, M. J., (2013). The effectiveness of psychotherapy. In M. J. Lambert (Ed), *Bergin and Garfield's handbook of psychotherapy and behavior change* (6th ed., pp. 169–218). New York, NY: Wiley.

Lambert, M. J., Masters, K. S., & Ogles, B. M. (1991). Outcome research in counseling. In C. E. Watkins & L. J. Schneider (Eds.), *Research in counseling* (pp. 51–83). Hillsdale, NJ: Erlbaum.

Lassiter, P. S., & Chang, C. Y. (2006). Perceived multicultural competency of certified substance abuse counselors. *Journal of Addictions and Offender Counseling, 26*, 73–83. doi:10.1002/j.2161-1874.2006.tb00009.x

Laudet, A. B. (2008). The road to recovery: Where are we going and how do we get there? Empirically driven conclusions and future directions for service development and research. *Substance Use and Misuse, 43*, 2001–2020. doi:10.1080/10826080802293459

Lawson, G. (2007). Counselor wellness and impairment: A national survey. *Journal of Humanistic Counseling, Education and Development, 46*(1), 20–34. doi:10.1002/j.2161-1939.2007.tb00023.x

Lazarus, A. A., & Beutler, L. E. (1993). On technical eclecticism. *Journal of Counseling & Development, 71*, 381–385. doi:10.1002/j.1556-6676.1993.tb02652.x

Leahy, R. L. (2012). *Overcoming resistance in cognitive therapy*. New York, NY: Guilford Press.

LeBlanc, M., & Ritchie, M. (2001). A meta-analysis of play therapy outcomes. *Counseling Psychology Quarterly, 14*, 149–163. doi:10.1080/09515070110059142

Lee, C. C., & Rodgers, R. A. (2009). Counselor advocacy: Affecting systemic change in the public arena. *Journal of Counseling & Development, 87*, 284–287. doi:10.1002/j.1556-6678.2009.tb00108.x

Lee, D., Olson, E. A., Locke, B., Michelson, S. T., & Odes, E. (2009, May/June). The effects of college counseling services on academic performance and retention. *Journal of College Student Development, 50*, 305–319. doi:10.1353/csd.0.0071

Lee, F., & Bednar, R. L. (1977). Effects of group structure and risk taking disposition on group behavior, attitudes, and atmosphere. *Journal of Counseling Psychology, 24*, 191–199. doi:10.1037/0022-0167.24.3.191

Lee, G. K., & Matteliano, M. A. (2009). *A guide to cultural competence in the curriculum: Rehabilitation counseling*. Buffalo, NY: Center for International Rehabilitation Research Information and Exchange.

Lee, J. B., & Bartlett, M. L. (2005). Suicide prevention: Critical elements for managing suicidal clients and counselor liability without the use of a no-suicide contract. *Death Studies, 29*, 847–865. doi:10.1080/07481180500236776

Lemberger, M. E., Wachter Morris, C. A., Clemens, E. V., & Smith, A. (2010). A qualitative investigation of the referral process from school counselors to mental health providers. *Journal of School Counseling, 8*(32). Retrieved from http://jsc.montana.edu/articles/v8n32.pdf

Lent, J., & Schwartz, R. C. (2012). The impact of work setting, demographic characteristics, and personality factors related to burnout among professional counselors. *Journal of Mental Health Counseling, 34*, 355–372. doi:10.17744/mehc.34.4.c3k8u2k552515166

Lent, R. W., & Brown, S. D. (1996). Social cognitive approach to career development: An overview. *Career Development Quarterly, 44*, 310–321.

Lent, R. W., Brown, S. D., & Hackett, G. (1994). Toward a unifying social cognitive theory of career and academic interest, choice, and performance. *Journal of Vocational Behavior, 45*, 79–122. doi:10.1006/jvbe.1994.1027

Lenz, A. S., & Hollenbaugh, K. M. (2015). Meta-analysis of trauma-focused cognitive behavioral therapy for treating PTSD and co-occurring depression among children and adolescents. *Counseling Outcome Research and Evaluation, 6*, 18–32. doi:10.1177/2150137815573790

Lewis, M., Haviland-Jones, J. M., & Barrett, L. F. (Eds.). (2010). *Handbook of emotions* (3rd ed.). New York, NY: Guilford.

Lewis, M. W., & Lewis, A. C. (1996). Peer helping programs: Helper role, supervisor training, and suicidal behavior. *Journal of Counseling and Development, 74,* 307–313.

Linde, L. E. (2015). Ethical, legal and professional issues in school counseling. In B. T. Erford (Ed.), *Transforming the school counseling profession* (4th ed., pp. 70–89). Columbus, OH: Pearson.

Lipp, A. (2011). Universal school-based prevention programmes for alcohol misuse in young people. *International Journal of Evidence-Based Healthcare, 9,* 452–453. doi:10.1111/j.1744-1609.2011.00244.x

Lipsey, M. W., & Wilson, D. B. (2001). *Practical meta-analysis.* Thousand Oaks, CA: Sage.

Littrell, J. M., Malia, J. A., & Vanderwood, M. (1995). Single-session brief counseling in a high school. *Journal of Counseling & Development, 73,* 451–458. doi:10.1002/j.1556-6676.1995.tb01779.x

Livneh, H., & Bishop, M. L. (2012). The psychosocial impact of chronic illness and disability. In R. M. Parker & J. B. Patterson (Eds.), *Rehabilitation counseling: Basics & beyond.* (pp. 167–197). Austin, TX: Pro-ed.

Livneh, H., & Parker, R. M. (2005). Psychological adaptation to disability: Perspective from chaos and complexity theory. *Rehabilitation Counseling Bulletin, 49,* 17–28. doi:10.1177/00343552050490010301

Loeber, R., Pardini, D., Homish, D. L., Wei, E. H., Crawford, A. M., Farrington, D. P.,…Rosenfeld, R. (2005). The prediction of violence and homicide in young men. *Journal of Consulting and Clinical Psychology, 73,* 1074–1088. doi:10.1037/0022-006X.73.6.1074

Loesch, L. C., & Ritchie, M. H. (2004).*The accountable school counsellor.* Austin, TX: Pro-Ed.

Logan, D. E., & Marlatt, G. A. (2010). Harm reduction therapy: A practice-friendly review of research. *Journal of Clinical Psychology, 66,* 201–214. doi:10.1002/jclp.20669

Lopez-Baez, S. I., & Paylo, M. J. (2009). Social justice advocacy: Community collaboration and systems advocacy. *Journal of Counseling & Development, 87,* 276–283. doi:10.1002/j.1556-6678.2009.tb00107.x

Lowinger, R. J. (2012, December). College students' perceptions of severity and willingness to seek psychological help for drugs and alcohol problems. *College Student Journal, 46,* 829–833.

Lu, L., Inman, A. G., & Alvarez, A. N. (2018). Individuals and families of Asian descent. In D. G. Hays & B. T. Erford (Eds.), *Developing multicultural counseling competence: A systems approach* (3rd ed., pp. 246–276). Columbus, OH: Pearson.

Ma, D., Zhang, Z., Zhang, X., & Li, L. (2014). Comparative efficacy, acceptability, and safety of medicinal cognitive-behavioral therapy, and placebo treatments for acute major depressive disorder in children and adolescents: A multiple-treatments meta-analysis. *Current Medical Research and Opinion, 30,* 971–995. doi:10.1185/03007995.2013.860020

MaCarn, S. R., & Fessinger, R. E. (1996). Revisioning of sexual minority identity formation: A new model of lesbian identity and its implications for counseling and research. *Counseling Psychologist, 24,* 508–534. doi:10.1177/0011000096243011

Maddi, S. R. (2004). Hardiness: An operationalization of existential courage. *Journal of Humanistic Psychology, 44,* 279–298. doi:10.1177/0022167804266101

Manhas, C., & Bakhshi, A. (2011). Gender differences in burnout among HIV/AIDS counselors in North India. *Public Policy and Administration Research, 1,* 1–7.

Maples, M., & Abney, P. (2006). Baby boomers mature and gerontological counseling comes of age. *Journal of Counseling & Development, 84,* 3–9. doi:10.1002/j.1556-6678.2006.tb00374.x

Martin, D. J., Garske, J. P., & Davis, M. K. (2000). Relation of the therapeutic alliance with outcome and other variables: A meta-analytic review. *Journal of Consulting and Clinical Psychology, 68,* 438–450. doi:10.1037/0022-006X.68.3.438

Martin, P. J. (2015). Transforming the school counseling profession. In B. T. Erford (Ed.), *Transforming the school counseling profession* (4th ed., pp.45–65). Columbus, OH: Pearson.

Maslach, C., Schaufeli, W. B., & Leiter, M. P. (2001). Job burnout. In S. T. Fiske, D. L. Schacter, & C. Zahn-Waxler (Eds.), *Annual Review of Psychology, 52,* 397–422. doi:10.1146/annurev.psych.52.1.397

Maslow, A. H. (1968). *Toward a psychology of being* (2nd ed.). New York, NY: Van Nostrand.

Matthews, C. (2014). *Wealth inequality in America: It's worse than you think.* Retrieved from http://fortune.com/2014/10/31/inequality-wealth-income-us/

Maxwell, M. (2007). Career counselling is personal counselling: A constructionist approach to nurturing the development of gifted female adolescents. *Career Development Quarterly, 55,* 206–225. doi:10.1002/j.2161-0045.2007.tb00078.x

May, R. (1977). *The meaning of anxiety* (rev. ed.). New York, NY: Norton.

McCubbin, H. I., & Patterson, J. M. (1983). The family stress process: The double ABCX model of adjustment and adaptation. In H. I. McCubbin, M. B. Sussman, & J. M. Patterson (Eds.), *Social stress and the family: Advances and developments in family stress theory and research* (pp. 7–37). New York, NY: Haworth Press.

McDermit, W., Miller, I. W., & Brown, R. A. (2001). The efficacy of group psychotherapy for depression: A meta-analysis and review of the empirical research. *Clinical Psychology: Science and Practice, 8,* 98–116.

McDevitt. T. M., & Ormrod, J. E. (2012). *Child development and education* (5th ed.). Upper Saddle River, NJ: Pearson.

McGothlin, J. (2008). *Developing clinical skills in suicide assessment prevention, and treatment.* Alexandria, VA: American Counseling Association.

McGlothlin, J., Erford, B. T., & Jackson-Cherry, L. R. (2018). Overview of crisis intervention. In L. R. Jackson-Cherry & B. T. Erford (Eds.), *Crisis assessment, intervention and prevention* (3rd ed., pp. 1–25). Columbus, OH: Pearson Merrill.

McIntosh, P. (1988). *White privilege and male privilege: A personal account of coming to see correspondences through work in women's studies.* Working papers #189, Wellesley College Center for Research on Women, Wellesley, MA.

McLeod, A., & Muldoon, J. (2018). Intimate partner violence. In L. R. Jackson-Cherry & B. T. Erford (Eds.), *Crisis assessment, intervention and prevention.* (3rd ed., 157–191). Columbus, OH: Pearson Merrill.

McMahon, H. G., Paisley, P. O., & Skudrzyk, B. (2018). *Individuals and families of European descent.* In D. G. Hays & B. T. Erford (Eds.), *Developing multicultural counseling competence: A systems approach* (3rd ed., pp. 333–366). Columbus, OH: Person.

McMinn, M. R., Staley, R. C., Webb, K. C., & Seegobin, W. (2010). Just what is Christian counseling anyway? *Professional Psychology: Research and Practice, 41,* 391–397. doi:10.1037/a0018584

McRoberts, C., Burlingame, G. M., & Hoag, M. J. (1998). Comparative efficacy of individual and group psychotherapy: A meta-analytic perspective. *Group Dynamics: Theory, Research, and Practice, 2,* 101–117. doi:10.1037/1089-2699.2.2.101

McWhirter, E. H., (1991). Empowerment in counseling. *Journal of Counseling & Development, 69,* 222–227. doi:10.1002/j.1556-6676.1991.tb01491.x

Meece, J., & Daniels, D. H. (2008). *Child and adolescent development for educators* (3rd ed.). New York, NY: McGraw-Hill.

Meloy, J. R., Hoffmann, J., Guldimann, M. A., & James, D. (2012). The role of warning behaviors in threat assessment: An exploration and suggested typology. *Behavioral Strategies and the Law, 30,* 256–279. doi:10.1002/bsl.999

Miller, P. H., & Scholnick, E. K. (2000). *Toward a feminist developmental psychology.* New York, NY: Routledge.

Milsom, A., & Bryant, J. (2006). School counseling departmental websites: What message do we send? *Professional School Counseling, 10,* 210–216.

Mitchell, K. E., Levin, S., & Krumboltz, J. D. (1999). Planned happenstance: Constructing unexpected career opportunities. *Journal of Counseling & Development, 77,* 115–124.

Mitte, K. (2005). Meta-analysis of cognitive-behavioral treatments for generalized anxiety disorder: A comparison with pharmacotherapy. *Psychological Bulletin, 131,* 785–795. doi:10.1037/0033-2909.131.5.785

Moe, J. L., & Perera-Diltz, D. M. (2009). An overview of systemic-organizational consultation for professional counselors. *Journal of Professional Counseling: Practice, Theory, and Research, 37*(1), 27–37.

Monk, G., Winslade, J., Crocket, K., & Epston, D. (1997). *Narrative therapy in practice.* San Francisco, CA: Jossey-Bass.

Moodley, R., Lengyell, M., Wu, R., & Gielen, U. (2015). *International counseling case studies handbook.* Alexandria, VA: American Counseling Association.

Moores, L., & Popadiuk, N. (2011). Positive aspects of international student transitions: A qualitative inquiry. *Journal of College Student Development, 52,* 291–306. doi:10.1353/csd.2011.0040

Moorhead, H., Gill, C., Barrio Minton, C., & Myers, J. E. (2012). Forgive and forget? Forgiveness, personality, and wellness among counselors-in-training. *Counseling and Values, 57*(1), 81–95. doi:10.1002/j.2161-007X.2012.00010.x.

Morse, G., Salyers, M. P., Rollins, A. L., Monroe-DeVita, M., & Pfahler, C. (2012). Burnout in mental health services: A review of the problem and its remediation. *Administration and Policy in Mental Health, 39*, 341–352. doi:10.1007/s10488-011-0352-1

Munsch, R. (1995). *Love you forever*. Ontario, CA: Firefly.

Murphy, B. C., & Dillon, C. (2014). *Interviewing in action in a multicultural world* (5th ed.). Belmont, CA: Brooks/Cole, Cengage Learning.

Murphy, L. L., Geisinger, K. F., Carlson, J. F., & Spies, R. A. (2011). *Tests in print* (Vol. VIII). Lincoln, NE: University of Nebraska Press.

Musci, R. J., Bradshaw, C. P., Maher, B., Uhl, G. R., Kellam, S. G., & Ialongo, N. S. (2014). Reducing aggression and impulsivity through school-based prevention programs: A gene by intervention interaction. *Prevention Science, 15*, 831–840.

Myer, R. A., James, R. K., & Moulton, P. (2010). *This is not a fire drill: Crisis intervention and prevention on college campuses.* Hoboken, NJ: Wiley.

Myers, J. E., Luecht, R. M., & Sweeney, T. J. (2004). The factor structure of wellness: Reexamining theoretical and empirical models underlying the wellness evaluation of lifestyle (WEL) and the five-factor WEL.*Measurement and Evaluation in Counseling and Development, 36*, 194–208.

Myers, J. E., & Sweeney, T. (2004). Advocacy for the counseling profession: Results of a national survey. *Journal of Counseling & Development, 82*, 466. doi:10.1002/j.1556-6678.2004.tb00335.x

Myers, J. E., & Sweeney, T. J. (2005). *The Five Factor Wellness Inventory.* Palo Alto, CA: Mindgarden, Inc.

Myers, J. E., Sweeney, T. J., & White, V. E. (2002). Advocacy for counseling and counselors: A professional imperative. *Journal of Counseling & Development, 80*, 394–402. doi:10.1002/j.1556-6678.2002.tb00205.x

Myers, J. E., Sweeney, T. J., & Witmer, J. M. (2000). The wheel of wellness counseling for wellness: A holistic model for treatment planning. *Journal of Counseling & Development, 78,* 251–267. doi:10.1002/j.1556-6676.2000.tb01906.x

Myrick, R. D. (2010). *Developmental guidance and counseling: A practical approach* (5th ed.). Minneapolis, MN: Educational Media.

Nassar-McMillan, S. C. (2014). A framework for cultural competence, advocacy, and social justice: Applications for global multiculturalism and diversity. *International Journal for Educational and Vocational Guidance, 14*, 103–118. doi:10.1007/s10775-014-9265-3

National Board for Certified Counselors. (2012). *NBCC policy regarding the provision of distance counseling services*. Retrieved from http://www.nbcc.org/Assets/Ethics/NBCCPolicyRegardingPracticeofDistanceCounselingBoard.pdf

National Board for Certified Counselors. (NBCC). (2014, Winter). NBCC international news. *National Certified Counselor, 30,* 12–14.

National Board for Certified Counselors. (NBCC). (2015a). *More information on TRICARE.* Retrieved from http://www.nbcc.org/InnerPageLinks/MoreInformationOnTRICARE

National Board for Certified Counselors (NBCC). (2017). *NBCC guide to advocacy communication.* Retrieved from http://www.nbcc.org/Assets/NBCC_GuideToAdvocacyCommunication.pdf

National Board for Certified Counselors. (2018). *Home.* Retrieved from http://www.nbcc.org

National Career Development Association. (2016). *Policy and procedures manual 2015–16.* Retrieved from http://www.ncda.org/aws/NCDA/pt/sp/guidelines

National Center for Education Statistics. (2014a). *Post baccalaureate enrollment. The condition of education.* Retrieved from https://nces.ed.gov/programs/coe/pdf/coe_cha.pdf

National Center for Education Statistics. (2014b). *Undergraduate enrollment. The condition of education.* Retrieved from https://nces.ed.gov/programs/coe/pdf/coe_cha.pdf

National Center for Educational Statistics (2018). *Crisis data management: A forum guide to collecting and managing data about displaced students.* Retrieved from https://nces.ed.gov/pubs2010/crisisdata/app_b.asp

National Comorbidity Survey Replication. (2005). *Lifetime prevalence of DSM-IV/WHM-CIDI disorders by sex and cohort.* Retrieved from http://www.hcp.med.harvard.edu/ncs

National Institute of Mental Health. (2015). *Any anxiety disorder among adults.* Retrieved from http://www.nimh.nih.gov/health/statistics/prevalence/any-anxiety-disorder-among-adults.shtml

National Institute of Mental Health. (2017). *Fact sheet on stress.* Retrieved from http://www.nimh.nih.gov/health/publications/stress/index.shtml

National Institute of Mental Health. (2018). *Statistics.* Retrieved from http://www.nimh.nih.gov/health/statistics/index.shtml

National Registry for Evidence-based Programs and Practices. (NREPP). (2018). *Evidence based programs*

(NREPP). Retrieved from http://www.samhsa.gov/data/evidence-based-programs-nrepp

National Vital Statistics System. (2015). *10 Leading causes of death by age group, United States – 2013.* Retrieved from http://www.cdc.gov/injury/wisqars/pdf/leading_causes_of_death_by_age_group_2013-a.pdf

Nauta, M. M. (2010). The development, evolution, and status of Holland's theory of vocational personalities: Reflections and future directions for counseling psychology. *Journal of Counseling Psychology, 57*(1), 11–22. doi:10.1037/a0018213

Neft, D. I. (2005). Social and emotional profiles of bullies and victims: Implications for school-based prevention programs. *Dissertation Abstracts International: Section B: The Sciences and Engineering, 67*(11-B), 6742.

Neswald-Potter, R., Blackburn, S. A., & Noel, J. J. (2013). Revealing the power of practitioner relationships: An action-driven inquiry of counselor wellness. *Journal of Humanistic Counseling, 52,* 177–190. doi:10.1002/j.2161-1939.2013.00041.x

Neukrug, E. (2012). *The world of the counselor: An introduction to the counseling profession* (4th ed.). Belmont, CA: Brooks/Cole.

Newell, J., & MacNeil, G. (2010). Professional burnout, vicarious trauma, secondary traumatic stress, and compassion fatigue: A review of theoretical terms, risk factors, and preventive methods for clinicians and researchers. *Best Practices in Mental Health.* Chicago, IL: Lyceum Books.

Newman, B. J., & Newman, P. R. (2014). *Development through life: A psychosocial approach* (12th ed.). Boston, MA: Cengage.

Newton, N. C., Vogl, L. E., Teesson, M., & Andrews, G. (2009). CLIMATE schools: Alcohol module: Cross-validation of a school-based prevention programme for alcohol misuse. *Australian and New Zealand Journal of Psychiatry, 43,* 201–207.

Nichols, M. P. (2013). *The essentials of family therapy* (6th ed.). Upper Saddle River, NJ: Pearson.

Nochajski, S. M., & Matteliano, M. A. (2008). *A Guide to Cultural Competence in the Curriculum: Rehabilitation Counseling.* Retrieved from http://cirrie.buffalo.edu/culture/curriculum/guides/ot.pdf

No Child Left Behind Act of 2001. (NCLB, 2001). Pub. L. 107–110, 115 Stat. 1425.

Nolen-Hoeksema, S. (2001). Gender differences in depression. *Current Directions in Psychological Science, 10,* 173–176. doi:10.1111/1467-8721.00142

Norcross, J. C. (2000). Toward the delineation of empirically based principles in psychotherapy: Commentary on Beutler (2000). *Prevention and Treatment, 3,* Article 28. doi:10.1037/1522-3736.3.1.328c

Norcross, J. C., & Goldfried, M. R. (2005). The future of psychotherapy integration: A roundtable. *Journal of Psychotherapy Integration, 15,* 392–471. doi:10.1037/1053-0479.15.4.392

Norcross, J. C., Krebs, P. M., & Prochaska, J. O. (2011). Stages of change. *Journal of Clinical Psychology, 67,* 143–154. doi:10.1002/jclp.20758

Norcross, J. C., & Lambert, M. J. (2013). Compendium of empirically supported therapy relationships. In G. P. Koocher, J. C. Norcross, & S. S. Hill, III (Eds.), *Psychologists' desk reference* (3rd ed., pp. 171–207). New York, NY: Oxford University Press.

Norcross, J. C., & Prochaska, J. O. (1983). Clinicians' theoretical orientations: Selection, utilization, and efficacy. *Professional Psychology, 14,* 197–208. doi:10.1037/0735-7028.14.2.197

Nouwen, H. J. (1979). *The wounded healer.* New York, NY: Image Books.

Obama, B. H. (2015, January 20). *Remarks by the president in state of the union address: January 20, 2015.* Retrieved from https://www.whitehouse.gov/the-press-office/2015/01/20/remarks-president-state-union-address-january-20-2015

O'Brien, M., & Graham, M. (2009). Rehabilitation counseling in the state or federal program: Is there a future? *Rehabilitation Counseling Bulletin, 52,* 124–128. doi:10.1177/0034355208323948

O'Hanlon, W. H., & Weiner-Davis, M. (2003). *In search of solutions: A new direction in psychotherapy* (rev. ed.). New York, NY: Norton.

Okun, B. F., & Kantrowitz, R. E. (2014). *Effective helping: Interviewing and counselling techniques.* Boston, MA: Cengage.

Oliver, L. W., & Spokane, A. R. (1988). Career intervention outcome: What contributes to client gain? *Journal of Counseling Psychology, 35,* 447–462. doi:10.1037/0022-0167.35.4.447

O*NET. (2015). *Summary report for: 21-1014.00 - Mental health counselors.* Retrieved from www.onetonline.org/link/summary/21-1014.00

Organization for Economic Cooperation and Development. (2004). *Career guidance: A handbook for policy makers.* Retrieved from http://www.oecd.org/edu/innovation-education/34060761.pdf

Orr, J. (2018). Alternative approaches to counseling theories. In D. G. Hays & B. T. Erford (Eds.), *Developing multicultural counseling competence: A systems approach* (3rd ed., pp. 389–405). Columbus, OH: Pearson.

Oser, C. B., Biebel, E. P., Pullen, E, & Harp, K. (2013). Causes, consequences and prevention of burnout among substance abuse treatment counselors: A rural versus urban comparison. *Journal of Psychoactive Drugs, 45*, 17–27. doi:10.1080/027910 72.2013.763558

O'Toole, M. E. (2000). *The school shooter: A threat assessment perspective.* Quantico, VA: National Center for the Analysis of Violent Crime (NCAVC) FBI Academy.

Owen, J., Imel, Z., Adelson, J., & Rodolfa, E. (2012). 'No-show': Therapist racial/ethnic disparities in client unilateral termination. *Journal of Counseling Psychology, 59*, 314–320. doi:10.1037/a0027091

Oxman, E. B., & Chambliss, C. (2003). Tailoring inpatient group psychotherapy to patients' needs: Size matters! *Research Reports, 143*, 1–9.

Özabacı, N. (2011). Cognitive behavioural therapy for violent behaviour in children and adolescents: A meta-analysis. *Children and Youth Services Review, 33*, 1989–1993. doi:10.1016/j.childyouth. 2011.05.027

Padula, M. A. (1994). Reentry women: A literature review with recommendations for counseling and research. *Journal of Counseling & Development, 73*, 10–16. doi:10.1002/j.1556-6676.1994.tb01703.x

Palmer-Olsen, L., Gold, L. L., & Woolley, S. R. (2011). Supervising emotionally focused therapists: A systematic research-based model. *Journal of Marital & Family Therapy, 37*, 411–426. doi:10.1111/ j.1752-0606.2011.00253.x

Papalia, D. E., Feldman, R. D., & Martorelli, G. (2012). *Experience human development* (12th ed.). New York, NY: McGraw-Hill.

Parikh, S. J. T., & Morris, C. A. W. (2011). Integrating crisis theory and individual psychology: An application and case study. *Journal of Individual Psychology, 67*, 364–379.

Paris, J. (2002). Implications of long-term outcome research for the management of patients with borderline personality disorder. *Harvard Review Psychiatry, 10*, 315–323. doi:10.1080/ 10673220216229

Park, W. J., Park, S. J., & Hwang, S. D. (2015). Effects of cognitive behavioral therapy on attention deficit hyperactivity disorder among school-aged children in Korea: A meta-analysis. *Journal of Korean Academy of Nursing, 45*, 169–182. doi:10.4040/jkan.2015.45.2.169

Parsons, F. (1909). *Choosing a vocation.* Boston, MA: Houghton Mifflin.

Patterson, C. L., Anderson, T., & Wei, C. (2012). Clients' pretreatment role expectations, the therapeutic alliance, and clinical outcomes in outpatient therapy. *Journal of Clinical Psychology, 70*, 673–680. doi:10.1002/jclp.22054

Patterson, J. B. (2009). Professional identity and the future of rehabilitation counseling. *Rehabilitation Counseling Bulletin, 52*, 129–132. doi:10.1177/ 0034355208323949

Patterson, J. B., Bruyére, S. M., Szymanski, E. M., & Jenkins, W. M. (1998). Philosophical, historical, and legislative aspects of the rehabilitation counseling profession. In R. M. Parker & E. M. Szymanski (Eds.), *Rehabilitation counseling: Basics and beyond* (5th ed., pp. 27–54). Austin, TX: Pro-Ed.

Patterson, W. M., Dohn, H. H., Bird, J., & Patterson, G. A. (1983). Evaluation of suicidal patients: The SAD PERSONS Scale. *Psychomatics, 24*, 343–349.

Pedro-Carroll, J. L., & Alpert-Gillis, L. J. (1997). Preventive interventions for children of divorce: A developmental model for 5 and 6 year old children. *Journal of Primary Prevention, 18*, 5–23. doi:10.1023/A:1024601421020

Pedro-Carroll, J. L., Sutton, S. E., & Wyman, P. A. (1999). A two-year follow-up of a preventive intervention for young children of divorce. *School Psychology Review, 28*, 467–476.

Perls, L. (1970). One Gestalt therapist's approach. In J. Fagan & I. Shepherd (Eds.), *Gestalt therapy now* (pp. 125–129). New York, NY: Harper & Row (Colophon).

Peter D. Hart Research Associates. (2012, October). *The College Board 2012 national survey of school counselors and administrators.* New York, NY: College Board Advocacy and Policy Center.

Pew Research Center. (2012). *U.S. foreign-born population: How much change from 2009 to 2010?* Retrieved from http://pewresearch.org/pubs/2163/ foreign-born-population-census-bureau-american-community-survey

Piaget, J. (1967). *Six psychological studies.* New York, NY: Random House.

Poll, J. B., & Smith, T. B. (2003). The spiritual self: Toward a conceptualization of spiritual identity development. *Journal of Psychology and Theology, 31*, 129–142.

Ponzo, Z. (1974). A counselor and change: Reminiscences and resolutions. *Personnel and Guidance Journal, 53,* 27–32. doi:10.1002/j.2164-4918.1974.tb04128.x

Pope, M., Briddick, W. C., & Wilson, F. (2013). The historical importance of social justice in the founding of the National Career Development Association. *Career Development Quarterly, 61,* 368–373. doi:10.1002/j.2161-0045.2013.00063.x

Poston, W. S. C. (1990). The biracial identity development model: A needed addition. *Journal of Counseling & Development, 60,* 152–155. doi:10.1002/j.1556-6676.1990.tb01477.x

PostTraumatic Growth Research Group. (2014). *What is PTG?* Retrieved from https://ptgi.uncc.edu/what-is-ptg/

President's New Freedom Commission on Mental Health. (2003). *Achieving the promise: Transforming mental health care in America* (Publication No. SMA 03-3832). Retrieved from http://govinfo.library.unt.edu/mentalhealthcommission/reports/FinalReport/downloads

Preston, J., O'Neal, J. H., & Talaga, M. C. (2013). *Handbook of clinical psychopharmacology for therapists* (7th ed.). Oakland, CA: New Harbinger.

Prochaska, J. O., & DiClemente, C. C. (1982). Transtheoretical therapy: Toward a more integrative model of change. *Psychotherapy: Theory, Research, and Practice, 20,* 161–173. doi:10.1037/h0088437

Protection of Pupil Rights Amendment. (1978). 20 U.S.C. § 1232h; 34 CFR Part 98.

Prout, S. M., & Prout, H. T. (1998). A meta-analysis of school-based studies of counseling and psychotherapy: An update. *Journal of School Psychology, 36,* 121–136. doi:10.1016/S0022-4405(98)00007-7

Pruett, S. R., & Chan, F. (2006). The development and psychometric validation of the Disability Attitude Implicit Association Test. *Rehabilitation Psychology, 51,* 202–213. doi:10.1037/0090-5550.51.3.202

Pryor, R. G. L., Amundson, N. E., & Bright, J. E. H. (2008). Probabilities and possibilities: The strategic counseling implications of the chaos theory of careers. *Career Development Quarterly, 56,* 309–318. doi:10.1002/j.2161-0045.2008.tb00096

Pryor, R. G. L., & Bright, J. E. H. (2007). Applying chaos theory to careers: Attraction and attractors. *Journal of Vocational Behavior, 71,* 375–400. doi:10.1016/j.jvb.2007.05.002

Pryor, R. G. L., & Bright, J. E. H. (2008). Archetypal narratives in career counselling: A chaos theory application. *International Journal for Educational and Vocational Guidance, 2,* 71. doi:10.1007/s10775-008-9138-8

Pryor, R. G. L., & Bright, J. E. H. (2014). The chaos theory of careers (CTC): Ten years on and only just begun. *Australian Journal of Career Development, 23*(1), 4. doi:10.1177/1038416213518506

QPR Institute. (2010). *Question, persuade, refer: Gatekeeper training for suicide warning signs.* Spokane, WA: Author.

Rathus, S. A. (2010). *Children and adolescence: Voyages in development* (4th ed.). Florence, KY: Wadsworth Cengage Learning.

Ratts, M. J. (2009). Social justice counseling: Toward the development of a "fifth force" among counseling paradigms. *Journal of Humanistic Counseling, Education, and Development, 48,* 160–172. doi:10.1002/j.2161-1939.2009.tb00076.x

Ratts, M. J., & Hutchins, A. M. (2009). ACA advocacy competencies: Social justice advocacy at the client/student level. *Journal of Counseling & Development, 87,* 269–275. doi:10.1002/j.1556-6676.2009.tb00106.x

Ratts, M. J., Singh, A. A., Nassar-McMillan, S., Butler, S. K., & McCullough, J. R. (2015). *Multicultural and social justice counseling competencies.* Retrieved from http://www.counseling.org/docs/default-source/competencies/multicultural-and-social-justice-counseling-competencies.pdf?sfvrsn=20

Raue, K., & Lewis, L. (2011). *Students with disabilities at degree-granting postsecondary institutions* (NCES 2011–018). U.S. Department of Education, National Center for Education Statistics. Washington, DC: U.S. Government Printing Office.

Ray, D. C., Armstrong, S. A., Balkin, R. S., & Jayne, K. (2015). Child-centered play therapy in the schools: Review and meta-analysis. *Psychology in the Schools, 52,* 107–123. doi:10.1002/pits.21798

Reicherzer, S. (2008). Evolving language and understanding in the historical development of the gender identity disorder diagnosis. *Journal of LGBT Issues in Counseling, 2,* 326–347. doi:10.1080/15538600802502035

Remley, T. P., Jr. (1992, August). Perspectives from the Executive Director: Are counselors unique? *ACA Guidepost,* 4.

Remley, T. P., & Herlihy, B. (2016). *Ethical, legal, and professional issues in counseling* (5th ed.). Upper Saddle River, NJ: Pearson.

Renger, R. F., Midyett, S. J., Mas, F. G., Erin, T. E., McDermott, H. M., Papenfuss, R. L., . . . Hewitt, M. J. (2000). Optimal Living Profile: An inventory to assess health and wellness. *American Journal of Health Promotion, 24*, 403–412. doi:10.5993/ AJHB.24.6.1

Resilience Research Centre. (2015). *What is resilience?* Retrieved from http://resilienceresearch.org/

Reynolds, S. (2000). Evidenced based practice and psychotherapy research. *Journal of Mental Health, 9*, 257–266. doi:10.1080/jmh.9.3.257.266

Rhode, R. I., & Stockton, R. (1994). Group structure: A review. *Journal of Group Psychotherapy, Psychodrama, and Sociometry, 46*, 151–158.

Rice, D. P., Kelman, S., Miller, L. S., & Dunmeyer, S. (1990). *The economic costs of alcohol and drug use and mental illness: 1985*. Report from the Office of Financing and Coverage Policy of the Alcohol, Drug Abuse and Mental Health Administration, U. S. Department of Health and Human Services. San Francisco, CA: Institute for Health and Aging, University of California.

Rimehaug, T., & Helmersberg, I. (2010). Situational consultation. *Journal of Educational and Psychological Consultation, 20*, 185–208. doi:10.1080/10474412. 2010.500509

Roach, L. F., & Young, M. E. (2007). Do counselor education programs promote wellness in their students? *Counselor Education and Supervision, 47*(1), 29–45. doi:10.1002/j.1556-6978.2007.tb00036.x

Robinson, L. A., Berman, J. S., & Neimeyer, R. A. (1990). Psychotherapy for the treatment of depression: A comprehensive review of controlled outcome research. *Psychological Bulletin, 108*, 30–49. doi:10.1037/0033-2909.108.1.30

Roe-Sepowitz, D. (2007). Adolescent female murderers: Characteristics and treatment implications. *American Journal of Orthopsychiatry, 77*, 489–496. doi:10.1037/0002-9432.77.3.489

Rogers, C. (1951). *Client-centered therapy*. Boston, MA: Houghton Mifflin.

Rogers, C. (1957). The necessary and sufficient conditions of therapeutic personality change. *Journal of Consulting Psychology, 21*, 95–103. doi:10.1037/ h0045357

Rogers, C. (1961). *On becoming a person: A therapist's view of psychotherapy*. Boston, MA: Houghton Mifflin.

Roget's New Millennium™ Thesaurus, Third Edition. (2018). *Advocacy*. Retrieved from http:// www.thesaurus.com/browse/advocacy?s=t

Rongione, D., Erford, B. T., & Broglie, C. (2010). Alcohol and other drug abuse counseling outcomes for school-aged youth: A meta-analysis of studies from 1990–2009. *Counseling Outcome Research and Evaluation, 1*, 19–43. doi:10.1177/ 2150137809356682

Rønnestad, M. H., & Skovholt, T. M. (2003). The journey of the counselor and therapist: Research findings and perspectives on development. *Journal of Career Development, 30*, 5–44. doi:10.1023/A:1025173508081

Roscoe, L. J. (2009). Wellness: A review of theory and measurement for counselors. *Journal of Counseling and Development, 87*, 216–226. doi:10.1002/j.1556-6678.2009.tb00570.x

Rothschild, B. (2006). *The psychophysiology of compassion fatigue and vicarious trauma help for the helper: Self-care strategies for managing burnout and stress*. New York, NY: Norton.

Rothschild, B. (2011). *Trauma essentials: The go-to guide*. New York, NY: Norton.

Rotter, J. B. (1946). Thematic Apperception Test: Suggestions for administration and interpretation. *Journal of Personality, 15*, 60–73. doi:10.1111/ j.1467-6494.1946.tb01052.x

Rowan-Kenyon, H. T., Perna, L. W., & Swan, A. K. (2011). Structuring opportunity: The role of school context in shaping high school students' occupational aspirations. *Career Development Quarterly, 59*, 330–344. doi:10.1002/j.2161-0045. 2011.tb00073.x

Rowan-Kenyon, H. T., Swan, A. K., & Creager, M. F. (2012). Social cognitive factors, support, and engagement: Early adolescents' math interests as precursors to choice of career. *Career Development Quarterly, 60*, 2–15. doi:10.1002/j.2161-0045. 2012.00001.x

Rowley, W. J., Stroh, H. R., & Sink, C. A. (2005). Comprehensive guidance and counseling programs' use of guidance curricula materials: A survey of national trends. *Professional School Counseling, 8*, 296–304.

Rubel, D., & Ratts, M. (2010). Diversity and social justice issues in counseling and psychotherapy. In D. Capuzzi & D. R. Gross (Eds.), *Counseling and psychotherapy: Theories and interventions* (5th ed., pp. 29–58). Alexandria, VA: American Counseling Association.

Rubinstein, G. (1995). The decision to remove homosexuality from the *DSM*: Twenty years later. *American Journal of Psychotherapy, 49,* 416–427.

Rudd, M. D. (2006). *The assessment and management of suicidality practitioner's resource.* Sarasota, FL: Professional Resource Exchange.

Rudd, M. D., Joiner, T. E., and Rajab, M. H. (2004). *Treating suicidal behavior: An effective, time-limited approach (Treatment manuals for practitioners).* New York, NY: Guilford Press.

Russell, K., Gillis, H. L., & Lewis, T. G. (2008). A five-year follow-up of a survey of North American outdoor behavioral healthcare programs. *Journal of Experiential Education, 31*(1), 55–77. doi:10.1177/105382590803100106

Ruzek, J. I., Brymer, M. J., Jacobs, A. K., Layne, C. M., Vernberg, E. M., & Watson, P. J. (2007). Psychological first aid. *Journal of Mental Health Counseling, 29,* 17–49. doi:10.17744/mehc.29.1.5racqxjueafabgwp

Saarni, C., Campos, J. J., Camras, L. A., & Witherington, D. (2006). Emotional development: Action, communication, and understanding. In W. Damon & R. M. Lerner (series eds.), & N. Eisenberg (vol. ed.), *Handbook of child psychology (Vol. 3): Social, emotional, and personality development* (6th ed., pp. 226–299). New York, NY: Wiley.

Safran, J. D., Muran, J. C., & Eubanks-Carter, C. (2011). Repairing alliance ruptures. *Psychotherapy, 48,* 80–87. doi:10.1037/0033-3204.38.4.406

Sales, A. (2007). *Rehabilitation counseling: An empowerment perspective.* Austin, TX: Pro-Ed.

Sampson, J. P., Hou, P.-C., Kronholz, J. F., Dozier, V. C., McClain, M.-C., Buzzetta, M., . . . Kennelly, E. L. (2014). A content analysis of career development theory, research, and practice-2013. *Career Development Quarterly, 62,* 290–326. doi:10.1002/j.2161-0045.2014.00085.x

Sandoval, J. (Ed.). (2013). *Crisis counseling, intervention and prevention in the schools* (3rd ed.). New York, NY: Routledge.

Sandoz, J. (2010a). Providing pastoral counseling for alcoholism recovery: Understanding mind and spirit in the AA 12 Step Program. *Sacred Spaces: The e-Journal of the American Association for Pastoral Counselors, 2,* 86–106.

Sandoz, J. (2010b). Reexamining the brain, addiction and neuro-spirituality. *Sacred Spaces: The e-Journal of the American Association for Pastoral Counselors, 2,* 107–144.

Sankaranarayanan, A. (2013). *Suicide risk assessment made easy.* Retrieved from http://ispub.com/IJMH/5/2/4081

Santrock, J. (2013). *Life-span development* (14th ed.). Boston, MA: McGraw-Hill.

Satcher, D. (1996). *Mental health: A report of the Surgeon General—Executive summary.* Retrieved from http://www.surgeongeneral.gov/library/mentalhealth/home.html

Savage, T. A., Harley, D. A., & Nowak, T. M. (2005). Applying social empowerment strategies as tools for self-advocacy in counseling lesbian and gay male clients. *Journal of Counseling & Development, 83,* 131–137. doi:10.1002/j.1556-6678.2005.tb00589.x

Savickas, M. L. (2003). Advancing the career counseling profession: Objectives and strategies for the next decade. *Career Development Quarterly, 52*(1), 87–96.

Savickas, M. L. (2013). Career construction theory and practice. In S. D. Brown & R. W. Lent (Eds.), *Career development in counseling: Putting theory and research into work* (pp. 147–186). New York, NY: John Wiley & Sons.

Schein, E. (1978). The role of the consultant: Content expert or process facilitator? *Personnel and Guidance Journal, 56,* 339–345. doi:10.1002/j.2164-4918.1978.tb04644.x

Schein, E. (1991). Process consultation. *Consulting Psychology Bulletin, 43,* 16–18.

Scherer, M. J. (2000). *Living in the state of stuck: How technology impacts the lives of people with disabilities* (3rd ed.). Cambridge, MA: Brookline Books.

Schlossberg, S. M., Morris, J. D., & Lieberman, M. G. (2001). The effects of a counselor-led guidance intervention on students' behaviors and attitudes. *Professional School Counseling, 4,* 156–174.

Schmidt, J. J. (2002). *Intentional helping: A philosophy for proficient caring relationships.* Upper Saddle River, NJ: Merrill Prentice Hall.

Schmitz, W., Jr., Allen, M., Feldman, B., Gutin, N., Jahn, D., Kleespies, P., Quinnett, P., & Simpson, S. (2012). Preventing suicide through improved training in suicide risk assessment and care: An American Association of Suicidology Task Force report addressing serious gaps in U.S. mental health training. *Suicide and Life-Threatening Behavior, 42,* 292–304. doi:10.1111/j.1943-278X.2012.00090.x

Scott, D., Royal, C., & Kissinger, D. (2014). *Counselor as consultant.* Thousand Oaks, CA: Sage.

Seligman, L. (2004). *Technical and conceptual skills for mental health professionals.* Upper Saddle River, NJ: Pearson Merrill Prentice Hall.

Seligman, L. (2009). *Fundamental skills for mental health professionals.* Upper Saddle River, NJ: Pearson.

Seligman, L., & Reichenberg, L. W. (2012). *Selecting effective treatments: A comprehensive, systematic guide to treating mental disorders* (4th ed.). New York, NY: Wiley.

Sexton, T. L. (1999). *Evidence-based counseling: Implications for counseling practice, preparation, and professionalism.* Greensboro, NC: ERIC Clearinghouse on Counseling and Student Services (ERIC Identifier: ED435948).

Sexton, T. L., Whiston, S. C., Bleuer, J. C., & Walz, G. R. (1997). *Integrating outcome research into counseling practice and training.* Alexandria, VA: American Counseling Association.

Shapiro, S. L., Brown, K. W., & Biegel, G. M. (2007). Teaching self-care to caregivers: Effects of mindfulness-based stress reduction on the mental health of therapists in training. *Training and Education in Professional Psychology, 1,* 105–115. doi:10.1037/1931–3918.1.2.105

Sharf, J., Primavera, L. H., & Diener, M. J. (2010). Dropout and therapeutic alliance: A meta-analysis of adult individual psychotherapy. *Psychotherapy: Theory, Research, Practice, Training, 47,* 637–645. doi: 10.1037/a0021175

Sharfstein, S. S. (2005). Commentary on "Constituting community: Creating a place for oneself": The healing power of relationships. *Psychiatry, 3,* 212–213.

Shea, S. C. (2011). *The practical art of suicide assessment: A guide for mental health professionals and substance abuse counselors.* Hoboken, NJ: John Wiley.

Sheu, H. B., & W. E. Sedlacek. (2002). Help-seeking attitudes and coping strategies among college students by race. Counseling Center Research Report #7-02. University of Maryland College Park.

Shi, Q., & Erford, B. T. (2016). Outcomes research on school counseling. In B. T. Erford (Ed.), *Professional school counseling: A handbook of theories, programs and practices* (3rd ed., pp. 35–46). Austin, TX: Pro-ed.

Siegler, R., DeLoache, J. S., & Eisenberg, N. (2011). *How children develop* (3rd ed.). New York, NY: Worth Publishers.

Singh, A. A., Hays, D. G., & Watson, L. S. (2011). Strength in the face of adversity: Resilience strategies of transgender individuals. *Journal of Counseling & Development, 89,* 20–27. doi:10.1002/j.1556-6678.2011.tb00057.x

Singh, A. A., & Mingo, T. (2018). Gender and sexism. In D. G. Hays & B. T. Erford (Eds.), *Developing multicultural counseling competence: A systems approach* (3rd ed., pp. 94–112). Columbus, OH: Pearson Merrill.

Sink, C. A., & Stroh, H. R. (2003). Raising achievement test scores of early elementary school students through comprehensive school counseling programs. *Professional School Counseling, 6,* 350–364.

Sklare, G. B. (2014). *Brief counseling that works: A solution-focused therapy approach for school counselors and other mental health professionals* (3rd ed.). Thousand Oaks, CA: Corwin.

Skovholt, T. M. (2001). *The resilient practitioner: Burnout prevention and self-care strategies for counselors, therapists, teachers, and health professionals.* Needham Heights, MA: Allyn & Bacon.

Skovholt, T. M., Grier, T. L., & Hanson, M. R. (2001). Career counseling for longevity: Self-care and burnout prevention strategies for counselor resilience. *Journal of Career Development, 27,* 167–176. doi:10.1023/A:1007830908587

Smart, J. F., & Smart, D. W. (2011). Models of disability: Implications for the counseling profession. *Journal of Counseling & Development, 84,* 29–40. doi:10.1002/j.1556-6678.2006.tb00377.x

Smith, H. L., Robinson, E. H., III, & Young, M. E. (2007). The relationship among wellness, psychological distress, and social desirability of entering master's-level counselor trainees. *Counselor Education and Supervision, 47,* 96–109. doi:10.1002/j.1556-6978.2007.tb00041.x

Smith, K. M., Chesin, M. S., & Jeglic, E. L. (2014, April). Minority college student mental health: Does majority status matter? Implications for college counseling services. *Journal of Multicultural Counseling and Development, 42,* 77–92. doi:10.1002/j.2161-1912.2014.00046.x

Smith, S. D., Reynolds, C. A., & Rovnak, A. (2009). A critical analysis of the social advocacy movement in counseling. *Journal of Counseling & Development, 87,* 483–491. doi:10.1002/j.1556-6678.2009.tb00133.x

Smith, S. L., Myers, J. E., & Hensley, L. G. (2002). Putting more life into life career courses: The benefits of a holistic wellness model. *Journal of College Counseling, 5,* 90–95.

Smolenski, D. J., Reger, M. A., Bush, N. E., Skopp, N. A., Zhang, Y., & Campise, R. L. (2015). *Department of Defense suicide event report.* Retrieved from http://www.suicideoutreach.org/Docs/suicide-data/2013-DoDSER-Annual-Report.pdf

Snyder, C. R. (2000). *Handbook of hope: Theory, measures, and applications.* San Diego, CA: Academic Press.

So, D. W., Gilbert, S., & Romero, S. (2005). Help-seeking attitudes among African American college students. *College Student Journal, 39,* 806–816.

Solomon, S. D., & Johnson, D. M. (2002). Psychosocial treatment of posttraumatic stress disorder: A practice-friendly review of outcome research. *Journal of Clinical Psychology/In Session: Psychotherapy in Practice, 58,* 947–959. doi:10.1002/jclp.10069

Sommers Flanagan, J., & Sommers Flanagan, R. (2009). *Clinical interviewing* (4th ed.). Hoboken, NJ: Wiley.

Sperry, L., Carlson, J., & Kjos, D. (2003). *Becoming an effective therapist.* Boston, MA: Allyn & Bacon.

Spokane, A. R., & Oliver, L. W. (1983). Research integration: Approaches, problems and recommendations for research reporting. *Journal of Counseling Psychology, 30,* 252–257. doi:10.1037/0022-0167.30.2.252

Stage, S. A., & Quiroz, D. R. (1997). A meta-analysis of interventions to decrease disruptive classroom behavior in public education settings. *School Psychology Review, 26,* 333–369.

Staudt, M., & Williams-Hayes, M. (2011). A state survey of child advocacy center therapists' attitudes toward treatment manuals and evidence-based practice. *Journal of Child Sexual Abuse, 20*(1), 1–13. doi:10.1080/10538712.2011.539999

Stebleton, M. J., Soria, K. M., & Huesman, R. L. (2014, April). First-generation students' sense of belonging, mental health, and use of counseling services at public research universities. *Journal of College Counseling, 17,* 6–20. doi:10.1002/j.2161-1882.2014.00044.x

Stein, D. M., & Lambert, M. J. (1995). Graduate training in psychotherapy: Are therapy outcomes enhanced? *Journal of Consulting and Clinical Psychology, 63,* 182–196. doi:10.1037/0022-006X.63.2.182

Steinberg, L. (2014). *Adolescence* (10th ed.). New York, NY: McGraw-Hill.

Stenovec, T. (2015). Facebook is now bigger than the largest country on earth. *Huffington Post,* (January 28, 2015). Retrieved from http://www.huffingtonpost.com/2015/01/28/facebook-biggest-country_n_6565428.html

Stinchfield, T. A., Hill, N. R., & Kleist, D. M. (2010). Counselor trainees' experiences in triadic supervision: A qualitative exploration of transcendent themes. *International Journal for the Advancement of Counseling, 32,* 225–239. doi:10.1007/s10447-010-9099-8

Stoltenberg, C. D., & McNeill, B. W. (2010). *IDM supervision: An integrative developmental model of supervision* (3rd ed.). New York, NY: Routledge.

Stoltenberg, C. D., & McNeill, B. W. (2012). Supervision: Research, models, and competence. In N. A. Fouad (Ed.), *APA handbook of counseling psychology: Vol. 1. Theories, research, and methods* (pp. 295–327). Washington, DC: American Psychological Association.

Stone, C. B. (2013). *School counseling principles: Ethics and law* (3rd ed.). Alexandria, VA: American School Counselor Association.

Streed, T. (2011). A template for the investigation of suicidal behavior and subject precipitated homicide. *Investigative Sciences Journal, 3,* 35–66.

Strike, D. L., Skovholt, T. M., & Hummel, T. J. (2004). Mental health professionals' disability competence: Measuring self-awareness, perceived knowledge, and perceived skills. *Rehabilitation Psychology, 49,* 321–327. doi:10.1037/0090-5550.49.4.321

Stuart, S., & Robertson, M. (2012). *Interpersonal psychotherapy: A clinician's guide* (2nd ed.). London, UK: Edward Arnold.

Substance Abuse and Mental Health Services Administration. (SAMHSA). (2013). *Results from the 2012 National Survey on Drug Use and Health: Summary of National Findings,* NSDUH Series H-46, HHS Publication No. (SMA) 13-4795. Rockville, MD: Author.

Substance Abuse and Mental Health Services Administration. (SAMHSA). (2014a). *Highlights of the National Mental Health Services Survey.* Retrieved from http://www.samhsa.gov/data/sites/default/files/NMHSS-SR191-2010Highlights2014/NMHSS-SR191-2010Highlights2014.pdf

Substance Abuse and Mental Health Services Administration. (SAMHSA). (2014b). *Prevention of substance abuse and mental illness.* Retrieved from http://www.samhsa.gov/prevention

Sue, D. W., Arredondo, P., & McDavis, R. J. (1992). Multicultural counseling competencies and standards: A call to the profession. *Journal of Counseling & Development, 70,* 477–486. doi:10.1002/j.1556-6676.1992.tb01642.x

Sue, D. W., & Sue, D. (2013). *Counseling the culturally diverse: Theory and practice* (6th ed.). New York, NY: Wiley.

Suicide Prevention Resource Center. (2016). *Assessing and managing suicide risk: Core competencies for mental health professionals.* Retrieved from http://www.sprc.org/sites/sprc.org/files/AMSRcompetencies.pdf

Sukhodolsky, D. G., Bloch, M. H., Panza, K. E., & Reichow, B. (2013). Cognitive-behavioral therapy for anxiety in children with high-functioning autism: A meta-analysis. *Pediatrics, 132*(5), e1341–e1350. doi:10.1542/peds.2013-1193

Super, D. (1976). *Career education and the meaning of work: Monographs on career education.* Washington, DC: Office of Career Education, U.S. Office of Education.

Super, D. (1990). A life-span, life-space approach to career development. In D. Brown, L. Brooks, & Associates (Eds.), *Career choice and development: Applying contemporary theories to practice* (2nd ed., pp. 197–261). San Francisco, CA: Jossey-Bass.

Svartberg, M., & Stiles, T. C. (1991). Comparative effects of short-term psychodynamic psychotherapy: A meta-analysis. *Journal of Consulting and Clinical Psychology, 59,* 704–714. doi:10.1037/0022-006X.59.5.704

Sweeney, T. J. (2012). Leadership for the counseling profession. In C. Y. Chang, C. A. Barrio Minton, A. L. Dixon, J. E. Myers, & T. J. Sweeney (Eds.), *Professional counseling excellence through leadership and advocacy* (pp. 3–20). New York, NY: Routledge.

Sweeney, T. J., & Witmer, J. M. (1991). Beyond social interest striving toward optimum health and wellness. *Individual Psychology, 47,* 527.

Sweet, S., & Moen, P. (2007). Integrating educational careers in work and family: Women's return to school and family life. *Community, Work and Family, 10,* 231–250. doi:10.1080/13668800701270166

Szymanski, D. M., & Owens, G. P. (2008). Do coping styles moderate or mediate the relationship between internalized heterosexism and sexual minority women's psychological distress? *Psychology of Women Quarterly, 32,* 95–104. doi:10.1111/j.1471-6402.2007.00410.x

Tang, M., & Erford, B. T. (2016). The history of school counseling. In B. T. Erford (Ed.), *Professional school counseling: A handbook of theories, programs and practices* (3rd ed., pp. 9–22). Austin, TX: Pro-Ed.

Tarasoff v. Regents of the University of California, 17 Cal. 3d 425, 551 P.2d 334 (Cal. 1976).

Taylor-Ritzler, T., Balcazar, R. E., Suarez-Balcazar, Y., Kilbury, R., Alvarado, F., & James, M. (2010). Engaging ethnically diverse individuals with disabilities in the vocational rehabilitation system: Themes of empowerment and oppression. *Journal of Vocational Rehabilitation, 33,* 3–14. doi:10.3233/JVR-2010-0511

Teesson, M., Newton, N. C., & Barrett, E. L. (2012). Australian school-based prevention programs for alcohol and other drugs: A systematic review. *Drug and Alcohol Review, 31,* 731–736. doi:10.1111/j.1465-3362.2012.00420.x

Thackeray, R., & Hunter, M. (2010). Empowering youth: Use of technology in advocacy to affect social change. *Journal of Computer-mediated Communication, 15,* 575–591. doi:10.1111/j.1083-6101.2009.01503.x

Thompson, R., & Littrell, J. M. (1998). Brief counseling for students with learning disabilities. *Professional School Counseling, 2,* 60–67.

Tillitski, L. (1990). A meta-analysis of estimated effect sizes for group versus individual versus control treatments. *International Journal of Group Psychotherapy, 40,* 215–224.

Tobler, N. S., & Stratton, H. H. (1997). Effectiveness of school-based drug prevention programs: A meta-analysis of the research. *Journal of Primary Prevention, 18,* 71–128. doi:10.1023/A:1024630205999

Toporek, R. L., Lewis, J. A., & Crethar, H. C. (2009). Promoting systemic change: Through the ACA advocacy competencies. *Journal of Counseling & Development, 87,* 260–268.

Toporek, R. L., & Williams, R. A. (2006). Ethics and professional issues related to the practice of social justice in counselling psychology. In R. L. Toporek, L. H. Gerstein, N. A. Fouad, G. Roysircar, & T. Israel (Eds.), *Handbook for social justice in counselling psychology: Leadership, vision, and action* (pp. 17–34). Thousand Oaks, CA: Sage.

Town, J. M., Diener, M. J., Abbass, A., Leichsenring, F., Driessen, E., & Rabung, S. (2012). A meta-analysis of psychodynamic psychotherapy outcomes: Evaluating the effects of research-specific procedures. *Psychotherapy, 49,* 276–290. doi:10.1037/a0029564

Trusty, J., & Brown, D. (2005). Advocacy competencies for professional school counselors. *Professional School Counseling, 8,* 259–265.

Turner, S. L., Conkel, J., Starkey, M. T., & Landgraf, R. (2011). The career beliefs of inner-city adolescents. *Professional School Counseling, 15*(1), 1–14. doi:10.5330/PSC.n.2011-15.1

Tyler, L. E. (1969). *The work of the counselor* (3rd ed.). New York, NY: Appleton-Century-Crofts.

United Healthcare. (2014). *Mental health conditions: Partial hospital/day treatment program.* Retrieved from http://www.uhccommunityplan.com/content/dam/communityplan/healthcareprofessionals/providerinformation/TN-PartialHospitalDayTreatment.pdf

U.S. Census Bureau. (2011a). *Profile of general population and housing characteristics* [Data file]. Retrieved from http://factfinder2.census.gov/faces/tableservices/jsf/pages/productview.xhtml?pid=DEC_10_DP_DPDP1&prodType=table

U.S. Census Bureau. (2011b). *2010 census counts of American Indians, Eskimos, or Aleuts and American Indian and Alaska Native areas.* Washington, DC: Author.

U.S. Department of Education. (2015). Retrieved from http://nces.ed.gov/pubs2015/2015025.pdf

U.S. Department of Health and Human Services. (2002). *Standards for privacy of individually identifiable health information; final rule. 45 CFR parts 160 and 164.* Retrieved from http://www.hhs.gov/ocr/privacy/hipaa/administrative/privacyrule/privrulepd.pdf

U.S. Department of Health and Human Services. (2012, November). *Report to Congress on the prevention and reduction of underage drinking.* Retrieved from http://files.eric.ed.gov/fulltext/ED540217.pdf

U.S. Department of Health and Human Services. (2014). *Bulletin: HIPAA privacy in emergency situations.* Retrieved from http://www.hhs.gov/ocr/privacy/hipaa/understanding/special/emergency/emergencysituations.pdf

U.S. Department of Health and Human Services. (2015). *Annual update of the HHS poverty guidelines.* Retrieved from https://www.federalregister.gov/articles/2015/01/22/2015-01120/annual-update-of-the-hhs-poverty-guidelines

U.S. Department of Health and Human Services. (2018). *Vocational rehabilitation services.* Retrieved from http://dhs.sd.gov/drs/vocrehab/vr.aspx

U.S. Department of Labor. (2014). *Occupational outlook handbook.* Retrieved from http://www.bls.gov/ooh/

U.S. Department of Labor. (2017). *WIOA overview.* Retrieved from http://www.doleta.gov/WIOA/Overview.cfm

U.S. Equal Employment Opportunity Commission. (2008). *ADA Amendments Act of 2008.* Retrieved from https://www.eeoc.gov/laws/statutes/adaaa.cfm

Ursa, M., & Koehn C. (2015). Young women's experience of coping with violence in intimate relationships. *Journal of Mental Health Counseling, 37,* 250–267. doi:10.17744/1040-2861-37.3.250

Vacha-Haase, T., Davenport, D. S., & Kerewsky, S. D. (2004). Problematic students: Gatekeeping practices of academic professional psychology programs. *Professional Psychology: Research and Practice, 35,* 115–122. doi:10.1037/0735-7028.35.2.115

Van der Kolk, B. (2006). Clinical implications of neuroscience research in PTSD. *Annals New York Academy of Sciences, 1,* 1–17. doi:10.1196/annals.1364.022

Van Dernoot Lipsky, L., & Burk, C. (2009). *Trauma stewardship: An everyday guide to caring for self while caring for others.* San Francisco, CA: Berrett-Koehler.

Van Etten, M. L., & Taylor, S. (1998). Comparative efficacy of treatments for posttraumatic stress disorder: A meta-analysis. *Clinical Psychology and Psychotherapy, 5,* 126–144. doi:10.1002/(SICI)1099-0879(199809)5:3<126::AID-CPP153>3.0.CO;2-H

van Wormer, K., & Davis, D. R. (2012). *Addiction treatment: A strengths perspective* (3rd ed.). Pacific Grove, CA: Brooks/Cole.

Vernon, A. (1998a). *The passport program: A journey through emotional, social, cognitive, and self-development (grades 6–8).* Champaign, IL: Research Press.

Vernon, A. (1998b). *The passport program: A journey through emotional, social, cognitive, and self-development (grades 9–12).* Champaign, IL: Research Press.

Vernon, A. (2002). *What works when with children and adolescents: A handbook of individual counseling techniques.* Champaign, IL: Research Press.

Vernon, A. (2006). *Thinking, feeling, behaving: An emotional education curriculum for children.* Champaign, IL: Research Press.

Vernon, A. (2010). *Counseling children and adolescents* (4th ed.). Denver, CO: Love Publishing.

Villalba, J. (2018). Individuals and families of Hispanic descent. In D. G. Hays & B. T. Erford (Eds.), *Developing multicultural counseling competence: A systems approach* (3rd ed., pp. 245–269). Columbus, OH: Pearson.

Walker, L. E. (1979). *The battered woman.* New York, NY: Harper and Row.

Walter, J. L., & Peller, J. E. (2014). *Becoming solution-focused in brief therapy* (reprint ed.). New York, NY: Routledge.

Walz, G. R., Gazda, G. M., & Shertzer, B. (1991). *Counseling futures.* (Report No. ISBN: 56109-005-0). Ann Arbor, MI: ERIC/CAPS. (Eric Document Reproduction Service No. RI88062011)

Wampler, K. S., Reifman, A., & Serovich, J. M. (2005). Meta-analysis in family therapy research. In D. H. Sprenkle & F. P. Piercy (Eds.), *Research methods in family therapy* (2nd ed., pp. 318–338). New York, NY: Guilford Press.

Wampold, B. E. (2011). *Qualities and actions of effective therapists.* Washington, DC: American Psychological Association.

Wampold, B. E., Imel, Z. E., Bhati, K. S., & Johnson-Jennings, M. D. (2007). Insight as a common factor. In L. G. Castonguay & C. Hill (Eds.), *Insight in psychotherapy* (pp. 119–139). Washington, DC: American Psychological Association.

Washington, K. T., Bickel-Swenson, O., & Stephens, N. (2008). Barriers to hospice use among African Americans: A systematic review. *Health & Social Work, 33,* 267–274. doi:10.1093/hsw/33.4.267

Wechsler, D. (2008). *Manual for the Wechsler Adult Intelligence Scale* (4th ed., WAIS-IV). San Antonio, TX: Pearson.

Wechsler, D. (2009). *Manual for the Wechsler Individual Achievement Test* (3rd ed., WIAT-III). San Antonio, TX: Pearson.

Wechsler, D. (2014). *Manual for the Wechsler Intelligence Scale for Children* (5th ed., WISC-V). San Antonio, TX: Psychological Corporation.

Weed, R. O., & Field, T. F. (2012). *Rehabilitation consultant's handbook* (4th ed.). Athens, GA: Elliott & Fitzpatrick.

Weinberg, M. S., Williams, C. J., & Pryor, D. W. (1995). *Dual attraction: Understanding bisexuality.* New York, NY: Oxford University Press.

Weiss, C. (1998). *Evaluation:* Methods for studying programs and policies (2nd ed.). Upper Saddle River, NJ: Prentice Hall.

Weisz, J. R., Weiss, B., Alicke, M. D., & Klotz, M. L. (1987). Effectiveness of psychotherapy with children and adolescents: A meta-analysis for clinicians. *Journal of Consulting and Clinical Psychology, 55,* 542–549. doi:10.1037/0022-006X.55.4.542

Weisz, J. R., Weiss, B., Han, S. S., Granger, D. A., & Morton, T. (1995). Effects of psychotherapy with children and adolescents revisited: A meta-analysis of treatment outcome studies. *Psychological Bulletin, 117,* 450–468.

Welfel, E. R., & Patterson, L. E. (2005). *The counseling process: A multitheoretical integrative approach* (6th ed.). Belmont, CA: Thomson Brooks/Cole.

West-Olatunji, C., & Gibson, D. (2012). A global and historical introduction to social class. In D. C. Sturm & D. Gibson (Eds.), *Social class and the helping professions: A clinician's guide to navigating the landscape of class in America* (pp. 3–15). New York, NY: Routledge.

Whaley, A. L., & Davis, K. E. (2007). Cultural competence and evidenced-based practice in mental health services: A complementary perspective. *American Psychologist, 62,* 563–574. doi:10.1037/0003-066X.62.6.563

Whiston, S. C., Brecheisen, B. K., & Stephens, J. (2003). Does treatment modality affect career counseling effectiveness? *Journal of Vocational Behavior, 62,* 390–410.

Whiston, S. C., Feldwisch, R., & James, B. (2015). Outcomes research on school counseling interventions and programs. In B. T. Erford (Ed.), *Transforming the school counseling profession* (3rd ed., pp. 132–144). Columbus, OH: Pearson Merrill.

Whiston, S. C., & Sexton, T. L. (1993). An overview of psychotherapy outcome research: Implications for practice. *Professional Psychology: Research and Practice, 24*(1), 43–51. doi:10.1037/0735-7028.24.1.43

Whiston, S. C., Sexton, T. L., & Lasoff, D. L. (1998). Career intervention outcome: A replication and extension of Oliver and Spokane (1988). *Journal of Counseling Psychology, 45,* 150–165. doi:10.1037/0022-0167.45.2.150

Whiston, S. C., Tai, W. L., Rahardja, D., & Eder, K. (2010). School counseling outcome: A meta-analytic examination of interventions. *Journal of Counseling & Development, 89,* 37–55.

White, M., & Epston, D. (1990). *Narrative means to therapeutic ends.* New York, NY: Norton.

Wilkerson, K., & Bellini, J. (2006). Intrapersonal and organizational factors associated with burnout among school counselors. *Journal of Counseling & Development, 84,* 440–450. doi:10.1002/j.1556-6678.2006.tb00428.x

Wilson, D. B., Gottfredson, D. C., & Najaka, S. S. (2001). School-based prevention of problem behaviors: A meta-analysis. *Journal of Quantitative Criminology, 17*, 247–272. doi:10.1023/A:1011050217296

Wilson, D. K., & Williams, J. E. (2005). A conceptual model for school-based prevention programs in children and adolescents in the next frontier. In L. C. James & R. A. Folen (Eds.), *The primary care consultant: The next frontier for psychologists in hospitals and clinics* (pp. 191–214). Washington, DC: American Psychological Association.

Wilson, S. J., Lipsey, M. W., & Derzon, J. H. (2003). The effects of school-based intervention programs on aggressive behavior: A meta-analysis. *Journal of Consulting and Clinical Psychology, 71*, 136–149. doi:10.1037/0022-006X.71.1.136

Witmer, J. M., & Granello, P. F. (2005). Wellness in counselor education and supervision. In J. E. Myers & T. J. Sweeney (Eds.), *Counseling for wellness: Theory, research and practice* (pp. 261–271). Alexandria, VA: American Counseling Association.

Wolin, S. J., & Wolin, S. (1993). *The resilient self.* New York, NY: Villard Books.

Wood, J. T. (2010). *Gendered lives: Communication, gender, and culture* (9th ed.). Belmont, CA: Wadsworth.

Woodcock, R., Schrank, F. A., Mather, N., & McGrew, K. (2014). *Woodcock-Johnson IV Tests of Achievement* (WJ IV). Itasca, IL: Riverside.

World Health Organization. (2011, June). *World report on disability.* Retrieved from http://whqlibdoc.who.int/hq/2011/WHO_NMH_VIP_11.01_eng.pdf

World Health Organization. (2013). *Investing in mental health: Evidence for action.* Geneva, Switzerland: Author

World Health Organization. (WHO). (2016). *International classification of diseases (tenth revision) with clinical modification* (ICD-10 CM). Geneva, Switzerland: Author.

World Health Organization. (WHO). (2017). *The international statistical classification of diseases,* (eleventh edition) (ICD-11). Geneva, Switzerland, Author.

Wrenn, C. G. (1962). *The counselor in a changing world.* Washington, DC: American Personnel and Guidance Association.

Wright, S. L., Perrone-McGovern, K. M., Boo, J. N., & White, A. V. (2014). Influential factors in academic and career self-efficacy: Attachment, supports, and career barriers. *Journal of Counseling & Development, 92*, 36–46. doi:10.1002/j.1556-6676.2014.00128.x

Wubbolding, R. E. (1991). *Understanding reality therapy.* New York, NY: HarperCollins.

Yager, G. G., & Tovar-Blank, Z. G. (2007). Wellness and counselor education. *Journal of Humanistic Counseling, Education, and Development, 46*, 142–153. doi:10.1002/j.2161-1939.2007.tb00032.x

Yalom, I. D. (2002). *The gift of therapy: An open letter to a new generation of therapists and their patients.* New York, NY: Harper Collins.

Yalom, I. D., & Leszcz, M. (2005). *The theory and practice of group psychotherapy* (5th ed.). New York, NY: Basic Books.

Yanos, P. T., Vreeland, B., Minsky, S., Fuller, R. B., & Roe, D. (2009). Partial hospitalization: Compatible with evidence-based and recovery-oriented treatment? *Journal of Psychosocial Nursing, 47*(2), 41–47. Retrieved from http://JPNonline.com

Young, M. A., Lindsey, C. V., & Kolodinsky, W. P. (2010). The role of live supervision in counselor education training clinics. In A. Mobley & J. Myers (Eds.), *Developing and maintaining counselor education laboratories* (2nd ed.). Alexandria, VA: Association of Counselor Education and Supervision.

Young, M. E. (2013). *Learning the art of helping: Building blocks and techniques* (5th ed.). Upper Saddle River, NJ: Pearson Education.

Young, M. E., & Lambie, G. W. (2007). Wellness in school and mental health settings. *Journal of Humanistic Counseling, Education and Development, 46*, 9–16.

Young, R. A., Marshall, S. K., & Valach, L. (2007). Making career theories more culturally sensitive: Implications for counseling. *Career Development Quarterly, 56*, 4–18. doi:10.1002/j.2161-0045.2007.tb00016.x

Young, R. A., Valach, L., & Collin, A. (2002). A contextualist explanation of career. In D. Brown & Associates (Eds.), *Career choice and development* (4th ed., pp. 206–254). San Francisco, CA: Jossey-Bass.

Zanskas, S. A., & Leahy, M. J. (2008). Importance of consultation content and instructional proficiency in rehabilitation counselor education. *Rehabilitation Education, 22*(1), 59–72. doi:10.1891/088970108805059507

Zunker, V. G. (2015). *Career counseling: A holistic approach* (9th ed.). Pacific Grove, CA: Brooks/Cole.

CREDITS

Chapter 1: Page 4 (Table 1.1): Bradley T. Erford, *Orientation to the Counseling Profession: Advocacy, Ethics, and Essential Professional Foundations* © 2018. Pearson Education, Inc., New York, NY; Page 5: From *What is Professional Counseling?* © 2017. Published by the American Counseling Association; Pages 10–12 (Table 1.2): Bradley T. Erford, *Orientation to the Counseling Profession: Advocacy, Ethics, and Essential Professional Foundations* © 2018. Pearson Education, Inc., New York, NY; Page 13: From *A Mind That Found Itself,* by Clifford Whittingham Beers © 2015. Published by Sheba Blake Publishing; Page 19: From *Counseling and the Future: Some Views of Editorial Board Members,* by James R. Barclay, Beverly M. Brown, Samuel T. Gladding, Rodney K. Goodyear, Donald G. Hays, Thomas H. Hohenshil, Darrell Smith, and James R. Barclay © 1981. Published by John Wiley & Sons, Inc.; Page 26: From "Do Formalized Gatekeeping Procedures Increase Programs' Follow-up with Deficient Trainees?" in *Counselor Education and Supervision, 41*(4), 294–305. By Michael D. Gaubatz, Elizabeth M. Vera © 2002. Published by John Wiley & Sons, Inc.; Page 27–28: From "Advocating for the Counseling Profession: My Path to Becoming an Advocate for the Field of Counseling," by Gregory Pollock. Pulbished by permission of Gregory Pollock; Page 33: From "Lack of Self-Care and Lorna Doones," by Nicole Bradley. Published by permission of Nicole Bradley.

Chapter 2: Page 36 (Figure 2.1): Bradley T. Erford, *Orientation to the Counseling Profession: Advocacy, Ethics, and Essential Professional Foundations* © 2018. Pearson Education, Inc., New York, NY; Page 38 (Figure 2.2): Bradley T. Erford, *Orientation to the Counseling Profession: Advocacy, Ethics, and Essential Professional Foundations* © 2018. Pearson Education, Inc., New York, NY; Pages 39–40: From "The Importance of Joining Professional Associations as a Graduate Student," by Carolyn Berger. Copyright © by Carolyn Berger; Page 41: From American Mental Health Counselors Association (AMHCA). Published by American Mental Health Counselors Association; Page 41–42: Excerpt from AADA. http://www.aadaweb.org/. Published by Association of Adult Development and Aging © 2016; Page 42: Excerpt

from "About Us." http://aarc-counseling.org/. Published by Association for Assessment in Counseling and Education © 2016; Page 43: Excerpt from *Code of Professional Ethics For Rehabilitation Counselors* (2009) http://ethics.iit.edu/ecodes/node/4596. Published by Association for Creativity in Counseling; Page 43: Excerpt from The Association for Humanistic Counseling (AHC). https://www.counseling.org/about-us/divisions-regions-and-branches/divisions Published by The Association for Humanistic Counseling (AHC). © 2016; Page 44: Excerpt from ASERVIC; Page 45: Excerpt from International Association of Marriage and Family Counselors (IAMFC). https://www.counseling.org/about-us/divisions-regions-and-branches/divisions Published by International Association of Marriage and Family Counselors (IAMFC) © 2016; Page 46: Excerpt from National Career Development Association. Published by National Career Development Association; Page 45: Excerpt from Counselors for Social Justice (CSJ). https://www.counseling.org/about-us/divisions-regions-and-branches/divisions Published by Counselors for Social Justice (CSJ). © 2016; Page 45: Excerpt from International Association of Addictions and Offender Counselors (IAAOC). https://www.counseling.org/about-us/divisions-regions-and-branches/divisions Published by International Association of Addictions and Offender Counselors (IAAOC). © 2016; Pages 49–50: Kelly Duncan; Page 49–50: From "Getting Involved: Joining and Promoting Professional Counseling Organizations," by Kelly Duncan. Copyright © by Kelly Duncan.

Chapter 3: Page 74–76 (Table 3.1): Bradley T. Erford, *Orientation to the Counseling Profession: Advocacy, Ethics, and Essential Professional Foundations* © 2018. Pearson Education, Inc., New York, NY; Page 77–78: From "Managing Boundary Issues in Counseling," by Victoria E. Kress. Copyright © by Victoria E. Kress; Pages 78–79: From "Ethics Case Study: Sarah," by Nadine Hartig. Copyright © by Nadine Hartig; Page 85: From *A Practitioner's Guide to Ethical Decision Making.* Copyright © 1996. Published by permission of American Counseling Association; Page 95–96: Based on *Counseling Ethics and Decision*

Making, 3rd ed., by Robert R. Cottone and Vilia M. Tarvydas. Published by Pearson Education, 2007; Page 99: From "Garnering a License," by James R. Rough. Copyright © by James R. Rough; Page 101: From 2014 ACA Code of Ethics, P.3. Published by permission of American Counseling Association © 2014; Page 106: Excerpt from Protection of Pupil Rights Amendment (PPRA), 1978; Pages107–108: From "Client Records: A Common Ethics Problem," by William L. Hegarty. Copyright © by William L. Hegarty; Page 111: From Eisel v. Board of Education, published by Court of Appeals of Maryland © 1991.

Chapter 4: Page 118 (Table 4.1): Bradley T. Erford, *Orientation to the Counseling Profession: Advocacy, Ethics, and Essential Professional Foundations* © 2018. Pearson Education, Inc., New York, NY; Page 118–119 (Table 4.2): Bradley T. Erford, *Orientation to the Counseling Profession: Advocacy, Ethics, and Essential Professional Foundations* © 2018. Pearson Education, Inc., New York, NY; Page 123–124 (Table 4.3): Bradley T. Erford, *Orientation to the Counseling Profession: Advocacy, Ethics, and Essential Professional Foundations* © 2018. Pearson Education, Inc., New York, NY; Page 128–129 (Table 4.4): Bradley T. Erford, *Orientation to the Counseling Profession: Advocacy, Ethics, and Essential Professional Foundations* © 2018. Pearson Education, Inc., New York, NY; Page 132 (Figure 4.1): Bradley T. Erford, *Orientation to the Counseling Profession: Advocacy, Ethics, and Essential Professional Foundations* © 2018. Pearson Education, Inc., New York, NY; Page 134–135: From *Working with the Problem Drinker: A Solution-focused Approach,* by Insoo Kim Berg and Scott D. Miller © 1992. Published by W.W. Norton; Pages 137–138 (Table 4.5): Bradley T. Erford, *Orientation to the Counseling Profession: Advocacy, Ethics, and Essential Professional Foundations* © 2018. Pearson Education, Inc., New York, NY; Pages 140–141 (Table 4.6): Bradley T. Erford, *Orientation to the Counseling Profession: Advocacy, Ethics, and Essential Professional Foundations* © 2018. Pearson Education, Inc., New York, NY; Page 143–144: From "Narrative Therapy with Children Who Have Been Abused," by Victoria E. Kress. Copyright © by Victoria E. Kress; Page 149–150 (Table 4.7): Bradley T. Erford, *Orientation to the Counseling Profession: Advocacy, Ethics, and Essential Professional Foundations* © 2018. Pearson Education, Inc., New York, NY; Page 152 (Table 4.8): Adapted from "Transtheoretical Therapy: Toward a More Integrative Model of

Change," by J. O. Prochaska and C. C. DiClemente, 1982, *Psychotherapy: Theory, Research, and Practice,* 20, pp. 161–173; Page 157 (Figure 4.2): Bradley T. Erford, *Orientation to the Counseling Profession: Advocacy, Ethics, and Essential Professional Foundations* © 2018. Pearson Education, Inc., New York, NY; Page 157 (Figure 4.3): Bradley T. Erford, *Orientation to the Counseling Profession: Advocacy, Ethics, and Essential Professional Foundations* © 2018. Pearson Education, Inc., New York, NY; Page 157–158: From "How My Counseling Theory Has Informed My Practice," by Randall M. Moate. Copyright © by Randall M. Moate.

Chapter 5: Page 162: Bradley T. Erford, *Orientation to the Counseling Profession: Advocacy, Ethics, and Essential Professional Foundations* © 2018. Pearson Education, Inc., New York, NY; Page 171: From "Trust in the Process and Yourself," by Nicole Bradley. Copyright © by Nicole Bradley; Page 174: Bradley T. Erford, *Orientation to the Counseling Profession: Advocacy, Ethics, and Essential Professional Foundations* © 2018. Pearson Education, Inc., New York, NY; Page 177 (Figure 5.1): Bradley T. Erford, *Orientation to the Counseling Profession: Advocacy, Ethics, and Essential Professional Foundations* © 2018. Pearson Education, Inc., New York, NY; Page 177–178: From "Different Strokes for Different Folks," by Nicole Adamson. Copyright © by Nicole Adamson; Page 187–188: From "Working within Multiple Systems While Remaining Focused on the Client's Welfare," by Amanda M. Evans. Copyright © by Amanda M. Evans; Page 189–190: From "Empathy and Patience," by F. Robert Wilson. Copyright © by F. Robert Wilson.

Chapter 6: Page 196: Bradley T. Erford, *Orientation to the Counseling Profession: Advocacy, Ethics, and Essential Professional Foundations* © 2018. Pearson Education, Inc., New York, NY; Page 204: Bradley T. Erford, *Orientation to the Counseling Profession: Advocacy, Ethics, and Essential Professional Foundations* © 2018. Pearson Education, Inc., New York, NY; Page 206 (Table 6.1): Bradley T. Erford, *Orientation to the Counseling Profession: Advocacy, Ethics, and Essential Professional Foundations* © 2018. Pearson Education, Inc., New York, NY; Page 208: From "Reflection of Feeling," by Larissa Carpenter. Copyright © by Larissa Carpenter; Page 213: Bradley T. Erford, *Orientation to the Counseling Profession: Advocacy, Ethics, and Essential Professional Foundations* © 2018. Pearson Education, Inc., New York, NY; Page 214: From *Learning the Art* of *Helping: Building Blocks and Techniques*, 5th ed., by Mark E. Young © 2013. Published by Pearson Education; Page 215–216: From "Applying Microskills to the Real World," by Nicole Adamson. Copyright © by Nicole Adamson.

Chapter 7: Page 219: From "Coping Strategies Used by School Staff After a Crisis: A Research Note" in *Journal of Loss and Trauma, 18*(5): 472–481. By Rachel Cole,Ben Hayes, Dan Jones, and Sonia Shah. Published by Taylor & Francis Group © 2013; Page 219–220: From "Voices from the Field 7.1," by Doreen S. Marshall. Copyright © by Doreen S. Marshall; Page 220–221: From "Psychological First Aid" in *Journal of Mental Health Counseling, 29*(1), 17-49. By Josef I. Ruzek, Melissa J. Brymer, Anne K. Jacobs, Christopher M. Layne, Eric M. Vernberg, and Patricia J. Watson. Published by American Mental Health Counselors Association © 2007; Page 221: From *Early Interventions Following Exposure to Traumatic Events: Implications for Practice From Recent Research,* by Atle Dyregrov and Stephen Regel © 2011. Published by Taylor & Francis Group; Page 224: From "Young Women's Experiences of Coping with Violence in Intimate Relationships," in *Journal of Mental Health Counseling, 37, 3,* 250- 267. By Marina Ursa and Corinne Koehn. Published by American Mental Health Foundation, Inc. © 2015; Page 226 (Table 7.1): Bradley T. Erford, *Orientation to the Counseling Profession: Advocacy, Ethics, and Essential Professional Foundations* © 2018. Pearson Education, Inc., New York, NY; Page 228: *Code of Ethics*, American Association for Marriage and Family Therapy. January 2015; Page 231 (Table 7.2): Bradley T. Erford, *Orientation to the Counseling Profession: Advocacy, Ethics, and Essential Professional Foundations* © 2018. Pearson Education, Inc., New York, NY; Page 235: From Gatekeeper Training for Suicide Warning Signs. Published by QPR Institute; Page 239–241 (Table 7.3): Bradley T. Erford,*Orientation to the Counseling Profession: Advocacy, Ethics, and Essential Professional Foundations* © 2018. Pearson Education, Inc., New York, NY; Page 242 (Table 7.4): Summarized from O'Toole, M. E. (2000). *The School Shooter: A Threat Assessment Perspective.* Quantico, VA: National Center for the Analysis of Violent Crime (NCAVC) FBI Academy; Page 245: From *Crisis Assessment, Intervention, and Prevention*, 2nd ed., by Lisa R. Jackson-Cherry and Bradley T. Erford. Published by Pearson © 2014; Page 246: From "The Role of Warning Behaviors in Threat Assessment: An Exploration

and Suggested Typology," in *Behavioral Strategies and the Law,* 30, 256-279. By John Reid Meloy, Jens Hoffmann, Angela Guldimann, and David V James. Published by John Wiley & Sons, Ltd © 2011.

Chapter 8: Page 249: From "20/20: A Vision for the Future of Counseling: The New Consensus Definition of Counseling," p. 02, by David M. Kaplan, Vilia M. Tarvydas, and Samuel T. Gladding. Published by the American Counseling Association; Page 251–252: From "Mental Health Counseling," by Greg E. Bechtold. Published by permission of Greg E. Bechtold; Page 254: Amy L. McLeod; Page 256: David C. Hill; Page 266: Excerpt from Brenda J. Edwards; Page 268 (Table 8.1): Bradley T. Erford, *Orientation to the Counseling Profession: Advocacy, Ethics, and Essential Professional Foundations* © 2018. Pearson Education, Inc., New York, NY; Page 269: From "Rehabilitation," in *International Encyclopedia of Rehabilitation*, 3rd ed., p. 9, by Maurice Blouin and Luz Elvira Vallejo Echeverri. Published by the Center for International Rehabilitation Research Information and Exchange © 2012; Page 269: From Americans with Disabilities Act. (2008). Americans with Disabilities Act of 1990, as amended. http:// www.ada.gov/pubs/adastatute08.pdf, http:// www.eeoc.gov/laws/statutes/adaaa.cfm; Page 269: From Rehabilitation Counseling Scope of Practice, https://www.crccertification.com/scope-of-practice. Published by Commission on Rehabilitation Counselor Certification © 2016; Page 269: From "Code of Professional Ethics for Rehabilitation Counselors." Published by Commission on Rehabilitation Counselor Certification, © 2002; Pages 269–270: From World Report on Disability, p.7. http:// apps.who.int/iris/bitstream/10665/70670/1/ WHO_NMH_VIP_11.01_eng.pdf. Published by World Health Organization. © 2011, June; Page 270: Excerpt from Brad Smith; Page 272: Excerpt from Tracy Roberts; Page 273 (Table 8.2): Bradley T. Erford, *Orientation to the Counseling Profession: Advocacy, Ethics, and Essential Professional Foundations* © 2018. Pearson Education, Inc., New York, NY; 274: From "Psychological Adaptation to Disability: Perspectives from Chaos and Complexity Theory," in *PRO-ED Journals*, by Hanoch Livneh, Randall M Parker. Published by Sage Publications (US) © 2008; Page 275 (Table 8.3): Bradley T. Erford, *Orientation to the Counseling Profession: Advocacy, Ethics, and Essential Professional Foundations* © 2018. Pearson Education, Inc., New York, NY; Page 277: From Psychological

Adaptation to Disability: Perspectives from Chaos and Complexity Theory. Published by Commission on Rehabilitation Counselor Certification, © 2009; Page 300: Edward T. Markowski.

Chapter 9: Page 300: Excerpt from Career Guidance: A Handbook for Policy Makers. http://www.oecd.org/edu/innovation-education/34050171.pdf. Published by Organization for Economic Cooperation and Development, p. 19 © 2004; Page 300: Excerpt from Career Education and the Meaning of Work, by Donald E. Super, 1976. http://catalog.hathitrust.org/Record/002532521; Page 281: From "Elementary School Counseling," by Jason Baker. Copyright © by Jason Baker; Page 282: From "Middle School Counseling," by Corissa Fetrow. Copyright © by Corissa Fetrow; Page 283: From "High School Counseling," by Eric Shellenberge. Copyright © by Eric Shellenberge; Page 286: From Glossary of Terms, Advocacy. Published by the American Counseling Association © 2014; Page 292 (Table 9.1): Bradley T. Erford, *Orientation to the Counseling Profession: Advocacy, Ethics, and Essential Professional Foundations* © 2018. Pearson Education, Inc., New York, NY; Page 293: From "College Counseling," by Joseph F. Lynch. Copyright © by Joseph F. Lynch; Page 296: From "Universal Design for Learning and Instruction: Perspectives of Students with Disabilities in Higher Education," in *Exceptionality Education International*, 25, 2, p. 3, by Robert D. Black, Lois A. Weinberg, and Martin G. Brodwin. Published by Exceptionality Education International © 2015; Page 300 (Table 9.2): Bradley T. Erford, *Orientation to the Counseling Profession: Advocacy, Ethics, and Essential Professional Foundations* © 2018. Pearson Education, Inc., New York, NY; Page 300: From *Introduction to the Counseling Profession*, 3rd ed., by Duane Brown and David J. Srebalus. Published by Pearson Education © 2003; Page 300: From *Introduction to the Counseling Profession*, 3rd ed., by Duane Brown and David J. Srebalus. Published by Pearson Education © 2003; Page 300: Excerpt from *Introduction to the Counseling Profession*, 3red ed., by Duane Brown and David J. Srebalus. Published by Pearson Education © 2003; Page 300: From *Introduction to the Counseling Profession*, 3rd ed., by Duane Brown and David J. Srebalus. Published by Pearson Education , © 2003; Page 300: From *Career Information, Career Counseling, and Career Development*, 11th ed., by Duane Brown. Published by Pearson Education © 2016; Page 300: Excerpt from *Advancing the Career Counseling*

Profession: Objectives and Strategies for the Next Decade, by Mark L. Savickas. Published by National Career Development Association © 2003; Page 300: From Policy and Procedures Manual 2015–16. Retrieved from http://www.ncda.org/aws/NCDA/pt/sp/guidelines; Pages 307–308: From "Voices from the Field 9.5" by Steve Sharp. Copyright © by Steve Sharp.

Chapter 10: Pages 314, 332: Excerpt from *Development Through Life: A Psychosocial Approach,* by Barbara M. Newman and Philip R. Newman, 12th ed., pp. 194, 553. Published by Cengage Learning, © 2014; Page 318–319: From "Working with Young Children: Generalization from One Context to Another," by Nicole Bradley. Copyright © by Nicole Bradley; Page 329: From *Development Across the Life Span*, 7th ed., by Robert S. Feldman. Published by Pearson Education © 2014; Page 335: Bradley T. Erford, *Orientation to the Counseling Profession: Advocacy, Ethics, and Essential Professional Foundations* © 2018. Pearson Education, Inc., New York, NY.

Chapter 11: Page 338 (Table 11.1): Bradley T. Erford, *Orientation to the Counseling Profession: Advocacy, Ethics, and Essential Professional Foundations.* © 2018. Pearson Education, Inc., New York, NY. Page 342: From "Cultural Competence and Evidence-Based Practice in Mental Health Services: A Complementary Perspective," in *American Psychologist*, Vol. *62(6)*, Sep 2007, 563-574. By Arthur L. Whaley and King E. Davis. Published by the American Psychological Association © 2007. Page 343 (Figure 11.1): Bradley T. Erford, *Orientation to the Counseling Profession: Advocacy, Ethics, and Essential Professional Foundations* © 2018. Pearson Education, Inc., New York, NY. Page 346 (Table 11.2): Bradley T. Erford, *Orientation to the Counseling Profession: Advocacy, Ethics, and Essential Professional Foundations* © 2018. Pearson Education, Inc., New York, NY. Page 352: From "Connecting with Multiculturalism," by Nicole Adamson. Copyright © Nicole Adamson. Page 364: From *ACA Code of Ethics 2004*, p. 3. Published by the American Counseling Association © 2004. Pages 364–365: From Competencies for Integrating Spirituality into Counseling, published by permission of Association for Spiritual, Ethical, and Religious Values in Counseling, 2016. Page 365: From "My Experience with Multicultural Counseling," by Nicholette Leanza. Copyright © by Nicholette Leanza. Page 369: From *Why Social Justice is a Counseling*

Concern, by Hugh C. Crethar and Manivong J. Ratts. published by Counselors for Social Justice (CSJ) ©.

Chapter 12: Page 380 (Table 12.1): Bradley T. Erford, *Orientation to the Counseling Profession: Advocacy, Ethics, and Essential Professional Foundations* © 2018. Pearson Education, Inc., New York, NY; Page 384: From "Suicide Prevention: Critical Elements for Managing Suicidal Clients and Counselor Liability without the Use of a No-Suicide Contract," in *Death Studies*, 29: 847–865, by Jeane B. Lee and Mary L. Bartlett. Published by Taylor & Francis Inc. © 2005; Page 387: From "Considering Client Contextual Factors in Assessment," by Amanda C. Healey. Copyright © by Amanda C. Healey; Page 388–389: From "A Case of Mistaken Identity," by Meghan Brown. Copyright © by Meghan Brown; Page 392–393: From "Case Management and Assessment in the Schools," by Bella Bikowsky and Christopher Sink. Copyright © by Bella Bikowsky and Christopher Sink; Page 402 (Table 12.2): Bradley T. Erford, *Orientation to the Counseling Profession: Advocacy, Ethics, and Essential Professional Foundations* © 2018. Pearson Education, Inc., New York, NY; Page 403 (Table 12.3): Bradley T. Erford, *Orientation to the Counseling Profession: Advocacy, Ethics, and Essential Professional Foundations* © 2018. Pearson Education, Inc., New York, NY.

Chapter 13: Page 407: From *The Counseling Dictionary: Concise Definitions of Frequently Used Terms*, 3rd ed., p. 150, by Samuel T. Gladding. Published by Pearson Education © 2011; Page 407: From *Psychological Consultation and Collaboration in School and Community Settings,* 6th ed., p. 8, by Michael Dougherty. Published by Pearson Education © 2013; Page 408: Bradley T. Erford, *Orientation to the Counseling Profession: Advocacy, Ethics, and Essential Professional Foundations* © 2018. Pearson Education, Inc., New York, NY; Page 418: Bradley T. Erford, *Orientation to the Counseling Profession: Advocacy, Ethics, and Essential Professional Foundations* © 2018. Pearson Education, Inc., New York, NY; Page 420: Used by Permission of Melanie E. Morlan; Page 421: Bradley T. Erford, *Orientation to the Counseling Profession: Advocacy, Ethics, and Essential Professional Foundations* © 2018. Pearson Education, Inc., New York, NY; Page 422 (Figure 13.1): Bradley T. *Erford, Orientation to the Counseling Profession: Advocacy, Ethics, and Essential Professional Foundations* © 2018. Pearson Education, Inc., New York, NY; Page 423: From "Consultation and Supervision," by Kami Wagner. Copyright © by Kami Wagner; Page 423: Kami Wagner; Pages 427–428: Bradley T. Erford, *Orientation to the Counseling Profession: Advocacy, Ethics, and Essential Professional Foundations* © 2018. Pearson Education, Inc., New York, NY; Page 429: Bradley T. Erford, *Orientation to the Counseling Profession: Advocacy, Ethics, and Essential Professional Foundations* © 2018. Pearson Education, Inc., New York, NY; Pages 431–432: From "Consultation Is Essential to Effective Practice," by Megan Kidron. Copyright © by Megan Kidron.

Chapter 14: Pages 436–437: From *ACA Code of Ethics*, published by the American Counseling Association © 2005; Page 438: Used by permission of Rob Rhodes; Pages 439–440: Excerpt from *Making An Impact: A Handbook on Counselor Advocacy*, by Karen Eriksen, p.1. Published by Taylor & Francis © 1997; Pages 440: Used by permission of Stephanie Burns; Pages 450–451: Used by permission of Stephanie Burns; Page 455: Used by permission of Stephen Kennedy.

Chapter 15: Page 477: Excerpt from "Counselor Advocacy: Affecting Systemic Change in the Public Arena," in *Journal of Counseling and Development,* 87(3), pp. 284–287, by Courtland C. Lee and Roe A. Rodgers. Published by John Wiley & Sons, Inc. © 2009; Page 480: Excerpt from "Counselor Advocacy: Affecting Systemic Change in the Public Arena," in *Journal of Counseling and Development,* 87(3), pp. 284–287, by Courtland C. Lee and Roe A. Rodgers. Published by the American Counseling Association © 2009; Page 481 (Table 15.7): Bradley T. Erford; Page 458: From "What Is Social Justice in Counselling?" https://counseling-csj.org/. Published by Counselors for Social Justice © 2016; Page 461 (Figure 15.1): Ratts, M. J., Singh, A. A., Nassar-McMillan, S., Butler, S. K., & McCullough, J. R. (2015). *Multicultural and social justice counseling competencies*. By the Association for Multicultural Counseling and Development. Used by permission of Manivong Ratts; Page 462 (Table 15.1): Ratts, M. J., Singh, A. A., Nassar-McMillan, S., Butler, S. K., & McCullough, J. R. (2015). *Multicultural and social justice counseling competencies*. By the Association for Multicultural Counseling and Development. Used by permission of Manivong Ratts; Page 462: Ratts, M. J., Singh, A. A., Nassar-McMillan, S., Butler, S. K., & McCullough, J. R. (2015). *Multicultural and social justice counseling competencies*. By the Association for Multicultural Counseling and Development. Used by permission of Manivong

Ratts; Page 465: From "Empowering Young Clients to Self-Advocate," by Danielle L. Geigle. Copyright © by Danielle L. Geigle; Page 467 (Table 15.2): Ratts, M. J., Singh, A. A., Nassar-McMillan, S., Butler, S. K., & McCullough, J. R. (2015). *Multicultural and social justice counseling competencies*. By the Association for Multicultural Counseling and Development. Used by permission of Manivong Ratts; Page 469: Bradley T. Erford, *Orientation to the Counseling Profession: Advocacy, Ethics, and Essential Professional Foundations* © 2018. Pearson Education, Inc., New York, NY; Page 470 (Table 15.3): Ratts, M. J., Singh, A. A., Nassar-McMillan, S., Butler, S. K., & McCullough, J. R. (2015) *Multicultural and social justice counseling competencies*. By the Association for Multicultural Counseling and Development. Used by permission of Manivong Ratts; Pages 472–473: From "Student and Community Advocacy: A View from the Schools," by Lacey Wallace. Copyright © by Lacey Wallace; Page 474 (Table 15.4): Ratts, M. J., Singh, A. A., Nassar-McMillan, S., Butler, S. K., & McCullough, J. R. (2015). *Multicultural and social justice counseling competencies*. By the Association for Multicultural Counseling and Development. Used by permission of Manivong Ratts; Page 476: From "New Professional Roles and Advocacy Strategies for School Counselors: A Multicultural/ Social Justice Perspective to Move beyond the Nice Counselor Syndrome," in *Journal of Counseling and Development,* 86(3), 372–381 by Fred Bemak and Rita Chi-Ying Chung. Published by John Wiley & Sons © 2008; Page 477: Bradley T. Erford, *Orientation to the Counseling Profession: Advocacy, Ethics, and Essential Professional Foundations* © 2018. Pearson Education, Inc., New York, NY; Page 478 (Table 15.5): Ratts, M. J., Singh, A. A., Nassar-McMillan, S., Butler, S. K., & McCullough, J. R. (2015). *Multicultural and social justice counseling competencies*. By the Association for Multicultural Counseling and Development. Used by permission of Manivong Ratts; Page 479 (Tabl15.6): From "Multicultural and Social Justice Counseling Competencies Conceptual Framework," © 2015 by M. J. Ratts, A. A.Singh, S. Nassar-McMillan and J. R.McCullough. Association for Multicultural and Development Multicultural Counseling Competencies Revisions Committee; Page 481: Bradley T. Erford, *Orientation to the Counseling Profession: Advocacy, Ethics, and Essential Professional Foundations* © 2018. Pearson Education, Inc., New York, NY; Page 481–482: From "DATA-DRIVEN DECISION MAKING: How Your Voice Can Influence Change," by Tracy Macdonald. Copyright © by Tracy Macdonald; Pages 482–483: From "USING DATA: Campus Advocacy for Students Who Self-Injure," by Victoria E. Kress. Copyright © by Victoria E. Kress; Page 484 (Table 15.8): Ratts, M. J., Singh, A. A., Nassar-McMillan, S., Butler, S. K., & McCullough, J. R. (2015). *Multicultural and social justice counseling competencies*. By the Association for Multicultural Counseling and Development. Used by permission of Manivong Ratts; Page 485:Bradley T. Erford, *Orientation to the Counseling Profession: Advocacy, Ethics, and Essential Professional Foundations* © 2018. Pearson Education, Inc., New York, NY.

Chapter 16: Page 493 (Table 16.2): Bradley T. Erford; Page 490 (Table 16.1): Bradley T. Erford, *Orientation to the Counseling Profession: Advocacy, Ethics, and Essential Professional Foundations* © 2018. Pearson Education, Inc., New York, NY; Page 494 (Figure 16.1): Bradley T. Erford, *Orientation to the Counseling Profession: Advocacy, Ethics, and Essential Professional Foundations* © 2018. Pearson Education, Inc., New York, NY; Page 496 (Table 16.3): Bradley T. Erford, *Orientation to the Counseling Profession: Advocacy, Ethics, and Essential Professional Foundations* © 2018. Pearson Education, Inc., New York, NY; Page 499 (Topic 16.2): Bradley T. Erford, *Orientation to the Counseling Profession: Advocacy, Ethics, and Essential Professional Foundations* © 2018. Pearson Education, Inc., New York, NY; Page 501 (Table 16.4): Bradley T. Erford, *Orientation to the Counseling Profession: Advocacy, Ethics, and Essential Professional Foundations* © 2018. Pearson Education, Inc., New York, NY; Page 503–504: From "Accountability in Counseling," by Annette Bohannon. Copyright © by Annette Bohannon; Page 505. Except From The ASCA National Model: A Framework for School Counseling Programs. http://www.lehman.edu/ academics/education/counselor-education/documents/SSE-program-audit.pdf. Published by ASCA National Model (American School Counselor Association), © 2003; Page 506 (Figure 16.3): Bradley T. Erford, *Orientation to the Counseling Profession: Advocacy, Ethics, and Essential Professional Foundations* © 2018. Pearson Education, Inc., New York, NY; Page 509 (Figure 16.4): Bradley T. Erford, *Orientation to the Counseling Profession: Advocacy, Ethics, and Essential Professional Foundations* © 2018. Pearson Education, Inc., New York, NY; Page 511 (Table 16.5): Bradley T. Erford, *Orientation to the Counseling Profession: Advocacy, Ethics, and Essential Professional Foundations* ©

2018. Pearson Education, Inc., New York, NY; Page 514 (Table 16.6): Bradley T. Erford, *Orientation to the Counseling Profession: Advocacy, Ethics, and Essential Professional Foundations* © 2018. Pearson Education, Inc., New York, NY; Page 515 (Figure 16.5): Bradley T. Erford, *Orientation to the Counseling Profession: Advocacy, Ethics, and Essential Professional Foundations* © 2018. Pearson Education, Inc., New York, NY; Page 517: From "Accountability for What I Do," by Carol Kulbeck and Christopher Sink. Copyright © by Carol Kulbeck and Christopher Sink.

Chapter 17: Page 526: From "Outcome Research in Counseling," by Annie Carmona and Christopher Sink. Copyright © by Annie Carmona and Christopher Sink; Page 527 (Table 17.1): Bradley T. Erford, *Orientation to the Counseling Profession: Advocacy, Ethics, and Essential Professional Foundations* © 2018. Pearson Education, Inc., New York, NY; Page 530 (Table 17.2): Bradley T. Erford, *Orientation to the*

Counseling Profession: Advocacy, Ethics, and Essential Professional Foundations © 2018. Pearson Education, Inc., New York, NY; Page 531: From *Integrating Outcome Research into Counseling Practice and Training*, by Thomas L. Sexton, Susan C. Whiston, Jeanne C. Bleuer, and Garry Richard Walz. Published by the American Counseling Association © 1997; Pages 532–533: From "Secondary Benefits of Outcome Assessment," by Nicole Adamson. Copyright © by Nicole Adamson; Page 535 (Table 17.3): Bradley T. Erford, *Orientation to the Counseling Profession: Advocacy, Ethics, and Essential Professional Foundations* © 2018. Pearson Education, Inc., New York, NY; Page 539 (Table 17.4): Bradley T. Erford, *Orientation to the Counseling Profession: Advocacy, Ethics, and Essential Professional Foundations* © 2018. Pearson Education, Inc., New York, NY; Page 543 (Table 17.5): Bradley T. Erford, *Orientation to the Counseling Profession: Advocacy, Ethics, and Essential Professional Foundations* © 2018. Pearson Education, Inc., New York, NY.

INDEX

A

AA. *See* Alcoholics Anonymous (AA)
AACD. *See* American Association for Counseling and Development (AACD)
AADA. *See* Association for Adult Development and Aging (AADA)
AAMFT. *See* American Association for Marriage and Family Therapy (AAMFT)
AAPC. *See* American Association of Pastoral Counselors
AARC. *See* Association for Assessment and Research in Counseling (AARC)
AARC Newsnotes, 42
AAS. *See* American Association of Suicidology (AAS)
ABAB design, 515
ABCD model (audience, behavior, conditions, and description model), 502
ABC-X model, 221, 225
AB design, 515
Abney, P., 368
Abstinence, 265
ACA. *See* American Counseling Association (ACA)
ACA Advocacy Competencies, 20
ACAC. *See* Association for Child and Adolescent Counseling (ACAC)
ACA Foundation, 50
ACCA. *See* American College Counseling Association (ACCA)
ACC Newsletter, 43
Accountability, 23, 489–520
  advantages and challenges, 490
  counseling program advisory committee, 491–492
  data-driven needs assessment, 492–496
  needs assessment, 492
  perceptions-based needs assessment, 497–503
  reporting results, 516–517
  social justice counseling and, 518
  stakeholder, 492
  technological innovations, 518
Accreditation
  history, 19
  international, 60
  mergers, 30
  national, 58–59, 67–68
  state, 60–61, 67–68

Acculturation, 345, 354
ACEG Newsletter, 46
ACHA. *See* American College Health Association (ACHA)
Achenbach System of Empirically Based Assessment, 512
Achievement tests, 378
ACPA. *See* American College Personnel Association (ACPA)
ACS. *See* American Community Survey
Action plan, 475
Action research, 170
Action stage of change, 167, 390
Active listening skill, 201
Active placebo, 163, 174
Activist, 45
Acute risk of suicide, 237–238
ADA. *See* Americans with Disabilities Act (ADA)
Adamson, N., 177–178, 215–216, 352, 532
Addictions
  adolescents, 266–267
  characteristics, 263–264
  culturally diverse clients, 267–268
  interpersonal advocacy, 468–469
  treatment approaches, 263–268
Adler, A., 15–16, 18, 122, 220
Adlerian counseling, 122–123
  "I" messages, use of, 122
  limitations, 122–123
  social interest, concept of, 122–123
  in wilderness therapy programs, 258
Administration on Aging, 244
Adolescence, early
  cognitive development, 323
  developmental interventions, 323–324
  development of abstract thinking, 323
  emotional development, 322
  formal-operational-stage thinking, 323
  physical changes, 321
  social development, 321–322
Adolescence, late (emerging adulthood)
  cognitive development, 326–327
  developmental interventions, 327–328
  drug/alcohol use, 266–267
  reflective judgment, 327
  self-development, 327
  social development, 327

Adolescence, middle. *See* Midadolescence
Adulthood, early. *See also* Adolescence, late
  (emerging adulthood)
  becoming a parent, 329
  developmental interventions, 329–330
  early-career stage, 328
  intimate relationship, 328–329
  marriage, 328–329
Adulthood, later
  accepting life and achieving satisfaction,
    333
  cognitive changes, 334
  dealing with loss in, 334
  developmental interventions, 334–335
  period of reinvention, 332–333
  physical changes, 333
  quality of life, 333
  redirecting energy to new roles and activities
    in, 333
  speed of processing information, 334
Adulthood, middle
  cognitive changes, 330
  developmental interventions, 332
  generativity, 331
  intimacy and relationships, 331
  key developmental tasks, 331
  physical changes, 330
  stagnation, 331
  working conditions, 331
Adultspan, 23, 42
Advisory committee, 491–492
Advocacy counseling, 458–485
  barriers encountered by clients, 458
  client advocacy, 458–459
  community collaboration, 469–473
  counselor competencies, 459, 461
  empowerment of clients, 458, 462–466
  explanation of, 338, 458
  future of, 20, 26–27
  for GLBTQ students, 286
  institutional and systems advocacy, 473–477
  international and global advocacy, 483–485
  interpersonal, 466–469
  intrapersonal, 462–466
  multicultural and social justice competencies,
    460–461
  problem assessment, 463
  public information activities, 477–478
  public policy advocacy, 477–482
  when to advocate, 459–460
Advocate consultant role, 427

Advocating for counselors. *See* Professional
  advocacy
African Americans, 355–356
AFSP. *See* American Foundation for Suicide
  Prevention (AFSP)
Ageism, 368
Aggregated data, 492
Aggregated hierarchical model, 508–509
AHC. *See* Association for Humanistic
  Counseling (AHC)
Alabama Suicide Prevention & Resources
  Coalition, 237
Alcohol. *See* Drug and alcohol treatment
  approaches
Alcoholics Anonymous (AA), 16, 258, 265
ALGBTIC. *See* Association for Lesbian, Gay,
  Bisexual, and Transgender Issues in
  Counseling (ALGBTIC)
ALGBTIC News, 43
Alicke, M. D., 533
Allen, M., 234
AMCD. *See* Association for Multicultural
  Counseling and Development (AMCD)
AMCD Multicultural Counseling
  Competencies, 339
American Association for Counseling and
  Development (AACD), 20, 37
American Association for Marriage and Family
  Therapy (AAMFT), 228
American Association of Pastoral Counselors, 257
American Association of State Counseling Boards
  (AASCB), 20–21, 30, 63–64
American Association of Suicidology (AAS), 220,
  236, 237, 260
American Association of University Women, 287
American College Counseling Association (ACCA),
  40–41, 289
American College Health Association (ACHA),
  290, 292
American College Personnel Association (ACPA),
  18, 37, 289
American Community Survey, 270
American Counseling Association (ACA), 36–49,
  286. *See also* Code of Ethics (ACA)
  advocacy, 286
  branches, 49–50
  college/university counseling, 289
  community service by counselors, 452–453
  conference, 37
  continuing-education courses, 51–52
  crisis counseling protocols, 232

discord and splintering, 29, 446
divisions, 29, 36, 38, 39–48, 249 (*See also* specific divisions)
history of, 19–20, 37
media kits and public relations, 449, 454
member benefits, 52–55
Member Services Committee, 46–47
mentoring and leadership training, 29
mission statement, 37
American Counseling Association Foundation (ACAF), 50
Graduate Student Essay Contest, 53
American Foundation for Suicide Prevention (AFSP), 220, 237
American Mental Health Counselors Association (AMHCA), 21, 29, 41
American Personnel and Guidance Association (APGA), 18, 19–20, 37, 43
American Psychological Association (APA), 7, 22, 56, 289, 530
American Rehabilitation Counseling Association (ARCA), 36–49, 269
American School Counselor Association, 21, 41, 245
Ethical Standards, 83–85
American School Counselor Association (ASCA), 21, 29, 41, 72, 289, 438, 475
Americans with Disabilities Act (ADA), 269, 271, 367
Americans with Disabilities Amendments Act of 2008, 271–272
AMHCA. *See* American Mental Health Counselors Association (AMHCA)
Androcentricism, 358
Androgyny, 146
Anorexia nervosa, 262
Anxiety, 261
APA. *See* American Psychological Association (APA)
APGA. *See* American Personnel and Guidance Association (APGA)
Appreciation stage, 347
Approved clinical supervisor (ACS) certificate, 66
Aptitude tests, 378
ARCA. *See* American Rehabilitation Counseling Association (ARCA)
Armstrong, S. A., 533
Army Alpha/Beta tests, 14
Arredondo, P., 277
ASCA. *See* American School Counselor Association (ASCA)

ASCA National Model: A Framework for School Counseling Programs, 21, 283–286, 475, 476, 497, 505
ASCA School Counselor magazine, 53
ASEBA. See Achenbach System of Empirically Based Assessment
ASERVIC Competencies for Integrating Spirituality into Counseling, 364–365
ASGW. See Association for Specialists in Group Work (ASGW)
Asian Americans, 356
Assessing and Managing Suicidal Risk for Clinicians, 237
Assessment, 374–389. See also Needs assessment
comprehensive models of, 402–404
cycle, 497, 506–507, 517
environmental, 386–387
explanation of, 373
problem, 463
service, 505–506
suicide, 384–385
Assistive technology (AT), 274–275
Association for Adult Development and Aging (AADA), 36, 41–42
Association for Assessment and Research in Counseling (AARC), 42, 381
Association for Child and Adolescent Counseling (ACAC), 42
Association for Counselor Education and Supervision (ACES), 42–43, 410
Association for Counselors and Educators in Government (ACEG), 45–46
Association for Creativity in Counseling (ACC), 43
Association for Humanistic Counseling (AHC), 18, 43
Association for Lesbian, Gay, Bisexual, and Transgender Issues in Counseling (ALGBTIC), 43, 362
Association for Multicultural Counseling and Development (AMCD), 44, 339
advocacy competencies, 460
counseling advocacy competencies, 459
Association for Specialists in Group Work (ASGW), 44
Association for Spiritual, Ethical, and Religious Values in Counseling (ASERVIC), 44–45, 364
Associative play, 316
AT. See Assistive technology (AT)
Attachment theory, 147
Attending skills, 193–196

Attorney General opinion, 92
Autonomy, 71, 313, 347
Awakening phase, 349
Ayers, W. A., 533

B

Bachar, E., 535
BAI. *See Beck Anxiety Inventory (BAI)*
Baker, J., 281–282
Balkin, R. S., 533
Baltes, P., 332
Bandura, A., 129, 303
Barber, S., 444
Bardhoshi, G., 533
Barrett, R., 229
Barrett-Lennard Relationship Inventory, 182
Bartlett, M. L., 384
Baseline assessment data, 507, 515
Basham, A., 427–429
Basic counseling paradigm, 166
Basic listening sequence, 196–197
Bass, D., 533
Bateson, G., 142
Battle fatigue, 17
Bauer, S. R., 537
BDI-II. *See Beck Depression Inventory, Second Edition*
Bechtold, G. E., 251–252
Beck, A., 131
Beck Anxiety Inventory (BAI), 495
Beck Depression Inventory, Second Edition, 379, 512
Bedi, R. P., 193
Bednar, R. L., 537
Beeferman, D., 537
Beers, C. W., 13
Behavioral/cognitive-behavioral paradigm,
        127–141
    behavioral counseling, 129–130
    choice theory, 133–134
    cognitive-behavioral-therapy (CBT) approach,
        130–131
    family systems, 136–141
    rational emotive behavior therapy (REBT),
        131–133
    reality therapy, 133–134
    solution-focused brief counseling (SFBC),
        134–136
    strategies and interventions, 137–138
Behavioral observations, 386
Behavior/appearance in mental status examination,
        383–384
Behaviorism, 127, 129–130

Bem, S. L., 146, 358
Bemak, F., 474
Beneficence, 71
Berg, I. K., 134
Berger, C., 39–40
Berk, L. E., 316, 319
Berke, D., 522
Bernal, G., 342
Bernard, J., 409, 413
Berne, E., 19
Best-practice guidelines, ethical and legal issues, 72
Best Practices in Clinical Supervision, 409–410, 421
Beutler, L. E., 530
Bikowsky B., 392–394
Binder, J. L., 532
Binet-Simon Scale, 14
Binge eating disorder, 262
Binswanger, L., 126
Biracial identity development, 347
Bird, J., 385
Bisexual identity development, 349
Bisexuals. *See* Gay, lesbian, bisexual, transgendered,
        and questioning (GLBTQ)
Bleuer, J. C., 522
Blewitt, P., 327, 330, 334
Blogs, 454–455
Board-qualified supervisors, 62–63
Body position, 194–195
Bohannon, A., 503–504
Bonadaptation, 221
Borders, L. D., 538
Boss, P.G., 222
Boulder Conference, APA, 22
Bowen, M., 139
Bowen family systems theory, 139, 257
Bradley, N., 33, 171, 318–319
branches, 49–50
Bretherton, D., 146
Broderick, P. C., 327, 330, 334
Broglie, C., 533
Broverman, D., 359
Broverman, I., 359
Brown, M., 388–389
Brymer, M. J., 220
Buckley Amendment. *See* Family Educational
        Rights and Privacy Act (FERPA)
Bug-in-the-ear (BITE) supervision, 415–416
Bulimia nervosa, 262
Burck, H. D., 541
Burk, C., 229
Burlingame, G. M., 536

Burnout, 32. *See also* Wellness and self-care
Burns, S., 440, 450–451
Bush, G. W., 251
Butler, S. F., 532
Butler, S. K., 339

C
CACREP. *See* Council for Accreditation of Counseling and Related Educational Programs (CACREP)
California Coalition for Counseling Licensure, 49
Callanan, P., 407
Campbell, D. T., 510
Caplan, G., 220, 424
Card sort technique, 145
Career choices in counseling, 249–250
Career counseling. *See also* Professional counselors
   career development theories, 299–307
   diversity issues in (*See* Diversity)
   lifespan context for, 298–299
   professional organizations, publications, and websites, 309
   social justice issues, 309–310
   technological tools, 308
Career counselors, 46
Career Development Quarterly, 23, 46
Career Developments, 46
Career development theories, 299
   constructivist or postmodern, 304–306
   developmental stages of life, 301–302
   learning theory, 303–304
   trait-factor/person-environment congruence, 299–301
Career interventions, 541–542
Carlozzi, B., 151
Carmona, A., 526
Carpenter, L., 208
Cartwright, B. Y., 278
Cartwright, S., 396
Case conceptualizations, 373, 390–398
Case consultation, 430
Cass, V., 348
Cattell, J., 14
Cavanaugh, J. C., 332
CBT. *See* Cognitive-behavioral therapy (CBT)
CDC. *See* Centers for Disease Control and Prevention (CDC)
CE. *See* Continuing education (CE)
Ceasar, P. T., 363
Center for International Rehabilitation Research Information and Exchange (CIRRIE), 277

Centers for Disease Control and Prevention (CDC), 222, 243, 266
Centration, 317
Certification
   Commission on Rehabilitation Counselor Certification (CRCC), 66–67
   for professional school counselors, 64–65
   state, 60–61
   for title restrictions, 61
Certified addictions counselor, 61
Certified clinical mental health counselor (CCMHC), 66
Chan, F., 277
Change, stages of, 167, 390–391
Chen, J., 245
Chen, T., 245
Chen-Hayes, S. F., 361
Chester, A., 146
Child abuse, 109–110, 243–244
Child Behavior Checklist, 379
Child-guidance demonstration clinics, 15
Childhood, early
   cognitive development, 317
   developmental interventions in, 318
   emotional development, 316, 318
   language development, 317
   social development, 316, 318
Childhood, middle
   cognitive development, 320
   developmental interventions, 321
   emotional development, 319–320
   social development, 319
Children's Depression Inventory-Second Edition, 512
Chi Sigma Iota (CSI), 50–51, 439
Chodorow, N., 359
Choice of group categorization stage, 347
Choosing a Vocation, 13, 299
Chronic illness and disability (CID), 274
"Chronic risk" of suicide, 238
Chung, C., 474
CID. *See* Chronic illness and disability (CID)
CIRRIE. *See* Center for International Rehabilitation Research Information and Exchange (CIRRIE)
Civilian Conservation Corps, 16
Civil liability, 96–97
Civil rights, 287
Clarkson, F., 359
Classical conditioning, 130
Client advocacy, 458–459
Client-centered counseling, 17

Client characteristics, 164–165
Client-counselor relationship, 125, 126
  in behavioral counseling, 130
  countertransference in, 181
  helping relationship, 169
  narrative therapy, 142–143
  point of termination, 185–187
Clinical efficacy studies, 524
Clinical trials, 524
Closed questions, 199–201
Code of Ethics (AAMFT), 228
Code of Ethics (ACA), 57, 116
  assessment and diagnosis issues, 375
  confidentiality and privacy, 77, 100–102
  counseling relationship, 73–79
  evaluation, assessment, and interpretation, 80
  interaction and relationships between
      counselors, 80
  Internet-based distance counseling, technology,
      and social media, 81–83
  professional responsibility, 78
  research and publication, 81
  research-based practices, 169
  resolution of ethical issues, 82
  school counselors, 83–84
  scope and history, 72–82
  on self-care in practice, 30, 32, 228
  six moral principles, 71
  supervision, training, and teaching, 81
  technological issues, 25–26
  test administration and interpretation, 381–382
Code of Ethics (NBCC), 66
Code of Professional Ethics for Rehabilitation Counselors
      (2010), 277
CogAT. *See* Cognitive Abilities Test
Cognitive Abilities Test, 378
Cognitive-behavioral model, 410
Cognitive-behavioral therapy (CBT), 131, 170
Cognitive development
  assimilation and accommodation, 317
  concrete operational thought, 320
  early adolescence, 323
  early-childhood, 317
  formal operational-stage, 320
  in infancy and toddlerhood, 315–316
  late adolescence (emerging adulthood), 326–327
  midadolescence, 325
  middle childhood, 320
Cognitive theories, 390
Cohen, J., 525
Cole, R., 219, 246

Collaborative consultation, 425
Collaborator role, 427
Collective counseling, 15–16
College counseling
  advocacy competencies, 471–473
  background and trends, 290
  multicultural and social justice issues, 297
  professional identity, 289
  role of, 290–293
  student-life services vs., 289
  for students with disabilities, 296–297
College counselors, 290
College health assessment data, 292
Comfort zone, 195
Coming-out process, 361
Commission on Rehabilitation Counselor
      Certification (CRCC), 66–67, 277
Common law, 91
Communication theory, 147
Community/agency setting, 251–252
Community-based mental health counseling
      programs, 497
Community collaboration advocacy counseling,
      469–473
Community disasters, prevention and intervention,
      244–245
Community Mental Health Centers Act, 19
Community service, 452–453
Compassion fatigue, 228
Competencies. *See* Outcomes
Competencies for Counseling with Transgender
      Clients, 360
Comprehensive Suicide Prevention Resource
      Directory, 237
Computer-administered tests, 381
Computers, 25–26
Conceptualizations. *See* Case conceptualizations
Concrete operational thought, 320
Confidentiality, 178–179
  duty-to-warn standard, 101–102
  educational records, 104–108
  ethical and legal issues, 100–103
  issues with minors, 103–104
  limits to, 101–102
  minor-consent law and, 103–104
  personal notes, 108
  privileged communication, 102–103
  professional-school-counselor-student, 100
  technology, 26
Connors 3 Rating Scales, 379
Constitutional law, 91

Constructivist or postmodern career development theories, 304–306
Constructivist theory, 144–145
Construct validity of tests, 380
Consultation in counseling, 406–409, 423–432
    consultant roles, 426–427
    internal vs. external role, 430–431
    models of, 424–425
    settings, 429–431
    skills, 428–429
    supervision vs., 406–409
Contact status, 347
Contemplation stage, 167
Contemplation stage of change, 390
Continuing education (CE), 37, 51–53, 58
Control groups, 512, 527
Convergent validity of tests, 380
CORE. *See* Council on Rehabilitation Education (CORE)
Core Competencies for Mental Health Professionals, 237
Corey, C., 407
Corey, G., 71, 232, 407
Corey, M., 407
Corey, M. S., 232
Cormier, S., 166
Corrections, 254–255
Cottone, R. R., 95
Council for Accreditation of Counseling and Related Educational Programs (CACREP), 376
    accreditation of university programs, 19
    advocacy for professional counselors, 436–439
    ALGBTIC competencies and, 362
    licensure standards and, 21
    merger with CORE, 30, 269
    professional discord, 29–30
    scientific methodology, 169
    specialty-area standards, 249
    tests, counselor knowledge of, 376
    2016 standards, 30, 376
    types of national accreditation, 58–59
    veterans health programs, 20
Council for the Accreditation of Educator Preparation (CAEP), 59
Council on Rehabilitation Education (CORE), 30, 51, 59, 269
Counseling. *See also* Career counseling; College counseling; Crisis counseling; Rehabilitation counseling; Social justice counseling
    accountability, 489–519
    assessment, 373

    basic paradigm of, 166
    case conceptualization, 373
    current issues in, 56–58
    current status of, 3–6
    definitions of, 4–5
    diagnosis, 373
    Emic perspective of, 340
    feminist, 145–147
    future challenges, 22–30, 56–58
    goals, 153, 171
    history of, 4, 9–21
    integrative, 155–158
    interpersonal psychotherapy (IPT), 147–148
    licensure for, 61–62
    multicultural considerations, 163
    person-centered, 125–126, 153
    philosophy of, 7–9
    psychotherapy vs., 4–5
    reasons clients seek, 171–174
    relational competence, 175
    specialties, 5–6
    treatment planning, 373
Counseling and Psychotherapy, 17
Counseling and Values, 45
Counseling Association for Humanistic Education and Development (C-AHEAD), 43
Counseling Awareness Month, 443–444, 454
Counseling Corner, 50
Counseling effectiveness
    facets of, 528–530
    group work with adults, 537–538
    group work with children, 536–537
    individual counseling, 533–535
Counseling Futures, 436
Counseling Outcomes Research and Evaluation, 42
Counseling process
    environment for, 174–175
    goal setting, 182–183
    helping relationship in, 168–171, 175–177
    information gathering, 179–180
    initiating, 171–174
    integration and termination, 185–187
    outcomes, 182–183
    relationship exploring, 180–182
    resistance, 183–185
    stages of change, 166–167
    structure and expectations, 178–179
    theory, role of, 177–178
Counseling program advisory committee, 491–492
Counseling supervision, 406–422
    Bug-in-the-ear (BITE), 415–416

Counseling supervision (*continued*)
Bug-in-the-eye (BITE), 415–416
confidentiality, 414–415, 421
consultation breaks, 416
consultation vs., 406–409
co-therapy, 415
digital recording review, 415
direct observation, 415
disclosure statement, template, 421–422
formats, 412–414
group, 413–414
individual, 412–413
interventions, 414–418
live supervision, 415, 418
models of, 412–414
peer supervision, 409
self-report, 414
triadic, 414
in vivo, 416
Counseling theory. *See also* Theories
application, 151–155
ethics of applying, 116–117
five components of a good, 117
integration, 155–158
Counseling Today, 37, 52, 93
Counseling & Values, 23
Counselor characteristics, 164
Counselor Education & Supervision, 23, 43
Counselors. *See also* Professional counselors;
School counselors
beginning, 162–164
college, 290
education for, 6
elementary school, 281
high school, 283
middle school/junior high school, 282
paraprofessional, 441
psychologists vs., 442
social workers vs., 442
Counselors for Social Justice (CSJ), 29, 45
Counselor wellness, 30–33
Countertransference, 122, 181
Court of Appeals, 91–92
Court order, 98–99
Court system, 91–92
CRCC. *See* Commission on Rehabilitation
Counselor Certification (CRCC)
Crisis, 232
Crisis counseling
basic protocols, 232
community disaster, 244–245

coping, 223–224
coping abilities, 223–224
counselor safety, 247
counselor wellness and self-care, 227–231, 247
multicultural awareness, 232
personal safety, 247
privacy issues, 233
resilience and post-traumatic growth, 224–227
school crises, 245–246
school system adaptions, 245–247
seven resiliencies, 226
stress, 222–223
theory of, 219–221
trauma, 223
Crisis counseling protocols, 232
Criterion-referenced tests, 377
Criterion-related validity, 379–380
Cross-cultural counseling. *See* Multicultural
counseling
Crouch, T., 443
Crystal Meth Anonymous, 265
CSJ. *See* Counselors for Social Justice (CSJ)
Cultural encapsulation, 338
Cultural fairness in testing, 381
Cultural identity development models, 344–346
Culturally competent counselor, 339–340
Culturally diverse individuals, 350–358
African Americans, 355–356
Asian Americans, 356
elderly, 368
European Americans, 352–353
gender differences, 358–359
gender-sensitive counseling practices, 361
Hispanic Americans, 353–355
individuals with disabilities, 367
multiracial individuals, 357
Native Americans, 357
poverty status, 350–352
racism, 357–358
sexism, 359–360
sexual minorities, 361–362
socioeconomic status, 350–352
spirituality, 363–365
transgender individuals, 362
Culturally encapsulated counselor, 24
Cultural pluralism, 338
Culture. *See also* Multicultural counseling;
Multiculturalism
explanation of, 338
test fairness and, 381
Curran, L. A., 231

D

Data collection procedures, 510–514
Data-driven needs assessment, 492–496
Data points, 515
Daughhetee, C., 247
Davenport, D. S., 26
Davis, J. B., 12–13
Davis, T. E., 246
Defense mechanisms, 121
Dependent variable, 515
Depression, 259–261, 379
De Shazer, S., 134
Despair, 314
Despenser, S., 247
Detoxification, 265
Developmental career development theories, 301–302
Developmental classroom guidance, 539
Developmental considerations, 387–388
Developmental interventions
    early adolescence, 323–324
    early adulthood, 329–330
    early-childhood, 318
    late adolescence (emerging adulthood), 327–328
    later adulthood, 334–335
    midadolescence, 325–326
    middle adulthood, 332
    middle childhood, 321
Developmental perspective, 7–9, 387–388
Dewey, J., 15
Diagnosis, 394–398
    DSM-5 used in clinical mental health settings, 394–395
    explanation of, 394
    social justice counseling, 396
Diagnostic and Statistical Manual of Mental Disorders, Fifth Edition (DSM-5), 23–24, 223
DiCaccavo, A., 161
DiClemente, C. C., 152
Dictionary of Occupational Titles, 16
Differentiation of self, 139
Dik, B. J., 310
Dillon, C., 165
Dinsmore, J. D., 444
Direct observation supervision, 415
Disabilities Education Improvement Act, 106
Disability
    college students with, 296–297
    explanation of, 269–270, 367
    Section 504 (Rehabilitation Act) plan, 392–394

Disaggregated, 495
Disclosure statement to clients, 74–76
Discord and splintering, 29, 446
Discrimination, 338, 411–412
Disidentification, 355
Disintegration status, 347
Distress, 222
Divergent validity of tests, 380
Diversion programs, 254
Diversity, 338. *See also* Multicultural counseling; Multiculturalism
Divisions, 29, 36, 38, 39–48, 249. *See also* specific divisions
Division 17 (Society of Counseling Psychology), 18
DO A CLIENT MAP model, 403–404
Doctor-patient model. *See* Prescriptive consultation model
Doctor-patient/prescription model, 424
Dohn, H. H., 385
Dostoyevsky, F., 126
DOT. See Dictionary of Occupational Titles
Double ABC-X model, 221, 227
Doubt, 313
Dougherty, A., 407
Downing, N. E., 348
Drapetomania, 396
Drug and alcohol treatment approaches, 264–267
DSM-5. See Diagnostic and Statistical Manual of Mental Disorders, Fifth Edition (DSM-5)
DSM diagnosis, 394–396
    benefits of, 397–398
    drawbacks of, 397–398
Duffy, R. D., 310
Duncan, K., 49–50
Duty to warn, 101–102
Dyregrov, A., 221

E

Eating disorders, 262–263
EBP. *See* Evidence-based practices (EBP)
Eclecticism, 155–156
Educational records, 104–108
Education for all Handicapped Children's Act, 271
Edwards, B. J., 266
Effective Advocacy with Members of Congress, 447–448
Effectiveness. *See* Counseling effectiveness
Effectiveness research, 524
Effect size (ES), 525
Egan, G., 176, 194

Ego, 121
Egocentrism, 317
Ego integrity, 314
Ego psychology, 123
Eighteenth Mental Measurement Yearbook, 382
Eisel, N., 111
Eisel, S., 111
Eisel v. Board of Education, 111
Eisengart, S., 533
Elder abuse, 243–244
Electra complex, 122
Elementary school counselors, 281
Elkind, D., 313
Ellis, A., 19, 120, 131
Emerging adulthood. *See* Adolescence, late
        (emerging adulthood)
Emic perspective of counseling, 340
Emotional development
    early adolescence, 322
    early-childhood, 316, 318
    in infancy and toddlerhood, 315
    midadolescence, 325
    middle childhood, 319–320
Empathy, 125, 177
Empirically based treatment five-step model, 545
Empowerment
    advocacy counseling, 462
    explanation of, 8
Empowerment model of rehabilitation
        counseling, 273
Empty-chair technique, 120
Enmeshment, 342
Enmeshment/denial stage, 347
Environmental assessment, 386–387
Environmental stressors, 397
Environment for counseling, 174–175
Epston, D., 142
Erford, B. M., 245–246, 533
Erford, B. T., 5, 74–76, 219, 245, 312, 314, 323, 326,
        333, 335, 383, 493, 502, 511, 515, 516, 533, 534
Erford, M. R., 533
Eriksen, K. P., 439, 444, 446–449, 451, 452
Erikson, E., 18, 313–314, 331
ES. *See* Effect size (ES)
Ethical standards and laws, 70–91
    American School Counselor Association Ethical
        Standards, 72, 83–85
    boundary issues, 77–79
    confidentiality, 101–103
    crisis prevention and intervention, 232–233
    decision making using, 85–91

local, 92–93
    minor-consent law, 103–104
    privileged communication, 102–103
    professional counselor organizations, 54
    professional licensure, 61–62
    psychotropic medications, 465–466
    questions and dilemmas, 93–95
Ethics Case Study Competition, 53
Ethnicity, 338
Etic perspective of counseling, 340
European Americans, 352–353
European Board for Certified Counselors, 439
Eustress, 222
Evans, A. M., 187–188
Evans, D. R., 214
Evans, J. H., 541
Event-topic counts, 505
Evidence, 507–508
Evidence-based practices (EBP)
    future challenges, 22
    in multicultural counseling, 342
Examinations, licensure, 63
Exceptions, 135
Existential anxiety, 126
Existentialism, 18, 19, 126
Existential vacuum, 126
Expert consultant, 426
Expert consultation model, 424–425
Expert/provision model, 424
Expert witnesses, 97
External consultation, 430
Eye contact, 193–194
Eysenck, H., 129, 547

F

Face-to-face supervision, 62–63
Facilitative consultation, 425
FACT. *See* Fair Access Coalition on Testing (FACT)
Fair Access Coalition on Testing (FACT), 49, 66, 375
Familism, 353–354
Family Adjustment and Adaptation Response
        model, 225
Family development, 139
The Family Digest, 45
Family Educational Rights and Privacy Act
        (FERPA)
    conflicts between HIPAA and, 109
    emergency situations, 233
    ethical and legal issues, 105
    provisions, 105
    right of consent, 105

The Family Journal, 45
Family systems theory, 136–141
Federal court system, 92
Federal Emergency Management Agency
	(FEMA), 245
Feldman, B., 234
Feldman, R. S., 315, 326, 329–331
Feldwisch, R., 537
FEMA. *See* Federal Emergency Management
	Agency (FEMA)
Feminist counseling, 145–147
Feminist identity development, 348
Feminist movement, 145–146
FERPA. *See* Family Educational Rights and Privacy
	Act (FERPA)
Fessinger, R. E., 348
Fetrow, C., 282
Fidelity, 71
Field, T. F., 278
Figley, C. R., 224
First-year experience in college, 295
Fitzpatrick, J. L., 501
Five Factor Wellness Evaluation of Lifestyle, 31
Flagging the minefield technique, 135–136
Fleming, C. L., 278
Focusing summaries, 214
Formal operational-stage cognitive
	development, 320
Formative evaluation, 507
Foster, L. H., 376
Frankel, Z. F., 164
Frankl, V., 18, 126
Freud, S., 14, 121
Fromm, E., 18
Fully functioning, 7

G

Gallagher, R. P., 292
Gallessich, J., 424
Gamblers Anonymous, 265
Gatekeeping, 26
Gateslippers, 26
Gaubatz, M. D., 26
Gay, lesbian, bisexual, transgendered, and
	questioning (GLBTQ), 286–287, 361–362
Gazda, G. M., 436
Geigle, Danielle L., 465–466
Gender role analysis, 146
Generativity, 314, 331
Genogram, 139
Genuineness (or congruence), 125

Gerber, S., 540
Gestalt therapy, 120, 127
Gibson, D., 469, 481, 485
Gilbert, L. A., 146
Gilchrist, L. A., 444
Gilligan, C., 146, 359
Gingerich, W. J., 533
Gladding, S., 435
Gladding, S. T., 19, 424, 436
Glasser, W., 133
GLBTQ. *See* Gay, lesbian, bisexual, transgendered,
	and questioning (GLBTQ)
Goals
	counseling, 153, 171
	outcomes and, 508
	setting, 153, 182–183
Goodyear, R., 409, 413
Gottfredson, L., 301, 302–303
Grade point average (GPA), 512, 514
Graduate Record Examination (GRE), 380
Granger, D. A., 533
Great Depression, 15–16
Group counseling, 14
Group outcomes research, process issues,
	535–536
Group supervision, 413–414
Group therapy with adults, outcomes,
	537–538
The Group Worker, 44
Group work with children, outcomes,
	536–537
Guidance movement, 4, 15–16
*A Guide to Cultural Competence in the Curriculum:
	Rehabilitation Counseling*, 277
Guillot-Miller, L., 93
Guilt, 313
Guldimann, M. A., 246
Gunther, C., 534
Gutin, N., 234
Guttmacher Institute, 103

H

Hackney, H., 166
Hall, G. S., 14
Han, S. S., 533
Hansen, J. C., 117
Hansen, J. T., 142
Hardiman, R., 345–347
Hardiness, 224
Haring-Hidore, M., 169
Harm reduction, 265

Harrington, J. A., 255
Hartig, N., 78–79
Hatch Amendment. *See* Protection of Pupil Rights
    Amendment (PPRA)
Hayes, B., 219
Hays, D. G., 444
Healey, A. C., 387
Health Insurance Portability and Accountability
    Act (HIPAA) of 1996, 109, 233
Hegarty, W. L., 107–108
Helmersberg, I., 430
Helms, J. E., 345–347
Helping, 168–171
    art of, 168–169
    common factors in, 170–171
    relationship, 175–177
    as a science, 169–170
    three-stage model for, 176
Henry, W. P., 532
Here and now, 126
Herlihy, B., 7, 71, 86, 100, 111, 232
Hershenson, D. B., 7
Heterosexism, 464
HHS. *See* U.S. Department of Health and Human
    Services (HHS)
High school counselors, 283
Hill, D. C., 256
Hill, R., 221
Hill-Burton Act, 271
HIPAA. *See* Health Insurance Portability and
    Accountability Act (HIPAA) of 1996
Hispanic Americans, 353–354
History of counseling, 4, 9–21
Hoag, M. J., 536
Hof, D. D., 444, 445
Hoffmann, J. R., 246
Hogan, T., 522
Holland, J. L., 299–300
Holland's Self-Directed Search, 379
Homicidal ideation (harming others), 234, 243
Homicide risk. *See* Suicide and homicide risk
Homophobia, 361
Hooks, bell (Gloria Jean Watkins), 146
Horney, K., 18
Hospitals, 252
Howard, K. I., 528
Humane Society of the United States, 241
Humanistic/existential paradigms,
    125–129
    development, 18
    existentialism, 126

Gestalt therapy, 127
    person-centered therapy, 125–126
    strategies and interventions, 128–129
Human nature, view of, 152
Hummel, T. J., 268
Humor, 133, 134
*The Hurried Child: Growing Up Too Fast Too
    Soon*, 313

I

IAAOC. *See* International Association of Addictions
    and Offender Counselors (IAAOC)
IAAOC Newsletter, 45
ICD-10, 394
ICD-11, 394
Identity, mistaken, 388–389
Identity, role confusion vs, 313
Identity development, cultural models for,
    345–350
IDM. *See* Integrated developmental model (IDM)
Id (pleasure principle), 121
Illinois Counseling Association, 49
Immersion-emersion status, 347
Impairment of professional counselor, 230
Individual supervision, 412–413
Individuals with Disabilities Education Act
    (1991), 271
Individuals with Disabilities Education
    Improvement Act (2004), 106, 271
Individuals with disability, 367
Indivisible Self: An Evidence-Based Model of
    Wellness (IS-WEL), 31
Infancy and toddlerhood
    cognitive/language development, 315–316
    emotional development, 315
    emotional differentiation, 315
    explanation of, 314
    fine motor skills development, 314–315
    motor development, 314–315
    Piaget's cognitive-developmental theory, 315
    preoperational stage, 315
    sensorimotor stage, 315
    terrible twos, 315
Inferiority feelings, 313
Infochange, 43
Informed consent, 107, 178–179
Initiative, 313
Inpatient treatment, 252
Inputs, 507
Inspection, 61
Institutional accreditation, 58–59

Institutional and systems advocacy, 473–477
  action plan, 475
  counselor competencies, 478
Intake, 179–180, 237–238, 382–385
Integrated developmental model (IDM),
      411–412
Integration stage, 349
Integrative-awareness, 347
Intellectual functioning, in mental status
      examination, 384
Intelligence tests, 377–378, 387
Intensive outpatient treatment, 253
Intentionality, 117
INTERACTION, 45
Interest inventories, 378–379
Internal consultant, 430
Internalization, 347
Internal Revenue Service (IRS) rules, 105
International and global advocacy, 483–485
International Association of Addictions and
      Offender Counselors (IAAOC), 45
International Association of Marriage and Family
      Counselors (IAMFC), 45
*International Classification of Diseases, Tenth Revision,
      with Clinical Modification* (ICD-10 CM), 394
International Registry of Counsellor Education
      Programs (IRCEP), 60, 439
*International Statistical Classification of Diseases,
      Eleventh Edition* (ICD-11), 394
Internet counseling. *See* Technology-assisted
      distance counseling
Interpersonal psychotherapy (IPT),
      147–148
Interventions, 23, 399. *See also* Developmental
      interventions
Intimacy, 313
Intimate partner violence (IPV), 243
In vivo supervision of counseling, 416
Iowa Tests of Basic Skills (ITBS), 378
IPV. *See* Intimate partner violence (IPV)
IQ scores, 387
IRCEP. *See* International Registry of Counsellor
      Education Programs (IRCEP)
Isolation, 313
IS PATH WARM, 261, 384–385
"I" statements
  Adlerian counseling, 122
  Bowenian counseling, 139
  Gestalt therapy, 127
IS-WEL. *See* Indivisible Self: An Evidence-Based
      Model of Wellness (IS-WEL)

Ivey, A. E., 193
Ivey, M. B., 193

J
Jackson-Cherry, L.R., 219, 222, 245
Jacobs, A. K., 220
James, B., 537
James, D., 246
James, R. K., 229
James, W., 14
Jayne, K., 533
Jobes, D. A., 236–238
Johnson, D., 537
Johnson, D. M., 534
Joiner, T. E., 236
Joint Committee on Testing Practices' Code of Fair
      Testing Practices in Education, 381
Jones, D., 219
Jordan, J., 146
*Journal for Social Action in Counseling and
      Psychology*, 45
Journal for Specialists in Group Work, 23, 44
Journal of Addictions & Offender Counseling, 45
Journal of College Counseling, 23, 289
Journal of Counseling & Development, 14, 23,
      37–39, 52, 52
Journal of Creativity in Mental Health, 43
Journal of Employment Counseling, 23, 46
Journal of Humanistic Counseling, 23, 43
Journal of LGBT Issues in Counseling, 43
Journal of Mental Health Counseling, 22, 23
Journal of Military and Government Counseling, 46
Jung, C. G., 123, 161, 332
Junior high counseling, 282
Justice, 71

K
Kaplan, D. M., 436
Karpiak, C., 522
Kazdin, A. E., 533
Keeping Children and Families Safe Act,
      109–110
Kelly, G., 144
Kennedy, R., 226
Kennedy, S., 455
Kentucky Counseling Association, 49
Kerewsky, S. D., 26
Kidron, M., 431–432
Kierkegaard, S., 126
Kinship care, 107
Kitchener's model of reflective judgment, 327

Kleespies, P.M., 234, 242
Klotz, M. L., 533
Koehn, C., 224
Kopta, S. M., 528
Kottler, J. A., 163, 164, 169
Krause, M. S., 528
Krebs, P. M., 390
Kress, V. E., 77–78, 143–144, 482, 533
Krumboltz, J., 129
Kulbeck, C., 517

L

Labouvie-Vief, G., 326
Lambert, M. J., 22, 527, 530, 545
Large-scale math achievement test, 493
Lattanzi, G., 533
Laws and ethical standards, 70–91. *See also* Ethical standards and laws
Layne, C. M., 220
Lazarus's BASIC ID Model, 402–403
LCMHC. *See* Licensed clinical mental health counselor (LCMHC)
LCSWs. *See* Licensed clinical social workers (LCSWs)
Leader characteristics, 536
Leadership, training, 29
Leanza, N., 365–366
Learning Institute, 52
Learning theory, 303–304
LeBlanc, M., 534
Lee, C. C., 479
Lee, D., 293
Lee, F., 384, 536
Lee, J. B., 277
Legal questions and dilemmas, 93–95
Legislation. *See also* Ethical standards and laws
Lesbian identity development, 348
Lesbians. *See* Gay, lesbian, bisexual, transgendered, and questioning (GLBTQ)
Levitt, H. M., 164
Lewis, A. C., 540
Lewis, L., 296
Lewis, M. W., 540
Liability insurance, 53, 55
Licensed clinical mental health counselor (LCMHC), 21
Licensed clinical social workers (LCSWs), 6
Licensed professional counselors (LPCs), 20, 21, 62, 64
Licensure
    accreditation and, 30

American Association of State Counseling Boards (AASCB), 63
    benefits and drawbacks, 65
    educational qualification for, 62
    education and training standards for, 21
    examination qualification, 63
    laws, 21, 61–62
    navigating the process, 99
    portability of, 21, 64
    practice acts, 61
    for professional school counselors, 64–65
    state counseling boards and, 63–64
    supervised experience for, 62–63
    title acts, 62
Life span developmental theory
    career development, 301–302
    psychosocial development, stages of, 311–314
Likert-type scales, 502, 514
Lindemann, E., 220
Lipsey, M. W., 525
Listening skills
    basic listening sequence, 196–215
    paraphrasing, 201–205
    questions, open vs. closed, 197–201
    reflecting feelings, 205–209
    reflecting meaning, 209–213
    summarizing, 214–216
Littrell, J. M., 540
Live supervision, 415, 417, 418
Livneh, H., 274
Local laws, regulations, and policies, 92–93
Locke, B., 293
Love You Forever, 312
Lowinger, R. J., 290
LPCs. *See* Licensed professional counselors (LPCs)
Lynch, J. F., 293

M

MAC. *See* Master addictions counselor (MAC)
MaCarn, S. R., 348
Macdonald, T., 481–482
Machismo, 359
MacNeil, G., 228
Maine Counseling Association, 49
Maintenance stage, 167, 390
Making an Impact: A Handbook for Counselor Advocacy, 456
Malia, J. A., 533
Malpractice, 96–98
Managed care, 22–23

Mandated reporters, 285
Maples, M., 368
Marianismo, 359
Markowski, E. T., 275–276
Marriage and family counseling, 257
Marshall, D. S., 219–220
Maslow, A., 18, 126
Maslow, A. H., 7
Master addictions counselor (MAC), 66
Masters, K. S., 527
Matteliano, M. A., 277
May, R., 18, 126
MBTI. *See* Myers Briggs Type Indicator (MBTI)
McCubbin, H. I., 224, 225
McCullough, J. R., 339
McDavis, R. J., 277
McGlothlin, J., 219
McLeod A., 243
McLeod A. L., 254
MCMI-III. *See* Millon Clinical Multiaxial
    Inventory-III (MCMI-III)
McRoberts, C., 535, 536
*Measurement and Evaluation in Counseling and
    Development*, 23, 42
Media kits and public relations, 449, 454
Mediation model, 424
Medical conditions, 398
Medical model, drug/alcohol treatment, 264–265
Meichenbaum, D., 131
Meloy, J. R., 246
Member Services Committee, 46–47
Mental health counselors, 6, 95
    expert witnesses, 97
    resources for, 268
Mental Health First Aid Act of 2015, 251
Mental health issues, 259–268
    addictions, 263–268
    anxiety, 261
    depression, 259–261
    eating disorders, 262–263
    social media impact on, 262
Mental Health Parity and Addiction Equity Act of
    2008, 251
Mental Health Report, 398
Mental health treatment settings, 250–259
    community/agency, 251–252
    corrections, 254–255
    history of, 250–251
    hospitals, 252–253
    inpatient treatment, 252
    intensive outpatient treatment, 253

level of care, 254
    marriage and family counseling, 257
    outpatient treatment, 253
    partial hospitalization, 252
    pastoral counseling, 257–258
    private practice, 255–256
    residential treatment, 253
    wilderness therapy, 258
Mental-hygiene movement, 13
Mental status examination, 383–384
Mental test, 14
Mentoring, 29
Mentoring and leadership training, 29
Meta-analysis, 525, 527
MGCA. *See* Military and Government Counseling
    Association (MGCA)
Michelson, S. T., 293
Microskills
    basic listening sequence, 196–215
    hierarchy, 192–193
    nonverbal attending skills, 193–196
    vocal tone, 195
Midadolescence. *See also* Adolescence, early;
    Adolescence, late (emerging adulthood)
    cognitive development, 325
    developmental interventions, 325–326
    emotional development, 325
    intimate friendships, 324
    sexual experimentation, 324
    social development, 324
Middle school/junior high school
    counselors, 282
Military and Government Counseling Association
    (MGCA), 45–46
Miller, S., 134
Millersville University, 292, 294
Millon Clinical Multiaxial Inventory-III
    (MCMI-III), 378
A Mind That Found Itself, 13
Minnesota Multiphasic Personality Inventory-2
    (MMPI-2), 378
Minor-consent laws, 103–104
Minority model of disability, 276–277
Miracle question, 135
Miranti, J. G., 363
Mirroring, 194
Mission statement, 37
Mistaken identity, 388–389
Mistrust, 313
MMPI-2. *See* Minnesota Multiphasic Personality
    Inventory-2 (MMPI-2)

Moate, R. M., 157–158
Mood/affect in mental status examination, 384
Moreno, J. L., 16
Morlan, M., 420
Morris, C. A. W., 220
Morton, T., 533
Motor development, in infancy and toddlerhood, 314–315
Moulton, P., 229
Muldoon, J., 243
Multicultural and Social Justice Counseling Competencies (MSJCC), 277–278, 339–340
Multicultural counseling, 337–340
    alcohol and drug use issues, 267–268
    assessment and treatment, issues with, 341–342
    case conceptualization, 390
    in college and student-life services, 297
    competencies, 277, 460–461
    critique of, 20, 341
    cultural identity development and, 342–350
    of culturally diverse individuals, 350–368
    culturally sensitive environment for, 269–270
    debate on definition of, 341
    drug/alcohol use, 267–268
    etic vs. emic debate, 340
    evidence-based practices in, 342
    key terms, 338
    rehabilitation, 276–278
    in schools, 286–287
    social justice principles in, 368–369
Multiculturalism, 24–25
Multicultural organizational development, 369–370
Munsch, R., 312
Murphy, B. C., 165
Myer, R. A., 229
Myers, J. E., 436, 445
Myers Briggs Type Indicator (MBTI), 378

N

NA. *See* Narcotics Anonymous (NA)
NAGCT. *See* National Association of Guidance and Counselor Trainers (NAGCT)
Narcotics Anonymous (NA), 265
Narrative theory, 142–144
NASPA. *See* National Association of Student Personnel Administrators (NASPA)
Nassar-McMillan, S., 339
Nassar-McMillan, S. C., 483

National Action Alliance for Suicide Prevention, 237
National Association for Social Work (NASW), 7
National Association of Guidance and Counselor Trainers (NAGCT), 18, 37
National Association of Student Personnel Administrators (NASPA), 289
National Board for Certified Counselors (NBCC), 29, 30, 49, 51, 65–66, 437, 439
    code of ethics, 66
    specialty-area certifications, 249
    technology-assisted distance counseling guidelines, 66, 83
National Career Development Association (NCDA), 46
National Catholic Guidance Conference, 44
National Center for Education Statistics (NCES), 233, 290
National Center for the Analysis of Violent Crime (NCAVC), 241, 242
National certification of professional counselors, 65–66
National certified school counselor (NCSC), 66
National Child Abuse Prevention and Treatment Act, 109
National Climate Survey of 2013, 287
National Clinical Mental Health Counselor Examination (NCMHCE), 63
National Council for Accreditation of Teacher Education (NCATE), 59
National Council on Rehabilitation Education (CORE), 50, 59
National Counselor Examination (NCE), 63
National Defense Authorization Act, 437
National Defense Education Act, 18
National Employment Counseling Association (NECA), 46
National Institute of Mental Health (NIMH), 222, 250–251, 521
National Mental Health Act, 17
National Mental Health Association, 13
National Mental Health Services Survey, 251
National Office for School Counselor Advocacy (NOSCA), 284–285
National percentile rank, 493
National Registry for Evidence-based Programs and Practices (NREPP), 530
National Rehabilitation Association, 269
National Rehabilitation Counseling Association (NRCA), 269
National Screening Day initiatives, 453

National Standards and National Model (American School Counselor Association), 21, 283–284, 475, 476, 497, 505

National Standards for School Counseling Programs (ASCA), 280

National Suicide Prevention Lifeline (NSPL), 237

National Survey on Drug Use and Health (SAMHSA), 259

National Vocational Guidance Association (NVGA), 14, 18, 37, 46

Native Americans, 357

Nature vs. nurture, 312

NBCC. *See* National Board for Certified Counselors (NBCC)

NCAVC. *See* National Center for the Analysis of Violent Crime (NCAVC)

NCES. *See* National Center for Education Statistics (NCES)

NCSC. *See* National certified school counselor (NCSC)

NECA Newsletter, 46

Needs assessment, 492–503
  data-driven, 492–496
  design, 498–502
  explanation of, 492
  frequency of, 497
  perceptions-based, 497–503
  populations to be assessed, 497–498
  program goals and objectives, 502–503
  questionnaire and survey guidelines, 501

Negligence, 96

Neukrug, E., 341

Neuville, T., 276

Newell, J., 228

New Jersey Association for Adult Development and Aging (NJAADA), 36

New Jersey Counseling Association (NJCA), 36

Newman, B. J., 315, 325, 328–329

Newman, P. R., 315, 325, 328–329

Nietzsche, F., 126

NIMH. *See* National Institute of Mental Health (NIMH)

NJAADA. *See* New Jersey Association for Adult Development and Aging (NJAADA)

NJCA. *See* New Jersey Counseling Association (NJCA)

No Child Left Behind Act (NCLB), 106, 283

Nonmaleficence, 71, 520

Nonstandardized tests, 377

Nonverbal attending skills, 193–196

Norcross, J. C., 22, 390, 522

Norm-referenced tests, 377

Nouwen, H. J., 228

NRCA. *See* National Rehabilitation Counseling Association (NRCA)

NVGA. *See* National Vocational Guidance Association (NVGA)

O

OA. *See* Overeaters Anonymous (OA)

Obama, B., 286

OBH. *See* Outdoor behavioral health programs (OBHs)

Object-relations theory, 123

Occupational Outlook Handbook, 6

O'Connor, B. P., 332

OCR. *See* Office for Civil Rights (OCR)

ODD. *See* Oppositional defiant disorder (ODD)

Odes, E., 293

Oedipus complex, 122

Office for Civil Rights (OCR), 287

Off time events, 8

Ogles, B. M., 527

O'Hanlon, W. H., 134

Oliver, L. W., 541, 542

Olson, E. A., 293

O'Neal, J. H., 400

O*NET (Occupational Information Network), 251, 308, 378

Online counseling. *See* Technology-assisted distance counseling

On time events, 8

Open questions, 197–201

Oppositional defiant disorder (ODD), 258

Oppression, 463

Orlinsky, D. E., 528

Orvaschel, H., 537

Otis-Lennon School Ability Test, Eighth Edition, 378

O'Toole, M. E., 241, 242

Outcomes, 507

Outcomes evaluation, 506–516
  action research, 516
  aggregated outcomes, 508–510
  baseline, 515
  designing, 510–513
  evidence, 507
  formative evaluation, 507
  human factors influencing, 22
  inputs, 507
  post-test, 507

Outcomes evaluation (*continued*)
  practical value, 508
  pretest, 507
  secondary benefits, 532–533
  single-subject research design (SSRD), 513–516
  sources of evidence, 508
  stakeholder, 507
  summative evaluation, 507
  value-added assessment, 507
Outcomes research
  accountability, 520
  assessment, secondary benefits of, 532–533
  clinical efficacy studies, 524
  clinical trials, 524
  collaborating on, 542–544
  definition, 524
  effectiveness of counseling, 527–528
  effectiveness of group counseling and, 535–538
  effectiveness research, 524
  effect size (ES), 525
  facets of counseling, 528–530
  five-step model for using, 544–545
  funding for, 544
  future of, 546–547
  literature, 544–546
  meta-analysis, 525, 527
  methodology, 524–526
  need for and barriers to, 520–523
  nonmaleficence, 520
  qualitative analysis, 524
  school-based interventions, effectiveness of, 538–542
  scientist-practitioner model, 523
Outdoor behavioral health programs (OBHs), 258
Outpatient treatment, 253
Overeaters Anonymous (OA), 265
Overshooting, 206

P
Paradigms, 117. *See also* Theoretical paradigms
Paradox, 134
Paraphrasing. *See* Reflecting skills
Paraprofessional counselors, 441
Parental rights, 105–106
Parent-teacher organizations, 491
Parikh, S.J.T., 220
Park, C., 245
Parker, R. M., 274
Parsons, F., 13, 299, 309
Partial hospital/day treatment program, 252
Partin, P. W., 93

Partner organizations, 50–51
Passion divisions, ACA, 39
Pastoral psychotherapy, 257
Patient-therapist match, 529
Patterson, G. A., 385
Patterson, J. M., 225
Patterson, L. E., 398
Patterson, W. M., 385
Pavlov, I., 130
Pedersen, P., 164
Peer supervision, 409
Peller, J. E., 135
"People first" language, 273
People of color racial identity development, 347
Percentile rank, 493
Perceptions-based needs assessment, 497–503
  designing, 498–502
  frequency of, 497
  populations to be assessed, 497–498
  program goals and objectives, 502–503
  questionnaire and survey guidelines, 501
  tallying, 500
Perls, F., 127
Perls, L., 127
Perry, W., 327
Personal constructs, 144
Personal identity model, 342–344
Personal identity stage, 347
Personality development
  psychoanalytic perspective, 121–122
  role of childhood in, 122–123
Personality disorders, 395
Personality tests, 378
Personalization skills, 411
Personal notes and confidentiality, 108
Person-centered supervision, 410
Person-centered therapy, 125–126
The Personnel and Guidance Journal, 19
Pew Research Center, 339
PFA. *See* Psychological first aid (PFA)
Piaget, J., 317
  cognitive-developmental theory, 315
  concrete operational thought, 320
Placebo treatments, 527
Planning summaries, 214
Pluralism, 19
Poll, J. B., 349
Pollock, G., 27–28
Ponzo, Z., 467
Positive counseling outcomes (PCO), 183
Postformal thought, 326

Post-test, 507
Post-traumatic growth, 224–227
Post-traumatic stress disorder (PTSD), 17, 223, 545
Poverty status and counseling, 350–352
Power, P. W., 7
Practice acts, 61
Precontemplation stage, 166–167
Precontemplation stage of change, 390
Pre-encounter status, 347
Premack principle, 130
Premature termination, 529
Preparation stage in counseling, 167
Preparation stage of change, 390
Prescriptive consultation model, 424
Presidential Task Force on Evidence-based Practice, 530
President's New Freedom Commission on Mental Health, 251
Preston, J., 400
Pretest, 507
Prevention, 287
Prioritization, 502
Privacy rule, 109, 233
Privileged communication, 102–103
Proactive advocacy, 443–444
Proactive process, counseling as, 9
Problem assessment, 463
Problem-free and preferred future dialogue, 135
Process consultation/collaboration model, 425
Process evaluation, 505
Process-oriented consultant, 425
Process specialist role, 427
Prochaska, J. O., 152, 390, 522
Professional advocacy, 7, 286, 435–456
   administrative tasks, 443
   agendas, 437–439
   celebrating accomplishments, 451
   communicating with policymakers, 456
   community service, 452–453
   credentials, displaying, 451–452
   explanation of, 286
   future of, 20, 26–27
   history, 436–437
   implementing plans, 450–451
   media kits and public relations, 443, 454–455
   need for, 27–28, 439–444
   prerequisites to effective, 444–446
   prioritizing problems, 447
   proactive approach, 443–444
   process, steps in, 446–451

professional counselor organizations and, 7, 49–50, 54
   public awareness, 451
   resource availability, 447–448
   skills used in, 444
   strategic-planning activities, 448–449
   training on, 449
   websites, blogs and social media, 454–455
Professional competence, 95–96
Professional Counselor, 66
Professional counselor organizations. *See also specific organizations*
   American Counseling Association (ACA), 7, 36–39
   American Counseling Association Foundation (ACAF), 50
   Association for Adult Development and Aging (AADA), 36
   Chi Sigma Iota (CSI), 50–51
   Council for Accreditation of Counseling and Related Educational Programs (CACREP), 51
   Council on Rehabilitation Education (CORE), 51
   ethical standards and laws, 54
   member benefits, 52–55
   National Board for Certified Counselors (NBCC), 51
   New Jersey Association for Adult Development and Aging (NJAADA), 36
   pursuing professional credentials and, 54
Professional counselors. *See also* Counselors
   addressing of androgyny, 146
   applying theory to practice, 153
   challenges with, 104, 110
   characteristics, 161–162
   client characteristics and, 164–165
   community service activities, 452–453
   confidentiality and, 179
   creating climate for change, 176
   cross-cultural counseling competence of, 165
   decision making, 93–95
   difference between ethical standards and laws, 70–71
   duty to warn, 110–111
   education and training for, 6–7
   effective, 160, 188
   elements of empathy, 177
   establishing rapport, 192
   ethical standards and, 70–71
   expert witnesses and, 97
   as healers with clients, 175–177

Professional counselors (*continued*)
 informed consent and, 178–179
 legal actions against, 97–98
 legal considerations, 95–99
 licensed, 21
 microskills, 192–216
 personal strengths and challenges, 188–189
 psychodynamic-oriented, views of, 115–116, 121–122
 psychologists vs., 4–6, 56
 purpose of, 4
 role/functions of, 35–36
 school counselors, 538
 self-awareness aspect, 116–117
 skilled, 161
 social workers vs., 5, 6
 steps to receive a subpoena, 98–99
 test, 376
 theoretical integration and, 155–158
 therapeutic alliance, 181
 unique position of, 160
Professional development, 51–52
Professional identity
 advocacy competencies, 444–445
 advocate role, 459
 college counseling vs. student-life services, 289
 evolving, 56–57
 professional advocacy and, 27–28
 supervised experience and, 63
 threats, 446
Professional licensure laws, 61–62
Professional School Counseling, 23, 53
Professional school counselors. *See* School counseling; School counselors
Program audit, 505
Program evaluation, 504–506
Program evaluator, 427
Protection of Pupil Rights Amendment (PPRA), 105–106
Prout, H. T., 538
Prout, S. M., 538
Pruett, S. R., 277
Pseudo-independence status, 347
Psychoanalytic counseling, 121–122
Psychodrama, 16
Psychodynamic paradigm
 Adlerian counseling, 122–123
 basis for, 121
 Jungian theory, 123
 psychoanalysis, 121–122

strategies and interventions, 123–124
Psychological first aid (PFA), 221–222
Psychological trauma, 223
Psychologists, 6–7
Psychometrics, 14
Psychometrists, 14
Psychosocial history, 179–180
Psychosocial stressors, 395
Psychotherapy, 4, 5
Psychotropic medications, 465–466
PTSD. *See* Post-traumatic stress disorder (PTSD)
Publications, 37
Public information activities, 477–478
Public policy, 54
Public relations, 449

Q
Qualitative analysis, 524
Quartile, 493–494
Questioning, open vs. closed, 197–201
Quiroz, D. R., 540

R
Race, 338
Racial identity development models, 345–347
 acculturation, 345
 biracial identity development, 347
 people of color racial identity development, 347
 self-identification, 345
 white racial identity development (WRID), 345–347
Racism, 338
Rajab, M. H., 236
Rank, O., 18
Rapport, 192
Rational emotive behavior therapy (REBT), 131–133
Rational-emotive therapy (RET), 19
Ratts, M. J., 339, 477
Raue, K., 296
Ray, D. C., 533
Reciprocity, 21
Recovery from alcoholism, 265
Recovery Inc., 16
Reentry women, 297
Reflecting skills, 201–213
 feelings, 205–209
 meaning, 209–213
 paraphrasing, 201–205
Regel, S., 221
Regions, 38, 48

Registration, 61
Rehabilitation, Comprehensive Services, and Developmental Disabilities Act, 271
Rehabilitation Acts, 271
Rehabilitation counseling, 41, 269–278
  assistive technology for, 274–275
  chronic illness and disability, 274
  eligibility and demographics, 272–273
  empowerment model of, 273
  explanation of, 269–270
  history of, 270–272
  multicultural and social justice issues, 276–278
  psychosocial adaptation models, 274
  vocational, 275–276
Rehabilitation Counseling Bulletin, 41
Rehabilitation counseling resources, 273
Rehabilitation counselors, 41
  expert witnesses, 97
  explanation of, 269
  as external consultants, 430
  resources for, 273
Reintegration status, 347
Relapse, 265
Relational competence, 175, 183–184
Reliability, examination, 384
Religiosity, 363
Remley, T. P., 7, 100, 111, 232
Remley, T. P., Jr., 7, 86, 111
Researcher consultant, 426–427
Residential treatment, 253
Resilience
  crisis, 224–227
  seven resiliencies, 224
Resilience Research Centre, 227
Resistance, 184
Response maintenance, 130
Responsive services, 540
Results evaluation. *See* Outcomes evaluation
RET. *See* Rational-emotive therapy (RET)
Return rate of assessment surveys, 498
Rhodes, R., 438
Rimehaug, T., 430
Ritchie, M., 534
Roberts, T., 272
Rodgers, A., 533
Rodgers, R. A., 479
Rogers, C., 7, 15, 17, 18, 30–31, 125, 415
Role confusion, 313
Rongione, D., 533
Ronnestad, M. H., 162
Rorschach Inkblot Test, 378

Rosenkrantz, P., 359
Ross Trust Graduate Student Scholarship Competition, 53
Rothschild, B., 230, 231
Rough, J. R., 99
Roush, K. L., 348
Rozell, C., 522
Rudd, M. D., 236, 237
Ruzek, J. I., 220

S
SAD PERSONS suicide assessment tool, 385
Saez-Santiago, E., 342
SAFE-T suicide assessment tool, 385
Safety concerns, 247
SAMHSA. *See* Substance Abuse and Mental Health Services Administration (SAMHSA)
Sanders, J. R., 501
Sandoval, J., 220, 223
Santrock, J., 315
Sapp, M., 537
Satcher, D., 398
SAT Reasoning Test, 377
Savickas, M. L., 304
Scaling, 135
Schacht, T. E., 532
Schaie, K. W., 326, 332
Schein, E., 424
Schein, H., 533
Schizophrenia, 395
Schmitz, W., Jr., 234
Scholarships, 53
School-based interventions, for children and adolescents, 538–542
  career interventions, 541–542
  crisis prevention, 245–246
  developmental classroom guidance, 539
  responsive services, 540
  types of, 539–541
School counseling. *See also* Professional school counselors
  advocacy competencies, 475–476
  crisis prevention and intervention, 245–246
  current issues affecting, 283–286
  elementary, 281
  high school, 283
  history of, 280
  middle school/junior high school counseling, 282
  multicultural and social justice issues, 286–288
  program assessment tools, 517
  school policies, procedures, and guidelines and, 93

School counselors, 378
    code of ethics for, 83–91
    collaborative relationships with parents/
        guardians, 84
    handling ethical dilemmas, 85
    internal vs. external role, 430–431
    maintaining physical and mental self-care and
        wellness, 84–85
    policies related to research and program
        evaluation, 85
    release-of-information processes, 84
Science of helping, 169–170
Scientist-practitioner, 22, 169
Scientist-practitioner model, 523
Scofield, T. R., 444
Scope of Practice for Rehabilitation Counseling, 270
SDS. *See* Holland's Self-Directed Search
Secondary traumatic stress, 228–229
Self-actualization, 7, 125, 131
Self-advocate, 462
Self-care. *See* Wellness and self-care
Self-injury, 472, 474–475, 482–483
Self-report, tutorial relationship, 414–415
Seligman, L., 211
Sensorium in mental status examination, 384
Service assessments, 505–506
SES. *See* Socioeconomic status
Settings, consultation, 429–431
Sex and Love Addicts Anonymous, 265
Sexton, T. L., 522, 523, 528, 530, 531, 538
Sexual diversity, 361
Sexual identity development, 348–349
SFBT. *See* Solution-focused brief therapy (SFBT)
Shah, S., 219
Shame, 313
Sharfstein, S. S., 168
Sharp, S., 307–308
Shea, S. C., 236, 237
Shellenberger, E., 283
Shell shock, 17
Shertzer, B., 436
Signal summaries, 214
SII. See Strong Interest Inventory
Singh, A. A., 339
Single case research design, 513
Single-subject research design, 513–516
Sink, C., 392–394, 517, 526
Sink, C. A., 538
Situational consultation, 430
Skillful questioning, 134
Skills. *See also* Microskills

    advocacy for counseling profession, 444
    conceptualization, 411
    fine motor, 314–315
    intervention, 411
    personalization, 411
Skinner, B. F., 14, 129
Sklare, G. B., 135
Skovholt, T. M., 162, 268
Slavery abolitionist movement, 145
Smith, B., 270
Smith, J. E., 444
Smith, T. B., 349
Smith-Fess Act of 1920, 271
Smith-Hughes Act of 1917, 15, 271
Snyder, C. R., 225
Social development
    early adolescence, 321–322
    early-childhood, 316, 318
    late adolescence (emerging adulthood), 326
    midadolescence, 324
    middle childhood, 319
Social interest, 122
Social justice counseling
    accountability and, 518
    career, 309–310
    competencies, 460–461
    counseling, 286–288, 297
    diagnosis and normality concept, 396
    future of, 24–25
    principles in multicultural counseling, 368–369
    in rehabilitation counseling competencies,
        276–278
Social-learning theory, 130
Social media, 25, 81–82
    impact on mental health, 262
    in professional advocacy, 454–455
    in public policy advocacy, 477–478
Social support system, 147, 148
Social theory, 148
Social workers, 6–7, 442
Socioeconomic status, 495
SOLER nonverbal listening skills, 196
Solomon, S. D., 534
Solution-focused brief counseling (SFBC), 134–136
Solution-focused brief therapy (SFBT), 533
Sparkling moments, 143
SPATE. *See* Student Personnel Association for
        Teacher Education (SPATE)
Specialties, counseling, 5–6
Spectrum, 43
Speech patterns, in mental status examination, 383

Spiritual identity development, 349–350

Spirituality, 7

Spokane, A. R., 541, 542

SPRC. *See* Suicide Prevention Resource Center (SPRC)

Spread phenomenon, 367

Sputnik, 18

SSRD. *See* Single-subject research design

Stage, S. A., 540

Stages of change, 152

Stagnation, 314, 331

Stakeholder group, 492

Standardized scores, curve, 494–495

Standardized tests, 375–377

Standard of practice, 97

Standards, 508

Standards for Ethical Practice of Internal Counseling, 66

Stanford Achievement Test, 378

Stanford-Binet scale, 14

Stanley, J. C., 510

State accreditation, 60

State and local agency regulations and policies, 92–93

State credentialing, 60–63

State-Federal Rehabilitation Program, 270–271

State of the Union Address (2015), 286

State Policies in Brief, 103

Statutory law, 91–92

Staudt, M., 532

Steger, M. F., 310

Steinberg, L., 323, 325

Stevic, R. R., 117

Stone, A., 16

Stone, C. B., 85

Stone, H., 16

Stratton, H. H., 541

Strengths-based approaches to drug/alcohol treatment, 265–266

Stress management needs assessment, 499, 501

Strike, D. L., 268

Stringer, M., 444

Stroh, H. R., 538

Strong, E. K., Jr., 15

Strong Interest Inventory, 376, 379

Strong Vocational Interest Blank, 15

Strupp, H. H., 532

Student-assistance programs, issues with, 103–104

Student-life services, 294
    background and trends, 290
    college counseling vs., 289
    multicultural and social justice issues, 297
    role of, 293–295

Student Personnel Association for Teacher Education (SPATE), 18, 37, 43

Subpoenas, 98–99

Substance Abuse and Mental Health Services Administration (SAMHSA), 237, 530

Substance use disorder, 263

Substitute maker, 108

Sue, D. W., 277

Suhr, R., 444

Suicidal ideation (self-harm), 234, 243, 261

Suicide and homicide risk, 234–244
    assessment principles, 236–237
    child and elder abuse, 243–244
    clinical interviewing, 237–238, 384–385
    duty to warn, 110–111, 234, 238
    groups, 234–236
    homicide risk assessments, 238–243
    intimate partner violence, 243
    societal significance, 234–236
    suicide assessment resources, 237
    threat levels of homicidal behavior, 242

Suicide assessment, 384–385

Suicide Intent Checklist, 384

Suicide Prevention Resource Center (SPRC), 220, 236, 237

Suicide Risk Assessment Interview, 239–241

Summarizing, 214–215

Summative evaluation, 507

Super, D., 19, 301, 302

Superego, 121

Supervised experience for licensure, 62–63

Supervision. *See* Counseling supervision

Supervisory consultation breaks, 416

Supervisory relationship, 418–423

Surveys of students, 105–106

Sweeney, T. J., 123, 436, 445

Symptom checklists, 379

System-centered consultation, 424–425

T

Talaga, M. C., 400

Tallying, 500

Tarvydas, V. M., 95

Task Force on Counselor Wellness and Impairment, 230

Taylor, S., 534

Taylor-Ritzler, T., 277

Teacher/trainer/educator, 427

Technology-assisted distance counseling, 25–26, 66, 81–83

Termination, 185

Terra Nova, 378
Terrible twos, 315
Terry-Day, B., 540
Tests
  Army Alpha/Beta, 14
  counselor knowledge of, 376
  cultural fairness, 381
  ethical considerations with, 381–382
  evaluating usefulness of, 379–380
  intake interviews, 382–383
  reliability of scores, 380
  resources, 382
  standardized/nonstandardized, 376–377
  types of, 377–378
  using computers, 381
  validity, 379–380
Tests in Print (VIII), 382
Texas Counseling Association, 49
Theater of Spontaneity, 16
Thematic Apperception Test, 378
Theoretical integration, 155–158
Theoretical paradigms
  behavioral/cognitive-behavioral, 127–141
  common factors, 120
  emergent, 142–151
  humanistic/existential, 125–129
  major theories and theorists, 118–119
  multicultural considerations, 118–119
  psychodynamic, 121–124
  summaries, 118–119
  systems, 136–141
  techniques, 118–119
Theories, 117–151
  common factors, 120
  constructivist, 144–145, 304–306
  crisis, 219–221
  existential, 126
  family systems, 136–141
  feminist, 145–147
  Gestalt, 127
  integration of, 155–158
  interpersonal psychotherapy (IPT),
    147–148
  learning theory, 303–304
  narrative, 142–144
  psychoanalysis, 121–122
  role of, 177
  selection of, 153–154
  significance, 115–117
  specific factors distinguishing, 117–120
  strategies and interventions, 149–150

Theory application, 151–155
  counseling goals, 153
  flexibility, 154
  professional counselor's role, 153
  techniques and approaches, 153–154
  view of human nature, 152
Theory of intellectual and ethical development in
    college years, 327
Therapeutic alliance, 120, 181, 530
The Self-Directed Search, 301
Thompson, R., 540
Thought process, in mental status
    examination, 383
Ticket to Work and Work Incentives Improvement
    Act, 271
Time log, 505
Timing-of-events model, 8
Title acts, 62
Title IX, 287
Tobler, N. S., 541
Toddlerhood. *See* Infancy and toddlerhood
Token economy, 130
Tolerance, substance use disorder, 263
Tone of voice, 195
Toporek, R. L., 470
Trainer/educator consultation model, 425
Training
  code of ethics and, 81
  counselor, 6–7
  leadership, 29
  licensure standards and, 21
  professional advocacy, 449
Trait theory, 13
Transcrisis, 229
Transference, 122, 181
Transforming the School Counseling Profession, 286
Transgendered. *See* Gay, lesbian, bisexual,
    transgendered, and questioning (GLBTQ)
TransTheoretical Model (TTM), 166–167
Trauma, 223
Trauma Essentials: Go To Guide, 231
Treatment-adherence technique, 135–136
Treatment efficacy, 183–185
Treatment manuals, 532
Treatment planning, 398–404
  BASIC ID model, 402–403
  DO A CLIENT MAP models, 403–404
  goals, 399
  interventions, 399
  objectives, 399
  Section 504 (Rehabilitation Act) plan, 392–394

Treatment plan/protocol, 182
Triadic supervision, 414
Triangulation in population needs assessment, 498
TRICARE health plan, 20, 438
True experimental designs, 511–512
Trust, 313
Twelve-step programs, 258, 265
20/20: A Vision for the Future of Counseling committee, 5, 20–21, 56
Twenty Things I Want To Do lists, 334–335

U

Unconditional positive regard, 125
Undershooting, 206
Unfinished business, 127
Unification, 30
University counseling. *See* College counseling
Urbanization, 9
Ursa, M., 224
U.S. Census Bureau, 339
U.S. Department of Defense, 437–438
U.S. Department of Health and Human Services (HHS), 233
U.S. Department of Homeland Security, 245
U.S. Department of Labor, 6
U.S. Employment Service, 16

V

VA. *See* Veterans Administration (VA)
Vacc, N. A., 169
Vacha-Haase, T., 26
Validity, of tests, 379–380
Vallerand, Robert J., 332
Value-added assessment, 507
Van Dernoot Lipsky, L., 229
Vanderwood, M., 533
Van Etten, M. L., 534
V codes, 395
Vera, E. M., 26
Veracity, 71
Verbal underlining, 195
Vernbert, E. M., 220
Vertinsky, I., 245
Veterans Administration (VA), 20, 30, 437–438
Vicarious traumatization, 229
VISTAS Online, 53
Vocal tone, 195
Vocational Bureau of Boston, 13
Vocational rehabilitation, 275–276
Vocational Rehabilitation Act of 1954, 271
Vogel, S., 359

Voice recognition technology (VRT), 274
Voting rights (suffrage) movement, 145
VRT. *See* Voice recognition technology (VRT)

W

Wagner, K., 423
Wagner-Peyser Act, 16
WAIS-IV. *See* Wechsler Adult Intelligence Scale-IV (WAIS-IV)
Waldo, M., 7
Walker, A., 146
Walker, L. E., 243
Wallace, L., 472–473
Walter, J. L., 135
Walz, G., 443
Walz, G. R., 436, 522
Wampold, B. E., 162
Warner, R. W., 117
War neurosis, 17
War Risk Insurance Act of 1914, 271
Watson, J. B., 129
Watson, P. J., 220
Website, 37
Wechsler Adult Intelligence Scale-IV (WAIS-IV), 377
Wechsler Individual Achievement Test, Third Edition (WIAT-III), 378
Wechsler Intelligence Scale for Children, Fifth Edition, 377
Weed, R. O., 278
Weiner-Davis, M., 134
Weiss, B., 533
Weiss, C., 513
Weisz, J. R., 533
Welfel, E. R., 398
Weller, J., 533
Wellness and self-care, 3
    burnout, 32, 228
    commitment to, 30–33
    compassion fatigue, 228
    during crisis counseling, 227–231
    crisis counseling and, 247
    resources, 231
    school counselors' ethical responsibility, 84–85
    secondary traumatic stress, 228–229
    vicarious traumatization, 229
Wellness perspective, 7, 9
Wertheimer, M., 14
Wheel of wellness, 31
Whiston, S. C., 522, 536–542
White, M., 142

White, V. E., 436

White privilege, 353

White racial identity development (WRID), 345–347

Who are LPCs?, 443

WIAT-III. *See* Wechsler Individual Achievement Test, Third Edition (WIAT-III)

Wilderness therapy programs, 258

Williams, J. E., 541

Williams, R. A., 470

Williams-Hayes, M., 532

Williamson, E. G., 15, 17

Wilson, D. B., 525, 541

Wilson, D. K., 541

Wilson, F. R., 189–190

Wilson, S. J., 540

WISC-V. *See* Wechsler Intelligence Scale for Children, Fifth Edition

Withdrawal, substance use disorder, 263

Wolin, S., 225

Wolin, S. J., 225

Wolpe, J., 129

Wood, C., 444

Woodcock-Johnson Tests of Achievement, Third Edition [WJ-III], 378

Workforce Innovation and Opportunity Act of 2014, 272

Working alliance, 181–182

Works Progress Administration, 16

World Health Organization (WHO), 269–270

Worldview, 338

World War II, 17–18

Worthen, B. B., 501

The Wounded Healer, 228

Wounded healers, 31

Wubbolding, R. E., 134

Wundt, W., 14

Y

Yalom, I., 126

Yalom, I. D., 126

Young, M., 418, 421

Young, M. E., 211

Yumangulov, L., 245